DATE DUE

JY 8 04			
JY 27 04			
JE 1 06			

DEMCO 38-296

An Encyclopedia of Keynesian Economics

An Encyclopedia of Keynesian Economics

Edited by

Thomas Cate

Associate Professor of Economics, Northern Kentucky University, USA

Associate Editors

Geoff Harcourt

Reader in the History of Economic Theory, Faculty of Economics and Politics, University of Cambridge and Fellow, Jesus College, Cambridge and Professor Emeritus, University of Adelaide, South Australia

David C. Colander

Christian A. Johnson Distinguished Professor of Economics, Middlebury College, Vermont, USA

Edward Elgar
Cheltenham, UK • Brookfield, US

publication may be reproduced, stored in a
form or by any means, electronic, mechanical,
without the prior permission of the publisher.

Cheltenham
Glos GL50 2HU
UK

Edward Elgar Publishing Company
Old Post Road
Brookfield
Vermont 05036
US

A catalogue record for this book is available from the British Library

Library of Congress Cataloging-in-Publication Data
An encyclopedia of Keynesian economics/edited by Thomas Cate;
associate editors, Geoff Harcourt, David C. Colander.
Includes bibliographical references.
1. Keynesian economics—Encyclopedias. I. Cate, Thomas, 1945–
II. Harcourt, Geoff. III. Colander, David C.
HB99.7.E528 1997
330.15'6'03—dc20   96–23171
                                                           CIP

ISBN 1 85898 145 X

Typeset by Manton Typesetters, 5-7 Eastfield Road, Louth, Lincolnshire LN11 7AJ, UK.
Printed and bound in Great Britain by
Biddles Ltd, Guildford and King's Lynn

Contents

Contributors to This Volume and Their Entries

Adams, John, Economics, Northeastern University, Boston, MA, USA
Dillard, Dudley

Aguirre, Maria Sophia, Economics, The Catholic University of America, Washington, DC, USA
Balance of Payments: Keynesian and Monetarist Approaches

Amsler, Christine, Economics, Michigan State University, East Lansing, MI, USA
Life Cycle Hypothesis

Anderson, David A., Economics, Centre College, Danville, KY, USA
Accelerator Principle, The; *Multiplier Effect*

Aschheim, Joseph, Economics, George Washington University, Washington, DC, USA
Money

Azari-Rad, Hamid, Business Administration, Alabama State University, Montgomery, AL, USA
Aggregate Demand–Aggregate Supply Model and Diagram

Barbour, James, Economics, Elon College, Elon College, NC, USA
Pigou, Arthur C.

Barkai, Haim, Economics, Hebrew University of Jerusalem, Jerusalem, Israel
Niemeyer, Sir Otto E.

Bechtold, Brigitte, Economics, Central Michigan University, Mt Pleasant, MI, USA
Myrdal, Gunnar

Beck, Stacie E., Economics, University of Delaware, Newark, DE, USA
Sharpe, William F.

Besomi, Daniele, Economics, Lugaggia, Switzerland
Harrod, Sir Roy

Black, Robert A., Economics, Houghton College, Houghton, NY, USA
Cambridge Circus

Bohanon, Cecil E., Economics, Ball State University, Muncie, IN, USA
Consumption and the Consumption Function; *Keynesian Economics, Deficit Finance in*

Bolch, Ben W., Economics, Rhodes College, Memphis, TN, USA
Tarshis, Lorie

Bordo, Michael D., Economics, Rutgers University, New Brunswick, NJ, USA
Leijonhufvud, Axel

Bowden, Elbert V., Finance, Appalachian State University, Boone, NC, USA
Neutrality of Money: The Keynesian Challenge

Braun, Bradley M., Economics, University of Central Florida, Orlando, FL, USA
Grossman, Herschel I.

Breit, William, Economics, Trinity University, San Antonio, TX, USA
Stone, Sir John Richard N.

Brems, Hans, Economics, University of Illinois at Urbana-Champaign, Urbana, IL, USA
Stockholm School of Economics

Burczak, Theodore A., Economics, Denison University, Granville, OH, USA
Interest, Theories of

Burnett, Nancy J., Economics, University of Wisconsin–Oshkosh, Oshkosh, WI, USA
Solow, Robert M.

Campbell, D.A., Economics, University of Utah, Salt Lake City, UT, USA
Aggregate Demand–Aggregate Supply Model and Diagram

Canterbery, E. Ray, Economics, Florida State University, FL, USA
Davidson, Paul; *Neo-Keynesianism*

Caporale, Tony, Economics, Ohio University, Athens, OH, USA
Tobin, James

Carey, Catherine, Economics, Western Kentucky University, Bowling Green, KY, USA
Johnson, Harry Gordon

Cate, Tom, Economics, Northern Kentucky University, Highland Heights, KY, USA
Crowding out; Economics of Keynes and of his Revolution, The Key Elements of the; Economics, The Art of; Keynes and Probability; Markowitz, Harry M.; Meltzer, Allan H.; Ohlin, Bertil; Quantity Theory of Money; Real Balance Effect; Schwartz, Anna J.; Wicksell, Knut

Chapple, Simon, Economics, NZ Institute of Economic Research (Inc.), Wellington, New Zealand
Kalecki, Michał

Christensen, Harold R., Economics, Centenary College, Shreveport, LA, USA
Treasury View

Churchman, Nancy, Economics, University of British Columbia, Vancouver, British Columbia, Canada
Ricardian Equivalence

Clayton, Gary E., Finance, Northern Kentucky University, Highland Heights, KY, USA
Keynesian Indicators

Clower, Robert W., Economics, University of South Carolina, Columbia, SC, USA
Dual Decision Hypothesis

Colander, David, Economics, Middlebury College, Middlebury, VT, USA
Functional Finance; IS/LM; Lerner, Abba P.; Post Walrasian Economics

Cornwall, John, Economics, Dalhousie University, Nova Scotia, Canada
Keynes?, What Remains of

Darity Jr., William, Economics, University of North Carolina at Chapel Hill, Chapel Hill, NC, USA
Gesell, Silvio

Davidson, Audrey B., Economics, University of Louisville, Louisville, KY, USA
Expectations, Theories of; Henderson, Sir Hubert Douglas

Davis, John B., Economics, Marquette University, Milwaukee, WI, USA
Government Investment Programs (The Socialization of Investment)

Dimand, Robert W., Economics, Brock University, St Catherine's, Ontario, Canada
Bretton Woods; White, Harry D.

Dornbusch, Rudiger, Economics, Massachusetts Institute of Technology, Cambridge, MA, USA
Mundell, Robert A.

Dow, Sheila, Economics, University of Stirling, Stirling, Scotland, UK
Harcourt, Geoff

Dutt, Amitava Krishna, Economics, University of Notre Dame, Notre Dame, IN, USA
Robinson, Joan

Elmslie, Bruce T., Economics, University of New Hampshire, Durham, NH, USA
Viner, Jacob

Findlay, David W., Economics, Colby College, Waterville, ME, USA
Business Cycle Theory (I)

Fleck, Juergen, Economics, Hollins College, Roanoke, VA, USA
Relative Income Hypothesis

Ford, J.L., Economics, University of Birmingham, Birmingham, UK
Shackle, G.L.S.

Fraley, C. Sean, Economics, College of Mount St Joseph, Delhi, OH, USA
Absolute Income Hypothesis; *Ackley, Hugh Gardner*

Frazer, William, Economics, University of Florida, Gainesville, FL, USA
Monetarist School of Economics

Gallman, Robert E., Economics, University of North Carolina at Chapel Hill, Chapel Hill, NC, USA
Kuznets, Simon

Gamber, Edward N., Economics, Lafayette College, Easton, PA, USA
Heller, Walter W.

Gapinski, James H., Economics, Florida State University, Tallahassee, FL, USA
Technological Change

Garrison, Roger W., Economics, Auburn University, Auburn, AL, USA
Cassel, Gustav

Giesbrecht, Martin Gerhard, Economics, Northern Kentucky University, Highland Heights, KY, USA
Boulding, Kenneth E.

Gilbert, Geoffrey, Economics, Hobart and William Smith Colleges, Geneva, NY, USA
International Clearing Union

Gootzeit, Michael J., Economics, University of Memphis, Memphis, TN, USA
Lipsey, Richard G.

Gramm, Warren S., Economics, Washington State University, Pullman, WA, USA
Samuelson, Paul A.

Groenewegen, Peter, Economics, University of Sydney, Sydney, New South Wales, Australia
Marshall and Keynes

Guthrie, William, Economics, Appalachian State University, Boone, NC, USA
Keynesian Cross

Haber, Lawrence J., Economics, IUPU-Ft Wayne, Ft Wayne, IN, USA
Hansen, Alvin H.

Hammes, David L., Economics, University of Hawaii–Hilo, Hilo, HI, USA
Hahn, Frank H.

Hansen, Ann, Economics, Westminster College, Salt Lake City, UT, USA
Deficits: Cyclical and Structural

Harcourt, Geoff C., Economics, Cambridge University, Cambridge, UK
Keynes, John Maynard

Hetzel, Robert L., Economic, Federal Reserve Bank of Richmond, Richmond, VA, USA
Friedman, Milton

Hoaas, David J., Economics, Centenary College, Shreveport, LA, USA
Weintraub, Sidney

Hobbs, Bradley K., Economics, Bellarmine College, Louisville, KY, USA
Okun, Arthur M.; Okun's Law

Holt, Richard P.F., Economics, Southern Oregan State College, Ashland, OR, USA
Post Keynesian School of Economics

Hooks, Linda M., Economics, Washington and Lee University, Lexington, VA, USA
Brunner, Karl

Horowitz, John B., Economics, Ball State University, Muncie, IN, USA
Demand Management

Humphrey, Thomas M., Economics, Federal Reserve Bank of Richmond, Richmond, VA, USA
Chicago School of Economics

Hutchinson, William K., Economics, Miami University, Oxford, OH, USA
Machlup, Fritz

Jacobsen, Joyce P., Economics, Wesleyan University, Middletown, CT, USA
Haavelmo, Trygve; Malinvaud, Edmond

Jacobsen, Sally A., Literature, Northern Kentucky University, Highland Heights, KY, USA
Bloomsbury Group

Jansen, Dennis W., Economics, Texas A & M University, College Station, TX, USA
Lucas, Jr., Robert E.

Janssen, Maarten C.W., Economics, Erasmus Universiteit, Rotterdam, The Netherlands
Microfoundations of Macroeconomics

John, Andrew, Economics, University of Virginia, Charlottesville, VA, USA
Coordination Failure and Keynesian Economics

Johnson, L.E., Economics, Bemidji State University, Bemidji, MN, USA
Baumol, William J.; Domar, Evsey D.; Economics of Keynes and of his Revolution, The Key Elements of the; Grossman, Herschel I.; Quantity Theory of Money

Jonung, Lars, Economics, Cabinet Office: Chief Economic Advisor to the Prime Minister, Stockholm, Sweden
Leijonhufvud, Axel

Kapuria-Foreman, Vibha, Economics, Colorado College, Colorado Springs, CO, USA
Econometric Models, Macroeconomic

Kumar, Vikram, Economics, Davidson College, Davidson, NC, USA
Clower, Robert W.

Laird, William E., Economics, Florida State University, Tallahassee, FL, USA
Monetizing the (Federal) Debt

Landreth, Donna, Economics, Centre College, Danville, KY, USA
Keynesianism in America

Landreth, Harry, Economics, Centre College, Danville, KY, USA
Keynesianism in America

Larson, John C., Economics, Loyola College, Baltimore, MD, USA
Keynes's Economics, National Income Accounting Activism and

Leeson, Robert, Economics, Murdoch University, Perth, Western Australia
Phillips, A.W.H.; Phillips Curve

Ley, Robert D., Economics, Bemidji State University, Bemidji, MN, USA
Baumol, William J.; Crowding Out; Domar, Evsey D.; Quantity Theory of Money; Real Balance Effect

Maneschi, Andrea, Economics, Vanderbilt University, Nashville, TN, USA
Kahn, Lord Richard F.

Marshall, James N., Economics, Muhlenburg College, Allentown, PA, USA
Fellner, William J.; Sraffa, Piero

Matthews, Peter Hans, Economics, Middlebury College, Middlebury, VT, USA
Lucas Critique

McCrickard, Myra J., Economics, Bellarmine College, Louisville, KY, USA
Keynes, John N.

McCulloch, Rachel, Economics, Brandeis University, Waltham, MA, USA
Mundell–Fleming Model

McKenna, Edward J., Economics, Connecticut College, New London, CT, USA
Neoclassical Synthesis (Bastard Keynesianism)

McLean, Paula, Economics, University of Prince Edward Island, Charlottetown, Prince Edward Island, Canada
Cagan, Phillip

Mehdizadeh, Mostafa, Economics, Miami University–Middletown, Middletown, OH, USA
Klein, Lawrence R.

Mizen, Paul, Economics, University of Nottingham, Nottingham, UK
Hawtrey, Sir Ralph

Moggridge, D.E., Economics, University of Toronto, Toronto, Ontario, Canada
Robertson, Sir Dennis H.

Montgomery, Michael R., Economics, University of Maine, Orono, ME, USA
Jorgenson, Dale W.

Moore, Geoffrey H., Economics, Center for International Business Cycle Research, Columbia University, New York, NY, USA
Burns, Arthur F.

Morgan, Jack, Economics, University of Louisville, Louisville, KY, USA
Automatic Stabilizers

Morris, Clair E., Economics, US Naval Academy, Anapolis, MD, USA
Say's Law

Moshtagh, Ali R., Economics, Eastern Illinois University, Charleston, IL, USA
Full Employment Budget

Moss, Laurence S., Economics, Babson College, Babson Park, MA, USA
Ricardo Effect; *von Hayek, Friedrich A.*

Noble, Nicholas R., Economics, Miami University, Oxford, OH, USA
Liquidity Trap

Noyd, Lou, Economics, Northern Kentucky University, Highland Heights, KY, USA
Employment Act of 1946

Obar, Ruth I., Economics, Hood College, Frederick, MD, USA
Townsend, Robert

Palivos, Theodore, Economics, Louisiana State University, Baton Rouge, LA, USA
Meade, James E.

Papadimitriou, Dimitri B., Economics, Bard College, Annadale–Hudson, NY, USA
Dornbusch, Rudiger

Payne, James E., Economics, Eastern Kentucky University, Richmond, KY, USA
Permanent Income Hypothesis

Pitzer, John S., Economics, US Department of Commerce, Washington, DC, USA
Clark, Colin

Potiowsky, Thomas P., Economics, Portland State University, Portland, OR, USA
Adjustment Mechanisms of the Basic Classical and Keynesian Models

Presley, John R., Economics, Loughborough University of Technology, Loughborough, Leicestershire, UK
Champernowne, David G.

Pulikonda, Naga, Economics, Indiana University Kokomo, Kokomo, IN, USA
Inflation

Rahnama-Moghadam, Mashalah, Economics, Texas Tech University, Lubbock, TX, USA
Incomes Policies

Rashid, Salim, Economics, University of Illinois, Champaign, IL, USA
Kaldor, Lord Nicholas

Rotheim, Roy J., Economics, Skidmore College, Saratoga Springs, NY, USA
New Keynesian Macroeconomics

Samavati, Hedayeh, Economics, IUPU-Ft Wayne, Ft Wayne, IN, USA
Leontief, Wassily W.

Samuels, Warren J., Economics, Michigan State University, East Lansing, MI, USA
Hicks, Sir John R.

Samuelson, Paul A., Economics, Massachusetts Institute of Technology, Cambridge, MA, USA
Stein, Herbert

Sandilands, Roger J., Economics, University of Strathclyde, Glasgow, Scotland, UK
Currie, Lauchlin

Sato, Kazuo, Economics, Rutgers University, New Brunswick, NJ, USA
Fischer, Stanley

Schneider, Friedrich, Economics, Johannes Kepler University of Linz, Linz, Austria
Rothschild, Kurt W.

Serven, Luis, Economics, World Bank, Washington, DC, USA
Metzler, Lloyd A.

Shionoya, Yuichi, Economics, Hitosubashi University, Tokyo, Japan
Schumpeter, Joseph A.

Simkins, Scott, Economics, North Carolina A and T State University, Greensboro, NC, USA
New Classical School of Economics

Skaggs, Neil T., Economics, Illinois State University, Normal, IL, USA
Monetary Policy

Skidelsky, Robert, Economics, University of Warwick, Coventry, UK
Keynes, The Influence of Burke and Moore on

Solow, Robert M., Economics, Massachusetts Institute of Technology, Cambridge, MA, USA
Swan, Trevor W.

Sorensen, Philip E., Economics, Florida State University, Tallahassee, FL, USA
Edgeworth, Francis Y.; Robbins, Lord Lionel

Spector, Lee C., Economics, Ball State University, Muncie, IN, USA
Fiscal Policy

Steindl, Frank G., Economics, Oklahoma State University, Stillwater, OK, USA
Keynesian Revolution

Syll, Lars Pålsson, Economics, Lund University, Lund, Sweden
Lundberg, Erik

Tarascio, Vincent J., Economics, University of North Carolina at Chapel Hill, Chapel Hill, NC, USA
Modigliani, Franco

Tavlas, George S., Special Advisor, Bank of Greece, Athens, Greece
Money

Turgeon, Lynn, Economics, Hofstra University, Hamstead, NY, USA
Keyserling, Leon

Uzawa, Hirofumi, Economics, The Japan Academy, Tokyo, Japan
Arrow, Kenneth J.

Vaughn, Karen I., Economics, George Mason University, Fairfax, VA, USA
Austrian School of Economics

Veramallay, Ashton I., Economics, Indiana East University, Richmond, IN, USA
Galbraith, John K.

Walker, Donald A., Economics, Indiana University of Pennsylvania, Indiana, PA, USA
Lausanne, The School of

Waller, Christopher, Economics, Indiana University, Bloomington, IN, USA
Brown, Arthur J.

Weinberg, David, Economics, Xavier University, Cincinnati, OH, USA
Minsky, Hyman P.

Whitaker, John, Economics, University of Virginia, Charlottesville, VA, USA
Marshall, Alfred

Wilson, Loretta S., Economics, Radford University, Radford, VA, USA
Frisch, Ragnar

Wood, J. Stuart, Economics, Loyola University, New Orleans, LA, USA
Business Cycle Theory (II)

Wray, L. Randall, Economics, University of Denver, Denver, CO, USA
Kregel, Jan A.

Yohe, William P., Economics, Duke University, Durham, NC, USA
Depression, The Great

Young, Jeffrey T., Economics, St Lawrence University, Canton, NY, USA
Classical Economics

Zannoni, Diane C., Economics, Trinity College, Hartford, CT, USA
Neoclassical Synthesis (Bastard Keynesianism)

Introduction

John Maynard Keynes was a man of many talents and great influence. He has played a significant role in shaping both modern economic policy and theory. He is, if not the most, then certainly one of the most important economists of the twentieth century. His most famous book is *The General Theory of Employment, Interest and Money*, a book written partly in response to the events associated with the Great Depression. While not everyone agrees with his explanation of why that event occurred or his public policy proposal for improving the average level of performance of an economic system, most would agree that *The General Theory* constituted an extraordinarily fruitful research agenda. A partial list of the research projects that have emerged from the discussion in which economists of all persuasions debated the merits of Keynes's theoretical model include the National Income and Product Accounts, for which Kuznets and Stone were awarded the Nobel Prize, the consumption function for which Friedman and Modigliani were awarded the Nobel Prize, and the revival of growth theory for which Solow was awarded the Nobel Prize.

Many of Keynes's writings have attained classic status (talked about, but not read) and his name is both deified and vilified by modern economic pundits. He remains with the profession today; he is a phoenix who has 'died' and been 'resurrected' more than any other economist. His collected writings are available in 30 volumes, including an index, but even that multitude of volumes does not include all of his letters and correspondence. A listing of books about him would itself be book length. This *Encyclopedia* is designed to be an introduction into that enormous literature.

The *Encyclopedia* has three general categories of entries. First, there are brief biographies of economists who have contributed to the debate about the merits of Keynes's message, to the development of the macroeconomic tools which are essential to carrying on the debate and to the implementation of public policies which follow from the models based on *The General Theory* or of critiques of those models. With a few exceptions, these biographies are of equal length, approximately 900 to 1100 words. Second, there are brief sketches of the basic principles, models and tools used by the participants in the conversation about the economic consequences of *The General Theory*. For the most part, these sketches are of equal length, about 900 to 1500 words. Third, there are longer pieces, 4000 to 6000 words, which deal with specific topics associated with Keynes and the Keynesian revolution. The purpose of these longer pieces is to provide the reader with a review of some of the principal factors which contributed to *The General Theory*, the economics of Keynes and the rise and apparent decline of Keynesian economics. Combined, these contributions give the reader a good introduction to Keynes and Keynesian ideas and provide a reader with both a summary of enormous knowledge for reference and an introduction to the debates for those who are unfamiliar with Keynes

While the central theme of the *Encyclopedia*, as its name implies, is the impact of John Maynard Keynes on the economics profession, the intention is not to ignore all other schools of economic thought. Rather, the intention is to provide readers with a review of some aspects of the ongoing debate about the continued viability of the approach to economics developed by Keynes, expanded and modified by his followers and commented on by his critics.

Absolute Income Hypothesis

The absolute income hypothesis is the name given to the consumption function described by John Maynard Keynes in *The General Theory of Employment, Interest and Money*. Keynes states the logic behind the formulation of the consumption function as follows:

> The fundamental psychological law, upon which we are entitled to depend with great confidence both *a priori* and from our knowledge of human nature and from the detailed facts of experience, is that men are disposed, as a rule and on the average, to increase their consumption as their income increases, but not by as much as the increase in their income.

Keynes viewed the consumption function as one of the two primary components of aggregate demand (the other being investment) which corresponds to a certain level of employment. The level of consumption depended upon the amount of income given in terms of wage units, objective circumstances and the subjective psychological habits of individuals. Keynes believed the psychological influences upon consumption to be stable and likely to change only during unusual or out-of-the-ordinary circumstances. The consumption decision made by an individual was not one of consumer maximization but rather was based on a psychological premise.

The objective factors of the consumption function focus on the following variables: changes in the wage unit, changes in the difference between income and net income, windfall capital gains or losses, interest rate fluctuations, fiscal policy changes and changes in the expectations between present and future levels of income. The subjective factors or psychological motives included protection against emergencies and unexpected expenses and plans for increased future consumption. Keynes viewed the normal circumstances of a consumption function to be of a short-run or cyclical nature, where the objective and subjective factors do not have enough time to change the consumption habits of the individuals.

From this cyclical view of stable consumption behavior, Keynes tells of the widening gap between the levels of consumption and income as the level of absolute income rises. That is, as real income increases there will not be an equal increase in the absolute level of consumption, but the absolute level of savings is likely to rise. Keynes viewed this absolute consumption behavior as a stabilizing factor for an economy. Allowing for changes in the objective and subjective factors of consumption, Keynes acknowledges that a consumption–income relation shifts upward (downward) as income increases (decreases) are foreseen or expected to continue for extended periods of time. However, this view of a long-run consumption function was not the primary concern of Keynes; rather he focused on the short-run or cyclical nature of consumption behavior, because it was the short-run cyclical nature of consumption which directly led to the multiplier, and the way increases in employment can only come from increases in investment, unless there is a shift upward in the propensity to consume (Minsky, 1975).

Keynes viewed consumption as the ultimate outcome of economic activity. He believed that aggregate demand that was derived from consumption spending was the primary source of employment for society. Consumption could take the form of aggregate demand for currently produced goods or of savings for consumption in the future. As the level of income rises and present needs for current consumption diminish, the gap between income and consumption for currently produced goods widens. Thus an increase in employment can only come from an increase in investment during periods of rising incomes, if the consumption function does not shift upward, which Keynes viewed as unlikely. New investment is generated during times of rising incomes because the public are increasing their savings during this same period. It is this absolute income consumption behavior that makes possible the added investment spending.

The absolute income hypothesis can be stated by the following four postulates: (1) real income is a stable function of real disposable income; (2) the marginal propensity to consume is a positive fraction close to but less than unity; (3) the marginal propensity to consume is less than the average propensity to consume and the average propensity to consume declines as income rises; and (4) the marginal propensity to consume declines as income rises. The postulate that the marginal propensity to consume is a fraction reflects Keynes's psychological law of consumption behavior and the falling average propensity to consume as the level of income rises refers to the widening gap between the changes in the absolute level of income and consumption (Speight, 1989).

The absolute income hypothesis has been empirically tested to determine its form. Estimates made by A. Smithies for the period 1924–40 supports the absolute income hypothesis that the cyclical consumption function is stable and linear. However, Simon Kuznets, using time series data from 1869 to 1938, found a stable consumption function that did not support the hypothesis that the marginal propensity to consume was less than the average propensity to consume. Kuznets found the average and marginal propensities to consume to be equal. This discrepancy between estimates of the propensity to consume using short-run and long-run periods of data led to the development of two alternative hypotheses about consumption.

M. Friedman's permanent income hypothesis rejects the psychological basis of consumption behavior and replaces it with an optimal process of maximizing the utility of consumption. Whereas Keynes found consumption to be the total expenditure on consumer goods, Friedman defines consumption as the value of the service flow consumed over time by the consumer. Friedman finds that long-run and short-run propensities to consume are equal.

Ando and Modigliani's life cycle hypothesis relates consumption spending to levels of wealth. Over time, individuals experience an income path that is low in the early years, rises and reaches a peak in the middle years, and falls with old age or retirement. The individual dissaves in youth, retirement and old age. This life cycle hypothesis explains why cross-sectional studies show the marginal propensity to consume as less than the average propensity to consume, and the consumption to income ratio falls as the level of income rises.

Neither the permanent income hypothesis nor the life cycle hypothesis fully explains the form of the consumption function. However, they do seriously challenge Keynes's view of an absolute income consumption function and its structural form. Keynes's absolute income hypothesis does leave us with an understanding of the psychological foundations of consumption behavior and the subsequent role of savings and investment in determining the level of employment for society.

C. Sean Fraley

See also:

Consumption and the Consumption Function; Friedman, Milton; Life Cycle Hypothesis; Modigliani, Franco; Multiplier Effect; Permanent Income Hypothesis.

Bibliography

Ando A. and F. Modigliani (1963), 'The Life-Cycle Hypothesis of Saving: Aggregate Implications and Tests', *American Economic Review*, **53**, (1), March, pp. 55–84.

Friedman, M. (1957), *A Theory of the Consumption Function*, Princeton NJ: Princeton University Press.

Keynes, John Maynard (1936), *The General Theory of Employment, Interest and Money*, New York: Harcourt, Brace.

Kuznets, Simon (1946), *National Product Since 1869*, New York: National Bureau of Economic Research.

Minsky, Hyman P. (1975), *John Maynard Keynes*, New York: Columbia University Press.

Smithies, A. (1945), 'Forecasting Postwar Demand', *Econometrica*, **13**, (1), January, pp. 1–14.

Speight, Allan E.H. (1989), *Consumption, Rational Expectations and Liquidity*, New York: St Martin's Press.

Accelerator Principle

The accelerator principle relates changes in net private investment to changes in consumption. The principle is based on the theory that businesses adjust their capital stocks in proportion to their expected sales. As sales increase, producers may increase plant capacity, not only to keep up with demand, but in anticipation of a continued upward trend in sales. Likewise, a decrease in the growth of consumption may yield decreases in expenditures on buildings and equipment. The accelerator value, sometimes called the *relation*, is the numerical coefficient for the increase in net investment (the change in desired capital stock) by business firms induced by each additional dollar of consumer purchases.

John M. Clark (1917) developed the simplest form of the accelerator while studying the relationship between boxcar production and preceding changes in railroad traffic. According to Clark's theory, net investment for a firm equals a fixed accelerator coefficient multiplied by the change in sales over the previous period. If the accelerator is two and sales increased by $2000 last year, net investment would be $4000. The value of the accelerator depends on capacity utilization, the importance of capital and the psychology of management in the industry and firm in question. Increases in consumption will translate into larger increases in investment in firms operating at capacity than in firms with excess capacity. Investment is more responsive to increases in consumption in capital-intensive industries than in labor-intensive industries. And managers will place differing levels of faith in the predictive power of past and present consumption trends.

More realistic models of the accelerator relax the rigid assumptions of Clark's accelerator to accommodate further contingencies. For example, managers are likely to consider trends that began prior to the previous period when predicting sales volume. Rather than being a constant, the accelerator is likely to depend on interest rates and the taxation of capital, among other factors. And firms cannot instantly bring their capital stocks to the desired level as the simple model suggests. Although investment does appear to mimic GNP in historical data, lags between changes in GNP and changes in investment are significant and inconsistent. As an alternative to the simple accelerator, a *flexible accelerator* can vary with interest and tax rates. Variants on these models can also allow for an adaptive learning process that considers several years of consumption rather than just the previous year and acknowledge that the construction of new buildings and the acquisition of new capital can extend over a period of several years.

The accelerator principle helps to explain instability in investment and the existence of business cycles. Consider a computer manufacturer with annual sales of one million dollars in its first year that requires five dollars' worth of machinery for every one dollar's worth of computers produced. At current sales levels, five million dollars' worth of capital is needed. If sales are constant, investment in new capital occurs only at the rate necessary to replace broken or out-of-date machines. If sales increase by one million dollars in the second year, investment will increase by five million dollars. In order to sustain the level of investment made in the second year, sales must continue to grow by one million dollars per year. If sales decrease, *or increase by less than one million dollars* in year three, investment will decrease. For example, if sales increase by only one-half million dollars in year three, induced capital investment will decrease from five million to two and one-half million dollars that year. The accelerator's ability to yield decreases in investment even when sales are increasing is a possible source of business cycles.

While the Keynesian multiplier describes the income resulting from an increase in investment, the total effect of a change in income may be broader than that described by the multiplier owing to the interaction between consumption and investment embodied in the accelerator. Alvin Hansen (1938) was the first to integrate the accelerator into the Keynesian system and develop the interactions between the multiplier and the accelerator. In his article on the same topic, Paul Samuelson (1939) demonstrated that business cycles can result from a constant annual government expenditure given various values for the multiplier and the accelerator. Other important figures in the development and formalization of the accelerator principle include A. Aftalion, C.W. Bickerdike, Evsey D. Domar, Ragnar Frisch, Roy F. Harrod and Ralph G. Hawtrey.

More recent students of the accelerator have studied the underlying reasons for the effect. Daron Acemoglu (1993) suggests that the accelerator is caused by technical externalities – firms having increased marginal productivity of investment as the result of increases in total investment in the economy. In other words, when consumption and output increase in the economy, the drive for more than proportional increases in investment may stem from spillover effects as from training and innovation that allow firms to benefit from each other's growth. Rational expectations models hold that the processes behind the demand for investment are determined concurrently with the demand for consumption. Thomas Sargent (1989) explains the success of accelerator theories under the scrutiny of empirical tests with measurement errors in the data.

Although theoretically sound, there is less evidence to support the existence of an *employment accelerator* analogous to the investment accelerator that would relate changes in consumption to magnified increases in job offerings. In one of the relatively few discussions of the employment accelerator, Acemoglu (1993) finds that the employment accelerator is more important in the United States and the investment accelerator is more important in the United Kingdom.

DAVID A. ANDERSON

See also:

Business Cycle Theory (I) and (II); Consumption and the Consumption Function; Domar, Evsey D.; Expectations, Theories of; Frisch, Ragnar; Hansen, Alvin H.; Harrod, Sir Roy; Hawtrey, Sir Ralph; Multiplier Effect; Samuelson, Paul A.

Bibliography

Acemoglu, Daron (1993), 'Learning About Others' Actions and the Investment Accelerator', *Economic Journal*, **103**, (1), March, pp. 318–28.
Clark, John M. (1917), 'Business Acceleration and the Law of Demand', *Journal of Political Economy*, **25**, (1), March, pp. 217–35.
Hansen, Alvin H. (1938), *Full Recovery or Stagnation*, New York: W.W. Norton & Co.
Samuelson, Paul A. (1939), 'Interaction Between the Multiplier Analysis and the Principle of Acceleration', *Review of Economic Statistics*, **21**, (2), May, pp. 75–8.
Sargent, Thomas (1989), 'Two Models of Measurements and the Investment Accelerator', *Journal of Political Economy*, **97**, (2), April, pp. 251–87.

Ackley, Hugh Gardner

Hugh Gardner Ackley was born on 30 January 1915 in Indianapolis, Indiana. Ackley received a BA degree in economics from the University of Western Michigan in 1936. He received his MA and PhD from the University of Michigan in 1937 and 1940, respectively. He was also awarded an Honorary LLD from Kalamazoo College in 1967. Ackley began his academic career at Ohio State University (1939–40). He then spent the majority of his academic life at the University of Michigan, from 1940 to his retirement in 1984. Ackley's distinguished performance earned him the appointment as the Henry Carter Adams Distinguished University Professor from 1969 until his retirement.

Gardner Ackley also worked in various government positions, which caused him to leave academic life for various periods while he was a faculty member at the University of Michigan. The following is a list of the offices, awards and appointments held by Ackley:

> Economist, Natural Resource Planning Board, 1940–41
> Economist, US Office of Price Administration, 1941–3, 1944–6
> Economist, US Office of Strategic Services, 1943–4
> Consultant, US Economic Stabilization Agency, 1950–51
> Economic Advisor and Assistant Director, Office of Price Stabilization, 1951–2
> Member (Chairman), Council of Economic Advisors, 1962–8 (1964–8)
> US Ambassador to Italy, 1968–9
> Member, National Advisory Council on Social Security, 1978–80
> Trustee, Joint Council on Economic Education, 1971–7
> Director, National Bureau of Economic Research, 1971–80
> Cavaliere del Gran Croce, Ordine della Merita, Republica d'Italia

Ackley's tenure on the Council of Economic Advisors occurred during the time of the John F. Kennedy presidency. It was during these years that economists believed that the economy could be turned by the appropriate fiscal policy action. The Kennedy Tax Cut was an implementation of Keynesian demand management policies. Ackley was in agreement that the economy could be manipulated by the fiscal tools of the government and the tax cut was successful in generating one of the longest periods of peacetime economic expansion in US history. However, during 1966 the US economy began to experience increases in the Consumer Price Index. Ackley's past work experience with price controls convinced him that the government could play an active role in curbing inflationary pressures.

In Ackley's book, *Macroeconomic Theory and Policy* (1978), which was an update of his *Macroeconomic Theory* (1961), we find his views concerning price control and the behavior of markets clearly written:

> Thus, beyond some point, further efforts to alter market structures and institutions may need to be supplemented by attempting to influence wage and price behavior directly – through some kind of an 'incomes policy'. This may be fully as effective as altering structures or institutions. For, as we have argued, in modern industrial societies, most wage- and price-setting behavior does not simply reflect inevitable market pressures: almost no wage rates, and very few prices are either automatically allowed, or deliberately adjusted, to 'clear the market'.

Ackley viewed the government role as alerting society to the fact that inflation created social costs and preventing inflation from getting out of control was in the best interest of society as a whole. Ackley believed the government would fail its role if an incomes policy was not undertaken to control inflation. Government intervention was necessary to prevent instability in the economic system due to inflationary pressures, real or expected. Powerful government stabilizers were needed to dampen the unstable and painful economic business fluctuations that were occurring in highly industrialized economies. He also noted that the role of institutions and traditions must be taken into account to understand the movement of prices and wages when conducting income policies. Wage and price controls on a large scale would be difficult to administer in any fair or equitable manner.

However, Ackley viewed economic growth as the primary cause of economic fluctuations. Income policies that could be used to dampen fluctuations must be such that there is no change in the distribution of income between wages and profits. He states that, if wage rates can be held to a rate of increase equal to that of the average rate of productivity gains for the economy as a whole, then the average price level or inflation rate can be held steady. He also recognized that, once the incomes policy is removed, there will be an immediate increase in wages and prices.

The other unique feature of Ackley's book centered on his belief that economic knowledge has a unique nature of its own and that this knowledge must relate to relationships that exist in the real world; that any knowledge that is brought forth should and must be used for the betterment of society. He used examples whenever possible to illustrate the applied solutions of economic theory. Economic theory was not to be taught only in the abstract, but in the application of the theory, subject to empirical testing.

Gardner Ackley's first book was concerned with price controls during the Korean War and he felt this was his best written book. The majority of Ackley's writings were concerned with the understanding of inflation and the role of social institutions in wage and price determination in an economic society. Of the hundreds of his publications, some of the most notable that relate to Ackley's focus on income policy and inflation are 'An incomes policy for the 1970's', *Research and Statistics*, **54**, (3), August 1972; 'The future of wage and price controls', *Atlanta Economic Review*, **22**, April 1972; *Policies for the Promotion of Economic Growth* (US Department of Labor, 1966) and *Stemming World Inflation* (Atlantic Institute, 1971).

It is for Gardner Ackley's active role as a government economist and teacher to presidents and students alike that we remember him. His belief in the role and application of economic theory to improve the lives of society is his greatest legacy.

C. SEAN FRALEY

See also:
Currie, Lauchlin; Demand Management; Dillard, Dudley; Fiscal Policy; Hansen, Alvin H.; Heller, Walter W.; Keynes's Economics, National Income Accounting Activism and; Keynesian Economics, Deficit Finance in; Neoclassical Synthesis (Bastard Keynesianism).

Bibliography
Ackley, Hugh Gardner (1961), *Macroeconomic Theory*, New York: Macmillan.
Ackley, Hugh Gardner (1971), *Macroeconomic Theory and Practice*, New York: Macmillan.
Sobel, Robert and Bernard S. Katz (1988), *Biographical Directory of the Council of Economic Advisors*, New York: Greenwood Press.
Stein, Herbert (1990), *The Fiscal Revolution in America*, Washington, DC: American Enterprise Institute Press.

Adjustment Mechanisms of the Basic Classical and Keynesian Models

The events of the Great Depression cast numerous doubts on the economic theories of the day. In the *General Theory*, Keynes suggested a model to address these doubts and give a fuller explanation for persistent unemployment. Keynes's model went through a number of modifications at the hands of John Hicks, Alvin H. Hansen, Lawrence R. Klein, Paul A. Samuelson and others. Through these revisions Keynes's original model evolved into today's standard textbook presentation known as the neoclassical synthesis, or simply the Keynesian model. As the first name suggest, this model shares similarities with the very model it was meant to replace – the classical model. Concepts of market equilibrium, demand and supply of labor, the production function, investment and savings are common to both models. However, the route taken by the economy to reach new market-clearing equilibriums, the adjustment mechanism, is quite distinct in the two models. The classical model depends upon a self-adjusting economy where the movement of prices assures real output equilibrium at full employment. The Keynesian model relies on real income or output movements to bring the economy to a new equilibrium, which may or may not be at full employment.

To describe the adjustment mechanism in these two models, a simple closed economy (no international sector) can be represented by three sectors, the labor, financial and goods markets. These three markets/sectors are represented in the analytical framework of aggregate demand and supply, which together establish an equilibrium or resting point for the economy. The labor market and an aggregate production function form the basis of aggregate supply; the financial and goods markets will determine aggregate demand.

The labor market formulation is almost identical in the two models. In the classical model, the level of employment is the result of perfectly working market mechanisms that bring together the demand and supply of labor at an equilibrating wage. Firms' demand for labor stems from the productivity of labor used in the production process. Workers relate their supply to the marginal disutility of work. Both demand and supply of labor are thus functions of the real wage. Firms compare the payment of the real wage to the productivity of labor while labor sees the real wage as compensation for the disutility of work. Similar to an auction market (not one of slavery but rather like the Chicago Board of Trade), the real wage is freely determined by the firms who want to hire and the workers who supply their labor services. Full employment is achieved as everyone who wishes to work at the equilibrium wage will be employed.

Once this full employment level is determined, this level of labor resource determines the level of output through the production function. For the short run, labor is the only variable input with other resources (for example, capital) being fixed. Since labor is fully employed, the level of output (or real income) generated is usually referred to as the full employment level of output (or real income).

The labor market in the Keynesian model is very similar in all respects except for the specification of perfectly flexible markets. Wages are assumed to be rigid downward. This rigidity can prevent the labor markets from clearing, resulting in unemployment. But if wages were allowed to be perfectly flexible in clearing labor markets, no discernible difference would exist between the classical and Keynesian model views of the labor market.

On the demand side, the role of the financial and goods markets also distinguishes the two models. In the Classical Model the real interest rate is determined in a loanable funds market and is separate from the aggregate demand in the goods market. The Keynesian model portrays the financial side through a money market which combines with the goods markets as the basis for aggregate demand.

In the classical model, the real interest rate is determined by the demand and supply for credit. Investment by firms and government financing needs form the demand for loanable funds while savings by individuals provide the supply of loanable funds. Demand is negatively affected by the real interest rate, while the supply will increase with a rise in the interest rate. This market-clearing adjustment by the interest rate prevents both investment demand and government financing needs from affecting employment or output. For example, if investment suddenly increases as the result of favorable expectations by firms, this increase in the demand for loanable funds will cause the interest rate to rise to coax out more savings. Any increase in investment spending will be matched by an equal drop in consumption spending, since savings must increase and real income (output) remains the same.

The Quantity Theory of Money is the anchor for aggregate demand in the classical model. Stated briefly, $MV = PY$ represents aggregate demand through the spending of money (MV) on nominal output (PY). Note that MV is called aggregate demand in the sense that an overall level of demand is related to the nominal output; any time spending is increased for one item, it must be decreased for another. The mix of goods and services is thus determined by relative prices but the aggregate demand stays the same as long as PY is unchanging. This relationship forms the basis for the demand for money known as the Cambridge equation:

$$M^d = kP\overline{Y} \tag{1}$$

where k represents the inverse of V (the velocity of money) and is assumed to remain constant. Money is held to complete transactions, so the demand for money is a demand for the medium of exchange. For equilibrium in the money market, money demand must equal money supply. Given a fixed level of output, $\overline{Y}$,

$$M^s = kP\overline{Y} \tag{2}$$

since k and Y are fixed in the short run, the level of money supply, M^s, will determine the price level, P. Finally, the real equilibrium wage established in the labor market joins with the price level, P, established by money supply, to set the level for money wages ($W/P \times P = W$, money wage).

The Keynesian model, as previously noted, is very much a product of the classical model. This neoclassical synthesis embraces the same concepts of labour markets and production functions for the economy. The same factors have an impact upon aggregate demand. The difference lies in two areas: (1) linking of the money market and loanable funds market to aggregate demand and (2) market imperfections that either prevent the flexibility of prices or result in a demand deficiency.

Aggregate demand in the Keynesian model follows from the circular flow of income and expenditures. Central to this concept is the consumption function, whereby income determines consumption which generates new income which sets off yet more consumption. This flow of income and expenditures has leakages in the form of savings and taxes and injections of investment and government spending. Unlike the case of the classical model, the decisions to invest and save are separate. That is, rather than both being a function of the interest rate, savings is postulated to be influenced by the income level whereas investment is either exogenously given or remains related to the rate of interest. Breaking this link between savings and investment necessitates a new determination of the rate of interest. This is accomplished in the money market with a new demand for money, or liquidity preference. The demand for money retains its feature as a medium of exchange but gains a function as a store of wealth. Demand for money is influenced by income, as in the classical model, but also is a function of the interest rate. The money market becomes a companion to the loanable funds market. As the money supply increases, the amount of loanable funds increases and interest rates start to fall. This lowers the return on bonds and lowers the opportunity cost of holding money, on the simplifying assumption that money pays no rate of return, or at least always less than paid on bonds. The increased money supply is then held by the public. Lowering of the interest rate will stimulate investment but will not lower savings. Investment enters the income and expenditure flow, raising incomes, which in turn raises savings to match the increase in investment. Adjustment to a new equilibrium level of real income (output) occurs as the result of an increase in income to satisfy the equality between investment and savings.

The Keynesian model incorporates the money supply, investment and the government budget as influences on aggregate demand. When one of the determinates of demand changes, income must change to bring about a new equilibrium if prices are held constant. Constant prices are a result of market imperfections. For example, if the economy is in a depressed stage no one expects prices to fall further; as demand increases, the income adjustment can raise output using unemployed resources without putting capacity constraint pressure on prices to rise.

Figure 1 illustrates both the classical and the Keynesian adjustment mechanisms using the analytic framework of aggregate demand and supply. The aggregate demand (AD) curve represents total demand for the output of the economy. The aggregate supply (AS) curve represents the total supply of output produced by the factors of production, most notably that of labor. Equilibrium in the economy occurs where the two curves intersect.

In the classical model, the relevant section of the AS curve is the vertical section that passes through points C and B down to the horizontal axis at full employment real output (Q) or real income (Y_{FE}). The vertical AS curve represents perfectly flexible prices that will always clear the labor market and assure full employment of resources. The curved aggregate demand curve, AD_C – a rectangular hyperbola – is derived from the quantity theory of money. Movement of aggregate demand caused by money supply disturbances will simply change aggregate prices, leaving unchanged all real variables including employment, output and real income, real wages and the real interest rate. Note that a disturbance in demand caused by changes in investment or government financing are completely absorbed in the loanable funds market and cause no movement in AD_C.

The Keynesian model is characterized by the AD_K curve for aggregate demand and the horizontal section of the AS curve, the range P_O to A. The downward-sloping AD_K curve is a caricature of the income and expenditure

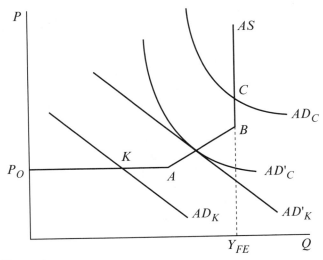

Figure 1

flow coupled with a variable price level. The flat *AS* curve represents the condition of constant output prices. The AD_K curve can shift along this flat section according to changes in investment, government financing needs, money supply or other factors that can affect spending, especially consumption. Point *K* represents only one of many possible equilibrium points for output or real income. As AD_K moves to the right with no change in prices, it is the change in real income that adjusts to bring the income–expenditure flow into equilibrium. Because prices do not adjust, demand determines the level of production, which in turn determines the level of employment, which may or may not be at full employment.

The similarity between the two models is depicted by point *K′*, *C′*. If prices are somewhat flexible or somewhat rigid, the relevant section of *AS* will be *AB*. As the AD_K curve increases, it could move to AD'_K and experience a partial rise in prices. The AD_C curve could decline to AD'_C and experience less than a complete market equilibrium drop in prices. Thus, under the right conditions, the models can result in the same equilibrium aggregate prices and output.

Although the models may generate the same outcome, the processes by which the equilibrium is reached are quite different. The classical model relies on price movements, even when subject to constant price conditions, while the Keynesian model relies on adjustments through real income or output, even when subject to perfectly flexible price conditions. The different adjustment mechanisms have profound consequences for policy prescriptions. The classical model supports measures to allow the free working of markets, to reduce impediments to the price system. The Keynesian model advocates policy to affect demand, to bolster spending in a recession or decrease spending in an inflationary state in order to bring the economy to full employment with stable prices.

THOMAS P. POTIOWSKY

See also:

Aggregate Demand–Aggregate Supply Model and Diagram; Classical Economics; Consumption and the Consumption Function; Depression, The Great; Hansen, Alvin, H; Hicks, Sir John R.; IS/LM Model and Diagram; Keynesian Revolution; Klein, Lawrence R.; Modigliani, Franco; Quantity Theory of Money; Samuelson, Paul A.; Say's Law.

Bibliography

Cochrane, James L. (1970), *Macroeconomics Before Keynes*, Glenview, Ill.: Scott, Foresman and Company.

Froyen, Richard T. (1993), *Macroeconomics, Theories and Policies*, 4th edn, New York: Macmillan.

Hansen, Alvin H. (1953), *A Guide to Keynes*, New York: McGraw-Hill.

Hicks, John (1967), *Critical Essays in Monetary Theory*, Oxford: Clarendon Press.

Hicks, Sir John (1974), *The Crisis in Keynesian Economics*, New York: Basic Books.

Klein, Lawrence R. (1966), *The Keynesian Revolution*, 2nd edn, London, Macmillan.

McConnell, Campbell R. and Stanley L. Brue (1990), *Economics: Principles, Problems and Policies*, 11th edn, New York: McGraw-Hill.
Samuelson, Paul A. and William D. Nordhaus (1989), *Economics*, 13th edn, New York: McGraw-Hill.

Aggregate Demand–Aggregate Supply Model and Diagram

Determining the price level and output of the macroeconomy

Aggregate demand (*AD*) and aggregate supply (*AS*) are macroeconomic concepts for studying output and price level determination. The aggregate demand function indicates how demand for the aggregate output varies with the economy's price level. The aggregate supply function indicates how the aggregate output which firms wish to produce varies with the economy's price level. The intersection of the two curves representing these functions determines the equilibrium price level P_o and real output level Y_o for the economy. Figure 1 shows typical aggregate demand and supply curves. The vertical axis P represents the economy's price level while the horizontal axis Y represents the level of real output.

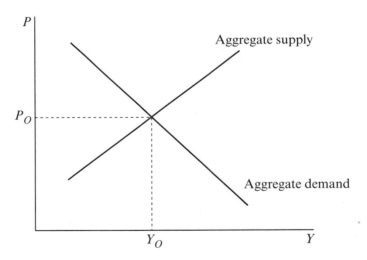

Figure 1   Typical aggregate demand and aggregate supply curves

The essentials of macroeconomics (leaving trade aside) 'lie in the interactions among the goods, labor and assets markets of the economy' (Dornbusch and Fischer, 1990, p. 3). We will now investigate the relation of the *AD–AS* model to this general three-market foundation of macroeconomics.

The relation of the aggregate demand function to the goods and money markets and the IS/LM model

The demand side of the economy arises from the interaction of the goods market and the money market. Equilibrium in the goods market can be characterized by:

$$Y = C + I + G$$

where Y represents the real output or income, C the consumption, I the investment and G the government spending. The standard approach is to take consumption as a function of income (and possibly the interest rate) and investment as a function of the interest rate i. That is:

$$C = C(Y, i)$$

and

$$I = I(i)$$

Combining these equations and taking the government spending as a parameter yields the following equation for the goods market:

$$Y = C(Y, i) + I(i) + \overline{G} \tag{1}$$

The money market gives the relationship of the real money supply (M/P) to the real money demand called the liquidity function L, which is a function of income and the interest rate. Therefore the money market equilibrium is

$$\frac{\overline{M}}{P} = L(Y, i) \tag{2}$$

Assuming G and M to be exogenous variables, we will have equations (1) and (2) for goods and money markets, respectively, and three unknowns Y, i and P. Equation (1) characterizes the equilibrium in the goods market (*IS*), while equation (2) characterizes the equilibrium in the money market (*LM*).

For any given level of P, equation (1) can be graphed as an *IS* curve in Y–i space, and equation (2) as an *LM* curve. Together they will give a solution for an equilibrium Y_0 and i_0, for that P. This is the standard IS/LM model, where P is taken as an exogenous variable or parameter.

Now let us consider varying P. For each level of P, there will be an *IS* curve from equation (1), which will be the same curve for all levels of P, since the equation is not dependent on P. The *LM* curve from equation (2), on the other hand, will move as P changes. This is illustrated in Figure 2.

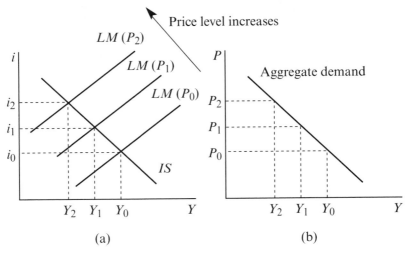

Figure 2   Derivation of the aggregate demand function

Part (a) of Figure 2 shows the *IS* and *LM* schedules for different price levels and their corresponding intersections. When the price level is P_0 the goods and money markets are simultaneously in equilibrium at the interest rate i_0 and the aggregate demand for the output Y_0. The same applies to all of the other intersections of the *IS* and *LM* curves. As the price level rises from P_0 to P_1, and on to P_2, the *LM* schedule shifts up to the left since the real value of the money stock falls. This will give rise to a corresponding decline in aggregate demand for the output from Y_0 to Y_1 and on to Y_2. Part (b) of Figure 2 shows the locus of all equilibrium demands for output from the IS/LM curves at different price levels. It is immediately obvious that the IS/LM model which traces the equilibrium conditions for the goods and money markets can be the building-block of the aggregate demand schedule.

Many economists find that graphical representations such as the one we have just provided promote intuition concerning the aggregate demand curve. A different approach would be to proceed algebraically from equations (1) and (2). Given two equations and three unknowns, Y, i and P, one can combine these equations to eliminate any one of the three variables. Choosing to eliminate i yields a single equation relating P and Y, and this equation is the aggregate demand function.

The relation of the aggregate supply function to the labour market and the production function

The supply side of the economy arises from the interaction of the labour market and the production function. To acquire the aggregate supply function, let us first consider the production function. The production function establishes the output as a function of labor and capital, and we will take capital to be fixed. Thus the production function is:

$$Y = F(N, \overline{K}) = F(N) \tag{3}$$

where N is the employment and K is the capital.

The second component required for the construction of the aggregate supply function is the labor market. The demand for labor is taken to be a function of the real wages or the marginal productivity of labor. It is economically clearer if we write out the inverse function, since that is simply the derivative of the production function:

$$W = PF'(N^D) \quad \text{or} \quad \frac{W}{P} = F'(N^D) \tag{4}$$

where W is the money wage, N^D is the labor demand and $F'(N)$ is the marginal productivity of labor.

The equilibrium condition for the labor market is:

$$N^D = N^S = N \tag{5}$$

where N^S is the labor supplied and N is a label for the common labor demanded and supplied. This allows us to rewrite (4) as:

$$\frac{W}{P} = F'(N) \tag{6}$$

The 'Classical case'
The supply of labor can be taken as a function of either the real wage or the nominal wage. In the former case we have.

$$N^S = L^S\left(\frac{W}{P}\right) \tag{7}$$

or by (5):

$$N = L^S\left(\frac{W}{P}\right) \tag{8}$$

The standard graphical solution to (3), (6) and (8) for N, (W/P) and Y is shown in Figure 3. Here (6) and (8) solve for N_0 and $(W/P)_0$ and that N_0 gives

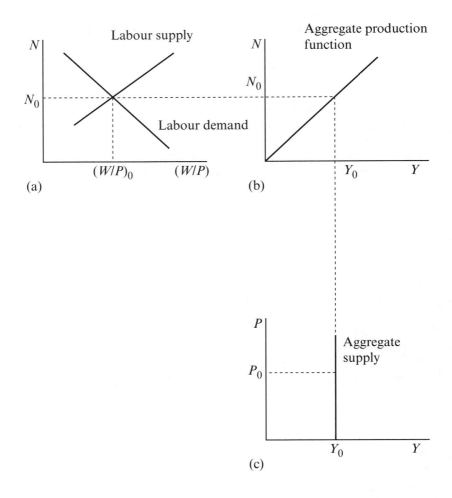

Figure 3   Derivation of the Classical aggregate supply function

Y_0 by (3). For any equilibrium P_0, one gets the same Y_0 (W must adjust by some mechanism, not specified here, to give the unchanging $(W/P)_0$ as P changes). This is referred to as the *Classical case*, or the *vertical supply curve case*. Total output Y_0 is determined strictly on the supply side by the interaction of the labor market and the production function. The *AD–AS* graph shown in Figure 4 illustrates that in this case the aggregate demand then determines the price level in the economy.

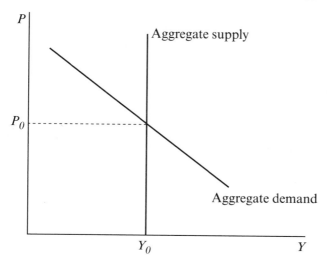

Figure 4   The Classical aggregate demand and aggregate supply

The 'Keynesian case'
Finally we return to consider the case where the supply of labor is affected by the nominal wage. Let

$$N^S = L^S(W) \quad with \quad (L^S)' > 0 \tag{9}$$

or, letting g be the inverse of the function of L^S,

$$W = g(N^S) \quad where, from\ (9) \quad g' > 0 \tag{10}$$

Dividing by P and using (5) then gives:

$$\frac{W}{P} = \frac{1}{P} g(N) \tag{11}$$

For a given P, we can find the intersection of the labor supply and demand curves as before, and then get Y_0 from the N_0 by the production function. This will give one point P_0, Y_0 on the supply curve, as shown in Figure 5. Now consider an increase in price level to P_1. The labor demand curve is unaffected in the (W/P)–N space, but from equation (11) we see that the labor supply curve will move as indicated in Figure 5. This yields new equilibrium values N_1 and Y_1 and a second point (P_1, Y_1) on the aggregate supply curve. This is referred to as the *Keynesian case*. The resulting Keynesian *AD–AS* graph, shown in Figure 1, indicates that now demand does affect real output. Output and price level are

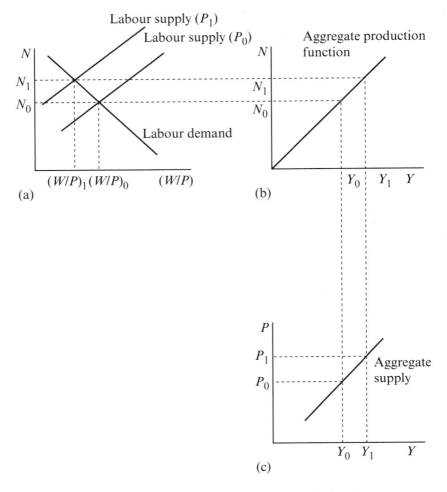

Figure 5   Derivation of the Keynesian aggregate supply function

determined simultaneously by the interaction of the supply and demand sides of the economy. In particular, expansionary fiscal or monetary policies which move the *AD* curve out will result in expansion of the real output in the Keynesian case, where such policies would only generate inflation in the Classical case considered above. Stripped to its barest essentials, the *AD–AS* presentation brings out the heart of the debate between the 'interventionist Keynesian' and the 'laissez-faire Classical' approaches.

HAMID AZARI-RAD
D.A. CAMPBELL

See also:

Classical Economics; Fiscal Policy; Hansen, Alvin H.; Hicks, Sir John R.; IS/LM Model and Diagram; Keynesian Cross; Keynesian Revolution; Monetary Policy; Neoclassical Synthesis (Bastard Keynesianism).

Bibliography

Dornbusch, R. and S. Fischer (1990), *Macroeconomics*, 5th edn, New York: McGraw-Hill.
Levačić R. and A. Rebmann (1989), *Macroeconomics: An Introduction to Keynesian–Neoclassical Controversies*, 2nd edn, London: Macmillan.

Arrow, Kenneth J.

Kenneth J. Arrow was born in New York City in 1921. After graduating from the City College of New York in 1940, he went to study at Columbia University, receiving his MA in 1941 and PhD in 1951. He worked as Research Associate at the Cowles Commission for Research in Economics in the University of Chicago from 1947 to 1949, and was appointed in 1949 Associate Professor and later Professor of Economics and Statistics at Stanford University. He was Professor of Economics at Harvard University from 1968 to 1979 and then returned to Stanford University as Joan Kenney Professor of Economics and Professor of Operations Research, from which post he retired in 1991. He received the Nobel Prize in the Economic Sciences in 1972.

Kenneth Arrow stands as one of the most profound and influential economists in the entire history of economic doctrines, celebrated for his originality, clarity of mind and technical ability. His contributions to economics cover virtually every branch of economic theory, ranging from social choice and justice to general equilibrium theory, from production and capital to individual choice under uncertainty, and areas in applied economics such as the economics of information and the economics of medical care. The magnificent scope of his accomplishments is exemplified in *Collected Papers of Kenneth J. Arrow*, published by Harvard University Press, 1983–5.

Arrow's work harmoniously blends his deep concern regarding social problems, indelibly written in his heart from the Depression, during which he grew to maturity, with logical precision and coherence, areas in which he was blessed with innate propensity and ability. He was first concerned with problems regarding the development of economic planning, a task he saw as synthesizing economic equilibrium theory, statistical methods and criteria for social decision making. His earliest works, however, went far beyond the narrowly defined scope of the development of economic planning, bringing about a decisive enlargement and deepening of the premises of economic theory as a whole, and, concurrently, bringing to economic reasoning the highly advanced mathematics and sophisticated logic which would be indispensable in solving the complex problems arising in the new realm of economic theory as posited by Arrow.

Social Choice and Individual Values (1951), Arrow's first major work, concerns the problem of how social choice may consistently be made in a democratic society. It is set in an inspiring model of formal logic, clarifying the logical and social implications of two basic modes of social choice: voting, typically used to make 'political' decisions, and the market mechanism, traditionally used to make 'economic' decisions. Arrow's conclusions are summarized as the pessimistic *Impossibility Theorem*, precluding the processes of consistent social choice, excepting the cases of dictatorship and convention. Arrow's *Social Choice and Individual Values* opened an entirely new dimension and vista, bringing to the fore the traditional concern of economists with the issues of justice and equity, and initiating a new and important branch in economic theory, which has since attracted an ever-increasing number of first-rate economists and philosophers, from I.M.D. Little, John Rawls and Robert Nozick to Ken-ichi Inada, A.K. Sen and Kotaro Suzumura.

Arrow's concern with general equilibrium and related topics led to the publication of a large number of articles from the late 1940s to the early 1980s, each noted for the scope and depth of the economic problems handled and for the ingenuity of the analytical methods which effectively solved the problems posed. Among them, particularly important is the seminal paper jointly written with Gerard Debreu, 'Existence of an Equilibrium for a Competitive Economy' (1954). In this paper, the general equilibrium for a competitive economy, originally introduced by Léon Walras, is formulated in terms of a logically consistent mathematical model, which captures the essential working of the capitalist market economy and illuminates the intricate processes of the market mechanism. The Arrow–Debreu paper also introduced new and powerful mathematical concepts and analytical tools, which have since come to play a crucial and indispensable role in economic theory.

Arrow has since extended this analysis of competitive equilibria to include such matters as dynamic processes for achieving a maximum and the stability of competitive equilibria, as described in *Studies in Resource Allocation Processes* (1977), jointly edited with Leonid Hurwicz.

Arrow has also given considerable attention to the problems of individual choice. He has written a number of articles which bring together the interest in choice shown in economics and in other social and behavioral sciences, particularly psychology. He has also worked on an extension of the theory of individual choice to include cases in which the consequences of actions are uncertain.

Arrow has written extensively on the subjects of production and capital, which are central to economic theory. Only a few articles may be noted here:

'Capital–Labor Substitution and Economic Efficiency', jointly written with H.B. Chenery, B.S. Minhas and R.M. Solow (1961, pp. 225–50); the famous CES function; 'Optimal Capital Adjustment' (1962a, pp. 1–17); 'The Economic Implications of Learning by Doing' (1962b, pp. 155–73); 'Criteria for Social Investment' (1965, pp. 1–8); 'Optimal Capital Policy with Irreversible Investment' (1968, pp. 1–20); and 'Uncertainty and the Evaluation of Public Investment Decisions' (1970, pp. 364–78).

The economics of information is another area in which Arrow has made substantial contributions. From his earlier years at Columbia, he has maintained an active interest in the foundations of statistical methods, mainly influenced by the works of Jerzy Neyman, Egon Pearson and, particularly, by Abraham Wald's *Statistical Decision Functions* (1950). Recognizing the inherent difficulties of framing the general theory of information as an economic commodity, primarily due to the absence of a common unit to measure different kinds of information, Arrow has nevertheless written prolifically on the economics of information, setting up the dimensions of the problems involved and proposing insightful approaches to certain specific cases.

Arrow has also written on a diverse range of topics drawn to his attention by the concerns of the time. Among these, his contributions to the economics of medical care and related subjects have not only had a permanent and decisive impact upon the way these problems are theoretically handled, but have also helped those engaged in the profession of medicine and health to orient themselves in the proper choice of actions to be taken.

This brief summary may not do justice to the depth, scope and ingenuity of Arrow's great works, or to his deep and compassionate concern with social and cultural issues. It is no exaggeration to say that the whole profession of economics owes a great debt to him; any economist today working in any subject in economics is strongly influenced by his thought and analysis.

HIROFUMI UZAWA

See also:

Government Investment Programs (the Socialization of Investment); Post Walrasian Economics.

Bibliography

Arrow, Kenneth J. (1951), *Social Choice and Individual Values*, New York: John Wiley.

Arrow, Kenneth J. (1962a), 'Optimal Capital Adjustment', in K.J. Arrow, S. Karlin and H. Scarf (eds), *Studies in Applied Probability and Management Science*, Palo Alto, CA: Stanford University Press.

Arrow, Kenneth J. (1962b), 'The Economic Implications of Learning by Doing', *Review of Economic Studies*, **29**, (86), June, pp. 155–73.

Arrow, Kenneth J. (1965), 'Criteria for Social Investment', *Water Resources Research*, **1**, pp. 1–8.

Arrow, Kenneth J. (1968), 'Optimal Capital Policy with Irreversible Investment', in J.N. Wolfe (ed.), *Value, Capital and Growth: Papers in Honour of Sir John Hicks*, Edinburgh: Edinburgh University Press.

Arrow, Kenneth J. and Gerald Debreu (1954), 'Existence of an Equilibrium for a Competitive Economy', *Econometrica*, **22**, (3), July, pp. 265–90.

Arrow, Kenneth J. and Leonid Hurwicz (eds) (1977), *Studies in Resource Allocation Processes*, New York: Cambridge University Press.

Arrow, Kenneth J., H.B. Chenery, B.S. Minhas and R.M. Solow (1961), 'Capital–Labour Substitution and Economic Efficiency', *Review of Economics and Statistics*, **43**, (3), August, pp. 225–50.

Lind, Robert C. and Kenneth J. Arrow (1970), 'Uncertainty and the Evaluation of Public Investment Decisions', *American Economic Review*, **60**, (3), June, pp. 364–78.

Wald, Abraham (1950), *Statistical Decision Functions*, New York: John Wiley.

Austrian School of Economics

The Austrian School of economics was a name given to the group that formed around the leadership of Carl Menger at the University of Vienna, beginning in the 1870s. Menger's pre-eminence was established as a consequence of his publishing *Principles of Economics* in 1871. In this book Menger demonstrated, in contradistinction to the British Classical School, that value was a relationship between the needs of individuals and the importance that they attached to the goods they believed would satisfy those needs. Value originated not in the good itself but in the subjective assessments of human beings. This insight, combined with his development of the notion that the value of an individual unit of a good declined as more units were acquired, led to Menger's being hailed, along with Jevons and Walras, as instigators of the marginal revolution.

Menger's initial subjectivist and marginalist perspective led him to develop theories of value, exchange and prices that seemed eminently compatible with similar developments in England and at Lausanne. It also inspired his two most famous associates, Friedrich von Wieser and Eugen von Böhm-Bawerk, to further develop aspects hinted at in Menger's work. Wieser developed the notion of opportunity cost, and extended marginalism to include a notion of diminishing marginal product of factors of production. Böhm-Bawerk is most noted for his development of a theory of capital that argued for the superior productivity of time-consuming methods of production, an approach inspired by Menger's discussion of capital as 'goods of a higher order'. Böhm-Bawerk's theory of capital later became the cornerstone of the Austrian theory of the business cycle as developed by a later generation of Austrian economists, Ludwig von Mises and Friedrich von Hayek.

The Austrian School has undergone significant evolution since the early days of Menger, Wieser and Böhm-Bawerk. During the 1920s the dominant figure in Vienna was Ludwig von Mises, whose early work on money and credit established him as a rising star of the Austrian School. For more than a decade, Mises conducted a regular seminar from his offices at the Austrian

Chamber of Commerce which attracted virtually all of the important economists in Vienna at one time or another. Among the regular participants were Fritz Machlup, Oscar Morgenstern, Gottfried Haberler and Friedrich von Hayek. While Machlup, Morgenstern and Haberler all acknowledged their ties to Austrian ideas, it was Hayek who emerged in the 1930s, upon his move to the London School of Economics, as the major representative of the Austrian School to the English-speaking world.

Hayek's move to England was precipitated by interest in his work on capital theory and his 'Austrian' theory of the trade cycle. Hayek's capital theory builds on Böhm-Bawerk to explain production as a series of time-consuming states that are at various distances from final production. His trade cycle theory explains booms and busts as the consequences of artificially low interest rates, brought about by excessive money expansion, that distort the structure of production and make current investment projects unsustainable in the long run. Until the publication of *The General Theory of Employment, Interest and Money* in 1936, Hayek was regarded as Keynes's major rival in macroeconomic matters. After 1936, Keynes's aggregate macroeconomics, with its interventionist policy implications, soon came to dominate Hayek's view that depressions were necessary corrections to previous malinvestment. Nevertheless, Hayek's approach has become a staple of modern Austrian economics.

Hayek's debate with Keynes and his followers over macroeconomic questions was only one of his two major preoccupations during his days at the London School of Economics. During the 1930s and early 1940s, Hayek also engaged in a lengthy debate with economists such as Oskar Lange, Abba Lerner and H.D. Dickinson over the economics of central planning that arguably led to his most important contribution to economics – Austrian or any other variety. The nub of Hayek's critique of central planning was an epistemological one: central planners could never garner enough information to allow them to bring about an effective plan that would take the place of market forces. Hayek's elaboration of this insight became known to Austrian economists as 'the knowledge problem'. In a nutshell, it posed the problem of the market order as follows: how is it that a decentralized decision-making regime based on a legal system of property and contract can generate order by allowing people to profit from their specialized and often tacit knowledge? This problem led Hayek, and Austrians in general, to conceive of market competition as a 'discovery procedure', a means of generating information about market data through a process of trial and error where profitability is a sign of success and loss is a sign of error. This process is assumed away in neoclassical economics with its assumption of 'given data'. As a consequence, neoclassical economics misunderstands the most important function of markets: to make it possible for actors to discover the information that is necessary to inform efficient action.

The Austrian School went into eclipse after 1945. By the end of the 1930s, most Austrian economists of a liberal persuasion left Austria to avoid Nazi persecution. Mises migrated first to Geneva and then to the United States in 1940. He settled in New York, where he began a weekly economics seminar at New York University which was to last two decades. Hayek left England in 1950 and moved to the University of Chicago, where he devoted his time to philosophy, political and social theory and psychology rather than economics.

During his American years, Mises's major scholarly contribution was his mammoth treatise on economics, *Human Action*. An attempt to deduce economic principles from the axiom 'all human action is purposeful', *Human Action* nevertheless emphasized the importance of uncertainty and entrepreneurship in explaining an ongoing market process in a way that was foreign to contemporary economic thinking. It also provided a defense of free markets that was unusual for its time. Mises's most famous American students, Israel Kirzner and Murray Rothbard, developed these aspects of his work, Kirzner in his lifelong work on entrepreneurship and Rothbard in his dedication to expounding the theory of the free market. Together, Rothbard and Kirzner generated enough academic interest in Mises's ideas and, by association, the ideas of the rest of the Austrian School for us now to be able to speak of an 'American Austrian School', as peculiar as that sounds. Austrian economics now stands for a set of ideas rather than the nationality of the economists.

Major tenets of the Austrian School
Modern Austrian economics is an attempt to elaborate the implications of a set of presumptions about the way human beings cope with the limitations of their environment. It is sometimes defined as 'radical subjectivism', to call attention to the fact that all human interaction with the environment is a process of interpretation that takes place within the individual's consciousness. Human beings not only make choices in the face of resource constraints, as neoclassical economics recognizes; they also make choices within a context of real time and with only limited knowledge about their circumstances. The knowledge they do possess, furthermore, is mostly concrete, particularized and sometimes tacit knowledge of time and place, as Hayek called it. The passage of time implies that action that is conceived in the present only unfolds in an unpredictable future. Hence all human action has an element of fundamental uncertainty about it. The passage of time also implies, however, that learning is a constant, endogenous process that continually affects human actions. The future may be unknowable and fraught with surprise, but human beings learn from their experiences to revise their plans to better achieve their purposes. In such a world, where knowledge is constantly changing, and actions adapt to new knowledge, Austrians argue that the

achievement of static equilibrium states is at best only a conceptual organizing tool of analysis.

Austrian economists have traditionally been dissatisfied with conventional equilibrium constructs. Mises argued that equilibrium was at best an analytic fiction that can be used as a foil to examine real market processes. Hayek tried to redefine equilibrium as the coherence of economic plans to bring some dynamism into the construct. More recently, Kirzner has argued that economic systems tend toward equilibrium without ever reaching such a state. To Kirzner, entrepreneurs, through their alertness to unexploited profit opportunities, are the equilibrators of the economic system. His further assumption that profit opportunities are endless guarantees a continuing, orderly market process.

A more radical note in Austrian economics has been sounded by Ludwig Lachmann and his followers, who argue that notions of equilibrium are inappropriate to explicating continual change. Rather we should view markets as a kaleidoscopic combination of order and change. Order is maintained by the existence of social institutions that allow individuals' expectations to be fulfilled in large measure. Change comes about because of continual learning that leads to innovative action. Currently, Austrians are divided on this issue, some siding with Kirzner and others with Lachmann. All agree, however, on the importance of entrepreneurial action, as well as on the central role of economic institutions in explaining how humans pursue their purposes. Furthermore, whatever metaphor is employed to capture the notion of economic order, unlike Post Keynesians who are also sensitive to the problems of real time in economic analysis, Austrians agree that market economies are in fact more orderly than not. Hayek has called the economy a 'spontaneous order', the unintended product of human action directed towards individual ends, thereby linking the Austrian School with Adam Smith and the Scottish Enlightenment, on the one hand, and with the new theories of self-ordering systems, on the other. Austrians further argue that the existence of progressive economic order depends on 'the rules of the game', a legal regime of property and contract, thus demonstrating their affinity with constitutional economics.

KAREN I. VAUGHN

See also:
Classical Economics; Interest, Theories of; Machlup, Fritz; Marshall, Alfred; Ricardo Effect; von Hayek, Friedrich A.

Bibliography
Hayek, F.A. (1948), *Individualism and Economic Order*, Chicago: University of Chicago Press.
Hayek, F.A. (1978), 'Competition as a Discovery Procedure', in *New Studies in Philosophy, Politics, Economics and the History of Ideas*, Chicago: University of Chicago Press.

Keynes, John M. (1936), *The General Theory of Employment, Interest and Money*, London: Macmillan.

Kirzner, Israel (1973), *Competition and Entrepreneurship*, Chicago: University of Chicago Press.

Lachmann, Ludwig (1971), *The Legacy of Max Weber*, Berkeley, CA: Glendessary Press.

Menger, Carl (1981) [1871], *Principles of Economics*, ed. J. Dingwall, trans. B.F. Hoselitz, New York: New York University Press.

Mises, L. von (1966), *Human Action: a Treatise on Economics*, 3rd edn, New York: Henry Regnery & Co.

O'Driscoll, Gerald P. Jr. and Mario J. Rizzo (1985), *The Economics of Time and Ignorance*, Oxford: Basil Blackwell.

Vaughn, Karen I. (1995), *Austrian Economics in America: The Migration of a Tradition*, Cambridge: Cambridge University Press.

Automatic Stabilizers

The General Theory of Employment, Interest and Money, first published in 1936, provided the foundation that led to Keynesian macroeconomic policies. Beginning with the market crash of 1929 and continuing through the 1930s, the world was in the midst of a severe economic depression and there was worry that western economies had matured and might be unable to maintain economic growth. Geographic expansion and colonization appeared to be at a halt; moreover, no new technological advances, like the steam engine, electricity or the automobile, seemed visible in the future.

Many economists feared economic stagnation during which nations might continue in depression indefinitely. Along these lines Keynes argued that governments should play a major role in stabilizing the economy and promoting full employment; that governments should divide their budgets into two parts, a current budget which is always in balance and a capital budget which would be used to stabilize national investment; and that the increased role of governments could be justified by the multiplier process.

The multiplier demonstrates the chain reaction in spending, or the magnified effect that occurs when a change in autonomous spending occurs. When discussing the multiplier process there are at least three important points to keep in mind: first, there are only two things which can be done with an increment of income – you may spend it or you may save it; second, one person's spending is someone else's income; third, in its most simple form, the value of the multiplier is a function of the marginal propensity to consume. For example, if autonomous spending were to increase by one dollar and if the marginal propensity to consume is equal to 0.75, then income will eventually increase by four dollars. The principle of the multiplier coupled with Keynes's ideas for government investment projects form the basis of Keynesian countercyclical policy: increase expenditures during a recession for the purpose of increasing employment and decrease expenditures during an expansion for the purpose of decreasing the rate of inflation.

There are two types of government fiscal intervention that can be used to stabilize the economy: discretionary intervention and non-discretionary intervention. Discretionary stabilizers, such as increases in government expenditures in the form of public works projects, require that laws be passed and carried out. When discretionary policies are employed, there is usually a time lag between the occurrence of a recession, its recognition and, finally, the application of appropriate fiscal policy. These time lags tend to make the discretionary fiscal policy ineffective.

Non-discretionary stabilizers, also called 'automatic' or 'built-in' stabilizers, are distinguished from discretionary stabilizers in that they operate without any government deliberation about policy, and therefore without any decision-making lag time. For this reason, economists believe automatic stabilizers are more effective than discretionary stabilizers. Examples of automatic stabilizers include the progressive income tax, unemployment insurance, social security and some farm subsidies.

With a progressive income tax, the higher the income, the larger the percentage of that income that is paid in taxes, the smaller the percentage of income that is available to consumers and investors, and the smaller the multiplier effect. During periods of declining economic activity, the percentage of income paid in taxes is less and, conversely, the multiplier is increased. To illustrate the effectiveness of the progressive income tax as an automatic stabilizer, it has been estimated that total tax receipts decrease by about two and a half billion dollars for every decrease of 10 billion of gross domestic product (GDP). The higher the progressive income tax rate, the greater the automatic stabilizer effect.

Unemployment insurance is another example of an automatic stabilizer. Total unemployment insurance payments increase when more people are unemployed, thus giving the unemployed money to spend they otherwise would not have, which, in turn, stimulates the economy. Unemployment insurance payments are usually provided for up to 26 weeks, but during times of high, prolonged unemployment they may be extended for additional weeks. In the United States this extension of unemployment insurance payments requires Congressional action. In this instance, there is in effect a combination of an automatic stabilizer with discretionary fiscal policy.

Other US automatic stabilizers include social security payments to the elderly, food stamps for the poor, Medicaid, support for families with dependent children and selective farm support programs. Similar to unemployment payments, these direct transfers offset the lowness or absence of income, and the consequent expenditures stimulate the economy. Income support payments are greater during periods of low economic activity. In contrast, when GDP is growing, there are fewer people in need of income support, and payments of this kind are less.

The first major fiscal intervention in the US economy occurred during the Great Depression. Roosevelt increased government expenditures in order to stimulate employment and production. Expansion of federal expenditures did indeed occur in a variety of programs, such as the Civilian Conservation Corps, the Public Works Administration and others, but the total was only approximately the same as the amount of decreases in expenditures by state and local governments during the depression. The advent of World War II provided a more comprehensive test of Keynes's theory. The total commitment of resources including government spending resulted in civilian unemployment dropping from 14.6 per cent in 1940 to a record low of 1.2 per cent in 1944.

Keynesian fiscal policy, including the operation of automatic stabilizers, is given significant credit for economic stability and growth after World War II. The actual institutionalization of a role for government in the management of the economy came with the Employment Act of 1946 and the creation of the Council of Economic Advisors. Albert Hart, economist for the Committee on Economic Development (CED), was influential in making automatic stabilizers an important part of a CED study report that same year. The idea of built-in flexibility was especially appealing and there was widespread public acceptance of the need for stabilization policies as well as the belief that they could be successful (Collins, 1981, p. 143).

Arthur Okun, Chairman of the President's Council of Economic Advisors in the 1960s, found that periods of expansion for the 30 years after the war were approximately twice as long as those experienced during the period 1854–1937. Postwar contractions were only about half as long in comparison with those of the same prewar period. Since 1950, there have been recessions in 1953–4, 1957–8, 1960–61, 1969–70, 1973–5, 1980, 1981–2 and 1990 (Peterson, 1987, p. 1591). According to Keynes, government would have deficits during years of recessions and build up surpluses during periods of recovery or peaks. In fact, that has not occurred, owing to many other factors that have caused the federal government to operate with deficits in almost every year since 1950.

Today, automatic stabilizers have come to be an accepted form of government intervention in the United States. They are believed to be effective in reducing the severity of economic fluctuations; they are less subject to political debates once the machinery for making the fiscal actions automatic is in place; and they avoid the injurious time lag problem of discretionary fiscal policy.

JACK MORGAN

See also:

Demand Management; Depression, The Great; Fiscal Policy; Hansen, Alvin H.; Keynes, John Maynard; Multiplier Effect; Okun, Arthur M.; Real Balance Effect; Samuelson, Paul A.; Tobin, James; Treasury View.

Bibliography

Collins, Robert M. (1981), *The Business Response to Keynes, 1929–1964*, New York: Columbia University Press.

Estey, James A. (1956), *Business Cycles: Their Nature, Cause and Control*, 3rd edn, Englewood Cliffs, NJ: Prentice-Hall.

Keynes, John M. (1936), *The General Theory of Employment, Interest and Money*, London: Macmillan.

McCracken, Harlan L. (1961), *Keynesian Economics in the Stream of Economic Thought*, Kingsport, TN: Kingsport Press.

Peterson, Wallace C. (1987), 'Macroeconomic Theory and Policy in an Institutionalist Perspective', *Journal of Economic Issues*, **21**, (4), December, pp. 1587–1621.

Tobin, James (1983), 'Keynes' Policies in Theory and Practice', *Challenge*, **26**, (5), November–December, pp. 5–11.

Balance of Payments: Keynesian and Monetarist Approaches

Introduction

The balance of payments (BOP) summarizes a country's trade of goods, services and financial assets with the rest of the world. It can be understood as an accounting statement. Credit entries reflect inflows of foreign currency in a country and debit entries record outflows. It is divided into three parts: the current account, which captures the movements of goods, services and unilateral transfers of funds; the capital account, which registers the purchase and sales of financial assets including both official and private transactions; and changes in foreign reserves. Any difference that remains is allocated to statistical discrepancies. The BOP balance is zero since any transaction in it involves a debit and a credit in one of its accounts. BOP equilibrium exists when the current and capital account balances have a zero balance. Thus no change in foreign reserves take place. Any other position would imply that a deficit in one of the accounts is financed by the other accounts.

Two main approaches have been taken to analyse the dynamics of the BOP position: the Keynesian approach (KA) and the monetarist approach (MA). The approaches and the debate over them are summarized in Cooper (1969) and Caves and Johnson (1968). The KA, following Keynes's analysis, finds in income a determinant factor of the BOP. As a consequence, this approach emphasizes the trade balance and gives less importance to the capital account in explaining the behavior of the BOP. The MA sees in the supply and demand for money the main determinant of the BOP position. Thus disequilibria in the money market affect the level of national income and the different components of the BOP, especially foreign exchange reserves.

The focus of both schools is on the relationship that exists among income, prices, output, interest rates and the BOP. The difference is found in the mechanisms by which these variables affect the BOP.

The Keynesian Approach

Fritz Machlup (1943) adapted the basic Keynesian approach of income determination to an open economy, thus providing foreign trade multipliers. These are used to show how economic fluctuations, spread between countries, affect the BOP and could be countered by economic policy.

In a simple open-economy Keynesian model of income determination, the basic assumptions are sticky prices, fixed exchange rates, unemployment and a money supply that adjusts to variations in the aggregate demand for money. Aggregate expenditure (E) could be defined as:

$$E = C(Y, p) + I + G + (X(Y^*, p) - M(Y, p^*))$$

where * indicates foreign. Consumption (C), imports (M) and exports (X) are a function of disposable income (Y) and prices (p). Consumption and imports are endogenous since they depend on domestic income. Exports (X), investment (I) and government expenditures (G) are taken as exogenous. E will be equal to Y only if full employment exists. Following the standard Keynesian model, we can define consumption and imports as follows:

$$C = a + mpcY$$
$$M = m + mpiY$$

where a and m are the autonomous consumption and imports, respectively, and mpc and mpi are the marginal propensity to consume and marginal propensity to import. By manipulating these three formulas we can derive the basic multiplier:

$$Y = \frac{1}{mps + mpi}(a + I + G + X - m)$$

The above formula shows that the introduction of the foreign sector reduces the value of the multiplier by increasing the value of the denominator by mpi, but increases the value of the numerator by $(X - m)$. Thus the economy receives an expansionary stimulus from a trade surplus and a contractionary stimulus from a trade deficit. We can write the current account balance $(X - M)$ as:

$$(X - M) = X - m - \frac{mpi}{mps + mpi} \times (a + I + G + X - m)$$

To analyse the effect of the exogenous variables in the BOP, we could obtain the value of the multipliers by taking first derivatives of Y and $(X - M)$ with respect to the exogenous variable. An increase in one of the exogenous variables leads to multiplied increases in national income through the multiplier which now incorporates foreign repercussions. While the multiplier increases the level of domestic income, it worsens the trade balance by the fraction of increase in imports. An increase in exports will improve the level of income but this is partially offset by the increase in imports induced by the rise in income.

If we incorporate the role of savings (S) and government deficit (tax revenues $T - G = D$), then we can rewrite the previous equation by recalling the approach of leakages ($S + T + M$) and injections ($I + G + X$) as

$$S - D = S + (T - G) = (X - M)$$

The right-hand side shows that the current account is balanced by the difference between savings and government deficit. An important point that emerges, then, is that, even though the economy may be in equilibrium, it is not necessary that the current account be zero. Thus an important result proposed by this model is that, under a fixed exchange rate, domestic equilibrium does not require external balance. Furthermore, there are two major implications of the Keynesian analysis. The first is that the income effects are an important part of the balance of payment analysis and, therefore, of macroeconomic policy. The second is that it is possible to explain the international transmission of economic disturbances. This is so because, while exports are exogenous to one country, they are endogenous to another.

The monetary approach

The monetary approach to the balance of payments can be traced back to David Hume in the eighteenth century. It was revived first in the 1950s by James Meade, in the 1960s by Harry G. Johnson and Robert Mundell, and in the 1970s by Jacques Polak.

A simplified version of the typical monetary model considers a small economy operating at full employment with a fixed exchange rate and full integration of goods and financial markets. Under this system, interest rates and prices are taken from world values and, therefore, they are exogenously determined. The money supply (M_s) is typically defined as the product of the money multiplier (m_e) and the monetary base which is composed of bank reserves (BR) and the currency held by the public outside the banks (C).

$$M_s = m_e (BR + C)$$

These two terms, BR and C, are balanced by the assets of the central bank which are composed of foreign exchange holdings, acceptable international assets and domestic assets holdings. Thus central bank foreign exchange operations affect international reserves and the M_s because the seller (buyer) operates through commercial banks, thus expanding (contracting) the monetary base by the amount of the operation times the multiplier.

The money demand (M_d) is defined as the product of prices (p) and a function (F) which is determined by the level of real income (Y), interest rates (i) and expected inflation $(E\pi)$.

$$M_d = (p)[F(Y, i, E\pi)]$$

The M_d is positively related to Y, inversely related to i, the opportunity cost of money, and negatively related to $E\pi$. The higher the inflation, the lower is the real value of money and, therefore, the less willing people are to hold money. Equilibrium in the market is reached where $M_s = M_d$ or

$$me\,(BR + C) = (p)[F(Y, i, E\pi)]$$

This last formula shows that an increase in M_s would lead to an excess of money supply. This, in turn, leads to an increase in Y and expending which, in turn, increases domestic prices. This increase in prices under a fixed exchange rate leads to a deterioration of the balance of trade owing to a fall in exports and an increase in imports.

The presence of excess money also affects the capital account. The alternative to holding cash is to hold other financial assets, including foreign assets. As this happens, the capital account falls into a deficit which is balanced out by a decrease in foreign reserves. Foreign reserves decrease since they have to be sold to keep the exchange rate from devaluating. Thus this model contains an automatic mechanism by which equilibrium is restored in the money market: foreign reserves. Deficit or surplus do not exist in the long run.

The degree of international capital mobility and the share of non-tradable goods in the GNP also affect the adjustment in foreign reserves. If the first one is low and/or the second is high, then the speed of adjustment to monetary disturbances will be reduced. Thus monetary imbalance effects in the BOP will be affected by the exchanged rate system and by the degree of openness of both the goods and capital markets. Growth and external shocks will also have a direct effect in the BOP through their effect on the M_d. An increase in the country rate of growth tends to improve the BOP provided that domestic credit does not expand accordingly. Similarly, a positive external shock will affect the BOP through the effect is has on prices and consequently on the money demand. Trade policy can also be analysed by the same mechanism.

Differences, similarities and policy implications

Harry Johnson has seen in the changes in reserve the basic challenge to the KA. Keynesians predict that an increase in income and prices will increase imports and decrease exports, worsening the BOP, while an increase in domestic interest rates will improve it through capital inflows. The MA, however, will predict exactly the opposite. An increase in income or prices will increase the demand for money and so increase reserves, while an increase in interest rates will decrease the demand for money, causing a deficit in the BOP. In fact this opposition is only apparent. There is no contradiction in the underlying behavioral relations proposed by these two systems. There are, however, policy differences regarding the effects of changes in income on prices or output. With full employment and in the absence of capital mobility, no conflict exists between the two approaches. Keynesians will predict changes in output when income changes while monetarists will predict changes in prices. If income, price and interest are not considered exogenous, they will be determined within the equilibrium system, and this could be solved in both models. If they are exogenous, however, as the monetarists have proposed, p and i are determined by the world market, while Y reaches full employment through adjustments in domestic wages. Under these conditions, then, the MA best describes the BOP adjustment since the Keynesian model cannot explain the changes in reserves.

Conclusion

Monetarist and Keynesian approaches to the BOP do not necessarily imply different conclusions. Once the behavior of p, Y and i are determined in a given context, the effect of a change in an exogenous variable within that context can be analysed. If this is the case, the models will provide the same answer.

MARIA SOPHIA AGUIRRE

See also:
Adjustment Mechanisms of the Basic Classical and Keynesian Models; Davidson, Paul; Dornbusch, Rudiger; Friedman, Milton; Johnson, Harry Gordon; Keynes, John Maynard; Meade, James E.; Metzler, Lloyd A.; Mundell, Robert A.; Mundell–Fleming Model.

Bibliography
Caves, R.E and H.G. Johnson (eds) (1968), *Readings in International Economics*, Homewood, Ill.: Irwin.
Cooper, R.N. (1969), 'Macroeconomic Policy Adjustment in Interdependent Economics', *Quarterly Journal of Economics*, **83**, (1), February, pp. 1–24.
Johnson, H.G. (1961), 'Towards a General Theory of the Balance of Payments', *International and Economic Growth*, Cambridge, Mass.: Harvard University Press.
Kreinin, M.E. and L.H. Officer (1978), 'The Monetary Approach to the Balance of Payments: A Survey', *Studies of International Finance No. 43*, Princeton: Princeton University Press.
Machlup, F. (1943), *International Trade and the National Income Multiplier*, Philadelphia: Blakiston.
Meade, J.E. (1951), *The Theory of International Economic Policy, Vol. I: The Balance of Payments*, Oxford: Oxford University.
Mundell, R. (1968), *International Economics*, New York: Macmillan.
Mussa, M.L. and J.A. Frenkel (1985), 'Asset Markets, Exchange Rates and The Balance of Payments', in R.W. Jones and P.B. Kenen (eds), *Handbook of International Economics, Vol. II*, New York: Elsevier.
Polak, J.J. (1957), 'Monetary Analysis of Income Formation and Payment Problems', *International Monetary Fund Staff Papers*, **6**, (4), November, pp. 1–50.
Taylor, M.P. and R. McDonald (1992), 'Exchange Rate Economics: A Survey', *International Monetary Fund Working Papers*, **39**, pp. 1–57.

Baumol, William J.

William Jack Baumol was born in New York City in 1922, the son of Solomon and Lillian (Itzkowitz) Baumol. As they were Jewish immigrants from Russia, Baumol's family background disposed him to a belief in the analytical and redemptive power of Marxism. Although his parents' view of the Soviet Union had been soured by the Hitler–Stalin pact, their commitment to human dignity and belief in the liberating potential of economic progress was adopted by their son. A pragmatist, Baumol's acceptance of neoclassicism has more to do with its explanatory power than with any ideological predisposition.

Baumol married Hilda Missel in 1941, while an undergraduate at City College of New York, and is the father of a daughter and a son. After graduating (1942), he working for the US Department of Agriculture (1942–3, 1946) and completed his PhD at London University in 1949. Baumol went to Princeton in 1949. He is at present a senior research economist there, having received the emeritus rank in 1992. Baumol also has an appointment at New York University, and has commuted between Princeton and New York City since 1971. Baumol has been awarded a number of honorary degrees from both European and American Institutions.

Over the course of his academic career, Baumol has received a number of fellowships and academic awards. He has also provided leadership to professional associations, including the presidencies of the Atlantic Economic Society, the American Economic Association, the Eastern Economic Association and the Association of Environmental Resource Economists, and the vice-presidency of the American Association of University Professors.

Baumol has made numerous theoretical contributions to welfare theory (1979(b); 1969; 1972, with Bradford). Moreover, a common theme of his work has been the application of welfare economics to situations of market failure such as the well known sales maximization hypothesis (1961) and the concept of contestable markets, which views easy entry and exit rather than numerous sellers as the prerequisite to efficient (that is, competitive) behavior, (1982; 1983, with Panzar and Willig; 1984, with Baile; 1986, with Willig; 1988, with Panzar and Willig; 1991, with Lee). Environmental policy also has emerged as an area to which Baumol devoted considerable thought after 1970 (1971(a); 1974; 1976; 1986(a); 1980, with Blackman; 1971, with Oates; 1988, with Oates), while problems of natural monopoly and regulation (1979(b); 1987, with Fischer; 1988, with Ordover; 1973, with Walton; 1988, with Wolff; 1994, with Wolff) and the economics of the arts (1969; 1971(a); 1986(d); 1980, with Baumol; 1992, with Rubenstien and Baumol) – a domain in which Baumol is also a practitioner – have been continuing concerns.

Baumol has made two major contributions to the analysis of stability and growth. The first involves his analysis of the demand for money (1952), an area where he, with Tobin, refined and extended the discussion in *The General Theory* (Keynes, 1936). Baumol viewed money as an inventory. He posited that holdings of cash will respond to the level of expenditures, and pointed out that, if cash is held to cover gaps between expenditures and receipts, scale economies will obtain, so that optimal cash holdings will increase only with the square root of receipts. Cash holdings also respond to interest rates and to the cost of exchanging cash for financial assets. This framework preserves the inverse relationship between money demand and the interest rate, but without Keynes's awkward distinction between speculative and transaction balances. Baumol's analysis is also consistent with the quantity theory's emphasis on the relationship between national income and the demand for money, but without the rigidity of the crude quantity theory.

The importance of Baumol's money model is evidenced by the fact that it was still an active topic in the literature more than 30 years after its initial publication (Baumol, 1989, with Tobin; Beckman and Forman, 1988). In the evolution of macroeconomics, moreover, it marks the beginning of mainstream efforts to reintegrate macro- and microeconomic theory using Marshall's convention of the representative agent. Whether efforts to put Keynesian analysis in individual maximizing terms are helpful is debatable, but the path has certainly been followed by many.

While Baumol has made several assorted contributions to macroeconomic theory and method, including the use of input/output analysis, chaos theory and the Phillips Curve analysis (1989, with Benhabib; 1985, with Quant; 1994, with Sidak), his second major contribution centers on the issue of economic growth. Logically, an interest in growth can be traced back to an article which argued that productivity growth differentials between sectors have important fiscal implications (1967).

Although he had examined the relationship between productivity, growth and R&D (1983, with Panzar and Willig) and produced a series of works related to US productivity growth during the mid-1980s (1984; 1983, with Wolff), an article on productivity growth and the income convergence hypothesis marked the emergence of growth as a principal research focus for Baumol (1986(b)). That Baumol's attention was thus captured is not surprising. Many economists in the 1980s came to see the core of US economic problems as relating to trend more than the cycle. Baumol's interest in growth continued in a later series of papers (1988, with Wolff; 1989, with Wolff; 1989, with Blackman and Wolff).

Not surprisingly, in the light of the recent interest in Schumpeter, Baumol turned to the consideration of the sources of growth and developed a hypothesis concerning entrepreneurship (1990). The argument was expanded in a book (1993) which held that social incentives determine entrepreneurs' economic contribution by drawing them into productive activity or else into non-productive, even destructive occupations, such as rent seeking or crime. This work is of interest in demonstrating Baumol's willingness to use historical observation to demonstrate relationships, displaying a methodological eclecticism. The notion that social institutions can influence the effective supply of entrepreneurs does not require a rejection of income convergence, but it at least raises the possibility of endogenous growth, thus indicating Baumol's willingness to expand or modify his views in the light of logical and/or empirical evidence.

An additional area of continuing interest for Baumol, which has both macroeconomic and microeconomic dimensions, is equity. A principal work here is his text *Superfairness* (1986(c)), in which Baumol develops a theory for explicitly considering distributional concerns in economic analysis. In it distributional goals are tied to the preferences of individuals in the same way that consumer preferences underlie the theory of consumer choice. Baumol believes that fairness can and should occupy a larger place in economic analysis and offers suggestions on how that might be accomplished.

It would be remiss to summarize Baumol's contribution without mentioning his role as a teacher of economics. Former students consistently praise his skill and enthusiasm in the classroom. He is the co-author of a principles text, the success of which was due in part to pedagogical innovations in the presentation of the macroeconomic analysis (1979, with Blinder). His *Economic Dynamics* (1951) and *Operations Research and Economic Analysis* (1961) were familiar resources to a generation of graduate students. Beyond attracting people to the discipline, he has almost certainly succeeded in persuading many that economics is not an intellectual puzzle or game, but a tool to be used in solving human problems.

ROBERT D. LEY
L.E. JOHNSON

See also:

Interest, Theories of; Keynes, John Maynard; Markowitz, Harry M.; Money; Schumpeter, Joseph A.; Sharpe, William F.; Tobin, James.

Bibliography

Baumol, William J. (1951), *Economic Dynamics*, New York: Macmillan.
Baumol, William J. (1952), 'The Transaction Demand for Money: An Inventory Theoretic Approach', *Quarterly Journal of Economics*, **66**, November, pp. 545–56.
Baumol, William J. (1961), *Operations Research and Economic Analysis*, Englewood Cliffs, NJ: Prentice-Hall.
Baumol, William J. (1966), *Performing Arts, The Twentieth Century Fund*, New York: The Twentieth Century Fund.
Baumol, William J. (1967), 'Macroeconomics of Unbalanced Growth: The Anatomy of Urban Crisis', *American Economic Review*, **57**, pp. 414–26.
Baumol, William J. (1969), 'On the Social Rate of Discount: Comment on the Comments', *American Economic Review*, **59**, (5), December, p. 30.

Baumol, William J. (1971a), 'Economics of Athenian Drama: Its Relevance for the Arts in a Small City Today', *Quarterly Journal of Economics*, **85**, (3), August, pp. 365–76.

Baumol, William J. (1971b), 'Environmental Protection at Minimum Cost', *American Journal of Economics and Sociology*, **30**, (4), October, pp. 337–44.

Baumol, William J. (1974), 'On Taxation and the Control of Externalities: Reply', *American Economic Review*, **64**, (3), June, p. 472.

Baumol, William J. (1976), 'It takes two to Tango, or Sind "Separable Externalities" Überhaupt Möglich?', *Journal of Political Economy*, **84**, (2), April, pp. 381–7.

Baumol, William J. (1979a), 'Quasi Optimality: The Price We Must Pay for a Price System', *Journal of Political Economy*, **87**, (3), June, pp. 578–99.

Baumol, William J. (1979b), 'Quasi-Permanence of Price Reductions: A Policy of Prevention of Predatory Pricing', *Yale Law Journal*, **89**, (1), November, pp. 1–26.

Baumol, William J. (1982), 'Contestable Markets: An Uprising in the Theory of Industry Structure', *American Economic Review*, **72**, (1), March, pp. 1–15.

Baumol, William J. (1984), 'On Productivity Growth in the Long Run', *Atlantic Economic Journal*, **12**, (3), September, pp. 5–10.

Baumol, William J. (1986a), 'On the Possibility of Continuing Expansion of Finite Resources', *Kyklos*, **39**, (2), pp. 167–79.

Baumol, William J. (1986b), 'Productivity Growth, Convergence and Welfare: What the Long Run Data Show', *American Economic Review*, **76**, (5), December, pp. 1072–85.

Baumol, William J. (1986c), *Superfairness*, Cambridge and London: MIT Press.

Baumol, William J. (1986d), 'Unnatural Value: or Art Investment as Floating Crap Game', *American Economic Review*, **76**, (2), May, pp. 10–14.

Baumol, William J. (1990), 'Entrepreneurship: Productive, Unproductive and Destructive', *Journal of Political Economy*, **98**, (5), part 1, October, pp. 893–921.

Baumol, William J. (1993), *Entrepreneurship, Management, and the Structure of Payoffs*, Cambridge and London: MIT Press.

Baumol, William J. and Elizabeth E. Baile (1984), 'Deregulation and the Theory of Contestable Markets', *Yale Journal of Regulation*, **1**, (2), pp. 111–37.

Baumol, William J. and H. Baumol (1980), 'On Finances of the Performing Arts during Stagflation: Some Recent Data', *Journal of Cultural Economics*, **4**, (2), December, pp. 1–14.

Baumol, William J. and Jess Benhabib (1989), 'Chaos: Significance, Mechanism and Economic Applications', *Journal of Economic Perspectives*, **3**, (1), Winter, pp. 77–105.

Baumol, William J. and Sue Anne Blackman (1980), 'Modified Fiscal Incentives in Environmental Policy', *Land Economics*, **56**, (4), November, pp. 417–31.

Baumol, William J. and Alan S. Blinder (1979), *Economics Principles and Policies*, New York: Harcourt Brace Jovanovich.

Baumol, William J. and David F. Bradford (1972), 'Detrimental Externalities and Non-Convexity of the Production Set', *Economica*, **39**, (154), May, pp. 160–76.

Baumol, William J. and Dietrich Fisher (1987), 'Peak Pricing Congestion and Fairness', in R. George Feiwel (ed.), *Arrow and the Foundations of the Theory of Economic Policy*, New York: New York University Press.

Baumol, William J. and Kyu Sik Lee (1991), 'Contestable Markets, Trade and Development', *World Bank Research Observer*, **6**, (1), January, pp. 1–17.

Baumol, William J. and Wallace E. Oates (1971), 'The Use of Standards and Prices for Protection of the Environment', *Swedish Journal of Economics*, **73**, (1), March, pp. 42–54.

Baumol, William J. and Wallace E. Oates (1988), *The Theory of Environmental Policy*, 2nd edn, with contributions by V.S. Bawa and David Bradford, Cambridge New York and Sydney: Cambridge University Press.

Baumol, William J. and Janusz A. Ordover (1988), 'Antitrust Policy and High-Technology Industries', *Oxford Review of Economic Policy*, **4**, (4), Winter, pp. 13–34.

Baumol, William J. and Richard E. Quandt (1985), 'Chaos Models and Their Implications for Forecasting', *Eastern Economic Journal*, **11**, (1), January–March, pp. 3–15.

Baumol, William J. and J. Gregory Sidak (1994), *Toward Competition in Local Telephony*, Cambridge and London: MIT Press/Washington, DC: American Enterprise Institute for Public Policy Research.

Baumol, William J. and James Tobin (1989), 'The Optimal Cash Balance Proposition: Maurice Allais' Priority', *Journal of Economic Literature*, **27**, (3), September, pp. 1160–62.

Baumol, William J. and Alfred G. Walton (1973), 'Full Costing Competition and Regulatory Practice', *Yale Law Journal*, **82**, (4), March, pp. 639–55.

Baumol, William J. and Robert D. Willig (1986), 'Contestability: Developments Since the Book', *Oxford Economic Papers*, NS, **38**, (0), Supplement, November, pp. 9–36.

Baumol, William J. and Edward N. Wolff (1983), 'Feedback from Productivity Growth to R & D', *Scandinavian Journal of Economics*, **85**, (2), pp. 147–57.

Baumol, William J. and Edward N. Wolff (1988), 'Productivity Growth, Convergence and Welfare: Reply', *American Economic Review*, **78**, (5), December, pp. 1155–9.

Baumol, William J. and Edward N. Wolff (1989), 'Three Fundamental Productivity Concepts: Principles and Measurement', in George R. Feiwel (ed.), *Joan Robinson and Modern Economic Theory*, New York: New York University Press.

Baumol, William J. and Edward N. Wolff (1994), 'A Key Role for Input–Output Analysis in Policy Design', *Regional Science and Urban Economics*, **24**, (1), February, pp. 93–113.

Baumol, William J., Sue Ann Blackman and Edward N. Wolff (1989), *Productivity and American Leadership: The Long View*, Cambridge and London: MIT Press.

Baumol, William J., John C. Panzar and Robert D. Willig (1983), 'Contestable Markets: An Uprising in the Theory of Industry Structure: Reply', *American Economic Review*, **73**, (3), June, pp. 491–6.

Baumol, William J., John C. Panzar and Robert D. Willig (1988), *Contestable Markets and the Theory of Industry Structure*, rev. edn, San Diego, London, Sydney, and Toronto: Harcourt Brace Jovanovich and Academic Press.

Baumol, William J., A.J. Rubenstien and Hilda Baumol (1992), 'On the Economics of the Performing Arts in the Soviet Union and the USA: A Comparison of Data', *Journal of Cultural Economics*, **16**, (2), December, pp. 1–23.

Beckman, Steve R. and Joshua N. Forman (1988), 'An Experimental Test of The Baumol–Tobin Transactions Demand for Money', *Journal of Money Credit and Banking*, **20**, (3), part 1, August, pp. 291–305.

Keynes, John M. (1936), *The General Theory of Employment, Interest and Money*, London: Macmillan.

Bloomsbury Group

The Bloomsbury Group takes its name from the Bloomsbury district of London, the area surrounding the British Museum, principally 46 Gordon Square. The term is a convenience for scholars and historians as well as for detractors when alluding to the collective ideals and conduct of the group. For some, the group is remembered principally for its outrageous behavior. Members of the group included Virginia and Leonard Woolf, Vanessa and Clive Bell, Lytton Strachey, John Maynard Keynes, Saxon Sydney Turner, Molly and Desmond MacCarthy, Adrian Stephen, Roger Fry, Duncan Grant, David 'Bunny' Garnett and E.M. Forster. They chafed against the stultifying norms of Victorian respectability, and the lengths to which they went to throw off its shackles, particularly in their sexual conduct, 'shocked' the nation, which is another way of saying that the group were avant-garde. The Bloomsbury Group was important because its individual achievements affected Britain's modernist taste in art and literature and its outlook towards economics and philosophy.

Upon the death in 1904 of Sir Leslie Stephen, founder of the *Dictionary of National Biography* (1882) and the foremost historian of nineteenth-century British intellectual life, his four children, Vanessa, Thoby, Virginia and Adrian, sold their house at the respectable Kensington address of 22 Hyde Park Gate and moved to 46 Gordon Square in bohemian Bloomsbury. The Bloomsbury Group formed in 1905 when Thoby Stephen began inviting friends who had been with him at Cambridge for 'Thursday Evening' conversations about current events in the world of art, literature and philosophy. Membership in the group can be traced back to at least three sources: the four children of Leslie Stephen; the Apostles (the Cambridge Conversazione Society), an intellectual society; and the Midnight Society play-reading group at Cambridge.

Thoby Stephen's tragic death of typhoid in 1906 drew the group closer together and precipitated Vanessa's marriage to Clive Bell. World War I and its dislocations interrupted the meetings. The group reformed in 1920, calling itself 'The Memoir Society', and began the practice of one of them reading a memoir, often a witty one, at each gathering. One of Keynes's contributions was 'My Early Beliefs', in which he questioned his belief in G.E. Moore's philosophy. This process of questioning is one step in Keynes's long journey from his *Treatise on Probability* (1921), based on a philosophy which espoused the reliance on personal choice as opposed to following rules in the pursuit of an objective good, to his position at the time of the *General Theory* (1936) that individuals were irrational, pursued multiple goals, held subjective degrees of belief about the future which were subject to sudden and violent shifts, and needed some rules in their lives.

In the area of economics, Keynes became a major force in shaping people's views of the workings of the economy. Of the four books which Keynes wrote during the inter-war period, two created a great deal of controversy. The first was *The Economic Consequences of the Peace* (1920), in which Keynes denounced the Versailles Peace Treaty as being a Carthaginian peace, a treaty which ignored the fact that the European economy performed well prior to the war because of the principle of the international specialization and division of labor, a treaty that would destroy friend and foe alike. The second was the *General Theory* , which argued that the traditional methods of political economy embodied in the phrase '*laissez faire* economics' did not promote full employment. If the private sector were unable or unwilling to do what was necessary to move the economy to full employment and to increase the average level of performance of the economic system, then the government was obliged to step in to do the job. The importance of these works is still being debated today.

In each of those books Keynes argued that the 'good' of the nation was no longer being served. Keynes's view of what was 'good' was influenced by the philosophy of G.E. Moore, who suggested that 'good' was a non-material property of things and that we 'intuit' its presence (Skidelsky, 1992). Moore's *Principia Ethica* in 1903 codified an ethic which Bloomsbury recognized as having been arrived at through two generations of discussions of the Cambridge Apostles, led by Moore. Desmond MacCarthy recalls that the Apostles discussed 'those "goods" which were ends in themselves ... the search for truth, aesthetic emotions and personal relations – love and friendship' (Gadd, 1974, pp. 21–2). Leonard Woolf calls Moore 'the only really great man whom I have ever ... known,' and says, 'Moore and the Society were the focus of my existence [at Cambridge]. They dominated me intellectually and emotionally' (1960, pp. 145, 171). The *Principia Ethica* blended Platonic ideal 'goods' with 'the divine voice of plain common sense' (L. Woolf, 1960, p. 162) from nineteenth-century Utilitarian realism (Rosenbaum, 1983, pp. 14–17). Woolf emphasized that the appeal of Moore's approach lay in its practicality. He rejected the impracticality of 'absolute good' (as in Plato's philosophy) in the formation of an ethic and insisted that each person inquire into what seemed to him 'intrinsically good' in order to shape his conduct (Regan, 1986, pp. 159–60). This is the source of the nonchalance with which Bloomsbury overthrew Victorian moral prescriptions. Moore held that an authority's declaration that something is 'good' ought not to be viewed as a 'command', but as a proposition to be proved by each person's experience (or intuition) (Regan, 1986, pp. 157, 159).

Moore's philosophy placed a premium on friendship unusual in formal ethical systems, and the Bloomsbury Group's practice of this ethic resulted in their closeness and loyalty. The nature of love was a favorite topic with the Apostles – Maynard Keynes says that it 'came a long way first' (Gadd, 1974, p. 53). Moore viewed friendship and 'affection' as 'organic unities', that is, as supreme 'goods' containing components that are less that beautiful, good or ideal: 'A whole composed of two great goods, even though one of these be obviously inferior to the other, may yet be ... decidedly superior to either by itself,' he wrote (Regan, 1986, p. 186). E.M. Forster evokes the synthesis of intellectual conversation and love that characterized Bloomsbury relationships. He says that, in his experience with the Apostles, 'People and books reinforced one another, intelligence joined hands with affection, speculation became a passion and discussion was made profound by love' (1934, p. 35). Forster's description is a fair account of the intensity of Bloomsbury friendships. The Bloomsbury Group perpetuated the Apostles' belief that their friendship and loves were supreme goods.

Bloomsbury conversations followed the Apostles' style of inquiry, and their discipline of speaking the truth of one's experience and insight translated in Bloomsbury into candor in expressing one's opinion; participants understood that speaking frankly was a higher 'good' than remaining silent because of consideration for a listener's feelings or conventional decorum. E.M. Forster's novel, *A Room With a View* (1923), portrays the 'goods' of which young characters' lives will be robbed if they are forced to observe conventions of respectability and refrain from speaking the truth of their affections. Virginia Woolf explores this theme in *To the Lighthouse* (1927). Candor in discussing sexual matters in mixed company reached unprecedented heights in Bloomsbury conversations. Also, as in the Apostles' debates, wit was prized almost as highly as truth. Lytton Strachey combined truth and wit in *Eminent Victorians* (1918); he wrote a factual account of the accomplishments of such Victorian heroes as General Gordon and Florence Nightingale, but at the same time satirized flaws in their personalities, effectively knocking them off their pedestals.

The group's mutual affection, frequent conversation and sharing of cultural events, reinforced by the intensity of love relationships that sprang up amongst them, go far to explain their impact in the formation of the aesthetics of modernism and Britain's post-World War I outlook in social philosophy as well as in economics. Maynard Keynes, Virginia Woolf and E.M. Forster are the only Bloomsbury members whose international fame will persist among laypersons into the twenty-first century, but it may be argued that the pursuits of all the group provided an environment that contributed to their accomplishments.

In aesthetics, the Bloomsbury Group introduced Modernist art to Britain. The First and Second Post-Impressionist Exhibitions mounted by Roger Fry at the Grafton Galleries in 1910 and 1912 inaugurated Formalism in British art – and outraged the British public. Fry had been curator of the Metropolitan Museum of Art in New York until 1909, a post he was forced to leave because he disapproved of the habit of J. Pierpont Morgan, when he accompanied Fry on European trips, of snapping up for his own collection the paintings Fry authenticated that the Metropolitan's budget could not accommodate. Since the Metropolitan's budget was largely funded by Morgan, there was little Fry could do to prevent his expertise being commandeered. The First Post-Impressionist Exhibition held in 1910 illustrated Fry's ideal of Significant Form, the 'attractions which draw the eye along a central line' in a picture – in other words, its hidden geometrical design. 'We may dispense once for all with the idea of likeness to Nature in art,' proclaimed Fry (1990, pp. 22, 27). The artists in the exhibition that so offended the critics were Cézanne, Van Gogh, Gauguin, Matisse and (as a sop to the public) Manet. Duncan Grant and Vanessa Bell helped Fry mount the 1910 exhibition, and Desmond MacCarthy acted as secretary–treasurer. Undeterred by the outrage of established British artists, Fry mounted a second exhibition in 1912, this time including British artists such as Vanessa Bell, Duncan Grant, Frederick and Jessie Etchells, and Wyndham Lewis, along with Cézanne, Picasso, Matisse, Derain and several

Russian painters. Leonard Woolf acted as secretary–treasurer of the exhibition. The 1912 exhibition was also greeted with shock and dismay but was nevertheless a financial success. One of the reasons for this success may be traced to the influence of Lady Ottoline Morrell, an art patron with close ties to Bloomsbury, who had raised interest in the exhibitions amongst her aristocratic acquaintances. 'Lady Ott' (for decades the mistress of Bertrand Russell, while also amusing herself with young artists and authors) contributed significantly to the survival of needy artists in Bloomsbury and Soho. She hung their pictures in her house, then invited the artists to soirees at which they not only could meet potential buyers, but were also liberally fed.

After the second exhibition, Fry was invited to publish a book defining his ideals of Significant Form, but he was too caught up in establishing the Omega Workshops to write the book. From 1913 to 1919, artists associated with the Omega subsidized their painting by designing fabrics, furniture, crockery and wallpaper for British interiors. Hence Fry turned the project of a book on Significant Form over to Clive Bell, who published *Art* in 1914. To make the situation even more complex, during the intensity of the Second Post-Impressionist Exhibition Vanessa Bell and Roger Fry fell furiously in love and began a two-year affair. Clive Bell, ever the *bon vivant*, had taken a string of mistresses and by 1912 the Bells were married in name only. They never divorced but remained close friends, maintaining the fiction of their marriage for the children's sake. Vanessa was temperamentally more suited to living and working with fellow artist Duncan Grant than with the frenetic and domineering Fry, however. At the beginning of World War I she took a lease on Charleston Farm in Firle, Sussex, where she gave shelter as conscientious objectors to Duncan Grant and his lover, 'Bunny' Garnett. Duncan and Vanessa were thereafter lifelong companions. Vanessa bore her third child to him in 1918, although Grant, like many of the Bloomsbury men, was primarily homosexual. The Woolfs' country cottage was nearby in Rodmell. Maynard Keynes had a bedroom at Charleston until his marriage to Lydia Lopokova, after which he leased Tilton Farm, also in Firle. Maynard, who had had an affair with Grant in 1908, admired Vanessa for the creativity and calm efficiency of her domestic arrangements, which may be viewed as a model of the sort of self-created ethic G.E. Moore endorsed. Keynes commissioned Duncan and Vanessa to decorate his rooms at Cambridge. (The male classical figures in their design were nude, the female ones clothed.) Keynes was also Vanessa's financial advisor. In 1920 he speculated, at first brilliantly, with Vanessa's and Duncan's modest assets as well as his own in the fluctuating European currency market he had predicted in *The Economic Consequences of the Peace*, but then his syndicate formed for this purpose went bankrupt and he had to perform fancy financial footwork to retrieve their money (Spalding, 1983, pp. 186–8).

Maynard Keynes wielded power in the political and financial worlds and was able to tap Leonard Woolf to draft documents upon which the League of Nations was based; in 1923, when Keynes became a publisher of the *Nation*, he chose Woolf as literary editor. There is no question of undeserved patronage here. Rather, their intimacy in the Bloomsbury Group gave Keynes a livelier appreciation than he otherwise would have had of Woolf's character, abilities, and accomplishments, as an assistant governor in Ceylon from 1904 to 1911, author of *Empire and Commerce in Africa* (1918), activity in the Labour Party, editor of the *International Review* and reviewer for the *Athenaeum* and the *Nation*. The Bloomsbury Group provided Keynes with the knowledge necessary to choose the right man for the job.

Virginia Woolf is recognized as one of the giants of British literary modernism (along with James Joyce, D.H. Lawrence, T.S. Eliot and Joseph Conrad – E.M. Forster escapes this classification because, although his themes are modernist, his technique has been viewed as conventional). Because of this eminence, Woolf has continued to be influential in literary aesthetics, whereas Bloomsbury Formalism in visual art has given way to later developments. Virginia Woolf and James Joyce concurrently explored the stream-of-consciousness technique, through which characters' unspoken thoughts and feelings are portrayed alongside what they say and do. Thus stream-of-consciousness added a layer of reality to the novel which had never before been available to readers, but which is instantly perceived as being 'true' to the reality we experience. Woolf is credited with surpassing Joyce in the portrayal of characters' depths of feeling, whereas Joyce excels in an erudite intellectual cleverness (another hallmark of literary modernism, promulgated by T.S. Eliot) that Woolf believed interfered with an emotional aesthetic response. In contrast to Joyce's intellectual complexity, Woolf held that characters should satisfy our common sense, a criterion that stems in part from Bloomsbury discussions of G.E. Moore's aesthetic. Her appeal to the common sense of the ordinary reader made her popular as a book reviewer, beginning in 1916, long before her fiction was widely noticed. Woolf recognized the ordinary reader's perceptions in entitling her essays collected into a volume *The Common Reader* (1925). Before *Mrs. Dalloway* (1925) made her famous, she reviewed books for a living. Her reviews appeared in the *Times Literary Supplement* as well as in the papers for which Leonard wrote. From the Woolfs' incessant reviewing of books came their authority in the literary world and the success of the Hogarth Press, which they started in 1917. Many works that are now well known, notably T.S. Eliot's *The Wasteland* (1923) and Sigmund Freud's *Collected Papers* (1924), were first published in volume form in England by the Hogarth Press.

SALLY A. JACOBSEN

See also:
Keynes, John Maynard; Keynes, The Influence of Burke and Moore on.

Bibliography
Forster, E.M. (1934), *Goldsworthy Lowes Dickinson*, London: Edward Arnold.
Fry, R. (1920), *Vision and Design*, reprinted 1990, ed. J.B. Bullen, London: Oxford University Press.
Gadd, D. (1974), *The Loving Friends: A Portrait of Bloomsbury*, New York: Harcourt Brace Jovanovich.
Keynes, John Maynard (1938), 'My Early Beliefs', in S.P. Rosenbaum (ed.), *The Bloomsbury Group: A Collection of Memoirs. Commentary and Criticism*, Toronto: University of Toronto Press.
Moore, G.E. (1903), *Principia Ethica*, reprinted 1968, Cambridge: Cambridge University Press.
Regan, T. (1986), *Bloomsbury's Prophet: G.E. Moore and the Development of his Moral Philosophy*, Philadelphia: Temple University Press.
Rosenbaum, S.P. (1983), 'Virginia Woolf and the Intellectual Origins of Bloomsbury', in E.K. Ginsberg and L.M. Gottlieb (eds), *Virginia Woolf: Centennial Essays*, Troy, NY: Whitson.
Skidelsky, Robert (1992), *John Maynard Keynes Hopes Betrayed 1883–1920*, New York: Viking.
Spalding, F. (1980), *Roger Fry: Art and Life*, Berkeley: University of California Press.
Spalding, F. (1983), *Vanessa Bell*, New Haven: Ticknor & Fields.
Woolf, L. (1960), *Sowing: An Autobiography of the Years 1880 to 1904*, New York: Harcourt Brace Jovanovich.
Woolf, V. (1985), *Moments of Being: Unpublished Autobiographical Writings*, ed. J. Schulkind, San Diego: Harcourt Brace Jovanovich.

Boulding, Kenneth E.

'Economist, philosopher, poet' is what the *New York Times Biographical Service* obituary called Kenneth Boulding, who died at the age of 83 in 1993. In fact, he was more than that: religious leader, romantic, wit, pacifist, enthusiastic public speaker (in spite of his stutter), teacher, author, family man and even water colorist, sculptor and composer. But all of these callings were integrated into the same function, which was the creation of the unique presence that gains him admission to this volume.

He was born to lower middle-class, politically active, Methodist parents in Liverpool, England. (His middle name, Ewart, memorializes the then Liberal Party leader, William Ewart Gladstone.) His intellectual brilliance was noticed early in his schooling and, at the age of 12, he won the Earl of Sefton Scholarship to Liverpool Collegiate School. In 1927, he won a scholarship to Liverpool University, but stayed on at the Collegiate School to enroll at New College, Oxford a year later, with an Open Major Scholarship in Natural Sciences. One year into his studies at Oxford, he switched from the study of chemistry to the humanities. In 1930, he won the Webb-Medley Junior Scholarship in Economics and by 1931 he had earned his BA with first class honours from the School of Philosophy, Politics and Economics.

It was to be his last truly earned degree. His MA, awarded from Oxford in 1939, was granted – as was the practice then – simply on the basis of elapsed time since graduation and the payment of a fee. His application for a DLitt degree from Oxford, based on his significant contributions to economics in the preceding years, was turned down in 1944. Academic respectability was to come his way, not through advanced degrees, although he eventually accumulated several dozen honorary doctorates, but through the power of his mind and pen. Already in 1938, while enjoying some early recognition in the United States, he wrote to a friend, 'How thankful I am that the special privilege I enjoy as a distinguished (?) foreigner makes me immune from the Ph. D. plague' (Kernan, 1974, p. 28).

And significant these writings were! In 1931, at the age of 22, he published his first article, 'The Place of the "Displacement Cost" in Economic Theory', in the *Economic Journal*, then under the editorship of John Maynard Keynes. From then on, the writings never stopped. His bibliography contains well over one thousand titles. (At one time he even proposed the formation of a Writers Anonymous for people like himself). So it is the reader's choice which are his most important contributions. Certainly among the most seminal, however, would be *Economic Analysis*, first published in 1941 and reissued through various editions until 1966. It integrated Keynesian macroeconomic analysis with classical microeconomics, establishing the pattern for virtually all textbooks to come for the rest of the twentieth century and setting the foundation for all future work dealing with the so-called 'neoclassical synthesis'. Perhaps even more important, its intellectual wit and humane charm gave the lie to the reputation of economics as a plodding or even dismal pursuit and must have recruited legions of good minds to the profession.

Economic Analysis was followed in quick succession through the years by such major works as *Economics of Peace* (1945), *A Reconstruction of Economics* (1950), *The Organizational Revolution* (1953), *The Image* (1956), *Principles of Economic Policy* (1958), *The Skills of the Economist* (1958), *Conflict and Defense* (1962), *The Meaning of the Twentieth Century* (1962), *Impact of the Social Sciences* (1966), *Beyond Economics* (1970), *Economics as a Science* (1970), *A Primer on Social Dynamics* (1970), *The Economy of Love and Fear* (1973), *Ecodynamics* (1981), *Human Betterment* (1985), *Towards a New Economics* (1992) and *The Structure of a Modern Economy* (1993) among many articles, religious writings and poems. As the titles indicate, questions of war and peace were a major concern. He had become a member of the Society of Friends (Quakers) in 1931 and, together with his wife, Elise Bjorn-Hansen, a professional sociologist, remained an active participant throughout his life, supporting, among many other such events, the Pugwash conferences of the 1960s.

After receiving his BA, Kenneth Boulding continued his studies on a Commonwealth Fellowship at the University of Chicago (1932–4) but interrupted them to take an appointment to teach at the University of Edinburgh in 1934. He returned to North America to teach at Colgate University (1937–41), to work for the league of Nations Economic and Financial Section in Princeton, New Jersey (1941–2), to teach again at Fisk University (1942–3) and Iowa State College (1943–6), to become Professor and Chairman of the Department of Economics at McGill University (1946–7), to return to Iowa State College (1947–9) – becoming a US citizen in 1948, and finally to settle for a while as Professor of Economics at the University of Michigan (1949–68). By that time, he had been recognized for his publications and been awarded the 1949 John Bates Clark Medal of the American Economic Association. During his Michigan years, he was to receive a Ford Foundation Fellowship, serve a year's fellowship at the Center for Advanced Study in Behavioral Sciences at Stanford University, form the Society for General Systems Research, establish the Center for Research on Conflict Resolution, together with its publication, the *Journal of Conflict Resolution*, and serve as visiting professor at the University College of the West Indies in Jamaica and as Danforth Visiting Professor at the International Christian University in Japan. He was also elected vice president – later to become president and chairman of the board – of the American Association for the Advancement of Science and President of the American Economic Association.

During these years, his far-ranging interests noticeably pulled him away from the narrowly orthodox concerns of the economics profession. 'The pursuit of any problem in economics always draws me into some other science before I can catch it', he wrote in *The Skills of the Economist* (p. 131). Some colleagues groused that 'He is much admired as an economist – by noneconomists' (Kernan, 1974, p. 22). And when confronted with the question, he responded, 'Oh, yes, I'm an economist – I *must* be – I'm President of the American Economic Association' (ibid.). In any case, his wit and charm distinguished him from the grayer practitioners of the profession, as when he deflated the neoclassical synthesists with his introductory verse to *Principles of Economic Policy*:

Our policy, to be effective,
Must chase a suitable objective,
So, our economy should be
Both Growing, Stable, Just, and Free.
The Dog would surely be a Dunce,
Who tried to chase four things at once,
Yet this is just the way we plan
The task of Economic Man!

By 1968, Kenneth Boulding had moved to the University of Colorado, where both he and his wife could teach. His writing and speaking tours continued unabated, while at the Institute of Behavioral Science and as Professor Emeritus of Economics there. During these Colorado years, he served as visiting professor at the University of Natal, South Africa, at the University of Edinburgh, Cornell University, Wellesley College, at the Lyndon B. Johnson School of Public Affairs of the University of Texas and at Dartmouth College. Nominated, but not designated, for both the Nobel Peace and Economics Awards, he was recognized by many other awards for his work for peace and his contributions to economics, including the Lentz International Peace award (1976), the Frank E. Seidman Distinguished Award in Political Economy (1976), the John R. Commons Award of the International Honor Society in Economics (1985), the eighteenth Boise Peace Quilt (with Elise Boulding, 1988) and the Mahatma Gandhi Prize for Non-violent Peace (1993).

In the obituary referred to above, Wassily Leontief said of Kenneth Boulding, 'He left economics. He became a universal philosopher.' If Kenneth Boulding did, indeed, leave conventional economics, he took it to new horizons, and many other economists went with him, to the eternal benefit of the science and of humanity.

MARTIN GERHARD GIESBRECHT

See also:
Keynes, John Maynard; Keynesian Cross; Keynesian Revolution; Neoclassical Synthesis (Bastard Keynesianism).

Bibliography
Boulding, Kenneth E. (1958), *The Skills of the Economist*, Cleveland, OH: Howard Allen.
Boulding, Kenneth E. (1958), *Principles of Economic Policy*, Englewood Cliffs, NJ: Prentice-Hall.
Kernan, Cynthia Earl (1974), *Creative Tension, The Life and Thought of Kenneth Boulding*, Ann Arbor: University of Michigan Press.
Nasar, Sylvia (1993), 'Kenneth Boulding, an Economist, Philosopher and Poet, Dies at 83', *New York Times Biographical Service*, 20 March, p. 389.
Solo, Robert A. (1994), 'Kenneth Ewart Boulding: 1910–1993. An Appreciation', *Journal of Economic Issues*, **28**, (4), December, pp. 1187–2000.
Wilson, Vivian (1985), *Bibliography of Published Works by Kenneth E. Boulding*, Boulder, CO: Colorado Associated University Press.
Wilson, Vivian (1993), *Curriculum Vitae* for Kenneth Boulding, correspondence with the author.

Bretton Woods

The United Nations Monetary and Financial Conference at Bretton Woods, New Hampshire, 1–22 July 1944, established the International Monetary Fund (IMF) and the International Bank for Reconstruction and Development (the World Bank) as cornerstones of a system of international cooperation for orderly balance of payments adjustments and postwar reconstruction. Exchange rates would be fixed, but adjustable in case of fundamental balance of payments disequilibrium, and IMF lending would help member countries to weather temporary payments problems. The Bretton Woods system was a gold exchange standard, with other central banks (but not the public) able to present their US dollar reserves to the Federal Reserve for gold at US$35 per ounce. Exchange controls were to be phased out, except in unusual circumstances. The major industrialized countries enjoyed a quarter-century of exchange rate stability, low inflation and near-full employment under the Bretton Woods system before its collapse in the early 1970s.

The fifth draft of Lord Keynes's 'Proposals for an International Currency Union' (1983, XXV) was published as an unsigned white paper on 7 April 1943, the same day as the US Treasury (prompted by a leak in a London newspaper) published Harry Dexter White's draft outlines of an International Stabilization Fund and a Bank for Reconstruction and Development. A Canadian plan (termed 'off White' by Keynes) appeared in June.

As in his 1925 opposition to Britain's return to the prewar gold parity, Keynes's wartime plan rejected the gold standard's straitjacket on domestic stabilization, while it would also avoid a return to the competitive, beggarthy-neighbor devaluations of the 1930s. Central bank management of a gold exchange standard went back in Keynes's thought as far as *Indian Currency and Finance* (1913). The proposed International Clearing Union creating *bancor*, an international currency supplementing gold in central bank reserves (like the Special Drawing Rights eventually issued by the IMF), revived Keynes's suggestion in *A Treatise on Money* (1930; 1983, VI, pp. 358–64) that the then new Bank for International Settlements issue such 'paper gold' to increase world liquidity. White's proposed international unit of account, unitas, would have been a receipt for gold deposited with the Fund, and would not have increased world liquidity as Keynes envisaged bancor doing.

The British delegation to Washington to discuss postwar monetary cooperation was led by Richard Law and included James Meade, Lionel Robbins and Dennis Robertson as well as Keynes, but their nine meetings with the US Treasury in September and October 1943 were dominated by Keynes and White. White's position in charge of foreign relations of the US Treasury in World War II resembled Keynes's role in the British Treasury in the previous war. Keynes and White displayed great mutual respect, yet sometimes behaved with extraordinary rudeness to each other, unnerving other negotiators at times, but not themselves. Keynes and White also took the lead at the preliminary meeting of experts from 15 countries at Atlantic City in June 1944 and at the Bretton Woods conference of 45 countries in July. At Bretton Woods, White chaired the commission on the IMF, Keynes the commission on the World Bank, and Eduardo Suarez of Mexico the commission on other forms of financial cooperation, with US Treasury Secretary Henry Morgenthau, Jr. chairing the full conference. Despite a mild heart attack on 19 July, Keynes delivered an impressive closing speech, amid much applause.

The agreement signed at Bretton Woods was a modified version of the White plan, establishing a fund for exchange rate stabilization and balance of payments adjustment, and a bank to make reconstruction and development loans. The initial quotas subscribed to the fund were greater than proposed by White, less than suggested by Keynes. The agreement was ambiguous on whether drawing by deficit countries on their fund quotas of foreign exchange would be automatically granted by a passive fund, as urged by Keynes, or subject to discretion by an activist fund, as preferred by White. The Keynes plan proposed penalizing creditor countries (expected to be primarily the United States) to encourage them to share in payments adjustment by expanding their economies. In place of these penalties, the White plan offered the Scarce Currency Clause: other member countries could impose exchange controls on a country whose currency was declared scarce.

The internationalism of Bretton Woods, and of the Anglo-American Financial Agreement of 6 December 1945, was criticized in Britain both by those, such as Thomas Balogh and Nicholas Kaldor, who favored greater state control of capital and trade movements, and by defenders of Imperial Preference such as Lord Beaverbrook. Keynes's defense of the agreements and the Lend-Lease settlement in the House of Lords on 18 December contributed to Parliamentary ratification.

As the first British governor of the World Bank, Keynes attended the first meeting of the IMF and World Bank in Savannah, Georgia, in March 1946. There he unsuccessfully protested against American plans to locate both fund and bank in the political atmosphere of Washington, rather than the financial center, New York city, and to make positions on the IMF board full-time and highly paid. Keynes suffered a heart attack on the train from Savannah to Washington. According to Sir George Bolton of the Bank of England, the first British executive director of the fund, Keynes drafted an angry article on board ship back to England, 'condemning American policy with extraordinary ferocity and passionately recommending H.M. Government to refuse to ratify the Fund and Bank agreement; such action would automatically have frustrated the U.S. and Canadian Loan Agreements'. Keynes was dissuaded from publication by Bolton and by Ernest Rowe-Dutton of the Treasury (Bolton, 1972, p. 1387). Britain had already ratified the agreement, so the advice, if given, would have been for withdrawal. No draft of this article survives, only that of a soberer Treasury memorandum on the conference by Keynes. Keynes died the next month.

The Bretton Woods system did not develop entirely as its founders had hoped. The Anglo-American Financial Agreement negotiated for Britain by Lords Halifax and Keynes, extending a $3750 million line of credit to Britain, required restoration of free convertibility of sterling within a year. (A Canadian credit of $1250 million carried no such conditions.) Britain's premature restoration of convertibility in 1947 was soon reversed, after defence of the sterling–dollar parity absorbed much of Britain's dollar reserves. The pound was devalued from $4.03 to $2.80 in 1949, remaining at that rate until 1967. The World Bank was overshadowed in postwar reconstruction by the US European Recovery Program (the Marshall Plan) and comparable US aid to Japan. Commercial policy discussions beginning with the Law Mission of 1943 led to the signing of the General Agreement on Tariffs and Trade (GATT) in 1947, but the United States did not ratify the 1948 charter of the International Trade Organization, intended to join the IMF and World Bank as one of the three pillars of international economic cooperation. A few currencies were allowed to float by their governments, as was the Canadian dollar from 1950 to 1962 and again after 1970. Overall, however, the Bretton Woods system provided 25 years of exchange rate stability, a period of low inflation, high employment and economic growth in the major industrial countries.

As Keynes predicted in his final, posthumous article on 'The Balance of Payments of the United States', the dollar shortage was not permanent, though it lasted longer than he expected. American foreign aid, overseas military spending and foreign investment combined with the US propensity to import as a high-income country and the growing export capacity of the recovering Japanese and West German economies to convert the much-feared dollar shortage into a dollar glut. Ultimately, even the creation of Special Drawing Rights (SDRs) to supplement the reserve assets of the system could not keep up with the growth of dollars in external circulation (Eurodollars). After a quarter-century of exchange rate stability, it proved impossible for central banks to continue defense of fixed exchange parities against speculative attack. US President Richard Nixon suspended the gold convertibility of the dollar and imposed a 10 per cent surcharge on American imports in August 1971. Devaluation of the dollar against gold in the Smithsonian Agreement of December 1971 and again in February 1973 was followed by general abandonment of fixed exchange rates in March 1973. That marked the end of the Bretton Woods system devised primarily by Keynes and White, but the International Monetary Fund and World Bank survive as its institutional legacy.

ROBERT W. DIMAND

See also:

Balance of Payments: Keynesian and Monetarist Approaches; Davidson, Paul; Dornbusch, Rudiger; Friedman, Milton; International Clearing Union; Johnson, Harry Gordon; Keynes, John Maynard; Machlup, Fritz; Meade, James E.; Mundell, Robert A.; Mundell–Fleming Model; Ohlin, Bertil; Viner, Jacob; White, Harry D.

Bibliography

Black, Stanley W. (1991), *A Levite Among the Priests: Edward M. Bernstein and the Origins of the Bretton Woods System*, Boulder, CO: Westview Press.

Bolton, Sir George (1972), 'Where Critics Are as Wrong as Keynes Was', *The Banker*, **100**, (549), November.

Bordo, Michael D. and Barry Eichengreen (eds) (1993), *A Retrospective on the Bretton Woods System*, Chicago and London: University of Chicago Press for National Bureau of Economic Research.

de Vries, Margaret Garritsen (1976), *The International Monetary Fund, 1966–1971*, 2 vols, Washington, DC: International Monetary Fund.

de Vries, Margaret Garritsen (1987), *Balance of Payments Adjustment, 1945 to 1986: The IMF Experience*, Washington, DC: International Monetary Fund.

Dostaler, Gilles (1995), 'Keynes et Bretton Woods', *Cahiers de recherche du département des sciences économiques de l'Université du Québec à Montréal*, no. 9502.

Gardner, Richard N. (1969), *Sterling–Dollar Diplomacy*, rev. edn, New York and London: McGraw-Hill.

Horsefield, J. Keith (ed.) (1969), *The International Monetary Fund, 1945–65*, 3 vols, Washington, DC: International Monetary Fund.

Johnson, M.E. (1993), *The International Monetary Fund, 1944–92: A Research Guide*, New York and London: Garland.

Keynes, John Maynard (1946), 'The Balance of Payments of the United States', *Economic Journal*, **56**, (2), pp. 172–87.

Keynes, John Maynard (1983), *Collected Writings*, ed. E.A.G. Robinson and D.E. Moggridge; vols XXV and XXVI, ed. D.E. Moggridge, London: Macmillan; New York: Cambridge University Press, for the Royal Economic Society.

Moggridge, Donald E. (1992), *Maynard Keynes: An Economist's Biography*, London and New York: Routledge.

Pressnell, Leslie S. (1987), *External Economic Policy Since the War*, Vol. I, *The Post-War Financial Settlement*, London: HMSO.

Thirlwall, A.P. (ed.) (1976), *Keynes and International Monetary Relations*, New York: St Martin's Press.

Van Dormael, Armand (1978), *Bretton Woods: Birth of a Monetary System*, New York: Holmes & Meier.

Brown, Arthur J.

Arthur Joseph Brown (born 8 August 1914) is Professor Emeritus of Economics, University of Leeds. He spent the bulk of his professional career at the University of Leeds (1949–79) where he focused on macroeconomic and regional economic issues.

Personal background and the early years

Brown was the son of working-class parents who served as managers of the Liberal Club of Bradford where he grew up. His early eduction took place at

Bradford Grammar School. While neither his mother nor his father attended university (in fact, his father's formal schooling ended at age 10 with the death of his father) they valued higher education and were determined that A.J. should have a university education. Therefore, he entered Queen's College of Oxford University in 1933 with a scholarship to study natural sciences. Shortly thereafter he asked and was given permission to change his academic path to philosophy, politics and economics, and chose to specialize in economics. He excelled in this newfound pursuit and won the junior and senior university prizes, the George Webb Medley Prizes, in his second and third years at Oxford.

Four months before his final degree examination, Keynes published *The General Theory*, which had a profound impact on A.J.'s desire to pursue a career in economics. Upon finishing his undergraduate degree, he entered the newly formed Oxford Institute of Statistics, where he completed the work for his DPhil under the supervision of Jacob Marschak. His thesis was entitled 'Liquidity Preference; a Study of Investment'. His thesis work was published in two articles in the inaugural issues of *Oxford Economic Papers* (October 1938 and May 1939). The first article was an empirical piece that estimated the demand function for idle money balances. The second was an attempt to analyse the asset holdings of the London clearing houses.

With the outbreak of World War II, Brown's attention was directed to supporting the war effort and the economic problems that are associated with wartime economies and problems. Most of his research during this time was published in 1947 in a book entitled *Applied Economics: Aspects of the World Economy in War and Peace.*

The academic years
In 1947, Brown took a position in the economics department at the University of Leeds. In the decade that followed, he spent most of his time working on macroeconomic issues, particularly inflation. The culmination of this research was the publication of his book, *The Great Inflation 1939–51* (1955). In this book, Brown attempted to explain the causes of the outbreak of inflation that occurred in the United Kingdom, beginning with the start of World War II. He attributes the source of inflation during this period to: (1) the war and wartime shortages, (2) increases in import prices, which served as the impulse for increases in the price level, and (3) an upward bias in factor prices of finished goods (that is, nominal wage inflation). Brown views the main contribution of this book to be 'a clarification of the price–wage spiral (together with an adumbration of the Phillips Curve) and a strengthening of the case for incomes policy'.[1] In 1985, after the oil price shocks of the 1970s, the collapse of Bretton Woods and the rise of neoclassical macroeconomic theories, he returned to the theme of investigating British inflation

with a follow-up book to *The Great Inflation* entitled *World Inflation Since 1950.* In this book, Brown again reaches the conclusion that, while monetary control may play a key role in containing inflation, the wage–price spiral is ultimately driven by an upward bias in nominal wage inflation, which could only be understood and dealt with by examining labor market institutions. Thus, while giving monetarists and neoclassicals their due, he nevertheless came to the conclusion that the Keynesian view of the inflation process was still the correct one.

After the publication of *The Great Inflation*, he entered the field of text-book writing and wrote *Introduction to the World Economy*, which appeared in 1959. The text reflects the optimism of the times regarding the use of Keynesian policy prescriptions for stabilizing the economy – an optimism that would fade over time. As Brown sees it today, the text is 'evidence of how completely my generation discounted the possibility of a return to mass unemployment and the rejection of Keynesian policies'.[2] During the 1950s he also published several articles in scholarly journals, including an *Economic Journal* article in 1958 on British inflation.

The Service Years
As often happens with successful scholars, in the 1960s and 1970s Brown became involved in public service work for the government, research agencies and professional organizations. He served on several government committees to study regional economic issues, thus beginning a change in the direction of his research from straight macroeconomics to regional economics. He served on committees whose objective was to investigate federalism in East and Central Africa, to study British regional problems and to work on British 'intermediate' areas. He also served on a United Nations Committee which focused on the economic and social consequences of disarmament. His work on regional economic problems led to his publishing two books on the subject, *The Framework of Regional Economics in the United Kingdom* in 1972 and *Regional Economic Problems* (with E.M. Burrows) in 1977.

In addition to government service, he also served as President of the Royal Economic Society from 1976 to 1978 and became heavily involved in British university matters, serving as a member of the University Grants Committee and serving as Pro-Vice-Chancellor of Leeds University. During this time he also served on an EEC study group that looked at public finance issues for European economic integration and the results of this effort were included in the 1977 'MacDougal Report', which had a profound effect on the European integration process.

Professor Brown retired in 1979 but has remained active to this day, contributing chapters to several edited volumes in recent years. His intellectual legacy lives on in his published work and in his son, W.A. Brown, who is Professor of Industrial Relations at Cambridge.

CHRISTOPHER WALLER

Notes

1 Letter from A.J. Brown to Christopher Waller, dated 14 December 1994.
2 Ibid.

See also:

Incomes Policies; Inflation; Keynes, John Maynard; Phillips Curve.

Bibliography

Brown, A.J. (1938), 'The liquidity-preference schedules of the London clearing banks', *Oxford Economic Papers* (Old Series), **1**, (1), October, pp. 49–82.
Brown, A.J. (1939), 'Interest, prices and the demand schedule for idle money', *Oxford Economic Papers* (Old Series), **1**, (2), May, pp. 46–69.
Brown, A.J. (1947), *Applied Economics: Aspects of the World Economy in War and Peace*, London: George Allen & Unwin.
Brown, A.J. (1955), *The Great Inflation 1939–1951*, London: Oxford University Press.
Brown, A.J. (1958), 'Inflation and the British Economy', *Economic Journal*, **68**, (271), September, pp. 449–63.
Brown, A.J. (1959), *Introduction to the World Economy*, London: George Allen & Unwin.
Brown, A.J. (1972), *The Framework of Regional Economics in the United Kingdom*, London: George Allen & Unwin.
Brown, A.J. (1985), *World Inflation Since 1950*, Cambridge: Cambridge University Press.
Brown, A.J. and E.M. Burrows (1977), *Regional Economic Problems*, Cambridge: Cambridge University Press.

Brunner, Karl

Karl Brunner contributed most notably to economics as one of the leaders of the monetarist school of macroeconomics. His efforts helped to initiate debates on the choice of targets and indicators of monetary policy and on the usefulness of a constant money-growth rule for monetary policy.

Brunner was born on 16 February 1916, in Zurich, Switzerland. After completing his doctorate in economics in 1943 at the University of Zurich, he spent a semester at Harvard University before moving to the University of Chicago for a year and a half. At Chicago, he met Milton Friedman, among other economists, who exposed him to '"new and astounding" vistas' (Brunner, 1980) for applications of economics. In 1951, Brunner moved to UCLA, where he met Armen Alchian, a colleague with whom he discussed applications of economics to a range of social issues, and Allan Meltzer, then a UCLA graduate student and later a frequent collaborator. Brunner's career led him to Ohio State University in 1966, and then to the University of Rochester in 1971, where he spent the remainder of his career. He died in 1989.

Brunner's best-known works develop the monetarist view of macroeconomics. (One often cited summary of the monetarist view is his 1968 article.) Brunner (in Klamer, 1984) defines monetarism broadly as 'the reassertion of the relevance of price theory to understand what happens in aggregate economics'. He applied this definition to a range of issues, using it to explain the appearance of money in an economy and to explain the tenets of monetarism for monetary economics. Finally, he used the theory of monetarism to analyse current monetary policy decisions.

To explain the presence of money in an economy, Brunner and Meltzer (1971) theorize that money evolves endogenously because it lowers the uncertainty and information costs inherently associated with transactions in an economy. The asset or assets most likely to become money are those that best help economic agents to overcome the uncertainty and information costs of transactions.

As Brunner himself noted, one important shortcoming of this theory of the evolution of money is that it does not explain why only one asset generally becomes recognized as money. However, the paper does establish the broad outline of Brunner's approach to macroeconomics: it explicitly acknowledges uncertainty and information costs; it illustrates the importance of social or institutional arrangements (in this case, money) in an economy; and it recognizes the relevance of price theory in explaining a broad range of economic phenomena.

In criticizing the prevailing Keynesian view of macroeconomics, Brunner emphasized his alternative theory of the transmission mechanism for monetary policy. The standard Keynesian argument that monetary policy affected the substitution between money and financial assets was narrow-sighted, according to Brunner. Instead, monetary policy affects relative prices, so it affects not only the substitution between money and financial assets, but also the substitution between money and real assets.

The necessary and sufficient condition for transmission of monetary policy to the real sector, then, depends not on the interest elasticity of money demand, as held by Keynesians, but on 'an order relation, irrespective of absolute magnitudes, between interest elasticities on the credit market and on the money market' (Brunner, 1980). As an increase in the money supply initially decreases the relative price of credit for a firm, it simultaneously increases the relative capital value of the firm's future streams of income. Thus a firm chooses to increase current output, and monetary policy has a temporary effect on real economic activity.

Brunner's transmission mechanism is certainly one of his most original contributions to monetary economics. It is also the basis for his unwillingness to portray the Keynesian–monetarist debates in an IS/LM model, because the Brunner transmission mechanism did not lead to the standard LM curve. On the basis of this theory of the transmission mechanism, Brunner also evaluated the accuracy of different indicators of the stance of monetary policy. Brunner and Meltzer (1967) showed that their model implies that the level of free reserves, an indicator in use at the time, is not a reliable measure of the stance of monetary policy. They suggested that a more reliable indicator would be the monetary base.

Brunner's concern with applying price theory to a range of social phenomena also led to a view of government that was distinct from the Keynesian view. Brunner held that Keynesian analysis ascribed to government the motive of public interest or goodwill. But Brunner argued that economic theory suggested that government should be modeled using a theory of motivation through private-interest or self-interest. This economic-based theory of government led Brunner to advocate the adoption of a constant money-growth rule for monetary policy. Initially, however, he based his support of a rule on the issue of information problems in an economy. Brunner and Meltzer (1969) argue that the choice between either a rule or a discretionary policy depends primarily on the severity of the information problem. They conclude that, if information problems are severe, a rule will be preferable; if not, discretionary policy may be helpful. In later writings, Brunner combined the issue of information problems with his economic analysis of government motives to support the adoption of a rule. He also recognized possible shortcomings of a money-growth rule due to changes in velocity or real income growth, and therefore supported a rule that would adjust for these changes (Brunner and Meltzer, 1993).

Finally, one of Brunner's major contributions to economics was his life-long devotion to encouraging the dialogue on economic issues. He founded three journals: the *Journal of Money, Credit and Banking*, the *Journal of Monetary Economics* and the *Carnegie–Rochester Conference Series on Public Policy*. He was also one of the founders of the Shadow Open Market Committee, which analyses Federal Reserve policy decisions. Each of these institutions has played a key role in the debate on monetary policy.

LINDA M. HOOKS

See also:

Chicago School of Economics; Depression, The Great; Friedman, Milton; Inflation; Meltzer, Allan H.; Monetarist School of Economics; Monetary Policy; Monetizing the (Federal) Debt; Money; Quantity Theory of Money; Schwartz, Anna J.

Bibliography
Brunner, Karl (1968), 'The Role of Money and Monetary Policy', *Federal Reserve Bank of St. Louis Monthly Review*, **50**, (7), July, pp. 9–24.
Brunner, Karl (1980), 'A Fascination with Economics', *Banca Nazionale del Lavoro Quarterly Review*, **33**, (135), December, pp. 403–26.

Brunner, Karl and Allan H. Meltzer (1967), 'The Meaning of Monetary Indicators', in G. Horwich (ed.), *Monetary Process and Policy – A Symposium*, Homewood, Ill.: Richard Irwin.

Brunner, Karl and Allan H. Meltzer (1969), 'The Nature of the Policy Problem', in K. Brunner (ed.), *Targets and Indicators of Monetary Policy*, San Francisco: Chandler.

Brunner, Karl and Allan H. Meltzer (1971), 'The Uses of Money: Money in the Theory of an Exchange Economy', *American Economic Review*, **61**, (5), December, pp. 784–805.

Brunner, Karl and Allan H. Meltzer (1993), *Money and the Economy: Issues in Monetary Analysis*, Cambridge: Cambridge University Press.

Klamer, Arjo (1984), *Conversations with Economists*, Totawa, NJ: Rowman and Allanheld.

Burns, Arthur F.

Arthur F. Burns was born in Stanislau, Austria on 27 April 1904. In 1914, his family emigrated to the United States, settling in Bayonne, New Jersey. Burns became a member of the economics faculty at Rutgers University in 1927, leaving in 1941 to accept an appointment at Columbia University, where he taught for many years and became John Bates Clark Professor of Economics. He joined the staff of the National Bureau of Economic Research in New York in 1930, was director of research in 1945–53 and president in 1957–67. In Washington, Burns served as chairman of the Council of Economic Advisors, 1953–6; Counsellor to the President, 1969–70; chairman of the Federal Reserve System, 1970–78; and member of the President's Economic Policy Advisory Board, 1981–7. From 1981 to 1985 he was US Ambassador to the Federal Republic of Germany. In 1978–80 and 1985–7 he was a distinguished scholar in residence at the American Enterprise Institute.

Burns's economic studies were primarily concerned with economic growth, business cycles, inflation and economic policies bearing upon these phenomena. In his book, *Production Trends in the United States Since 1870*, published in 1934, he examined growth rates in individual industries, noting the nearly universal tendency towards retardation. An initial stage of rapid growth in a new industry is usually followed by slower growth as it loses part of its market or its resources to still newer industries. Despite the tendency towards slower growth and eventual decline of most industries, Burns noted that this did not imply that growth in total output of the country would slow. The underlying cause, that is, the rise of new industries, would itself help to maintain rapid growth in total output.

Burns's collaboration with Wesley Mitchell in the study of business cycles led to many innovations in measurement techniques and to a vast accumulation of knowledge about the characteristics of cycles and the economic interactions that generated them. In 1938, for example, Burns and Mitchell published the first list of leading economic indicators, in response to a request by the Secretary of the Treasury for a forecasting tool for the next recession. Such indicators are still widely used and have been applied to inflation cycles as well as business cycles.

The Burns–Mitchell studies have also led to a more realistic view of what business cycle theory had to explain and what economic policy could be expected to accomplish. This in turn helped to prepare Burns for his later role as an economic policy-maker, as advisor to the President and chairman of the Federal Reserve. It enabled him to write in 1953, in his last annual report to the National Bureau before taking on these responsibilities, 'It is reasonable to expect that contracyclical policy will moderate the amplitude and abbreviate the duration of business contractions in the future ... But there are no adequate grounds, as yet, for believing that business cycles will soon disappear, or that the government will resist inflation with as much tenacity as depression.' Subsequently, his efforts were largely directed to improving the anti-recession, anti-inflation and growth-promoting policies of government. In 1978, Burns discussed many of these experiences in his last, *Reflections of an Economic Policy Maker*.

His testimony before Congress in March 1979 concerning a balanced budget amendment to the Constitution remains highly relevant to an issue still under discussion in 1995. Burns argued in favor of the balanced budget requirement. He noted that the historical record showed that government spending needed better control and that surpluses and deficits could be used to stabilize the business cycle and reduce the dangers of inflation.

Although Arthur Burns died on 26 June 1987, much of his work will continue to survive and be applied for many years.

GEOFFREY H. MOORE

See also:
Business Cycle Theory (I) and (II); Fiscal Policy; Friedman, Milton; Galbraith, John K.; Inflation; Monetary Policy; Money; Quantity Theory of Money.

Bibliography
Burns, Arthur F. (1930), *Stock Market Cycle Research*, New York: Twentieth Century Fund.
Burns, Arthur F. (1934), *Production Trends in the United States Since 1870*, New York: National Bureau of Economic Research.
Burns, Arthur F. (1946), *Economic Research and the Keynesian Thinking of Our Times*, New York: National Bureau of Economic Research, 26th Annual Report.
Burns, Arthur F. (1954), *The Frontiers of Economic Knowledge*, Princeton, NJ: Princeton University Press.
Burns, Arthur F. (1957), *Prosperity Without Inflation*, New York: Fordham University Press.
Burns, Arthur F. (1966), *The Management of Prosperity*, New York: Columbia University Press.
Burns, Arthur F. (1969), *The Business Cycle in a Changing World*, New York: Columbia University Press.
Burns, Arthur F. (1978), *Reflections of an Economic Policy Maker*, Washington: American Enterprise Institute.
Burns, Arthur F. (1985), 'Interview: An Economist's Perspective Over 60 Years', *Challenge*, **27**, (6), Jan.–Feb., pp. 17–25.

Burns, Arthur F. (1988), *The Ongoing Revolution in American Banking*, Washington, DC: American Enterprise Institute.
Burns, Arthur F. and Wesley C. Mitchell (1938), *Statistical Indicators of Cyclical Revivals*, New York: National Bureau of Economic Research, Bulletin 69.
Burns, Arthur F. and Wesley C. Mitchell (1946), *Measuring Business Cycles*, New York: Columbia University Press.

Business Cycle Theory (I)

Introduction

The Great Depression continues to have significant impact on the research agenda of macroeconomists. The search for an explanation of this event, as Bernanke (1995, p. 1) notes, 'remains a fascinating intellectual challenge'. An analysis of the Great Depression also sheds light on the recent debate between new Keynesian and new classical macroeconomists and on the historical development of modern business cycle theory. Specifically, the inability of the classical model to explain both the reduction in output and the increase in unemployment in the early 1930s suggested that an alternative framework was required to explain macroeconomic fluctuations. Keynes's analysis in *The General Theory of Employment, Interest and Money* and Hicks' (1937) subsequent development of the now familiar IS/LM model provided such a framework. In particular, the assumed inflexibility of nominal wages and prices (in contrast to the classical assumption of wage and price flexibility) could yield situations where equilibrium output would remain below the full employment level of output.

Through much of the 1960s the study of macroeconomic fluctuations continued to follow the Keynesian model. The IS/LM model, combined with the Phillips curve, served as a useful framework to explain fluctuations in output and inflation. The assumed, fixed position of the Phillips curve provided policy makers with what was then believed to be a stable trade-off between inflation and output. To increase economic activity, policy makers simply needed to stimulate aggregate demand and, incidentally, accept the subsequent increase in inflation. Alternatively, to reduce inflation, a reduction in aggregate demand would cause a movement along the Phillips curve and a subsequent reduction in inflation and output. More generally, the business cycle was believed to be caused by changes in aggregate demand and, therefore, represented movements along the Phillips curve. The stable trade-off between inflation and unemployment during the 1950s and 1960s gave the impression that the Keynesian explanation of the business cycle worked quite well.

This Keynesian interpretation of the business cycle, however, was rejected by many economists in the 1970s, as noted by Mankiw (1990, p. 1647), for two reasons: first, the Keynesian model simply could not explain the simultaneous increase in inflation and unemployment observed during this period (that is, the collapse of the Phillips curve); second, many macroeconomists became uneasy with the absence of a microeconomic principles-based foundation of the Keynesian model. This collapse of the Phillips curve had, in fact, been predicted by both Friedman (1968) and Phelps (1968). The then-Keynesian belief that the Phillips curve was negatively sloped even in the long run was soundly rejected by the Friedman–Phelps development of the natural rate hypothesis. They argued that nominal wages and, therefore, the aggregate price level would be a function of individuals' expectations of the aggregate price level. As expectations of inflation changed, the Phillips curve would also shift. For example, a permanent, one-time increase in aggregate demand would only increase output in the short run since expectations of prices would adjust, causing output to return to the natural level of output. Furthermore, policy makers could maintain output above the natural level only if actual inflation remained permanently above the constantly adjusting (and increasing) rate of expected inflation. The view of Keynesian economics and its policy recommendations at the time is best summarized by Lucas (1981, p. 559) who argued that 'Keynesian orthodoxy is in deep trouble, the deepest kind of trouble in which an applied body of theory can find itself: it appears to be giving seriously wrong answers to the most basic questions of macroeconomic policy.' By the end of the 1970s, the new classical (or, as some also describe it, the rational expectations) revolution was under way.

New Classical business cycle theory[1]
In all of the new classical theories of the business cycle, three key assumptions are typically found: (1) households and firms optimize objective functions subject to resource and technology constraints; (2) all agents possess rational expectations; and (3) relative prices and wages automatically adjust to maintain market equilibrium. The earliest work on new classical theories of the business cycle was conducted by Lucas (1972, 1973) who attempted to generate monetary policy-induced business cycles. In these models, agents were assumed to possess better information about the price of goods they produced than about the prices of goods they consumed. In this imperfect information setting, an unexpected increase in the aggregate price level would cause agents to increase production as they attributed (incorrectly) some of the increase in the price of their product to changes in local demand. Business cycles were then believed to be caused by price surprises. Sargent and Wallace (1975) extended this analysis by using the assumption of rational expectations developed by Muth (1961) to argue that systematic monetary policy would have no effects on output; any expected change in the money supply would be matched by a proportionate change in all nominal variables, thus rendering systematic monetary policy ineffective. The new classical prescrip-

tion for monetary policy would be to follow some announced rule where a monetary aggregate would increase by, say, 6 per cent each year. Any attempt to 'fine-tune' the economy would have destabilizing effects.[2]

Kydland and Prescott (1982) along with the numerous papers that followed took the new classical theory one step further by arguing that fluctuations in output are caused solely by changes in the productive capacity of the economy. In these real business cycle (RBC) models in which perfectly competitive markets always clear, changes in output represent the aggregate response of optimizing agents to changes in an economy's productive capacity and, therefore, represent Pareto efficient fluctuations in aggregate economic activity. In much of this literature, changes in monetary aggregates (expected or unexpected) are irrelevant. Hence there is no role for monetary policy in such an economy.

These RBC models are based on a representative agent framework and draw heavily on the neoclassical growth model of Solow (1956). The earlier RBC models assumed that fluctuations in output were determined solely by technology shocks. As Stadler (1994, p. 1770) notes, a reduction in output would then be caused by a *reduction* in 'the stock of knowledge'. The more recent RBC models provide a broader interpretation of technology shocks which include, for example, the effects of energy price shocks, tighter pollution laws and changes in the legal and regulatory system. The most recent RBC models also consider the effects of government, the open economy, the labor market and even money on the macroeconomy.[3]

New Keynesian business cycle theory

In stark contrast to the new classical interpretations of the business cycle, new Keynesian (and, for that matter, 'old' Keynesian) analysis indicates that changes in economic activity are caused by some type of market failure (generally the failure of wages and/or prices to adjust instantly to maintain market equilibrium) and, therefore, do not represent Pareto efficient responses to shocks. Specifically, Blinder (1988, p. 279) states that 'Keynesian economics is a theory of aggregate demand and of the effects of aggregate demand on real output and inflation.' Blinder continues with a list of (his) six principal tenets of Keynesian economics, the first three of which shed light on the new Keynesian theory of the business cycle: tenet 1 – a Keynesian believes that aggregate demand is affected by both private and public sector behavior; tenet 2 – changes (expected or unexpected) in aggregate demand have their greatest short-run effect on output, not on prices; and tenet 3 – the goods and labor markets respond slowly to shocks.

The emergence of the new Keynesian theory of business cycles occurred not just because of a more clearly articulated list of principal tenets, but because of the work of some macroeconomists to resurrect the Phillips curve and, most importantly, to develop a stronger microtheoretic foundation. While new Keynesian economists acknowledge that business cycles can be caused by 'real' shocks, they also believe that output can deviate from its 'natural' level because of shocks to aggregate demand. The majority of research in this area has focused on providing a theoretically consistent explanation for firms, for example, cutting production in response to a reduction in aggregate demand.[4]

The research of Mankiw (1985) and Akerlof and Yellen (1985) focused attention on the effects of monopolistically competitive firms. In the presence of costs of adjusting prices, these price-setting firms might not change prices in response to a change in demand. Even if these 'menu costs' are small, it is argued that they may be sufficiently large to cause business cycles. For example, suppose aggregate demand were to fall in an economy in which these menu costs exist. In this situation, profit-maximizing firms might not find it profitable to cut their price. This failure to cut price causes output at the firm level and, therefore, at the aggregate level to fall. Alternatively, if all firms were to cut their prices simultaneously, output would not change.[5] In addition to these output price rigidities, the work by Yellen (1984) and others on efficiency wage models has provided a rigorous explanation of wage rigidity. Regardless of the source, any market failure that prevents wages and/ or prices from adjusting instantly to shocks will allow changes in aggregate demand to have real effects in the short run.[6]

Summary

The policy implications of the new Keynesian view of the business cycle are quite clear. Since changes in output are not viewed as Pareto-efficient responses to economic disturbances, new Keynesians generally believe, as argued by Blinder (1988, p. 280) that 'stabilization policy [should be used] to reduce the amplitude of business cycles'. These policy recommendations are in conflict with the implications of the RBC models. As Prescott (1986a, p. 21) notes, RBC theory indicates that 'costly efforts at stabilization are likely to be counterproductive'. He therefore suggests that 'attention should be focused not on fluctuations in output but rather on determinants of the average rate of technological advance'. While a consensus has not yet emerged concerning business cycle theory, the research conducted by both new Keynesian and new classical economists has increased our understanding of the causes, consequences and policy implications of fluctuations in economic activity.[7]

DAVID W. FINDLAY

Notes

1   There are some differences in the classification of the theories of the business cycle. For example, Stadler (1994) describes three separate schools of thought: (1) new Keynesian; (2)

new classical (that is, imperfect information models); and (3) real business cycle. Mankiw (1990), on the other hand, includes the imperfect information models and real business cycle models in his description of new classical macroeconomics. The discussion found below follows the Mankiw classification approach.

2   It is also during this period that Lucas (1976) clearly articulated the now familiar 'Lucas critique'.

3   There are two additional areas of research in the new classical framework that should be mentioned. One of the criticisms of the RBC theory is that unemployment is viewed as a voluntary response of labor market participants. Lilien (1982) developed a model that could explain unemployment in a RBC model. Specifically, sectoral shift theory assumes that shocks to particular sectors of the economy (such as defense-related industries) will cause increases in unemployment and reductions in output as unemployed workers spend time searching for employment in other sectors of the economy. Second, research by Romer (1986a, 1986b) and Lucas (1988) renewed interest in the theory of economic growth. Their work on endogenous growth theory has served as a catalyst for more careful examination of the determinants of technical progress.

4   Two papers that should be mentioned here but which do not fit neatly into any of the following categories are the studies by Fischer (1977) and Taylor (1980). Both of these papers illustrated that systematic monetary policy is not necessarily ineffective in the presence of rational expectations. What drives this result is the existence of either Fischer's long-term contracts or Taylor's staggered contracts. Neither paper provides a theoretical explanation for the existence of such contracts.

5   This situation is an example of a coordination failure that can result in aggregate demand-induced business cycles. For a more detailed discussion of coordination failures and their macroeconomic consequences, see Diamond (1982).

6   In addition to these areas of research on the theoretical foundations of new Keynesian economics, Blanchard and Summers (1986) and others have developed models of hysteresis which allow for changes in aggregate demand (and other shocks) to have real and persistent effects on economic activity. These models have been used to explain, for example, the persistent unemployment in Europe.

7   A number of survey articles exist which provide an overview of recent developments in these two areas of macroeconomics. See, for example, Gordon (1990), Huh and Trehan (1991), Mankiw (1989), Manuelli (1986), McCallum (1994), Plosser (1989), Prescott (1986b) and Summers (1986).

See also:

Business Cycle Theory (II); Coordination Failures and Keynesian Economics; Depression, The Great; Expectations, Theories of; Friedman, Milton; Hicks, Sir John R.; IS/LM Model and Diagram; Keynes, John Maynard; Lucas Jr., Robert E.; New Classical School of Economics; New Keynesian Macroeconomics; Phillips Curve.

Bibliography

Akerlof, G. and J. Yellen (1985), 'A Near-Rational Model of the Business Cycle, with Wage and Price Inertia', *Quarterly Journal of Economics*, **100**, (supplement), pp. 823–38.

Bernanke, B. (1995), 'The Macroeconomics of the Great Depression: A Comparative Approach', *Journal of Money, Credit and Banking*, **27**, (1), February, pp. 1–28.

Blanchard, O. and L. Summers (1986), 'Hysteresis and the European Unemployment Problem', *NBER Macroeconomics Manual*, pp. 15–78.

Blinder, A. (1988), 'The Fall and Rise of Keynesian Economics', *Economic Record*, **64**, (187), December, pp. 278–94.

Diamond, P. (1982), 'Aggregate Demand Management in Search Equilibrium', *Journal of Political Economy*, **90**, (5), October, pp. 881–94.

Fischer, S. (1977), 'Long-Term Contracts, Rational Expectations, and the Optimal Money Supply Rule', *Journal of Political Economy*, **85**, (1), February, pp. 191–205.

Friedman, M. (1968), 'The Role of Monetary Policy', *American Economic Review*, **58**, (1), March, pp. 1–17.

Gordon, R. (1990), 'What is New-Keynesian Economics?', *Journal of Economic Literature*, **28**, (3), September, pp. 1115–71.

Hicks, J. (1937), 'Mr. Keynes and the "Classics"', *Econometrica*, **5**, (2), April, pp. 147–59.

Huh, C. and B. Trehan (1991), 'Real Business Cycles: A Selective Survey', *Economic Review*, Federal Reserve Bank of San Francisco, Spring, no. 2, pp. 3–14.

Keynes, John M. (1936), *The General Theory of Employment, Interest and Money*, London: Macmillan.

Kydland, F. and E. Prescott (1982), 'Time to Build and Aggregate Fluctuations', *Econometrica*, **50**, (6), November, pp. 1345–70.

Lilien, D. (1982), 'Sectoral Shifts and Cyclical Unemployment', *Journal of Political Economy*, **90**, (4), August, pp. 777–93.

Lucas, R., Jr. (1972), 'Expectations and the Neutrality of Money', *Journal of Economic Theory*, **4**, (2), April, pp. 103–24.

Lucas, R., Jr. (1973), 'International Evidence on Output–Inflation Tradeoffs', *American Economic Review*, **63**, (3), June, pp. 326–34.

Lucas, R., Jr. (1976), 'Econometric Policy Evaluation: A Critique', in K. Brunner and A. Meltzer (eds), *The Phillips Curve and Labor Markets*, Carnegie–Rochester Conferences on Public Policy, vol. 1.

Lucas, R., Jr. (1981), 'Tobin and Monetarism: A Review Article', *Journal of Economic Literature*, **19**, (2), March, pp. 558–67.

Lucas, R., Jr. (1988), 'On the Mechanics of Economic Development', *Journal of Monetary Economics*, **22**, (1), July, pp. 3–42.

Mankiw, G. (1985), 'Small Menu Costs and Large Business Cycles: A Macroeconomic Model', *Quarterly Journal of Economics*, **100**, (2), May, pp. 529–38.

Mankiw, G. (1989), 'Real Business Cycles: A New Keynesian Perspective', *Journal of Economic Perspectives*, **3**, (3), Summer, pp. 79–90.

Mankiw, G. (1990), 'A Quick Refresher Course in Macroeconomics', *Journal of Economic Literature*, **28**, (4), December, pp. 1645–60.

Manuelli, R. (1986), 'Modern Business Cycle Analysis: A Guide to the Prescott–Summers Debate', *Quarterly Review*, Federal Reserve Bank of Minneapolis, **10**, (4), Fall, pp. 3–8.

McCallum, B. (1994), 'Macroeconomics After Two Decades of Rational Expectations', *Journal of Economic Education*, **25**, (3), Summer, pp. 219–34.

Muth, J. (1961), 'Rational Expectations and the Theory of Price Movements', *Econometrica*, **29**, (3), July, pp. 315–35.

Phelps, E. (1968), 'Money-Wage Dynamics and Labor Market Equilibrium', *Journal of Political Economy*, **76**, (4, Part II), July/August, pp. 687–711.

Plosser, C. (1989), 'Understanding Real Business Cycles', *Journal of Economic Perspectives*, **3**, (3), Summer, pp. 51–77.

Prescott, E. (1986a), 'Theory Ahead of Business Cycle Measurement', *Quarterly Review*, Federal Reserve Bank of Minneapolis, **10**, (4), Fall, pp. 9–22.

Prescott, E. (1986b), 'Response to a Skeptic', *Quarterly Review*, Federal Reserve Bank of Minneapolis, **10**, (4), Fall, pp. 28–33.

Romer, P. (1986a), 'Dynamic Competitive Equilibria with Externalities, Increasing Returns and Unbounded Growth', doctoral dissertation, University of Chicago.

Romer, P. (1986b), 'Increasing Returns and Long Run Growth', *Journal of Political Economy*, **94**, (5), October, pp. 1002–37.

Sargent, T. and N. Wallace (1975), '"Rational Expectations", the Optimal Money Instrument and the Optimal Money Supply Rule', *Journal of Political Economy*, **83**, (2), April, pp. 241–54.

Solow, R. (1956), 'A Contribution to the Theory of Economic Growth', *Quarterly Journal of Economics*, **70**, (1), February, pp. 65–94.

Stadler, G. (1994), 'Real Business Cycles', *Journal of Economic Literature*, **32**, (4), December, pp. 1750–83.

Summers, L. (1986), 'Some Skeptical Observations on Real Business Cycle Theory', *Quarterly Review*, Federal Reserve Bank of Minneapolis, **10**, (4), Fall, pp. 23–7.

Taylor, J. (1980), 'Aggregate Dynamics and Staggered Contracts', *Journal of Political Economy*, **88**, (1), February, pp. 1–23.

Yellen, J. (1984), 'Efficiency Wage Models of Unemployment', *American Economic Review*, **74**, (2), May, pp. 200–205.

Business Cycle Theory (II)

Characteristics of business cycles

The secular increase of total national output which we characterize as 'economic growth' does not show a continuous, uninterrupted trend upward year after year, but rather a wave-like movement of business activity around its average annual increase or trend, during which a period of rapid progress or increase is followed by a period of stagnation. These wave-like changes are generally called 'business cycles'. *A business cycle is a cyclical (increase, then decrease, then increase) fluctuation in the aggregate economic activity of a nation, or a cyclical change in the rate of economic growth.* Business cycles involve coherent changes in output quantities and prices of consumer goods and capital goods, input costs, employment and wage rates, profits, productivity, investment, total and per capita income, the quantity of money, volume of credit and interest rates. The sizes of changes are greater in the capital goods industries than in the consumer goods industries. Business cycles are not the same as seasonal movements within the year, or erratic irregular disturbances caused by wars, cartelization of oil supplies or other exogenous shocks.

A 'cycle' consists of 'expansions' or 'booms' (increased rates of increase or 'growth') occurring at about the same time in many economic activities, followed by similarly general 'recessions' or 'contractions', in which the same activities suffer reductions in growth rates, or actual decreases, and then revivals which merge into the expansion phase of the next cycle. The 'boom' period consists in a general increase in the volume of production and income, with increasing job creation and employment; then, in the 'recession' (the descending portion of the wave), a general decline in the volume of production (total output), income, employment and trade volume, or at least decreases in their rates of growth, accompanied by shrinking income and, in the case of many firms, losses and bankruptcies, and widening unemployment and declining incomes. During the recession, reduced employment and output occur in many different lines of business, and firms in many different lines of business contract and fail, showing that the cause and effects of the cycle are economy-wide. The recession may involve either large absolute decreases in output, employment and wages, involving great numbers of project abandonments and business failures, or merely reductions in the rate of increase in output, employment and income.

Prices generally rise during the boom and fall during the recession; interest rates follow a similar pattern, but not in phase. Not only is there a general increase in the numbers and quantities of goods during the expansion, but there is also an increase in the volume of payments in the financial markets and on the stock exchange as well during the boom, and a contraction in the volume of payments during the recession (Haberler, 1932, p. 299). Such a change in the volume of payments requires some combination of changes in the quantity of means of payment (money and credit) and the velocity of exchange.

This sequence of expansions and contractions is not 'cyclic' in the sense of having regular periods or consistent amplitudes, like a sine wave; rather, cyclic fluctuations merely accelerate, slow, pause and reverse. To be 'cyclic', such fluctuations must be pervasive throughout many, if not all, sectors of the economy, affecting labor demand and wages in many industries, productivity of capital in many industries, and interest rates and most prices as well. Also to be 'cyclic', the seeds of the next phase must be sown during the present phase; that is, the recession must be caused by the preceding boom. Business cycles vary in duration from more than one year to 10 or 12 years; a business cycle is not divisible into shorter cycles of similar character.

Business cycles could not exist in a barter economy (Dauten and Valentine, 1974, p. 83) or in an economy using only commodity money and warehouse receipts for money issued by banks (ibid., p. 84). It is legal tender currency, fractional reserve banking, central control of the quantity of money and central government deficit financing which appear to be the common elements causing business cycles. No general expansion in employment and output could occur without an expansion of the quantity or velocity of media of exchange and fiduciary media; likewise, no general contraction of output and employment could occur without a reduction in the quantity of media of exchange and fiduciary media, or a reduction in their velocity of use. For example, recall the expansion of fiduciary media and money in the United States during the 1920s boom and the 33 per cent drop in the quantity of money in the United States between 1929 and 1933.

The cyclic fluctuations are more pronounced in the capital goods industries than in the consumer goods industries, and the fluctuations appear larger the farther the industry is from consumer goods (Haberler, 1974, pp. 41–6).

The business cycle has had certain definite features: first, there is a boom period, when prices and productive activity expand. There is a greater boom in the heavy capital-goods and higher-order industries – such as industrial raw materials, machine goods and construction, and in the markets for titles to these goods, such as the stock market and real estate. Then, suddenly, without warning, there is a 'crash'. A financial panic with runs on banks ensues, prices fall very sharply, and there is a sudden piling up of unsold inventory, and particularly a revelation of great excess capacity in the higher-order capital-goods industries. A painful period of liquidation and bankruptcy follows, accompanied by heavy unemployment, until recovery to normal conditions gradually takes place. (Rothbard, 1962, p. 745)

Business cycles are not unique to the United States, but plague the entire industrialized world – or at least that portion of it with central banks and collection facilities for nationwide economic data (Moore, 1983, p. 167). Business cycles differ from one another in many respects, so no single theory, factor or mechanism has convinced all economists that it explains all business cycles.

The end of the expansion phase of a business cycle was historically characterized by glaring breakdowns of business activity, bankruptcies and financial panics, constituting an unanticipated 'crisis' (Haberler, 1932, p. 297). Aside from the greater intensity of cyclical changes in the capital goods industries than in the consumer goods industries, the striking characteristic of business cycles is the great unanimity of *entrepreneurial error* pervading the economy: entrepreneurs have previously undertaken activities which now turn out to be unprofitable, leading to the crisis and manifested as the great number of business failures in the following recession.

Every boom period is characterized by an extension of investments of capital goods. It is primarily the construction of fixed capital goods and the materials used for them, where the largest changes occur: the greatest expansion during the boom and the most violent contractions during the recession (ibid., p. 309). The reduction in the relative height of interest rates which normally precedes and accompanies a boom benefits especially those branches of industry which are capital-intensive and which have large interest expense. If the cost of capital is reduced, there is a general tendency to replace labor with machinery: the roundaboutness of production is increased. If this productive expansion is not financed by real, voluntary saving of individuals or corporations, but by *artificially created* credit, a reaction will inevitably set in, when interest rates rise, showing that these new capital investments are not going to be profitable: their net present values are negative with the higher interest rates. A relative credit inflation will therefore induce the same cyclical movements as an absolute inflation (ibid., p. 310). All business cycle theories share the assumption that the quantity of money or its rate of growth expands during the boom, through credit expansion by banks and other financial intermediaries. Such expansions of money and credit provide the financing for the increased investment which characterizes the boom (Rothbard, 1962, p. 763).

The data suggest that no two 'cycles' are alike; each 'cycle' has many elements of uniqueness. Furthermore, the character of cycles has undergone

secular changes: 'Perhaps the most obvious change is that business recessions – periods of actual decline in economic activity – have become less
frequent, shorter and milder. Interruptions to a steady rate of growth are more
often simply slowdowns rather than actual declines in aggregate economic
activity' (Moore, 1983, p. 161). 'Moreover, different industrial segments experience different intensity of fluctuation, with manufacturers of durable
goods and mining experiencing the greatest fluctuation in trade; [while]
consumption-good sellers, services and finance experience the smallest fluctuation' (ibid., p. 162).

> The crucial phenomenon of the crisis is the most elusive of explanation: why is
> there a sudden revelation of business error, and what caused these generally
> pervasive errors that remained undetected until the crisis? Suddenly, nearly all
> businessmen find that their investments and estimates have been in error, that they
> cannot sell their products for the prices which they had anticipated. This is the
> central problem of the business cycle, and this is the problem which any adequate
> theory of the cycle must explain. No real businessman is equipped with perfect
> foresight; all make errors. But the market process precisely rewards those busi-
> nessmen who are equipped to make a minimum number of errors. Why should
> there suddenly be a cluster of errors? Furthermore, why should these errors
> particularly pervade the capital-goods industries? (Rothbard, 1962, p. 746)

Since the eighteenth century there has been an almost regular pattern of
consistent clusters of error which always follow a boom and expansion of
money and prices. Prior to the eighteenth century, business crises rarely
followed upon booms in this manner. Crises took place suddenly, in the midst
of normal activity, generally as the result of some obvious and identifiable
external event: famine, plague, seizures of goods in war, bad harvests, royal
manipulations in the cloth trade, seizures of bullion by the King, a sudden
burst of hoarding or a sudden rise in individual time preferences and a
decrease in saving. Since the late seventeenth century, however, it is obvious
that the crisis and ensuing depression could no longer be attributed to some
single external event of single act of government (ibid.).

During the second half of the nineteenth century there was a marked
tendency for these disturbances to become milder. The crisis events, such as
bankruptcies and panics, became less numerous and there were some cycles
which lacked such crises at their peaks (Haberler, 1932, p. 7). Following the
Great Depression of the 1930s, which was a worldwide event and which was
characterized by the intense and spectacular crisis of 1929, the severity of
crises declined again, so that most recent cycles have reached their peak
without a profound crisis, though business failures and widening unemployment are still common during the recession.

Theories

Apart from Mises's explanation of the causes of business cycles in *The Theory of Money and Credit* in 1912, business cycle theory prior to the late 1920s was primitive and ad hoc owing to the neglect in those early theories of most of what had already been learned in economics. Mostly, these early theories ignored the normal planning by entrepreneurs and assumed uncharacteristic foolishness and short-sightedness on the part of business managers, who never learned from past events, and who were driven by skittish emotions to replicate unprofitable activities (Mitchell, 1927, pp. 11–53). In the 1930s, Hayek, at the London School of Economics, and Keynes, in *The General Theory of Employment, Interest and Money*, stimulated a flurry of activity on cycle theory. Hayek, in several books and articles, developed in detail the theory proposed by Mises in 1912, which ascribed cyclic phenomena to activities of the centralized banking system which led entrepreneurs to invest in incorrect assets, while Keynes ascribed cyclic phenomena to defects in the market mechanism causing inconsistencies between consumers' and producers' responses to economic data, especially to the alleged 'gap' between savings and investment, which Hayek and Mises argued was equilibrated by the rate of interest. Between the followers of these two opposing views is an immense gulf, as the following summaries of the major theories show.

Exogenous theories

Early theories of business cycles were often concerned with outside events which affected commerce. Cycles in agricultural yields could be produced by periodic changes in weather, which could be brought about by the sunspot cycle or periodicities in planetary approaches to Earth, which affected crop yields through light, heat or rainfall. Changes in agricultural activity then influenced general business conditions, since agriculture was at that time the dominant economic activity. Bumper crops, for example, reduced prices, thereby lowering costs in industries using these products as inputs, and the increased profits led to increased investment. Increased exports of the plentiful crops led to increases in the domestic money supply and therefore reductions in interest rates, which stimulated business investment further. A general boom ensued. The reverse effect on crops produced the recession. Empirical investigation, however, does not support this theory and the theory neglects the processes of storage and speculation, both of which mitigate price changes, so it has been abandoned.

The Cobweb Theorem

The 'Cobweb Theorem' arose from the long-standing observation of regularly recurring cycles in prices and production of various commodities (Ezekiel, 1938). Cobweb theory assumes that producers, primarily of agricultural products, being short-sighted, decide what quantity of goods to supply in the future on the basis of the current price, without regard to the way the price may change during the period of production. Therefore, a 'shock' to supply (such as loss of part of a crop because of weather or disease, or some other exogenous event) which causes a price increase automatically causes producers to respond to the higher price by increasing production for the next period by increasing their purchases of factors of production, thereby creating a boom. In the next period, then, the higher than equilibrium quantity causes a general fall in prices, producing the recession. The shortcoming of the theory is that it requires that there be initially unemployed factors in all fields which can be hired by some lines of production without reducing the output of other goods, so it is more applicable to the production of a single product, such as corn or hogs, than it is to the entire economy, and Samuelson states that statistics support such a corn–hog cycle (Samuelson, 1976).

Underconsumption theories
These are ancient theories which have been abandoned by many economists, but they underlie the more modern theories of Keynes and Hansen and much modern opinion. Mostly, these theories are invoked to explain the downturn and depression in terms of an insufficient quantity of purchasing power in the hands of consumers. Some include various portions of modern theory, such as the periodic hoarding of money or a slowing down of the velocity of money. The most recent proponent of these ideas was C.H. Douglas, who argued that an insufficient quantity of purchasing power was paid to consumers because of a diversion of a portion of the sales revenues to capital goods producers and banks (Douglas, 1933). These diverted funds are not spent on current output, causing the recession. The theories explain the boom as being due to a lag of wage income behind profit income; profit receivers are assumed to save a larger portion of their incomes than do wage earners, so an investment boom accompanies the growth of saving. After a time, the saving growth becomes too fast and total consumption spending can no longer support output, causing the crisis and depression. As incomes fall, saving decreases more rapidly, since profits fall faster than wages, and the decreased saving exacerbates the recession in the capital goods industries. A variant of the underconsumption theory argues that the quantity of money does not increase fast enough to keep up with increases in economic production and commerce so that a shortfall occurs in people's ability to purchase all of the social output; such a view, of course, depends on the downward stickiness of all prices and the failure of merchants to lower prices in response to unsold inventories. Another variant, argued by Hobson, was that modern productivity so outran increases in consumption that the ever-greater portions of income were diverted into saving rather than consumption,

leading to unsold inventories and depression (Dauten and Valentine, 1974, pp. 72–3).

Psychological theories

A.C. Pigou (1927), Wesley Mitchell and Keynes all argued that unified emotional responses of businessmen to economic events cause the observed general fluctuations in economic activity. Changes in economic conditions cause pervasive changes in businessmen's attitudes which bring about the unified alterations of decisions which cause the recession and boom. Responses of businessmen to real changes in economic conditions (such as bumper or short agricultural crops, changes in the rate of investment or new mineral discoveries) may be mistaken because of incorrect feelings of optimism or pessimism. Such errors are worse when businessmen have incomplete information, leading them to respond emotionally. In an expansion, entrepreneurs will overestimate the demand for their products, both the price and the quantity, and underestimate the costs of production, including the cost of capital (the interest rate), resulting in mistakenly large capital outlays on capital goods which are not really as profitable as they appear because of the underestimated discount rate and overestimated quantities and prices of output, ultimately causing entrepreneurs to suffer losses and bring on the recession. In a recession, entrepreneurs will underestimate demand and overestimate costs, including the cost of capital, thereby underinvesting in factors (investing only in those factors which will be wildly profitable) and increasing profitability of capital generally, so causing the boom. Also in an expansion, with its heady optimism, entrepreneurs overorder goods, casting a veil over the true state of demand and causing general overproduction of goods. Pigou argued that the errors would be larger, the larger the 'period of gestation' of the goods; that is, the period of time required to produce them, once the decision to produce them had been made. This led to wilder fluctuations in the capital goods industries because of the longer periods of gestation of capital goods. During the gestation period, bank credit is expanded, thereby increasing purchasing power beyond the expansion of consumer goods, increasing prices of consumer goods during the boom and leading entrepreneurs to believe that demand is far stronger than it actually is; during the expansion, errors of optimism feed on themselves and cause overbuilding in excess of what is required by the true state of demand. After the completion of the long-gestating capital goods causes an expansion in the quantity of consumer goods, their prices fall, revealing the mistakes of entrepreneurs who had anticipated that higher prices would continue and who, therefore, overbuilt the production structure; this revelation of error constitutes the crisis and brings on the recession as a period of necessary constriction of the production structure to bring it back into coordination with the true state of demand;

during the recession, errors of pessimism feed on themselves and spread, causing more of a constriction than is necessary. The expansion of bank credit during the gestation period was critical to Pigou's theory because it was this expansion of bank credit which led to the unified errors of entrepreneurs overestimating demand which caused the boom and the consequent recession. The expansion of bank credit distorts intertemporal prices, which are expressed as interest rates, leading entrepreneurs to overbuild the production structure of long-gestating capital goods. Also necessary is the assumed tendency of businessmen to adopt the overly pessimistic or overly optimistic views which are gathering strength around them, and the competitive tendency of businessmen to mimic the actions of others in their industry, as by reducing interest charges or terms of credit, or ordering more supplies in response to increased demand for one's product. Thus Pigou argued that a wave of optimism led to a wave of pessimism, which in turn led to a new wave of optimism. It seems reasonable to believe that emotional or psychological responses of businessmen are important in contributing to cyclic behavior, but since these alleged waves of emotion were responses to bank credit expansion and other pure economic variables, it is probably claiming too much to argue that psychological factors cause the business cycle.

Mitchell

Wesley C. Mitchell spent more time than anyone else studying business cycles and his view was that a multitude of factors contributed in different amounts and proportions to different cycles, leading to great differences between cycles in their length, amplitude and specific industries and firms affected. Mitchell's eclectic view was close to Pigou's, however, but with glances at time series seasoning his picture. Mitchell emphasized the cumulative nature of expansionary or contractionary forces, which would begin in a small sector of the economy and spread to more and more sectors. He also emphasized that the data indicated that finished goods' prices tended to rise by larger proportions than do costs of goods during the boom, leading to increases in profit rates during the boom which cause expansions of investment activity. The increased investment causes greater output which ultimately stops and reverses the price increases on goods, thereby sowing the seeds for a cumulative recession. As the expansion proceeds, costs increase faster than selling prices owing to the bringing into production of less efficient factors, increased wages due to overtime, and increased raw materials costs, which themselves are observed to rise more rapidly than selling prices. Profit rates are thereby reduced. Interest rates rise during the expansion and, when expired contracts must be renegotiated at higher interest rates, wage rates, rental rates and supply costs, profits are squeezed further and the volume of new loans contracts, all causing the abandonment of production plans because of the reduced profit expected.

Mitchell argued that the differential rates of decline of prices and profits in wholesale and retail sectors during the recession then sowed the seeds of the subsequent recovery. Prices of capital goods and raw materials fall faster than the prices of consumers goods, thereby raising profit rates; then interest rates fall during the recession, raising the profitability of capital goods, and eventually a trough is reached and expansion begins again.

Non-monetary overinvestment theory

This theory argues that the greater severity of fluctuations in investment spending compared to other spending components in the economy indicates that investment spending is the primary cause of cycles. This independent tendency of investment to fluctuate causes the remainder of the economy to fluctuate in response. In this theory the money supply expands during booms and contracts during busts only in response to the influence of the general economy, which is driven by fluctuations of investment spending which themselves respond to the relative quantities of 'fixed capital' (material goods) and 'free capital' (stores of cash) in the economy at any time. Free capital is converted into fixed capital by investment during the boom, which ends when all free capital has been converted. During the recession, depreciation charges allow the conversion of fixed capital into free capital and, when a sufficient pressure of free capital is built up, another expansion begins. A refinement of this theory by Speithoff suggested that innovations created new profit opportunities and thereby ended the recession by stimulating the demand for capital goods, and that the ceasing of innovations caused the end of the expansion.

Schumpeter: innovations as the cause of cycles

Schumpeter's theory attempted to integrate an explanation of the business cycle within an analysis of the entire economic system. The theory was presented first in his *Theory of Economic Development*, in 1912, and it formed the basis of the 'first approximation' of his more elaborate theory, presented in the two-volume *Business Cycles*, published in 1939. Schumpeter attempted to explain the general business cycle by postulating three superimposed periodic cycles, which were thought of as independent entities, combining in various ways to yield the aggregate cyclical pattern which is actually observed. Schumpeter thought that only clusters of innovation financed by newly expanded bank credit, could begin a general cyclical departure from the pre-existing general equilibrium (Schumpeter, 1935). Such clusters of innovation would begin each new boom period and, when a slackening of innovative activity occurred and their effects faltered, the recession would occur.

Monetary theories

Changes in the quantity of money or in its rate of change are essential to any cyclic phenomena; the differences between theories is only in the relative importance placed on these factors and whether these factors are considered sufficient to produce cycles, or whether monetary factors must interact with non-monetary factors, such as investment spending. Even in the 'non-monetary' theories considered above, changes in the quantity of money, and their effects on interest rates, are important causal variables; even a 'cobweb' could not occur in a barter economy without lending and borrowing. The difference is in whether or not monetary factors initiate the cycle.

The 'purely monetary' theory is most closely associated with Ralph Hawtrey; he argued that monetary changes were necessary and sufficient to bring about business cycles. Hawtrey emphasized the time lags between different flows of forms of money into and out of the banking system (Hawtrey, 1928, 1937). At the trough, the banking system has excess reserves and so lowers interest rates and credit requirements in the attempt to expand loans and bank profitability. The lower interest rates stimulate business borrowing for increased inventories and investment among the first hardy souls who overcome the prevailing pessimism. Hawtrey emphasized the use of borrowing for inventories at this stage over its use for capital goods. Larger inventories lead to a greater market share and improved profits, and then to increases in orders which spread to other firms. The expansion process cumulates just as for Mitchell. Increased orders lead to increased production and higher wage incomes, hence to greater disposable income to consumers, and thus to correspondingly increased demand for goods. Prices rise with the brisk demand, further stimulating production. As prices rise, the expectation of further price rises causes people to reduce their cash balances to accelerate their purchases before prices rise further, and this accelerates the boom unsustainably. Cash withdrawals for business needs and consumption, as well as new business loans, have eliminated the banks' excess reserves.

The boom ends when the banks become alarmed at the state of their depleted reserves and restrict new credit by raising interest rates and stiffening credit requirements. This causes a reduction of loan volume as firms restrict their new orders in order to repay inventory-carrying loans, and scale back their expansion plans. Owing to the holding of higher cash balances, there is a gap between the banks' assets and liabilities, ultimately leading excess (loanable) reserves to drop below zero. The banks must constrict their loans to retrieve their solvency. They do this by raising interest rates on renewals of debt, thereby reducing the amount of borrowing, and by increasing borrowing requirements, forcing the constriction of some inventories through lower prices and subsequently smaller orders from suppliers, and thereby reduced production and incomes, and hence reduced consumer purchasers, exacerbating the inventory surpluses. And the contraction cumulates.

The Austrian or monetary malinvestment theory

The 'Austrian' theory was built on the basis of general economic theory primarily by Ludwig von Mises and Friedrich A. von Hayek. It argues that business cycles arise from the institution of fractional reserve central banking, and the theory is unique in its consideration of the heterogeneous nature of real capital goods and how this structure of capital goods is altered by changes in the relationship between the money rate of interest and the natural rate of interest (Batemarco, 1994).

In *The Theory of Money and Credit*, originally published in 1912 (Mises, 1981, pp. 377–404, 437), Mises first explained how expansion in the quantity of money and credit artificially lowered the rate of interest, thereby causing misdirected investments in particular capital goods, and led to expansions; later, because the malinvestments could not be maintained when the interest rate rose back to its natural height, contractions ensued. Mises gave a more direct and concise explanation in a 1936 paper, in which he emphasized that the expansion is not sustainable because it consists, not of genuinely new factors, but of transferred factors of production and labor removed from lower orders of production and applied to higher orders (Mises, 1936). Mises argued that only two conclusions to the artificially induced boom were possible: if the inflation was not stopped, the flight into real values of the 'crack-up boom' and the collapse of the economy, as happened in Germany in 1923; or else, if the inflation was stopped in time, a recession involving the liquidation of some of the malinvestments which would be revealed to be unprofitable.

Several years before 1931, when he came to the London School of Economics, Friedrich A. von Hayek began the elaboration of Mises's theory of business cycles by considering the alteration in the structure of production which accompanies an increase in saving or an expansion of bank credit: namely, the distribution of productive resources between capital goods and consumption goods and the importance of the system of relative prices, particularly the relative prices of capital goods and consumption goods (Hayek, 1933, pp. 119–35). For Mises and Hayek, the crucial element necessary for the analysis of cycles was the 'elasticity of the volume of money' and its effect on the height of interest rates (ibid., pp. 139–42). Expansion of credit lowers the money, or nominal, rate of interest below the 'natural' or 'equilibrium' rate of interest (ibid., pp. 133, 139, 141, 145–9). The artificially lowered rate of interest which results from the expansion of credit raises first the prices of capital goods and only subsequently the prices of consumption goods, causing a differential shift in the production structure towards more highly specialized capital goods and more capital-intensive production, embodied in a greater number of 'stages' of production (ibid., pp. 175–6). The reduced interest rate causes new investment in new capital goods which lengthen the structure of production. Entrepreneurs have been fooled by normally reliable systems of prices and interest rates into simultaneously making mistakes in the wrong direction (Hayek, 1939, pp. 141–9). Because the lengthened structure is due to the expansion of bank credit, consumers suffer 'forced saving' which is not the result of a reduction in time preferences: they have not really increased the proportion of income which they seek to save, which is the normal cause of a reduction of the interest rate, and which would allow entrepreneurs to complete their investment projects; but the expansion of credit has allowed entrepreneurs to bid factors away from consumer goods industries and into capital goods industries, thereby causing an effective reduction in the portion of consumer incomes spent on consumption (ibid.). The money rate of interest can remain below the equilibrium rate only so long as the volume of money and credit continues to increase (Hayek, 1933, p. 176). Once the rate of growth of the volume of credit diminishes, consumers are able to reassert their unchanged time preferences, and undo some of the forced saving, thereby causing the new investments which had lengthened the production structure to become unprofitable. The liquidation of the unsupported new investments constitutes the crisis. (Hayek, 1931, pp. 54–104).

Keynes

Keynes's view in the *General Theory* (1936, ch. 22, 'Notes on the Trade Cycle'), seems to have been that the essential character of the trade cycle is a cyclical change in the (homogeneous) *marginal efficiency of capital*, or the uniform rate of return of all new capital goods (Keynes, 1936, p. 313). Keynes's theory of 1936 appears to be similar in some regards to that of Mises and Hayek; but Keynes argued that there was no market mechanism which could bring the supply of savings into equality with the demand for borrowed funds for investment, and Keynes assumed that capital goods are homogeneous, neglecting the heterogeneity of capital goods which Mises and Hayek saw as the essential cause of the recession. Therefore, Keynes argued, total spending on consumption plus investment might be less than business expenditures on production and, with business revenues falling short of total costs, business losses would result, causing business failures and unemployment. Keynes apparently saw a disparity between saving and investment, as Mises and Hayek had seen; but whereas Mises and Hayek argued that the quantity of investment outstripped the quantity of savings, Keynes argued that the quantity of savings was larger than the quantity of investment, thereby causing a reduction in 'aggregate demand'.

In the Austrian theory, the quantity of voluntary savings is too small to support the new investments because of the 'forced saving' portion caused by the artificial enhancement of investment arising from the expansion of bank credit. Keynes thought that the full quantity of saving was not directed into new investment because saving and investment were accomplished by different groups of people, so that the quantity of investment fell short of the quantity of savings withdrawn from the national circulation, and this gap in overall spending caused the crisis.

Keynes also found, as did Hayek, disappointed expectations to be important in the cycle: 'A monetary economy ... is essentially one in which changing views about the future are capable of influencing the quantity of employment and not merely its direction' (ibid., p. vii). (Aside from Keynes, the only other mainstream economist to emphasize the importance of expectations before the 'rational expectations' school arose was Sir John Hicks; the Austrians – Mises, Hayek and Lachmann – and also G.L.S. Shackle, have always emphasized the importance of patterns of expectations in understanding business cycles.) Keynes also contrasted the peak of the cycle, which had a crisis associated with it, with the trough, which had no such sharp turning-point or sudden transformation associated with it (ibid., p. 314). The crisis, said Keynes, is characterized by 'a sudden collapse in the marginal efficiency of capital', (ibid., p. 315). That is, the rate of profit on capital goods (which Keynes thought to be uniform throughout the economy in the consumer goods industries and capital goods industries as well) falls below the market interest rate, just as in the crisis mechanism described by Hayek; but for Hayek it was the profitability of particular capital goods, especially those of longer life and higher orders of production, which fell and caused the crisis. Although Keynes did not elaborate on the cause of this sudden collapse, what this must mean is that the expected prices of consumer goods fall, thereby reducing the rate of return expected on capital goods which will be used to make them. Expectations of profitability of capital goods dissolve into pessimism, liquidity preference increases and the interest rate rises sharply. The increased interest rate reduces the net present values of capital goods, causing losses to their manufacturers, who have already manufactured them in anticipation of sale to consumer goods manufacturers, since now the consumer goods industries no longer wish to purchase these capital goods. But if this is to choke off investment spending, we must be talking about investment outlays *not yet made*, and not about existing and already producing capital goods which are now perceived to have been mistakes because the prices of the goods they are manufacturing are lower than had been expected. (In the latter case, the best course of action would be to continue producing, since the outlay for the capital goods had already been made.) Keynes argues that, at this time, no reduction in the rate of interest would be sufficient to cause recovery because the expectations of profitability of capital goods are so dismal – presumably because of depressed prices of consumers goods to be manufactured by these capital goods; that is, entrepreneurs realize that they have made serious mistakes in investing in the particular capital goods they chose (ibid., pp. 316–18). Again we see the cluster of entrepreneurial error manifested, when entrepreneurs realize that their prior expectations of great profitability from these investments, which had fueled the prior boom, were incorrect, and they now expect these same investment projects to be unprofitable. They do what they can to cut their losses – abandon incomplete projects, lay off labor, lower prices to stimulate sales of existing inventories – and the recession follows. Associated with the fall in the marginal efficiency of capital is a decline in stock market prices of shares and a decline in the marginal propensity to consume. Keynes said that the disappointed expectations of the entrepreneurs who invested in capital goods arise because the capital goods gave the temporary appearance of profitability only because of the unstable and unmaintainable conditions of the boom period, and the entrepreneurs discover that this profitability cannot be maintained. But Keynes thought that *all* capital goods suffered this sudden loss of profitability compared to the rate of interest, whereas Hayek thought that it was particularly long-lived and high-order capital goods which suffered the relative decline in profitability compared with shorter-lived capital goods and lower-order capital goods. Hayek argued that it cannot be that a *general* 'overinvestment' occurred and characterized the boom; rather it seems that particular inappropriate capital goods were invested in, which should not have been. Investment was misdirected into goods whose rates of return were overestimated during the boom. The crisis occurs when the true rates (lower) of return of these particular projects are realized; however, a new crisis of pessimism causes entrepreneurs now to underestimate the true rates of return of these projects and abandon them altogether (ibid., pp. 321–2). Keynes then concluded that the proper policy is to lower the interest rate sufficiently to keep the boom from ending (ibid., p. 322); presumably this would be accomplished by further expansions of credit by the central bank. It was this policy prescription that the Austrians rejected as destined to lead to a 'crack-up boom' like that of Germany in 1923 (Mises, 1936, p. 293). Keynes did not think that the cause of the increased investment of the boom was a relevant consideration and dismissed the Austrian view that the true culprit of the mistaken investments which constituted the boom was an artificial lowering of the rate of interest caused by an expansion of money and credit by banks which made higher-order investments appear relatively more profitable than lower-order investments (Keynes, 1936, pp. 328–9). Keynes's theory also requires multi-period outlays for capital goods, or otherwise these outlays are but sunk costs, and there is no need to abandon exiting capital goods, even though the prices of the goods they manufacture have fallen. However much one infers about Keynes's theory by filling in the explicit gaps, however, it is clear that

Keynes himself did not fill in these gaps in capital theory and differential prices (Garrison, 1989). Sir Roy Harrod considerably extended and somewhat corrected Keynes's analysis (Harrod, 1936).

Multiplier–accelerator theory

The 'accelerator' principle describing the supposed leveraged relationship between consumption and investment spending is very old (Clark, 1917), and has been used as an explanation of the greater fluctuation in investment than in consumption during the cycle (Mitchell, 1923, pp. 5–18). 'Keynesian' theories of the business cycle generally begin with the simple Keynesian model of $Y = C + I + G$ and the IS/LM mechanism. The *multiplier–accelerator* theory, which was an offshoot of Keynes's investment and government-spending multipliers of the *General Theory*, was developed by Keynes, Hansen, Hicks and Samuelson (Samuelson, 1939). The most comprehensive explanation was presented by Sir John Hicks in his 1950 book, which worked in terms of real quantities, rejecting money as an important factor in the cause of cycles, in favor of the accelerator (Hicks, 1950, p. 136). Hicks brought in the effects of money only through his 'IS/LM' diagram, which considers only economy-wide aggregates and the 'price level' rather than the structure of relative prices (ibid., pp. 136–54). This theory is consistent with the characteristic of business cycles that investment fluctuates more violently than does consumption, and the cyclical amplitude of production of durable goods and producer goods is greater than that of non-durables and consumer goods. *Net investment* (additions to the stock of capital during a year) is due to *growth* in income, so a period of prosperity can end merely as the result of a decline in the rate of growth of consumption: consumption must continue to increase at the same rate unabated for investment spending to remain constant from year to year (Samuelson, 1976, pp. 260–3). If consumption growth weakens, investment spending will decline; consequent to this reduction in investment spending, the Keynesian 'multiplier' causes widespread reductions in other areas of the economy, in greater dollar volume than the original decline in consumption growth, and a widespread recession occurs.

Modern monetarist theory

The difference between the modern monetary theory and the older monetary theory is twofold: first, the utilization of empirical statistical evidence from time series which has been gathered in support of the modern theory, and second, the refinements made in understanding of time lags. Friedman and Schwartz found close correspondence between rates of growth of monetary aggregates and business conditions: rapid growth rates of the quantity of money were associated with booms, and slower or negative growth of money was associated with recessions (Friedman and Schwartz, 1963). However, there is a variable time lag between the occurrence of leading changes in money growth rates and the associated lagging business cycle effects. The changes in the growth rates of the money stock are the result of changes of monetary policy of the central bank, which may be related to government fiscal policy. Open market purchases of securities by the central bank feed new reserves into the banking system and increase the quantity of money, causing a business expansion which cumulates through the economy in the usual way. Should the central bank reduce the growth rate of the quantity of money by reducing the rate of purchase of government securities, or if it should sell securities, a recession would ensue. One might call this a 'central bank' theory instead of a 'monetary' theory.

Political cycles

Errors in government fiscal and monetary actions are seen as causes of cycles. Government policies cause unintended consequences, at least partly because of inappropriate lags in action relative to the conditions the policies are intended to ameliorate, so the effects of particular laws and regulations may be contrary to the goals of such activities. Government policies encouraging investment and consumption must ultimately be restrained to avoid hyperinflation and the 'crack-up boom', and the recession occurs when government-led expansionary activities are slowed or stopped.

J. STUART WOOD

See also:

Business Cycle Theory (I); Coordination Failures and Keynesian Economics; Depression, The Great; Expectations, Theories of; Friedman, Milton; Keynes, John Maynard; Lucas, Jr., Robert E.; New Classical School of Economics; New Keynesian Macroeconomics; Schwartz, Anna J.; von Hayek, Friedrich A.

Bibliography

Batemarco, Robert J. (1994), 'Austrian Business Cycle Theory', in Peter J. Boettke (ed.), *The Elgar Companion to Austrian Economics*, Aldershot: Edward Elgar.

Clark, J.M. (1917), 'Business Acceleration and the Law of Demand', *Journal of Political Economy*, **25**, (3), March, pp. 217–35.

Dauten, Carl A. and Lloyd M. Valentine (1974), *Business Cycles and Forecasting*, 4th edn, Cincinnati: South-Western Publishing Co.

Douglas, C.H. (1933), *Social Credit*, New York: W.W. Norton.

Ezekiel, Mordecai (1938), 'The Cobweb Theorem', *Quarterly Journal of Economics*, **52**, (1), February, pp. 255–80.

Friedman, Milton and Anna J. Schwartz (1963a), *A Monetary History of the United States, 1867–1960*, New York: National Bureau of Economic Research.

Friedman, Milton and Anna J. Schwartz (1963b), 'Money and Business Cycles', *Review of Economics and Statistics*, **45**, (1), February, Supplement, pp. 32–64.

Garrison, Roger (1989), 'The Austrian Theory of the Business Cycle in the Light of Modern Macroeconomics', in Murray N. Rothbard and Walter Block (eds), *The Review of Austrian Economics*, vol. 3, Lexington: Heath, Lexington Books.

Haberler, Gottfried (1932 [1990]), 'Money and the Business Cycle', reprinted in Stephen

Littlechild (ed.), *Austrian Economics*, Vol. II, Part IV, 'The Business Cycle and Macroeconomics', Brookfield, Vermont: Edward Elgar.

Haberler, Gottfried (1974), *Economic Growth & Stability*, Los Angeles: Nash Publishing Company.

Harrod, R.F. (1936), *The Trade Cycle*, Oxford: Clarendon Press.

Hawtrey, Ralph G. (1928), *Trade and Credit*, London: Longmans, Green & Co.

Hawtrey, Ralph G. (1937), *Capital and Employment*, London: Longmans, Green & Co.

Hayek, F.A. (1931), *Prices and Production*, London: George Routledge & Sons; reprinted New York: Augustus M. Kelley, 1967.

Hayek, F.A. (1933), *Monetary Theory and the Trade Cycle*, New York: Harcourt, Brace & World; reprinted New York: Augustus M. Kelley, 1966.

Hayek, F.A. (1939), *Profits, Interest and Investment*, London: Routledge & Sons.

Hicks, J.R. (1950), *A Contribution to the Theory of the Trade Cycle*, Oxford: Oxford University Press.

Keynes, John M. (1936), *The General Theory of Employment, Interest and Money*, London: Macmillan.

Mises, Ludwig von (1936 [1990]), 'The "Austrian" Theory of the Trade Cycle', reprinted in Stephen Littlechild (ed.), *Austrian Economics*, Vol. II, Part IV, 'The Business Cycle and Macroeconomics', Brookfield, Vermont: Edward Elgar.

Mises, Ludwig von (1981), *The Theory of Money and Credit*, New York: Foundation for Economic Education (translation of the second German edition, 1924; originally published in 1912).

Mitchell, Wesley Clair (1913), *Business Cycles*, Berkeley: University of California Press.

Mitchell, Wesley Clair (1923), *Business Cycles and Unemployment*, New York: McGraw-Hill and National Bureau of Economic Research.

Mitchell, Wesley C. (1927), *Business Cycles: The Problem and Its Setting*, New York: National Bureau of Economic Research.

Moore, Geoffrey H. (1983), *Business Cycles, Inflation and Forecasting*, 2nd edn, National Bureau of Economic Research Studies in Business Cycles No. 24, Cambridge, Mass.: Ballinger.

Pigou, A.C. (1927), *Industrial Fluctuations*, London: Macmillan.

Rothbard, Murray (1962), *Man, Economy and State*, Princeton, NJ: Van Nostrand.

Samuelson, Paul A. (1939), 'Interactions between the Multiplier Analysis and the Principle of Acceleration', *Review of Economic Statistics*, **21**, (2), May, pp. 75–8.

Samuelson, Paul A. (1976), *Economics*, New York: McGraw-Hill.

Schumpeter, Joseph A. (1935), 'The Analysis of Economic Change', *Review of Economic Statistics*, **17**, (4), May, pp. 2–10.

Cagan, Phillip

Phillip Cagan was born on 30 April 1927 in Seattle, Washington to Herman Solomon and Lillian (Leviason). After completing his undergraduate education at the University of California at Los Angeles in 1948, he made a choice which might well have been the defining one of his academic career – to pursue graduate education at the University of Chicago. There he received both his master's and doctoral degrees, in 1951 and 1954, respectively. For the next several years, he was on the faculty at the University of Chicago and at Brown University in Providence. In 1966, he joined the faculty of Columbia University, New York City, where he continues to work. During his long career, Cagan has also served for many years as a member of the senior research staff with the National Bureau of Economic Research and as an adjunct scholar of the American Enterprise Institute in Washington, DC. His published work includes seven books and over 50 major papers spanning five decades of research.

Cagan has long been known as a monetarist through his association with Milton Friedman, first as a doctoral student and then as an associate in the National Bureau's monetary studies. As with other monetarists, Cagan's research emphasizes the role of money in influencing economic activity and the price level. Specifically, much of his research has dealt with two principal issues: the stability of the demand for money and the question of whether the supply of money and the demand for money are independent. Cagan's 1956 study, 'The Monetary Dynamics of Hyperinflation' (an expanded version of his PhD dissertation conducted under the supervision of Friedman), provided important evidence on the stability of the demand for money.

Hyperinflation is characterized by an extremely rapid rise in the general level of prices of goods and services, typically lasting several years before moderating or ending. Cagan's pioneering 1956 study set out to examine the monetary characteristics of hyperinflation as displayed in seven such episodes. He theorized that variations in real money balances would depend inversely on variations in the expected rate of change of prices, offering the following explanation. The depreciation of money during inflation greatly increases the cost of holding it; this leads the public to reduce its holdings of a rapidly depreciating money; these efforts result in a large reduction in money balances in real terms and a sharp rise in monetary velocity. Cagan's results were entirely consistent with the monetarist assertion of a stable money demand function – the sharp rise in the velocity of circulation of money being a predictable response to the changes in the expected rate of change of prices.

This classic analysis of hyperinflation not only contributed significantly to the vast literature on monetary dynamics, but also renewed interest in the role of inflationary expectations. In order to relate the demand for real cash balances to the expected rate of price rise, it was first necessary to model inflationary expectations. In Cagan's model, expectations were formed adaptively, whereby next period's expectations of price increase were adjusted by some proportion of the difference between last period's expected and actual outcomes. Expressed in this way, the adaptive expectations hypothesis was also referred to as the 'error learning hypothesis'. The implication of this approach was that expected inflation would be estimated as a weighted average of all past inflation rates, where the weights declined geometrically. Such adaptive expectations lagged behind the changes actually realized, which had the potential to explain why hyperinflations characteristically tended to escalate. The adaptive expectations hypothesis, popularized by Cagan's work on hyperinflation, remained the dominant proposition concerning the formation of expectations of inflation (and a large number of other macroeconomic variables) from the mid-1950s to the late 1960s. Yet the approach had its weaknesses and the hypothesis was eventually abandoned, in the 1970s, in favor of the rational expectations hypothesis.

Cagan's 1965 monograph, 'Determinants and Effects of Changes in the Stock of Money, 1875–1960' (a companion piece to that of Friedman and Schwartz, 1963), addressed a number of propositions related to the general topic of the supply of money, perhaps the most important of which was the question of whether the observed money–output relationship was due to the exogeneity or endogeneity of money. His examination of the determinants of the money stock helped to clarify the direction of influence – the covariation observed was largely the result of influence from money to prices and output. The monetarist view that monetary changes were responsible for business cycles was widely contested, but, in large measure owing to the efforts of Cagan, Friedman and others, the view that monetary policy had important effects on economic activity came to be generally accepted by the end of the 1960s, restoring money to the center of macroeconomic inquiry.

Like many Chicago-trained economists, Cagan believed strongly in rigorous empirical testing of theoretical generalizations. His 1965 monograph, covering nearly a century of US history, best exemplified the systematic, careful conduct of his analyses. As Friedman writes in the Foreword to that work, 'There does not yet exist any other study of conditions determining the supply of money that is remotely comparable to Cagan's in its empirical scope and thoroughness' (Cagan, 1965, p. xxvii).

In the conduct of his analyses and in his emphasis on the role of money, Cagan followed the Chicago tradition. Yet the Chicago tradition encompassed much more. It was a philosophy, a perspective on the economic system, a methodology emphasizing statistical rigor and a policy prescription which was associated with the department of economics at the University of Chicago. It was a manner of looking at things, one which Cagan adopted. Today, Cagan continues the Chicago tradition, directing his attention to policy-oriented analyses of the role of monetary policy, the nature of inflation and the problems of controlling it (see, for example, Cagan, 1989).

PAULA A. MCLEAN

See also:

Brunner, Karl; Friedman, Milton; Inflation; Meltzer, Allan H.; Monetary Policy; Money; Quantity Theory of Money; Schwartz, Anna J.

Bibliography

Cagan, Phillip (1956), 'The Monetary Dynamics of Hyperinflation', in M. Friedman (ed.), *Studies in the Quantity Theory of Money*, Chicago: University of Chicago Press.

Cagan, Phillip (1965), *Determinants and Effects of Changes in the Stock of Money, 1875–1960*, New York: Columbia University Press for the National Bureau of Economic Research.

Cagan, Phillip (1989), 'The Uncertain Future of Monetary Policy', in F. Capie and G. Wood (eds), *Monetary Economics in the 1980s*, London: Macmillan.

Friedman, Milton and Anna Schwartz (1963), *A Monetary History of the United States, 1867–1960*, Princeton: Princeton University Press for the National Bureau of Economic Research.

Cambridge Circus

Following publication of Keynes's *Treatise on Money* on 31 October 1930, the Cambridge 'Circus' worked closely with Keynes as he moved from ideas in the *Treatise* to a reformulation of those ideas in what was to be *The General Theory* (1936). Also known as 'Keynes's Circus' or simply the 'Circus', its membership consisted of his close associates at Cambridge University, mainly the younger generation of economists, including Richard Kahn, Piero Sraffa, Austin and Joan Robinson, and James Meade. While Keynes also discussed the *Treatise* with Dennis Robertson and A.C. Pigou at Cambridge, these communications with older members of the faculty were separate, though not of course unrelated.

Piero Sraffa is said to have urged the formation of the Circus in the autumn of 1930 when the small group of faculty began to gather weekly in Richard Kahn's rooms in Gibb's Building, King's College. The gathering 'met the alternative dictionary definition of [a circus as] a scene of lively action and a group of people engaged in a common activity – in this case trying to understand and, later, to criticize the *Treatise*' (Moggridge, 1992, p. 533). During the winter and spring of 1931, until examinations in May, the Circus gathered as a larger 'seminar', meeting by invitation in the Old Combination

Room of Trinity College. A few undergraduates received invitations after satisfactory interviews with Kahn, Sraffa and Austin Robinson.

Keynes did not join the Circus at its regular meetings. He communicated with its members through Kahn, their 'secretary', who conversed directly with Keynes and who carried questions, issues and answers back and forth. Luigi Pasinetti considered Keynes's collaboration with the Circus 'extraordinary and unprecedented', saying further that 'Keynes knew how to write books. He was a world-famous economist; and yet he was submitting every proposition he was putting forward to the discussion of this group' (see Pasinetti's 'Discussion' in Kahn, 1984, p. 223). Kahn (1984, p. 106) noted that it would be 'astonishing' only to those 'who did not know Keynes'; Kahn recalled that Austin Robinson had credited this behavior to 'Keynes' "extraordinary magnanimity"'.

Formal records of the Circus's proceedings were not kept, but Donald Moggridge's editorial comments in Vol. XIII of *The Collected Works* (Keynes, 1973 pp. 337–43) summarize personal memories of five (at that time) living members of the Circus some 40 years after its work on the *Treatise* concluded. Kahn himself (1984) has added an eyewitness account as well as reflections on the Moggridge account of events and a response to Don Patinkin's revisionist history of how and when the new ideas in *The General Theory* took shape. A key question is whether and to what extent Kahn and the Circus influenced Keynes's change of emphasis after the *Treatise*.

Joseph Schumpeter (1954, p. 1172) contended that, during this period, Kahn's 'share in the historic achievement' of *The General Theory* 'cannot have fallen very far short of co-authorship'. Although Kahn (1984, p. 178) called this 'clearly absurd', Pasinetti (Kahn, 1984, p. 223) found a contradiction between this denial and Kahn's other remarks on the work of the Circus leading up to the publication of *The General Theory*. The issue of 'co-authorship' is closely related to the issue of where and when Keynes developed the new ideas contained in *The General Theory*. Patinkin (1982) has argued that Keynes's 'crucial breakthroughs' came much later than 1931, thereby 'disputing the importance commonly attributed to [the Circus] in assisting Keynes' (Kahn, 1984, p. 105). Kahn and Moggridge have argued for earlier dates which include the influence of the Circus.

As members of the Circus read the *Treatise*, met weekly for discussion and communicated back and forth with Keynes through Kahn, the give and take generated comments and criticisms which are said to have significantly shaped his exposition of ideas in *The General Theory*. The Circus (along with Ralph Hawtrey), for instance, assisted Keynes in moving from a theory emphasizing price fluctuations with constant output, an idea found in the *Treatise*, to the theory emphasizing adjustment through output and employment fluctuations found in *The General Theory*.

The Circus, primarily Austin Robinson, first pointed out to Keynes the nature of his 'widow's cruse' fallacy and its dependence on the assumed constancy of national output. The complaint was with the idea found in the *Treatise* that entrepreneurs' profits were 'a widow's cruse which remains undepleted however much of them may be devoted to riotous living' (the reference here is to the widow's jar of oil which did not run dry, in the days of the prophet Isaiah; see Moggridge, 1992, p. 533). Kahn (1984, p. 108) later came to see that Keynes's *Treatise* had not assumed at every point an 'inelastic supply' and he was 'mystified' as to 'why [he and other members of the Circus] did not see this for ourselves'. Nevertheless, Kahn claimed that, by June 1931, when Keynes was in Chicago to address a Harris Foundation Conference, the 'members of the Circus were entitled to feel that Keynes was responding to their criticisms with remarkable speed' (1984, p. 109). As Keynes began to give more emphasis to fluctuating output, he also began to integrate Kahn's and Hawtrey's separate investigations of a multiplier effect into what was becoming the structure of *The General Theory*.

The Circus was not the only source of fruitful criticism for Keynes at that time; Roy Harrod and Ralph Hawtrey, along with other Cambridge outsiders, contributed. The Circus served as a filter for ideas, though. If comments 'came from outside, and ... were taken up or echoed by members of the circus or merely by Richard Kahn ... they were more likely to strike home' (Moggridge, 1992, p. 532). Harry Johnson (Johnson and Johnson, 1978, p. 76) points to another use which Keynes made of the Circus, in his disagreement with 'the monetary theory specialists' over causes of Britain's economic difficulties in the 1920s. Holding 'that the key to the problem lay in the behavior of entrepreneurs', Keynes 'encouraged his "Circus" at Cambridge to ridicule the concept of hoarding and the Robertsonian "loanable funds" approach to interest rate theory in which it was embedded'.

While the Circus concluded formal meetings in 1931, Pasinetti has claimed that similar meetings went on for years. Similarly, Johnson notes (1978, p. 143) that Kahn was still holding weekly sessions in his rooms at King's, by invitation only, when Johnson lectured there at Cambridge in the 1950s. By then, the purpose of the seminars was to defend the liquidity preference theory and to test 'the technical analysis of Joan Robinson's *The Accumulation of Capital*'.

The Circus should be distinguished from the Political Economy Club at Cambridge, or 'Keynes's Club', which Keynes initiated in October 1909 and which gathered in his own rooms at King's. This group met on Monday evenings until 1937, except for a period during World War I. The Club was mainly for undergraduate students, who read and discussed each other's papers there, while the Circus was composed predominantly of the young faculty discussing Keynes's *Treatise*.

ROBERT A. BLACK

See also:

Kahn, Lord Richard F.; Keynes, John Maynard; Keynesian Revolution; Meade, James E.; Pigou, Arthur C.; Robertson, Sir Dennis H.; Robinson, Joan; Sraffa, Piero.

Bibliography

Dimand, Robert (1988), *The Origins of the Keynesian Revolution*, Stanford: Stanford University Press.

Harrod, Roy (1951), *The Life of John Maynard Keynes*, New York: W.W. Norton.

Johnson, Elizabeth S. and Harry G. Johnson (1978), *The Shadow of Keynes: Understanding Keynes, Cambridge and Keynesian Economics*, Chicago: University of Chicago Press.

Kahn, Richard F. (1984), *The Making of Keynes's General Theory*, Cambridge: Cambridge University Press.

Keynes, John Maynard (1973), *The Collected Writings of John Maynard Keynes*, especially *Vol. XIII – The General Theory and After: Preparation*, ed. Donald Moggridge, London: Macmillan, for the Royal Economic Society.

Moggridge, D.E. (1992), *Maynard Keynes: An Economist's Biography*, London: Routledge.

Patinkin, Don (1982), *Anticipations of the General Theory? and Other Essays on Keynes*, Chicago: University of Chicago Press.

Schumpeter, Joseph A. (1954), *History of Economic Analysis*, New York: Oxford University Press.

Cassel, Gustav

Karl Gustav Cassel (1866–1945) was a founding member, along with Knut Wicksell and David Davidson, of the Swedish School of economics. Cassel came to economics from mathematics. After earning an advanced degree in mathematics from the University of Uppsala, he taught in Stockholm during the late 1890s but went to Germany before the turn of the century to study economics. His publications in economics date from 1899 and span a period of nearly four decades. He taught economics at the University of Stockholm from 1903 until 1936. Gunnar Myrdal and Bertil Ohlin were his most prominent students.

Despite the formal training in Germany, Cassel's perspective on economic reality, and especially on the role of interest, was rooted in British neoclassicism and in the nascent Swedish school, which was given shape by Wicksell's early writings. Cassel's facility with mathematics and his use of it to describe the interconnectedness of markets created a strong kinship between his theories and those of Leon Walras. In addition to his major works on interest rate determination and general equilibrium theory, Cassel popularized the purchasing power parity theory of exchange rates and contributed to the current debates on monetary stability and currency reform. (Keynes incorporated the idea of purchasing power parity in his *Tract on Monetary Reform* (1923). In 1922, Cassel and Keynes, along with two other economists, were signatories of the majority report of a commission on currency reform submitted to the German government.) Cassel also wrote extensively for the popular press and was a staunch supporter of free markets and free trade. A summary of his ideas is offered in his own *Fundamental Thoughts in Economics* (1925).

The Nature and Necessity of Interest (1903) advanced and soon came to exemplify Swedish thought on the fundamental economic realities that underlie the relationship between saving and investment. If the interest rate is conceived as a price, it is the price of a factor of production called 'waiting'. Casselian waiting has the dual dimensions of value and time, as might be measured in dollar-years. Two hundred dollars relinquished to a borrower for a period of three years constitutes, if compounding is ignored, six hundred dollar-years of waiting. A positive rate of interest entices income earners to wait to consume what they could in fact consume now; it entices investors to economize on resource utilization that involves waiting. Alfred Marshall had used the term 'waiting' to similar effect – preferring it to the older term, 'abstinence' (which has moral connotations); William Stanley Jevons had introduced the units of pound-years on the basis of his own dimensional analysis. Critical of Böhm-Bawerk's time-preference theory for its special treatment of intertemporal exchange, Cassel drew on Marshall and Jevons to emphasize that the theory of interest was on equal footing with price theory in general.

Cassel's most ambitious work, *Theoretische Sozialökonomie* (1918), translated into English in 1923 as *The Theory of Social Economy*, sets out the conditions for a general equilibrium in the sense of Walras. Cassel's formulation was simpler than Walras's in that money prices rather than the underlying values or utilities served as the basic building-blocks of the system. (Critics, including Wicksell, held that this analytical simplicity came at the expense of economic understanding and that the strong link to Walras's system of equations was never sufficiently acknowledged.) Cassel dealt first with the static state, in which secular change is ruled out by assumption, and then with the progressive state, which is characterized by uniform growth. Considerations of dynamics, including cyclical variation, were offered as a supplement to the more fundamental economics of the static and progressive states. Cassel was an eclectic on the issue of the trade cycle: money, credit, trade flows and speculation in securities markets were all accorded causal roles. In the final analysis, however, movements in the interest rate and corresponding changes in the profitability of fixed capital are central, according to Cassel, to our understanding of trade cycles in modern times.

In several respects, Cassel's theory of general equilibrium – more so than Walras's – represents the relevant foil against which Keynes's own ideas were presented. When Keynes dealt on an exegetical level with alternative theories of interest, he categorized the theories of Marshall, Cassel and Walras as 'classical' in the sense that they took interest to be a real, rather than monetary, phenomenon and took the interest rate as the market's device for bringing saving and investment into equality. Cassel's formulation was the more obvious foil if only because it was a clear and direct outgrowth of Marshall's. Also the theory of interest, so central to Keynes's thinking, was given due prominence in Cassel's. The system of general equilibrium equations, as set out in Cassel's 1918 work, was built up around the theory of interest he had developed a decade and a half earlier. By comparison, Walras's *Elements of Pure Economics*, as first published in 1874, contained no theory of interest at all. The utility theory of saving and a treatment of capital goods pricing were not introduced until the fourth edition, which appeared in 1900. Finally, Walras was neither well received nor even widely read in England at the time that Keynes's ideas were developing; there was no English translation of *Elements* until 1954.

One of Keynes's objections to the classical theory of interest makes direct use of Cassel's treatment of the relationship between saving and the interest rate. The saving function may be backward-bending – and *will* be if people save with an eye towards accumulating a set amount by some future date. (This point is also made by Marshall). Keynes argues that a downward-sloping demand for loanable funds and a backward-bending supply may have no intersection, a possibility that, in his judgement, should have warned the classical economists away from Cassel's (and Marshall's) supply-and-demand approach.

Probably the most sweeping contrast between Cassel's and Keynes's frameworks derives from differing perceptions of the scope for a general theory of the particular phenomena that give macroeconomics its subject matter. According to Cassel, there can be no such thing as a general theory of unemployment. The system of equations of a truly general theory determine simultaneously all prices and quantities in both product and factor markets and provide a full solution in which, for example, unemployment and distribution of income have no independent, or separate, existence – and hence in which demand management policies have no justification. This was Cassel's summary judgment in his 1937 review of Keynes's *General Theory*. For Keynes, however, the inherent unknowability of the future and the inherent subjectivity of expectations about the future were enough to render Cassel's system of equations irrelevant and give scope for the 'dark forces of time and ignorance' to affect the performance of real-world market economies.

ROGER W. GARRISON

See also:

Arrow, Kenneth J.; Classical Economics; Interest, Theories of; Keynes, John Maynard; Lausanne, The School of; Marshall, Alfred; Myrdal, Gunnar; Ohlin, Bertil; Stockholm School of Economics; Wicksell, Knut.

Bibliography

Cassel, Gustav (1903), *The Nature and Necessity of Interest*, New York: Macmillan.
Cassel, Gustav (1918), *Theoretische Sozialökonomie*, Leipzig: C.F. Winter; English translation 1923: *The Theory of Social Economy*, London: T.F. Unwin.
Cassel, Gustav (1921), *The World's Monetary Problems*, London: Constable and Co.
Cassel, Gustav (1922), *Penningväsendet efter 1914*, Stockholm: P.A. Norstedt; English translation 1922: *Money and Foreign Exchange after 1914*, London: Constable and Co.
Cassel, Gustav (1925), *Fundamental Thoughts in Economics*, London: T.F. Unwin.
Cassel, Gustav (1936), *The Downfall of the Gold Standard*, Oxford: Clarendon Press.
Cassel, Gustav (1937), 'Keynes' *General Theory*', *International Labor Review*, **36**, (4), October, pp. 437–45.

Champernowne, David G.

Born into an academic family in Oxford, David Champernowne attended school at Winchester, from where he became a student at King's College, Cambridge. As a schoolboy he excelled at mathematics and this became his first course of study at university. However, his pre-university reading of Marshall's *Principles of Economics*, an early encounter with Dennis Robertson at Cambridge, and a persuasive John Maynard Keynes led him to take the mathematics Part II tripos in one year, allowing him to proceed to the economics tripos. His ability was demonstrated by the fact that he gained a first in both economics and mathematics. An MA at Cambridge in 1938 was followed by an MA at Oxford University in 1945.

His academic career was almost entirely focused in Oxford and Cambridge. Between 1945 and 1959, he worked in Oxford, becoming Professor of Statistics, and was Director of the Oxford Institute of Statistics. From 1959, he moved to Cambridge, first as Reader in Economics and then Professor of Economic Statistics from 1969 to 1978. Since 1979, he has become Emeritus Professor at Cambridge. During World War II he worked first in the statistical section of the prime minister's office, then transferred to the Ministry of Aircraft Production; here again he worked in the Department of Statistics and programming under John Jewkes. He became co-editor of the *Economic Journal* (1971–5) and was elected a Fellow of the British Academy in 1970.

It would be incorrect to label Champernowne purely as an economic statistician; although he made significant contributions in economic statistics, he was equally productive in adding to economic theory. He first turned his attention to income distribution in his dissertation at King's in 1936. This much later became *The Distribution of Income between Persons* (1973), which must be regarded as remarkable now for its use of stochastic processes in the analysis of income distribution. He also provided a scientific approach to the relative merits of different 'indexes of inequality' (1974). There was no one 'best coefficient of inequality'. He believed that there were a variety of aspects of inequality which were of interest and different coefficients were better suited to reflect different aspects. Using inappropriate coefficients could lead to 'seriously wrong conclusions' (1974, p. 787) when investigating particular aspects of inequality. He demonstrated this via an exhaustive enquiry into six general inequality indexes, using certain maps and triangular diagrams to investigate, amongst other things, the sensitivities of the indexes to different types of inequalities.

His early acquaintance with probability theory led him to apply Bayesian analysis to anti-regressive series at a time when other economists had taken alternative approaches. As a consequence his three-volume work, *Uncertainty and Estimation*, published in 1969, looks decidedly modern; it is also remarkable for its clarity, comprehensiveness and originality – the latter quality not often associated with what at first sight appears to be a basic textbook. But it is much more than this; Champernowne succeeds in providing perhaps the first major work which offers an understanding of the nature and influence of uncertainty in many areas of economics. In addition, the trilogy of volumes offers a methodology for analysis, given the existence of uncertainty. It is particularly important for the insight which it gives to economic behavior when decision making occurs under conditions of imperfect knowledge.

What is often less appreciated of Champernowne, frequently disguised from view, is the stimulus he provided to others in pioneering work. There are other examples of this: Joan Robinson benefited in her working out of the relation between capital and growth; Pigou was influenced on the theory of output; Van Neumann's work was interpreted for a wider audience. As an example of this, let us take Champernowne's contribution to our understanding of Kaldor's growth model (Champernowne, 1973) and also his interpretation of Keynes. In his usual painstaking fashion, he sets out the conditions which make the growth part of Kaldor's model stable; essentially, if there is some restyling of the model as a continuous-time model, it is possible for it to become stable. In his 1936 paper, before the publication of Hicks's seminal work on Keynes and the Classics, Champernowne goes a long way to producing the IS/LM framework, and this may well have influenced Hicks (see Warren Young, 1987).

JOHN R. PRESLEY

See also:
IS/LM Model and Diagram; Kaldor, Lord Nicholas; Keynes, John Maynard; Robertson, Sir Dennis H.

Bibliography

Champernowne, D.G. (1936), 'Unemployment, Basic and Monetary: the Classical Analysis and the Keynesian', *Review of Economic Studies*, 3, (3), pp. 201–16.

Champernowne, D.G. (1958), 'Capital Accumulation and the Maintenance of Full Employment', *Economic Journal*, **68**, (270), June, pp. 211–44.

Champernowne, D.G. (1969), *Uncertainty and Estimation in Economics*, 3 vols, Edinburgh: Oliver and Boyd.

Champernowne, D.G. (1973), *The Distribution of Income Between Persons*, Cambridge: Cambridge University Press.

Champernowne, D.G. (1974), 'A Comparison of Measures of Income Distribution', *Economic Journal*, **84**, (336), December, pp. 787–816.

Young, W. (1987), *Interpreting Mr Keynes*, Oxford: Polity Press in association with Basil Blackwell.

Chicago School of Economics

The term 'Chicago School' refers to a singular approach to economic analysis and policy established by economists associated with the University of Chicago. The school originated in the 1930s, gained formal recognition in the mid-1950s and achieved intellectual prominence in the 1960s, 1970s and 1980s.

At least five hallmarks distinguish the school. First is its interpretation of all economic behavior in terms of the perfectly competitive model of neoclassical price theory. Non-Chicagoans protest that the model's assumption of price-taking maximizing agents, flexible prices and continuously clearing markets are too unrealistic to be taken seriously. But Chicagoans contend that the test of a theory is its predictive power rather than the realism of its assumptions. Chicagoans believe the competitive model better predicts business behavior than do monopoly and imperfect competition models. They argue that such market-power models cannot account for the all-pervasive drive for efficiency and cost cutting found even in oligopolistic and monopolistically competitive firms. Moreover, modern Chicagoans insist that market-power considerations are largely irrelevant in a world in which freedom of entry renders monopoly positions ephemeral.

A second hallmark is the school's belief in free markets as the solution to economic and social problems. Chicagoans hold that free markets allocate resources, distribute incomes and organize activity far more efficiently than do non-market mechanisms such as the government. The role of the government is not to interfere with the market but rather to provide a stable framework of law and order within which it can flourish.

A corollary hallmark, therefore, is the school's aversion to government intervention. Chicagoans oppose such intervention on the grounds that it replaces voluntary cooperation with coercion, distorts prices, subverts incentives, promotes monopoly and is the source of macroeconomic policy errors that destabilize the economy. Chicagoans hold that market economies are inherently stable and would tend to operate close to capacity were it not for policy mistakes emanating from discretionary fine-tuning. Inept policy, not market failure, precipitates inflations and depressions.

A fourth hallmark is the school's monetarist approach to macroeconomic analysis and policy. In contrast to the Keynesian investment-saving or aggregate demand model of income determination, Chicagoans employ a quantity-theoretic, or money supply and demand, approach. This approach they regard as nothing other than neoclassical value theory applied to money. They stress the notions of exogenous (that is, central bank-determined) money, direct money-to-price causality, inflation as a monetary phenomenon, velocity as a stable function of a few key variables and controllability of money through the high-powered monetary base. They advocate rules rather than discretion in the conduct of monetary policy.

A fifth identifying hallmark is the school's extension of price theory to areas traditionally regarded as beyond the jurisdiction of economics. Politics, corporate finance, the legal system, crime, punishment, marriage and divorce – no subject is too alien to elude the school's imperialistic reach. Chicago brings all within the compass of price theory.

Although any economist adhering to the foregoing propositions qualifies as a Chicagoan, that label most often attaches to the leaders of the school. These include Frank Knight and Henry Simons, progenitors of the school in the 1930s, Milton Friedman and George Stigler, who brought it into intellectual prominence in the 1950s and 1960s, and others such as Gary Becker, Robert Lucas, Robert Fogel, Merton Miller, Eugene Fama and Ronald Coase who keep the tradition alive today.

Knight, although skeptical of the ethical basis of free-market capitalism, nevertheless denounced all social engineering schemes and so defined the school's aversion to government intervention. And in his famous 1924 *Quarterly Journal of Economics* article on 'Some Fallacies in the Interpretation of Social Cost', he enunciated the school's case for property rights and free-market pricing. Addressing the problem of highway congestion, he argued that such overcrowding requires no corrective intervention. Instead it requires privatization and the establishment of property rights so that the owner can charge a market-clearing toll and thus eliminate the congestion.

Simons outlined the school's case for confining the government to the task of maintaining a stable framework within which markets could flourish. He saw stable money as well as progressive income taxation and government ownership of natural monopolies as components of that framework. He likewise foreshadowed some monetarist doctrines of the school. With his colleague, Lloyd Mints, he used the quantity theory framework (although he never treated its velocity component as a stable function). He held that monetary mismanagement had worsened the Great Depression and that rules – in his case a price-stabilization rule – should replace discretion in the conduct of monetary policy. In response to the Keynesian view that fiscal policy replaces ineffective monetary policy in depressions, he argued that, on the contrary, fiscal deficits are merely the means by which powerful countercyclical expansions of the money stock can be injected into circulation.

Friedman, whose name is synonymous with the school, contributed more than all the others to establish Chicago's price-theoretic, monetarist, free-market foundations. He strove to render price theory more operational by using it to construct simple models yielding testable hypotheses. As the world's leading monetarist, he deployed a resuscitated quantity theory to attack the Keynesian notions that money does not matter, that fiscal policy constitutes the dominant stabilization tool, that real shocks precipitated the Great Depression, that inflation is a cost-push phenomenon, that velocity is an infinitely malleable will-o'-the-wisp, that monetary policy is passive and accommodating rather than active and controlling, and that discretionary fine-tuning outperforms policy rules. With his permanent income hypothesis he refuted Keynes's notion that consumption is a function of current, as opposed to lifetime or permanent, income. He combined his adaptive expectations hypothesis with his natural rate hypothesis to demolish the Keynesian notion of a stable long-run Phillips curve trade-off between inflation and unemployment. He showed that the trade-off is between inflation's *rate of rise* and unemployment such that Keynesian full-employment policies require ever-accelerating inflation. As the foremost proponent of free-market solutions to social problems, he crusaded tirelessly for such reforms as the negative income tax, the all-volunteer army, educational vouchers, flexible exchange rates and the abolition of rent controls and licensure of physicians (Friedman and Friedman, 1979).

Finally, the work of Stigler, Becker, Fogel, Miller, Fama, Coase and Lucas epitomizes the Chicago's disciplinary imperialism. Stigler extended the competitive model to the fields of industrial organization, public regulation and political activity where it had not been used before. Becker applied price theory to the analysis of labor market discrimination, crime and punishment, allocation of time and the economics of marriage, divorce and child-rearing. Miller and Fama extended the neoclassical axioms to financial analysis just as Fogel did to the study of economic history. Coase demonstrated that externalities are efficiently internalized when rights to inflict damage can be bought and sold. Lucas, building on work of John Muth, extended the rational-agent assumption to the theory of expectations formation and thence to macro-policy analysis. The result was the policy ineffectiveness proposition: rational agents fully anticipate systematic future policy actions and so adjust their wages and prices accordingly. Consequently, when the policy actions occur, they have no real effects. When incorporated into Friedman's expectations-augmented Phillips curve, Lucas's rational expectations hypothesis rules out even temporary trade-offs between inflation and its time derivatives and unemployment.

Chicago's hallmarks distinguish it from rival schools. Its notions of continuously clearing markets, perfect competition, long-run neutrality of money and rigorous empirical testing differentiate it from the Austrian School. Its opposition to the ideas of endogenous (demand-determined) money, reverse causality, cost-push or supply-shock inflation, infinitely malleable velocity and monopoly market power set it apart from the Post Keynesian school. Its belief in the monetary theory of the cycle and the short-run non-neutrality of money distinguish it from the Real Business Cycle school. And so forth.

As for the future, a race between persuasion and innovation will determine the school's survival. For Chicago loses its distinctiveness as it persuades others to accept its doctrines. But it regains that uniqueness as it finds new applications for its ideas. Its 40-year survival despite its great influence is testament to its inventiveness.

THOMAS M. HUMPHREY

See also:

Austrian School of Economics, The; Expectations, Theories of; Friedman, Milton; Lucas, Jr., Robert E.; Money; New Classical School of Economics; Quantity Theory of Money.

Bibliography
Friedman, Milton and Rose Friedman (1979), *Free to Choose*, New York: Harcourt Brace Jovanovich.
Patinkin, Don (1981), *Essays On and In the Chicago Tradition*, Durham, NC: Duke University Press.
Reder, Melvin W. (1982), 'Chicago Economics: Permanence and Change', *Journal of Economic Literature*, **20**, (1), March, pp. 1–38.
Reder, Melvin W. (1987), 'Chicago School', John Eatwell, Murray Milgate and Peter Newman (eds), *The New Palgrave: A Dictionary of Economics*, Vol. 1, New York: Stockton Press.
Stigler, George J. (1988), *Memoirs of an Unregulated Economist*, New York: Basic Books.

Clark, Colin

Colin Clark enjoyed a long and productive career in economics. The initial period of his career focused on the methodological development and compilation of national income statistics for several countries and their use to analyse growth and development within a Keynesian framework. He then published in many fields of economics over a long span of years.

Clark was born in London in 1905 and died in Brisbane, Australia in September 1989, at the age of 83. After attending Oxford University, graduating with an honours degree in chemistry in 1928, and a fleeting career in politics as an unsuccessful Labour Party candidate for Parliament, Clark entered economics in 1930 as a staff member of the newly formed Economic Advisory Council. In 1931, he became a lecturer in statistics at Cambridge University. In 1937, he moved to Australia, first as a visiting lecturer, and then as director of the Bureau of Industry, the state statistician and the financial adviser to the Treasury, all of the Queensland state government. Clark left Australia in 1952 to be a visiting professor at the University of Chicago. In 1953, he returned to the United Kingdom as the director of the Institute of Agricultural Economics at Oxford University. In 1969, he again moved to Australia, first to Monash University until retirement in 1977, then to the University of Queensland as a research consultant (Arndt, 1979; Higgins, 1989).

Clark played leading roles in the concurrent revolutions of national economic statistics and macroeconomic theory in the 1930s. His first book (1932) and associated journal articles preceded the publication of Keynes's *General Theory*, but provided estimates of national product and investment with which to begin testing the theory. In subsequent publications, he presented estimates in the Keynesian final demand format that laid the foundation for the creation of British government statistical programs during World War II and further extensions of macroeconomic theory (Clark, 1937). In this process he played a role parallel to that of Simon Kuznets in the United States (Patinkin, 1976). Clark is often credited with being the first to use the term 'gross national product' rather than national income. He later extended his work to estimates of the national income and product of New Zealand, Australia and the Soviet Union (Higgins, 1989).

From the beginning, Clark recognized that the value of national economic statistics was to test theories and support policy. Keynes and others commended him for posing important questions and answering them by ingenious use of inadequate statistics (Arndt, 1979). For example, he used his data to estimate values for theoretical concepts such as the marginal propensity to save, the multiplier and changes in product per man-year. More practically, he applied Keynesian macroeconomics to advise the Queensland government in the late 1930s and 1940s (Kenwood, 1988).

Clark greatly expanded the scope of his work in the book for which he is probably most widely known, *The Conditions of Economic Progress* (1940, revised in 1951 and 1957). As summarized by Arndt (1979),

The book is a seminal work in at least three respects. First, it was one of the first systematic attempts to use national accounts data for a wide range of countries to test macroeconomic hypotheses and in this sense a pioneering contribution to modern macroeconomic econometrics. Second, it was the first major work, after decades of almost exclusive preoccupation of the Western economic profession with static problems of resource allocation and latterly with economic fluctuations, that turned attention back to the classical problem of economic growth and was thus a starting point of modern development economics. Third, by supplying the first substantial statistical evidence of the gulf in living standards between rich and poor countries, it help awaken Western opinion to the problems of the under-developed.

In order to make international economic comparisons, Clark not only collected estimates for many countries and converted them to constant prices, but also invented the International Unit as a means to convert each country's data to a single set of prices, a forerunner of the work of Gilbert and Kravis and others years later. Beyond this major methodological breakthrough, Clark used the data to make international comparisons of labour productivity, industrial structures and price elasticities of consumption.

Clark was also a pioneer in forecasting. In *The Economics of 1960* (1942), he built an econometric model for the world economy. He boldly predicted, although incorrectly as it turned out, that the terms of trade would move strongly in favor of primary products between the end of World War II and 1960, largely on the basis of optimistic estimates of how rapidly China and India would industrialize. In another path-breaking analysis, Clark suggested that, whenever taxes exceeded 25 per cent of national income, there will be a strong resistance to additional taxes and governments will be more likely to accept higher rates of inflation (Perkins and Van Hoa, 1988). He later admitted that the correlation between tax incidence and inflation was weak (Perkins and Powell, 1990), but his analysis opened an important new field for others to plough.

Clark's wide-ranging interests and, according to Arndt (1979), his conversion to Roman Catholicism led him into many important fields. One field was demographic economics. He believed that population growth was economically beneficial and that there was no practical limit on the ability of the food supply to expand to support any size of world population. He disagreed with the Club of Rome forecast of a rapid exhaustion of natural resources, partly on the basis of the rationale that mining companies did not waste money discovering reserves that they would not use for many years (Higgins, 1989). Arndt (1979) believes that Clark 'provided much of the economic rationale for the hard line against birth control by contraceptive devices of the papal encyclical *Humanae Vitae*'.

JOHN S. PITZER

See also:

Demand Management; Econometric Models, Macroeconomic; Fiscal Policy; Keynes's Economics, National Income Accounting Activism and; Keynesian Revolution; Kuznets, Simon; Multiplier Effect; Shackle, G.L.S.; Stone, Sir John Richard N.

Bibliography

Arndt, H.W. (1979), 'Colin Clark', in *International Encyclopedia of the Social Sciences Biographical Supplement*, New York: The Free Press.

Clark, Colin (1932), *The National Income, 1924–1931*, London: Macmillan.

Clark, Colin (1937), *National Income and Outlay*, London: Macmillan.

Clark, Colin (1940, 1951, 1957), *The Conditions of Economic Progress*, London: Macmillan

Clark, Colin (1942), *The Economics of 1960*, London: Macmillan.

Higgins, Christopher I. (1989), 'Colin Clark: An Interview', *Economic Record*, **65**, (190), pp. 296–310.

Kenwood, George (1988), 'The Use of Statistics for Policy Advising: Colin Clark in Queensland, 1938–52', in D. Ironmonger, J.O.N. Perkins and Tran Van Hoa (eds), *National Income and Economic Progress: Essays in Honour of Colin Clark*, New York: St Martin's Press.

Patinkin, Don (1976) 'Keynes and Econometrics: On the Interaction between the Macroeconomic Revolutions of the Interwar Period', *Econometrica*, **44**, (6), pp. 1091–1123.

Perkins, J.O.N. and Alan A. Powell (1990), 'Colin Clark, 1905–1989: An Affectionate Memoir', *Economic Record*, **66**, (195), pp. 329–41.

Perkins, J.O.N. and Tran Van Hoa (1988), 'Twenty-Five Per Cent Forty Years On', *National Income and Economic Progress: Essays in Honour of Colin Clark*, New York: St Martin's Press.

Classical Economics

Karl Marx first used the term 'classical' to refer to a type of political economy which he claimed 'investigated the real relations of production in bourgeois society' (Marx, 1971, p. 85n). For him this tradition spanned the writers from Petty to Ricardo, ending around 1830 with the rise of 'vulgar economy', a pseudo-scientific form of economic thought which concentrated on appearances only. As is so frequently the case, Marx was guilty of writing the history of economics 'backwards' and, as a result, his view of what constitutes classical economics is heavily influenced by a desire to find his own intellectual roots. A 'classical' economist, then, is someone who contributed to Marx's class conflict model of the laws of motion of the capitalist economy. This view thrives today among Marxist historians of economics who emphasize the break with Ricardian value theory which occurred after 1830 as a significant watershed after which capitalist apologetics in the form of subjective value theory and supply and demand price theory achieved hegemony.

In the twentieth century, Keynes and the Keynesians appropriated the term 'classical' and used it in a pejorative sense to refer to those economists who came under the thrall of Say's Law and, therefore, failed to appreciate Keynes's principle of effective demand and its concomitant unemployment macroeconomic equilibrium. In this view Marshall, Walras and Pigou become 'classical' economists, despite the usual tendency to label them 'neoclassical'.

Although controversy continues to surround the interpretation of the classical school, neither Marx's nor Keynes's meaning is the dominant one today. Marx's view is so intimately dependent on his view of intellectual activity as subservient to class interests that it is not much help to those who reject his model of the social formation of ideas. Moreover, the Keynesian approach, with its preoccupation with Say's Law and full employment, can only be sustained at the expense of seriously misrepresenting the ideas of the economists in question. Most historians treat classical economics as spanning a period of roughly 100 years, from the publication of the *Wealth of Nations* in 1776 to the marginal revolution in 1870. Smith, Ricardo and J.S. Mill are the dominant figures of the school, with dozens of lesser lights of which the most prominent are Malthus and J.B. Say. In broadest terms these economists shared an interest in the process of economic growth and viewed economics, or political economy as it was called, as a science of the creation and distribution of wealth. Microeconomics played an important role in their theories, but it was developed within the context of their primary concerns about social wealth. They were generally free traders and shared a crusading spirit to debunk the mercantilist fallacies. Even Malthus, who opposed the Ricardians in the Corn Law controversies, viewed corn as an exception to the free trade position.

The core of classical economics is a dynamic model of value, distribution and growth. Building on the Physiocrats, Adam Smith first constructed such a model, and the *Wealth of Nations* became the fountainhead from which the classical theories of the nineteenth century emerged. Using the Physiocratic concept of capital as goods, such as food, seeds, implements and buildings, advanced to the production process, Smith built a model in which saving behavior, frugality, created capital which in turn expanded both the division of labor and the percentage of the workforce productively employed. The latter meant those employed in agriculture, manufacturing and trade. This was the basis of economic growth. As long as the economy was growing, the demand for labor would rise faster than the supply. The force of increasing returns as the division of labor expanded and lowered the real price of goods in conjunction with the rising population and the 'savings-is-investment' assumption assured that aggregate demand grew apace with aggregate supply without short-term disruptions. At the end of Book I, Smith proposed a model of the dynamic trend of the distributive shares predicting rising wages and rents along with falling profits. The predictions for rent and profits, but not wages, became commonplace in the nineteenth century, albeit for different reasons than Smith's.

One of the key differences between Smith and his followers was the introduction of the theory of the long-run subsistence wage based on Malthusian population dynamics (which were in Smith) in the context of diminishing returns in agriculture (which was not in Smith). This alone did much to convert Smith's optimism into the dismal science. With appropriate caveats about rational reconstructions and the dangers of generalizations, especially as interpretations of any one person's thought, it would be appropriate to examine a modern reconstruction of what Samuelson (1978) has called the 'canonical classical' model.

Consider a twice differentiable production function in which corn output is a function of capital, also measured in units of corn (although not necessarily all corn). Capital consists of homogeneous labor and other inputs combined in fixed proportions and, therefore, measured as doses of capital, K, along the horizontal axis of Figure 1. Average and marginal products fall as successive doses are applied to the intensive margin, and they fall as the extensive margin moves into ever more infertile land. Ow is the per person subsistence wage and w_s represents the long-run labor supply if we assume instant adjustment of population to wage changes. k_s is the long-run supply of capital if wk/Ow is the rate of profit which just compensates risk such that capital accumulation ceases when the rate of profit falls to that level.

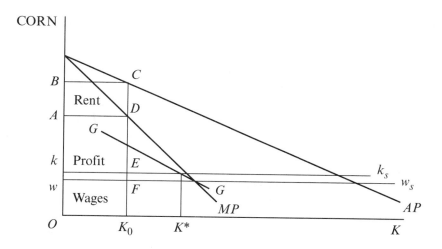

Figure 1

The economy is initially at K_0 with rent determined as the difference between average and marginal products. The marginal product of the composite dose determines the wage plus profit share. With instant adjustment of population, the subsistence wage determines the wage share, leaving $wADF$ as profits. Since this is above the minimum, capital accumulates, the economy grows, increasing the demand for food, short-run wages and population until we reach the stationary state at K^*. Corn wages are constant, rent rises and profits fall as a result of rising population pressing up against scarce land.

Although we have assumed instant adjustment of the population/labor supply/real wage segment of the model, it is attractive to allow wages to rise above subsistence as capital accumulates since this is actually necessary to explain the rising population. As recent interpretations have shown, there is textual evidence to support such a variation of the model (Casarosa, 1985; Hollander, 1987). In this case the model is easily modified to show the dynamic path of wages and profits falling along a locus such as *GG* (Samuelson, p. 1427). Capital and labor grow at the same rate along *GG* until they once again reach their long-run equilibrium values. In fact, with appropriate reproductive restraint, frequently expressed in the classical literature as the workers acquiring a taste for luxuries, improvements in the wage goods sector, and/or free importation of corn, the classical model will yield substantially more optimistic results. The stationary state was not necessarily inevitable (although J.S. Mill, for one, thought it a good state of the world).

This reconstruction of a classical-like model is helpful in reproducing classical dynamic results. Rents rise while profits fall. One has to be careful, however, with wages. The long-run commodity wage is constant. The cost of producing wage goods rises, causing the monetary payment of wages to rise. From this definition of wages we get the inverse wage/profit relation, or fundamental theorem of distribution, which was central to classical theory. In the intermediate run, which could actually last a long time, commodity wages are above subsistence and tend to fall at the same time that money wages are rising.

Understanding these more intricate effects, which underpin the fundamental theorem, requires a knowledge of classical value theory. This in turn developed as an integral part of the total model. Value and distribution were interdependent phenomena and cannot be understood separately. There was, however, no single classical theory of value. Labor time, cost of production, supply and demand, and nascent utility theories were all advanced by one or more of the classical economists. There was, however, widespread agreement on the Smithian distinction between natural and market prices and his analysis of the process by which the market price adjusted in the long run to equality with the natural price. Classical value theory for the most part aimed at explaining the determinants of natural price.

Ricardo is fairly typical in this regard. In brief, assuming constant returns in manufacturing and diminishing returns in agriculture, he argued that the cost of production measured in labor time determined manufacturing prices while the same principle at the no-rent margin determined agricultural prices. J.S. Mill produced similar results, although he moved away from the labor theory towards a more modern supply and demand framework.

There were numerous points of contention among economists of this era in the area of value theory. Malthus contended with Ricardo and the Ricardians on the role of labor time and the cost of production in the determination of prices. Samuel Bailey criticized Ricardo's concept of absolute values (inherent in the labor theory approach) on the grounds that value is an entirely relative concept. In addition, Say, for example, advanced the notion that value was subjective, residing in the utility of the final consumer. These discussions ultimately generated some progress towards a modern conception of the supply and demand apparatus. J.S. Mill made a major contribution by clearly distinguishing the quantity from the schedule concepts of supply and demand. In addition, the introduction of abstinence as an element of cost in the supply of capital moved the cost of production away from physical labor time to a subjective conception of sacrifice. However, much of the classical debate appears frustrating and unfruitful from the modern perspective. Virtually all of the classical theories are valid and mutually compatible within the context of the assumptions of their models. For example, given constant returns to scale, equal capital/labor ratios across industries and factor price equalization in competitive markets, that is free mobility of labor and capital, labor values are the same as cost of production values, which in turn are the same as supply and demand values in long-run competitive equilibrium. Labor and cost theories are special cases of supply and demand theories and, in fact, require the equilibrating mechanism of supply and demand analysis. Though he is not usually given credit for his contributions to value theory, Malthus saw very clearly that Ricardo was talking about a special case. Given Ricardo's understanding of supply and demand as quantities, not schedules, he was unable to make sense of what Malthus was saying.

It is important to understand that value theory, especially for Ricardo, had a very important role to play in the aggregate analysis of distribution and growth. Indeed, the theoretical requirements of the growth model essentially determined the direction he and his followers, including J.S. Mill, pursued. The fundamental theorem of distribution is at bottom a relative price phenomenon, and it is the determination of the relative price structure, therefore, which is at the center of the Ricardian system. Diminishing returns in agriculture, coupled with rising demand for food, cause agricultural prices to rise relative to manufacturing prices. Ricardo could most clearly deduce this if he looked at relative labor inputs in the two sectors – hence his preoccupation with the labor theory of value. A generalized supply and demand framework can produce the same result. Since food entered the manufacturing process via its impact on wages, diminishing returns which depressed agricultural profits then depressed profits generally as the money price of wages rose to squeeze manufacturing profits. The falling rate of profit and the inverse wage/profit relation of the classical model are ultimately relative price phenomena in a general equilibrium framework.

Piero Sraffa advanced an alternative interpretation in the early 1950s in which the falling rate of profit occurs as the surplus corn output falls relative to corn capital at the margin in agriculture. In agriculture the surplus-to-capital ratio is a physical one, independent of prices and distribution. From this Sraffa explained the determining role of agricultural profits as a logical necessity of the model. Sraffa's interpretation remains powerful, and it is at the heart of a view which treats classical economics as a surplus-orientated tradition, in sharp contrast to the allocative economics of the neoclassicals. Controversy continues to surround Sraffa's reading. His case has always been circumstantial, as it is based on things Ricardo must have said in conversation or in unknown letters (Sraffa, 1951, p. xxxi). In the extant material Ricardo did, of course, measure inputs and outputs in terms of corn, but this is by no means the same thing as assuming that corn is both the only input and the only output in the agricultural sector (Peach, 1984, p. 737).

Lying behind classical dynamics is a monetary theory in which money is gold, a produced commodity, the exchange value of which depends on the relative amount of labor embodied in it. This view then sits somewhat ambiguously and uncomfortably alongside Say's Law and the quantity theory of money. It is beyond the scope of this entry to investigate the meaning of these theories in the classical school. Suffice it to say that the quantity theory, along with the labor theory of relative value, was necessary to support the contention that the increase in the relative price of food would not be inflationary as it could not be passed on in the form of higher money prices for manufactured goods. Say's Law then supported Ricardo's belief that only diminishing returns in agriculture could cause the declining rate of profit.

The model developed in the context of policy debates over the Corn Laws and consequently the theoretical conclusions became closely associated with the dominant classical view that free trade in corn would improve the long-run growth potential of the economy. To allay fears about cheap foreign labor, Ricardo developed the principle of comparative advantage as an extension of Smith's theory of absolute advantage. He was thus able to show that a country with absolute disadvantage in all goods could still trade with another country, to the benefit of both, as long as there was a commodity in which it had a relatively smaller disadvantage. In modern terms, a country with absolute disadvantage, that is high total resource cost, would be the lowest opportunity cost producer of the good for which its absolute disadvantage is least. Domestic comparative cost ratios determined a range within which mutually beneficial international trade could occur at agreed prices.

Ricardo recognized international price determination as an exception to his general theory of value which depended on the assumption of labor and capital mobility. However, it remained for J.S. Mill to complete the Ricardian theory with the concept of reciprocal demand. The result was a determinate theory of international prices and quantities which remains largely unchanged at the core of trade theory today.

The emphasis of the mainstream economists shifted with the marginal revolution of the 1870s. The marginal utility theorists, Jevons, Menger and Walras, tended to denigrate the classical focus on labor and costs to the exclusion of demand. Despite Marshall's attempt to soften the blow, the fact remains that the issues of growth, population and distribution which concerned the classicals faded from view in the late nineteenth and early twentieth centuries. With an analytically superior microeconomic theory emerging, and with the failure of the classical dismal predictions to materialize, it is not surprising that characteristically classical modes of analysis fell into disrepute. Whether these developments constitute a paradigm shift of revolutionary proportions remains controversial. Classical theories have had a profound impact on mainstream neoclassical theory as well as on Marx and on the Post Keynesians. It is not surprising, therefore, that all camps claim to be the true heirs of classical economics.

They are a truly impressive group to want to claim. From Smith to J.S. Mill the classics built an engine of economic analysis to investigate the aggregate relations between people, land and capital. Although economists have eschewed their long-run predictions as depending too much upon an empirically discredited Malthusianism, they have nonetheless renewed their interest in these aggregate relations with the postwar revival of interest in economic development and the recent emergence of concern about environmental limits to economic growth. Ironically, the contemporary relevance of classical economics is also reflected in the way neo-Malthusian environmentalists have embraced the classical conclusion that growth will end in an impoverished stationary state. Modern economics has progressed beyond this, but the classical theories still offer inspiration as we once again grapple with the classical problems of economic growth in the face of scarce natural resources.

JEFFREY T. YOUNG

See also:

Keynes, John Maynard; Marshall, Alfred; New Classical School of Economics; Pigou, Arthur C.; Say's Law; Sraffa, Piero.

Bibliography

Casarosa, Carlo (1985), 'The "New View" of the Ricardian Theory of Distribution and Economic Growth', in Giovanni A. Caravale (ed.), *The Legacy of Ricardo*, Oxford: Basil Blackwell.

Hollander, Samuel (1987), *Classical Economics*, Oxford: Basil Blackwell.

Marx, Karl (1971), *Capital*, Vol. I, Moscow: Progress Publishers.

Peach, Terry (1984), 'David Ricardo's Early Treatment of Profitability: A New Interpretation', *Economic Journal*, **94**, (376), December, pp. 733–51.

Samuelson, Paul (1978), 'The Canonical Classical Model of Political Economy', *Journal of Economic Literature*, **16**, (4), December, pp. 1415–34.

Sraffa, Piero (1951), 'Introduction', *The Works and Correspondence of David Ricardo*, Vol. I, Cambridge: Cambridge University Press.

Clower, Robert W.

Born in 1926 to Fay Walter and Mary Valentine Clower in Pullman, Washington, Robert Wayne Clower has arguably been one of the most distinguished exponents of Keynesian economics in recent decades. Upon leaving the US Army in 1946 as a Warrant Officer (JG), Clower studied at Washington State University, graduating with a BA in economics (Phi Beta Kappa) in 1948 and an MA in economics in 1949. In 1952, he earned a Bachelor of Letters, and 26 years later a Doctor of Letters, from Oxford University. He has been the Hugh C. Lane Professor of Economic Theory at the University of South Carolina since 1986. He served as Professor of Economics at the University of California at Los Angeles (1971–86) and at Northwestern University (1964–71). Over the years he has served as a visitor in institutions around the globe: Orleans (France), Siena and Perugia (Italy), Canterbury (New Zealand), Vienna (Austria), Kampala (Uganda), Lahore (Pakistan) and Liberia. In addition he has spent time at Oxford, Essex and Cambridge. Robert Clower has seven children. He and his wife, Georgene, reside in Columbia, South Carolina.

This Rhodes scholar's long and notable career is marked by numerous contributions to the study of the working of markets. His fundamental insights have paved the way for a whole class of research in disequilibrium theory. It will be readily agreed that Clower's *tour de force* was his 1965 paper, 'The Keynesian Counterrevolution: A Theoretical Appraisal', a path-breaking paper which significantly strengthened the fundamental arguments of Keynesian economics and permanently transformed the landscape for the succeeding generation of economists.

By providing, for the first time, firm micro-theoretic foundations for a macroeconomic equilibrium compatible with unemployment, Clower swept away the general unease with the original interpretation of Keynes wherein union-induced wage rigidity prevented adjustments to equilibrium in the labor market. The centerpiece of Clower's formulation, the key to explaining a less-than-full-employment equilibrium, is the dual-decision hypothesis. In general terms it postulates that, if agents are rationed in one market, they will be rationed in other markets as well. Clower defined as *notional demand* the commodity demand at prices consistent with a full employment equilibrium. If, however, households are rationed in the labor market, they will revise downwards their spending decisions in the goods market. Thus their *effective demand* will be less than their notional demand since their actual income will be less than their notional income. Conversely, it may be argued that, if firms are rationed in the goods market, they will, in turn, ration the demand for labor regardless of the wage rate: the firms' *effective demand* for labor will be less than their *notional demand*. Of course, wage reductions could clear the labor market but they would not necessarily increase the effective demand for commodities which the firms face.

In this disequilibrium scenario, therefore, firms would increase employment in response to increased effective demand for goods rather than to declining wages: it would be quantity adjustments and not price adjustments which would absorb the shocks to the economy. Thus Clower's argument was that prices would not convey the correct information about market pressures to producers and consequently the burden of adjustment to equilibrium would be assigned to income, not to the price of labor relative to goods. His thrust, therefore, was the very essence of the Keynesian counterrevolution and his particular insight was to show that the main impediments to the smooth functioning of markets were rooted in privately optimal decision making by individual units quite apart from union-type institutions. These privately optimal decisions significantly weaken the self-correction mechanism of the economy and impose macroeconomic externalities in the form of output fluctuations which tend to be persistent.

The concept of the dual-decision hypothesis spawned a large volume of literature and has since become a mainstay of numerous disequilibrium models and of what may be loosely called the New Keynesian economics. While the great debate continues over the efficacy of the price system, Clower's work remains a defining contribution in the annals of the intellectual developments of the discipline.

His compelling interest in Keynes is evident in a selection of his recent articles (Clower, 1988a, 1988b, 1990, 1991). For a selection of his philosophical papers, see Clower (1973, 1974, 1975, 1988c). Clower (1967, 1971, 1985) are representative of his extensive work on monetary theory.

Numerous honors have come Clower's way. He was the managing editor of the *American Economic Review* (1981–5) and of *Economic Inquiry* (1973–80) and has served as the president of both the Southern and the Western Economic Associations. In 1978, he was elected Fellow of the Econometric Society and was made an Honorary Fellow of Brasenose College, Oxford. He is a past recipient of fellowships from both the Guggenheim and the Ford Foundations.

VIKRAM KUMAR

See also:

Dual Decision Hypothesis; Keynesian Revolution; Microfoundations of Macroeconomics; Neoclassical Synthesis (Bastard Keynesianism); New Keynesian Macroeconomics; Post Walrasian Economics.

Bibliography

Blaug, M. (1985), *Great Economists Since Keynes*, Totowa, NJ: Barnes and Noble Books, pp. 33–35.

Clower, Robert W. (1965), 'The Keynesian Counterrevolution: A Theoretical Appraisal', in F.H. Hahn and F.P.R. Brechling (eds), *The Theory of Interest Rates*, London: Macmillan.

Clower, Robert W. (1967), 'A Reconsideration of the Microfoundations of Monetary Theory', *Western Economic Journal*, **6**, (1), December, pp. 1–8.

Clower, Robert W. (ed.) (1969), *Monetary Theory*, London: Penguin.

Clower, Robert W. (1971), 'Theoretical Foundations of Monetary Policy', in G. Clayton, J.C. Gilbert and R. Sedgwick (eds), *Monetary Theory and Monetary Policy in the 1970s*, London: Oxford University Press.

Clower, Robert W. (1973), 'Snacks, Quarks and Other Fictions: The Role of Formal Theory in Economic History', in L.P. Cain and P.J. Uselding (eds), *Business Enterprise and Economic Change*, Youngstown, OH: Kent State University Press, pp. 3–14.

Clower, Robert W. (1974), 'Reflections on Science and Economics', *Intermountain Economic Review*, **5**, (1), Spring, pp. 1–12.

Clower, Robert W. (1975), 'Reflections on the Keynesian Perplex', *Zeitschrift für Nationalökonomie*, **35**, (1), July, pp. 1–24.

Clower, Robert W. (1984), *Money and Markets: Selected Essays of R.W. Clower*, ed. D.A. Walker, Cambridge: Cambridge University Press; paperback edn, 1986.

Clower, Robert W. (1985), 'Monetary Theory and Macroeconomics: A Perspective', *Keizai Shushi*, **54**, (3), Nihon University.

Clower, Robert W. (1988a), 'Keynes and the Classics Revisited', in O.F. Hamouda and J.N. Smithin (eds), *Keynes and Public Policy After Fifty Years*, Aldershot: Edward Edgar.

Clower, Robert W. (1988b), 'Keynes's *General Theory*: The Marshall Connection', *Perspectives in the History of Economic Thought*, Cambridge: Cambridge University Press.

Clower, Robert W. (1988c), 'The Ideas of Economists', in A. Klamer, D. McCloskey and R.M. Solow (eds), *The Consequences of Economic Rhetoric*, New York: Cambridge University Press.

Clower, Robert W. (1990), 'Keynes's *General Theory*: A Contemporary Perspective', *Greek Economic Review*, **12**, Supplement, Autumn, pp. 73–84.

Clower, Robert W. (1991), 'Ohlin and the *General Theory*', in Lars Jonung (ed.), *The Stockholm School after Fifty Years*, New York: Cambridge University Press.

Clower, Robert W. and J.F. Due (1966), *Intermediate Economic Analysis*, 7th edn, Homewood, Ill.: Richard D. Irwin.

Clower, Robert W. and J.F. Due (1972), *Microeconomics*, Homewood, Ill.: Richard D. Irwin.

Clower, Robert W. and John Harris (1965), *Puerto Rico Shipping and the U.S. Maritime Laws*, Evanston, Ill.: Transportation Center, Northwestern University.

Clower, Robert W., Phil Graves and Robert Sexton (1988), *Intermediate Microeconomics*, San Diego: Harcourt Brace & Jovanovich.

Clower, Robert W., G. Dalton, A. Walter and M. Harwitz (1966), *Growth Without Development: An Economic Survey of Liberia*, Evanston, Ill.: Northwestern University Press.

Consumption and the Consumption Function

A textbook definition of consumption states: 'Consumption is the part of GNP used by households for their own current use' (Hall and Taylor, 1986, p. 5). A more detailed definition distinguishes between household purchases of durable goods (goods expected to last more than one year) and non-durable goods (goods expected to last less than one year) but notes that spending on new houses is excluded from consumption because it is by convention considered investment.

Viewed from the perspective of economic expenditure in a closed economy, *consumption* is one type of expenditure as opposed to *investment*, which is defined as the purchase of final investment goods by firms (but including the proviso for new house construction), or *government spending*, which is defined as any purchase of resources by a government entity. Consumption is the largest component of aggregate expenditure. Measures of consumer confidence and consumer spending are scrupulously followed by economic forecasters.

Households allocate their income between *consumption, savings and taxes.* The tax component is generally exogenous to the household. The consumption and savings components are endogenous to the household. How this household income allocation problem is solved is central to Keynesian macroeconomics. The attention economists have given to the issue is one of the enduring legacies of Lord Keynes.

In a strict Classical Model, this household allocation between consumption and savings is irrelevant to the level of aggregate demand, or to the determination of national income. As J.S. Mill stated in 1848, 'consumption never needs encouragement ... The person who saves his income is no less a consumer than he who spends it: he consumes in a different way.' Increased savings imply increased investment, and a dollar spent on investment has an identical contribution to aggregate demand to that of a dollar spent on consumption.

The mechanism that ensures savings are channeled to investment in the Classical Model is the interest rate. If savings and investment are not in equilibrium, then the operation of Say's Law will correct the situation. The rate of interest is one of many prices within the economic system which is infinitely flexible, and its task is to maintain savings and investment in equilibrium.

Wicksell (1898) modified Say's Law, suggesting that there were two rates of interest, the market rate and the natural rate of interest. The central bank could determine, within limits, the market rate of interest. The real forces of the economic system determined the natural rate of interest. If the market rate and the natural rate of interest were equal, then savings and investment would be in equilibrium. If, however, the market rate and the natural rate were not equal, then savings and investment would not be in equilibrium and a cumulative change in all wages and prices would continue to occur until the central bank took action to make the market rate of interest equal to the natural rate of interest.

Nevertheless, insufficient consumption is logically impossible in the Classical Model. That a government might want to encourage consumption would seem bizarre to the classical economists. If anything, in the Classical Model saving is *preferred* to consumption, because it provides a basis for more capital accumulation, which is viewed as the key to rising wealth.

The Keynesian income–expenditure model, however, turns the Classical Model on its head. First, consumption and saving are primarily functions of *income.* The interest rate simply does not play an important role in determining the amount of spending or saving undertaken by a household. Second, investment decisions are not automatically driven by interest rates. The interest rate becomes an awkward and less than perfect mechanism to coordinate aggregate economic activity. The simple investment savings equality inherent and automatic in the Classical Model is not forthcoming in a Keynesian formulation.

Put another way, Keynes's separation of the income allocation decision (C, S and T), from the expenditure allocation decision (C, I and G) allows for the household consumption–savings decision to *determine* the level of national income, compared to *being determined by* the level of national income. A shift in household allocation from consumption to savings, that would simply imply a different kind of consumption to Mill, triggers a decline in aggregate spending which causes a decline in national income that leads to further declines in consumption (and savings!) and income. This is the important contribution of Keynes's model. (See Patinkin, 1987).

The famous 45 degree line income–expenditure model, or the simple Keynesian algebra of $C + I + G = C + S + T$ are both familiar manifestations of this consumption-based view, a view that is practically universal to modern macroeconomic pedagogy. In this simple Keynesian model, variations in national income are caused by changes in aggregate demand. These changes are amplified by household consumption habits; particularly through the role of marginal propensity to consume (MPC) in the income determination process. The marginal propensity to consume refers to the change in consumption expenditures which occurs when an individual's income changes. The average propensity to consume (APC) refers to the ratio of consumption expenditures to income.

An increase in spending that generates an increase in household income induces households to spend more, which in turn generates additional income generation for other households and additional spending. This is the well-known 'spending multiplier'. If households spend a large fraction of their new income on consumption, that is, they have a high marginal propensity to consume, then the multiplier effect is larger than if the marginal propensity to consume is lower. Far from being irrelevant, household consumption habits are crucial for both the level and dynamics of macroeconomic activity in the Keynesian system.

Keynes's basic model of household consumption posits that consumption = autonomous consumption + (marginal propensity to consume) × (income) or the standard $C = a + bY$ equation. Keynes suggested that the marginal propensity to consume is greater than zero but less than one, that it declines as income rises, that it is less than the average propensity to consume and that the average propensity to consume declines as income rises.

The decreasing tendency to consumption as income rises was seen as a potential source of economic stagnation (Hansen, 1939). If the MPC declines as income rises, market economies may be subject to persistent deficiencies in aggregate demand. A new role for government is envisioned. The ratio of government expenditures to income must increase in order to fill this 'expenditure gap' and to keep the economy growing. Keynes argued that the use of 'monetary policy in conjunction with the stabilization of investment by means of a permanent increase in the proportion of income spent by governments' (Blaug, 1994) would result in an average level of output and employment in Britain that was higher and more stable than had been the case in the past. If, on the other hand, the marginal propensity to consume is constant as income rises then the scope of government activity is limited because the fear of insufficient aggregate expenditures will not materialize.

It is not surprising, given this elevation of the importance of consumption by Keynesians, that investigation into the nature of the household consumption function became a central item on the research agenda of postwar economists. Early empirical evidence which provided some support for Keynes's theory of consumption came from cross-section analysis of family budgets. A by-product of the studies undertaken to test the validity of 'Engel's Law' was a consumption function that 'acted' and 'looked' like the one described by Keynes. The major problem with these studies was that, in order to support Keynes's theory of consumption, an inappropriate transformation of the data must take place. Family budget data relate how consumption expenditures differ as income differs at the level of the individual, whereas Keynes's theory of consumption attempts to explain how consumption expenditures change as income changes at the aggregate level. Unless the income variable measures 'relative income' as opposed to 'absolute income', these studies cannot be used to support Keynes's theory of consumption (Duesenberry, 1949).

A second source of early empirical evidence in support of Keynes's theory came from the time series analysis of consumption and income figures for the period 1929–41. These studies suggest that the marginal propensity to consume is positive and less than one, is less than the average propensity to consume, and that consumption is a stable function of income. These studies, however, did not support the idea that the marginal propensity to consume declines as the level of income increases. Furthermore, these studies raised more questions than they answered. Should income be measured in real or nominal terms? Should the income variable be total income or disposable income? Should the income variable be in aggregate terms or per capita terms? And what is the direction of causation – from consumption to income or the other way around? (See Haavelmo, 1947.)

Collectively these questions about Keynes's theory of consumption are known as the 'consumption puzzle'. Empirical work conducted by Kuznets revealed that the ratio of consumption to income is fairly constant as income rises, which calls into question the need for an increase in the ratio of government expenditures to income (Kuznets, 1946a).

Friedman's (1957) permanent income hypothesis, and Modigliani and Brumberg's (1954) life-cycle hypothesis refine the simple Keynesian model. Both theories emphasize that it is *wealth*, not current income per se, that drives the household consumption decision. Because changes in wealth are less apparent than changes in income, the short-run marginal propensity to consume out of rising (or falling) income may be less than the long-run propensity. Correspondingly, the multiplier effect may well be less profound than what long-run savings would imply. Friedman argues that income can be divided into two categories: permanent income, income which individuals expect to receive, and temporary income, income which is a surprise to the individual. Friedman suggests that individuals plan to consume about 90 per cent of permanent income. Modigliani approaches the problem in a slightly different manner. He argues that, while during some time periods individuals consume more than their income and during other periods they consume less than their income, when these different patterns of consumption and income are analysed individuals, over their lifetime, consume about 90 per cent of their income.

Perhaps the most dramatic implication of Keynes's view of consumption in the *General Theory* is his insistence that the consumption–savings decision is not particularly normative. Thrift, one of those fine Victorian values, was considered virtuous in its own right in Keynes's time. However, in Keynes's model the individual virtue of savings can aggregate into the social malady of stagnation and underemployment. Underinvestment is only aggravated by increased savings because increased savings reduce aggregate demand, which reduces national output. An increased desire to save, therefore, can paradoxically lead to fewer aggregate savings.

In the *General Theory*, Keynes, the talented expositor, outlined the conventional motives for saving as being aligned primarily with virtues such as precaution, enterprise, improvement, independence and calculation (although the pride and avarice motives go against this grain). The consumption motive, on the other hand, is aligned primarily with vices such as enjoyment, short-sightedness, miscalculation, ostentation and extravagance (although generosity is an exception) (Keynes, 1936, p. 316). He then outlines an example of the paradox of thrift: increased savings lead to reduced national income that reduces the actual level of savings: 'The more virtuous we are, the more deliberately thrifty ... the more our incomes will have to fall ... the actual rates of aggregate savings and spending do not depend on precaution, foresight, calculation, improvement, independence, [or] enterprise ... *virtue and vice play no part*' (pp. 317–18, emphasis added).

The policy implications of this are profound. Encouraging thrift and savings are no longer overwhelming important policy goals, while encouraging consumption and expenditure can be a socially prudent policy. Government deficits are not an indication of irresponsible government 'living beyond its means', but are instead part of a policy to allow society to live up to its full employment potential. To many in Keynes's day (as well as the present) this is shocking. Undermining thrift, prudence and precaution are often seen as a legacy of Keynes by his critics, inevitably for the bad. Buchanan and Wagner (1977) for example, argue that the rise of Keynesian macroeconomics contributed to the decline in the implicit fiscal constraint that required the federal government to run a balanced budget.

The resurgence of classical economics and so-called 'supply-side approaches' argue against viewing consumption as an unmitigated good. Concern over the aggregate savings rate is perhaps as profound in the late 1990s as the concern for apparent underconsumption was in the 1930s. Independent of one's views on either the historical or the contemporary economic issue, it is universally agreed that the economist's view of *consumption* was inalterably changed by the Keynesian revolution.

CECIL E. BOHANON

See also:

Absolute Income Hypothesis; Clark, Colin; Classical Economics; Friedman, Milton; Keynesian Cross; Keynesian Revolution; Kuznets, Simon; Life Cycle Hypothesis; Modigliani, Franco; Multiplier Effect; Permanent Income Hypothesis; Relative Income Hypothesis; Stone, Sir John Richard N.

Bibliography

Blaug, Mark (1994), 'Recent Biographies of Keynes', *Journal of Economic Literature*, **32**, (3), September, pp. 1204–15.
Buchanan, James and Richard Wagner (1977), *Democracy in Deficit*, New York: Academic Press.
Duesenberry, James S. (1949), *Income, Saving and the Theory of Consumer Behavior*, Cambridge, MA: Harvard University Press.
Friedman, Milton (1957), *A Theory of the Consumption Function*, NBER General Series, Volume 63, Princeton: Princeton University Press.
Haavelmo, T. (1947), 'Methods of Measuring the Marginal Propensity to Consume', *Journal of the American Statistical Society*, **42**, (237), March, pp. 105–22.
Hall, Robert and John B. Taylor (1986), *Macroeconomics*, New York: W.W Norton.
Hansen, A.H. (1939), 'Economic Progress and Declining Population Growth', *American Economic Review*, **29**, pp. 1–15.
Keynes, John Maynard (1936), *The General Theory of Employment, Interest and Money*, London: Macmillan.
Kuznets, Simon (1946a), *National Income: A Survey of Findings*, New York: National Bureau of Economic Research.
Kuznets, Simon (1946b), *National Product Since 1869*, New York: National Bureau of Economic Research.

Mill, John Stuart (1848 [1960]), 'Of the Influence of Consumption on Production', reprinted in Henry Hazlitt (ed.), *Critics of Keynesian Economics*, New York: D. Van Nostrand, 1960.

Modigliani, Franco and R. Brumberg (1954), 'Utility Analysis and the Consumption Function: An Interpretation of Cross-Sectional Data', in K.E. Kurihara (ed.), *Post-Keynesian Economics*, New Brunswick, NJ: Rutgers University Press.

Patinkin, Don (1987), 'John Maynard Keynes', in John Eatwell, Murray Milgate and Peter Newman (eds), *The New Palgrave*, Vol. 3, New York: Stockton Press.

Wicksell, Knut (1898), *Interest and Prices*, reprinted New York: A.M. Kelley, 1965.

Coordination Failures and Keynesian Economics

Thus ... the economic system may find itself in stable equilibrium with [employment] at a level below full employment. ... This analysis supplies us with an explanation of the paradox of poverty in the midst of plenty. For the mere existence of an insufficiency of effective demand may, and often will, bring the increase of employment to a standstill before a level of full employment has been reached. The insufficiency of effective demand will inhibit the process of production in spite of the fact that the marginal utility of labour still exceeds in value the marginal disutility of employment. (Keynes, 1936, pp. 30–31)

Keynes believed that economies can get trapped indefinitely in equilibria with undesirable social properties. Such a view assuredly does not correspond to modern textbook Keynesianism. For example, when discussing the Keynesian model, Barro (1993, p. 569) writes that 'the economy adjusts automatically toward the market-clearing levels of output and employment' and Mankiw (1994, p. 302) writes that, 'in the long run ... output returns to the natural rate'. Since the development of the Neoclassical Synthesis, the orthodox Keynesian view has been that price rigidities cause short-run deviations from full employment, and that price flexibility restores the economy to the natural rate in the long run (but see Tobin, 1975, for a dissenting argument). The idea that the economy could get *permanently* stuck in a bad equilibrium all but disappeared from the Keynesian mainstream in the heyday of Keynesian economics.

Some modern macroeconomists have returned to the notion that the economy can get trapped in bad equilibria. The authors in this new literature are not usually formalizing the ideas of the *General Theory*, and would not necessarily describe themselves as Keynesians. Still, their models do capture some of the ideas exemplified by the above quotation from Keynes. The following paragraphs briefly summarize some of the significant contributions to this literature, but should not be viewed as a comprehensive survey.

A *coordination failure*, in modern macroeconomic usage, occurs when the economy gets stuck in a bad equilibrium even though a better equilibrium is attainable. In other words, coordination failures can arise if the economy exhibits *multiple, Pareto-ranked* equilibria. Such a precise usage of this terminology is relatively recent. Earlier writers (for example, Weintraub, 1979;

Leijonhufvud, 1981) used 'coordination failure' more loosely to mean lack of market clearing or mismatch of saving and investment.

The underlying intuition of recent models is illustrated in Figure 1. The horizontal axis measures average output in an economy ($\bar{y}$). The vertical axis measures the output of a typical individual firm (y_i). If y_i depends positively upon $\bar{y}$, multiple equilibria are possible. In Figure 1, there are three equilibria, y_L, y_M and y_H, where the reaction function intersects the 45 degree line. If there are positive externalities, so higher levels of output by one firm benefit others, then the equilibria can be Pareto-ranked, with y_H, preferred. If the economy gets stuck at y_L or y_M, there is a coordination failure.

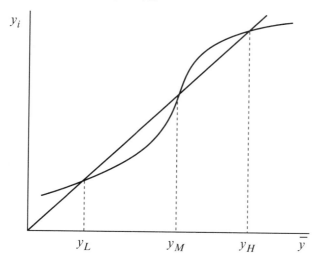

Figure 1

While the focus here is on modern formulations of Keynesian macroeconomics, the idea of coordination failure can be found in the writings of Rousseau (1773) and Schelling (1978), among others, and coordination failures have arisen in work on topics as diverse as motor insurance, the arms race and the pure theory of money. Kaldor (1940) and Leontief (1958), meanwhile, provided early macroeconomic examples.

Many authors have now supplied macroeconomic models of coordination failure based on explicit microeconomic underpinnings. Broadly speaking, there are three types of model, driven by technological externalities, search externalities or demand externalities. Technological externalities can cause the return to production at one firm to increase when output at other firms rises (Bryant, 1983). Search models abandon the Walrasian auctioneer and consider economies with thick-market externalities, meaning that the return to trading is higher when many others are also trading (Diamond, 1982). Pagano (1989) and Chatterjee (1988) apply this idea to asset markets and investigate the links between thick-market effects and asset price volatility.

Macroeconomic models with imperfect or monopolistic competition give rise to demand externalities: imperfectly competitive firms produce less when demand is low, and demand is low when output (hence income) is low (Heller, 1986). Such models have a particularly Keynesian flavor (and, indeed, imperfect competition is important in the so-called 'New Keynesian Economics'). Furthermore, price stickiness can arise as a coordination failure when monopolistically competitive firms face small costs of changing prices (Ball and Romer, 1991).

In all these examples, a necessary ingredient is *strategic complementarity*: a change in economic activity by one agent causes others to change their actions *in the same direction* (Cooper and John, 1988). Strategic complementarity implies that reaction functions slope upward, as in Figure 1. (Strategic complementarities also give rise to multiplier effects that amplify and propagate shocks, much as in traditional Keynesian models.)

Coordination failure models provide support for the Keynesian notion that 'animal spirits' might move the economy among equilibria. Optimistic agents expect a high level of economic activity and thus take actions that make a high level of activity self-fulfilling. The opposite is true if agents are pessimistic. The actual level of activity in an economy is then determined in part by the whim of capricious investors, much as Keynes argued (Bryant, 1987; Howitt and McAfee, 1992; Kiyotaki, 1988; Weil, 1989). But these examples also point to a fundamental difficulty with coordination failure models. Agents must form beliefs not just about other agents' actions, but also about their *beliefs*. Thus these models are incomplete without a theory of the way beliefs are formed. Or, to put much the same point another way, models with multiple equilibria lack a theory that explains which equilibrium will ultimately be chosen, and must be augmented by some theory of equilibrium selection.

A couple of possibilities can be dismissed easily. First, agents will not always succeed in coordinating on the best equilibrium. Experimental evidence reveals that, even with a small number of players, coordination failure games often yield Pareto-inferior outcomes (Van Huyck, Battalio and Beil, 1990; Cooper *et al.*, 1990). Second, introducing explicit dynamics into models does not always solve the equilibrium selection problem. In some cases multiple equilibria in a static model may correspond to multiple steady states in a dynamic model, and initial conditions determine the ultimate resting place of the economy. In other cases there may be multiple paths consistent with the same initial conditions (Howitt and McAfee, 1988).

Economists have sought various equilibrium refinements to restrict the set of equilibria. Some, drawing on evolutionary game theory, argue that learning behavior might pin down equilibrium (Crawford, 1995). Others suggest that history provides a natural focal point (R. Cooper, 1994). Still others conjecture that economic policies may select equilibrium: perhaps well-conceived government policies can guide the economy to a good equilibrium. There is much informal discussion of this possibility in the literature, but little formal work (but see Bohn and Gorton, 1933; Boldrin, 1992; Yavas, 1995). There is as yet no compelling theory of equilibrium selection in coordination games.

Coordination failures are related to various other lines of inquiry in macroeconomics. Much modern growth theory builds on technological externalities like those in the coordination failure literature. Such models can exhibit low-level steady states, sometimes called development traps (Azariadis and Drazen, 1990), or multiple growth paths (Evans, Honkapohja and Romer, 1994; Startz, 1994). Sufficiently strong externalities or monopolistic competition allow for the possibility of indeterminacy and sunspots (Benhabib and Farmer, 1994; Gali, 1994); indeed, sunspot equilibria resemble coordination failure equilibria. Finally, some researchers have suggested that coordination failure can arise in the adoption of new technologies; the now classic example is the adoption of the QWERTY keyboard (David, 1985). But despite these connections, it is as yet unclear how coordination failure models fit into modern business cycle theory. It is hard to test for the presence or absence of multiple equilibria using conventional econometric techniques, and it is hard to incorporate multiple equilibria into dynamic general equilibrium models that can be calibrated and simulated.

Notwithstanding the difficulties, there are indications that the effort to include coordination failures in standard macroeconomic models will ultimately prove worthwhile. The underlying ingredients – technological externalities, search or imperfect competition – have been successfully included in such models: Baxter and King (1991) and Cooper and Johri (1994), for example, show that such complementarities can improve the performance of a standard real business cycle model. There is evidence that technological externalities and imperfect competition are significant in the US and other economies. There is also some direct evidence of significant complementarities in the US economy (Cooper and Haltiwanger, 1993). Coordination failures provide one possible explanation of persistence in GDP (Durlauf, 1991). And, finally, there is some evidence that the GDP time series is well described by models that permit switching among multiple regimes (Hamilton, 1989; Perron, 1989; S. Cooper, 1994). Coordination failure models provide a promising avenue for explaining such features of the data.

ANDREW JOHN

See also:

Kaldor, Lord Nicholas; Keynesian Revolution; Leijonhufvud, Axel; Microfoundations of Macroeconomics; Post Walrasian Economics; Say's Law.

Bibliography

Azariadis, C. and A. Drazen (1990), 'Threshold externalities in economic development', *Quarterly Journal of Economics*, **105**, (2), May, pp. 501–26.

Ball, L. and D. Romer (1991), 'Sticky Prices as Coordination Failure', *American Economic Review*, **81**, (3), June, pp. 539–52.

Barro, R. (1993), *Macroeconomics*, 4th edn, New York: Wiley.

Baxter, M. and R. King (1991), 'Productive Externalities and Business Cycles', Institute for Empirical Macroeconomics Discussion Paper 53, Federal Reserve Bank of Minneapolis.

Benhabib, J. and R. Farmer (1994), 'Indeterminacy and Increasing Returns', *Journal of Economic Theory*, **63**, (1), June, pp. 19–41.

Bohn, H. and G. Gorton (1993), 'Coordination Failure, Multiple Equilibria and Economic Institutions', *Economica*, **60**, (239), August, pp. 257–80.

Boldrin, M. (1992), 'Dynamic Externalities, Multiple Equilibria and Growth', *Journal of Economic Theory*, **58**, (2), December, pp. 198–218.

Bryant, J. (1983), 'A Simple Rational Expectations Keynes-Type Model', *Quarterly Journal of Economics*, **98**, (3), August, pp. 525–9.

Bryant, J. (1987), 'The Paradox of Thrift, Liquidity Preference and Animal Spirits', *Econometrica*, **55**, (5), September, pp. 1231–5.

Chatterjee, S. (1988), 'Participation Externality as a Source of Coordination Failure in a Competitive Model with Centralized Markets', University of Iowa, Department of Economics Working Paper No. 88-15.

Cooper, R. (1994), 'Equilibrium Selection in Imperfectly Competitive Economies with Multiple Equilibria', *Economic Journal*, **104**, (426), September, pp. 1106–22.

Cooper, R. and J. Haltiwanger (1993), 'Evidence on Macroeconomic Complementarities', NBER Working Paper No. 4577.

Cooper, R. and A. John (1988), 'Coordinating Coordination Failures in Keynesian Models', *Quarterly Journal of Economics*, **103**, (3), August, pp. 441–64.

Cooper, R. and A. Johri (1994), 'Dynamic Complementarities: A Quantitative Analysis', mimeo, Boston University.

Cooper, R., D. DeJong, R. Forsythe and T. Ross (1990), 'Selection Criteria in Coordination Games: Some Experimental Results', *American Economic Review*, **80**, (1), March, pp. 218–33.

Cooper, S. (1994), 'Multiple Regimes in U.S. Output Fluctuations', mimeo, Kennedy School of Government, Harvard University.

Crawford, V. (1995), 'Adaptive Dynamics in Coordination Games', *Econometrica*, **63**, (1), January, pp. 103–43.

David, P. (1985), 'Clio and the Economics of QWERTY', *American Economic Review*, **75**, (2), May, pp. 332–7.

Diamond, P.A. (1982), 'Aggregate Demand Management in Search Equilibrium', *Journal of Political Economy*, **90**, (5), October, pp. 881–94.

Durlauf, S. (1991), 'Multiple Equilibria and Persistence in Aggregate Fluctuations', *American Economic Review*, **81**, (2), May, pp. 70–74.

Evans, G., S. Honkapohja and P. Romer (1994), 'Growth Cycles', mimeo.

Gali, J. (1994), 'Monopolistic Competition, Business Cycles and the Composition of Aggregate Demand', *Journal of Economic Theory*, **63**, (1), June, pp. 73–96.

Hamilton, J. (1989), 'A New Approach to the Economic Analysis of Nonstationary Time Series and the Business Cycle', *Econometrica*, **57**, (2), March, pp. 357–84.

Heller, W. (1986), 'Coordination Failure Under Complete Markets with Applications to Effective Demand', in W. Heller, R. Starr and D. Starrett (eds), *Equilibrium Analysis: Essays in Honor of Kenneth J. Arrow*, Vol. 2, New York: Cambridge University Press.

Howitt, P. and P. McAfee (1988), 'Stability of Equilibria with Externalities', *Quarterly Journal of Economics*, **103**, (2), May, pp. 261–77.

Howitt, P. and P. McAfee (1992), 'Animal Spirits', *American Economic Review*, **82**, (3), June, pp. 493–507.

Kaldor, N. (1940), 'A Model of the Trade Cycle', *Economic Journal*, **50**, (197), March, pp. 78–92.

Keynes, J.M. (1936), *The General Theory of Employment, Interest and Money*, London: Macmillan.

Kiyotaki, N. (1988), 'Multiple Expectational Equilibria under Monopolistic Competition', *Quarterly Journal of Economics*, **103**, (4), November, pp. 695–766.

Leijonhufvud, A. (1981), *Information and Coordination*, New York: Oxford University Press.

Leontief, W. (1958), 'Theoretical Note on Time Preference, Productivity of Capital, Stagnation and Economic Growth', *American Economic Review*, **48**, (1), March, pp. 105–11.

Mankiw, N.G. (1994), *Macroeconomics*, 2nd edn, New York: Worth.

Pagano, M. (1989), 'Endogenous Market Thinness and Stock Price Volatility', *Review of Economic Studies*, **56**, (186), April, pp. 269–88.

Perron, P. (1989), 'The Great Crash, the Oil Price Shock and the Unit Root Hypothesis', *Econometrica*, **57**, (6), November, pp. 1361–1401.

Rousseau, J.-J., (1773), 'A Discourse on the Origin of Inequality', *The Social Contract and Discourses*, London: J.M. Dent.

Schelling, T. (1978), *Micromotives and Macrobehavior*, New York: W.W. Norton.

Startz, R. (1994), 'Growth States and Sectoral Shocks', mimeo, Department of Economics, University of Washington.

Tobin, J. (1975), 'Keynesian Models of Recession and Depression', *American Economic Review*, **65**, (2), May, pp. 195–202.

Van Huyck, J., R. Battalio and R. Beil (1990), 'Tacit Coordination Games, Strategic Uncertainty, and Coordination Failure', *American Economic Review*, **80**, (1), March, pp. 234–48.

Weil, P. (1989), 'Increasing Returns and Animal Spirits', *American Economic Review*, **79**, (4), September, pp. 889–94.

Weintraub, E.R. (1979), *Microfoundations: The Compatibility of Microeconomics and Macroeconomics*, Cambridge: Cambridge University Press.

Yavas, A. (1995), 'Can Brokerage Have an Equilibrium Selection Role?', *Journal of Urban Economics*, **37**, (1), January, pp. 17–37.

Crowding Out

Crowding out refers to the process by which expansionary fiscal policy, especially debt-financed expenditures, displaces private spending – investment and/or exports. If that happens, the ability of fiscal policy to stimulate economic activity is compromised. If investment is reduced, it is also possible that policy may lessen the growth rate of potential growth output as well. Most often 'crowding out' is simply the result of expansionary fiscal policy raising interest rates. As used here, however, crowding out will include private-sector responses to policy-induced changes in relative asset prices and resulting changes in their yields as well as the size/composition of wealth portfolios. As such, it does not consider any of the effects policy may have on expectations, as expressed in Keynes's concern for the state of business confidence.

Crowding out is the sum of a 'transactions effect' and a 'portfolio effect', associated with bond-funded fiscal policy (Friedman, 1978). It occurs in both closed and open and large and small economies. The process of buying and selling of government bonds affects changes in the prices of these bonds and their effective yields. If investment spending is a function of 'the' rate of interest, then new government spending which is funded by bonds may affect private spending. The extent of the impact depends on the underlying assumption of the models used to examine the concept of crowding out.

This 'transactions effect' is illustrated in Figure 1. At Point A, the actual level of output, Y_A, is less than the potential level of output, Y_P. The effect of bond-funded fiscal policy is to shift the *IS* curve to the right, IS_1 to IS_2. The distance between Point A and Point B represents the full impact of the simple fiscal policy multiplier, which assumes that the rate of interest (r_1) does not change. Under the assumptions of the *IS–LM* model however, the rate of interest does change and the economy moves from Point A and Point C where both income and the rate of interest have increased. The 'transactions effect' shows that the increase in government spending associated with the bond-funded fiscal policy raises the rate of interest and therefore has crowded out some of the investment spending which would have occurred at r_1. Graphically, the reduction in private investment spending equals the horizontal distance between Point A and A_1 on IS_1.

Figure 1 makes clear that the conduct of monetary policy will be a critical determinant of whether or not crowding out occurs. If the central bank is committed to concentrating attention on the money supply, the *LM* curve will

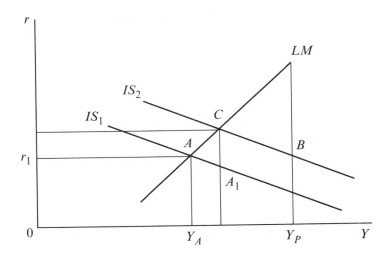

Figure 1

remain unchanged in the face of a fiscal exercise and bond-funded fiscal policy will have the results just described. If, on the other hand, the monetary authority is committed to concentrating on the interest rate, the fiscal stimulus which moves the *IS* curve will also induce an increase in the money supply large enough to shift the *LM* rightward far enough to leave the equilibrium interest rate unchanged. In that case, the monetary stimulus obviates the transaction effect and the central bank becomes the servant of the fiscal authorities.

'Portfolio effects' include the impact of changes in both the level and composition of private wealth as a result of the exercise of fiscal policy. A common assumption has been that government debt is considered net wealth by the public, so that debt-financed expenditures involve an increase in wealth. On the other hand, to the extent that Barro/Ricardo equivalence holds, the public perceives their government bond holdings to be matched by equal increases in future tax liabilities, so that net wealth is unaffected by changes in the government debt. While the matter is not completely settled, most economists do not believe the public to be indifferent between present and future tax liabilities. As a result, debt-financed fiscal policy is likely to have an effect on net wealth and will therefore affect the economy further as individuals adjust their portfolios.

To assess 'portfolio effects' requires that three issues be addressed. The first issue is what is the composition of the portfolio? The financial portfolio of the *General Theory* included only money and bonds, although elsewhere Keynes discussed adjustments of the capital stock (and so holdings of real capital) in response to changes in the interest rate on bonds. Recent investigations more often work with four assets: money, short-term debt, long-term debt and real capital.

The second issue concerns the degree of substitutability between the assets in the portfolio. If long-term debt and real capital are more substitutable than short-term debt and money, an increase in the public's bond holdings raises interest rates and reduces holdings of real capital. In this case the 'portfolio effect' will reinforce the 'transaction effect' to render fiscal policy less effective. On the other hand, if there is greater substitutability between bonds and money, fiscal policy can increase the public's desired holdings of real capital. In this case, 'crowding in' will reinforce the impact of fiscal policy. The evidence that wealth elasticities in demand for money studies are typically greater than zero would indicate that some crowding out through portfolios is not precluded.

The third question concerns the government's debt management policy. Since the question of the extent to which crowding out occurs hinges on the degree of substitutability between assets, the government's debt management policy becomes a matter of some importance. The government's debt management policy, therefore, cannot be separated from fiscal policy discussions.

The story just told may also be presented in an Aggregate Demand–Aggregate Supply *AD–AS* setting. If the government implements a bond-funded fiscal policy program, the aggregate demand curve shifts to the right, from AD_1 to AD_2 in Figure 2. At Point *B* the level of output and the price level are higher than at Point *A* and crowding out is 'measured' by the increase in the price level. If, however, the private sector's expectations incorporate the belief that one result of bond-funded fiscal policy is an increase in the price level, then, to protect itself, the private sector will adjust its wage demands accordingly. If expectations are adaptive, the aggregate supply curve will shift slowly to the left. If expectations are rational and are reinforced by a market-clearing hypothesis, the aggregate supply curve will shift instantaneously to the left. In either case, fiscal policy cannot permanently raise the level of output beyond the point associated with the equilibrium real wage (point *C*).

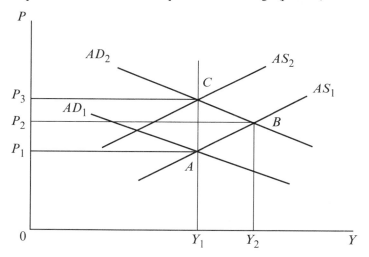

Figure 2

This long-run policy ineffective proposition of course excludes any possibility of hysteresis. Moreover, it does not really address the issue which concerned the Keynes of the *General Theory*. Keynes did not deny that real factors determined capacity output; he did, however, deny the effectiveness of price level adjustments in keeping the economy at that level in the face of negative demand shocks and believed that government expenditures could hasten recovery on those occasions.

To proponents of crowding out, the US experience in the early 1980s would seem a test case of the doctrine. Large government deficits were indeed associated with high real interest rates but, contrary to predictions, there was no discernible drop in private investment as a share of GDP. Rather than reject the crowding out hypothesis, however, some advocates were led to argue that, under the post-Bretton Woods international monetary regime, crowding out merely manifests itself through another channel, namely appreciation of the nation's currency which reduces exports. The results here are qualitatively similar to domestic crowding out: fiscal policy's effectiveness is reduced and the nation is poorer in the future than it might have been, but the mechanism is substantially different.

While 'international crowding out' has become standard textbook fare, exactly how, and if, it operates, depends on the nature of the international monetary system. The Fleming–Mundell (1962) model might be seen as an extension of the US case to a small open economy with a flexible exchange rate. Fiscal stimulus, with a fixed money supply, leads to currency appreciation strong enough to yield a multiplier of zero. On the other hand, with fixed exchange rates and perfect substitutability between assets internationally, the economy's *LM* curve becomes horizontal at the world interest rate for a small country, obviating the interest rate effects on which transactions crowding out depends.

The possibility raised here is conceptually different from the international repercussions inherent in the British 'Treasury View' of the 1920s and 1930s. The concern then was with a conflict between policy objectives and a fear that changes in the balance of the government budget might render unsustainable an exchange rate which was meant to be defended. That result assumes that the fiscal change succeeds in stimulating domestic activity. The message of international crowding out is that, because of foreign repercussions, fiscal policy's impact on the domestic economy will be muted.

The national income accounts provide a useful framework for assessing 'international crowding out'. It is true by definition that private savings (*S*) plus tax collections (*T*) must be sufficient to finance the sum of private domestic investment (*I*), private foreign investment (the current account balance *F*) and government expenditures (*G*). Thus:

$$S + T = I + F + G$$

The Kahn/Keynes multiplier analysis explains how any change in *G* would change the level of activity to produce an accommodating change in *S*. Proponents of crowding out argue that interest rate, portfolio and exchange rate effects will cause changes in *G* to lead to offsetting changes in *I* and/or *F*, reducing the fiscal exercise's impact on the level of activity. How powerful these effects are is, of course, an empirical question, but it would be unreasonable to assume that they are substantial. Over time and space, the evidence linking interest rates to budget deficits is weak at best, a condition which makes it hard to believe that either the direct or indirect effects of crowding out are likely to be substantial. On a practical level, considerations of crowding out may reduce the numerical value of the multiplier and make its estimation more difficult, but they do not overthrow the basic Keynesian insight concerning the ability of fiscal policy to affect output and employment in an economy operating at less than its capacity.

TOM CATE
ROBERT D. LEY

See also:

Aggregate Demand–Aggregate Supply Model and Diagram; Economics of Keynes and of his Revolution, The Key Elements of; Expectations, Theories of; Fiscal Policy; Friedman, Milton; IS/LM Model and Diagram; Keynesian Revolution; Lucas Critique; Pigou, Arthur, C.; Real Balance Effect; Ricardian Equivalence.

Bibliography

Barro, Robert (1974), 'Are Government Bonds Net Wealth?', *Journal of Political Economy*, **82**, (6), November/December, pp. 1095–1117.

Buiter, Willem H. (1977), 'Crowding Out and the Effectiveness of Fiscal Policy', *Journal of Public Economics*, **7**, (3), June, pp. 309–28.

Chrystal, K.A. (1983), *Controversies in Macroeconomics*, 2nd edn, Oxford: Philip Allan.

Fleming, J. Marcus (1962), 'Domestic Financial Policies Under Fixed and Flashing Exchange Rates', *IMF Staff Papers*, **9**, (4), November, pp. 369–79.

Friedman, Benjamin M. (1978), 'Crowding Out or Crowding In? Economic Consequences of Financing Government Deficits', *Brookings Papers on Economic Activity*, (3), pp. 593–641.

Friedman, Milton (1968), 'The Role of Monetary Policy', *American Economic Review*, **58**, (1), March, pp. 1–17.

Hicks, Sir John (1937), 'Mr. Keynes and the "Classics": A Suggested Interpretation', *Econometrica*, **5**, (2), April, pp. 147–59.

Hillier, Brian (1986), *Macroeconomics: Models, Debates and Developments*, New York: Basil Blackwell.

Keynes, John Maynard (1936), *The General Theory of Employment, Interest and Money*, London: Macmillan.

Lucas, Robert (1981), 'Econometric Policy Evaluation: A Critique', in R.E. Lucas, Jr., *Studies in Business Cycle Theory*, Cambridge, Mass.: MIT Press.

Mundell, Robert (1962), 'The Appropriate Use of Monetary and Fiscal Policy for Internal and External Stability', *IMF Staff Papers*, **9**, (1), March, pp. 70–77.

Muth, John (1961), 'Rational Expectations and the Theory of Price Movements', *Econometrica*, **29**, (3), July, pp. 315–35.

Pigou, A.C. (1943), 'The Classical Stationary State', *Economic Journal*, **53**, (211), December, pp. 343–51.

Pigou, A.C. (1947), 'Economic Progress in a Stable Environment', *Economica*, **14**, (54), August, pp. 180–88.

Sargent, Thomas J. and Neil Wallace (1976), 'Rational Expectations and the Theory of Economic Policy', *Journal of Monetary Economics*, **2**, (2), April, pp. 169–84.

Currie, Lauchlin

A native of Nova Scotia, Currie studied at the London School of Economics, 1922–5. His teachers included Edwin Cannan and Hugh Dalton, who tended to deprecate the economics taught at rival Cambridge. But the single most important thing he learned, from courses in logic, was the fallacy of composition. He thus delighted in Keynes's ridicule of Dalton's capital levy proposal, exposing the distinction between private and social accounting. While Cannan taught him the importance of getting behind the monetary veil to real things, Currie learned the importance of the veil itself from Keynes's *Economic Consequences of the Peace* and *Economic Consequences of Mr Churchill*.

In 1925, he moved to Harvard where, in 1931, he gained his PhD with a dissertation on 'Bank Assets and Banking Theory'. This was influenced by his Harvard mentor Allyn Young (who died in 1929) and by Keynes's *Treatise on Money* (1930). He served as instructor in courses led by Ralph Hawtrey, Joseph Schumpeter and John H. Williams and, between 1931 and 1934, he wrote pioneering papers in the *Journal of Political Economy* and *Quarterly Journal of Economics* on monetary theory and policy and constructed the first money supply series for the United States.

Currie blamed the Federal Reserve Board for the persistence and depth, if not for the onset, of the Great Depression of 1929–1933 (Sandilands, 1990; Laidler, 1993), exposing the errors of the commercial loan theory of central banking that gave too much attention to the stock market and too little to the real economy that started to decline some months before the October crash. He insisted that the stock market played only a minor and ambiguous role in the course of the business cycle, through its influence on aggregate savings relative to its influence on real investment. He rejected the view, held by his Harvard superiors and rivals, including Schumpeter and Seymour Harris (whom Currie regarded as a Johnny-come-lately to Keynesian economics), that the depression was the inevitable and salutary consequence of an unsustainable boom in the 1920s.

By 1932, Currie was convinced that monetary policy alone could not undo the damage. He applauded Roosevelt's decision to leave the gold standard in 1933, and urged deficit spending in his Harvard classes. His views cost him promotion and the prestigious Wells Prize (which went instead to his close friend, Harry White). J.K. Galbraith (1975), whom Currie was to recruit for New Deal Washington in 1940, has held Currie up as an object lesson of the dangers of being right too soon. In July 1934, he joined Viner's 'freshman brain trust' at the US Treasury to devise an 'ideal' monetary system for the United States. He proposed a 100 per cent reserve system. He teamed up with Marriner Eccles, another fierce advocate of deficit spending as the means to recovery, and prepared the memorandum on radical reform of the federal reserve system that Eccles presented to Roosevelt in November 1934, before accepting the post of governor. Eccles took Currie with him to the Fed and they drafted the 1935 Banking Act that created a true central bank for the United States.

First at the Treasury in 1934 and then at the Fed, Currie initiated a regular statistical series to measure the net contribution to economic activity of the public sector's income and expenditure. Because of the passion aroused at that time by the very word 'deficit', he used various names for the series to make clearer not only its quantitative but also its conceptual significance and usefulness as a policy tool. First it was called the 'pump-priming deficit', but because he did not believe a one-shot fiscal boost could meet the immensity of the problem at hand this was soon changed to 'federal net income-increasing expenditures', the 'government net contribution' and 'income-increasing deficit'. Alan Sweezy (1972) described this series as 'a semantic triumph of the first magnitude ... No one used to thinking in terms of the net contribution could advocate promoting recovery by increasing public works spending while at the same time cutting government salaries and raising tax rates'.

The analysis anticipated modern discussions of the relative effectiveness of expenditure increases compared with tax reductions in controlling aggregate demand and acting on motivations. In a 1935 memorandum and at the 1936 American Economic Association meetings in Chicago, Currie outlined an early version of a balanced-budget multiplier: 'By selecting income-increasing types of expenditures and non-income-decreasing methods of raising revenue, it is conceivable that a balanced budget could be maintained and at the same time a considerable stimulus be given to business.' For policy purposes, however, he believed that substantially unbalanced budgets would be indispensable for some years if full employment was to be restored. He worked out the magnitude of the government's net contribution, together with measures to revive the housing market, that would be needed to offset withdrawals from the circular flow at a 1929 level of income plus the potential increase due to technical change since then.

When the *General Theory* was published in 1936, he presented a summary to the top Treasury and Fed officers, but believed that some of the new concepts were unhelpful for policy purposes. He was one of the first economists to subject the supposedly stable investment multiplier to empirical test (Patinkin, 1976) and found that its value ranged from 20 to a negative number. He criticized Keynes's loose definition of money and disliked the use made of the concept of liquidity preference as a 'demand for money'. Currie preferred to distinguish demand for money proper, as a demand for command over goods and services, from demand for command over interest-bearing assets or demand for (interest) income. The former demand, together with the money supply, determined the price level; the latter the interest rate. The demand for *liquidity* could be satisfied by holding interest-bearing assets, albeit at shorter rather than longer term. There was no need to hold money itself for this purpose. He endorsed the controversial raising of reserve requirements by the Fed in late 1936 and early 1937, believing that the great increase in banks' excess reserves following massive gold inflows from Europe represented a potential threat to the Fed's ability to control the money supply in the future as the economy picked up steam. It was intended as a 'precautionary', not a deflationary, measure. The banks did in fact remain highly liquid, and interest rates increased only slightly.

But the move coincided with a very sharp reversal of fiscal stimulus in early 1937, as measured by the 'net contribution' series, which fell from $4.3 billion in 1936 to only $1.1 billion in 1937. Also an inventory buying boom (connected with fears about labor unions) at the end of 1936 presaged a working off of stocks a few months later, and the economy fell into a new recession. Treasury Secretary Morgenthau blamed a loss of business confidence due to unbalanced budgets, whereas Currie was able to use his series to blame the sharp decline in the fiscal deficit. In November 1937, he presented his evidence to the President in a four-hour meeting in the White House, and the following year was appointed to a fiscal and monetary advisory board that influenced the President's budget statement of January 1939. He kept in touch with the Hansen–Williams fiscal policy seminar at Harvard, and in 1939 recruited Hansen to appear with himself as star witnesses at the Temporary National Economic Committee (TNEC) Hearings. Tobin (1976) remarked that 'in the [Keynesian] crusade launched at the TNEC, Currie was Mr. Inside, and Hansen, Mr. Outside'. There followed the Works Financing Bill, popularly known as the Lend–Spend Bill, July 1939, that Currie drafted with legal and political help from Ben Cohen and Tom Corcoran. This, though defeated by a hostile Congress, indicated the extent to which Keynesian, or at least what has been called 'Curried-Keynesian' thinking, had gained intellectual acceptance among New Dealers who previously had embraced an activist approach to government more from their humanitarian instincts than from an understanding of its economics (Stein, 1969).

In July 1939, Currie became the first professional economic adviser in the White House when Roosevelt appointed him as his assistant on economic affairs. From there he continued his work as an unofficial recruiting agency for Keynesians in the New Deal, and did much to school the President in the new economics. He claimed (Currie, 1972) that the President finally grasped a firm understanding of the theory in long discussions on proposed revisions to the Social Security System in 1940. Currie remained in the White House until Roosevelt's death, with major wartime responsibilities for the Lend-Lease program to China and as acting director of the Foreign Economic Administration which, in 1943–4, included delicate negotiations with Keynes on US loans to Britain.

In 1949, Currie headed the World Bank's first full-scale country study mission, to Colombia. He was commissioned to serve on a committee to implement the mission's proposals for the integration of what had been a highly disarticulated country. He remained active as a top adviser to successive Colombian governments until his death in December 1993.

Currie's main theoretical explorations in the field of economic development were oriented towards the underlying nature of secular growth, emphasising the endogenous relationships between real market size and macroeconomic increasing returns that Allyn Young had emphasized. Deviations from secular growth he ascribed partly to Keynesian-type interruptions to spending, partly to major policy blunders such as inflation, overvalued exchange rates and confusion over the distinction between money and credit. In his 'leading sector' model of growth, this not only inhibited export-led growth but also disrupted the construction sector, so important in the urbanization of less developed countries. Currie disagreed with Keynesian emphasis on the interest rate as an influence on non-residential business investment, which, in net terms, is self-financed from retained profits. However, he emphasized that residential construction is peculiarly vulnerable to fluctuating interest rates and therefore requires special protection if it is to play its proper role both as a macroeconomic stabilizer and as an agent of growth.

He was still working on these ideas at the time of his death and his draft paper on endogenous growth was edited for publication in *History of Political Economy* (Currie, 1997).

ROGER J. SANDILANDS

See also:

Ackley, Hugh Gardner; Deficits: Cyclical and Structural; Depression, The Great; Fiscal Policy; Friedman, Milton; Hansen, Alvin H.; Keynesianism in America; Monetary Policy; Money; Multiplier Effect; Quantity Theory of Money; White, Harry D.

References

Currie, Lauchlin B. (1972), 'The Keynesian Revolution and its Pioneers: Discussion', *American Economic Review*, **62**, (2), May, pp. 139–41.

Currie, Lauchlin B. (1997), 'Implications of an Endogenous Theory of Growth in Allyn Young's Macroeconomic Concept of Increasing Returns', *History of Political Economy*, **29**, (3), Fall.

Galbraith, J.K. (1975), 'How Keynes Came to America', *Economics, Peace and Laughter*, Harmondsworth: Penguin.

Laidler, David (1993), 'Hawtrey, Harvard and the Origins of the Chicago Tradition', *Journal of Political Economy*, **101**, (6), December, pp. 1068–1103.

Patinkin, Don (1976), 'Keynes and Econometrics: On the Interaction between the Macroeconomic Revolutions of the Interwar Period', *Econometrica*, **44**, (6), November, pp. 1091–1123.

Sandilands, Roger J. (1990), *The Life and Political Economy of Lauchlin Currie: New Dealer, Presidential Adviser and Development Economist*, Durham, NC: Duke University Press.

Stein, Herbert (1969), *Fiscal Revolution in America*, Chicago: University of Chicago Press.

Sweezy, Alan (1972), 'The Keynesians and Government Policy, 1933–39', *American Economic Review*, **62**, (2), May, pp. 116–24.

Tobin, James (1976), 'Hansen and Public Policy', *Quarterly Journal of Economics*, **90**, (1), pp. 32–7.

Davidson, Paul

Paul Davidson, a child of the Great Depression, was born in New York City on 23 October 1930, about two months after the Harvard Economic Society had written that 'the present depression has about spent its force' (*Weekly Letters*, 30 August 1930). Davidson, like many of the economists of his generation, was a late-bloomer in economics. He majored in chemistry and biology at Brooklyn College, and graduated with a BS degree in 1950 without having had a single course in economics. He left the city for graduate training in biochemistry at the University of Pennsylvania from 1950 to 1952, easily completing most of his course work while working as an instructor in biochemistry at the Medical and Dental Schools. Although intending to do a PhD thesis on DNA, he quickly lost interest in biochemical research and withdrew from the program.

Returning to New York, and enrolling at City University, he began to prepare himself for a 'real job' in commerce by entering the business program. Exposed to a course in basic economics and not immune to the misuse of data, he was sickened by the misuse of data by economists. He decided then and there to make his mark in economics. After a stint in the US Army (1953–5) on a biochemical team, Davidson returned to complete the MBA program at City University, graduating in 1955. Thereafter he enrolled in the graduate economic program at the University of Pennsylvania where he first encountered the affable Sidney Weintraub. Sidney's influence can be felt in Paul's dissertation, published as *Theories of Aggregate Income Distribution* (1960). As a result, his early work was on the relationship between income distribution and macroeconomic analytics.

The real world has never been alien to Davidson. While working for Conoco in the 1960s, he developed expertise in natural resource economics. In collaboration with two graduate students (J.J. Seneca and C.J. Cicchetti) he published a landmark econometric analysis of the 'Demand and Supply of Outdoor Recreation'. Again, with the same co-workers, Davidson developed the first econometric cross-sectional analysis of the demand for communications. In turn, he has been a consultant to various organizations, ranging from Chase Econometrics Associates to the Central Bank of Venezuela.

Subsequent to a stint on the economics faculty at the University of Pennsylvania (1961–6), Davidson spent 20 years at Rutgers University (1966–86) and has since held the Holly Chair of Excellence in Political Economy at the University of Tennessee. One senses that he still loves New York; at the least, his voice retains a New York cadence. He and his mentor Weintraub were co-founders of the *Journal of Post Keynesian Economics*, a journal that Davidson continues to edit. He and his wife, Louise, comprise a strong, supportive team.

Davidson's bibliography reads like debate topics; this reflects a part of his personality, his enjoyment of verbal combat. Early on, his Keynesian instincts were honed in attacks on Milton Friedman, the founder of modern monetarism; more recently, he has engaged the New Classicals. His quick wit, intellect and ironic smile easily disarm his opponents. Vigorous in a disputation, he nonetheless displays no anger, only intellectual disagreement.

It is impossible in this small space to review Paul Davidson's contributions to 12 books and more than 105 professional journal articles. A summary of his major contribution to Post Keynesian economics must suffice. In this regard, he has not only carried the Keynesian torch for another generation but also has fully explicated what Keynes really meant while advancing his analytics.

The culmination and full synthesis of Davidson's work can be found in his *Post Keynesian Macroeconomic Theory: A Foundation for Successful Economic Policies for the Twenty-first Century* (1994). Davidson attacks the mainstream's acceptance of the ergodic hypothesis of stochastic economic processes as the *sine qua non* of scientific method. In an ergodic system, the future is always reliably predictable through a probabilistic analysis of past and current outcomes. Although risk can be calculated with a known distribution of probabilities, wherever uncertainty exists, it pre-empts knowledge of such distributions. Under conditions of uncertainty, people do not know what is going to happen, and know that they do not know.

Davidson's most powerful application of this principle is to money and its effects in the real world. Money comes into its own in the real world of uncertainty and past mistakes. People feel uneasy about committing their claims on resources to a path that can only be changed, if future events and actions require it, at significant costs (sometimes infinitely high). Money minimizes transactions' costs through its functions as a generally accepted medium of contractual settlement and a liquid store of value (or a time-machine vehicle, moving purchasing power to the future).

These properties of money create the possibility of unemployment in monetary economies. If, because of uncertainty, people decide to demand more time-machine vehicles to convey their purchasing power to an unspecified future to meet possible liquidity needs, the shift of funds away from produced goods can cause unemployment. The increase in demand for liquidity cannot cause an offsetting increase in employment in the production of money since money is not a produced good, nor does it cause an increase in the demand for produced goods.

Debt instruments enable the household or corporation to forgo the current purchase of produced goods and services while retaining liquid stores of value into the indefinite future. Since the saver's demand for such a liquidity time machine does not require the use of current resources, the decision to save does not create an equal value of real capital. The decision to buy machines and plant is a separate one, made by other parties, so that saving does not create investment: quite the contrary, real investment creates real saving.

As Davidson relates the story, Keynes added the finance motive to his other reasons for demanding money (ultimate liquidity) as the 'coping stone' for his liquidity preference theory. As an example, if profit expectations increase, entrepreneurs will demand more investment goods and willingly enter into more forward contracts to produce capital if they can obtain the finance. The demand for such finance – based as it is on 'planned' demand – will increase even before additional employment and income are forthcoming. Once this finance motive is introduced, the demand for money can change as a consequence of a change in planned spending (aggregate demand) of any kind. Then the income velocity of money is subject to more volatility while the real and monetary sectors of the economy become necessarily intertwined. The finance motive at once makes monetarism suspect, lifting the veil of money, and allows money to influence output and employment.

Youthful and energetic, Paul Davidson can be expected to continue his Post Keynesian crusade. By now he has enlisted many new recruits. His force will continue to be felt.

E. Ray Canterbery

See also:

Depression, the Great; Econometric Models, Macroeconomic; Economics of Keynes and of his Revolution, Key Elements of; Galbraith, John K.; Harcourt, Geoff; Kalecki, Michał; Keynes, John Maynard; Keynes and Probability; Kregel, Jan A.; Robinson, Joan; Shackle, G.L.S.; Weintraub, Sidney.

Bibliography

Davidson, Paul (1960), *Theories of Aggregate Income Distribution*, New Brunswick: Rutgers University Press.

Davidson, Paul (1969), 'Demand and Supply of Outdoor Recreation' (with C.J. Cicchetti and J.J. Seneca), New York: Bureau of Economic Research.

Davidson, Paul (1994), *Post Keynesian Macroeconomic Theory*, Aldershot: Edward Elgar.

Deficits: Cyclical and Structural

The size of the federal budget deficit or surplus is influenced by the level of economic activity as well as by fiscal policy. For this reason, the actual deficit is divided into two components: the cyclical deficit and the structural deficit.

The cyclical deficit is the result of the workings of the automatic stabilizers as the economy deviates from full employment. When the economy is operating at less than full employment, tax revenues are lower and transfer payments in the form of unemployment compensation and welfare benefits are higher than the levels which would prevail if the economy were operating without slack. Hence the cyclical deficit becomes larger as the unemployment rate increases and shrinks as the unemployment rate decreases. The cyclical budget may show a surplus if the economy operates at levels higher than full employment. By definition, the cyclical deficit is zero at full employment. In the Keynesian view, the countercyclical effects of cyclical deficits are desirable.

The structural portion of the deficit excludes the influence of cyclical fluctuations on tax revenues and transfer payments. It is an estimate of what the deficit would be, given existing expenditure and tax policies, if the economy were at full employment and producing at its potential GDP. Full employment is generally considered to be achieved when the unemployment rate is at the natural rate (which is also called the non-accelerating inflation rate of unemployment – NAIRU). This rate is currently estimated at approximately 5 to 6 per cent. The structural deficit is alternatively called the high employment, full employment, cyclically adjusted budget, or the standardized employment budget deficit. Because the structural deficit is uninfluenced by the actual level of employment and output achieved by the economy, it is the part of the deficit for which policy makers are directly responsible. The structural deficit is therefore used as a gauge of discretionary fiscal policy because it is the result of deliberate decisions of policy makers regarding tax rates, government spending levels and transfer payments.

The concept of the full employment budget has its roots in the Keynesian analyses of the 1930s. The Committee on Economic Development (CED) proposed fiscal policy in terms of the full employment budget in 1947. E. Cary Brown used the concept to demonstrate that the federal deficits of the 1930s were primarily the result of the automatic stabilizers rather than of discretionary expansionary policy. Arthur Okun and Walter Heller advocated using the full employment budget for policy purposes during the Kennedy administration. Beginning in 1955, the Bureau of Economic Analysis of the Department of Commerce constructed a series of high employment budget surpluses and deficits. Initially, an unemployment rate of 4 per cent was used as an estimate of the natural rate but this figure was subsequently raised. The first major refinements of the concept and measurement were provided by Arthur Okun and Nancy Teeters in 1970. A further refinement in the 1980s consisted of estimating automatic inflation effects on the high employment budget and estimating what budget deficits would be at a 6 per cent unemployment trend rate for GNP.

The structural deficit (or surplus) has several uses. The most widespread use is as a measure of discretionary fiscal policy because the structural deficit is uncontaminated by the influence of economic fluctuations on the budget. However, the size of the structural deficit or surplus may be a misleading indicator of the fiscal impact of the government sector on the economy. An expansionary influence would be exercised if expenditures and taxes were raised by the same amount so as to maintain the same structural deficit. The magnitude of government expenditures and taxes as well as the difference between the two affect the economy. Another use of the structural deficit is to provide a measure of budget trends. A cyclically adjusted budget is analogous to seasonal adjustment. Trends are more apparent when the 'noise' of cyclical fluctuations has been filtered out. The structural deficit may also be used to analyse whether large deficits, by absorbing a high proportion of private saving, crowd out private investment and thereby interfere with long-term growth. However, the possible long-run crowding out effect of the federal budget depends more on the stock of federal debt relative to the GDP than the current deficit. Finally, the size of the structural deficit or surplus may be used as a policy objective in its own right. Shortly after World War II, the CED advocated that fiscal policy be set to achieve a small surplus in the full employment budget.

Until 1974, actual deficits were relatively small and the full employment budget showed a surplus or a negligible deficit. However, from 1966 to 1969, owing to the stimulus of the Vietnam War, the economy operated at rates exceeding full employment and the actual deficit for 1966 to 1968 was less than the high employment deficit. Since 1975, both the actual deficit and the structural deficit have been substantial. Partly as a result of the severe recession of 1981–2, the actual deficit burgeoned to unprecedented levels in the early 1980s. As the economy recovered from this recession and the cyclical component of the deficit fell, actual deficits remained stubbornly high owing to a high structural deficit. These high structural deficits can be attributed to a number of causes, including the large 'supply-side' tax cuts and indexation of tax brackets to control 'bracket creep' instituted in the early 1980s, the rapid growth of defense spending enacted by the Reagan administration, high and rising interest costs to service the federal debt, which has risen concomitantly with deficits, rapidly rising Medicare costs and greater inflation sensitivity of many spending programs combined with lower inflation sensitivity of revenues.

Several economists have argued that the absolute size of the deficit and debt has generated unwarranted alarm. The debt and the deficit should be measured as a percentage of the GDP. Although the ratio of publicly held gross debt to the GDP increased from 26.8 per cent in 1980 to 51.6 per cent in 1993, this ratio is well below the post-World War II high of 113.8 per cent (1946). The ratio of the deficit to GDP was down from a 1983 high of 6.3 to 4.0 per cent in 1993 and remained significantly below its peak of 31 per cent of GDP in 1943. However, the peak percentages of the debt and the deficit to the GDP experienced during the 1940s were produced by the financing of World War II. The ensuing postwar prosperity reduced these ratios. The rising debt-to-GDP ratios over the 15 years since 1981 represent an ongoing trend with no foreseeable reversal. It should be noted that, were it not for the federal debt ballooning to $5 trillion and the over $200 billion interest expenditures to service this debt (accounting for 15 per cent of total budget outlays), the federal budget would have been balanced in 1994.

James Buchanan notes that large structural deficits are the predictable outcome of incentives facing politicians. Politicians seek to be re-elected, which requires pleasing their various constituents. The benefits of 'pork barrel' spending projects in their home districts are concentrated within the district, while the costs of these projects are dispersed. This, coupled with the fact that voters perceive tax increased unfavorably and are more inclined to re-elect legislators voting for tax decreases, gives politicians a strong motive to increase deficits in order to maximize their chances of re-election. Viewed from this perspective, there are two avenues to reducing the deficit. One is that voters become sufficiently convinced of the pernicious effects of high deficits for them to guide their votes accordingly. The other would be a constitutional amendment mandating a balanced budget. Such an amendment may provide politicians with immunity from voter reprisal for cutting expenditures and/or increasing taxes.

A balanced budget amendment is not viewed favorably by most economists. An annually balanced budget would require procyclical discretionary fiscal policy. During economic downturns, when tax revenues automatically decline and welfare and unemployment expenditures automatically rise, an increase in tax rates or a discretionary spending cut would be required. This contractionary fiscal policy would intensify the downturn. An alternative would be a constitutional amendment requiring that only the structural component of the budget be balanced. The cyclical budget may thereby be permitted to run either deficits or surpluses, as prescribed by Keynesian countercyclical Policy.

ANN HANSEN

See also:

Automatic Stabilizers; Demand Management; Economics of Keynes and of his Revolution, Key Elements of Employment Act of 1946; Full Employment Budget; Keynes, John Maynard; Keynes's Economics, National Income Accounting Activism and; Keynesian Revolution; Okun, Arthur M.; Okun's Law.

Bibliography

Brown, E.C. (1956), 'Fiscal Policy in the Thirties: A Reappraisal', *American Economic Review*, **46**, (5), December, pp. 857–79.

Buchanan, J.M., C.K. Rowley and R.D. Tollison (eds) (1987), *Deficits*, New York: Basil Blackwell.
Congressional Budget Office (1994), *The Economic and Budget Outlook: Fiscal Years 1995–1999*, Washington, DC: Government Printing Office.
de Leeuw, F. and T.M. Holloway (1983), 'Cyclical Adjustment of the Federal Budget and Federal Debt', *Survey of Current Business*, **63**, (12), December, pp. 25–40.
Eisner, R. (1986), *How Real is the Federal Deficit?*, New York: The Free Press.
Eisner, R. (1989), 'Budget Deficits: Rhetoric and Reality', *Journal of Economic Perspectives*, **3**, (2), Spring, pp. 73–93.
Levy, M.E. *et al.* (1984), *Federal Budget Deficits and the U.S. Economy*, New York: The Conference Board.
Okun, A.M. and N. Teeters (1970), 'The Full Employment Surplus Revisited', *Brookings Papers on Economic Activity*, **3**, pp. 77–110.
Teeters, N.H. (1965), 'Estimates of the Full-Employment Surplus, 1955–1964', *Review of Economics and Statistics*, **47**, (2), August, pp. 309–14.

Demand Management

In the United States the expression 'stabilization policy' is usually used instead of 'demand management'. The ideas of demand management comes from Keynes (1936) who offered an explanation why the aggregate demand for goods and services could be less than the capacity of the economy to produce. This insufficient aggregate demand, commonly known as a recessionary gap, causes unemployment. A recessionary gap can be remedied by an expansionary fiscal policy and/or an expansionary monetary policy. An expansionary fiscal policy would increase aggregate demand by increasing government expenditures and/or lowering taxes. An expansionary monetary policy would increase aggregate demand by lowering interest rates that in turn would stimulate investment. On the other hand, a contractionary fiscal policy and/or a contractionary monetary policy could remedy excess aggregate demand, commonly known as an inflationary gap. A contractionary fiscal policy would decrease aggregate demand by decreasing government expenditures and/or increasing taxes. A contractionary monetary policy would decrease aggregate demand by increasing interest rates and discouraging investment.

Demand management is aimed at returning the economy to where the aggregate demand equals the long-run capacity to produce. In other words, the purpose of demand management is to return the economy to a long-run equilibrium where there are no recessionary gaps or inflationary gaps. Demand management is not aimed at increasing the long-run output capacity of the economy. Increasing the long-run capacity of the economy is done by growth in the labor force, an increase in the stock of capital, an improvement of the incentives to produce and technological progress.

In practice, demand management requires an impressive understanding of the economy. Those responsible for fiscal and monetary policy must answer the following questions. Is the economy in an inflationary or recessionary gap? Where is the long-run equilibrium now and where will it be in the future? What will be the future changes in consumption, investment, net exports or wages? How will these changes affect gross domestic product and unemployment? How much should aggregate demand be increased or decreased to return to a long-run equilibrium? What effect will various changes in government spending, taxes and monetary policy have on the economy? What fiscal policies are other members of the government likely to accept? How long will it take to get them accepted? What will the details of the fiscal policy after it has been accepted? What monetary policies will the central bank likely accept? What will be the details of the monetary policy after it has been accepted? How will people and businesses respond to the changes in fiscal and monetary policy? If the central bank carries out the policies when will they take effect? What are the fiscal and monetary policies of other countries?

Besides the understanding of the economy inherent in demand management, the feasibility of intervening in the economy depends on a number of time lags. First, fiscal and monetary authorities must recognize whether the economy is in an inflationary or recessionary gap. Second, they must decide how to change the fiscal and monetary policies. Third, they must carry out these changes. Lastly, there is a lag between implementing the policies and when the policies affect the economy. Also the length of each lag is uncertain.

A problem facing demand management policies is cost inflation. Cost inflation is a decrease in the aggregate supply caused by an increase in input prices, such as oil prices and wages. If cost inflation is reduced by contractionary fiscal or monetary policies then unemployment will increase. However, if expansionary fiscal or monetary policies reduce the unemployment caused by the cost inflation then an inflationary spiral may occur. Another inhibition on demand management is that countries that unilaterally try to expand out of a recession face exchange rate depreciation. To offset this problem, countries must coordinate their national policies.

Neo-Keynesians argue that, though there are problems, there still is a place for demand management policies. They feel that wage and price rigidities make it so that the economy does not self-correct very quickly. However, most Neo-Keynesians do not believe in trying to 'fine-tune' the economy. Some Neo-Keynesians feel that part of the problem in using demand management in the 1970s and 1980s was that it was used to fight inflation rather than for its original purpose of reducing unemployment. Unfortunately, reducing unemployment may lead to renewed inflation. To avoid inflation some Neo-Keynesians argue that other policies should be used to fight inflation, such as policies to restrain the growth of nominal incomes.

Monetarists argue that demand management policies should not be used. They feel that wages and prices are fairly flexible, so that the economy will self-correct on its own. Also monetarists argue that many and uncertain time lags, the difficulty of forecasting recessions, and the many policy blunders made by government leaders make demand management unworkable. This is why Milton Friedman proposed a simple money growth rule.

Rational expectations implies that demand management policies do not affect the economy. Rational expectations assumes that all markets clear. In other words, wages and prices are always at their equilibrium.

JOHN B. HOROWITZ

See also:

Ackley, Hugh Gardner; Aggregate Demand–Aggregate Supply Model and Diagram; Crowding Out; Deficits: Cyclical and Structural; Expectations, Theories of; Fiscal Policy; Friedman, Milton; Full Employment Budget; Hansen, Alvin, H.; IS/LM and Diagram; Keynes, John Maynard; Keynesian Cross; Lucas Critique; Monetary Policy; Neo-Keynesianism.

Bibliography

Friedman, Milton (1960), *A Program for Monetary Stability*, New York: Fordham University Press.

Friedman, Milton (1968), 'The Role of Monetary Policy', *American Economic Review*, **58**, (1), March, pp. 1–17.

Keynes, John M. (1936), *The General Theory of Employment, Interest and Money*, London: Macmillan.

Worswick, G.D.N. (1987), 'Demand Management', John Eatwell, Murray Milgate and Peter Newman (eds), *The New Palgrave: a Dictionary of Economics*, Vol. 1, New York: Stockton Press.

Depression, The Great

The Great Depression of the 1930s was a catastrophe of such magnitude and complexity that it is the subject of continual research.[1] Work on the subject has centered on a number of issues, including the following: where did the Depression begin and how were its effects transmitted internationally; what were the causes of the Depression's onset, intensity and persistence; and was the Depression a short-run cyclical phenomenon or did it represent secular stagnation?

That the Great Depression largely originated in the United States and was primarily the result of internal disturbances has long been widely held (Lewis, 1949, p. 52; Romer, 1993, p. 20). Early blame for the Depression's onset was attributed to such things as the stock market crash of 24 October 1929, the effect of weather on agricultural prices, overinvestment in housing induced by easy credit, secular shifts in the terms of trade and the vagaries of the inter-war gold standard rules (Bernstein, 1987; Kindleberger, 1983; Meltzer, 1976). That 'deflationary impulses' caused declines in output and employment was widely attributed to the increasingly imperfect competition and 'sticky prices' that had come to prevail in both product markets and labor markets (Bernstein, 1987; Robbins, 1934).

Following the publication of John Maynard Keynes's *General Theory of Employment, Interest and Money* (1936), the majority of economists probably came to believe that the Great Depression of the 1930s was an aggregate demand (aggregate expenditures) phenomenon: downward shifts in private spending (for example, consumption, investment, and exports) that were not adequately offset by government spending and tax policy, with not only deflation but also, because of an upward-sloping aggregate supply at the time, protracted falls in output and high unemployment (more than 25 per cent at its peak) the consequences.[2] Representative of the Keynesian thinking was the study by E. Cary Brown (1956), which concluded: 'Fiscal policy, then, seems to have been an unsuccessful recovery device in the thirties – not because it did not work, but because it was not tried' (Brown, 1956, pp. 863, 866).

The economics profession's prevalent view was badly shaken by the 1963 publication of *A Monetary History of the United States, 1867–1960* by Milton Friedman and Anna J. Schwartz. A long chapter (Chapter 7) was devoted to 'The Great Contraction, 1929–33' (later published by itself as a paperback) and blamed the financial collapse and the resulting depression on the ineptitude of the Federal Reserve System in the conduct of monetary policy. In contrast to the 'sound general principle that great events have great origins' (p. 419), Friedman and Schwartz attributed the Federal Reserve's ineptitude to the shift of power in the system that occurred after the untimely death in 1928 of Benjamin Strong, governor of the Federal Reserve Bank of New York and staunch advocate of open market operations for countercyclical purposes.

Not until 1976 was there a systematic response from the Keynesians,[3] when Peter Temin published *Did Monetary Forces Cause the Great Depression?* Temin's book reasserted the importance of unexplained falls in aggregate demand (especially consumption spending) as the primary cause of the Depression and argued that the financial collapse (falling money stock and bank failures, in particular) was endogenous, that is, induced by the decreases in aggregate demand.

The next two decades saw a flurry of activity in response to the Temin–Friedman and Schwartz conflict (Mayer, 1978a, 1978b). Anderson and Butkiewicz's 1980 paper, 'Money, Spending and the Great Depression', was an attempt to build a small structural model encompassing government expenditures, consumption, housing and export shocks, as well as monetary policy shocks.[4] A major collection of original essays and comments on the topic, including papers by Anna Schwartz and Temin, appeared in 1981 under the editorship of Karl Brunner: *The Great Depression Revisited*. As Brunner pointed out (p. 3), the issues are far from completely resolved and the opportunities for further research are plentiful.

Among the lines of inquiry currently being explored intensively is the role that consumer and business debt played (see Anderson and Butkiewicz, 1980, p. 401). A factor strongly emphasized by Irving Fisher (1933), the 'debt-deflation theory', has been elaborated for some years by Hyman Minsky (1982) and applied to modern circumstances ('Can "It" Happen Again?'). More recently, this approach has been described as being concerned with the 'allocative effects of imperfections in capital markets', which provides a 'new paradigm of financial–real interaction'.[5]

In studying the 1930s (and earlier) periods in the United States, a major problem has always been the lack of quarterly and/or monthly data for many important variables needed to uncover short-run relationships. Fortunately, there has been a steady stream of estimates for the missing data over the past 30 years. Numerous time series have been collected in Moore (1961), estimates for monetary and related variables appear in Friedman and Schwartz (1963) and new quarterly estimates of the nominal and real GNP and GNP deflator have been made by Balke and Gordon (1986). A study by Dominguez, Fair and Shapiro (1988) sought to discover whether modern time series methods could have enabled either the Harvard Economic Service, with its 'speculation', 'business' and 'money' indexes, or Yale-based Irving Fisher, with his commodity price and stock market indexes, to have forecast successfully the Great Depression (the authors came to a negative conclusion). They also tested whether, had a variety of modern time series subsequently estimated for the period been available, as well as statistical methodology, the forecasts would have been more accurate (again, a negative conclusion).

An eclectic summary of the present state of knowledge about the Great Depression has been provided by Christina Romer:

> The United States slipped into recession in mid-1929 because of tight domestic monetary policy aimed at stemming speculation on the U.S. stock market. The Great Depression started in earnest when the stock market crash in the United States caused consumers and firms to become nervous and therefore to stop buying irreversible durable goods. The American Depression worsened when banking panics swept undiversified and overextended rural banks and the Federal Reserve failed to intervene. Finally, the American Depression ended when the Roosevelt administration chose to increase the money supply tremendously after 1933. (Romer, 1993, p. 37)

In short, the depths reached in the Great Contraction 'required a confluence of factors thus far unique in our history' (Anderson and Butkiewicz, 1980, p. 402).

WILLIAM P. YOHE

Notes

1   For example, the 1993 symposium on the Great Depression in *Journal of Economic Perspectives*: papers by Romer and Calomiris will be cited below.
2   There were many unbelievers in the Keynesian explanation, such as economists of the Austrian School (especially Friedrich von Hayek and Ludwig von Mises) and the American economists Clark Warburton and Irving Fisher. See Haberler (1958). The Austrian interpretation was popularly called the 'hangover theory'.
3   Some would cite Kindleberger's 1973 book as a major strike. There were, of course innumerable critical reviews of the Friedman and Schwartz book, such as Tobin (1965).
4   In Yohe (1991), the model is enlarged to include determination of the price level and unemployment, and opportunities are given to simulate the possible effects of counterfactual levels of government spending, monetary policy, excess supply of housing and exports.
5   Calomiris (1993, pp. 61 and 70, respectively). He credits work on the effects of debt-deflation on consumption by Mishkin and on investment by Bernanke and others as providing a 'new synthesis of early (and other) monetary shocks and long-run financial propagators' (p. 75). He credits Kindleberger with a similar approach in his explanation of the international transmission of disturbances (p. 71).

See also:

Brunner, Karl; Classical Economics; Currie, Lauchlin; Friedman, Milton; Galbraith, John K.; Hansen, Alvin H.; Harcourt, Geoff; Keynes, John Maynard; Keynesian Revolution; Meltzer, Allan H.; Minsky, Hyman P; Pigou, Arthur C.; Schwartz, Anna J.

Bibliography

Anderson, Barry L. and James L. Butkiewicz (1980), 'Money, Spending and the Great Depression', *Southern Economic Journal*, **47**, (2), October, pp. 388–403.
Balke, Nathan S. and Robert J. Gordon (1986), 'Appendix B: Historical Data', in Robert J. Gordon (ed.), *The American Business Cycle*, Chicago: University of Chicago Press for the National Bureau of Economic Research.
Barber, William J. (1985), *From New Era to New Deal*, Cambridge: Cambridge University Press.
Bernstein, Michael A. (1987), *The Great Depression*, Cambridge: Cambridge University Press.
Bolch, Ben W. and John D. Pilgrim (1973), 'A Reappraisal of Some Factors Associated with Fluctuations in the United States in the Interwar Period', *Southern Economic Journal*, **39**, (3), January, pp. 327–44.
Brown, E. Cary (1956), 'Fiscal Policy in the Thirties: A Reappraisal', *American Economic Review*, **46**, (5), December, pp. 857–79.
Brunner, Karl (ed.) (1981), *The Great Depression Revisited*, Boston/The Hague/London: Kluwer-Nijhoff.
Calomiris, Charles W. (1993), 'Financial Factors in the Great Depression', *Journal of Economic Perspectives*, **7**, (2), Spring, pp. 61–85.
Dominguez, Kathryn M., Ray C. Fair and Matthew D. Shapiro (1988), 'Forecasting the Depression: Harvard Versus Yale', *American Economic Review*, **78**, (4), September, pp. 595–612.
Fisher, Irving (1933), 'The Debt-Deflation Theory of Great Depressions', *Econometrica*, **1**, (4), October, pp. 337–57.
Friedman, Milton and Anna J. Schwartz (1963), *A Monetary History of the United States*, Princeton, NJ: Princeton University Press for the National Bureau of Economic Research.
Galbraith, John Kenneth (1972), *The Great Crash, 1929*, 3rd edn, Boston: Houghton Mifflin.
Haberler, Gottfried (1958), *Prosperity and Depression*, 4th edn, Cambridge, Mass.: Harvard University Press.
Haberler, Gottfried (1976), *The World Economy, Money and The Great Depression 1929–39*, Washington: American Enterprise Institute.
Keynes, John M. (1936), *The General Theory of Employment, Interest and Money*, London: Macmillan.

Kindleberger, Charles P. (1973), *The World in Depression, 1929–1939*, Berkeley, CA: University of California Press.

Lewis, William Arthur (1949), *Economic Survey, 1919–1939*, London: George Allen & Unwin.

Mayer, Thomas (1978a), 'Consumption in the Great Depression', *Journal of Political Economy*, **86**, (1), February, pp. 139–45.

Mayer, Thomas (1978b), 'Money and the Great Depression: A Critique of Professor Temin's Thesis', *Explorations in Economic History*, **15**, (2), April, pp. 127–45.

Meltzer, Allan H. (1976), 'Monetary and Other Explanations of the Start of the Great Depression', *Journal of Monetary Economics*, **2**, (4), October, pp. 455–71.

Minsky, Hyman P. (1982), *Can 'It' Happen Again?: Essays on Instability and Finance*, Armonk, NY: M.E. Sharpe.

Moore, Geoffrey H. (ed.) (1961), *Business Cycle Indicators*, Vol. II, Princeton, NJ: Princeton University Press for the National Bureau of Economic Research.

Robbins, Lionel (1934), *The Great Depression*, London: Macmillan.

Romer, Christina D. (1993), 'The Nation in Depression', *Journal of Economic Perspectives*, **7**, (2), Spring, pp. 19–39.

Temin, Peter (1976), *Did Monetary Forces Cause the Great Depression?*, New York: W.W. Norton.

Temin, Peter (1989), *Lessons from the Great Depression*, Cambridge, Mass.: MIT Press.

Tobin, James (1965), 'The Monetary Interpretation of History', *American Economic Review*, **55**, (3), June, pp. 464–85.

Wicker, Elmus R. (1966), *Federal Reserve Monetary Policy, 1917–1933*, New York: Random House.

Yohe, William P. (1991), *Simulating the Great Depression in the United States, 1929–1933*, vers. 3.0, Dubuque, Iowa: William C. Brown.

Dillard, Dudley

Keynes believed that the United States could serve as a crucial laboratory in which to test his trenchant policy thesis that a sufficient elevation in governmental spending will propel an economy out of a depression. In his broad assessment, even the stumbling fiscal efforts of the Roosevelt administration in the mid-1930s appeared to confirm the powerful income and employment multiplier effects of public expenditures. During this period, Keynes communicated directly with the President and many of his advisors, but thought that the real force of his ideas would be felt only when they had percolated throughout America's intellectual and political circles. The exigencies of wartime needs completed the post-depression recovery, but many in the United States feared that the end of hostilities would return the nation, and indeed the world, to the parlous economic fluctuations in incomes, employment and prices that had plagued the 1920s and 1930s.

At least one young economist, Dudley Dillard, was convinced that the postwar era could be faced with hope, if Keynes's message were widely disseminated and comprehensively understood (Dillard, 1946). This great teacher perceived that engaging new generations of students, and their uncommitted professors, would be the best means of advancing the Keynesian Revolution on American turf. Virtually all of Dillard's professional work was to fall within the compass of this pursuit.

Superficially, Keynes and Dillard had little in common. They never met. Keynes was a Cambridge aesthete, a Bloomsburyite and an advisor to prime ministers. Born in 1913 and junior by three decades, Dillard was a survivor of the scramble to survive in the American west. He and his family, including six brothers and sisters, saw the convulsions of the 1930s uncoil from the bottom, not the top (Adams, 1993). What Keynes and Dillard did share were three convictions, derived from their utterly different but practical experiences: very little unemployment is truly voluntary, money and finance play an upsetting role in industrial capitalism, and economic science should be directed at policy effectiveness, not theoretical elegance (Dillard, 1946, p. 121).

Dillard had been greatly influenced by his mentor at Berkeley, Leo Rogin, and believed with him, and with Keynes, that economic theory was significant only when it bore on addressing the social issues and policy tasks of the historical moment in which it had been incubated (Dyer, 1993, p. 572). Urged on by E.A.J. Johnson, Dillard completed a book that became the standard American interpretation of Keynes: *The Economics of John Maynard Keynes* (1948). In his bid to make Keynes intelligible to a wide audience and to enhance the influence of his ideas, Dillard had adopted an activist stance fully in accord with his notions of the way economic thought influenced the course of events. He stressed that he was writing about the 'economics of Keynes' (1948, p. vii), not about 'Keynesian economics', as it had so far developed, and was neither defending Keynes against his critics nor furnishing a partial biography. Dillard was brilliantly effective: his book went through a dozen printings, was translated into ten languages, and remains in print.

Fifty years on, *The Economics of John Maynard Keynes* is still the most lucid introduction to the novel insights of the man whom Dillard recognized as the greatest economist of the twentieth century. Drawing on *The General Theory* and later sources, Dillard deftly dissects Keynes's propensity to consume, the investment multiplier, liquidity preference and the impact of uncertainty on finance capital. He utilizes algebra, numerical examples and graphics to explicate Keynes's complex and not always fully formulated concepts and their relationships. The book succeeds magnificently as a pedagogic device and its writing could serve as a model today.

The Economics of John Maynard Keynes captures and espouses Keynes's economic radicalism and his calls for profound social improvement. A strong reformist fire burned underneath Dillard's placid demeanor throughout his life. For Dillard as for Keynes, the central conflict in capitalism was between financial capitalists and industrial capitalists. At root, capitalism was a monetary economy, one in which private and public choices about money mattered enormously (Wray, 1993, p. 547). Dillard took immense pride in having subtitled his book, *The Theory of a Monetary Economy*, believing that this fortified an often unappreciated aspect of Keynes. Contrasting with Marx's vision of a pending war of the classes, Keynes and Dillard thought that labor's often unhappy lot was a by-product of financiers' decisions taken when worry about future sales led them to idle factory capacity and shed workers in order to protect monetary profit. To offset such pusillanimous expectations, what was required was aggressive, compensating fiscal intervention, perhaps managed by a public investment board that would set levels but not the composition of investment; nor would public ownership of industrial capital be necessary. This socialization of investment would be accompanied by a lowering of the rate of interest and, critically, by the expunction of financial rentiers (Dillard, 1948, pp. 333–4) and a levelling of incomes.

Dillard chaired the Department of Economics at the University of Maryland, College Park, from 1951 to 1975, nurturing it into the ranks of the nation's top-rated programs (Adams, 1994). Afterwards, when he fully reactivated his program of writing, he reverted to the theme that capitalism is a monetary economic system and is consequently flawed and unstable. He spoke on the evolutionary economics of a monetary economy when presented with the Veblen–Commons Award of the Association for Evolutionary Economics (Dillard, 1987a). He found significantly similar convictions about the role of money in capitalism in Keynes, Veblen, Marx and Mitchell, and identified aspects of Copeland's study of money flows and Minsky's post-Keynesianism that he admired (Dillard, 1987b). His presidential address to the Eastern Economic Association (1988) had a wry theme, the barter illusion in classical and neoclassical economics. The *Eastern Economic Journal* published four Nobel Laureates' reminiscences of Dillard after his death in 1991, and in one of these James Tobin comments, 'I particularly admire and appreciate Dudley's 1988 article ... not least its title. His points are central to refutation of the classical propositions, recently once again all too popular in our profession' (Tobin *et al.*, 1995).

Dillard was an economic historian as well as an historian of thought, and saw the two fields as entirely intertwined. To him, economics comprised three levels of analysis: microeconomics, macroeconomics and economic history. Because all economics is contextual, the first two cannot be appreciated without knowledge of the third, which, in turn, can be illuminated by the two forms of theory (Dillard, 1982). This was not merely an abstract conception but was embodied in Maryland's undergraduate curriculum. Introductory students were required to take an economic history course prior to the standard principles sequence. Finding no text, Dillard (and his wife Louisa) devoted years of late nights to the composition of *Economic Development of the North Atlantic Community* (1967). More than a textbook, it has been called by Mayhew (1993) 'an original and significant contribution'. It refracts the history of capitalism through a Keynesian lens, underlining the importance of the rise of the system's unique commercial, financial and industrial institutions.

In appreciating the force of his career and contributions, Dillard should be venerated as an unflinching Keynesians' Keynesian and a splendid interpreter and advocate. More than this, he divined a deep and crucial parallel between Keynes and the other great heterodox critics of orthodox classicism at its most obdurate, such as Marx, Veblen and Mitchell. The evolving monetary institutions of capitalism must confound the fullest extraction of product from its industrial technologies. This expansive actuation of the historical meaning of Keynes is the most vibrant legacy of Dillard's life's work.

JOHN ADAMS

See also:

Currie, Lauchlin; Galbraith, John K.; Hansen, Alvin H.; Keynes, John Maynard; Keynesian Revolution; Keynesianism in America; Kuznets, Simon; Samuelson, Paul A.

Bibliography

Adams, John (1993), 'Reflections on Dudley Dillard's Career', *Journal of Economic Issues*, **27**, (2), June, pp. 579–92.

Adams, John (1994), 'The Maryland School of Institutional Economics', in Geoff Hodgson, Warren J. Samuels and Marc R. Tool (eds), *The Elgar Companion to Institutional and Evolutionary Economics*, Aldershot: Edward Elgar.

Dillard, Dudley (1946), 'The Pragmatic Basis of Keynes's Political Economy', *Journal of Economic History*, **6**, (2), November, pp. 121–52.

Dillard, Dudley (1948), *The Economics of John Maynard Keynes: The Theory of a Monetary Economy*, New York: Prentice-Hall.

Dillard, Dudley (1967), *Economic Development of the North Atlantic Community: Historical Introduction to Modern Economics*, Englewood Cliffs, NJ: Prentice-Hall.

Dillard, Dudley (1982), 'Rewriting the Principles of Economics', *Journal of Economic Issues*, **16**, (2), June, pp. 577–85.

Dillard, Dudley (1987a), 'The Evolutionary Economics of a Monetary Economy', *Journal of Economic Issues*, **21**, (2), June, pp. 575–85.

Dillard, Dudley (1987b), 'Money as an Institution of Capitalism', *Journal of Economic Issues*, **21**, (4), December, pp. 1623–47.

Dillard, Dudley (1988), 'The Barter Illusion in Classical and Neoclassical Economics', *Eastern Economic Journal*, **14**, (4), October–December, pp. 299–318.

Dyer, Alan. W. (1993), 'Dudley Dillard, Vision and the Meaning of Ideas', *Journal of Economic Issues*, **27**, (2), June, pp. 571–8.

Mayhew, Anne (1993), 'The Economic Development of the North Atlantic Community: Dudley Dillard and Economic History', *Journal of Economic Issues*, **27**, (2) June, pp. 561–9.

Tobin, James, Lawrence R. Klein, Paul A. Samuelson and Robert M. Solow (1995), 'Reminiscences of Dudley Dillard', *Eastern Economic Journal*, **21**, (1), Winter, pp. 1–6.

Wray, L. Randall (1993), 'The Monetary Macroeconomics of Dudley Dillard', *Journal of Economic Issues*, **27**, (2), June, pp. 547–60.

Domar, Evsey D.

Evsey David Domar was born in 1914 in Lodz, Poland (then Russia) to David and Sarah Domashevitsky. He spent most of his early life in Harbin and Dairen, Manchuria, finally moving to the United States in 1936. He became a naturalized citizen in 1942. Domar married Carola Rosenthal in 1946, and the couple had two children.

Domar was an undergraduate at the State Faculty of Law in Harbin, (1930–31) and received his BA from UCLA in 1939. He received an MA in mathematical statistics from the University of Michigan (1941) and did postgraduate work at the University of Chicago (summers of 1940 and 1941). Domar received his MA in economics from Harvard in 1943 and completed his PhD there in 1947.

Domar is at present the Ford International Professor of Economics, Emeritus, at MIT, a position he has held since 1984. Prior to completing his PhD he was a Teaching Fellow at the University of Michigan (1940–41) and at Harvard University (1941–3). He was a lecturer in economics at George Washington University (summer 1944) and at the University of Michigan (summer 1946). He also served on the research staff of the Board of Governors of the Federal Reserve System from 1943 to 1946.

Domar's first permanent academic positions were as an Associate Professor of Economics at the Carnegie Institute of Technology (1946–7), a research associate for the Cowles Commission and Assistant Professor of Economics at the University of Chicago (1947–8). He was then appointed Associate Professor of Political Economy at Johns Hopkins University (1948–55) and Professor of Political Economy, Johns Hopkins (1955–8). Domar moved to MIT as a Professor of Economics (1958–72), and became the Ford International Professor of Economics at MIT (1972–84).

In addition to his permanent faculty positions, Domar held numerous visiting positions in the United States and abroad. He was the Director, Russian Studies at the Operations Research Office (1949–51); Visiting Lecturer of Economics at the University of Buffalo (1949); Visiting Associate Professor of Economics at the Russian Institute of Columbia University (1951–3); and a Visiting Fulbright Professor at Oxford University (1952–3). He also held visiting professorships in Economics at Stanford University (summer 1957), MIT (1957), Harvard University (1962 and the summers of 1958 and 1976), Universidad de Los Andes (Bogota, Colombia, Summer 1965), UCLA (Summer 1968), Stockholm School of Economics (1972), La Trobe University (Melbourne, Australia, summer 1974) and Hebrew University (Jerusalem, 1979). He was also a Distinguished Exchange Scholar to the People's Republic of China (summer 1981), the Visiting Kathryn Wasserman Davis Professor of Slavic Studies at Wellesley College (1985) and a Visiting Professor of Economics at Brandeis University (1986–90).

Domar has also held various consulting positions during his long career. He was a consultant to the Rand Corporation (1951–81), the Ford Foundation (1954–8), the Brookings Institute (1956–9) and the National Science Foundation (1958 and 1967–9). Domar also consulted for the Batelle Memorial Institute (1959–60), OECD (1961–2) and the Institute for Defense Analysis (1961–2).

Domar's distinguished career is replete with academic awards. In addition to early teaching fellowships, he was a Fellow at Harvard's Russian Research Center (1958) and a Distinguished Fellow of the American Economic Association (1962–5, 1970 and 1984). Domar has been a Fellow of the American Academy of Arts and Sciences (1962 to the present), a Stanford Fellow at the Center of Advanced Study in the Behavioral Sciences (1962–3) and a Fellow of the Empirical Society (1968 to the present). He received the John R. Commons Award from Omicron Delta Epsilon (1965) and in 1970 served as the vice president of the American Economic Association, the same year in which he served as the president of the Association of Comparative Economics.

Domar believes that three early influences stimulated his interest in economic matters: first, there were the problems emanating from the multiple currencies used in Harbin during his youth; second, his father's small import business led to continuous discussions regarding interest rates, price stability and issues of international finance within his household; finally, the State Faculty of Law in Harbin was basically a commercial school where accounting, business mathematics, economic geography and political economy were taught. While Domar took a semester of economics at the State Faculty of Law, his primary lifelong interest has been history. This interest is apparent in his latter work on comparative economic systems and economic history.

When Domar moved to UCLA in 1936 he received little exposure to the *General Theory* (Keynes, 1936), and became uninterested in theory in general. Instead he emphasized empirical economics, taking a large number of courses in mathematics and statistics. At Michigan Domar's interest in theoretical economics was rekindled by Smithies, who provided his first real exposure to Keynesian economics. Moving to Harvard in 1941, Domar came under Hansen's strong influence, and his main interest shifted to employment stability.

Domar has published over 70 articles and working papers, written numerous books and has delivered numerous papers on empirical, historical–institutional and theoretical economics. In terms of the profession's present proclivity to define research in terms of very specialized categories, Domar has written on public finance, national income accounting, economic growth, comparative economic systems and economic history. However, the underlying theme in all of his work has been a concern with economic growth. His work thus includes research on growth modeling, risk taking, empirical studies on productivity and technological change, issues of measurement and various historical and institutional aspects of economic growth.

In his first published article (with R.A. Musgrave) Domar examined Lerner's idea that income taxes do not discourage risk taking. Domar and Musgrave demonstrated that, not only had Lerner been correct, but he had not carried the argument far enough. In the case of a proportional income tax, with complete and immediate loss offsets, the tax encourages risk taking since the taxing authority bears part of the loss (Domar and Musgrave, 1944).

In the same year, Domar developed his first formal growth model. This emerged as a result of his puzzlement over a diagram showing the impact of a constant stream of investment on national income in Hansen's *Fiscal Policy and the Business Cycles* (1941). In an article examining the burden of the national debt, Domar demonstrated that the debt was a direct function of the fraction of income borrowed, but an indirect function of the rate of growth of national income. As such, the problem of the national debt came down to the problem of economic growth (Domar, 1944).

In another series of articles in the 1940s, Domar independently derived his variant of the Harrod–Domar growth model, though his presentation was preceded by Harrod's (Harrod, 1939). Domar's growth model was developed as a long-run extension of Keynes, employing both the multiplier and accelerator principles. This is not surprising since Domar views himself as a lifelong Keynesian. While Keynes focused on the fact that unemployment today would result if ex ante savings exceeded ex ante investment, Domar argued that the increase in investment required to eliminate unemployment today would cause increased productive capacity and could create more unemployment tomorrow. His dynamic steady-state equilibrium growth model rests on the dual role of investment as a capacity creator and an income generator since it increased aggregate demand and national income and productive capacity. The solution to this dilemma rests on the economy's ability to generate a stream of investment that grows at a rate equal to the rate of savings multiplied by the capital–output ratio. Hence the solution to persistent unemployment is economic growth, with investment seen as the critical element in the growth process (Domar, 1946, 1947, 1948, 1952).

A number of specific criticisms have been directed at Domar's model. They include his assumptions that the rate of population growth is constant and that capital is the only factor input, and his exclusion of technological change. The population growth assumption is of little significance, however, since the capital–output ratio and the marginal propensity to save determine the unique rate of growth. Domar has addressed the other two criticisms, arguing that only investment affects both aggregate demand and supply, and that his assumption of a constant capital–output ratio implies substantial technological change. Despite criticisms, however, it is true that Domar's growth model, along with the work of Harrod, Kuznets and others, brought the issue of economic growth back to the forefront of orthodox economics in the 1950s and 1960s after its long hiatus following the demise of classical political economy.

Domar has continued to write on issues related to growth, but his emphasis has shifted from theoretical modeling to problems of measurement, recognizing that orthodox growth models rest on production functions whose inputs fail to account for significant portions of the historical growth of national income and output in various nations. This 'residual factor', as Domar called it, was explored in the work of Solow, Denison and others. Domar also made important contributions to the treatment of depreciation (Domar, 1953a, 1953b, 1955, 1957), index number theory (Domar, 1989) and the measurement of productivity and technological change (Domar, 1961, 1962, 1963, 1964a).

Much of Domar's work seems consistent with the orthodoxy of the 1950s, 1960s and much of the 1970s, where economic growth and economic development were viewed as largely one and the same process. While Domar did seem to equate the two in a number of works, it is important to realize that his notion of growth is considerably broader than that of most of his contemporaries. This may reflect his Russian heritage as well as his lifelong love of history. At any rate, Domar early on began to discuss certain historical and institutional aspects of the growth process, particularly as they related to capitalist and socialist economies. As early as the 1950s he wrote on a number of aspects of the Soviet economy (Domar, 1951, 1964b, 1966, 1970a, 1974a, 1974b, 1989, 1990). In addition, and partly in response to reading Kliuchevskii's five volumes of Russian history, Domar developed a historical model to explain the causes of serfdom and slavery. He argued as a general proposition that it is not possible to have free land, free labor and a non-working aristocracy. He then presented the view that the economic basis of serfdom (or slavery) was a low land-to-labor cost ratio (Domar, 1970b, 1984; Domar and Machina, 1985).

L.E. JOHNSON
ROBERT D. LEY

See also:

Frisch, Ragnar; Hansen, Alvin H.; Harcourt, Geoff; Harrod, Sir Roy; Hicks, Sir John R.; Keynes, John Maynard; Kuznets, Simon; Lerner, Abba P.; Lundberg, Erik; Schumpeter, Joseph A.; Solow, Robert M.; Swan, Trevor W; Technological Change.

Bibliography

Domar, Evsey, D. (1944), 'The Burden of the Debt', *American Economic Review*, **34**, (5), December, pp. 798–827.

Domar, Evsey, D. (1946), 'Capital Expansion, Rate of Growth, and Employment', *Econometrica*, **14**, (2), April, pp. 137–47.

Domar, Evsey, D. (1947), 'Expansion and Employment', *American Economic Review*, **37**, (1), March, pp. 34–55.

Domar, Evsey, D. (1948), 'The Problem of Capital Accumulation', *American Economic Review*, **38**, (5), December, pp. 777–94.

Domar, Evsey, D. (1951), 'The Economy of the Soviet Union: A Discussion', *American Economic Review*, **41**, (3), May, pp. 483–94.

Domar, Evsey, D. (1952), 'Economic Growth: An Econometric Approach', *American Economic Review*, **42**, (3), May, pp. 479–95.

Domar, Evsey, D. (1953a), 'The Case for Accelerated Depreciation', *Quarterly Journal of Economics*, **67**, (4), November, pp. 559–63.

Domar, Evsey, D. (1953b), 'Depreciation, Replacement and Growth', *Economic Journal*, **63**, (249), March, pp. 1–32.

Domar, Evsey, D. (1955), 'Accelerated Depreciation: A Rejoinder', *Quarterly Journal of Economics*, **69**, (2), May, pp. 299–304.

Domar, Evsey, D. (1957), 'Depreciation, Replacement and Growth, and Fluctuations', *Economic Journal*, **67**, (268), December, pp. 655–8.

Domar, Evsey, D. (1961), 'On the Measurement of Technological Changes', *Economic Journal*, **71**, (284), December, pp. 709–29.

Domar, Evsey, D. (1962), 'On Total Productivity and All That', *Journal of Political Economy*, **70**, (6), December, pp. 597–608.

Domar, Evsey, D. (1963), 'Total Productivity and the Quality of Capital', *Journal of Political Economy*, **71**, (6), December, pp. 586–8.

Domar, Evsey, D. (1964a), 'Economic Growth and Productivity in the United States, Canada, United Kingdom, Germany, and Japan in the Post-War Period', *Journal of Research and Statistics*, May, pp. 33–40.

Domar, Evsey, D. (1964b), 'Efficiency of the Soviet Union: A Discussion', *American Economic Review*, **54**, (3), May, pp. 516–22.

Domar, Evsey, D. (1966), 'The Soviet Collective Farm as a Producer Co-operative', *American Economic Review*, **56**, (4), September, pp. 734–57.

Domar, Evsey, D. (1970a), 'The Causes of Slavery or Serfdom: A Hypothesis', *Journal of Economic History*, **30**, (1), March, pp. 18–32.

Domar, Evsey, D. (1970b), 'Market and Price Mechanism in Socialist Countries: A Discussion', *American Economic Review*, **60**, (3), May, pp. 324–5.

Domar, Evsey, D. (1974a), 'On the Optimal Compensation of a Socialist Manager', *Quarterly Journal of Economics*, **88**, (1), February, pp. 1–18.

Domar, Evsey, D. (1974b), 'Poor Old Capitalism: A Review Article', *Journal of Political Economy*, **82**, (6), November–December, pp. 1301–13.

Domar, Evsey, D. (1989), *Capitalism, Socialism, and Serfdom: Essays*, Cambridge University Press.

Domar, Evsey, D. (1990), 'Privatization in Eastern Europe and the Soviet Union: A Discussion', *Jahrbuch-der-Wirtschaft-Osteuropas*, pp. 175–6.

Domar, Evsey, D. and Mark J. Machina (1944), 'On the Profitability of Russian Serfdom', *Journal of Economic History*, **44**, (4), December, pp. 919–55.

Domar, Evsey, D. and Mark J. Machina (1985), 'The Profitability of Serfdom: A Reply', *Journal of Economic History*, **45**, (4), December, pp. 960–2.

Domar, Evsey, D. and R.A. Musgrave (1994), 'Proportional Income Taxation and Risk-Taking', *Quarterly Journal of Economics*, **58**, (3), May, pp. 388–422.

Hansen, A.H. (1941), *Fiscal Policy and Business Cycles*, New York: W.W. Norton.

Harrod, R.F. (1939), 'An Essay in Dynamic Theory', *Economic Journal*, **49**, March, pp. 14–33.

Keynes, John, M. (1936), *The General Theory of Employment, Interest and Money*, London: Macmillan.

Dornbusch, Rudiger

Rudiger (Rudi) Dornbusch was born in Germany in 1942, studied political science at the University of Geneva, and did graduate work at the University of Chicago, where he was awarded his MA and PhD in 1969 and 1971, respectively. After two initial appointments on the faculty at the University of Rochester (1972–4) and the Graduate School of Business at the University of Chicago (1974–5), he moved to MIT in 1975, and since 1984 has been the Ford International Professor of Economics there.

His many honors and distinctions include Fellow of the Econometric Society, the American Academy of Arts and Sciences and the Finnish Academy of Sciences and Letters; John Simon Guggenheim Fellowship; delivery of Gaston Eykens Lectures (1984), Graham Lecture (1985), Lionel Robbins Lectures (1986), John R. Hicks Lecture (1988), Edmund James Lectures (1989), Geary Lecture (1990) and Okun Lectures (1992); and honorary doctorates from the University of Basle and Universidad del Pacifico, Lima, Peru. A vice president of the American Economic Association in 1990, member of the Brookings Panel of Economic Activity, SSRC Committee on Growth and Stability and McNamara Fellowship Panel of the World Bank, Dornbusch has authored or co-authored 20 books, over 250 papers, and has appeared as expert witness at hearings before various senate and House Committees of the US Congress and at the House of Commons in the United Kingdom.

Rudi Dornbusch's published books and papers include original and creative contributions in the areas of macroeconomics, international trade, public finance and, lately, on economic development and global warming. His theoretical and policy-oriented writings, including those of the popular genre such as the monthly 'Economic Viewpoint' column in *Business Week*, have had a profound impact on the theoretician, the policy maker and the layperson alike, a rare achievement for an economist of any generation. Last, but not least, he has influenced a score of undergraduates over the years with his exceptionally clear presentation of macroeconomics in the textbook he co-authored with Fischer. His scholarly work has addressed the most crucial macroeconomic issues of open economies from the theoretical and policy perspectives: exchange rates, inflation, stabilization policy, debts and deficits.

In the 1980s, when the LDC debt crisis became *the* international economic policy issue, Dornbusch occupied center stage in the debates, raising challenging questions that went much further than the superficial proposals of the US Treasury, which primarily aimed at averting an American financial industry crisis. The solution to the debt problem, Dornbusch argued, will be found neither in instituting a long-term moratorium on the debtor country, until it gains the capacity to negotiate a settlement, nor in letting the free market determine it. Dornbusch's option, more pragmatic and realistic, called for the 'recycling of interest' paid by the debtor country in its own currency, and allowing the creditor banks to invest in that country, thus strengthening the debtor country's potential for progress and ultimately preserving the bank's equity. This approach to policy, together with an environment of balanced budgets, market-oriented programs and some relief on the debt service, seemed preferable to the Baker or Brady plans (Felix, 1990). The LDC crisis is not front page news anymore, and the agreements between debtors and lenders involving long-term rescheduling and debt servicing have been thus far fulfilled, confirming the notion that the crisis is over. Dornbusch, however, has cautioned (1986, 1993) that the economic and social adjustments implemented to resolve the crisis entail heavy costs in the domestic economies of the debtor countries. 'These costs may well lead to political radicalization, which would threaten the new democratic institutions in Latin America and therefore ultimately create vast losses for the lending countries themselves' (1986, p. 88). Moreover, debt servicing assumes that developed economies will continue the high level of imports from LDCs that will yield the needed trade surpluses. Any trade protection overtures affecting these assumptions may therefore lead to the resurfacing of the crisis.

Dornbusch's expert advice was also sought when the transformation of the Eastern European command economies to the market began a few years ago. His approach in confronting the problems of transition (low productivity, production and distribution breakdowns, uncontrollable printing of money) was based on the experiences of similar situations in Latin America that his numerous writings, reports and Congressional testimonies have documented so well, and in precedents of past historical episodes, including that of the dismantling of the Austro-Hungarian empire. In his own words, 'The analogies are valuable because they give us a framework of analysis and tell us where to look for solutions' (Dornbusch, 1933, p. 9).

Rudi Dornbusch is a major economist and an independent thinker whose intellectual positions are not necessarily determined by any particular association. In the introduction to his last book, writing about inflation and stabilization policies, he advocates that the orthodox approach of fiscal responsibility is not enough, and that an incomes policy (a heterodox stance) is just as necessary: 'There are plenty of examples', he writes, 'of heterodoxy gone wrong, and there are examples of failed orthodoxy' as well (ibid., p. 2).

DIMITRI B. PAPADIMITRIOU

See also:

Balance of Payments: Keynesian and Monetarist Approaches; Bretton Woods; Econometric Models, Macroeconomic; International Clearing Union; Meade, James E.; Mundell, Robert A.; Mundell–Fleming Model; Ohlin, Bertil; Viner, Jacob.

Bibliography

Dornbusch, R. (1980), *Open Economy Macroeconomics*, New York: Basic Books.
Dornbusch, R. (1986), *Dollars, Debts and Deficits*, Cambridge, Mass.: MIT Press.
Dornbusch, R. (1988), *Exchange Rates and Inflation*, Cambridge, Mass.: MIT Press.
Dornbusch, R. (1993), *Stabilization, Debt and Reform*, Englewood Cliffs, NJ: Prentice-Hall.
Dornbusch, R. and S. Fischer (1990), *Macroeconomics*, New York; McGraw-Hill.
Dornbusch, R. and J.A. Frenkel (eds) (1979), *International Economic Policy: Theory and Evidence*, Baltimore: Johns Hopkins University Press.
Dornbusch, R. and J. Poterba (1992), *Global Warming: Economic Policy Responses*, Cambridge, Mass.: MIT Press.
Dornbusch, R., R. Layard, O. Blanchard and P. Krugman (1992), *East–West Migration*, Cambridge, Mass.: MIT Press.
Felix, David (ed.) (1990), *Debt and Transfiguration?*, Armonk, NY: M.E. Sharpe.

Dual Decision Hypothesis

The dual decision hypothesis was conceived by R.W. Clower as a device for introducing *realized* transaction variables into household demand functions, in an attempt to provide a formal bridge between Hicks–Arrow–Debreu–Patinkin general equilibrium theory and Keynes's 'effective demand' theory of national income determination (cf. Suits, 1963, pp. 12–13). The dual decision hypothesis first appeared in a paper presented at a conference on 'The Theory of Interest and Money' organized by the International Economic Association held at the Abbey of Royaumont (near Paris) in 1962, was first published in German translation in 1963 as 'Die Keynesianische Gegenrevolution: eine theoretische Kritik', and was then published in English in 1965 as 'The Keynesian Counterrevolution: A Theoretical Appraisal'.

Subsequently, a revised rendition of the dual decision hypothesis appeared in 1967 (as a 'dichotomized budget constraint model' – see Clower, 'Afterword', in Walker, 1984, pp. 264–7). Then the 1967 version of the hypothesis was converted by Lucas into a 'cash-in-advance' model (often called the 'Clower' model, though as restated by Lucas it owes nothing but its inspiration to Clower – see Howitt, 1992, pp. 318–19). Thereafter, the dual decision idea was disconnected entirely from its original purpose, which was to make analytical sense of Keynes's 'realized income' theory of the consumption function.

Since the 1980s, the dual decision hypothesis seems to have dropped out of sight, along with the original idea, which was that in money (Keynesian) economies, spending depends, not on earnings one might notionally hope to obtain from sales of factor services in continually clearing auction markets that guarantee absence of involuntary unemployment, but on earnings one might realistically expect to receive from actual employment obtained through markets for 'leased' labor services.

Although neither Clower nor other writers seem to have recognized this, a 'dichotomized budget constraint' version of the dual decision hypothesis was adumbrated by Lange in 1942 (Lange, 1942, p. 50, eqs (2.3) and (2.4)). Like most later writers, Lange (ibid., p. 52) mistakenly confused equality between planned money expenditure and planned money receipts with zero excess demand for money balances rather than with mere (planned) budget balance! In this connection, it merits emphasis that nothing in the dual decision hypothesis, or in the paper where it first appeared, implies anything about price flexibility or its absence, or deals with anything other than 'disequilibrium' in the most general sense. So research on so-called 'fix-price' models that was set in motion in the 1970s by the Clower paper has led a life of its own, most of it explicitly disavowed by Clower (Walker, 1984, p. 267).

ROBERT W. CLOWER

See also:

Arrow, Kenneth J.; Clower, Robert W.; Hicks, Sir John R.; Keynes, John Maynard; Leijonhufvud, Axel; Lucas Jr., Robert E.; Post Walrasian Economics; Say's Law.

Bibliography

Clower, Robert W. (1965), 'The Keynesian Counterrevolution: A Theoretical Appraisal', in F.H. Hahn and F.P.R. Brechling (eds), *The Theory of Interest Rates*, London: Macmillan.

Clower, Robert W. (1967), 'A Reconsideration of the Microfoundations of Monetary Theory', *Western Economic Journal*, 6, (1), December, pp. 1–8.

Howitt, Peter W. (1992), 'Cash in Advance Economy', in P. Newman, M. Milgate and J. Eatwell (eds), *The New Palgrave Dictionary of Money and Finance*, vol. 1, New York: Stockton.

Lange, O. (1942), 'Say's Law: A Restatement and Criticism', in O. Lange, F. McIntyre and T.O. Yutema (eds), *Studies in Mathematical Economics and Econometrics*, Chicago: University of Chicago Press.

Suits, Daniel B. (1963), 'The Determinants of Consumer Expenditure: A Review of Present Knowledge', in D.B. Suits (ed.), *Impacts of Monetary Policy*, Englewood Cliffs, NJ: Prentice-Hall.

Walker, Donald A. (1984), *Money and Markets: Selected Essays of R.W. Clower*, Cambridge: Cambridge University Press.

Econometric Models, Macroeconomic

In discussing the role of econometric models in macroeconomics one must distinguish between macroeconometric models, systems of equations that model the entire economy and single equation models, models that focus on one sector or set of relationships. Macroeconometric models are constructed for economic forecasting, the simulation of dynamic behavior and the evaluation of economic policies. Single equation models are intended for all of these purposes and, in addition, are employed to develop and evaluate competing economic theories. Macroeconometric models and single equation models will be discussed separately. Not considered here but also important are computable general equilibrium (CGE) models – intersectoral and inter-industry models of the economy.

The use of macroeconometric models can be dated from Jan Tinbergen's (1939) attempt to examine the cyclical behavior of the US economy and evaluate competing business cycle theories. Ragnar Frisch's (1933) model of the business cycle (solved using 'reasonable' parameter values) and Michael Kalecki's (1935) model containing crude parameter estimates are precursors of Tinbergen's work. Both Frisch and Kalecki attempted to verify that 'realistic' cycles could be derived from a system of dynamic equations. Tinbergen's model of the US economy was estimated using ordinary least squares for data for 1919–32. He concluded that most business cycle theories could not be tested because they were partial theories.[1]

J.M. Keynes's famous critique of Tinbergen revolved around issues of omitted variables bias, measurability of theoretical concepts by the statistics employed, questions of spurious correlation, multicollinearity, simultaneity, appropriate functional form and dynamic specification, as well as the likelihood of stability of estimated structural relationships. Considerable efforts were subsequently employed by econometricians to deal with these questions, so much so that most of these topics now form a chapter or more in standard econometric texts.

Structural models of the economy began to be constructed more frequently as technique and theory were developed and a probability basis for estimation was established. These developments included the solution to the identification problems (Koopmans, 1949; Koopmans, Rubin and Leipnik, 1950; Wegge, 1965; Fisher, 1966) and development of the full information maximum likelihood method (Koopmans, Rubin and Leipnik, 1950), the limited information maximum likelihood method (Anderson and Rubin, 1949), two-stage least squares (Theil, 1954, 1958; Basmann, 1957), instrumental variables (Reirsol,

1941, 1945; Geary, 1949; Sargan, 1958) and three-stage least squares (Zellner and Theil, 1962). These made possible the estimation of simultaneous systems of equations and thus cleared the way for the estimation of complete models of the economy (Christ, 1952; Epstein, 1987; Pesaran, 1987).

Meanwhile there was progress in the analysis of economic time series such as the description and solution to autocorrelated errors by Cochrane and Orcutt (1949) and the development by Durbin and Watson (1950, 1951) of the test for residual autocorrelation. In addition, distributed lag models such as the Koyck (1954) and Almon (1965) models began to be developed and employed to model macroeconomic relationships. Finally, Box and Jenkins (1970) proposed asymptotically efficient methods for the estimation of time series models.

These developments began to be applied to the analysis of macroeconomic relationships, stimulating further theoretical work. Notable among these were attempts to estimate the consumption function (Thomas, 1989) which led to the discovery of differences between the behavior of cross-sectional and time series consumption data. This, in turn, led to theoretical developments as the life cycle (Modigliani and Brumberg, 1954) and permanent income (Friedman, 1957) hypotheses were devised to explain these differences.

In addition, econometric techniques were employed to illuminate the relationship between the rate of unemployment and the rate of wage inflation (Phillips, 1958; Lipsey, 1960), leading to the Phillips curve. Many attempts were made to estimate investment functions (Roos and Szeliski, 1943; Roos, 1948; Klein, 1951; Koyck, 1954) as well as growth models, money demand functions and the term structure of interest rates (Cagan, 1956; Modigliani and Sutch, 1966).

Meanwhile macroeconometric models of increasing complexity began to be constructed and employed for prediction and policy analysis. Lawrence Klein constructed three models of the US economy (presented as Klein, 1950) while at the Cowles Commission and, with Arthur Goldberger, the Klein–Goldberger model (1955). The latter was estimated using limited information maximum likelihood for 1929–41 and 1946–52 and employed to create ex post and ex ante forecasts and simulations for the US economy.

During the 1960s and 1970s complete models of the economy – macroeconometric models – came into greater prominence and use with the Brookings model and the DRI, Wharton and Chase models as well as the Federal Reserve Board and Commerce Department models. These models contained a Keynesian structure but increasingly incorporated greater detail regarding the monetary behavior of the economy and frequently contained hundreds of equations and thousands of variables. Large macro models continue to be used for forecasting, though their use for purposes of policy analysis was somewhat checked by Robert Lucas's critique of econometric policy evaluation (1976), which argued from the perspective of rational expectations and competitive markets that the parameters of most macroeconometric models could not be invariant under changes in policy regimes. This appraisal was sharpened in Lucas and Sargent (1981), which concluded that 'modern macroeconomic models are of *no* value in guiding policy and this condition will not be remedied by modifications along any line which is currently being pursued' (Lucas and Sargent, 1981, p. 296). In addition there was other academic and growing non-academic criticism of macroeconometric models and their uses (Kmenta and Ramsey, 1981, p. vii).

There have been several responses to the Lucas critique. Sims (1980) has favored vector autoregressive (VAR) models, estimated by regressing each variable on its own and other variables' lagged values, which require imposing fewer assumptions than do macroeconometric models. VAR models usually empirically select a lag structure for the variables and have been employed for prediction and for comparisons with the forecasting performance of macroeconometric models (Kmenta and Ramsey, 1981)

Other responses to Lucas include a more explicit treatment of expectations, especially rational expectations, in macro models. In addition, real business cycle models (McCallum, 1989) and new-Keynesian models (Mankiw and Romer, 1991) can be seen as a response to the rational expectations revolution of the 1970s (Taylor, 1993). These models focus on the optimal design of policy rules, issues of credibility in the transition from one policy rule to another and the operation of policy rules.

Macroeconometric models continue to be constructed, estimated and employed for policy analysis.[2] However, it is difficult to compare macroeconometric models since they yield differing results depending upon the structure of the models as well as the nature of the assumptions embodied in them: specifically, differences in the treatment of particular variables as endogenous or exogenous. A recent attempt to compare the performance of US macroeconometric models discovered an astonishing variation and could not identify a consensus with respect to any policy simulation (see F.G. Adams and L.R. Klein, in Klein, 1991).

Concurrent work on single (and multiple) equation models that are not full macroeconometric models continues. A recent survey by the author found econometric estimation and testing of models of the labor market, the current account, exchange rates, import demand, interest rate spreads, the relationship between exchange rates and inflation, business cycles and saving functions. In the area of macroeconometric models, developments are proceeding on many fronts, including an expansion of multi-country modeling. Thus the use of econometric models in macroeconomics is diverse and controversial.

VIBHA KAPURIA-FOREMAN

Notes

1 See Bodkin, Klein and Marwah (1991) for a history of macroeconometric model building.
2 See R.C. Fair (1994), *Testing Macroeconomic Models*, Cambridge, Mass.: Harvard University Press, for continuing work in this area.

See also:

Frisch, Ragnar; Haavelmo, Trygve; Jorgenson, Dale W.; Klein, Lawrence R.; Kuznets, Simon; Schumpeter, Joseph A.

Bibliography

Almon, S. (1965), 'The distributed lag between capital appropriations and net expenditures', *Econometrica*, **33**, (1), January, pp. 178–96.
Anderson, T.W. and H. Rubin (1949), 'Estimation of the parameters of a single equation in a complete system of stochastic equations', *Annals of Mathematical Statistics*, **20**, pp. 46–63.
Basmann, R.L. (1957), 'A generalized classical method of linear estimation of coefficients in a structural equation', *Econometrica*, **25**, (1), January, pp. 77–83.
Bodkin, R.G., L.R. Klein and K. Marwah (1991), *A History of Macroeconometric Model Building*, Aldershot: Edward Elgar.
Box, G.E.P. and G.M. Jenkins (1970), *Time Series Analysis: Forecasting and Control*, San Francisco: Holden-Day.
Brown, T.M. (1952), 'Habit persistence and lags in consumer behavior', *Econometrica*, **20**, (3), July, pp. 355–71.
Cagan, P. (1956), 'The monetary dynamics of hyperinflation', in M. Friedman (ed.), *Studies in the Quantity Theory of Money*, Chicago: University of Chicago Press.
Chenery, H.B. (1952), 'Overcapacity and the accelerator principle', *Econometrica*, **20**, (1), January, pp. 1–28.
Christ, C.F. (1952), *Economic Theory and Measurement: A Twenty Year Research Report, 1932–52*, Chicago: Cowles Commission for Research in Economics.
Cochrane, D. and G.H. Orcutt (1949), 'Application of least squares regression to relationships containing autocorrelated errors', *Journal of the American Statistical Association*, **44**, (245), March, pp. 32–61.
Duesenberry, J.S. (1949), *Income, Saving and the Theory of Consumer Behavior*, Cambridge, Mass.: Harvard University Press.
Durbin, J. and G.S. Watson (1950), 'Testing for serial correlation in least squares regression I', *Biometrika*, **37**, (3 and 4), December, pp. 409–28.
Durbin, J. and G.S. Watson (1951), 'Testing for serial correlation in least squares regression II', *Biometrika*, **38**, pp. 159–78.
Epstein, R.J. (1987), *A History of Econometrics*, Amsterdam: North Holland.
Fisher, F.M. (1966), *The Identification Problem in Econometrics*, New York: McGraw-Hill.
Friedman, M. (1957), *A Theory of the Consumption Function*, Princeton: Princeton University Press.
Frisch, R. (1933) 'Propagation problems and impulse problems in dynamic economics', in *Economic Essays in Honour of Gustav Cassel*, 20 October, London: Frank Cass and Co., Ltd.
Geary, R.C. (1949), 'Studies in relations between economic time series', *Journal of the Royal Statistical Society*, Series B-10, pp. 140–48.
Kalecki, M. (1935), 'A macrodynamic theory of business cycles', *Econometrica*, **3**, (3), July, pp. 327–44.
Keynes, J.M. (1939), 'Professor Tinbergen's Method', *Economic Journal,* **49**, (195), September, pp. 558–68.
Klein, L.R. (1950), *Economic Fluctuations in the United States 1921–41*, Cowles Commission Monograph No. 11, New York: John Wiley.
Klein, L.R. (1951), 'Studies in investment behavior', in *Conference on Business Cycles*, New York: National Bureau of Economic Research.

Klein, L.R. (ed.) (1991), *Comparative Performance of U.S. Econometric Models*, New York: Oxford University Press.

Klein, L.R. and A.S. Goldberger (1955), *An Econometric Model of the United States, 1929–1952*, Amsterdam: North Holland.

Kmenta, J. and J.B. Ramsey (1981), *Large-Scale Macroeconometric Models*, Amsterdam: North Holland.

Koopmans, T.C. (1949), 'Identification problems in economic model construction', *Econometrica*, **17**, (2), April, pp. 125–44.

Koopmans, T.C., H. Rubin and R.B. Leipnik (1950), 'Measuring the equation systems of dynamic economics', in T.C. Koopmans (ed.), *Statistical Inference in Dynamic Economic Models*, Cowles Commission Monograph No. 10, New York: John Wiley.

Koyck, L.M. (1954), *Distributed Lags and Investment Analysis*, Amsterdam: North Holland.

Lipsey, R.G. (1960), 'The relation between unemployment and wage ratio', *Economica*, **27**, (105), February, pp. 1–31.

Lucas, R.E. (1976), 'Econometric Policy evaluation: A critique', in K. Brunner and A.H. Meltzer (eds), *The Phillips Curve and Labor Markets*, Carnegie–Rochester Conference Series on Public Policy, vol. 1, New York: North Holland.

Lucas, R.E. and T.J. Sargent (1981), 'After Keynesian macroeconomics' reprinted in R.E. Lucas and T.J. Sargent (eds), *Rational Expectations and Econometric Practice*, Boston: George Allen & Unwin.

Mankiw, N.G. and D. Romer (1991), *New Keynesian Economics*, Cambridge, Mass.: MIT Press.

McCallum, B. (1989), 'Real business cycle models', in R.J. Barro (ed.), *Modern Business Cycle Theory*, Cambridge, Mass.: Harvard University Press.

Modigliani, F. and R. Brumberg (1955), 'Utility analysis and the consumption function: An interpretation of cross-section data', in K.K. Kurihara (ed.), *Post-Keynesian Economics*, London: Allen & Unwin.

Modigliani, F. and R. Sutch (1966), 'Innovations in interest rate policy', *American Economic Review*, **56**, (2), May, pp. 178–97.

Pesaran, M.H. (1987), 'Econometrics', in John Eatwell, Murray Milgate and Peter Newman (eds), *The New Palgrave: A Dictionary of Economics*, Vol. 2, New York: Stockton Press.

Phillips, A.W. (1958), 'The relation between unemployment and the rate of change of money wage rates in the UK, 1861–1957', *Economica*, **25**, (100), November, pp. 283–99.

Reirsol, O. (1941), 'Confluence analysis by means of lag moment and other methods of confluence analysis', *Econometrica*, **9**, (1), January, pp. 1–24.

Reirsol, O. (1945), *Confluence Analysis by Means of Instrumental Sets of Variables*, Stockholm.

Roos, C.F. (1948), 'The demand for investment goods', *American Economic Review*, **38**, (2), May, pp. 311–20.

Roos, C.F. and von Szeliski, V.F. (1943), 'The demand for durable goods', *Econometrica*, **11**, (2), April, pp. 97–112.

Sargan, J.D. (1958), 'The estimation of economic relationships using instrumental variables', *Econometrica*, **26**, (3), July, pp. 393–415.

Sims, C. (1980). 'Macroeconomics and reality', *Econometrica*, **48**, (1), January, pp. 1–48.

Stone, R. and W.M. Stone (1938), 'The marginal propensity to consume and the multiplier: A statistical investigation', *Review of Economic Studies*, **6**, (1), October, pp. 1–24.

Taylor, John B. (1993), 'The use of the new macroeconometrics for policy formulation,' *American Economic Review*, **83**, (2), May, pp. 300–305.

Theil, H. (1954), 'Estimation of parameters of econometric models', *Bulletin of International Statistics Institute*, **34**, pp. 122–8.

Theil, H. (1958), *Economic Forecasts and Policy*, Amsterdam: North Holland.

Thomas, J.J. (1989), 'The Early Econometric History of the Consumption Function', *Oxford Economic Papers*, **41**, (1), January, pp. 131–49.

Tinbergen, Jan (1939), *Business Cycles in the United States of America, 1919–32*, Geneva: League of Nations.

Wegge, L.L. (1965), 'Identifiability criteria for a system of equations as a whole', *Australian Journal of Statistics*, **3**, (1), pp. 67–77.
Zellner, A. and H. Theil (1962), 'Three-stage least squares: simultaneous estimation of simultaneous equations', *Econometrica*, **30**, (1), January, pp. 54–78.

Economics of Keynes and of his Revolution, Key Elements of the

A review of the writings of J.M. Keynes reveals that he had two primary goals in the *General Theory*, one theoretical, one political. The fist was to explode the myth perpetuated by what he termed the 'classical' economists, that the perfectly competitive, self-adjusting, market-clearing model tends toward full employment. In this regard, Keynes's reference to the 'classical' economist was primarily to the neoclassical economists that preceded or were contemporary to him. However, Keynes was surely referring as well to Marshall's neoclassical version of Smith and Ricardo, since he centered his attack on Say's Law as it came to be incorporated into the market-clearing, neoclassical orthodoxy. Keynes's second goal was to provide understanding and guidance in trying to improve the average level of performance of the British economy as he saw its reality during the 1920s and 1930s.

In this effort, we believe that there are five key elements in Keynes's attack on Say's Law and the perfectly competitive, self-adjusting, market-clearing model. The first four elements relate to his theoretical criticisms, including (1) his analysis of equilibrium; (2) his theory of probability: expectations and uncertainty; (3) his critique of the neoclassical loanable funds theory of interest rate determination; and (4) his theory of money, liquidity preference and interest rate determination. His concern for improving the economy's performance is embodied in the final element: his public policy proposal.

Keynes's Equilibrium Analysis

In the *Treatise* and the *General Theory* Keynes develops a very simple yet elegant model of a closed economic system. He divides the economic system into two sectors, consumers and producers. Consumers decide how to divide their stream of income into two parts: spending on consumption goods and saving. Simultaneously, and yet independently of consumers, producers decide how to divide the stream of output into two parts; consumption goods and investment goods. Three outcomes are possible. First, if the decisions made by the consumers are consistent with the decisions made by the producers, the economic system is in equilibrium. This consistency of decisions, however, in no way implies that the economic system is operating at full employment. Full employment is but one of an infinite number of possible equilibria. Second, if the amount of income allocated for spending on consumer goods is greater than the dollar value of consumer goods which the producers have decided to produce, the two decisions are not consistent and the economic system is in disequilibrium. This situation cannot persist because inventories will decline below some critical level and producers will respond by increasing the production of consumer goods. This positive feedback mechanism moves the economic system toward an equilibrium position, which may, or may not, be consistent with full employment. Third, if the amount of income allocated for spending on consumer goods is less than the dollar value of consumer goods which the producers have decided to produce, the two decisions are not consistent and the economic system is in disequilibrium. This situation cannot persist because inventories will rise above some critical level and producers will respond by decreasing the production of consumer goods. This negative feedback mechanism moves the economic system toward an equilibrium, which may, or may not, be consistent with full employment.

There are four aspects of Keynes's equilibrium analysis that were both unique and sources of interpretive controversy. In part, this was because Keynes's concept of equilibrium differed in its structure, content and purpose from that of his English orthodox predecessors. The first aspect of uniqueness and controversy was the ex ante–ex post analysis used by Keynes. While this approach may have been novel to mainstream British economists, such was not the case for Hayek or Myrdal. Neither could understand the undue attention being paid to this aspect of Keynes's work since the ex ante–ex post sequence analysis, employed rather clumsily by Keynes, was an old friend to them.

The second aspect of uniqueness and controversy was the fact that the composition of national income and aggregate demand together determined the level of aggregate demand and, therefore, critically affected the determination of the equilibrium level of national income and employment (the very point that Domar elaborated in his theory of economic growth). With the direction of causation running from the labor market to the real goods market via aggregate supply, orthodox macroeconomics, using Say's Law, was able to demonstrate that the economic system always operated at its full employment level of output. Since Keynes did not believe that Say's Law was an accurate description of the way an economic system worked, he reversed the direction of causation established in orthodox macroeconomics. In his model, Keynes had causation running from aggregate demand and the real goods market to the labor market because he believed that the economic system rarely, if ever, operated at its full employment level of output.

The third aspect of uniqueness and controversy was Keynes's use of the term 'unemployment'. For the advocates of the perfectly competitive, market-clearing model, involuntary unemployment was unimportant because either it was not possible or it was only possible out of equilibrium. In a model with completely flexible wages and prices unemployment is voluntary, or is a short-run disequilibrium phenomenon which cures itself. In the long run, the economy operates at its potential level of output. Keynes's concept of involuntary unemployment was, therefore, foreign to the classical and neoclassical economists in the same sense that voluntary unemployment was foreign to him. Recent research has put forth the hypothesis that during the early stages of unemployment the individual feels that he or she is responsible for being unemployed; but as the duration of unemployment grows longer the blame for being unemployed is transferred from the individual to society (Goldsmith, Veum and Darity, 1994). That is to say, in the early stages of unemployment individuals behave according to 'classical' precepts and act as if they are voluntarily unemployed. As the duration of unemployment increases, however, they behave according to 'Keynes's' precepts and act as if they are involuntarily unemployed.

The final aspect of uniqueness and controversy was the fact that Keynes's concept of equilibrium reflected a purposive function, the ultimate purpose or goal pursued by practitioners of normal science, that differed in its maximand and normative content from the classical and neoclassical concepts of equilibrium (Johnson, 1980, 1983; Johnson and Ley, 1988). As used by the classical economists, Malthus and Marx excluded, the term 'equilibrium' implied that total social welfare measured in material terms (vendable commodities) was maximized with an ethically acceptable distribution of income. This reflected the fact that the classical purposive function was concerned with whether a perfectly competitive market–capitalist, economic system was capable of maximizing total social welfare over time. As such, the classical conception of equilibrium reflected the fact that the basic economic concerns were centered on economic growth and the distribution of income. As used by the neoclassical economists, the term 'equilibrium' implied that individual welfare measured in terms of utility should be maximized given any distribution of income. This reflects the fact that the neoclassical purposive function was concerned with whether a perfectly competitive market–capitalist, economic system was capable of maximizing individual welfare, defined subjectively in terms of utility, at any point in time. As such, the neoclassical conception of equilibrium reflected the fact that the basic economic concern was centered on allocative efficiency. As used by Keynes, the term 'equilibrium' was ethically neutral and did not imply that total social welfare, measured in terms of goods and services, should be maximized given any distribution of income. This reflected the fact that Keynes's purposive function was concerned with whether a perfectly competitive, market–capitalist, economic system was capable of increasing its average level of performance. As such, Keynes's conception of equilibrium reflected that fact that his basic economic concerns were centered on economic stability, as measured by unemployment and, to a certain degree, the distribution of income (Johnson, 1980, 1983, 1984, 1988, 1991, 1992, 1993a, 1993b; Johnson, Gramm and Hoass, 1980, 1991; Johnson and Ley, 1988).

Keynes's theory of probability: expectations and uncertainty

Keynes developed his theory of probability and ultimately his views regarding expectations and uncertainty in response to G.E. Moore's *Principia Ethica* (1903) and refined it in light of Ramsey's (1922, 1931) critique. This theory of probability describes three categories of logical propositions. These logical relationships may be expressed in the following manner: $a/h = p$, where a is the conclusion, h is premises and p is the resulting probability. The three categories of logical propositions which Keynes developed are universal induction, propositions that are either true ($a/h = 1$) or false ($a/h = 0$), statistical induction, propositions that are neither true nor false ($0 < a/h < 1$), and uncertainty, propositions where the probabilities are unknown. Keynes developed two versions of this theory, a subjective and an objective version.

In the objective version of his theory, Keynes argued that individuals were rational, pursued a single goal – that of maximizing the amount of good in the society – used induction to establish relationships between a and h, possessed objective degrees of belief in these relationships and were quite capable of deciding for themselves what is the best course of action. Keynes used this version of his theory of probability as a basis of attack on the idea that the quantity theory of money provided a reasonable guide for monetary policy. In his attack, Keynes examined the factors which affect the velocity of money, namely the ratio of cash to deposits and of reserves to deposits, and established the fact that the velocity of money is not stable over time. Given this conclusion, Keynes argued that monetary policy should be based on the discretion of the central bank and not on some rule association with the quantity theory of money (Keynes, 1924; Schumpeter, 1954).

In the subjective version of his theory, Keynes argued that individuals were irrational, pursued many goals, held subjective degrees of belief about a and h that were subject to sudden and violent shifts, and recognized the need to maintain certain conventions and rules (Bateman, 1990, 1991, 1995). With this version of his theory, Keynes concluded that consumption and saving are stable functions of disposable income and that the speculative demand for money and gross private domestic investment are unstable owing to the presence of uncertainty.

Even though individuals are confronted by uncertainty, they still must decide what to do. In these instances individuals fall back on conventions and rules. Embedded in these conventions and rules are expectations about the next occurrence of an event which form the basis of subjective probabilities about this event. These expectations, and hence the probabilities on which they rest, are subject to sudden and violent shifts. The existence of these factors led Keynes to conclude that gross private domestic investment and the speculative demand for money are unstable, with the result that the average level of performance of the British economy was below what it could be. The question, then, is what to do about this state of affairs. The answer to this question is discussed below in the section on Keynes's public policy proposals.

Keynes's critique of the loanable funds theory of interest rate determination

Among the many points of disagreement which Keynes had with the orthodox tradition, two dealt with consumption, saving and investment. According to the orthodox tradition, consumption, saving and investment are functions of the rate of interest. As such the loanable funds theory states that the rate of interest is determined in the loanable funds market where new financial assets for new investment projects are bought and sold. Saving is a direct function of the rate of interest because of consumers' positive time preferences, consumption is an indirect function of the rate of interest because of the dominant substitution effect between savings and consumption, and investment is an indirect function of the rate of interest because investment projects are ranked according to their expected rates of return which are governed by the value of the marginal product of capital and diminishing returns. The operation of perfect competition and Say's Law ensures that the supply of (saving) and demand for (investment) loanable funds is in long-run equilibrium with full employment as long as interest rates are flexible. Moreover, in such a theory, saving is automatically transformed into investment. This led the British neoclassical orthodoxy toward a positive view of saving that has its origin in the work of Adam Smith and his theory of growth. However, Keynes saw saving as a leakage from the income stream; hence it reduced aggregate demand, output and employment.

   With respect to consumption and saving, Keynes agreed with the neoclassical economists that, upon the receipt of an increment of income, consumers decided how much to spend on consumption and how much to save. Keynes disagreed, however, with the neoclassical economists that consumption and saving were functions of the rate of interest and argued instead that consumption and saving are stable functions of disposable income. After postulating the relationship between consumption expenditures and disposable income, Keynes examines thoroughly the factors which affect this relationship and establishes the fact that a stable pattern exists. This is important because the marginal propensity to consume plays an important role in Keynes's investment multiplier which is vital to his public policy proposals and the goal of the *General Theory* of increasing the average level of performance in the

British economy. This line of reasoning led some economists to investigate more thoroughly the exact nature of the consumption function, including the issue of proportionality between consumption and disposable income. Moreover, Keynes saw that changes in consumption, including changes in the distribution of income that could result from fiscal and non-fiscal policy changes, would affect changes in aggregate demand and equilibrium level of national income and employment. However, the primary reason for the unstable nature of aggregate demand was changes in investment.

While Keynes agreed with the neoclassical economists that investment was an indirect function of the rate of interest, he disagreed with their contention that the rate of interest was determined in the loanable funds market according to the principles set forth in the loanable funds theory. Instead, he argued that the rate of interest was determined in the secondary money market where existing financial assets were bought and sold, and that the rate of interest in question was the long-term rate on gilt-edged securities. Furthermore, Keynes argued that the level of output is less than optimal because investment is less than optimal. Investment is less than optimal because of the uncertainty associated with the future rate of return on invested capital. In the *General Theory* and in his critique of Tinbergen's work on investment activity, Keynes argues that a careful examination of the factors that affect investment activity yields establishes the existence of an unstable pattern in the underlying factors which affect gross private domestic investment. This result can be used as a partial explanation of the cyclical movements in employment, output and income (Keynes, 1936, 1939; Tinbergen, 1939)

As was the case with Keynes's consumption decision-making process, Keynes's hypothesis about the rate of interest and its relation to investment has stimulated a great deal of theoretical and empirical research. One aspect of this research involves the question of the stability of investment. Empirical research concludes that investment, especially investment in capital goods, is very volatile. Why is that the case? As we have indicated above, Keynes's theories of expectations and uncertainty offer one explanation.

Keynes's theories of liquidity preference, money and interest rate determination

Having disposed of the neoclassical notion that the rate of interest is determined according to the principles embodied in the loanable funds theory, Keynes explains the role of the secondary money market and the determination of the rate of interest. Of the three functions which money performs, Keynes focused his attention on the store of value function of money. Why would anyone want to hold money, a non-income-earning asset? Money, as Keynes patiently points out, is the bridge between the dead hand of the past and an unforeseen and less than certain future. Apart from the need for day-to-day transactions, individuals can be persuaded to part with their money – if the price is right. Keynes's liquidity preference theory of the rate of interest provides an explanation of what is necessary to get individuals to part with their money. According to Keynes, the rate of interest is determined in the secondary money market through the equilibrating forces of the demand for and supply of money. In Keynes's theory, money then becomes an integral part of the modern economic system.

Keynes's theory of the determination of the rate of interest accomplished four objectives. First, his theory attacks the neoclassical notion of full employment as being a real phenomenon determined completely by the interaction of saving and investment. In an economic system 'with a past as well as a future and in which contracts are made in terms of money, no equilibrium may exist' (Arrow and Hahn, 1971). Moreover, even if the economy did achieve equilibrium, there was certainly no assurance – or even a strong likelihood – that the resulting equilibrium would occur at full employment. Second, his theory introduces the concept of money into the economic system. Money is no longer a veil which covers the operation of the real sectors of the economic system. Third, his theory redefines the demand for money to include three component parts, a transaction component, a precautionary component and a speculative component. Keynes's examination of the factors which affect the speculative demand for money establishes the existence of an unstable pattern in these factors due mainly to the existence of uncertainty. The implications of the impact of uncertainty on the speculative demand for money have been discussed above. Fourth, his theory is a direct attack on the quantity theory of money. The principal role for monetary policy in the quantity theory of money as it was presented at that time was dealing with inflation. In the *Tract* (1924) Keynes distinguished between the equation of exchange and the assumptions necessary for the long-run conclusions of the quantity theory. After a careful examination of the factors which affect these assumptions, Keynes concluded that the quantity theory is not a useful guide for monetary policy. Rather, given his theory of interest rate determination, monetary policy in conjunction with government investment projects can be used to combat involuntary unemployment. Appropriate expansions of the money supply will reduce the interest rate, thereby increasing investment. The increase in investment and the resulting increase in aggregate demand will expand income and employment as long as the secondary money market is not caught in the 'liquidity trap'.

Keynes's public policy proposals

The goal of the *General Theory* is to increase the average level of performance of the economic system. To achieve this goal the government must implement public policies which establish and/or maintain conventions or rules acceptable to the business community (Bateman, 1995). Why the business community? This group of individuals undertake gross private domestic investment and, as we have shown above, Keynes argued that gross private domestic investment is unstable. Two such conventions and rules are balanced budgets and the idea that investment is related to the rate of interest. These conventions and rules guide Keynes's public policy proposal which, if implemented, will increase the stability of gross private domestic investment and achieve the goal of the *General Theory*.

There are four aspects of Keynes's public policy proposal. First, the government must use monetary policy to reduce the rate of interest. Such a policy will promote more gross private domestic investment. Second, the government must subdivide its budget into two parts, a current expenditures budget and a capital expenditures budget. Third, the current expenditures portion of the budget must be in balance, or in surplus, at the end of each fiscal year. The capital expenditures portion underwrites self-liquidating capital projects. Fourth, Keynes states that gross domestic investment is equal to the sum of gross private and gross public domestic investment and that these two components are complements and not substitutes. Keynes argues that problems associated with gross private domestic investment can be overcome if the government increases gross public domestic investment. To do this the government must develop an investment inventory, needs assessment mechanism which permits the government to identify what investments are in progress or scheduled to begin, by whom, for what purpose and how they are to be funded. Keynes's public policy proposal implies that the government must put the interests of the nation ahead of the pleadings of special interest groups and that the government must be comprised of leaders and statesmen and not politicians.

TOM CATE
L.E. JOHNSON

See also:
Classical Economics; Consumption and the Consumption Function; Expectations, Theories of; Government Investment Programs (The Socialization of Investment); Keynes, John Maynard; Keynes?, What Remains of; Keynesian Revolution; Liquidity Trap; Neoclassical Synthesis (Bastard Keynesianism); Neutrality of Money: The Keynesian Challenge; Post Keynesian School of Economics; Say's Law.

Bibliography
Arrow, Kenneth J. and F.H. Hahn (1971), *General Competitive Analysis*, San Francisco: Holden-Day.
Bateman, Bradley (1990), 'Keynes, induction and econometrics', *History of Political Economy*, **22** (2), Summer, pp. 359–80.
Bateman, Bradley (1991), 'The Rules of the Road: Keynes's Theoretical Rationale for Public Policy', in Bradley W. Bateman and John B. Davis (eds), *Keynes and Philosophy*, Brookfield, VT: Edward Elgar.

Bateman, Bradley (1995), 'Rethinking the Keynesian Revolution', in John B. Davis (ed.), *The State of Interpretation of Keynes*, Boston: Kluwer Academic.

Davis, John B. (1995), 'Keynes's Later Philosophy', *History of Political Economy*, **27**, (2), Summer, pp. 237–60.

Goldsmith, Arthur H., Jonathan R. Veum and William Darity, Jr. (1994), 'The Impact of Unemployment on Perceptions of Personal Efficacy: Do Gender and Race Differences Exist?', in Paul Davidson and J.A. Kregel (eds), *Employment, Growth and Finance,* Brookfield, VT: Edward Elgar.

Johnson, L.E. (1980), 'A Neo-Paradigmatic Model for Studying the Development of Economic Reasoning', *Atlantic Economic Journal*, **8**, (4), December, pp. 52–61.

Johnson, L.E. (1983), 'Economic Paradigm: A Mission Dimension', *Journal of Economic Issues*, **17**, (4), December, pp. 1097–1111.

Johnson, L.E. (1984), 'Ricardo's Labour Theory of the Determinant of Value', *Atlantic Economic Journal*, **21**, (1) March, pp. 50–59.

Johnson, L.E. (1988), 'The Legacy of Ricardo: A Review Article', *Rivisita Internazionale di Scienze Economiche e Commerciali*, **35**, (8), August, pp. 781–96.

Johnson, L.E. (1991), 'Ricardo's Labour Theory of the Determinant of Value', in Mark Blaug (ed.), *Pioneers in Economics*, vol. II, Aldershot: Edward Elgar.

Johnson, L.E. (1992), 'The Source of Value and Ricardo: A Historical Reconstruction', *Atlantic Economic Journal*, **20**, (4), December, pp. 21–31.

Johnson, L.E. (1993a), 'Professor Arrow's Ricardo', *Journal of the History of Economic Thought*, **15**, (3), Spring, pp. 54–71.

Johnson, L.E. (1993b), 'Professor Arrow and Mr. Ricardo's Geistesdeschichten', *Best Papers and Proceedings of the Atlantic Economic Society*, **3**, (1), January, pp. 23–7.

Johnson, L.E. and Robert D. Ley (1988), *Origins of Modern Economics: A Paradigmatic Approach*, Lexington, Mass.: Ginn Press.

Johnson, L.E., Warren S. Gramm and David J. Hoaas (1989), 'Marx's Law of Profit: The Current State of the Controversy', *Atlantic Economic Journal*, **17**, (4), December, pp. 55–62.

Johnson, L.E., Warren S. Gramm and David J. Hoaas (1991), 'The Falling Rate of Profit Debate in Marx: Alternative Line of Interpretation', in Giovanni A. Caravale (ed.), *Marx and Modern Economic Analysis*, vol. II, Aldershot: Edward Elgar.

Keynes, John Maynard (1921), *A Treatise on Probability*, London: Macmillan.

Keynes, John Maynard (1924), *A Tract on Monetary Reform*, London: Macmillan.

Keynes, John M. (1936), *The General Theory of Employment, Interest and Money*, London: Macmillan.

Keynes, John M. (1939), 'Professor Tinbergen's Method', *Economic Journal*, **49**, (194), September, pp. 558–68.

Keynes, John M. (1980), *Collected Writings of John Maynard Keynes*, vol. XXVII, *Activities 1940–1946: Shaping the Post-War World Employment*, New York: Cambridge University Press.

Keynes, John M. (1981), *Collected Writings of John Maynard Keynes*, vol. XIX, *Activities 1922–1929: The Return to Gold and Industrial Policy*, New York: Cambridge University Press.

Keynes, John M. (1983), *Collected Writings of John Maynard Keynes*, vol. XII, *Economic Articles and Correspondence: Investment and Editorial*, New York: Cambridge University Press.

Lerner, Abba (1943), 'Functional Finance and the Federal Debt', *Social Research*, **10**, (1), February, pp. 38–52.

O'Driscoll, Jr, Gerald P. (1977), *Economics as a Coordination Problem*, Kansas City: Sheed Andrews and McMeel.

Ramsay, Frank P. (1922), 'Mr. Keynes on Probability', *The Cambridge Magazine*, **11**, (1), January, pp. 3–5.

Ramsay, Frank P. (1931), 'Truth and Probability', in R.B. Braithwaite (ed.), *The Foundations of Mathematics*, London: Routledge & Kegan Paul.

Schumpeter, Joseph A. (1954), *History of Economic Analysis*, New York: Oxford University Press.

Sraffa, Piero (1926), 'The Laws of Return under Competitive Conditions', *Economic Journal*, **36**, (144), December, pp. 535–50.
Tinbergen, Jan (1939), *A Method and Its Application to Activity, Statistical Testing of Business-Cycle Theories*, I, Geneva: League of Nations.

Economics, The Art of

The distinction between positive economics, the study of what is, normative economics, the formation of societal goals, and the art of economics, the process of making economic policy, was introduced into the literature by J.N. Keynes (1890). According to Hutchison (1992) from the time of Petty to that of J.M. Keynes the aim of economics was to develop models that would provide useful guidelines for the creation of practical policy proposals, policies that would be considered seriously by politicians. This tripartite division of economic methodology was reintroduced into the literature by Friedman (1953) and Lipsey (1966) albeit with a very different emphasis and focus (Samuelson, 1963; Wong, 1973). Thus Hutchison (1992) suggests that since World War II the aim of economics has been to develop models that cannot provide useful guidelines for the creation of public policy but do result in publications designed to enhance the reputation of the author(s). Formalism, the name which Hutchison has given to this post-World War II process, has had at least two unintended outcomes: a breakdown in the consensus as to what constitutes the methodological foundation and basic principles of the discipline of economics and a neglect of the importance of accurate forecasts as they pertain to the development of practical policy proposals. The rise of the economist *qua* academician has been at the expense of the economist *qua* policy analyst, the primary role performed by economists outside of the university.

What can be done to assist the policy analyst? Colander (1994) begins his re-examination of this neglected aspect of economic methodology by asking the question, 'How can the insights of positive economics be translated into real-world policies which achieve society's goals, taking account of real-world institutions, as well as the sociological and political dimensions of the policy?' The answer to that question involves a two-step process. The first step is the careful examination of the assumptions on which the models rest. Are the assumptions too restrictive? By what process can these assumptions be made more realistic? This examination involves the integration of the three invisible forces which operate within the economic system: Smith's 'invisible hand', Okun's (1980) 'invisible handshake' and Brock and Magee's (1984) 'invisible foot'. The 'invisible handshake' and the 'invisible foot' represent the social, historical, legal and political forces of the economic system which modify the operation of the 'invisible hand'.

The second step is the empirical testing of these models in an effort to avoid the pitfalls associated with the 'activist paradise' (Okun, 1972). The forecasts and predictions on which policy is based need not be as accurate as the forecasts and predictions developed by chemists or physicists, as accurate as the predictions and forecasts arrived at by inductive logic; but they do need to be more accurate than 'back-of-envelope' calculations. The social, historical, legal and political institutional data included in these applied policy models do not lend themselves to tests of their second-order conditions. Rather than 'pumping-up the R^2', the policy analyst is interested in the answers to questions like 'Is the direction of change correct?' or 'Is the order of magnitude correct?' In short, are the test results reasonable? Several economists have examined this aspect of the art of economics and have developed 'rules' for conducting research in the area of applied policy economics (Colander, 1992, 1994; Kamarck, 1983; Mayer, 1992).

In addition to the task of making models which are more consistent with the real world, the policy analyst has a second task to perform: heeding Schultz's 'three rules' about policy making. First, 'the real task [of the policy analyst] is to know when to compromise and when to hold firm, how to move tactically while maintaining your strategy'. Second, the policy analyst must realize that 'cuts in government spending are easier to advocate than to execute'. Third, a successful policy analyst has learned that the 'key to a successful policy is often to get the right process going. While the economist is accustomed to the concept of lags, the politician likes instant results' (Schultz, 1995). Even if the policy analyst performs those two tasks expertly, the best laid plans come undone, as the following example illustrates.

During the early years of the Nixon administration, Nixon and his advisors were confronted with the problem of what to do about inflation, which was running at about 4.5–5 per cent per annum. Friedman advocated a reduction in the rates of growth of the money supply and government expenditures and a reduction in marginal tax rates. Galbraith argued for the immediate implementation of an 'incomes policy' as the only way to break the back of the inflation psychology. Stein, in his capacity as counselor to the President, wanted to reduce the rates of growth of the money supply and government expenditures, specifically the Great Society's programs and appropriations for the war in Vietnam. Nixon supported his counselor and the planned recession was given the green light. This might have solved the inflation problem, had Nixon not simultaneously decided to implement Moynihan's program of social activism. The situation became more complicated when the Vietnam War heated up once again.

Each of the policy options in this example had its own cast of supporters and detractors. After he was subjected to a cacophony of advice from his policy advisors, Nixon made a series of choices, the economic consequence of which was stagflation. No matter how skillful or knowledgeable the policy analyst is, she or he may not be able to stop the politician from making politically motivated decisions.

TOM CATE

See also:

Fiscal Policy; Friedman, Milton; Keynes, John N.; Lipsey, Richard G.; Monetary Policy; Okun, Arthur M.; Samuelson, Paul A.

Bibliography

Brock, William A. and Stephen Magee (1984), 'The Invisible Foot and the Waste of Nations: Redistribution and Economic Growth', in David Colander (ed.), *Neoclassical Political Economy: The Analysis of Rent-Seeking and DUP Activities*, Cambridge, Mass.: Ballinger.

Colander, David (1992), 'The Lost Art of Economics', *The Journal of Economic Perspectives*, **6**, (3), summer, pp. 191–8.

Colander, David (1994), 'The Art of Economics by the Numbers', in Roger Backhouse (ed.), *New Directions in Economic Methodology*, New York: Routledge.

Friedman, Milton (1953), 'The Methodology of Positive Economics', *Essays in Positive Economics*, Chicago: University of Chicago Press.

Hutchison, T.W. (1992), *Changing Aims in Economics*, Cambridge, Mass.: Blackwell.

Kamarck, Andrew (1983), *Economics and the Real World*, Philadelphia: University of Pennsylvania Press.

Keynes, John Neville (1890), *The Scope and Method of Political Economy*, London: Macmillan.

Lipsey, Robert (1966), *An Introduction to Positive Economics*, 2nd edn, London: Weidenfeld & Nicolson.

Mayer, Thomas (1992), *Truth and Precision in Economics*, Brookfield, VT: Edward Elgar.

Okun, Arthur (1972), 'Fiscal–Monetary Activism: Some Analytical Issues', *Brookings Papers on Economic Activity*, **3**, (1), pp. 123–63.

Okun, Arthur (1980), 'The Invisible Handshake and the Inflationary Process', *Challenge*, **22**, (6), January–February, pp. 5–12.

Samuelson, Paul A. (1963), 'Comment on Ernest Nagel's "Assumptions in Economic Theory"', *Papers and Proceedings of the American Economics Association*, **53**, (2), May, pp. 231–6.

Schultz, George P. (1995), 'Economics in Action: Ideas, Institutions, Policies', *American Economic Review*, **85**, (2), May, pp. 1–9.

Wong, Stanley (1973), 'The "F-Twist" and the Methodology of Paul Samuelson', *American Economic Review*, **63**, (3), June, pp. 312–25.

Edgeworth, Francis Y.

Francis Ysidro Edgeworth, one of the founders of mathematical economics and a pioneering economic theorist, was born in 1845 on his family's estate in Ireland. He was educated at home until he entered Trinity College, Dublin. He continued his studies at Balliol College, Oxford, where he earned first class honors in Lit. Hum. Edgeworth was fluent in many languages and quoted liberally from the classics in his lectures and writings. Unable initially to find a suitable academic position, he studied law in London and was admitted to the bar in 1877.

In his first book, *New and Old Methods of Ethics* (1877), Edgeworth made a brilliant but hopeless attempt to formulate a model of exact utilitarianism, combining the ethical precepts of Sidgwick with the mathematical and statistical methods of the physical sciences. The book elicited high praise from Jevons and he was encouraged to make a more ambitious attempt to work out a utilitarian calculus, these efforts culminating in the publication of *Mathematical Psychics* (1881), a book regarded as one of the classics of theoretical economics. Here Edgeworth introduced the indifference curve, the contract curve and the theory of pure exchange in markets with different numbers of traders, culminating in the equilibrium conditions achieved under perfect competition (or the 'core' of the competitive economy).

The qualities of originality and high imagination which characterize Edgeworth's writings are exemplified in this extract from *Mathematical Psychics*:

'Mécanique Sociale' may one day take her place along with 'Mécanique Céleste', throned each upon the double-sided height of one maximum principle, the supreme pinnacle of moral as of physical science ...
[M]athematics has long walked by the evidence of things not seen in the world of atoms (the methods whereof ... may illustrate the possibility of social mathematics). The invisible energy of electricity is grasped by the marvellous methods of Lagrange; the invisible energy of pleasure may admit of a similar handling. (pp. 12–13)

Mathematical Psychics was reviewed by Marshall, who recognized its originality but was dubious about excessive reliance upon mathematical reasoning in economics:

This book shows clear signs of genius and is a promise of great things to come ... The essay is devoted to the fundamental problem of the mathematical rendering of a 'Calculus of Pleasure' ... It is well put but there is a certain air of unreality about all such arguments ... The real question is not whether it is possible but whether it is profitable to apply mathematical reasonings in the moral sciences. When a man has cleared up his mind about a difficult economic question by mathematical reasoning, he generally finds it best to throw aside his mathematics and express what he has to say in [ordinary] language. (*The Academy*, 1933, XIX, p. 457)

With the support of Marshall, Edgeworth was appointed as Tooke Professor of Economic Science and Statistics at King's College, London, and then Drummond Professor of Political Economy and a Fellow of All Souls College, Oxford, where he remained to the end of his life. He became the first editor of the *Economic Journal*, in 1891, and continued in that position to the end of his career. He was joined by J.M. Keynes as co-editor in 1911. Keynes recalled this association in one of his memorable *Essays in Biography*:

> [Edgeworth] had a strong feeling for the solidarity of economic science through-
> out the world and sought to encourage talent wherever he found it ... His tolerance
> was all-embracing, and he combined a respect for established reputation ... with a
> natural inclination to encourage the youthful and unknown. All his eccentricity
> and strangeness found its outlet in his own writings. All his practical good sense
> and daily shrewdness was devoted to the *Economic Journal.*

Edgeworth never wrote a major treatise in economics. His ideas were
expressed in hundreds of articles and reviews, many of which were repub-
lished in his honor by the Royal Economic Society just prior to his death in
1926. He made notable contributions to the theory of international trade,
duopoly, taxation, income distribution and the laws of returns in production.
He also made pathbreaking contributions to statistics in the areas of index
numbers, the law of error and correlation.

Although he was introduced to economics by Jevons and followed the
utility principle almost exclusively in his early writings, he eventually moved
toward the neoclassical position and became a strong defender of both the
classical economists and Marshall.

Edgeworth was uneasy giving policy advice in economics because he saw
most issues in general equilibrium terms and thus disdained simple explanations. In general, he was a champion of free markets in the spirit of Ricardo
and Mill. In his later writings, he debated with the Austrians, Walras and
various socialist writers on methodological issues. He delighted in correcting
the propositions of others when he found them guilty of mathematical error,
but he also readily admitted his own mistakes. An obituary writer in *The
Times* said of him:

> To a courtly grace, derived perhaps from his Spanish mother, he added the Irish
> characteristics of humour, imagination, and generosity. A lifelong friend has never
> known him to be out of temper or speak an ill word of others ... His range of
> learning was astonishing for quite apart from economics he was an admirable
> classical scholar, an accomplished mathematician, and deeply read in foreign litera-
> ture, and he took a keen interest in the latest developments in the physical sciences.

By his highly original application of mathematical and statistical techniques, Edgeworth helped to establish the respectability of both mathematical
economics and econometrics. In one version or another, the 'Edgeworth Box'
analysis will likely remain an essential part of the training of young economists around the world, a suitable tribute to a pioneering economic theorist.

PHILIP E. SORENSEN

See also:

Arrow, Kenneth J.; Baumol, William J.; Frisch, Ragnar; Haavelmo, Trygve; Hahn, Frank H.;
Hicks, Sir John R.; Marshall, Alfred; Robbins, Lord Lionel; Samuelson, Paul A.; Say's Law.

Bibliography

Bonar, James (1926), 'Memories of F.Y. Edgeworth', *Economic Journal*, **36**, (144), December, pp. 647–53.

Edgeworth, F.Y. (1877), *New and Old Methods of Ethics*, London: Parker & Co.

Edgeworth, F.Y. (1881), *Mathematical Psychics*, London: Kegan Paul & Co.

Edgeworth, F.Y. (1925), *Papers Relating to Political Economy*, 3 vols, London: Macmillan for the Royal Economic Society.

Keynes, J.M. (1933), 'F.Y. Edgeworth', *Essays in Biography*, London: Macmillan.

The Times, London, 'Obituary, Professor F.Y. Edgeworth', 16 February 1926, p. 21.

Employment Act of 1946

Adam Smith's philosophy of political economy was influenced in part by Newtonian mechanics. Believing that the economy was self-correcting, Smith argued that there was no need for the government to take an active role in the operation of the economic system. Indeed Smith limited the role of the government to four functions or duties: to provide for the defense of the realm, to establish an equitable system of justice, to undertake those projects which the private sector find unprofitable, and to obtain enough revenues to cover the expenses incurred by performing the first three duties (Smith, 1776).

The idea that the economic system is self-correcting became the cornerstone upon which the Classical economists erected their economic theory. The phrases 'laissez faire' and 'Say's Law' may be seen as shorthand notation for a very sophisticated body of economic theory. This is not to say that individual economists did not develop theoretical arguments which identified instances where the interest of the commonweal would be served best by government intervention. One such set of arguments was developed by Pigou, who stated that, under certain conditions, market failures could emerge, and articulated a set of policies for dealing with these market failures. Pigou's theory held sway until the advent of Buchanan (public choice theory) and Coase (the Coase theorem). But even Pigou was an ardent defender of the self-correcting nature of the economic system.

The economic consequences of World War I and the Great Depression once again called into question the idea that the economic system is self-correcting. Out of the discussions about these two great events of the first part of the twentieth century came Keynesian economics and the call for a more active role for government. In particular, Keynesian economists believed that the economic system is not self-correcting, and that, if the private sector is unable or unwilling to take the steps necessary to promote full employment, the government must implement public policies which lead to full employment.

With the successful conclusion of World War II, the mood of the political leaders of the United States favored the idea that the government should take a more active role in the operation of the American economy. One of the pieces of legislation which embodied this new spirit was Public Law 79–304, The Employment Act of 1946. With this piece of legislation,

> The Congress declares that it is the continuing policy and responsibility of the federal Government to use all practical means consistent with its need and obligations and other essential considerations of national policy, with the assistance and cooperation of industry, agriculture, labor, and state and local governments, to coordinate and utilize all its plans, functions, and resources for the purposes of creating and maintaining, in a manner calculated to foster and promote free competitive enterprise and the general welfare, conditions under which there will be afforded useful employment opportunities, including self-employment, for those able, willing, and seeking work, and to promote maximum employment, production, and purchasing power. (Preamble of PL 79–304)

Much of the debate on the bill focused on having as a national policy the goal of full employment. The final version of the bill substituted the words 'maximum employment' for 'full employment'. The idea that the government must in some sense undertake steps to promote full employment sounded too much like socialism to members of Congress. Given the events in Eastern Europe in the postwar period, and later with the rise to power of the House Committee on Un-American Activities, the government acting as the employer of last resort was an idea whose time had not come in the United States.

On 20 February 1946, President Truman signed the bill into law. He confessed that he did not have a very clear grasp of the express purpose of the law but noted that 'occasionally, as we pore through the pages of history, we are struck by the fact that some incident, little noted at the time, profoundly affects the whole subsequent course of events. I venture the prediction that history, someday, will so record the enactment of The Employment Act of 1946' (Truman, 1956). The moral authority of this act has grown with the passage of time. Burns has put forth the idea that the act has acquired the force of an economic constitution (Burns, 1966).

Since the ideas for developing the policies necessary for promoting maximum employment originate in the Executive Branch, the act created the Council of Economic Advisors (CEA). Until the appointment of Lauchlin Currie in 1939 as an administrative assistant to the President, economists played only an informal advisory role. Although the President and members of his 'Brain Trust' were suspicious of 'compensatory finance', advocates like Marriner Eccles could be found within the government who favored the use of the budget to achieve a given level of national income. The CEA was charged with the task of analysing economic trends and formalizing the Executive Branch's economic policy. These findings and proposals were to be published in a document entitled *The Economic Report of the President*. In the spirit of checks and balances the act also created the Congressional Joint Economic Committee, which would provide the legislative branch of government with its staff of economic advisors.

The CEA would comprise three members appointed with the advice and consent of the Senate. The first CEA consisted of Edwin Nourse (Chicago) John D. Clark (Johns Hopkins) and Leon Keyserling (Columbia), with Nourse serving as the chairman. In addition to fulfilling their duty under the law, the members of the CEA were immediately confronted by a tricky issue: should the CEA serve as an advisory body to the President or should the CEA serve as an advocate of the President's economic policy? Nourse favored the former approach, while Clark and Keyserling, and, as it turned out, President Truman, favored the latter. Nourse, having discovered that what makes good economic sense may not coincide with the political needs of the President, resigned, and Keyserling replaced him as chairman. The confrontation between CEA Chairman Martin Feldstein and President Reagan over the future direction of the American economy is another example of the tension which exists between the CEA and the White House.

The Employment Act of 1946 has had a celebrated existence and has been duly toasted with formal remembrances by its political authors and subsequent economic practitioners with official Washington, DC-based meetings on its decennial anniversaries. A common conclusion of these meetings is that, while the act created a structure of policy making designed to coordinate economic policy and to provide maximum employment, production and purchasing power, it did not provide guidance on how this responsibility is to be discharged and on how to rank order conflicting economic objectives.

In the mid-1970s, the Joint Economic Committee sponsored a series of reports covering the topics of employment, energy, inflation and market structure, and economic planning in honor of the thirtieth anniversary of the act. Its chairman, Hubert H. Humphrey, stated that the findings of this study series were to be used to develop an expanded and improved means to achieve the goals of the Employment Act of 1946. This research resulted in the Full Employment and Balanced Growth Act of 1978, or The Humphrey–Hawkins Act. Three aspects of this piece of legislation are important. First, the 1978 act identified seven national goals to be pursued by the federal government: full employment and production, increased real income, balanced growth, a balanced federal budget, adequate productivity growth, an improved trade balance and reasonable price stability. Second, the 1978 act specified numerical values for the rates of inflation and unemployment of 4 per cent and 3 per cent, respectively by 1983 and zero inflation by 1988. Third, the 1978 act required that a representative of the Federal Reserve Board appear before Congressional banking committees to report on its intended monetary policy for the year. This requirement has become known in the financial industry as the Humphrey–Hawkins Testimony.

James Tobin (1986), an advocate of this type of legislation, stated on the fortieth anniversary of the Employment Act that Congress erred by incorporating in the Humphrey–Hawkins Act numerical goals for unemployment and inflation. Given the economic conditions of the 1970s, the 1978 act's goals for inflation and unemployment were patently unachievable, with the result that policy makers could ignore not only the numerical goals of the 1978 act but the spirit that motivated them. Furthermore the failure of Keynesian economics to develop politically acceptable policies for dealing with stagflation has led to the demise of activist fiscal policy, and a slow shift to a reliance on monetary policy and market forces. The reintroduction of competition manifested in redefining the telecommunications and transport industries and the proposal to wean farmers from government subsidies by the year 2000, for example, point to a return closer to Smith's position of 1776 and to the relegation of fiscal policy to the status of a junior partner to monetary policy.

This trend away from activist Keynesian economic macroeconomic policy has culminated in a proposal from the Joint Economic Committee, 'The Economic Growth and Price Stability Act of 1995'. This proposed piece of legislation replaces the multiple goals of the Humphrey–Hawkins Act with a single goal, that of price stability. The Fed is charged with the responsibility for defining, achieving and maintaining long-term price stability within the American economy. The Fed would be required to support some secondary goals such as low taxes, free markets, a respect for private property and stable money (*Annual Report* 1994).

LOU NOYD

See also:
Demand Management; Fiscal Policy; Keynes, John Maynard; Monetary Policy; New Classical School of Economics.

Bibliography
Annual Report (1994), Cleveland: Federal Reserve Bank of Cleveland.
Bailey, Stephen K. (1950), *Congress Makes a Law   The Story Behind the Employment Act of 1946*, New York: Columbia University Press.
Burns, Arthur (1966), 'Aggregate or Structural Approaches to Achieving Employment Act Objectives', in *US Congress Joint Economic Committee Twentieth Anniversary of the Employment Act of 1946. An Economic Symposium*, Washington, D.C.: US Government Printing Office.
Norton, Hugh S. (1973), *The Council of Economic Advisers: Three Periods of Influence*, Columbia, South Carolina: Bureau of Business and Economic Research, College of Business Administration, Essays in Economics No. 27.
Norton, Hugh S. (1977), *The Employment Act and the Council of Economic Advisers, 1946–1976*, Columbia, South Carolina: University of South Carolina Press.

Public Law 79-304 *Employment Act of 1946*, as recorded in United States Code: Congressional Service, Laws of 79th Congress, Second Session, St. Paul: West Publishing Company.

Public Law 95-523 *Full Employment and Balanced Growth Act of 1978*, as recorded in United States Code: Congressional Service and Administrative News, Laws of 95th Congress, Second Session, vol. 1, 92 STAT. St. Paul: West Publishing Company.

Smith, Adam (1776), *The Wealth of Nations*, reprinted 1965, New York: Modern Library.

Stein, Herbert (1969), *The Fiscal Revolution in America*, Chicago: University of Chicago Press.

Tobin, James (1986), 'High Time to Restore the Employment Act of 1946', *Challenge*, **29**, (2), May–June, pp. 4–12.

Truman, Harry S (1956), *Memoirs. Years of Trial and Hope. Vol. 2*, Garden City, New York: Double Day.

Expectations, Theories of

One of the underpinnings of New Classical Economics is rational expectations theory. In breaking from the classical tradition, adherents to the New Classical school maintain that individuals develop expectations regarding future prices and market behavior. This is in contrast to the classical position which maintained that all agents in the market had full information about the future. Expectations can be formed in various ways, giving rise to such distinctions as adaptive expectations theory and rational expectations theory. Clearly, different individuals have differing perceptions of the economy and its future behavior, which results in different sets of expectations. Individuals who form price expectations today which are determined by the recent and/or past behavior of prices are formulating expectations in accord with adaptive expectations theory. In such instances, more recent price behavior is more heavily taken into account than past behavior when arriving at an expectation. Rational expectations theory differs from adaptive expectations theory in that expectations about price behavior are generally formed in accord with the predictions of the prevailing economic theory.

The father of rational expectations theory is traditionally held to be John Muth, who in his 1961 article, 'Rational Expectations and the Theory of Price Movements', sought to develop a theory by which dynamic models would be made complete, thereby enhancing long-run analysis. Muth proposed that 'expectations, since they are informed predictions of future events, are essentially the same as the predictions of the relevant economic theory. At the risk of confusing this purely descriptive hypothesis with a pronouncement as to what firms ought to do, we call such expectations rational' (1961, p. 316). In other words, expectations of firms are, on average, consistent with the existing theory. From his hypothesis Muth asserts the following: first, that since information is not plentiful and readily available, it will not be wasted; second, that expectations will be formed differently, depending on the economic system or theory describing the economy at the time; and third, a generally held prediction will not significantly influence the functioning of the economic system (1961, p. 316). While Muth's colleague, Herbert A. Simon, disagreed with the theory of rational expectations and held to a theory of bounded rationality (a theory which emphasizes limitations in individual decision making) and others maintained that Muth's theory was lacking in its explanatory power of observed events, Muth believed that the existence of rational behavior was often underestimated and that expectations of economic variables could be formed by economic actors. In other words, people do not repeatedly ignore information that will aid in their decision making. Hence, on average, individuals will predict correctly in forming their expectations and, as a result, policy implications will be correctly anticipated. What followed was a revolution of sorts in the field of macroeconomics that persisted throughout the 1970s and 1980s, when expectations theory took hold, in large part due to the continuing work of Robert Lucas, Thomas Sargent and others.

Although economic actors have traditionally been regarded as rational by the classical economists (such as Smith, Mill and Pigou), their assumption was based on individuals having perfect information. This is distinctly different from the modern view of expectations theory in the sense that perfect information is no longer assumed. Rather, it is believed that people process information to form expectations. While Muth and his followers perhaps espoused the notion of rational expectations most clearly, there were precursors who clearly understood that there was an explanatory role for expectations in the economy. Adam Smith, for example, broadly touched upon the idea in his *Theory of Moral Sentiments* (1976), as did Tinbergen (1932) in his 'Ein Problem der Dynamik' (Keuzenkamp, 1991). Keynes, too, explored the issue of probability underlying expectations in his *A Treatise on Probability* (1921), while Austrian economist O. Morgenstern was against such claims of predictability owing to the likelihood that expectations become self-fulfilling prophecies. Morgenstern was not alone in his lack of enthusiasm for rational expectations theory. Proponents of the Austrian School oppose theories of expectations on the basis that economic agents cannot know the impact of policy changes on price since policy changes dismantle the existing expectations of economic agents. Hence, according to Austrian economists, individuals are constantly adapting and adjusting as they obtain new information, as opposed to being able immediately to determine the impact of a policy change on price. To take the latter view, according to the Austrian School, would be effectively to disregard the informational role of the price system. Keynesians also express opposition to rational expectations theory, claiming that the theory does not account for extended periods of unemployment and depression. The disagreement is perhaps due to the fundamental difference of opinion regarding the general state of the economy. Keynesians maintain that the economy is typically unstable, while expectations theorists believe that, once expectations are adjusted to take a policy change into account, the economy will return to equilibrium.

While theories of expectations remain a point of debate to this day, rational expectations theorists claim that one advantage of the theory for the economy is stability in the face of policy changes. However, critics suggest that such policy neutrality inferred by rational expectations theory is more aptly dubbed a non-existent approach to policy, since rational expectationists maintain that effects of policy changes are fully anticipated, so that a return to rational expectations equilibrium occurs by means of neutralizing policy changes via expectations. According to Sargent, rational expectations theory is often informally characterized as reflecting 'a process in which individuals are inspecting and altering their own forecasting records in ways to eliminate systematic forecast errors' (1993, p. 21). Undoubtedly the debate on the legitimacy of rational expectations theory will continue until more factual evidence exists.

AUDREY B. DAVIDSON

See also:

Chicago School of Economics; Classical Economics; Friedman, Milton; Lucas, Jr., Robert E.; Lucas Critique; Monetarist School of Economics; New Classical School of Economics.

Bibliography

Ekelund, Robert B., Jr. and Robert F. Hébert (1990), *A History of Economic Theory and Method*, third edn, New York: McGraw-Hill.
Keuzenkamp, Hugo A. (1991), 'A Precursor to Muth: Tinbergen's 1932 Model of Rational Expectations', *Economic Journal*, **101**, (408), September, pp. 1245–53.
Keynes, John M. (1922), *A Treatise on Probability*, London: Macmillan.
Lucas, R.E. Jr. and T.J. Sargent (eds) (1981), *Rational Expectations and Econometric Practice*, Minneapolis: University of Minnesota Press.
Muth, John F. (1961), 'Rational Expectations and the Theory of Price Movements', *Econometrica*, **29**, July, pp. 315–35.
Sargent, Thomas J. (1986), *Rational Expectations and Inflation*, New York: Harper & Row.
Sargent, Thomas J. (1993), *Bounded Rationality in Macroeconomics*, Oxford: Clarendon Press.
Schiller, Robert J. (1987), 'Expectations', in John Eatwell, Murray Milgate and Peter Newman (eds), *The New Palgrave: A Dictionary of Economics*, Vol. 2, New York: Stockton Press.
Sheffrin, Steven M. (1983), *Rational Expectations*, Cambridge: Cambridge University Press.
Smith, Adam (1976) [1759], *The Theory of Moral Sentiments*, Indianapolis: Liberty Press.

Fellner, William J.

William J. Fellner was born in 1905 to a wealthy Hungarian manufacturing family. Early in life he lived in Budapest and worked in the family businesses. An academic career followed. Late in life he served on the Nixon Council of Economic Advisors (CEA). He then joined the American Enterprise Institute (AEI) as a public policy analyst, remaining there until his death in 1983.

While his family permitted him to study economics at the University of Berlin, where he earned his PhD in 1929, it was with the firm expectation that, like his three brothers before him, he would go into one of the several family manufacturing enterprises. This he did, relegating his interest in economics to the status of a hobby to be shared with friends. Two revealing visits to the United States gave birth to the dream of an academic career in America. In 1938, with his wife Valerie, an accomplished scholar in her own right whom he had married two years earlier, and young daughter Anna, he won family approval to move to Berkeley, California to pursue the academic life.

US citizenship came in 1944, and the rank of full professor in 1947. Fellner was by any measure a prolific author, a side of him made evident early on. After an early book on war finance, he published *Monetary Policies and Full Employment* in 1946. It set the stage for many positions he held throughout his life: though government might pursue policies to encourage full employment, these should never take the form of a guarantee; this would invite monopoly elements to use their market power to raise prices and wages, and the inevitable result would be inflation. Wage and price controls were also unacceptable: they would limit important freedoms, while inhibiting the capacity of market capitalism to make a socially desirable allocation of resources. No full employment guarantee, no economic controls: these were to become enduring themes for Fellner.

Fellner bore personal witness to the great Continental hyperinflations of the 1920s. Some attribute his lifelong concern with inflation to this experience. He was never sympathetically disposed towards Keynes, whose policies he thought inflationary. Conceding little to Keynes, Fellner questioned his originality. Irma Adelman describes Fellner as a 'limited Keynesian'. Should an economy fall into a deep depression, he would accept government intervention, yet, in the same breath, he would surely tell us that a deep depression comes about only as a result of the ineptitude of policy makers: don't blame market capitalism; it's the fault of the fine-tuners. While highly opinionated, Fellner was unpredictable and non-ideological. Like his conservative colleagues, he viewed big government as a threat to fundamental freedoms. But he was willing to grant that a large government sector brought with it the automatic stabilizers which dampened the amplitude of macroeconomic fluctuations. What would he have had to say in the debate over the balanced budget amendment? His contempt for gimmicks and grudging appreciation for the automatic stabilizers would likely have led him to condemn the sophistry of the balanced budget amendment proponents.

Fellner's scholarly range was wide: macroeconomics, growth, oligopoly, technological progress, economic thought, decision theory and the international payments system. His *Competition Among the Few* (1949) introduced the notion of the reaction function and remains a standard work on oligopoly. *Trends and Cycles in Economic Activity* (1956) may be his most important book. No less an authority than Charles Schultze of the Brookings Institution believes it to contain the finest statement of the conditions necessary to ensure sustained economic growth. *Emergence and Content of Modern Economic Analysis* (1960) is Fellner's undiscovered gem. This *tour de force* demonstrates how contemporary theory is informed by the history of economic ideas. His last book, *Towards a Reconstruction of Macroeconomics* (1976), pours old wine into new bottles: inflation poses the gravest threat to market capitalism and so price stability is the single most important objective of macroeconomic policy. His beloved 'credibility effect' is the central idea: policies to restore non-inflationary growth can be credible only if policy authorities make clear their willingness to tolerate transitional unemployment. Fellner's hope that this would be his lasting contribution to macroeconomic policy was not fulfilled. Critics noted that the transitional unemployment required could prove to be deep and prolonged, posing as grave a danger as the inflation it was meant to cure.

By the early 1950s, tiring of the recriminations and loyalty oaths that the McCarthy era brought to Berkeley, Fellner looked eastward. In 1952, an offer from Yale was gladly accepted, as closer proximity to the nation's capital might afford new opportunities. At Yale he began his long and friendly debate with neo-Keynesian rival James Tobin.

Fellner was a blunt man, known for his integrity. Mark Blaug has recounted his interview for a faculty position at Yale in 1954. He had lost his previous job as the result of his support of a colleague's exercise of her Fifth Amendment rights at a Congressional hearing. Fellner, a member of the search committee, declared that 'what transpired ... a few years ago is of no concern to us'. Honors and public recognition were to come to Fellner. In 1969, he was elected president of the American Economic Association. The Nobel Prize in economics eluded him, but West Germany awarded him its Commander's Cross in 1979 and he received the Bernhard-Harms Prize from the University of Kiel in 1982. Over the years he served as a consultant to the

Treasury Department, the Federal Reserve, the Organization of European Economic Cooperation and the Congressional Budget Office.

Fellner's most public moment came in 1973, following his retirement from Yale. Enveloped by Watergate, Richard Nixon had to fill a vacancy on the CEA with a nominee of unquestioned competence and honesty. The CEA had been accused of manipulating the economic news in the previous election year. Fellner accepted the job, but on his terms. At a press conference he made clear his disapproval of the excessive demand stimulation in the two years leading up to the Nixon re-election bid and called for an end to the Nixon program of wage and price controls. Winning easy Senate confirmation, he was thought the likely successor to Herbert Stein as CEA chairman, but Alan Greenspan was appointed in August 1974 to replace Stein. During his Council service from 1973 to 1975, he was the principal author of the annual *Economic Report of the President*. Bringing demand-side management into disrepute, he made price stability through demand restraint the focus of policy.

After his CEA service in 1975, he joined the AEI as a Resident Scholar. In 1976, he started to direct and edit the AEI annual policy issues series, *Contemporary Economic Problems*. Fellner began to study the economic effects of 'tax bracket creep'. Believing that inflation was robbing the automatic stabilizers of their power, he crusaded for the indexation of the personal income tax. His tax indexation ideas became part of the tax bill passed in 1981. This contribution is his most lasting legacy to public policy.

Fellner defies categorization. Unconvinced of the predictability of the velocity of money, he was no strict monetarist. Seeing no sufficiently systematic component in government policy, he remained skeptical of rational expectations. Critical of its disdain for empirical evidence, Fellner was no friend to supply-side economics. He preferred his own eclectic band of conservative economics. James Tobin eulogized his friend's 'respect for evidence, and intellectual integrity', words of praise from the enemy in the macro wars.

JAMES N. MARSHALL

See also:

Demand Management; Expectations, Theories of; Fiscal Policy; Incomes Policies; Inflation; Lucas Critique; Monetary Policy; Phillips Curve; Stein, Herbert; Tobin, James.

Bibliography

Adelman, Irma (1987), 'Fellner, William John (1905–1983)', in John Eatwell, Murray Milgate and Peter Newman (eds), *The New Palgrave: A Dictionary of Economics*, Vol. 2, New York: Stockton Press.

Fellner, W.J. (1946), *Monetary Policies and Full Employment*, Berkeley: University of California Press.

Fellner, W.J. (1949), *Competition Among the Few: Oligopoly and Similar Market Structures*, New York: Knopf.

Fellner, W.J. (1956), *Trends and Cycles in Economic Activity: An Introduction to Problems of Economic Growth*, New York: Holt.

Fellner, W.J. (1960), *Emergence and Content of Modern Economic Analysis*, New York: McGraw-Hill.

Fellner, W.J. (1976), *Towards a Reconstruction of Macroeconomics: Problems of Theory and Policy*, Washington, D.C.: American Enterprise Institute.

Marshall, James N. (1988), 'Fellner, William J.', in Robert Sobel and Bernard S. Katz (eds), *Biographical Directory of the Council of Economic Advisers*, New York: Greenwood Press, pp. 67–75.

Marshall, James N. (1992), *William J. Fellner: A Bio-Bibliography*, Westport, Conn.: Greenwood Press.

Fiscal Policy

Fiscal policy can be defined as changes in the federal government's budget made for the express purpose of changing the level (or the growth rate) of economic activity. The underpinnings of fiscal policy stem from the idea, often attributed to Keynes, that the level of economic activity is positively correlated to aggregate spending.

This positive correlation suggests that the government can have a major impact on economic activity to the extent that it can alter the level of spending in the economy. The government's budget has outflows of spending and transfer payments and inflows of tax revenues and user fees. Fiscal policy primarily operates through changes in government spending and taxes. Changes in government spending affect aggregate spending directly, while changes in taxes affect aggregate spending indirectly through their influence on the spending patterns of households and firms.

Suppose, for example, economic activity is too low. As a response to this condition, the government could raise its spending and/or lower its taxes. This will translate into increases in the demand for goods and services facing firms. Firms respond by raising prices and/or output. To the extent that real output increases, there is an increase in real economic activity and fiscal policy has been successful.[1] For fiscal policy to be effective, three conditions must hold:

1. the change in government's budget must actually change aggregate spending and not just cause a redistribution of spending between the private and public sectors;
2. changes in aggregate spending must actually lead to changes in aggregate activity; and
3. any change in economic activity resulting from fiscal policy must occur in a timely fashion.

Fiscal policy has been challenged by its critics on each of these fronts.

Net changes in aggregate spending

Those who believe that changes in government spending or taxes have little impact on aggregate spending focus their attention on the fact that all government spending must be financed. Consider the case of an increase in government spending. The two primarily financing methods are tax increases and bond sales. Clearly any increase in taxes will have a substantial offsetting effect and will cause the expansion of aggregate spending to be minimal. Similarly any borrowing the government does to finance its expenditures will also limit the expansiveness of increases in government spending. This can be seen in Figure 1, which is a graph of the loanable funds market.

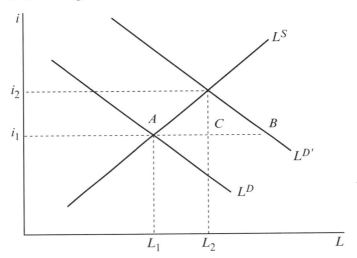

Figure 1

Suppose the government wishes to borrow \$AB to finance its expenditures. This causes an increase in the demand for loans to $L^{D'}$, an increase in the interest rate to i_2 and an increase in loans by \$AC. Thus total spending increases by \$AC rather than \$AB. Total loans do not increase by \$AB because the increase in the interest rate discourages consumers and firms from borrowing as much as previously. Thus, while government spending rises by \$AB, private spending falls by \$BC. That is, \$BC are said to be crowded out.

The amount aggregate spending increases, \$AC, depends on the elasticities of L^D and L^S. Critics of fiscal policy believe that L^D is quite elastic, L^S is quite inelastic and the net change in aggregate spending is small. Therefore they suggest that increases in government spending, rather than increasing aggregate economic activity, primarily redistributes resources from the private to the public sector.[2]

Long-run changes in economic activity

Some economists discount the relationship between aggregate spending and long-run changes in real economic activity. This criticism goes to the heart of the theory underlying fiscal policy and is focused on the labor market. As aggregate spending increases, these economists believe, the first response is an increase in the average price level. This causes the aggregate supply of labor (N^S) and the aggregate demand for labor (N^D) to pivot upward by the same proportion as the price change. This is shown in Figure 2, where W equals the nominal wage rate.

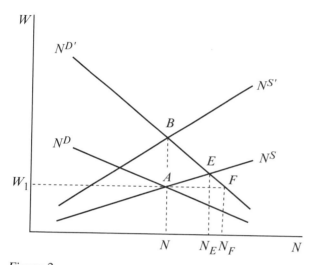

Figure 2

Then, if one believes that wages are flexible and price expectations are correct, the aggregate labor market moves from A to B and no change in employment and aggregate real activity occurs. Fiscal policy, even if it can increase aggregate spending, is totally ineffective.[3]

Other economists believe that flexible wages and/or perfect price expectations can only occur in the long run and therefore believe that fiscal policy has some short-run effects. In our example, the initial changes in L^D and L^S were caused by changes in the government's budget. Suppose these shifts were due to abnormal increases in private spending: then, if wages are fixed and employment is demand-determined in the short run, the aggregate labor market moves to F and employment and economic activity increase. Likewise, if price expectations are in error in the short run, the aggregate labor market moves to E and again employment and economic activity increase.[4]

Points *E* and *F*, however, are inferior to points *A* and *B* because they yield lower levels of utility. The government, these economist suggest, could then use fiscal policy to offset this increase in private spending and move the economy back towards the original employment level. Therefore fiscal policy, while not changing the long-run resting point of the economy, can help achieve this point faster and with less harm.

Timeliness
Even some who believe that the above criticisms of fiscal policy are unfounded still discount the usefulness of fiscal policy. They suggest that using fiscal policy is too cumbersome since all fiscal policy decisions are, in the end, made by the legislature. The size of this body, the differing viewpoints of its members and the political considerations underlying any spending or tax change make any fiscal policy decision a long-drawn-out process. Therefore these critics suggest that, even if fiscal policy could be useful in solving short-term economic problems, the practical reality is that the policy is unlikely to be passed in time.

Proponents of fiscal policy suggest that these legislators could be bypassed by embedding fiscal policy in the institutions of the economy to act automatically when an economic problem occurred. For example, consider the case of unemployment compensation. Whenever the economy goes on a down swing, people lose their jobs and as a result there is an increase in unemployment compensation. Thus government spending automatically rises when the economy falls into a recession.

Another example is income tax. Taxes automatically go down during a downturn in the economy. In other words, fiscal policy automatically goes into effect. These embedded policies are often called automatic stabilizers. Note, however, that these automatic stabilizers cannot take care of 100 per cent of the problem because they would destroy incentives. For example, to offset entirely a recession via unemployment compensation would require that the compensation be the same as the lost wages. If this were the case then few people would work.

Summary
In the end, a critical analysis of fiscal policy yields mixed results. To the extent that crowding out (in) can be avoided and policy changes can be initiated in a timely fashion, fiscal policy can be useful in offsetting 'abnormal' short-run changes in private spending. However fiscal policy is unlikely to have much of a long-run impact when expectations are perfect and wages and prices are flexible. Therefore any future discussion of fiscal policy should focus primarily on its short-run possibilities.[5]

LEE C. SPECTOR

Notes

1 It must be noted that not all changes in the government's budget can be considered to be fiscal policy because most of these changes are not for the purpose of changing economic activity. Defense spending is an example where the government's budget changes, economic activity changes and yet one would not normally consider defense spending as part of the government's fiscal policy.
2 A counterargument is based on the Ricardian equivalence hypothesis. In short, this hypothesis states that households take into account the future taxes they will have to pay when the government redeems these bonds. Consequently they increase their present savings and L^S increases simultaneously as L^D increases. The result is a much larger increase in the equilibrium quantity of loans.
3 Of course, so is monetary policy under these circumstances.
4 In this example, it is assumed that laborers see none of the price change. To the degree that they see any of the price change, the increase in employment will be lessened.
5 It must also be said, as a technical point, that, even if one believes in the possibility of short-run macroeconomic policy, the actual determination of how much government spending and/or taxes should be changed is not trivial. One problem, often identified as the Lucas Critique, is that government policy can change the behavior of economic agents. For example, the marginal propensity to consume out of present income may change as the government increases its spending. Therefore the impact on the economy may be quite different from what one predicted from the government's policy models.

See also:

Aggregate Demand–Aggregate Supply Model and Diagram; Automatic Stabilizers; Demand Management; Employment Act of 1946; Full Employment Budget; Functional Finance; Government Investment Programs (The Socialization of Investment); IS/LM Model and Diagram; Keynes, John Maynard; Keynesian Revolution; Lerner, Abba P.; Lucas Critique; Monetary Policy; Monetizing the (Federal) Debt; Multiplier Effect.

Fischer, Stanley

Stanley Fischer was born on 15 October 1943 at Lusaka, Northern Rhodesia (now Zambia). He went to the London School of Economics (BS 1965, MSc 1966) and then to the Massachusetts Institute of Technology (PhD 1969). After four years (1969–72) of teaching at the University of Chicago, he returned to MIT in 1973 and has stayed on there (serving as department head in 1993–4). During this time he visited Hebrew University (1972, 1976–7) and the Hoover Institute at Stanford University (1981–2). He worked at the World Bank (1988–90) as vice president and chief economist, development economics. In January 1995, he assumed deputy managing directorship at the International Monetary Fund.

He has been a fellow of the Econometric Society since 1977, a fellow of the American Academy of Arts and Sciences since 1981, a Guggenheim fellow in 1985, and associated with the National Bureau of Economic Research in various capacities, including the editorship of *NBER Macroeconomics Annual* from 1988. In 1988, he replaced James Tobin as honorary advisor to the Bank of Japan's Institute of Monetary and Economic Studies (1988–94).

In 1995, he was elected to the vice presidency of the American Economic Association.

Throughout his illustrious career, Fischer has been active in both original research and textbook writing in Keynesian macroeconomics. Of several textbooks (jointly authored with his MIT colleagues), the best known is *Macroeconomics*, co-authored with Rudiger Dornbusch (1978). He has also edited several books, including *Rational Expectations and Economic Policy* (1980). His book co-authored with Oliver Blanchard, *Lectures on Macroeconomics* (1989) is a comprehensive graduate-level survey of macroeconomic theory. He has written two extensive surveys on the state of macroeconomics (1976, with Barro; 1988).

In his original research, Fischer has maintained a steady stream of high-level articles since 1969, when he received his doctorate. In his own words, his main research interests 'are in economic growth and development, inflation and stabilization, indexation, and international macroeconomics' (*Macroeconomics*, 1994, p. v). We review his contributions to these subjects briefly below.

Since the time of his doctoral research, Fischer has been interested in the contributions that money makes to the growth process (for example, Fischer, 1972, 1979), concluding that, the more rapid the money growth, the faster the speed of capital accumulation in the transition path. Later on, particularly during his World Bank tenure, he turned to empirical aspects of economic growth and development (Fischer, 1993 and references therein).

The macroeconomic role played by long-term contracts with resultant wage stickiness in stabilizing nominal aggregate demand (in contrast to rational expectations models) attracted his analytical interest (Fischer, 1977a, 1980). This interest led him to consider wage indexation and its effects on macroeconomic stability (1977b).

Along with these studies, Fischer wrote several papers on inflation and money from the late 1970s to the 1980s, for example on the welfare cost of inflation (1978, with Modigliani) and on seigniorage (1982). He then widened his vista from national economics to international economics, especially open macroeconomics, such as the role of exchange rates (1980, with Dornbusch) and international comparison of monetary policy performances.

His interests in policy led him to study economic reforms for Eastern Europe. Since the collapse of communism in the late 1980s, he has been active writing on reform programs, suggesting prescriptions for quick transition to a market economy and emphasizing the roles of macroeconomic stabilization and market liberalization (for example, Fischer, 1992).

To sum up, Fischer has played an active part in developing New Keynesian macroeconomics. He has proved himself to be not only a superb theorist but a good empiricist and policy expert. In all these, he follows in the footsteps of the great predecessor, Keynes himself.

KAZUO SATO

See also:

Dornbusch, Rudiger; Incomes Policies; Inflation; Lucas Critique; Modigliani, Franco; Monetary Policy; Quantity Theory of Money.

Bibliography

Barro, R.J. and S. Fischer (1976), 'Recent Developments in Monetary Theory', *Journal of Monetary Economics*, **2**, (2), April, pp. 133–67.

Blanchard, O. and S. Fischer (1989), *Lectures on Macroeconomics*, Cambridge, Mass.: MIT Press.

Dornbusch, R. and S. Fischer (1994), *Macroeconomics*, 6th edn, New York: McGraw-Hill; first published 1978.

Fischer, S. (1972), 'Keynes–Wicksell and Neoclassical Models of Money and Growth', *American Economic Review*, **62**, (5), December, pp. 880–90.

Fischer, S. (1977a), 'Long-Term Contracts, Rational Expectations and the Optimal Money Supply', *Journal of Political Economy*, **85**, (1), February, pp. 191–206.

Fischer, S. (1977b), 'Wage Indexation and Macroeconomic Stability', in K. Brunner and K. Meltzer (eds), *Carnegie–Rochester Conference Series on Public Policy*, Amsterdam: North Holland.

Fischer, S. (1979), 'Capital Accumulation in the Transition Path in a Monetary Optimizing Model', *Econometrica*, **47**, (4), November, pp. 1433–9.

Fischer, S. (1980), *Rational Expectations and Economic Policy*, 2 vols, Chicago: University of Chicago Press.

Fischer, S. (1982), 'Seigniorage and the Case for a National Money', *Journal of Political Economy*, **90**, (1), April, pp. 295–313.

Fischer, S. (1988), 'Recent Developments in Macroeconomics', *Economic Journal*, **98**, (391), June, pp. 294–339.

Fischer, S. (1992), 'Stabilization and Economic Reforms in Russia', *Brookings Papers on Economic Activity*, No. 1, pp. 77–111.

Fischer, S. (1993), 'The Role of Monetary Factors in Growth', *Journal of Monetary Economics*, **32**, (3), December, pp. 485–512.

Fischer, S. and R. Dornbusch (1980), 'Exchange Rates and the Current Account', *American Economic Review*, **70**, (5), December, pp. 960–71.

Fischer, S. and F. Modigliani (1978), 'Towards an Understanding of the Real Effects and Cost of Inflation', *Weltwirtschaftliches Archiv*, **114**, (4), pp. 810–33.

Friedman, Milton

Milton Friedman was born in Brooklyn, New York on 31 July 1912, the son of Jewish immigrants from central Europe. Shortly thereafter Friedman's family moved to Rahway, New Jersey, where his parents ran a dry goods store. At Rutgers University he studied mathematics and took economics courses taught by Homer Jones and Arthur Burns. He did graduate work in economics at the University of Chicago, where he worked with Jacob Viner, Frank Knight, Henry Simons and Henry Schultz, and at Columbia, where he worked with Harold Hotelling and Wesley Mitchell. Friedman's first research involved statistical studies of consumption with the National Resources Committee in Washington from 1935 to 1937. He then went to the National Bureau of Economic Research to do a study with Simon Kuznets on the incomes of professionals. During World War II he initially worked with the Division of Tax Research in the Treasury and then with the Statistical Research Group at Columbia University, where he and W. Allen Wallis developed the statistical idea of sequential analysis to aid in the efficient testing of ordnance (Wallis, 1980). In 1946, Friedman began a teaching career at the University of Chicago that lasted until 1976.

At the University of Chicago, Friedman became a primary exponent of the Chicago School of economics, which emphasized the use of simple theoretical models to derive testable hypothesis. Its basic working hypothesis was that free markets work well to organize economic activity. At a microeconomic level, the price system allocates resources efficiently. The government does not need to intervene to defend individuals against monopoly and large concentrations of economic power, provided it allows free entry and refrains from imposing controls on prices. At a macroeconomic level, the economy is basically self-equilibrating. The government does not need to conduct countercyclical policies to offset economic instability and should concentrate on providing a stable monetary and fiscal framework.

Friedman's most important contribution to economic theory, the permanent-income hypothesis, was part of the mainstream program of macroeconomics at the time. Like other macroeconomists, he worked on giving the structural relationships in macroeconomic models a sound price-theoretic underpinning. In the permanent-income hypothesis, Friedman explained consumption as a function of wealth rather than contemporaneous income. Friedman's (1957) exposition reflected his desire to construct theories that could be contradicted by data. He used his permanent-income hypothesis to explain seemingly contradictory empirical evidence on the marginal propensity to consume coming from cross-section and time series data. Friedman (1969) also contributed significantly to monetary theory with his work on the optimum quantity of money.

In 1948, under the sponsorship of Arthur Burns, Friedman became a research associate at the NBER. Aided by Anna Schwartz, he carried on Wesley Mitchell's investigation of the interrelationship between money and the business cycle. The collaboration with Anna Schwartz ultimately led to a series of NBER monographs on monetary economics (Friedman and Schwartz, 1963a, 1970, 1982). Beginning in the early 1950s, Friedman began to challenge the prevailing Keynesian views of income determination. Specifically he used the quantity theory to attack the Keynesian income–expenditure view. Friedman and Meiselman (1963) contended that money rather than investment is more stably related to income. In a variety of papers, Friedman gave the quantity theory empirical content by arguing that money demand is a stable function of a small number of variables (Friedman, 1956). This version of the quantity theory, which was exposited also by Karl Brunner and Allan Meltzer, among others, came to be known as monetarism.

Friedman used the quantity theory to attack the prevailing Keynesian view of the price level as a non-monetary phenomenon. He summarized his views with the statement, 'Inflation is everywhere and always a monetary phenomenon' (Friedman, 1968a, p. 39). One of the earliest examples of Friedman's (1953b) use of the quantity theory is his defense of floating exchange rates as a way of avoiding the price level changes required to equilibrate trade balances under fixed exchange rates.

Friedman's most widely influential work derived from his research on the impact of monetary disturbances on cyclical fluctuations. In *A Monetary History of the United States*, Friedman and Schwartz substantially altered the standard view of the causes of the Depression. They rendered their monetary explanation convincing by showing that fluctuations in money could offer a general explanation for cyclical movements in the economy since 1867. This work also supplemented Friedman and Schwartz's (1963b) evidence on timing relationships between money and the business cycle with historical evidence indicating that money supply disturbances arose independently of money demand disturbances. Friedman (1959) used the evidence showing a 'long and variable lag' running from cyclical changes in money to cyclical changes in the economy to argue for steady growth of the money stock. He argued that, given the ignorance of economists about the structure of the economy, such a rule would work better to enhance macroeconomic stability than a policy of discretionary stabilization.

Friedman exercised significant influence on the policy debates of the 1960s and 1970s. Using the assumption of stability of money demand, he employed the behavior of money to predict successfully cyclical fluctuations and inflation. More than anyone else, he gave the business cycle its characterization in terms of stop–go monetary policy. Friedman's greatest success was his critique of the Phillips curve, an empirical relationship showing an inverse relationship between price or wage inflation and unemployment. Mainstream Keynesian economists presented this relationship as a trade-off facing the monetary policy maker who wanted to lower unemployment. Friedman (and Edmund Phelps) predicted that the true relationship was between unanticipated inflation and unemployment and that the inflation–unemployment relationship identified by Phillips would break down if the monetary authority attempted to exploit it. The stagflation of the 1970s fulfilled Friedman's prediction. Furthermore the marriage of the Friedman–Phelps expectations-augmented Phillips curve with rational expectations by Lucas and Sargent led to the New Classical macroeconomics of the 1970s.

In addition to his work as an economist, Friedman has been a tireless advocate of free markets. In *Capitalism and Freedom* (1962) and *Free to Choose* (Friedman and Friedman, 1980), along with numerous *Newsweek* columns, he criticized government intervention in the market-place and promoted free market reforms. These reforms have included the abolition of rent controls, the privatization of the education system through vouchers and a negative income tax. In order to appreciate fully the contributions of Milton Friedman, one must remember that in the 1950s and 1960s when he made his primary contributions, the intellectual environment overwhelmingly favored government intervention both to direct resource allocation in individual markets and to stabilize the aggregate economy. Friedman's challenge to economic orthodoxy and his defense of individual liberty combined individual brilliance with personal courage.

ROBERT L. HETZEL

See also:

Brunner, Karl; Cagan, Philip; Chicago School of Economics; Inflation; Lucas, Jr., Robert E.; Lucas Critique; Meltzer, Allan H.; Monetary Policy; Monetarist School of Economics; Money; New Classical School of Economics; Permanent Income Hypothesis; Quantity Theory of Money; Schwartz, Anna J.

Bibliography

Friedman, Milton (1953a), 'The Methodology of Positive Economics', in M. Friedman (ed.), *Essays in Positive Economics*, Chicago: University of Chicago Press.

Friedman, M. (1953b), 'The Case for Flexible Exchange Rates', in M. Friedman (ed.), *Essays in Positive Economics*, Chicago: University of Chicago Press.

Friedman, M. (1956), 'The Quantity Theory of Money – A Restatement', in M. Friedman (ed.), *Studies in the Quantity Theory of Money*, Chicago: University of Chicago Press.

Friedman, M. (1957), *A Theory of the Consumption Function*, Princeton: Princeton University Press.

Friedman, M. (1959), *A Program for Monetary Stability*, New York City: Fordham University Press.

Friedman, M. (1962), *Capitalism and Freedom*, Chicago: University of Chicago Press.

Friedman, M. (1968a), 'Inflation: Causes and Consequences', in M. Friedman (ed.), *Dollars and Deficits*, Englewood Cliffs, NJ: Prentice-Hall.

Friedman, M. (1968b), 'The Role of Monetary Policy', *American Economic Review*, **58**, (1), March, pp. 1–17.

Friedman, M. (1969), 'The Optimum Quantity of Money', in M. Friedman (ed.), *The Optimum Quantity of Money*, Chicago: Aldine.

Friedman, Milton and Rose Friedman (1980), *Free to Choose*, New York: Avon Books.

Friedman, Milton and David Meiselman (1963), 'The Relative Stability of Monetary Velocity and the Investment Multiplier in the United States, 1897–1958', in Commission on Money and Credit (ed.), *Stabilization Policies*, Englewood Cliffs, NJ: Prentice-Hall.

Friedman, Milton and Anna J. Schwartz (1963a), *A Monetary History of the United States, 1867–1960*, Princeton: Princeton University Press.

Friedman, Milton and Anna J. Schwartz (1963b), 'Money and Business Cycles', *Review of Economics and Statistics*, **45**, (1), February, pp. 32–64

Friedman, Milton and Anna J. Schwartz (1970), *Monetary Statistics of the United States*, New York: National Bureau of Economic Research.

Friedman, Milton and Anna J. Schwartz (1982), *Monetary Trends in the United States and the United Kingdom*, Chicago: University of Chicago Press.

Wallis, W. Allen (1980), 'The Statistical Research Group, 1942–1945', *Journal of the American Statistical Association*, **75**, (370), June, pp. 320–30.

Frisch, Ragnar

Ragnar Frisch was awarded the first Nobel Prize in economics in 1969, together with Jan Tinbergen. Frisch's contributions are numerous and span many branches of the economics discipline. The Swedish National Bank, in awarding the prize, cited Frisch's and Tinbergen's pioneering work in the application of mathematical and statistical methods to the development of dynamic models of the macro economy.

Frisch was born in Oslo, Norway on 3 March 1895. Following a long-standing family tradition, he assumed a goldsmith apprenticeship in an Oslo firm, where he worked while simultaneously pursuing undergraduate studies at the University of Oslo in economics, a course of study chosen by him because it appeared to be 'the shortest and easiest to study'. In 1919, he was awarded a BA in economics and in 1920 became a certified goldsmith. He subsequently embarked upon graduate study in economics which took him to France, the United States, Germany, Great Britain and Italy. After completing his dissertation on mathematical statistics, he was awarded a PhD in 1926 from the University of Oslo, where he had accepted a faculty appointment in 1925. While continuing to travel extensively, his base remained in Oslo for the rest of his life. He was one of the main founders of the Econometrics Society in 1931 and was chief editor of the journal, *Econometrics* until 1955. Intermittently during his career he served as economic advisor to a number of less developed countries. Frisch retired from his post of professor at the University of Oslo in 1965 and died in 1973 at the age of 78.

A major development in the economic discipline during the inter-war period was the increased use of mathematical and statistical modeling (econometrics) to analyse the economy. Frisch was a leader and pioneer in this effort to make economics a quantitative science. (It was Frisch, in fact, who coined the term 'econometrics'). That he and Tinbergen won the Nobel Prize was not only a tribute to their particular contributions, but also an indication of a general acceptance of the then new quantitative approach to economics (Samuelson, 1969).

The quantification of economic processes and their analysis by mathematical techniques is the common thread in Frisch's work throughout all of its phases. In the early phase, the 1920s, Frisch made significant contributions to the development of the traditional core of microeconomics. His work in this area, in particular on mathematical theories of consumer behavior and cost of living index numbers, proved to be highly influential and provided important foundations for subsequent research (Frisch, 1932, 1976).

Frisch is perhaps best remembered for his contributions in the 1930s to the analysis of business cycles. The object of this phase of his work was to explain the economic depression. The policy prescriptions to which his research gave rise were along what were later called Keynesian lines. Frisch, in fact, is credited with having developed many of the ideas that Keynes did, independently of him. In Frisch's classic contribution of 1933, 'Propagation Problems and Impulse Problems in Dynamic Economics', he constructed a dynamic model which simulated business cycles, a study which Kenneth Arrow called 'almost certainly the first careful study of a complete dynamic system' (Arrow, 1960 p. 180). Aggregate measures were interrelated into a system of simultaneous dynamic equations. The solution revealed the dynamics of business cycles, or the 'structural properties of the swinging system' (Frisch, 1933, p. 156). While simulation experiments with the model provided an explanation for the oscillatory nature of the economic system (the propagation mechanism), they also pointed to a tendency for damping: that is, the cycles tended to collapse. This finding conflicted with the undamped cycles which Frisch observed in reality. The explanation of what maintained the swings and caused persistent business cycles was the 'impulse problem'. Frisch believed that the energy necessary to maintain the swings was produced by erratic and random shocks, often endogenously generated by business cycles themselves. These would shift the value of one or more of the parameters in the model, producing disturbances in economic relations that would keep fluctuations alive.

Frisch's macrodynamic model gave rise to countercyclical policy prescriptions similar to policies advocated by Keynes. Frisch believed that, on the basis of the explanation of oscillations provided by the model, policy makers could apply countercyclical policy with a fairly high degree of precision. A study of the model's solution would indicate the relative strengths of various economic variables and their importance in producing fluctuations. Policy could then be applied to influence those variables in such a way as to steer the economy in the desired direction.

In the context of business cycle research in the 1930s, Frisch's approach was at odds with the institutionalist approach of, for example, Wesley C. Mitchell as well as with the theoretical approach employed by, for example, Keynes and Robertson. Unlike either, Frisch produced a model which simulated business cycles by means of equations. His work on business cycles in the 1930s was pathbreaking.

The development of econometric techniques is a third area in which Frisch is recognized for having made extremely valuable contributions. Several of his numerous published works in this area represented significant advances in the application of statistical techniques to economic data. His analyses of what later came to be known as the problems of identification and of multicollinearity were pioneering. Confluence analysis developed in Frisch (1934) was the first general theoretical treatment of econometric problems.

During World War II, Frisch was imprisoned in a Nazi concentration camp. After his release Frisch's research focused primarily on the development of macroeconomic planning models. This shift in focus was based upon Frisch's perception of a need to construct alternative systems that would not produce economic fluctuations such as occurred in the 1930s. A collection of some of his work in this area is contained in *Economic Planning Studies* (1976). The planning models and techniques developed by Frisch had a pervasive influence on later research in this area and also on economic policy. Believing his planning models to be particularly applicable to the problems of developing nations, he devoted much of his career after the war to serving as economic consultant in those nations, including India and Egypt.

LORETTA S. WILSON

See also:

Business Cycle Theory (I) and (II); Econometric Models, Macroeconomic; Haavelmo, Trygve; Schumpeter, Joseph A.

Bibliography

Andvig, Jens Christopher (1988), 'From Macrodynamics to Macroeconomic Planning, A Basic Shift in Ragnar Frisch's Thinking?', *European Economic Review*, **32**, (2/3), March, pp. 495–502.

Arrow, Kenneth J. (1960), 'The Work of Ragnar Frisch, Econometrician', *Econometrica*, **28**, (2), April, pp. 175–92.

Frisch, Ragnar (1932), *New Methods of Measuring Marginal Utility*, Tübingen: Verlag van J.C.B. Mohr.

Frisch, Ragnar (1933), 'Propagation Problems and Impulse Problems in Dynamic Economics', *Essays in Honour of Gustav Cassel*, London: Allen & Unwin, pp. 171–205; reprinted in Robert A. Gordon and Lawrence R. Klein (eds) (1965), *Readings in Business Cycles*, Homewood, Ill.: Irwin.

Frisch, Ragnar (1934), *Statistical Confluence Analysis by Means of Complete Regression Systems*, Oslo: University Institute of Economics.

Frisch, Ragnar (1936), 'Annual Survey of General Economic Theory: The Problem of Index Numbers', *Econometrica*, **4**, (1), January, 1–38.

Frisch, Ragnar (1976), *Economic Planning Studies: A Collection of Essays*, ed. Frank Long, Dordrecht: D. Reidel.

Samuelson, Paul A. (1969), 'On Two Remarkable Men', *Newsweek*, 17 November, p. 108.

Full Employment Budget

The major economic events of the 1930s, the Great Depression and the Keynesian Revolution, necessitated the federal government's commitment to economic stability. The Employment Act of 1946 made the executive branch of the federal government responsible for maintaining economic stability through monetary and fiscal policy. To assist the President in formulating appropriate programs and policies to carry out the mandates of the Employment Act so that the 'maximum levels of production, employment and purchasing power rise through time' (Heller, 1967, p. 64) the act established the Council of Economic Advisors (CEA). The CEA, which is made up of a group of economists hand picked by the President, educates the President, Congress and the public on economic matters, defends the economic policy of the federal government and prepares *The Economic Report of the President*. The idea of the full employment budget was first used officially by President Kennedy's Council of Economic Advisors in *The Economic Report of the President, 1962*. The late Professor Walter W. Heller, Professor of Economics at the University of Minnesota and Chairman of the Council of Economic Advisors under Presidents John F. Kennedy and Lyndon B. Johnson, and his colleagues on the Council were the first group of economists that officially adopted the full employment budget surplus (or deficit) as their fiscal gauge.

The idea of the full employment budget (also known as the high employment budget, or structural budget) originated with Beardsley Ruml in 1943. In a nationwide radio broadcast, Ruml pointed out the merits of tax policy, as compared with expenditure policy, as a means of stimulating the economy. In his speech, he outlined a position that was later adopted by the Committee on Economic Development (CED) and others in the 1940s:

> Our first goal is to get as much production and create as many jobs as we can. The best way we know of doing this is to keep private business as active as possible. Government policies should foster and encourage this at all times. But whenever private activity slackens, because of the business outlook, the policies of government should replace the purchasing power which has declined because of the falling off of private business. Thus government supports private activity and compensates for any falling below the high employment and production that we want. For this reason, such a policy is sometimes referred to as a 'compensatory' fiscal policy. (Stein, 1969, pp. 184–5)

Full employment budget refers to what the size of the government's surplus (or deficit) would be with the existing spending programs (government purchases of goods and services and transfer payments) and tax rates, if the economy were at full employment (the natural rate of unemployment). Full employment budget, then, is full employment government receipts (that is, the receipts that would be obtained with present tax rates if the economy were at the natural rate of unemployment) minus full employment government expenditures (that is, actual expenditures less expenditures directly associated with unemployment in excess of the natural rate of unemployment).

The full employment budget can specify whether a particular surplus (or deficit) in the budget stems from an active fiscal policy. According to Walter Heller, the full employment budget does not measure the actual budget surplus (or deficit) in any particular year; rather, it is a measure of the surplus (or deficit) that would prevail if the economy were actually operating at the natural rate of unemployment (the level of GNP associated with a 4 per cent rate of unemployment in the early 1960s). The full employment budget will give a much clearer indication of the active fiscal influence of a particular budget. A deficit in the full employment budget is a definite indication that the budget is expansionary (inflationary). Measuring the full employment surplus (or deficit) requires, first, estimating the economy's potential output (GDP at the natural rate of unemployment) and, second, determining the amount of revenue the federal tax rate structure will generate at the economy's potential output as well as the amount of expenditures forthcoming. 'The basic rationale for this budget concept is that the true inflationary or deflationary potential of any proposed federal budget is apparent only when the economy is at its full employment' (Peterson and Estenson, 1992).

Because the government's budget is guided by automatic stabilizers towards deficit during declining real GDP (due to falling tax revenues and rising transfer payments) and towards surplus during prosperity (due to larger tax collections and declining transfer payments), the state of the budget cannot be taken as a measure of the way fiscal policy has changed. For example, the deficits of 1931 to 1933 did not mean that President Herbert Hoover and his successor President Franklin Roosevelt were following a stimulative fiscal policy; the deficits persisted through the Depression because of the declining economy. To restore business confidence and to speed up economic recovery, Hoover sought to balance the budget. In 1932, he recommended fiscal restraints. The result was one of the largest peacetime tax increases in US history (Brown, 1956). The decrease in full employment deficit from $4 billion to a surplus of $2 billion from 1931 to 1933 is blamed for the deepening of the Great Depression.

In order to determine whether fiscal policy is moving in a stimulative or restrictive direction, economists divide the government's deficit into two components:

1. The part of the deficit that is attributable to cyclical downturns in the economy. As the economy moves into recession, tax receipts are automatically depressed while transfer payments are increased, and the deficit is thereby pushed up. This part of the deficit is called the *cyclical component*.
2. The part of the deficit that would occur even if there were no business cycles and the economy were always at its natural rate of unemployment.

This deficit is due to the structure of the tax and the government's spending programs. This part of the deficit is known as the *structural deficit*, the *full employment deficit* or the *cyclically adjusted deficit*.

The Bureau of Economic Analysis of the Department of Commerce has constructed a series of full employment budget surpluses and deficits for the US economy since 1955 (see Table 1). For that purpose, the initial natural rate of unemployment was set at 4 per cent, but that figure was subsequently raised to 5.1 per cent unemployment in 1983 and 1984 (Eisner, 1987, pp. 95–110). The full employment budget provides a measure of what is happening to fiscal policy because it changes only in response to changes in tax rates and spending programs and not in response to business cycles. Specifically, when the full employment budget is moving towards a larger deficit (or smaller surplus), fiscal policy is stimulative. Tax rates are being cut or government transfer payments are rising. When the full employment budget is moving towards a larger surplus (or smaller deficit), fiscal policy is restrictive. Movements in the full employment budget can be used to identify some important changes in fiscal policy.

Table 1   Actual and high employment federal budget surpluses and deficits, 1955–84 (billions of dollars)

Year	Actual	High	Year	Actual	High
1955	4.4	5.2	1970	−12.4	−4.6
1956	6.1	7.9	1971	−22.0	−11.3
1957	2.3	6.1	1972	−16.8	−12.1
1958	−10.3	0.0	1973	−5.5	−9.5
1959	−1.1	5.4	1974	−11.5	−0.3
1960	3.0	12.1	1975	−69.3	−29.1
1961	−3.9	7.1	1976	−53.1	−17.4
1962	−4.2	3.0	1977	−45.9	−20.4
1963	0.3	7.4	1978	−29.5	−15.9
1964	−3.3	1.1	1979	−16.1	−2.0
1965	0.5	0.9	1980	−61.2	−17.1
1966	−1.8	−5.6	1981	−64.3	−3.2
1967	−13.2	−15.1	1982	−148.2	−32.6
1968	−6.0	−11.0	1983	−178.6	−57.0
1969	8.4	4.9	1984	−175.8	−91.8

Source: Robert Eisner, 'Will the Real Federal Deficit Stand UP?', in Ben Bernanke (ed.), *Readings and Cases in Macroeconomics*, New York: McGraw-Hill, 1987, p. 100.

The decline of the surplus in the full employment budget in 1964 reflects the expansionary tax cut of that year. On the other hand, the full employment budget shows a swing from deficit to surplus in 1968–9 as a result of the policies designed to reduce inflationary pressure of high employment and increased military expenditures of 1965–6. The 1968 tax increase and restraints on government spending proved to be too little too late. When President Richard Nixon took office in 1969, he inherited high inflation and low unemployment (the unemployment rate was 3.4 per cent). In 1975, the full employment budget moved sharply into deficit as a result of the tax cut and increase in government spending designed to lift the economy out of the recession of 1973–5. The almost continuous deficit in the full employment budget since 1960 suggests that expansionary fiscal policy has been more prevalent than contractionary policy.

ALI R. MOSHTAGH

See also:

Currie, Lauchlin; Demand Management; Employment Act of 1946; Fiscal Policy; Hansen, Alvin H.; Heller, Walter W.; Keyserling, Leon; Monetary Policy; Okun, Arthur M.; Stein, Herbert.

Bibliography
Brown, Edgar Cary (1956), 'Fiscal Policy in the Thirties: A Reappraisal', *American Economic Review*, **46**, (5), December, pp. 857–79.
Eisner, Robert (1987), 'Will the Real Federal Deficit Stand Up?', in Ben Bernanke (ed.), *Readings and Cases in Macroeconomics*, New York: McGraw-Hill.
Heller, Walter W. (1967), *New Dimensions of Political Economy*, New York: W.W. Norton.
Peterson, Wallace C. and Paul S. Estenson (1992), *Income, Employment, Economic Growth*, 7th edn, New York: W.W. Norton.
Stein, Herbert (1969), *The Fiscal Revolution in America*, Chicago: University of Chicago Press.

Functional Finance

Functional finance is the name Abba Lerner gave to the theory of financing government according to the following three rules (Lerner, 1941):

1. The government shall maintain a reasonable level of demand at all times. If there is not enough spending and thus there is excessive unemployment, the government shall reduce taxes or increase its own spending. If there is too much spending the government shall prevent inflation by reducing its own expenditures or by increasing taxes.
2. By borrowing money when it wishes to raise the rate of interest and by lending money or repaying debt when it wishes to lower the rate of interest, the government shall maintain that rate of interest which induces the optimum amount of investment.

3. If either of the first two rules conflicts with the principles of 'sound finance' or of balancing the budget or of limiting the national debt, so much the worse for these principles. The government press shall print any money that may be needed in carrying out these rules.

Lerner's purpose in proposing these rules of functional finance was to change the focus of thinking about government finance from sound finance principles that made sense for individuals – such as balancing the budget – to sound finance principles that made sense for the aggregate economy in which government spending and taxing decisions had consequences on the level of economic activity. Because the secondary effects of spending decisions and savings decisions had to be taken into account in the aggregate economy, the two kinds of decisions were different. To those sound finance principles for the aggregate economy he gave the name 'functional finance'. In introducing functional finance his goal was to get economists to focus on the *consequences* of government financing, not on the then generally accepted, but little thought about, rules of sound finance and the quantity theory of money.

Lerner's stark presentation of these rules of functional finance caused much stir in the 1940s and 1950s when most Keynesians, including Keynes, were politically more circumspect about the implications of Keynesian ideas for policy. Thus, when Lerner first proposed these rules, and elaborated on them in his famous *Economics of Control* (1944), many Keynesians of the time, including Keynes, recoiled from them. This reaction led Lerner into many debates with Keynesians as well as with non-Keynesians. He won many of these debates, and Keynes, after his initial reaction to Lerner's presentation, later wrote him a letter telling him:

> It is a grand book worthy of one's hopes for you. A most powerful piece of well organized analysis with high aesthetic qualities, though written more perhaps than you see yourself for the cognoscenti in the temple and not for those at the gate.... I shall have to try when I get back to hold a seminar of the heads of the Treasury on Functional Finance. (Keynes, 1944)

These debates made the concept of functional finance well known and in the 1950s and 1960s Lerner's functional finance rules became the basis of most textbook presentations of Keynesian economics.

Some of the reaction to functional finance was less to the rules per se than to the way they were interpreted. The initial interpretation of the rules of functional finance was that an approximately 3 per cent unemployment rate should be the target rate of unemployment and that inflation would only become a problem at lower rates of unemployment. At levels of unemployment below 3 per cent, the deficit could be forgotten entirely. If unemployment were above 3 per cent, the government should increase spending or lower taxes; if unemployment were below 3 per cent, the government should increase taxes or lower spending. So, too, with the interest rate: if unemployment were above 3 per cent, the government should lower interest rates by increasing the money supply. If unemployment were below 3 per cent, the government should raise the interest rate by decreasing the money supply.

It is important to note that the initial interpretation is not inherent in the functional finance rules. Depending on how they are interpreted, the rules of functional finance can be compatible with many different types of government spending rules. Rule 1 does not state what is meant by excessive unemployment. Nor does it state what to do if one cannot achieve both a zero level of inflation and the desired rate of unemployment. As they were interpreted, however, the rules became synonymous with significant deficit spending. Functional finance was seen as having an expansionary and inflationary bias. As modern Keynesians gave up their belief that they could specify the desired inflation and unemployment rates independently of the actual functioning of the economy, they gave up the functional finance policy prescription; and in the 1990s the rules of functional finance are little discussed. That is unfortunate because there is still much sense in the rules. They lead to the policy questions of why a 3 per cent unemployment rate is inconsistent with a stable price level, and whether institutions could be changed to make them consistent.

By the 1970s Lerner, the originator of the rules, had recognized the inconsistency and had started work on designing some type of institutional control of inflation which would make them consistent. This work culminated in his proposal for MAP: a Market Anti-Inflation Plan (Lerner and Colander, 1980), under which property rights in prices were created and individuals were required to trade rights to raise prices. Anyone wanting to raise their price had to buy the right from someone willing to lower their price by an offsetting amount. Were functional finance still taken seriously, there would be much more current work on such institutional policies to control inflation than there is.

To many modern Keynesians who have essentially adopted a unique equilibrium interpretation of the aggregate economy, the rules of functional finance seem quaint, but they are consistent with some of the multiple equilibria interpretations of Keynesian economics that have ben put forward by some New Keynesians. As introducing policies to prevent inflation has become seen, by Keynesians as well as Classicals, as politically impossible, we observe Keynesian policies being discarded and replaced by calls for balanced budgets. In practice, however, few countries have been willing to accept the consequences of running balanced budgets and most discussions of fiscal policy are now conducted in reference to what percentage of GDP the deficit is. Thus, in a way, functional finance is the finance method that is currently being used, under different assumptions about what is achievable than early Keynesians had.

DAVID COLANDER

See also:
Ackley, Hugh Gardner; Currie, Lauchlin; Hansen, Alvin H.; Keynes, John Maynard; Keynesian Revolution; Keynesianism in America; Lerner, Abba P.; Meade, James E.; Multiplier Effect; Neoclassical Synthesis (Bastard Keynesianism); Samuelson, Paul A.; Tarshis, Lorie; Tobin, James.

Bibliography
Keynes, John Maynard (1944), personal correspondence to Abba Lerner 27 September.
Lerner, Abba (1941), 'The Economic Steering Wheel', *The University Review*, June.
Lerner, Abba (1943), 'Functional Finance and the Federal Debt', *Social Research*, **10**, (1), February, pp. 38–52.
Lerner, Abba (1944), *The Economics of Control*, New York: Macmillan.
Lerner, Abba and David Colander (1980), *MAP: A Market Anti-Inflation Plan*, New York: Harcourt Brace Jovanovich.

Galbraith, John K.

John Kenneth Galbraith was born on 15 October 1908 to William Archibald and Catherine Kendall Galbraith, a farming family of Scottish ancestry, in southwestern Ontario, Canada. He accompanied his father to political rallies and once described him as 'the leading Liberal of the community' in *The Scotch* (1964), an autobiographical account of Scottish life in that Ontario community. Galbraith's agrarian and puritanical background is reflected later in his prolific writings.

Upon graduation from Dunnon High School, Galbraith pursued animal husbandry at the Ontario Agricultural College, now the University of Guelph. In 1931, he received a BS degree and emigrated to the United States. He obtained his MS and PhD degrees in agricultural economics from the University of California at Berkeley in 1933 and 1934, respectively. In 1937, Galbraith married Catherine Atwater and became a United States citizen. Galbraith then began his long but frequently interrupted tenure at Harvard University. From 1934 to 1939, he was an instructor and tutor. In 1939, he became an assistant professor of economics at Princeton University, after which he entered public service. He worked with the Department of Agriculture during the New Deal and in the Office of Price Administration and Civilian Supply during World War II. His monograph, *A Theory of Price Control* (1952), was the nucleus for his major works.

In 1949, Galbraith returned to Harvard as Paul M. Warburg Professor of Economics and is now emeritus professor. At Harvard he wrote his major intellectual contributions to economic theory, *The Affluent Society* (1958), *The New Industrial State* (1967) and *Economics and the Public Purpose* (1973). He is one of the world's most widely read economists whose celebrity is attributable to his achievements as an author, advisor, public servant, diplomat and social critic. His writings attack the neoclassical system which omits the role of power in economic life. He argues that it is incompatible with the real world.

In *The Affluent Society*, Galbraith questioned the American obsession with higher consumption and production which are propelled by powerful vested interest and mass media advertising. This phenomenon not only increases the risk of inflation and recession as consumers overextend themselves but also neglects the provision of public goods and services which enhances the quality of life. Galbraith advised Americans in a Veblenian way to forgo conspicuous consumption, reject insatiability of wants and opt for environ-mental quality, decent housing, better education and support for the arts. The 'more is better' mentality inhibits economic progress. The author contends: 'The first task is to see the way our economic attitudes are rooted in the poverty, inequality and economic peril of the past.... We face here the greatest of vested interests, those of the mind.' Most literary critics praised Galbraith's *Affluent Society*, which is translated into several languages, for illuminating economics to lay people.

In *The New Industrial State*, Galbraith continued his onslaught on neoclassical economics by analysing the role of power in economic life. The market system of consumer sovereignty has spawned the planning system of producer sovereignty with massive wealth and power. 'One aspect of the relationships between the factors of production has, however, been less examined. That is why power is associated with some factors and not with others.' The 1000 largest industrial firms, especially the three automakers, produce a larger share of the gross domestic product than the remaining 12 million firms combined. The giant corporations' interest is to expand power in economic, political, social and cultural life through conscious manipulations. This dependence effect, in turn, negates conventional price theory that consumer demand is an autonomous phenomenon.

Apart from the planning system, the technostructure of technical and managerial experts makes decisions in order to control output and maximize corporate growth and prestige. The technostructure has other goals of job satisfaction and security. It is able to impose these goals on the giant corporations and on society through the 'principle of consistency'. Both entities benefit from state expenditures which perpetuate the status quo. For example, the munitions industry has a vested interest in an aggressive foreign policy. Corporations enjoy monopoly power by restricting output and charging higher prices above the competitive norm, thereby violating the efficiency criterion. The technostructure retains its virtuosity by serving society. Galbraith notes:

> A curiosity of modern life is the role of change. The economic system of the United States is praised on all occasions of public ceremony as a largely perfect structure. This is so elsewhere also. It is not easy to perfect what has been perfected. This is massive change, but, except as the output of goods increases, all remains as before. (1967, p. 13)

The planning system transcends the market system and rivals the power of the state. Consequently Galbraith advocates price and wage controls as a stabilization tool to neutralize the planning system. He also acknowledges the recent trends in corporate development as antithetical to his model.

In *Economics and the Public Purpose*, Galbraith again elaborated on the theme of power by noting the symbiosis between corporations and government agencies. Neoclassical microeconomics fails to explain this phenomenon under the 'imagery of choice'. It is inimical to the public interest since the 'whole deployment of power – over prices, costs, consumers, supplies, the government' – is what really counts. Under a 'new socialism', however, the public ownership of key sectors in the economy would weaken corporate power and technostructure elitism and strengthen the public purpose. Galbraith also called upon fellow economists to end the gadgetry of disguise and examine the uneven development in the American economy which spills into the realm of political economy. He argues that economists make the mistake of 'trying to place all problems within the framework of the market and all behavior subordinate to market command'. In doing so they fail to see the gestalt of integrating economy with society, polity and culture.

In addition to his major trilogy, Galbraith has written *American Capitalism: the Concept of Countervailing Power; The Great Crash; Economic Development; Money: Whence It Came, Where It Went; The Liberal Hour; How to Get Out of Vietnam; Ambassador's Journal; A Life in Our Times; The McLandress Dimension; The Triumph; A Tenured Professor; Indian Painting; The Anatomy of Power and Economics in Perspective: A Critical History.* He also hosted the BBC series on *The Age of Uncertainty*, was a confidant of presidents, particularly John F. Kennedy, and was president of the American Economic Association.

Unquestionably John Kenneth Galbraith is an intellectual giant who has elucidated the social imbalance in the American economy and the failure of neoclassical orthodoxy. His legacy is yet to be fully assessed and synthesized considering the plethora of contemporary problems with Galbraithian overtones.

ASHTON I. VERAMALLAY

See also:

Business Cycle Theory (I) and (II); Demand Management; Depression, The Great; Government Investment Programs (The Socialization of Investment); Incomes Policies; Keynesianism in America.

Bibliography

Bowles, Samuel, R. Edwards and W.G. Shepherd (1989), *Unconventional Wisdom*, Boston Mass.: Houghton Mifflin.
Eggenberger, David (ed.) (1987), *Encyclopedia of World Biography*, Palatine, Ill.: Jack Heraty & Associates.
Europa Publications (1995), *The International Who's Who 1995–96*, London.
Galbraith, John K. (1952), *A Theory of Price Control*, Cambridge, Mass.: Harvard University Press.
Galbraith, John K. (1958), *The Affluent Society*, Boston, Mass.: Houghton Mifflin.
Galbraith, John K. (1964), *The Scotch*, 2nd edn, Boston: Houghton Mifflin.
Galbraith, John K. (1967), *The New Industrial State*, Boston, Mass.: Houghton Mifflin.
Galbraith, John K. (1973), *Economics and the Public Purpose*, Boston, Mass.: Houghton Mifflin.
Galbraith, John K. (1977), *The Age of Uncertainty*, Boston, Mass.: Houghton Mifflin.
Galbraith, John K. (1981), *A Life in Our Times: Memoirs*, Boston, Mass.: Houghton Mifflin.

Moritz, Charles (ed.) (1975), *Current Biography Yearbook*, New York: The H.H. Wilson Company.
Reisman, David A. (1980), *Galbraith and Market Capitalism*, New York: New York University Press.

Gesell, Silvio

Silvio Gesell (1862–1930) was described by John Maynard Keynes (1936, pp. 353–4) as 'a successful German merchant in Buenos Aires who was led to the study of monetary problems by the crisis of the late eighties, which was especially violent in the Argentine'. Gesell's explorations of economic crises led him eventually to become a 'monetary doctor' with a comparatively small but fervent band of followers on both sides of the Atlantic, probably numbering in the thousands. Frequently dismissed by many as no more than a money 'crank', he was rescued from obscurity by the serious attention that Keynes devotes to his ideas and influence in Chapter 23 of *The General Theory*. In fact, Keynes's *General Theory* is the major English-language source of biographical information about Gesell.

Keynes himself could be classified legitimately as a Gesellist, on the basis of *The General Theory*, both in terms of his sense of the monetary origins of economic flux and in terms of his political philosophy vis-à-vis the relationship between state and economy (Darity, 1995). But earlier Keynes, too, had 'treated [Gesell's] profoundly original strivings as being no better than those of a crank' (Keynes, 1936 p. 353). It was not until later, when, according to Keynes (1936, p. 353), he had come to a similar position 'in his own way' that he recognized the importance of Gesell's contributions.

Gesell's works were first published in German, even those published in Argentina. Those published in Argentina included *Die Reformation in Munzwesen als Brücke zum socialen Staat* (1891), a study of the causes of the economic crisis in Argentina in the late 1880s, *Nervus rerum* (1891), Gesell's treatise on money, and several additional books and pamphlets on monetary reform. In 1906, having attained sufficient wealth in Argentina, Gesell went into retirement in Switzerland. In Keynes's words (1936, p. 354), Gesell was then 'able to devote the last decades of his life to the two most delightful occupations open to those who do not have to earn their living, authorship and experimental farming'.

His most significant work, the two-volume study entitled *The Natural Economic Order* in its English translation (translation by Philip Pye), was first published in Switzerland in German, volume one in 1906 and volume two in 1911. During 1919, Gesell served briefly as Minister of Finance in Bavaria's Soviet cabinet. Thereafter he was subjected to court-martial proceedings but did not suffer any permanent adversity as a result. The remainder of his life was given over to the promotion of his economic and political philosophy, by encouraging his followers and by promoting the development of organizations devoted to the dissemination and implementation of his ideas.

The English language translation of *The Natural Economic Order* was published in San Antonio, Texas by the Free Economy Publishing Company, an instrument of the core of Gesell's followers based in that city. The Free Economy Publishing Company also issued a newsprint periodical called *The Way Out* (presumably the 'way out' of economic crisis), which included articles celebrating Gesell's greatness as well as pieces that extolled his ideas, especially the stamped currency scheme, which so intrigued Keynes. In fact, one of Gesell's most committed followers, Hugo R. Fack (1931), set out in the pages of *The Way Out* actual steps to be followed in the United States to introduce stamped currency.

For Gesell the critical barrier to continuous full employment in a capitalist economy was the money/interest system: the tendency of individuals to hold their wealth in the form of money lent at interest inhibits their inclination to engage directly in productive investments. Moreover, in an environment where loan rates were perceived to be excessively low, they could hold onto their money, waiting for rates to rise, thereby denying the economy even an indirect stimulus to productive investment. Gesell's solution was a reform of the money/interest system that would decrease the tendency of individuals to hold their wealth as money. Gesell's money stamping scheme would impose a direct cost on money holders for refusing to part with money. Holders of currency would have to have their bills stamped at regular intervals at a fee to maintain its status as legal tender (see Dillard, 1942a).

Keynes found this idea to be especially interesting because a stamped money scheme would impose a carrying cost on money that would offset its liquidity premium and reduce the lure of holding it. However, Keynes argued (1936, p. 358), Gesell did not conceptualize liquidity-preference doctrine. Therefore Gesell failed to recognize 'that money was not unique in having a liquidity-premium attached to it, but differed only in degree from many other articles, deriving its importance from having a *greater* liquidity-premium than any other article'. To put a stamp on currency simply would mean that 'a long series of substitutes [would] step into [its] shoes – bank money, debts at call, foreign money, jewelry, and the precious metals generally'.

Despite Keynes's ultimate rejection of the stamped money scheme – Keynes preferred the state to be responsible for management of aggregate effective demand – he viewed Gesell as being squarely on the right track. And, in terms of social philosophy, Keynes found an authentic soulmate in Gesell. Both embraced a perspective that Gesell called 'anti-Marxian socialism' and Keynes called 'liberal socialism'. They shared in a philosophical tradition that reaches back to the nineteenth-century French libertarian socialist Pierre-Joseph Proudhon (see Dillard, 1942b; Darity, 1995). Both Gesell and Keynes opposed nationalization of industry and central planning (although Gesell did advocate nationalization of land in conjunction with stamped currency to prevent a flight to land as an alternative to a flight to money). Both were dissatisfied with capitalism on grounds of maldistribution of income and the waste of unemployment, and both rejected 'communism' as an alternative on grounds of destruction of individual liberties; Gesell and Keynes were champions of the 'middle way'. Both sought to reconcile individualism with the need for state action to maintain economic prosperity. And both saw the extension of prosperity – rather than social revolution – as the best avenue towards the end of capitalism and its attendant social ills.

WILLIAM DARITY, JR.

See also:
Liquidity Trap; Monetary Policy; Money; Real Balance Effect.

Bibliography
Darity, William Jr. (1995), 'Keynes' Political Philosophy: The Gesell Connection', *Eastern Economic Journal*, **21**, (1), Winter, pp. 27–41.
Dillard, Dudley (1942a), 'Gesell's Monetary Theory of Social Reform', *American Economic Review*, **32**, (2), June, pp. 348–52.
Dillard, Dudley (1942b), 'Keynes and Proudhon', *The Journal of Economic History*, **2**, (1), May, pp. 63–76.
Fack, Hugo R. (1931), 'The Age Old Secret of Money Power Revealed', *The Way Out*, December, pp. 7–10.
Gesell, Silvio (1934), *The Natural Economic Order: Money Part*, San Antonio: Free Economy Publishing Company.
Gesell, Silvio (1936), *The Natural Economic Order: Land Part*, San Antonio: Free Economy Publishing Company.
Keynes, John Maynard (1936), *The General Theory of Employment, Interest and Money*, London: Macmillan.

Government Investment Programs (the Socialization of Investment)

In the last chapter of *The General Theory* Keynes said that the 'outstanding fault of the economic society in which we live are its failure to provide for full employment and its arbitrary and inequitable distribution of wealth and incomes' (Keynes, 1936, p. 372). These problems were linked by the classical theory of the rate of interest that justified high interest rates as needed to generate savings for investment: high interest rates contributed to significant inequalities in fortunes accumulated by the rentier class and reduced investment below full employment levels. However, were interest rates low, it would be possible 'to increase the stock of capital up to a point where its marginal efficiency had fallen to a very low figure', so that 'capital instruments would cost almost nothing' (ibid., p. 375). Depriving capital of its scarcity value 'would mean the euthanasia of the rentier' or 'functionless investor' (ibid.) and would also imply a responsibility for the state to formulate policy regarding what inducements to investment and influence upon the propensity to consume were necessary to achieve a rate of accumulation sufficient for full employment. Keynes adds,

> it seems unlikely that the influence of banking policy on the rate of interest will be sufficient by itself to determine the optimum rate of investment. I conceive, therefore, that a somewhat comprehensive socialisation of investment will prove the only means of securing an approximation to full employment. (Ibid., p. 378).

This involved neither 'state socialism' nor state ownership of the means of production. Indeed, 'apart from the necessity of central controls to bring about an adjustment between the propensity to consume and the inducement to invest, there is no more reason to socialise economic life than there was before' (ibid., p. 379) – efficiency, freedom and private initiative being the likely casualties of attempting to do so.

Keynes's long-term economic policy thus focused on the state 'taking an ever greater responsibility for directly organising investment' (ibid., p. 164). In his wartime Treasury memoranda of 1943–4 concerning postwar economic adjustment he was more specific about the extent of this responsibility:

> If two-thirds or three-quarters of total investment is carried out or can be influenced by public or semi-public bodies, a long-term programme of a stable character should be capable of reducing the potential range of fluctuation to much narrower limits than formerly, when a smaller volume of investment was under public control and when even this part tended to follow, rather than correct, fluctuations of investment in the strictly private sector of the economy. (1973–89, XXVII, p. 322)

Thus Keynes allowed that the state could carry out programs of public investment itself, and/or encourage such programs being developed by organizations independent of the state but which still possessed some public character. There are two ways in which he apparently understood the latter, both deriving from views Keynes expressed much earlier in 'The End of Laissez-Faire' (1926).

On the one hand, Keynes emphasized the importance of a variety of 'semi-autonomous bodies within the state':

> I believe that in many cases the ideal size for the unit of control and organisation lies somewhere between the individual and modern state. I suggest, therefore, that progress lies in the growth and recognition of semi-autonomous bodies within the

State – bodies whose criterion of action within their own field is solely the public good as they understand it, and from whose deliberations motives of private advantage are excluded. (1973–89, IX, p. 288).

As examples Keynes cited 'the universities, the Bank of England, the Port of London Authority, even perhaps the railways companies', and suggested that these institutions were rooted in an ancient English tradition that regarded such bodies as 'a mode of government' (ibid., p. 289). On this view, then, 'semi-public bodies' were public-spirited in concerning themselves with the public good (rather than shareholder interests), but still not part of the state proper. They might be thought part of an extended state, as compared to the nuclear state made up of Parliament, the Cabinet, the civil service and the judiciary (Jensen, 1994).

On the other hand, Keynes also though that 'joint stock institutions', which had traditionally made shareholder interests primary, tended to undergo an evolution in nature when they increased in size over time:

> when they have reached a certain age and size, [they] approximate to the status of public corporations rather than that of individualistic enterprise. One of the most interesting and unnoticed developments of recent decades has been the tendency of big enterprise to socialise itself. A point arrives in the growth of a big institution ... at which the owners of the capital, i.e. the shareholders, are almost entirely dissociated from the management, with the result that the direct personal interest of the latter in the making of great profit becomes quite secondary. When this stage is reached, the general stability and reputation of the institution are more considered by the management than the maximum of profit for the shareholders. (Keynes, 1973–89, IX, p. 289)

While such 'joint stock institutions' would still typically be involved in forms of production less public in character than that carried out by Keynes's 'semi-autonomous bodies within the [extended] State', the separation of management and ownership allowed for greater retained earnings and thus potentially higher levels of investment. The state might then well anticipate some success in designing inducements to investment for organizations of this sort, as compared to the more traditional owner-managed firms that predominated in the nineteenth century.

Given these different strategies for carrying out and/or influencing investment, a further issue for Keynes was how the state might coordinate and guide investment across its own agencies, the 'semi-autonomous bodies with the [extended] State' and manager-operated 'joint stock institutions'. In 1939, he wrote that 'we need, if we are to enjoy prosperity and profits, ... much more central planning than we have at present' (1973–89, XXI, p. 492) and recommended creating a National Investment Board to assist in this purpose. Keynes, however, did not indicate clearly what proportions of public investment, semi-public investment and private investment he thought might be desirable. Presumably the point of having a National Investment Board was to determine what these shares ought to be on the basis of economic conditions.

An important philosophical theme in Keynes's thinking on these matters concerns the ethical goals underlying policy recommendation. Keynes was critical of utilitarian thinking from the time when he studied G.E. Moore's ethics as an undergraduate, and in a number of his early Apostles papers he discussed the ethical conflict between the goals of being good and doing good. In his post-*General Theory* 'My Early Beliefs' memoir, however, he defended rules and conventions – 'the extraordinary accomplishment of our predecessors in the ordering of life' (1973–89, X, p. 448) – as normatively valuable, because they helped individuals reconcile being good and doing good. Rules and conventions, moreover, were embodied in institutions in Keynes's view, and long-term economic policy could not but be concerned with the development of institutions (Davis, 1994). Thus we may infer that Keynes supported a socialization of investment, not just because he thought it would lead to higher levels of employment and reduce inequitable distributions of income and wealth, but also because he expected it would enable individuals increasingly to reconcile the twin moral requirements of being good and doing good. This theme is most prominent in his references to public-spiritedness in the 'semi-autonomous bodies within the [extended] State' and to the socializing of big enterprise. Essentially Keynes sought a closer blending of private and public purpose – a closer connection between being good and doing good, which should also be thought part and parcel of Keynes's liberal vision. Neither a state-commanded economy nor one driven by narrow self-interest was healthy either economically or ethically.

The socialization of investment summarized for Keynes a range of long-term policies meant to improve the functioning of the economy and raise the well-being of individuals in society generally. A first step involved the 'euthanasia of the rentier', and thus a shift in the balance of class power. A second step involved programs to enhance investment, including public investment, inducements for private investment and institutional change that would have an impact on investment decision-making practices. A third step involved embracing a new moral vision meant to overcome old dualisms produced by the historic shift from entrepreneurship to speculation. Generally these strategies and their rationales have been overlooked by economists since Keynes, who have restricted their understanding of his policy thinking to short-term policy issues. Keynes likely thought short-term policy operated within a long-term policy framework, and thus himself evaluated short-term proposals from this broader perspective.

JOHN B. DAVIS

See also:
Economics of Keynes and of his Revolution, Key Elements of the; Keynes, John Maynard; Keynes and Probability; Keynes, The Influence of Burke and Moore on.

Bibliography
Davis, J.B. (1994), *Keynes's Philosophical Development*, Cambridge: Cambridge University Press.
Jensen, H.E. (1994), 'Aspects of J.M. Keynes's Vision and Conceptualized Reality', in J.B. Davis (ed.), *The State of Interpretation of Keynes*, Boston/Dordrecht/London: Kluwer.
Keynes, John M. (1936), *The General Theory of Employment, Interest and Money*, London: Macmillan.
Keynes, John M., *The Collected Works of John Maynard Keynes*, vol. IX (1972), ed. Don Moggridge, *Essays in Persuasion*, London: Macmillan; vol. X (1972), ed. Don Moggridge, *Essays in Biography*, London: Macmillan; vol. XXI (1982), ed. Don Moggridge, *Activities 1931–1939: World Crises and Policies in Britain and America*, London: Macmillan; vol. XXVII (1980), ed. Don Moggridge, *Activities 1940–1946: Shaping the Post-War World Employment*, London: Macmillan.

Grossman, Herschel I.

Herschel I. Grossman was born in 1939 in Philadelphia, Pennsylvania. He received his BA (with highest honors) from the University of Virginia in 1960. Grossman also received a B. of Ph. from the University of Oxford (England) in 1962, and in 1965 he completed his PhD at Johns Hopkins University.

From 1964 to 1969, Grossman held the rank of assistant professor of economics at Brown, and was an associate professor of economics there from 1969 to 1973. He at present holds the Merton P. Stoltz Professorship in the Social Sciences at Brown University, where he has been a professor of economics since 1973.

During his distinguished career Grossman was a Fellow at the University of Essex (England) in 1969 and the Simon Sr. Research Fellow at the University of Manchester (England) in 1971. In addition he has held visiting positions at the State University of New York (1978), the Institute of Advanced Studies, Vienna (1979), the European University Institute, Florence (1980), the University Louis Pasteur, Strasbourg (1982) and the University of Bologna (1990).

Grossman also has a long and distinguished record as a research associate at the National Bureau of Economic Research, beginning in 1979, and was a John Simon Guggenheim Foundation Fellow during 1979–80. He was on the board of editors of the *American Economic Review* from 1980 to 1983, the board of editors for the *Journal of Monetary Economics* from 1977 to the present, and has served as the book review editor for this journal since 1984. In addition, Grossman has been a National Science Foundation grantee periodically since 1969, was a member of the Social Science Research Council in 1982, a Research Fellow at the United States Department of Labor in 1974 and 1980, and an IRIS scholar in 1991.

During his very productive career, Grossman's motivation (Blaug, 1986, pp. 346–7) has been to develop an analysis of the relationship between money and economic fluctuations that is consistent with individual maximizing behavior assumed in the neoclassical paradigm (Johnson, 1980, 1983; Johnson and Ley, 1990a, 1990b). In this effort he has authored or co-authored over 40 journal articles and approximately 40 papers for the Working Paper Series at both the National Bureau of Economic Statistics and Brown University. In addition, Grossman has contributed various articles for texts, and was co-author with Robert J. Barro of *Money, Employment and Inflation* (1976), a work which has been translated into Chinese, Japanese and Italian. He also wrote *Money, Expectations and Business Cycles: Essays in Macroeconomics* (Barro, 1981).

The general analytical framework employed by Grossman has been the general equilibrium neoclassical (Walrasian) model of allocative efficiency. He has modified this framework to take account of non-market clearance, risk sharing in labor markets, the analysis of incomplete information regarding monetary disturbances, rational bubbles and limitations on Walrasian recontracting. Motivated by his empirical concern for formal hypothesis testing, Grossman's recent analyses have employed the rational expectations hypothesis. These efforts have attempted to establish the theoretical and empirical foundations for a body of positive macroeconomic analysis that includes the choice-theoretic modeling of monetary policy.

The focus of Grossman's early research was the study of the microeconomic foundations of economic fluctuations. This varied body of scholarship included analysis of risk shifting and sharing among employers and workers in the face of incomplete information (Grossman, 1977, 1978, 1979b, 1981) and the maximizing behavior of the job searcher (Grossman, 1973, 1974b, 1979a, 1981). At the same time, Grossman explored a series of non-market clearing models (1969, 1971, 1974a, 1986b and, with Barro, 1971).

Grossman's early research also examined monetary theory. His work includes models with imperfect information concerning monetary disturbances and, in a general equilibrium, neoclassical framework, he has explored such issues as contemporaneous information and positive choice-theoretic models (Grossman, 1982 (with Boschen), 1986b). His work in monetary theory was capped by his review essay in monetary theory (Grossman, 1991b) and his book *Money, Expectations and Business Cycles: Essays in Macroeconomics* (1981).

Grossman's use of the neoclassical general equilibrium framework was further extended to include a body of work on the existence of rational asset bubbles and the implications for macroeconomic stability, particularly as regards the problem of inflation. This research was founded on maximizing behavior in individual markets, such as gold and equities (Grossman, 1988b, 1988c; 1988, with Diba).

Another aspect of Grossman's work has involved the political economy of political survival. His research has included reputational equilibrium models to describe seigniorage, inflation and nominal sovereign debt. Grossman's treatment of debt focused on default, contingent claims, repudiation and risk sharing (1986a, 1988c, 1990a; 1993, with Van-Huyck). In fact, he extended his analysis to a general theory of war finance (Grossman and Han, 1993). In a similar vein, his study of political survival led Grossman to explore positive models of public finance (Grossman and Noh, 1994). This body of research was based on a public choice model of the maximization behavior of politicians, where the objective of the incumbents is the extraction of political rents. In this model, the choice variable is fiscal policy, which in turn determines the incumbents' survival probability. As a further extension, he investigated political competition from legitimate rivals as well as from nonlegitimate rivals, such as the mafia (Grossman, 1990b).

Grossman's interest in issues of neoclassical political economy was further extended into the study of developing economies. Once again a neoclassical, general equilibrium, maximizing framework was employed. One topic of interest was his concern with the economics of insurrection. Employing a general equilibrium model of insurrection, Grossman looked more specifically at the relationship of insurrection to famine relief and land reform (Grossman, 1991a, 1992). His interest in the developing nations was also extended to the study of colonialism. The two main themes in this area dealt with the profitability of colonialism and the conditions under which colonial policies were abandoned.

L.E. JOHNSON

BRADLEY M. BRAUN

See also:
Business Cycle Theory (I) and (II); Microfoundations of Macroeconomics; Monetary Policy; Neoclassical Synthesis (Bastard Keynesianism).

Bibliography

Blaug, Mark (ed.) (1986), *Who's Who In Economics: A Biographical Dictionary of Major Economists, 1700–1986*, 2nd edn, Cambridge, Mass.: MIT Press.

Grossman, Herschel I. (1969), 'Theories of Markets Without Recontracting', *Journal of Economic Theory*, **1**, (4), December, pp. 476–9.

Grossman, Herschel I. (1971), 'Money, Interest and Prices in Market Disequilibrium', *Journal of Political Economy*, **79**, (5), September–October, pp. 943–61.

Grossman, Herschel I. (1973), 'Aggregate Demand, Job Search and Employment', *Journal of Political Economy*, **81**, (6), November–December, pp. 1353–69.

Grossman, Herschel I. (1974a), 'The Nature of Quantities in Market Disequilibrium', *American Economic Review*, **64**, (3), June, pp. 509–14.

Grossman, Herschel I. (1974b), 'The Cyclical Pattern of Unemployment and Wage Inflation', *Economica*, **41**, (164), November, pp. 403–13.

Grossman, Herschel I. (1977), 'Risk Shifting and Reliability in Labor Markets', *Scandinavian Journal of Economics*, **79**, (2), pp. 187–209.

Grossman, Herschel I. (1978), 'Risk Shifting, Layoffs and Seniority', *Journal of Monetary Economics*, **4**, (4), November, pp. 661–86.

Grossman, Herschel I. (1979a), 'Why Does Aggregate Employment Fluctuate?', *American Economic Review*, **69**, (2), May, pp. 64–9.

Grossman, Herschel I. (1979b), 'Employment Fluctuations and the Mitigation of Risk', *Economic Inquiry*, **17**, (3), July, pp. 344–458.

Grossman, Herschel I. (1981a), *Money, Expectations and Business Cycles: Essays in Macroeconomics*, New York: Academic Press.

Grossman, Herschel I. (1981b), 'Incomplete Information, Risk Shifting and Employment Fluctuation', *Review of Economic Studies*, **48**, (2), April, pp. 189–97.

Grossman, Herschel I. (1986a), 'Seigniorage, Inflation and Reputation', *Journal of Monetary Economics*, **18**, (1), July, pp. 21–31.

Grossman, Herschel I. (1986b), 'Money, Real Activity and Rationality (The Significance of Monetary Disequilibrium)', *Cato Journal*, **6**, (2), Fall, pp. 401–8.

Grossman, Herschel I. (1988a), 'Rational Inflationary Bubbles', *Journal of Monetary Economics*, **21**, (1), January, pp. 35–46.

Grossman, Herschel I. (1988b), 'Explosive Rational Bubbles in Stock Prices', *American Economic Review*, **78**, (3), June, pp. 520–30.

Grossman, Herschel I. (1988c), 'Sovereign Debt as a Contingent Claim: Excusable Default, Repudiation and Reputation', *American Economic Review*, **78**, (5), December, pp. 1088–97.

Grossman, Herschel I. (1990a), 'Inflation and Reputation with Generic Policy Preferences', *Journal of Money, Credit and Banking*, **22**, (2), pp. 165–77.

Grossman, Herschel I. (1990b), 'A Theory of Kleptocracy with Probabilistic Survival and Reputation', *Journal of Economics and Politics*, **2**, (2), July, pp. 157–71.

Grossman, Herschel I. (1991a), 'A General Equilibrium Model of Insurrections', *American Economic Review*, **81**, (4), September, pp. 912–21.

Grossman, Herschel I. (1991b), 'Monetary Economics: A Review Essay', *Journal of Monetary Economics*, **28**, (2), October, pp. 323–45.

Grossman, Herschel I. (1992), 'Foreign Aid and Insurrection', *Journal of Defense Economics*, **3**, (4), pp. 275–88.

Grossman, Herschel I. and Robert J. Barro (1971), 'A General Disequilibrium Model of Income and Employment', *American Economic Review*, **61**, (1), March, pp. 82–93.

Grossman, Herschel I. and Robert J. Barro (1976), *Money, Employment and Inflation*, New York: McGraw-Hill.

Grossman, Herschel I. and John F. Boschen (1982), 'Tests of Equilibrium Using Contemporaneous Monetary Data', *Journal of Monetary Economics*, **10**, (3), November, pp. 309–33.

Grossman, Herschel I. and Behzad T. Diba (1988), 'The Theory of Rational Bubbles in Stock Prices', *Economic Journal*, **98**, (392), September, pp. 746–54.

Grossman, Herschel I. and Taejoon Han (1993), 'A Theory of War Finance', *Journal of Defense Economics*, **4**, (1), February, pp. 33–44.

Grossman, Herschel I. and Kenneth Happy (1981), 'Fixed Wages, Layoffs, Unemployment Compensation and Welfare: Note', *American Economic Review*, **71**, (3), June, pp. 483–4.

Grossman, Herschel I. and Suk-Jae Noh (1994), 'Proprietary Public Finance and Economic Welfare', *Journal of Public Economics*, **53**, (2), February, pp. 187–204.

Grossman, Herschel I. and John B. Van-Huyck (1993), 'Nominal Sovereign Debt, Risk Shifting and Reputation', *Journal of Economics and Business*, **45**, (3–4), August–October, pp. 341–52.

Johnson, L.E. (1980), 'A Neo-Paradigmatic Model for Studying the Development of Economic Reasoning', *Atlantic Economic Journal*, **8**, (4), December, pp. 52–61.

Johnson, L.E. (1983), 'Economic Paradigms: A Missing Dimension', *Journal of Economic Issues*, **17**, (4), December, pp. 1097–1111.

Johnson, L.E. and Robert D. Ley (1990a), 'Selecting Social Goals: Alternative Concepts of Rationality', *The American Journal of Economics and Sociology*, **49**, (4), October, pp. 469–82.

Johnson, L.E. and Robert D. Ley (1990b), *Origins of Modern Economics: A Paradigmatic Approach*, Lexington, Mass.: Ginn Press/Prentice-Hall.

Haavelmo, Trygve

Trygve Haavelmo, 1989 Nobel laureate in economics, was born in 1911 in Skedsmo, Norway, a township in the county of Akershus outside Oslo, son of Halvar and Jennie Eugenie (nee Gundersen). He received his Examen artium (secondary school qualification) in 1930 and graduated from the University of Oslo with a Cand. oecon. (undergraduate degree) in Political Economy in 1933. He then spent the next five years working as a research assistant to Ragnar Frisch at the Institute of Economics at the University of Oslo. After a year spent as a lecturer in statistical theory at the University of Aarhus in Denmark, Haavelmo left Nazi-dominated Scandinavia in 1939 for the United States. Here he was primarily associated with the Cowles Commission in Chicago, but also spent much time in New York and Washington, DC in official positions related to Norwegian government-in-exile interests. He returned to Norway in 1947 and spent a year working in the Ministry of Commerce and Industry and Ministry of Finance. Then he became professor of economics at the University of Oslo, from which he had received his doctorate in 1946, serving from 1948 until his retirement in 1979.

It is almost impossible to conceive how the practice of empirical economics could have advanced without Haavelmo's contributions. Quantitative work prior to the 1940s had focused on two fundamental problems concerning how to test economic theories with available data. The first problem is that data never exactly conform to economic theory owing to many idiosyncratic fluctuations which it is not desirable to include explicitly in theory. The second problem is that economic data are never freed of mutually interacting effects which can hide the particular relationship the researcher is seeking to identify. So economists had no formal way of testing economic theories to decide if they were false. If collected data did not appear to conform to theory, it was held to be a problem with the data set, such as measurement error or omitted variables, rather than with the theory.

Haavelmo's most important research circulated originally as a bound mimeo entitled 'On the Theory and Measurement of Economic Relations' (1941). This manuscript was later published as a special supplement to *Econometrica* in 1944, entitled 'The Probability Approach in Econometrics'. In this work, Haavelmo persuasively demonstrated that these two fundamental problems were solvable if economists were willing to adopt probabilistic interpretations for economic theories. Haavelmo argued that, if the data were too far out of line to be consistent with the theory, yet did not appear to suffer unduly from measurement error or errors of omission, the theory should be rejected.

He opened the door for a wide range of tools to be used by economists in hypothesis testing, tools that had already been developed or were being concurrently developed by statisticians. Economic theories could now be tested according to statistical criteria. Additionally, by taking a broader view of the way economic variables interrelate, larger economic models can be estimated all at once and the interrelationship bias avoided.

This manuscript immediately created a stir. While many economists either professed not to be able to understand it, or did not think that Haavelmo's arguments were correct, others were convinced that he had found the key to correct estimation of statistical relations in economics. These new methods were adopted with extraordinary rapidity by major economists and statisticians of the time, including Jacob Marschak and Tjalling Koopmans, the leaders of the Cowles Commission. The methodology employed in practically all quantitative studies in economics today is structured according to the methodological development initiated by Haavelmo.

The second major contribution Haavelmo made was to solve the identification puzzle. In 'The Statistical Implications of a System of Simultaneous Equations' (1943), Haavelmo argued that economic systems are often too complex to be summarized by only one equation. Estimating the parameters of a single equation out of a multiple equation system leads to misestimation of the parameters on variables that appear in more than one equation. He suggested use of a more complicated estimating technique than the one commonly used with single equation models.

Subsequently Haavelmo used his method in a groundbreaking applied paper, 'Methods of Measuring the Marginal Propensity to Consume' (1947), but the news of the usefulness of his techniques had already spread widely and they were being used by many other researchers as well. While he also wrote one important theoretical paper during this period, 'Multiplier Effects of a Balanced Budget' (1945), dealing with the expansionary effects of a balanced increase in government spending and taxes, his main contributions in the early part of his career were methodological rather than theoretical.

Haavelmo has had great influence on the economics profession in Norway, educating generations of economists both directly through lecturing and advising, and indirectly through circulation of copies of his lecture notes on a variety of topics in economic theory. Haavelmo turned his attention to economic theory after returning to Norway, and published two books in this area, both based on his university lectures. The first book, *A Study in the Theory of Economic Evolution*, published in 1954, deals with growth theory. In it Haavelmo interrelates population growth, education, migration patterns and income redistribution problems in an imaginative yet precise framework. While this book has not had wide impact, it nonetheless stands as a unique contribution to the field of economics.

Haavelmo then turned to the study of investment theory and published a book on this topic in 1960, *A Study in the Theory of Investment*. Here Haavelmo was truly ahead of his time in seeking to provide firmer microeconomic foundations for the macroeconomic theory of what drives the demand for capital investment. He also clarified previous work in the area and provided the essential insight that an explanation of the way capital should optimally be used in an economy does not in itself lead to explaining how much investment will occur.

JOYCE P. JACOBSEN

See also:

Business Cycle Theory (I) and (II); Econometric Models, Macroeconomic; Frisch, Ragnar; Schumpeter, Joseph A.

Bibliography

Haavelmo, T. (1943), 'The Statistical Implications of a System of Simultaneous Equations', *Econometrica*, **11**, (11), January, pp. 1–12.
Haavelmo, T. (1944), 'The Probability Approach in Econometrics', *Econometrica*, **12**, (3), Supplement to July, pp. 1–118.
Haavelmo, T. (1945), 'Multiplier Effects of a Balanced Budget', *Econometrica*, **13**, (4), October, pp. 311–18.
Haavelmo, T. (1947), 'Methods of Measuring the Marginal Propensity to Consume', *Journal of the American Statistical Society*, **42**, (237), March, pp. 105–22.
Haavelmo, T. (1954), *A Study in the Theory of Economic Evolution*, Amsterdam: North Holland.
Haavelmo, T. (1960), *A Study in the Theory of Investment*, Chicago: University of Chicago Press.

Hahn, Frank H.

Frank Hahn was born in Berlin in 1925 to Dr Arnold and Mrs Maria Hahn. When he was six the Hahns left Berlin for Prague, in turn leaving Prague for England in 1938. In Prague their home was the scene of a fortnightly salon where intellectual discussion and heated debate ruled. Hahn's father, a chemist by training, increasingly turned his energies towards journalistic and literary pursuits, writing several novels, popular science books, and a book of poetry. Frank Hahn credits this upbringing for his 'voracious appetite for reading and intellectual speculation' (Hahn, 1992, p. 161).

Frank Hahn served in the RAF during World War II. While he was still in the service, M. Kalecki, a family friend, suggested Hahn read economics and this led Hahn to the London School of Economics. Hahn earned a BS (1945) and a PhD (1951) from the University of London. In his days at the LSE, and into his initial academic post in Birmingham, Hahn was an active participant in the fervour of postwar academic economics in England. He and others (such as Terence Gorman) insisted upon a mathematically rigorous grounding for all aspects of the discipline that was stimulated by Hicks's *Value and Capital*, Samuelson's *Foundations of Economic Analysis*, Lange's *Price Flexibility and Employment* and Arrow's *Social Choice and Individual Values*.

Teaching first at the University of Birmingham (1953 to 1960) Hahn then moved to Cambridge University, where he stayed until 1967, when he became professor of economics at the London School of Economics. In 1972, he returned to Cambridge University, where he is currently professor of economics (Churchill College).

Frank Hahn is best known for his work in general equilibrium theory and his work with Kenneth Arrow, *General Competitive Analysis* (1971), is a landmark in modern economics. Work in this field satisfied two of Hahn's interests: a lingering desire to be a mathematician, and a desire to set out carefully the requirements that must hold in order for the 'invisible hand' of Adam Smith to ensure that markets reach a coordinated, stable equilibrium. By delineating precisely what conditions must be true for a general competitive equilibrium to hold, Hahn and others have been able to show the gap between our theoretical knowledge and our practical knowledge. Further, he has forcefully argued that making public policy on the basis of a theory which is visibly at odds with reality is a role unbecoming to a serious economist.

The absence of complete, contingent futures markets in the world we live in, but which are logically necessary for the existence of a competitive general equilibrium in an Arrow–Debreu–Hahn 'world', gives Hahn pause for thought when making policy prescriptions based on the A–D–H– model: 'The limitations on the applicability of pure market theory are numerous and some of them quite serious... The Smithian vision still provides a reference point but an increasingly remote one' (Hahn, 1982a; reprinted in Hahn, 1984, p. 132). And 'Economic theory at its best is a powerful aid to thought about the world, not because it provides a very satisfactory description, but because it provides clear limits to understanding' (Hahn, 1992, p. 164).

At the same time as he was working on the question of *existence* of a general competitive equilibrium, Hahn was also working on the question of the *stability* of equilibrium. In work with T. Negishi (1962; reprinted in Hahn, 1985) it was shown under what circumstances processes allowing trading at 'false' (that is, disequilibrium) prices are stable. Given the view that economies can be out of equilibrium, or 'in' disequilibrium, providing a trading rule that led disequilibrium trades to be equilibrating was a necessary requisite to showing the stability of the system. Otherwise only trades at equilibrium prices – in equilibrium – would be allowable and, in a very real sense, the notion of disequilibrium would be vacuous.

Hahn (1984, 1985) used this way of viewing theory through reality to examine what changes theorists need to make in their models of competitive equilibrium in order to explain intrinsically worthless, but widely used, definitions of money. Hahn shows that making sense of money in competitive general equilibrium depends upon there being sequential markets, where trading does not occur simultaneously at a point in time; and that sequential markets, depending as they do upon the passage of time, require theorists to confront the issue of foresight, expectations and their formation.

This work complements Hahn's studies examining what have become known as 'non-Walrasian', or non-perfectly competitive, equilibria where strategic actions, coalitions, conjectures, and expectations are endogenously determined and give meaning to Hahn's 'learning-based' definition of equilibrium depending on the actions of individuals and in the aggregate, as follows:

> The concept of the equilibrium action of an agent... is such that if it is in fact the action pursued by the agent an outside observer, say the econometrician, could describe it by structurally stable equations. When the agent is learning, however, then there is a change in the regime so that one would require a 'higher level' theory of the learning process. (Hahn, 1973; reprinted in Hahn, 1984, p. 56)

For the economy as a whole: 'an economy is in equilibrium when it generates messages which do not cause agents to change the theories which they hold or the policies they pursue' (Hahn, 1984, p. 59). This vision also illuminates Hahn's work on economic growth theory, where he showed that limited foresight would not, in general, lead economies to Harrod's warranted rate of growth and the attainment of the steady state.

Hahn has emerged as a central figure in at least two debates within economics. The 'Two Cambridges' debate over the logical determinacy of marginal productivity theory saw Hahn defend neoclassical theory against Sraffa's followers, such as J.L. Eatwell, P. Garegnani and G.C. Harcourt, whom Hahn has named 'the neo-Ricardians' (Hahn, 1982b; reprinted in Hahn, 1984). Hahn has also publicly engaged 'monetarists' and 'New Classical economists' on the issue of whether or not changes in the nominal money supply logically lead to equiproportional changes in the aggregate price level (Hahn, 1981). Hahn's work in these and other areas have made him hard to 'label':

> In showing that neo-classical economics has nothing to fear from the neo-Ricardians I became in their eyes a dyed-in-the-wood neo-classical who considered Arrow–Debreu adequate for all of economics. I fear that, in just the same way, my dissatisfaction with the new macroeconomics will be regarded as a sign that I am an old Keynesian. In truth, I am none of those things: 'any school of thought which would accept me I should not care to join'. On the final truths of economics

I am completely agnostic. Until such final truth is unequivocably revealed I hold all coherent theorising as worthy of attention and respect. (Hahn, 1984, p. 18)

DAVID L. HAMMES

See also:

Arrow, Kenneth J.; Classical Economics; Clower, Robert W.; Dual Decision Hypothesis; Hicks, Sir John R.; Lausanne, The School of; Lucas, Jr., Robert E.; Lucas Critique; New Classical School of Economics; Post Walrasian Economics; Robbins, Lord Lionel; Samuelson, Paul A.; Say's Law; Wicksell, Knut.

Bibliography

Arrow, K.J. (1951), *Social Choice and Individual Values*, New Haven/London: Yale University Press.
Arrow, K.J. and F.H. Hahn (1971), *General Competitive Analysis*, San Francisco: Holden Day.
Hahn, F.H. (1973), 'On the Notion of Equilibrium in Economics', inaugural lecture, Cambridge: Cambridge University Press.
Hahn, F.H. (1981), *Money and Inflation*, Oxford: Basil Blackwell.
Hahn, F.H. (1982a), 'Reflections on the Invisible Hand', *Lloyds Bank Review*, (144), April, pp. 1–21.
Hahn, F.H. (1982b), 'The neo-Ricardians', *The Cambridge Journal of Economics*, **6**, (4), December, pp. 353–74.
Hahn, F.H. (1984), *Equilibrium and Macroeconomics*, Oxford: Basil Blackwell.
Hahn, F.H. (1985), *Money, Growth and Stability*, Oxford: Basil Blackwell.
Hahn, F.H. (1992), 'Autobiographical Notes with Reflections', in M. Szenberg (ed.), *Eminent Economists*, Cambridge: Cambridge University Press.
Hahn, F.H. and T. Negishi (1962), 'A Theorem on Non-tâtonnement Stability', *Econometrica*, **30**, (3), July, pp. 463–9.
Hicks, J.R. (1946), *Value and Capital*, 2nd edn, London: Oxford University Press.
Lange, O. (1944), *Price Flexibility and Employment*, Bloomington, Ind.: Principia Press.
Samuelson, P.A. (1947), *Foundations of Economic Analysis*, Cambridge, Mass.: Harvard University Press.
Szenberg, M. (ed.) (1992), *Eminent Economists*, Cambridge: Cambridge University Press.

Hansen, Alvin H.

Best known as an early advocate of Keynesian macroeconomic theory and policy, Alvin Hansen played an important role in the dissemination and extension of those theories in the United States. He accomplished his purposes through teaching at Harvard, through published research and through testimony before and service to various government agencies. The effects of these activities altered the terms of intellectual debate in the United States and elsewhere about the appropriate conduct of macroeconomic policy.

Alvin Hansen was born in Viborg, South Dakota in 1887. His upbringing and early education instilled him with lifelong interests in the social sciences and in history. He received his undergraduate education at Yankton College, where one of his instructors, George Warren, encouraged him to pursue graduate work in sociology. After a two-year hiatus spent as a school principal and superintendent, Hansen obtained sufficient financial resources to enroll at the University of Wisconsin in 1914. There, under the guidance of Richard T. Ely and John R. Commons, he decided to concentrate his efforts in economics. Commons's workshop proved particularly influential, imbuing Hansen with the faculty for careful analysis of data and institutions that characterized his later work.

Hansen married and accepted an instructorship at Brown University in 1916. Two years later, he defended his PhD thesis, a study of business cycles in the United States, Britain and Germany (Hansen, 1921). The following year (1919), Hansen accepted an appointment at the University of Minnesota, where he remained until the mid-1930s. While at Minnesota, Hansen continued his research in macroeconomics. His scholarly output there included *Business Cycle Theory* (1927), an interpretative survey that established Hansen's reputation as a macroeconomist of note. He received a Guggenheim Fellowship and spent some of 1928 and 1929 travelling abroad. During his travels he became acquainted with many English and Continental European economists who influenced his later work. With the arrival of the New Deal, Hansen applied his talents to policy making, serving in several advisory positions during Roosevelt's first term.

In 1937, Hansen accepted a position as the Littauer Professor of Political Economy, a joint appointment at Harvard University in the Department of Economics and the newly-created Graduate School of Public Administration. His teaching duties at Harvard centered around the Fiscal Policy Seminar that he conducted with John Williams, Dean of the Graduate School of Public Administration. The seminar provided the forum through which Hansen, Williams and a series of later to be eminent graduate students examined and debated different approaches to macroeconomic policy.

At the time of Hansen's arrival at Harvard, the Depression had reached unexpected depths. In this context, the publication of *The General Theory* by Keynes in 1936 received immediate critical attention. While Hansen was initially skeptical of Keynes's contribution, he changed his opinion once at Harvard. On the other hand, Williams remained wary of many Keynesian ideas. Through interplay with Williams and the graduate students (some of whom, as Littauer Fellows, already had public-service experience) Hansen developed, tested and refined his thoughts on appropriate macroeconomic policy, particularly where an economy is well below full employment.

Several themes run through much of Hansen's work. The first is that of underemployment of resources. Heavily influenced by Continental economists such as Cassel and Spiethoff, as well as by Keynes, Hansen used Hicks's IS/LM framework to explain why an unregulated economy would experience long periods of unemployment in the recessionary phase of its business cycle. Specifically, he was concerned that the forces that impel recovery might be weak and that, therefore, long periods of insufficient aggregate demand would persist. Hansen's depiction of the possibility of persistent unemployment using the IS/LM model (later known as the Hicks–Hansen Synthesis) proved so influential that it has become part of the canon through which macroeconomic theory is presented to graduate students.

The role of liquidity preference in determining aggregate demand was a second theme that Hansen emphasized. He elucidated the role of Keynes's speculative motive for holding money in determining the level of interest rates and, hence, the ex ante level of investment expenditure. If either the liquidity preference schedule were extremely interest-elastic (a liquidity trap) or the marginal efficiency of investment schedule were investment-inelastic, then monetary policy would not be efficacious in restoring full employment. Moreover Hansen believed that such situations routinely occurred in well-developed economies in a recession caused by 'a temporary saturation of investment opportunities following a pronounced upward surge of investment' (Hansen, 1949, p. 173). Like Keynes, then, Hansen advocated a compensatory program of government spending to offset the shortfall of private investment.

The third theme takes a longer view. Hansen believed that the developed economies of the world had reached a stage of maturity that would lead to economic stagnation if left unregulated. He attributed the tendency towards stagnation to declining population growth rates, the slowing of technological innovation and the closing of frontiers that spelled the end of abundant natural resources. While he analysed this trend, Hansen did not believe it to be either uniform or uncorrectable. When birth rates rose well above expectations, he correctly anticipated the postwar boom. Further, he suggested that the same active fiscal policies that mitigate the business cycle could also be employed to counteract stagnation.

Once Hansen decided that expansionary fiscal policy was needed to end the Depression, he sought the adoption of such a policy. His testimony before the Temporary National Economic Committee in 1939 placed him at the center of the policy debate. During World War II, he served as a Special Economic Advisor to the Federal Reserve Board and Chairman of the United States–Canadian Joint Economic Commissions. From these positions, and with the help of others, he advanced policies that promoted and managed the expansion of the wartime economy. Later Hansen fostered the adoption of Keynesian prescriptions that shaped not only the postwar economic environment (for example, the Employment Act of 1946 and the Bretton Woods Agreement) but also the fiscal policies of the Kennedy and Johnson administrations in the 1960s.

Although best known as an interpreter of Keynes (see Hansen, 1953), Hansen was an original thinker in his own right. For example, Samuelson attributed the original insight behind the multiplier–accelerator interaction to Hansen (Samuelson, 1976, pp. 29–30). Accordingly, as an interpreter, as a theorist and as a persuasive policy advocate, Alvin Hansen has left his indelible stamp on modern macroeconomics.

LAWRENCE J. HABER

See also:

Currie, Lauchlin; Dillard, Dudley; Employment Act of 1946; Fiscal Policy; Full Employment Budget; Keynes's Economics, National Income Accounting Activism and; Keynesian Economics, Deficit Finance in; Keynesian Revolution; Keynesianism in America; Keyserling, Leon; Metzler, Lloyd A.; Okun, Arthur M.; Okun's Law; Samuelson, Paul A.; Stein, Herbert; Tarshis, Lorie.

Bibliography

Breit, William and Roger L. Ransom (1971), 'Alvin H. Hansen – The American Keynes', *The American Scribblers*, New York: Holt, Rinehart & Winston, pp. 85–110.
Haberler, Gottfried (1976), 'Some Reminiscences', *Quarterly Journal of Economics*, **90**, (1), February, pp. 10–13.
Hansen, Alvin H. (1921), *Cycles of Prosperity and Depression in the United States, Great Britain and Germany: A Study of Monthly Data 1902–1908*, Madison: University of Wisconsin Press.
Hansen, Alvin H. (1927), *Business Cycle Theory*, New York: Ginn and Co.
Hansen, Alvin H. (1949), *Monetary Theory and Fiscal Policy*, New York: McGraw-Hill Book Company.
Hansen, Alvin H. (1953), *A Guide to Keynes*, New York: McGraw-Hill Book Company.
Musgrave, Richard A. (1976), 'Caring for the Real Problems', *Quarterly Journal of Economics*, **90**, (1), February, pp. 1–7.
Salant, Walter S. (1976), 'Alvin Hansen and the Fiscal Policy Seminar', *Quarterly Journal of Economics*, **90**, (1), February, pp. 14–23.
Samuelson, Paul A. (1976), 'Hansen as a Creative Economic Theorist', *Quarterly Journal of Economics*, **90**, (1), February, pp. 24–31.
Tobin, James (1976), 'Hansen and Public Policy', *Quarterly Journal of Economics*, **90**, (1), February, pp. 32–7.

Harcourt, Geoff

Geoff Harcourt was born in Melbourne, Australia in 1931 and has divided his life (primarily) between Australia and Cambridge, England. Following an upbringing in a 'middle-class assimilationist, agnostic Jewish household with right-wing political views' (as put by Geoff Harcourt in his Introduction to Sardoni, 1992, p. 1), he developed his own persona at the University of Melbourne as a democratic socialist and a Methodist; it was in this period also that he developed his abiding and infectious enthusiasm for economics. The inextricable links between political and religious beliefs and economics have been the hallmark of Geoff Harcourt's economics, and life, ever since. He and his wife, Joan, have four children and one granddaughter.

Having completed a Cambridge-oriented first degree and master's degree in economics from Melbourne (in 1954 and 1956, respectively), Geoff Harcourt spent 1955 to 1958 in Cambridge working on a PhD, initially under Kaldor, then under Ronald Henderson. In 1958, he returned to Australia, taking up a lecturing post at the University of Adelaide; he remained at Adelaide until 1982, and has since been made an emeritus professor. During this period in Australia, Geoff Harcourt was actively involved in politics, both with the Australian Labor Party and as a leader of the Campaign for Peace in Vietnam. He also kept up his contact with Cambridge during this period, returning in 1963 on leave from Adelaide, and being appointed to a university lectureship in economics and politics and as Trinity Hall's first Teaching Fellow in Economics. He returned to a readership at Adelaide in 1967, and was elected to a personal chair in the September of that year. He returned to Cambridge permanently in 1982. Geoff Harcourt is currently the Reader in the History of Economic Theory in the Faculty of Economics and Politics. In 1994, he was made an Officer in the General Division of the Order of Australia 'for service to economic theory and to the history of economic thought'.

Geoff Harcourt has published numerous books, articles and papers. Selections of his papers have been published in five volumes (Kerr, 1982; Hamouda, 1986; Sardoni, 1992; Harcourt, 1993, 1995). He has made notable contributions in a range of areas in economics, using a variety of methods of enquiry. Yet there is an overriding unity behind these contributions and a very strong sense in which the whole is more than the sum of the parts. We deal first with the detailed contribution, and conclude with an account of Geoff Harcourt's contribution as a whole.

A refusal to accept the conventional distinction between microeconomics and macroeconomics stemmed from work as an undergraduate which used accounting data to integrate the theory of price setting under oligopoly with the Keynesian theory of income determination. Influenced in Cambridge by Joan Robinson's *Accumulation of Capital*, Geoff Harcourt's doctoral research stressed the importance of accounting conventions for price setting and income measurement, respectively. At Adelaide, he pursued these ideas further in 'The accountant in a Golden Age', in a review article of Salter's work on vintage models and in a critique of the form of pricing behavior required by the full employment assumption in Kaldor's theory of growth and distribution. Back in Cambridge, in the company of Arrow, Meade, Solow, Sraffa, Kahn, Kaldor and Joan Robinson, Geoff Harcourt further developed his ideas in a two-sector growth model, in a satirical critique of the CES production function, incorporating Salterian vintages into the Robinsonian critique of the aggregate production function in econometric work, and on the question of investment decision rules and the choice of technique. One of the most pathbreaking papers coming out of this period is the *Kyklos* article, written with Peter Kenyon in 1976, which explained the size of mark-up terms of the financial requirements of the firm. The apogee of Geoff Harcourt's work on microfoundations was his chairing of the 1975 IEA conference on the subject and the Introduction he wrote to the conference volume (Harcourt, 1977).

The second strand in Geoff Harcourt's work is a direct outcome of his work on microfoundations, particularly regarding the production function and investment decisions. He was invited to write a survey article on the Cambridge capital theory controversies for the second issue of the *Journal of Economic Literature*; out of this work arose an invitation to write a book on the subject (Harcourt, 1972) and a series of further articles. With these contributions, written in his inimitable humorous style, Geoff Harcourt made meaningful and accessible an important, but to many obscure, debate apparently about reswitching and factor reversal, but actually about theorizing itself. In the process Geoff Harcourt played a key role in nurturing the growth concern with neoclassical economics which subsequently evolved as Post Keynesian economics.

The third strand of Geoff Harcourt's work took the form of engagement in policy debate, applying his theoretical ideas. The transition from theory to policy was relatively smooth since Geoff Harcourt has always sustained the view that policy making is the object of theorizing and that theories should be constructed with that end in view. In a series of papers published in the 1970s and early 1980s, he put together a policy package for Australia, reflecting his continuous involvement in politics and incorporating policies addressed to distribution as well as growth. In the 1990s, he has returned to policy with three articles, the first two addressing policy issues in Australia (Harcourt, 1992, 1993b) and the third addressing the issue of speculation on a world scale (Harcourt, 1994).

The fourth strand of Geoff Harcourt's work, in which he is currently most actively engaged, was sparked off by the request in the early 1970s from Angus Wilson, as the orator at the University of East Anglia, for a background paper on Joan Robinson for her honorary degree presentation, and by the tragic death in 1977 of his close friend and mentor in Adelaide, Eric Russell. His intellectual biographies of Joan Robinson and Eric Russell have been followed by a long series of intellectual biographies of great economists, and reflective papers tracing more general intellectual developments in economics. Geoff Harcourt has been uniquely placed for such an exercise in having such a vast and intimate knowledge of economics and economists. Implicit in these papers is the insistence that understanding the process of knowledge discovery is crucial to an understanding of that knowledge. His early work in this regard was before its time; only with the recent explosion of 'conversations' with economists has the worth of such an enterprise been properly appreciated. Geoff Harcourt is currently engaged in the huge enterprise of documenting the intellectual history of his long-time mentor and friend, Joan Robinson, and her circle in Cambridge.

It would do an injustice to Geoff Harcourt to assess his contribution to economics solely in terms of these elements, important though each of them is. All the elements are united by a commonality of purpose (the betterment of the human condition) and a coherent methodological stance which explicitly requires different methods for different purposes ('horses for courses' is the way Geoff Harcourt likes to put it, following Joan Robinson). As well as containing explicit statements of this methodology, his work provides an exemplar of how it can be put into practice. This exemplar goes beyond the specific methods and issues to be addressed; Geoff Harcourt provides a role model with his humor, warmth and courtesy, as well as his passionately held beliefs and his determination to promote the development of economics along constructive lines. The corpus of his work has been achieved at the same time as devoting himself tirelessly and selflessly to encouraging, inspiring and promoting the work of others. Geoff Harcourt has played a key role in fostering Post Keynesian economics, while working hard to keep open the lines of communication with other schools of thought.

SHEILA DOW

See also:

Davidson, Paul; Domar, Evsey D.; Harrod, Sir Roy; Hicks, Sir John R.; Kaldor, Lord Nicholas; Kalecki, Michał; Kregel, Jan A.; Malinvaud, Edmond; Microfoundations of Macroeconomics; Post Keynesian School of Economics; Robinson, Joan; Solow, Robert M.; Sraffa, Piero; Swan, Trevor W.; Technological Change; Weintraub, Sidney.

Bibliography

Hamouda, O.F. (ed.) (1986), *Controversies in Political Economy: Selected Essays by G.C. Harcourt*, New York: New York University Press.

Harcourt, G.C. (1972), *Some Cambridge Controversies in the Theory of Capital*, Cambridge: Cambridge University Press.

Harcourt, G.C. (1977), *The Microeconomic Foundations of Macroeconomics*, London: Macmillan.

Harcourt, G.C. (1992), 'Markets, Madness and a Middle Way', *Australian Quarterly*, **64**, Autumn, pp. 1–17.

Harcourt, G.C. (1993a), *Post Keynesian Essays in Biography: Portraits of Twentieth Century Political Economists*, London: Macmillan.

Harcourt, G.C. (1993b), 'Macroeconomic Policy for Australia in the 1990s', *Economic and Labor Relations Review*, **4**, (2), December, pp. 167–75.

Harcourt, G.C. (1994), 'A "Modest Proposal" for Taming Speculators and Putting the World on Course to Prosperity', *Economic and Political Weekly*, **29**, (28), 17 September, pp. 2490–92.

Harcourt, G.C. (1995), *Capitalism, Socialism and Post-Keynesianism: Selected Essays of G.C. Harcourt*, Aldershot: Edward Elgar.

Harcourt, G.C. and Peter Kenyon (1976), 'Pricing and the Investment Decision', *Kyklos*, **29**, (3), pp. 449–77.

Kerr, P. (ed.) (1982), *The Social Science Imperialists: Selected Essays of G.C. Harcourt*, London: Routledge & Kegan Paul.

Sardoni, C. (ed.) (1992), *On Political Economists and Modern Political Economy: Selected Essays of G.C. Harcourt*, London: Routledge.

Harrod, Sir Roy

Henry Roy Forbes Harrod was born on 13 February 1900 in Norwich. He was the son of Henry Dawes Harrod and Frances Forbes-Robertson. Under his mother's influence he was 'brought up in a literary and artistic home in which the tradition was that conversation was by far the greatest pleasure, if not the prime object, of life' (Harrod, 1959, pp. 39–40). This aspect of his upbringing was further nurtured during his schooldays at Westminster and as an undergraduate at New College, Oxford, where he read Greats from 1919 to 1921, and Modern History in 1922, in both cases getting a first. The characteristic Oxbridge process of learning through debates and conversation (Harrod, 1951, pp. 58–9) inevitably stimulated his wide range of interests.

His early philosophical and political concerns later played an important part in the development of Harrod's dynamic theory. Under the influence of Ramsey and Ayer he embraced a logicist attitude towards the cognitive status and the method of economics (Harrod, 1951, p. 321; 1959, pp. 62–5), while the empiricism he imbibed from Mitchell (Harrod, 1937, 1949) induced him to found the axiomatic basis of his dynamics on inductive generalizations (Harrod, 1938). Interestingly though, having been an 'ardent liberal' in the 1920s, after the 1931 electoral debacle of the Liberal Party Harrod – like Keynes, and possibly under his inspiration – looked with sympathy at the position of the Labour Party, and took part in the discussions between 'Keynesians' and 'Hayekians' within the New Fabian Research Bureau (Durbin, 1985). In spite of their theoretical divergences, they shared as an analytical postulate the assumption of a base of steady progress, which later characterized Harrod's notion of dynamic equilibrium (Harrod, 1934b, 1936, 1939).

Although Harrod did not receive a proper training in economics, Christ Church considered his qualification suitable to teach economics, elected him to a studentship (which he maintained until his retirement in 1967) and allowed him two terms away to study the subject. One of these was spent in Cambridge, where Harrod attended Keynes's lectures on Cambridge monetary theory (Harrod, 1951, p. 325, 341), wrote weekly essays for him covering the ground of Marshall's *Principles* (ibid., pp. 323–4) and participated in his Political Economy Club. On his return to Oxford, Harrod attended Edgeworth's 'absolutely fascinating lectures' (Harrod, 1937, pp. 79–80) and 'took essays to him on cost curves and international trade' (Phelps Brown, 1980, p. 8). His surviving notebooks certify that this was a period of intense reading, the subjects covering monopoly, monetary problems (of both theoretical and historical character), trade unionism, international trade and political science, besides of course the milestones of economic literature. His work for the British (later Royal) Institute of International Affairs as the Secretary of the Commission on Cartels made him well known within economic circles, and by 1926 his name was prophetically cited as one of a new generation of economists expected to make real contributions to the subject (Fisher, 1926).

In 1927, Keynes asked him to write something on international economics for the *Cambridge Economic Handbooks* series. The book, published in 1933, was praised for its originality and marks Harrod's introduction of the concepts of the crawling peg and the international trade multiplier (as they later came to be known). In the meantime, Harrod participated in the debates on imperfect competition and contributed the notion of *marginal returns*, which he independently discovered in 1928 (although the paper was only published in 1930: see Harrod, 1951, pp. 159–60n).

Besides their intrinsic interest, Harrod's reflections on imperfect competition also entailed important consequences for his dynamics. In Harrod's view, the principal difficulty for trade cycle theory is that of allowing for the *possibility* of economic change, which the assumption of stability of equilibrium negates. At first, Harrod saw the possibility of increasing returns as the condition which enables an economy to overcome the tendency to stay in a state of rest (Harrod, 1934a; Besomi, 1993). Although he later resorted to other specific mechanisms, the postulate that *instability* must be an essential ingredient of a dynamic model was consistently maintained through the subsequent evolution of his thought. This was later interpreted and discussed as an analytical *result* to be proved (the 'knife-edge'), while in reality it constituted a *premise* of his dynamics.

Harrod's first contributions to dynamics, *The Trade Cycle* (1936) and an 'Essay in Dynamic Theory' (1939), although differing in their emphasis on expectations and in their causal interpretation of the 'accelerator' (Besomi, 1995), relied on a similar mechanism for explaining the rate of growth of the economic system. In both cases this was interpreted as depending on the interaction between the multiplying effect of investment on income and the accelerating influence of the increase of income on the demand for investment goods, equilibrium being characterized by the mutual support of investment and increasing demand.

Harrod intended his dynamic determination of the equilibrium rate of growth to refer to a single instant of time. He knew, in fact, that growth itself affects both the multiplier and the accelerator coefficients, but as he was unable to work out the mathematics involved in this non-linearity he correctly insisted that the validity of his analysis be confined to the only domain warranting constancy of the parameters (Besomi, 1995, 1996). His result, however, was understood as describing the equilibrium growth *path*, and Harrod – together with Domar – was credited with the fatherhood of modern growth theory (for a discussion, see Kregel, 1980).

After the war, Harrod revised and refined his dynamic theory (Harrod, 1948, 1960, 1973; see Asimakopulos, 1985), further contributed to imperfect competition theory (1952), wrote the first biography of Keynes and a memoir of Lord Cherwell (1951, 1959), a book on induction (1956), several pieces on monetary theory and policy (1965, 1969) and was involved in the most important theoretical issues of the economics of his time. When he died on 8 March 1978, he left behind a monumental amount of writing (for a partial bibliography, see Eltis *et al.*, 1970; Scott, 1971) and his surviving papers testify to a life of intense exchanges of views with his most eminent contemporaries – economists, philosophers and politicians (Riley-Smith, 1982). In particular, since the early 1930s, people like Keynes, Robertson and Henderson – besides his contemporary fellows Meade, Joan Robinson, Kahn and Kaldor, to cite only a few – often asked for his opinion (see Young, 1989). In 1945, he took over the editorship of the *Economic Journal* from Keynes. From 1962 to 1964 he was president of the Royal Economic Society. He was knighted in 1959 and received several honorary degrees, although to his disappointment he was never elected to a Chair in Oxford (see, for further details on his life and career, Blake, 1970; Hinshaw, 1978; Phelps Brown, 1980).

DANIELE BESOMI

See also:

Cambridge Circus; Domar, Evsey D.; Economics of Keynes and of his Revolution, Key Elements of the; Hicks, Sir John R.; Kaldor, Lord Nicholas; Keynes, John Maynard; Keynesian Revolution; Multiplier Effect; Robinson, Joan; Swan, Trevor W.; Technological Change.

Bibliography

Asimakopulos, A. (1985), 'Harrod on Harrod: the evolution of "a line of steady growth"', *History of Political Economy*, **17**, (4), Winter, pp. 619–35.

Besomi, D. (1993), 'Roy Harrod, la concorrenza imperfetta e la possibilità di una teoria dinamica', *Studi Economici*, **50**, (2), pp. 41–70.

Besomi, D. (1995), 'From *The Trade Cycle* to the "Essay in Dynamic Theory". The Harrod–Keynes Correspondence, 1937–1938', *History of Political Economy*, **27**, (2), Summer, pp. 309–44.

Besomi, D. (1996), 'Harrod's Dynamics in 1938. An Additional Note on the Harrod–Keynes Correspondence', *History of Political Economy*, **28**, (2), Summer, pp. 245–52.

Blake, R. (1970), 'A Personal Memoir', in Eltis, Scott and Wolfe (1970, pp. 1–19).

Durbin, E.F. (1985), *New Jerusalems. The Labour Party and the Economics of Democratic Socialism*, London: Routledge & Kegan Paul.

Eltis, W.A., M.F. Scott and J.N. Wolfe (eds) (1970), *Induction, Growth and Trade. Essays in Honour of Sir Roy Harrod*, Oxford: Clarendon Press.

Fisher, I. (1926), Letter to R.F. Harrod, 15 December, in Harrod and Keynes, Notes and Memoranda, Tokyo University, item 154.

Harrod, R.F. (1930), 'Notes on Supply', *Economic Journal*, **40**, (158), June, pp. 233–41.

Harrod, R.F. (1933), *International Economics*, London: Nisbet; Cambridge: at the University Press; New York: Harcourt and Brace.

Harrod, R.F. (1934a), 'Doctrines of Imperfect Competition', *Quarterly Journal of Economics*, **48**, (3), May, pp. 442–70.

Harrod, R.F. (1934b), 'The expansion of Credit in an Advancing Community', *Economica*, NS 1, (3), August, pp. 287–99.

Harrod, R.F. (1936), *The Trade Cycle. An Essay*, Oxford: Clarendon Press.

Harrod, R.F. (1937), 'L'Université d'Oxford', in *L'Enseignement Économique en France et à l'Étranger*, Cinquantenaire de la *Revue d'Économie Politique*, Paris: Librairie du Recueil Sirey, pp. 79–90.

Harrod, R.F. (1938), 'Scope and Method of Economics', *Economic Journal*, 48, (191), September, pp. 383–412.

Harrod, R.F. (1939), 'An Essay in Dynamic Theory', *Economic Journal*, 49, (193), March, pp. 14–33.

Harrod, R.F. (1948), *Towards a Dynamic Economics*, London: Macmillan.

Harrod, R.F. (1949), 'Wesley Mitchell in Oxford', *Economic Journal*, 59, September, pp. 459–60.

Harrod, R.F. (1951), *The Life of John Maynard Keynes*, London: Macmillan.

Harrod, R.F. (1952), *Economic Essays*, London: Macmillan.

Harrod, R.F. (1956), *Foundations of Inductive Logics*, London: Macmillan.

Harrod, R.F. (1959), *The Prof. A Personal Memoir of Lord Cherwell*, London: Macmillan.

Harrod, R.F. (1960), 'Second Essay in Dynamic Theory', *Economic Journal*, 70, (278), June, pp. 277–93.

Harrod, R.F. (1965), *Reforming the World's Money*, London: Macmillan and New York: St Martin's Press.

Harrod, R.F. (1969), *Money*, London: Macmillan and New York: St Martin's Press.

Harrod, R.F. (1973), *Economic Dynamics*, London: Macmillan and New York: St Martin's Press.

Hinshaw, R. (1978), 'Sir Roy Harrod', *Journal of International Economics*, 8, (3), August, pp. 363–72.

Kregel, J.A. (1980), 'Economic Dynamics and the Theory of Steady Growth: An Historical Essay on Harrod's "Knife-Edge"', *History of Political Economy*, 12, (1), Spring, pp. 97–123.

Phelps Brown, H. (1980), 'Sir Roy Harrod: A Biographical Memoir', *Economic Journal*, 90, (357), March, pp. 1–33.

Riley-Smith, H. (1982), *Catalogue of the Papers of Sir Roy Harrod*, Norfolk: Riley-Smith Booksellers.

Scott, M.F. (1971), 'List of Articles and Letters by Sir Roy Harrod', mimeo (copy in Nuffield College, Oxford), March.

Young, W. (1989), *Harrod and his Trade Cycle Group. The Origins and Development of the Growth Research Programme*, London: Macmillan.

Hawtrey, Sir Ralph

Ralph George Hawtrey (1879–1975) was born on 22 November 1879 in Slough, England, the son of a preparatory schoolteacher. Although he proceeded to Eton, he was brought up in circumstances which reflected money worries, which were later to prove influential over his choice of career. From Eton he went to Trinity College, Cambridge in 1898 where he read mathematics, emerging as 19th wrangler with a first class degree in 1901.

In the following years he prepared himself for the civil service examinations at Cambridge, attending lectures on economics by G.P. Moriarty and J.H. Clapham, and duly entered the Admiralty in 1903. In many respects his life up to this point was similar to that of Keynes, who followed him from

Eton to Cambridge and the civil service four years later. Indeed Hawtrey, under the influence of the philosopher G.E. Moore, was involved in the Apostles and subsequently Bloomsbury, and retained a lifelong friendship with Keynes.

In terms of their careers, however, the two followed quite different paths, Hawtrey remaining in the civil service – now in the Treasury – until his retirement in 1947, while Keynes took an academic position in Cambridge. Only after his retirement (with the exception of a visiting professorship to Harvard in 1928–9 while on leave from the Treasury) did Hawtrey take an academic position at the Royal Institute of International Affairs as the Henry Price Professor of International Economics. However it would be misleading to suggest that he did not keep in close contact with the academic world, particularly Cambridge, and the influence of his publications in academic journals and books testifies to this. In particular, *Good and Bad Trade* (1913) and *Currency and Credit* (1919) were very influential in the theory of the relation between money and the trade cycle, and the latter was a standard work in Cambridge of the 1920s.

In total, Hawtrey published 21 books and seven articles, which appeared in the *Economic Journal*, with the sole exception of a paper published in *Economica*. He was made a Fellow of the British Academy, and of Trinity College, Cambridge and became the President of the Royal Economic Society for the years 1946–8.

Hawtrey will be remembered primarily for his views on the relation of monetary conditions to the trade cycle, psychological factors and real influences he believed to be secondary to monetary ones, and only relevant in circumstances where the monetary conditions were accommodating. As a consequence he will be recalled as the foremost advocate of the so-called 'Treasury View', in which public works were seen as liable to cause crowding out, and short-term interest rate adjustments were seen as the only dependable way to manage the cycle. Even to the end of his life he held this view, modifying it only slightly to account for the all-too-rare case of a severe depression, of which the 1930s, he conceded, was one example. Central to his theory of the cycle was the concept of the adjustment to monetary disequilibrium and the role of the manipulation of the short-term interest rate (the bank rate) through its effect on the banking intermediaries, traders and, ultimately, producers and consumers. It was the assumption that trader's demands were elastic with respect to rate of interest, determined by the banks, which made the management of new credit (under Hawtrey's definition the creation of *new* money) drive the cycle. On the upswing the consumers would demand more goods, the traders would find stocks falling and, owing to the delay in the response to new orders given to producers, would increase prices to choke off the excess demand. Banks would be commited to providing credit on terms already agreed, but, in response to the excess demand for credit in the face of falling reserves, would raise the interest rates on new credit. This would set in place the start of the downswing, since the demand for new credit at the higher interest rates would fall off. In the downswing, traders would be faced with excess stocks and would lower the prices of goods to attempt to stimulate sales, they would reduce their demand for goods from producers and a process of decline in output, prices and credit would occur. Ultimately the banks would accumulate excess reserves and on lowering their interest rates would start the cycle over again.

Therefore the key to the cycle was the instability of the banking system, which, in turn, occurred because of the lag in the responsiveness of the demand for money for trade to the changes in credit markets, and the lag in the production process which caused cycles in the stocks held by traders as demand for goods rose and fell.

It was because Hawtrey took a monetary view of the cycle, in which *new* money caused the variation in output, that he has been claimed by some as one of the first monetarists. However his solution was to be found in the control of the short-term interest rate, not in the control of the money stock itself. There are also many who have claimed him as a forerunner of Keynes, and Keynes himself claims to have thought of him (and Dennis Robertson) as 'parent and grandparent in errancy' from the classical view. Certainly he was influenced when corresponding with Keynes on the drafts of the *Treatise on Money* and on the *General Theory*, but he never really accepted that public works could be used to remedy the cycle. However, Davis (1971) makes a good case for Hawtrey having discovered the underemployment equilibrium concept, through the undesired accumulation of stocks when investment and saving are not equated, in his comments on the *Treatise* in 1932. In reality he was a Hawtreyan, a believer in quantity adjustments to shocks in goods markets and sensitivity of markets to the terms on which credit was extended from financial institutions. He believed that, as a result of the inherent lags in the transmission process by which traders, producers, consumers and financiers responded to shocks in turn, the economy was prone to cyclical behavior, and that the 'Treasury view' was the right view of the way to deal with it.

PAUL MIZEN

See also:

Automatic Stabilizers; Classical Economics; Crowding Out; Economics, The Art of; Inflation; Interest, Theories of; Keynes, John Maynard; Keynesian Revolution; Meltzer, Allan H.; Monetary Policy; Money; Niemeyer, Sir Otto E.; Pigou, Arthur C.; Quantity Theory of Money; Real Balance Effect; Treasury View; Viner, Jacob.

Bibliography

Davis, J. Ronnie (1971), *The New Economics and the Old Economists*, Ames: Iowa State University Press.
Hawtrey, R.G. (1913), *Good and Bad Trade*, London: Constable.
Hawtrey, R.G. (1919a), *Currency and Credit*, London: Longmans.
Hawtrey, R.G. (1919b), 'The Gold Standard', *Economic Journal*, **29**, pp. 428–42.
Hawtrey, R.G. (1921), *The Exchequer and the Control of Expenditure*, London: World of Today.
Hawtrey, R.G. (1922), 'The Genoa Resolutions on Currency', *Economic Journal*, **32**, pp. 290–304.
Hawtrey, R.G. (1923), *Monetary Reconstruction*, London: Longmans.
Hawtrey, R.G. (1924), 'Discussion on Monetary Reform', *Economic Journal*, **34**, pp. 155–76.
Hawtrey, R.G. (1925), 'Public Expenditure and the Demand for Labour', *Economica*, **5**, pp. 38–48.
Hawtrey, R.G. (1926), *The Economic Problem*, London: Longmans.
Hawtrey, R.G. (1927), *The Gold Standard in Theory and Practice*, London: Longmans.
Hawtrey, R.G. (1928), *Trade and Credit*, London: Longmans.
Hawtrey, R.G. (1930), *Economic Aspects of Sovereignty*, London: Longmans.
Hawtrey, R.G. (1931), *Trade Depression and the Way Out*, London: Longmans.
Hawtrey, R.G. (1932), *The Art of Central Banking*, London: Longmans.
Hawtrey, R.G. (1933), 'Saving and Hoarding', *Economic Journal*, **43**, pp. 701–8.
Hawtrey, R.G. (1934), 'Monetary Analysis and the Investment Market', *Economic Journal*, **44**, pp. 631–49.
Hawtrey, R.G. (1937), 'Alternative Theories of the Rate of Interest: Three Rejoinders', *Economic Journal*, **47**, pp. 436–43.
Hawtrey, R.G. (1938), *A Century of the Bank Rate*, London: Longmans.
Hawtrey, R.G. (1939), *Capital and Employment*, London: Longmans.
Hawtrey, R.G. (1944), *Economic Destiny*, London: Longmans.
Hawtrey, R.G. (1946a), *Economic Rebirth*, London: Longmans.
Hawtrey, R.G. (1946b), *Bretton Woods: For Better For Worse*, London: Longmans.
Hawtrey, R.G. (1949), *Western European Union*, London: Royal Institute for Economic Affairs.
Hawtrey, R.G. (1950), *Balance of Payments and the Standard of Living*, London: Royal Institute for Economic Affairs.
Hawtrey, R.G. (1954), *Towards the Rescue of Sterling*, London: Longmans.
Hawtrey, R.G. (1955), *Cross Purposes in Wages Policy*, London: Longmans.
Hawtrey, R.G. (1961), *The Pound at Home and Abroad*, London: Longmans.
Hawtrey, R.G. (1967), *Incomes and Money*, London: Longmans.

Heller, Walter W.

Born on 27 August 1915 in Buffalo, New York, Walter W. Heller was raised in Milwaukee, Wisconsin. His decision to pursue a career in economics and public policy was no doubt influenced by the devastating economic and social turmoil he witnessed during his formative years in the Great Depression. His economics training began at Oberlin College and was influenced by Benjamin Lewis who was, as Heller would later become, a devoted teacher and public servant. From the start, Heller saw economics as a tool to influence public policy.

Upon graduating from Oberlin in 1935, Heller entered the PhD program in economics at the University of Wisconsin to study public finance and taxation under Harold Groves. After completing his PhD in 1941, he sought to serve in the military but was rejected because of poor eyesight. Instead Heller went to work for the US Treasury Department in the division of tax research, where he helped develop an income tax withholding system. In 1946, he left Washington to take up a position as associate professor of economics at the University of Minnesota School of Business. His deep sense of public service and conviction that economic tools could serve the public good repeatedly drew him away from Minnesota to work on applied policy issues. His first leave from the University of Minnesota was after just one year. Heller traveled to West Germany to work as Chief of Finance for the American military government. While there he helped establish a tax system and worked on monetary policy issues. During the late 1940s and throughout the 1950s Heller established himself as an expert on the effects of taxation on economic growth, writing numerous articles and books on the subject and consulting for the US as well as foreign governments.

In 1960, Heller was called by President Kennedy to chair the Council of Economic Advisors. His most significant contribution while at the CEA was to design the tax cut legislation of 1963–4. He was the first chairman of the council to fully embrace the Keynesian prescription for eliminating the gap between the current growth in economic output and the full employment equilibrium. It was Heller's mastery of political persuasion that ensured a tax cut of $11.5 billion (1.8 per cent of GDP) in 1963–4.

Heller first met Kennedy in Minneapolis during his campaign. Hubert Humphrey introduced Heller as the best economist west of the Mississippi. During this brief encounter Kennedy expressed his concerns about how to get the economy, then in the midst of the 1960–61 recession, moving again. Heller was impressed with Kennedy's concern for economic issues, and Kennedy was impressed with Heller's belief that the federal government could steer the economy out of recession and his ability to communicate economic issues clearly. Kennedy next spoke to Heller after the election to offer him the position of chairman of the CEA. Heller accepted, acting on his belief that Kennedy would restore the CEA to the position outlined in the Employment Act of 1946. Heller chose James Tobin from Yale University and Kermit Gordon from Williams College to serve on the council with him.

At the time of Kennedy's election most economists agreed that economic growth had been below potential throughout the Eisenhower administration. What to do about this was unclear. Kennedy did not immediately accept Heller's massive tax cut prescription. His campaign platform emphasized sacrifice and early in his administration he even contemplated a tax increase to pay for military build-up in response to the Bay of Pigs and the Berlin Wall crises. In addition Kennedy, like most politicians, pursued a goal of a balanced budget. Heller was able to convince Kennedy that the deficit was due to slow economic growth and that the economy would actually generate a budget surplus at full employment. The education of Kennedy on this issue points to Walter Heller's greatest strength, his ability to translate economic theory into public policy. He was a superb communicator and skillful educator. Heller even boasted that he was able to teach Kennedy about multiplier analysis. By the middle of 1962, Heller had convinced Kennedy of the need for a tax cut. Heller estimated an income gap of $35 billion and multiplier in the range of two to three. His prescription was to cut taxes by $11.5 billion to bring the economy to full employment equilibrium.

The CEA under Heller exemplified the confidence of the economics profession in the early 1960s. Keynesian theory all but promised an end to large cyclical movements in the economy. The problem was no longer what to do about economic fluctuations but rather a matter of communicating the prescribed solutions to the public and the political leaders. Heller was well suited to this task. He firmly believed that economics could offer substantive improvements to the performance of the economy and he had the ability to persuade non-economists of the virtues of fiscal policy tools. Although he would later be criticized for his narrow approach to economic stabilization, that is the use of a tax cut rather than monetary policy to stimulate the economy, it is clear that the policies he advocated were right for the times. The international gold standard did not allow monetary policy sufficient flexibility to be effective. Further, given the conservative opposition to increasing spending, a tax cut was the only politically viable alternative. Although the structural changes of the 1970s changed the profession's view of the virtues of fiscal stabilization policy, the Kennedy–Johnson tax cut still remains the classic textbook example of fiscal policy stimulus.

Under Heller the CEA also developed wage and price guideposts and helped lay the groundwork for what later became part of President Johnson's War on Poverty. Shortly after the 1964 election Heller resigned from the council to return to the University of Minnesota. For the remainder of his career he continued to consult for US and foreign governments on fiscal policy matters. He served as president of the American Economic Association in 1974.

Edward N. Gamber

See also:

Ackley, Hugh Gardner; Burns, Arthur F.; Demand Management; Fellner, William J.; Fiscal Policy; Keynesian Revolution; Neoclassical Synthesis (Bastard Keynesianism); Okun, Arthur M.; Okun's Law; Phillips Curve; Samuelson, Paul A.; Tobin, James.

Bibliography

Biographical Directory of the Council of Economic Advisors (1988), ed. Robert Sobel and Bernard S. Katz, New York: Greenwood Press.

Friedman, Milton and Walter W. Heller (1969), *Monetary vs. Fiscal Policy*, New York: W.W. Norton.

Heller, Walter (1966), *New Dimensions of Political Economy*, Cambridge, Mass.: Harvard University.

Heller, Walter (1976), *The Economy: Old Myths and New Realities*, New York: W.W. Norton.

Heller, Walter (1986), *Perspectives on Economic Growth*, New York: W.W. Norton.

Heller, Walter, Joseph Penchman and N.J. Simler (1982), *Economics in the Public Service*, New York: W.W. Norton.

Rowen, Hobart (1964), *The Free Enterprisers*, New York: Putnam's.

Sobel, Robert (1980), *The World Economists*, New York: Free Press.

The President and the Council of Economic Advisors Interviews with CEA Chairmen (1984), ed. Erwin C. Hargrove and Samuel A. Morley, Boulder CO: Westview.

Henderson, Sir Hubert D.

Sir Hubert Henderson was born on 20 October 1890 to a Glasgow family. Following his education at Aberdeen Grammar School and Emmanuel College, Cambridge, where he studied economics, Henderson became secretary of the Cotton Control Board in 1917. Henderson was at Cambridge during the time when A.C. Pigou was a young professor and John Maynard Keynes was a lecturer. He went on to publish a history of the Cotton Control Board and, after World War I in 1919, he returned to Clare College, Cambridge as a lecturer in economics. While at Cambridge, Henderson met and married Faith Bagenal, an economics student, with whom he had three children.

For the most part, Henderson was generally opposed to formal theoretical systems, believing that they were too limiting to explain reality. He railed against completely mathematical deductions to explain economic theory, maintaining that it was too easy to deceive students and even the theorist himself. His method was primarily empirical and he embraced a dynamic rather than a static perspective in his analysis. One of Henderson's greatest assets, perhaps, was his ability to approach issues with an open mind. He was not a doctrinaire, like many economists, which meant he was able to analyse each situation unencumbered by prevailing doctrine. He was greatly admired for his moderation in debate, all the while holding fast to his convictions. Henderson was open to unconventional ideas and was often a sounding board for students and young colleagues as a result.

In 1922, Henderson published the first book in the *Cambridge Economics Handbook* series, *Supply and Demand*. His book, a small introductory text, was to remain popular for at least 30 years. At the age of 32, Henderson left his position as lecturer to become editor of the *Nation and Athenaeum*, a liberal paper run by J.M. Keynes. During Henderson's tenure as editor he worked closely with Keynes in setting forth the liberal agenda. Henderson wrote for the common man throughout his career, carefully avoiding any technical presentation of his ideas. He focused on economic affairs as editor, although he also wrote about political issues. Henderson wrote about monetary policy, maintaining that the gold standard was a contributing factor to the unemployment problem. In the 1920s, his attention turned to the coal strike and the General Strike, the two greatest economic happenings of the decade in England. He also addressed what he termed the 'New Industrial Revolution' beginning in 1926, as well as writing about international affairs. In sum, Henderson's seven-year editorship of the *Nation* may have produced his most influential writing on policy issues.

Leaving the *Nation* in 1930, Henderson went on to become the joint secretary of the Economic Advisory Council. In 1934, his involvement with Oxford began. He became chairman of the Economists' Research Group in 1936 and was one of the founders of *Oxford Economic Papers* in 1938, sitting on the editorial board and contributing the first article to the journal. Henderson became a delegate to the University Press (Clarendon) in 1941 by election and was also involved in international affairs. With the onset of war in 1939, he was on a committee with Lord Stamp and Henry Clay to examine the problems of wartime economies. Following the war, he was appointed to an advisory position in the Treasury, where he remained until 1934.

With his release from the Treasury, Henderson accepted a research fellowship at All Souls College, Oxford and in 1945 was appointed to the Drummond Chair of Political Economy at Oxford. Henderson was awarded a knighthood in 1942, in recognition of service to his country. He remained active in government affairs, however, serving as chairman of the Statutory Committee on Unemployment Insurance from 1945 to 1948 and serving on the Royal Commission on Population from 1944 to 1949, acting as chairman in his last five years. Henderson was elected Warden of All Souls, Oxford in June 1951.

When he arrived at All Souls in 1934, Henderson was unknown by the majority of the fellows at the college. His ease with conversation and debate made his transition from public life to the private, college environment smooth, and he was soon a popular addition to the All Souls community. Upon the establishment of the Oxford Economists' Research group at Oxford, Henderson took it upon himself to instill an appreciation for practical experience to substantiate economic theory. The group was primarily theoretical in focus and regularly interviewed businessmen, with Henderson acting as an intermediary. Henderson explained economic theories in practical terms to the businessmen and reformulated their practical problems into economic theory. In the main, the interviews entertained questions related to the impact of interest changes on the business environment as well as the means by which producers established the prices for their goods.

In 1945, Henderson was appointed Drummond Professor of Political Economy at Oxford. For the first series of lectures, his topic was 'The Economics of the Modern World', in which he addressed regulation of international trade. In the following years, Henderson lectured on economic and social problems, as well as the general status of the economy, including such topics as inflation, monetary policy and population. He also conducted a seminar for research students in which the format was more one of discussion than of lecture.

In addition to his lecturing, Henderson took his turn as chairman of the Economics sub-faculty. He was a faculty fellow at All Souls and Nuffield College, a member of the Board of Faculty of Social Studies, a member of the General Board of the Faculties, and was chairman of the Standing Committee of the Institute of Statistics. Henderson published no substantial research during his tenure as Drummond Professor, although he had been asked repeatedly to publish his inter-war years' lectures. (His untimely death, in 1952, prevented this work from being undertaken.) Henderson also delivered lectures outside Oxford, giving the Stamp Memorial Lecture in London in 1946, the Rede Lecture in Cambridge the following year, and in 1948, as president of the British Association, addressed Section F. His primary topic of concern was contemporary policy towards international problems.

Shortly after his election as Warden of All Souls, Henderson suffered a heart attack and was never able to take office. He resigned the wardenship in January 1952 and died shortly thereafter, on 22 February 1952.

AUDREY B. DAVIDSON

See also:

Keynes, John Maynard; Keynesian Revolution; Monetary Policy; Money.

Bibliography

Henderson, Hubert D. (1922), *Supply and Demand*, New York: Harcourt, Brace and Company.
Robertson, D.H. (1953), 'Sir Hubert Henderson', *Economic Journal*, **63**, (252), December, pp. 923–31.
Robinson, E.A.G. (1987), 'Henderson, Hubert Douglas', in John Eatwell, Murray Millgate and Peter Newman (eds), *The New Palgrave: A Dictionary of Economics*, Vol. 2, New York: Stockton Press.
Wilson, T. (ed.) (1953), 'Sir Hubert Henderson 1890–1952', supplement to *Oxford Economic Papers*, pp. 1–79.

Hicks, Sir John R.

John Richard Hicks was born 8 April 1904 in Warwick, England. He was the son of Edward and Dorothy (nee Stephens) Hicks, the oldest of three children. He attended Clifton Public School and Balliol College, Oxford, from which he received the BA in 1925, remaining an extra year for postgraduate research. He taught at the London School of Economics, Manchester University, The University of Cambridge and Nuffield College, Oxford, from which he retired in 1965. He married the economist Ursula Webb in 1935. Hicks became a fellow of the British Academy in 1942 and was knighted in 1964. He received the Nobel Prize in Economic Science, together with Kenneth Arrow, for 1972. He died 20 May 1985 at Blockley.

Although working largely on his own, a rather shy and diffident man who combined candor and humility with brilliance, Hicks became one of the handful of leading general theorists of his time, perhaps second only to Paul Samuelson in general influence. Almost no area of economic theory fails to contain and build upon his significant contributions. His was perhaps the most complete version of the British practice of neoclassical economics; with the US version, Hicks was rather uncomfortable.

Hicks was instrumental in the ascendancy of neo-Walrasian general equilibrium theory, which came to rival, if not eclipse, Marshallian partial equilibrium economics as the dominant paradigm or core of economic theory. He received the Nobel Prize for his contributions to both general equilibrium theory and welfare economics.

Hicks considered economic theory to be, not a definition of reality per se, but a set of tools, with which to analyse the economy. He was a methodological and theoretical pluralist, believing that no technique and no theory could answer every question into which economists might inquire. Believing that economics was a discipline and not strictly a science, he argued both that the claims of progress in economics were largely hubris and that progress came about through serious internal criticism, and refused to participate in the absolutist legitimation of the neoclassical paradigm. Although not a specialist historian of economic thought, he drew heavily upon the work of his predecessors, conducting what he considered a conversation with them as he modified and extended their insights, theories and models. He thereby enriched as well as modernized our understanding of the work of past economists. He himself created a number of conceptual tools which have become part of the standard apparatus of economics, including the indifference curve, IS/LM, fixprice and flexprice, income, elasticity of substitution, temporary equilibrium, income and substitution effects, Hicksian aggregation (the composite commodity theorem), compensated demand functions, compensated and equivalent variation, and duality.

Beyond, but often utilizing, the above tools, Hicks made basic contributions to the theories of demand, equilibrium and disequilibrium, expectations, market structure and its consequences (flexprice and fixprice), economic dynamics, business cycles, growth, the interpretation of the work of John Maynard Keynes (with whose work after 1936 Hicks had a continuing interpretive relationship), value, capital and accumulation, wages and labor markets, money and liquidity, and other fields. He also wrote, with less impact, on economic causation and history.

Among other results, Hicks's work both contributed to and reinforced the increasingly dominant Paretian (as opposed to the Pigovian) tradition of welfare economics, and likewise with the emphasis on liquidity, time and uncertainty that, in various and quite different formulations, increasingly became central issues in macroeconomics. He also contributed to the corpus of monetary theory in a manner that was richer and not as rigid as much of the modern quantity theory.

Hicks's intellect grew, or at least changed, with time. He insisted that his IS/LM model was neither an interpretation of Keynes's *General Theory* nor an exhaustive model of the macroeconomy, both of which it had conventionally been taken to be, only a means of relating Keynes's ideas to those of 'the classics'; indeed he came to identify what he considered fundamental flaws and limitations in it and in the general course of interpretation of Keynes and of macroeconomics itself. He felt that economists had not after all accepted what he had intended to be the most important part of his classic, *Value and Capital* (1939), namely the dynamics, and, notwithstanding the Nobel Prize awarded in part for this work, that he had outgrown it. He frequently found fault with his earlier work, for example his theory of wages. He differentiated himself from various methodological, epistemological and substantive orthodoxies in economics. From a pillar of economic orthodoxy Hicks became a quiet (as he always had been) critic and even heterodox economist, perhaps not least in his rejection, as unrealistic, of the flexprice markets of the conventional assumption of competition.

These to some extent later developments notwithstanding, Hicks was willy-nilly an architect of the modern pure, high-theory mode of practicing economics. The kinds of tools he molded, coupled with the types of theories he created, combined with abstract mathematical formalism (which he himself did not overwhelmingly practice), resulted in modern neoclassicism, with its emphasis on the techniques of identifying unique determinate optimal equilibrium solutions to problems. These features are not altogether absent from his writings but are not their centerpiece, which is, rather, the admittedly abstract analysis of the actual economy, with all its complexity and dynamic change. Hicks was this own man and was indeed by any criterion a success, but the result of his theorizing was neither completely foreseen nor intended by him.

WARREN J. SAMUELS

See also:

Arrow, Kenneth J.; Demand Management; Domar, Evsey D.; Hahn, Frank H.; Harcourt, Geoff; Harrod, Sir Roy; IS/LM Model and Diagram; Keynesian Revolution; Money; Neoclassical Synthesis (Bastard Keynesianism); Samuelson, Paul A.; Solow, Robert M.; Swan, Trevor W.; Technological Change.

Bibliography

Collard, D.A., N.H. Dimsdale, C.L. Gilbert, D.R. Helms, M.F.G. Scott and A.K. Sen (eds) (1984), *Economic Theory and Hicksian Themes*, Oxford: Clarendon Press.
Hamouda, O.F. (1993), *John R. Hicks. The Economist's Economist*, Cambridge, Mass.: Basil Blackwell.
Hicks, J.R. (1939), *Value and Capital*, Oxford: Clarendon Press.
Hicks, J.R. (1965), *Capital and Growth*, New York: Oxford University Press.
Hicks, J.R. (1977), *Economic Perspectives*, Oxford: Oxford University Press.
Hicks, J.R. (1981), *Wealth and Welfare*, Cambridge, Mass.: Harvard University Press.
Hicks, J.R. (1982), *Money, Interest and Wages*, Cambridge, Mass.: Harvard University Press.
Hicks, J.R. (1983), *Classics and Moderns*, Cambridge, Mass.: Harvard University Press.

Incomes Policies

Incomes policies are governmental controls applied to wages and prices. Wages are incomes to workers and prices determine what capital and other productive resources are paid. In other words, wage and price controls are really income controls. The purpose of incomes policies is to reduce or control inflation without creating recession. These policies are generally supplemental to, rather than substitutes for, more standard stabilization policies, such as fiscal and monetary policies.

Incomes policies may be the oldest of all economic policies. There is evidence that the Babylonians and Egyptians imposed controls on wages and prices as early as 1000 BC. The Persian empire routinely imposed wage and price controls on various industries and regions. In more modern times, the historical record shows that the Greeks, Romans and Byzantines also relied on incomes policies to control wages and prices. It is also evident that few lessons have been learned concerning these approaches in modern times.

There is a continuum of incomes policies that range from the informal to formal. Informal policies focus on programs designed to educate, monitor and persuade people to control increases in prices and wages. Formal policies are typically enacted as law and involve direct control of economic behaviors, often with enforcement mechanisms. The most informal income policies include little more than a government agency monitoring wages and prices and reporting this information to economic decision makers. Informal policies may also include voluntary wage and price guidelines to simply appeal for wage and price restraint. President Carter used a program or moral suasion to attempt to persuade producers and workers to refrain from escalating prices and wages, without success. Carter then proceeded with his voluntary anti-inflation program of guidelines in 1977 that also met with little or no success in controlling inflation. Few economists advocate the use of informal incomes policies because the underlying premise of microeconomic theory is that people will act in their own self-interest and persuasion to act for the commweal is generally ineffective.

Formal incomes policies may include actual governmental regulation of wages and prices. If formal wage and price controls are implemented, as during World War II, there are specific enforcement procedures and penalties for violations of the regulations included in the legislation. In general, when formal controls are implemented black-markets, shortages and surpluses often emerge, which, in turn, result in the controls becoming ineffective and eventually abandoned.

There are several types of incomes policies that fall between the most and least formal. For example, tax-based incomes policies (TIP), first proposed by Arthur Okun, encouraged compliance with established wage–price guidelines by using fiscal incentives for compliance. The TIP system was to rely on tax surcharges and rebates to encourage compliance. Firms that increase prices or wages in excess of the guidelines established by the government suffer a progressive tax surcharge. On the other hand, firms that hold the line on price and wage increases are rewarded with tax rebates. The TIP proposal was never enacted in the United States, but TIP has been used in the planned economies of eastern Europe, such as Hungary and Poland, with limited success. More penalty-based programs were proposed by Henry Wallich, Sidney Weintraub and Laurence Seidman that permitted the government a wide range of alternative penalties should producers not adhere to price controls. Abba Lerner also suggested a variant of TIP using wage-increase permits (WIP) that required firms to stay within the wage controls, or purchase on the open market a limited number of governmental licenses to increase wages above the government-imposed limits.

President Carter suggested a *real-wage assurance* program similar to TIP in 1980. Carter wanted unions to keep their wage demands within the administration's 7 per cent guidelines. What he suggested was that, if inflation exceeded the 7 per cent target of his voluntary guidelines, the loss of any earning power due to unions negotiating wage increases of 7 per cent or less would be made up by income tax credits. Carter's proposal also died in committee once it reached Congress.

In the planned economies of eastern Europe prior to 1991, incomes policies were built into the economic plans. Wage and price guidelines were established in five-year planning cycles. The industries that met the wage–price targets were often rewarded by additional resources and those failing to meet the targets would often be required to make adjustments to assure feature compliance. In capitalist economies of North America, Asia and Europe, there have been many variations on incomes policies. For the only time since World War II, President Nixon established mandatory wage and price controls. The inflationary pressures of the Vietnam War caused the Nixon administration to attempt to emulate the controls that were successful during World War II, but these policies were quickly undermined by the self-interest of various economic agents.

Most economists argue that incomes policies cannot be effective unless the government is willing to regulate a wide range of economic behaviors (and not just wages and prices). The allocative inefficiencies created by income policies have been exhibited in many ways. In the United States, during Nixon's abortive experiment with incomes policies, registered nurses in New York, rather than negotiate a labor agreement outside the wage controls, reduced their standard working week by 2.5 hours (thereby getting a legal overtime premium which effectively increased earnings by 3.125 per cent) and candy bar companies reduced the size of their product (yet sold them at the same price). Because these types of rather sophisticated market behaviors were not controlled, the mandatory wage and price controls failed to produce any desirable results. In the planned economies of the former Soviet Union, the shortages of consumer commodities were in large measure attributable to the incomes policies included in the five-year planning process. By controlling prices at artificially low levels, the Soviet planners were by necessity creating shortages.

Economists have been critical of incomes policies on other grounds. The cost of administering even voluntary controls that were attempted by the Kennedy, Johnson and Carter administrations was significant. Economists have argued that these administrative costs were not justified by the results of these programs. Perhaps more persuasively, economists have identified a *bubble effect* associated with wage and price controls. Wages and prices have a tendency to increase dramatically after the policy is announced and before it is implemented. Wages and prices also increase significantly at the time the policies are terminated. The result is that there are wage and price increases that occur in anticipation of controls and a second round of increases to recapture any value lost as a result of the controls once they are lifted.

These behaviors demonstrate the problems with government controls. If controls over wages and prices are attempted by a government, people and firms will generally find ways around the regulation that render income policies ineffective. The argument for incomes policies is founded on changing the inflationary expectations of producers and consumers. To the extent that income policies can dampen inflationary expectations, these policies may be an effective adjunct to fiscal and monetary policies.

Incomes policies have been the topic of debate in the economics profession for decades. However incomes policies are rarely used in market economics. With the exception of World War II, the experiments with incomes policies have been failures in the United States and western Europe. In planned economies incomes policies were significant factors that helped ensure the demise of the Eastern Bloc countries' economic systems. Several of the less developed countries of Latin America, the Middle East and Africa still use a variety of incomes policies, but none has yet produced evidence of success.

MASHALAH RAHNAMA-MOGHADAM

See also:

Demand Management; Lerner, Abba P.; Okun, Arthur M.; Post Keynesian School of Economics; Weintraub, Sidney.

Bibliography
Adam, Jan (1979), *Wage Control and Inflation in the Soviet Bloc Countries*, London: Macmillan.
Lerner, Abba P. (1977), 'Stagflation – Its Cause and Cure', *Challenge*, **20**, (4), October, pp. 14–19.
Okun, Arthur (1970), *The Political Economy of Prosperity*, New York: W.W. Norton.
Seidman, Laurence S. (1978), *Tax-Based Incomes Policies*, Washington, DC: Brookings Institution.
Wallich, H.C. and Sidney Weintraub (1971), 'A Tax-Based Incomes Policy', *Journal of Economic Issues*, **5**, (2), June, pp. 1–19.

Inflation

Inflation refers to a process of continuing increase in the general price level. It is measured as the percentage rate of change in a price level. While economists agree that inflation is a monetary phenomenon, they offer two rival explanations for it. Classical economists believe that money supply increases cause price increases because, given the potential supply, demand pulls prices up – the demand-pull theory. Keynesian economists, on the other hand, reason that it is price increases that cause the money supply to increase. They argue that institutional pressures cause production costs to increase, which pushes prices up – the cost-push theory.

Classical theory of inflation

According to the Classicals, inflation is the result of demand pull, that is, aggregate demand growing faster than aggregate supply at the prevailing price level. The most celebrated demand-pull explanation is the 'Quantity Theory of Money'. Fischer's equation of exchange succinctly expresses this view: $MV = PQ$, where M is the stock of money, V is the income velocity of money, P is the average price level of goods and services bought in the economy and Q is the real national output. The product MV is the money value of expenditure. The product PQ is the money value of the aggregate output. By making the strong classical assumption that the velocity, V, is constant, the dynamic form of the simple Quantity Theory can be written as:

$$(\% \text{ change of } M) = (\% \text{ change of } P) + (\% \text{ change of } Q)$$
$$\Delta M/M = \Delta P/P + \Delta Q/Q$$

or

$$\Delta P/P = \Delta M/M - \Delta Q/Q.$$

Therefore inflation ($\Delta P/P > 0$) results when money supply grows faster than real output ($\Delta M/M > \Delta Q/Q$).

The essence of the classical argument is that changes in the supply of money affect the public's ability to spend. If the economy's productive capacity is underutilized, the increase in effective demand results in an increase in real income and output. With no large-scale underutilization, money supply increases will contribute to higher real income and a higher price level. However, if there is no unused productive capacity and the money supply increases, only the price level will increase. Therefore, in the long run, inflation is everywhere and always a monetary phenomenon.

Keynesian theory of inflation

Economic institutions are central to Keynesian cost-push explanations of inflation. Keynesians argue that, because product markets are not entirely competitive, in order to reduce coordination costs firms adopt cost-based pricing policies, which depend on resource prices and resource productivity. Also, in the determination of wages, sociological and institutional forces are significant. All workers, whether unionized or not, look at the wage gains of their peers and seek to do as well or better. Employers pay the pattern wage increase knowing they will not jeopardize their competitive position since rivals will adopt the same wage stance.

In an imperfectly competitive system, prices and wages develop their own momentum because it is self-consistent and becomes habitual and expected. What starts inflation, whether wage or price increases, is difficult to tell. If input prices increase for any reason, however, producers are likely to increase the prices of their products to protect their profit margins. Rising prices in effect decrease the purchasing power of wages, so workers may apply pressure for wage increases. This leads to further price increases, which then develops into a wage–price spiral.

The Phillips curve

In 1958, A.W. Phillips of the London School of Economics documented that, for the United Kingdom from 1861 to 1957, a higher unemployment rate typically corresponded to lower wage rate growth, and vice versa. A plot of the trade-off between inflation and unemployment, the Phillips curve is curvilinear: quite flat at high unemployment rates and increasingly steep as unemployment declines.

Early on, it seemed that the Phillips curve presented policy makers with a stable trade-off by which they could choose a lower unemployment rate if they were willing to accept a higher inflation rate and vice versa. Theoretical developments and real world events suggest that, in the long run, there is no trade-off between inflation and unemployment and, in the short run, the relationship is not stable. In the late 1960s, Edmund Phelps (1967) and Milton Friedman (1968), in separate papers, raised serious theoretical questions about the Phillips curve and its implied trade-off. They argued that it is real wages and not money wages that matter in labor supply and labor demand decisions. Workers and employers, in setting wages, consider inflation and expected inflation; if actual inflation is equal to expected inflation, the rate of inflation, whether it is zero or 10 per cent, will not affect real wages and employment. That is, in the long run, unemployment is the same regardless of the rate of inflation.

Short-run response may be different, however. If the inflation rate rises unexpectedly and if workers suffer money illusion and do not realize the fall in real wages, they will not reduce their labor supply. The decrease in real wages will, however, increase labor demand. If the inflation rate stays at the new, higher level, workers will notice that their real wages have fallen and will bid for wage increases. When real wages rise back to the previous level, the demand for labor will fall and unemployment will rise to the previous level.

Expectations are important to Phillips curve analysis. Whenever actual inflation exceeds expected inflation, the short-run Phillips curve, which assumes constant expectations, will shift up until actual inflation equals expected inflation. When expectations have adjusted fully, there is no trade-off between inflation and unemployment, and the long-run Phillips curve is vertical. According to the Classicals, there is only one unemployment rate independent of the expectations of inflation and the rate of inflation, the 'natural rate' of unemployment. If the unemployment rate is held below the natural rate, it leads to actual inflation higher than expected inflation. Gradually expectations will adjust, future increases in inflation will be expected, the short-run Phillips curve will shift up and the unemployment rate will rise. According to the Classicals, in the long-run there is no trade-off between inflation and unemployment; regardless of the inflation rate, the economy returns to the natural rate of unemployment.

While the Keynesians do not disagree that the long-run Phillips curve is vertical, they believe that the long-run is too long in coming. Economic activity does not take place in a vacuum: institutional forces play a role. Prices are sticky because of implicit contracts and coordination failures. If prices are sticky, inflationary expectations may be held in check and even when actual inflation exceeds expected inflation, expectations may not adjust. In the Keynesian view, there is a trade-off between inflation and unemployment.

Inflation and economic policies
These divergent views on what causes inflation obviously lead to differing policy options to end inflation. Classical economists believe that wages and prices are flexible and, if unimpeded, markets function well. Inflation results

from expansionary policies that attempt to lower the unemployment rate below the natural rate, causing the actual inflation rate to exceed the expected inflation rate. The only remedy is to squeeze inflation out of the economy by pursuing contractionary monetary and fiscal policies to engineer a recession and force the unemployment rate above the natural rate. Then expectations of inflation will adjust, eventually falling to zero. Future policies are an important dimension of economic expectations, so the credibility of government policies is paramount to their success. Therefore the framers of monetary policy should announce and stick to the non-inflationary rates of monetary growth. Inflation expectations will fall quickly and the economy will gravitate to the natural rate.

If the natural rate of unemployment is too high, the Classicals argue, it is because public policies contribute to generous unemployment benefits, higher minimum wage rates, reduced labor mobility and poor education and training. To reduce unemployment, governments should concentrate more on microeconomic policies to promote labor market flexibility than on expansionary macroeconomic policies that only ignite inflation without reducing unemployment.

Keynesians argue that, because of the reluctance of business firms and the contractual nature of many employment relationships, prices and wages are sticky. To rid the economy of inflationary psychology, what is necessary is either a deep, short recession or a prolonged, shallow recession. Because recessions impose greater costs on lower-income individuals, Keynesians prefer an anti-inflationary policy, called incomes policies, to directly hold down individual wages and prices. These range from voluntary wage and price guidelines to compulsory wage and price controls to tax-based incomes policies (TIP). These might be used (1) to suppress demand-pull inflation; (2) to break exceptional inflation; and (3) to control permanent wage-cost inflation.

NAGA PULIKONDA

See also:

Aggregate Demand–Aggregate Supply Model and Diagram; Classical Economics; Davidson, Paul; Expectations, Theories of; Friedman, Milton; Galbraith, John K.; Incomes Policies; Keynes, John Maynard; Meltzer, Allan H.; Monetary Policy; Monetarist School of Economics; Phillips Curve; Post Keynesian School of Economics; Quantity Theory of Money; Schwartz, Anna J.; Weintraub, Sidney; Wicksell, Knut.

Bibliography

Friedman, M. (1968), 'The Role of Monetary Policy', *American Economic Review*, **58**, (1), pp. 1–17.
Laidler, D. and M. Parkin (1975), 'Inflation: A Survey', *Economic Journal*, **85**, (340), December, pp. 741–809.
Phelps, E.S. (1967), 'Phillips Curves, Inflation Expectations and Optimal Employment over Time', *Economica*, **34**, (135), August, pp. 254–81.

Phillips, A.W. (1958), 'The Relationship Between Unemployment and the Rate of Money Wage-Rates in the United Kingdom, 1861–1957', *Economica*, **25**, (100), November, pp. 283–99.

Trevithick, J.A and C. Mulvey (1980), *The Economics of Inflation*, New York: Wiley, A Halsted Press Book.

Interest, Theories of

Our understanding of the interest rate is intimately connected to the way we conceive the relationship between the monetary and real sectors of the economy. Theorists of the interest rate as a real phenomenon view money as a veil which flutters over the more fundamental and ultimately dominant forces of consumer preferences and the productivity of capital. Irving Fisher (1930) conceived the real interest rate to be the price that balanced consumers' time preferences – their preferences to consume now rather than in the future – with the 'waiting' that investors provide when they undertake 'roundabout' capital investment that promises a return of marketable consumer goods in the more distant future. Knut Wicksell's (1935) natural rate of interest likewise signals time preferences for consumption and the productivity of capital. From Fisher's and Wicksell's 'real' perspectives, any potentially disequilibrating monetary influences on the real or natural rate are temporary and/or inconsequential, so that real savings and investment will be equilibrated at full employment, in the long run, by fluctuations in the interest rate. An important component of Keynes's interest theory is that monetary forces on the interest rate are likely to be dominant in both the short and the long run, thereby disrupting the equilibrating role of interest. For Keynes, the interest rate was not determined by the forces of productivity and thrift but by speculative activity in financial markets. The attempt to articulate this view persuasively continues to engage economists working in the Keynesian tradition.

Wicksell's analysis of the relationship between the market and natural interest rate is the natural entry point into the issues raised by Keynes's interest theory, since Keynes was largely operating in a Wicksellian framework. Wicksell conceived the natural interest rate to be the rate of interest that equilibrated real saving and investment at full employment. In a monetary economy, real saving and investment are expressed by the supply and demand for loanable funds. Wicksell argued that, in a modern banking system with the ability to grant credit, the supply of loanable funds could exceed real savings, thereby lowering the market or money rate below the natural rate and stimulating investment expenditure. This monetary disturbance of the interest rate was, however, temporary as the monetarily induced increase in spending initiated a cumulative increase in the price level that would eventually begin to drain reserves from the banking system. Faced with the steady loss of reserves, banks would be forced to raise the market rate back to the level of the natural rate. The natural interest rate thus acted as a center of gravity anchoring the market rate and ensuring the ultimate stability of a monetary economy.

The task of articulating a monetary theory of interest is connected to demonstrating why market economies may not be self-equilibrating in either the short or the long run. Central to this task is to illustrate how the market interest rate is determined exogenously with respect to the income-generating process. In the *General Theory*, Keynes rejects the loanable funds theory, which grounds interest in the forces of productivity and thrift, and substitutes his liquidity preference theory of interest. Liquidity preference theory asserts that the interest rate is determined by the supply and demand for the stock of bonds and money, which Keynes provisionally defines as 'any command over general purchasing power which the owner has not parted with for a period in excess of three months' (Keynes, 1936, p. 167, fn). Keynes's theory reverses Wicksell's understanding of the relationship between the monetary and real sectors. For Keynes, the monetary economy is repeatedly following a particular sequential process of adjustment: the market interest rate is continuously determined by monetary factors, and the marginal efficiency of capital, a proxy for Wicksell's natural interest rate, then adjusts to the market interest rate. Given this sequential process, it is possible for the market interest rate to 'rule the roost' at considerable levels of unemployment.

It is increasingly clear to many Keynesian theorists that Hicks's (1937) well-known translation of liquidity preference into the IS/LM apparatus does Keynes's vision a disservice (Hicks, 1980–81). For one, IS/LM does not capture the sequential nature of Keynes's adjustment process. In addition, IS/LM suggests that the interest rate is ultimately determined by the real forces of productivity and thrift if wages and prices are flexible in the long run. Thus in the IS/LM model liquidity preference collapses into the real theory that sees interest as being an endogenous and equilibrating variable.

The attempt to develop a theory of interest as a variable determined exogenously with respect to the income-generating process has been developed in two different directions by followers of Keynes. One approach has been to stress the endogeneity of the supply of credit money (Moore, 1988). Adherents of this approach emphasize the evolution of overdraft facilities in modern banking systems. Firms regularly negotiate lines of credit with banks which they draw upon at their discretion to finance changing working capital requirements. As lenders of last resort, central banks stand ready to supply reserves to the banking system, at the price of their choosing, to accommodate the demand for credit. The money supply is therefore primarily driven by the demand for bank credit, and central banks control the price at which base money is supplied to the banks. In a credit money system, the short-term interest rate is then entirely a policy variable. Long-term interest rates are determined as the weighted sum of expected future short-term rates. Insofar as Keynes's presentation of liquidity preference relies upon an exogenously administered supply of money, many advocates of monetary endogeneity reject liquidity preference as an explanation of interest, although they do accept Keynes's insistence that the interest rate is a monetary variable.

The second approach to developing a monetary theory of interest is associated with Shackle's (1967, pp. 203–47) interpretation of Keynes. Those in the Shackleian tradition might accept the proposition that the short-term interest rate is a policy variable, but they doubt that long-term rates can be represented as merely the weighted sum of expected short-term rates. The Shackleian rearticulation of liquidity preference requires the following steps. First, it is necessary to reject the general equilibrium method. General equilibrium does not allow an essential role for money in developing an interest theory (Hahn, 1984, p. 162). Nor can general equilibrium capture the sequential nature of Keynes's understanding of the relationship between monetary forces and the real economy (Chick, 1983, pp. 14–33). Second, liquidity preference requires that the speculative activity of wealth-holders can dominate the impact savings and investment decisions have on the prices of financial assets. Finally, a reconstructed theory of liquidity preference recognizes the pervasive fact of uncertainty. Given this uncertainty, rational economic actors will respond to the expected value of nominal variables, particularly in financial markets (Rogers, 1989).

This tradition describes the interest rate as a conventional variable, a description that follows directly from the emphasis on the pervasiveness of uncertainty (Keynes, 1937, p. 203). Because bond-holders can never be certain of future bond values, they will often engage in speculation. Speculators are continually attempting to guess what average opinion will hold the interest rate to be in the future. If speculators think that average opinion will be such that bond-holders will make decisions causing the interest rate to decline, they will purchase bonds now in order to obtain an expected capital gain. If enough speculators expect the interest rate to fall, it actually will, as a consequence of speculative decisions to purchase bonds. At any moment the interest rate will be constituted by a competition among guessers, who of course will not all guess the same way. There will be bulls and bears, some who think bond prices will rise, others who think they will fall. The balance point that emerges between the bulls and bears will be nothing more than a convention, a value of interest around which speculator's expectations will be distributed, a point contingent upon conventional opinion of what conventional opinion will be.

Dennis Robertson (1940, p. 25) argued that the liquidity preference theory neglected a crucial point: what wealth-holders in fact speculated about were the future influences of productivity and thrift. That is, while liquidity preference might be able to explain temporary changes in the interest rate as a result of speculation about future changes in its value, it does not establish why interest exists – and what speculators guess about – in the first place. If we accept Robertson's view that interest exists because of consumers' time preferences and the productivity of investment, then perhaps speculation is like the boiling surface on a pan of soup, where the level of the soup is akin to the forces of productivity and thrift (Coddington, 1983, p. 81). This view is, however, fundamentally mistaken. Keynes called interest the 'reward for parting with liquidity for a specified period' (Keynes, 1936, p. 167). Interest can arise simply because wealth-holders expect that they might need to liquidate their wealth some time in the future at an unknowable price, and they need to be compensated for the possibility that these future prices might lead to capital loss. The greater the fear of capital loss, the greater the demand for liquid assets and the greater the long-term interest rate must be to entice wealth-holders to hold illiquid assets. Fear provoked by uncertainty over future prices of financial assets can explain the existence of interest, independently of productivity and thrift (Shackle, 1972, pp. 187–205).

Finally, it is important to make clear why changes in real forces, such as consumers' time preferences and productivity improvements, will not necessarily have an impact on long-term interest rates. In real theories of interest, an increase in saving will cause the interest rate to fall and bond prices to rise. A small drop in the interest rate initiated by the increase in savings may, however, be differently interpreted by speculative wealth-holders. If the rise in bond prices is interpreted as an indication that bond prices have reached their peak, speculators will sell bonds to avoid future expected capital losses. The speculative sale of bonds may absorb all the new savings without any corresponding increase in investment. If the rise in bond prices is interpreted as the start of a long-term trend, speculators may attempt to move wealth from money to bonds, thereby causing interest to fall by a greater amount than is warranted by the increase in savings. Consequently any impact changes in real forces might have on interest rates will depend on the firmness and nature of the conventional value of interest established in financial markets (Maclachlan, 1993, pp. 61–85).

THEODORE A. BURCZAK

See also:

Austrian School of Economics; Classical Economics; Friedman, Milton; Hahn, Frank H.; Harcourt, Geoff; Hawtrey, Sir Ralph; IS/LM Model and Diagram; Jorgenson, Dale W.; Kalecki, Michał; Keynes, John Maynard; Kregel, Jan A.; Lausanne, The School of; Liquidity Trap; Monetary Policy; Money; Sraffa, Piero; Wicksell, Knut.

Bibliography

Chick, Victoria (1983), *Macroeconomics after Keynes*, London: Philip Allan.
Coddington, Alan (1983), *Keynesian Economics: The Search for First Principles*, London: George Allan & Unwin.
Fisher, Irving (1930), *The Theory of Interest*, New York: Macmillan.
Hahn, Frank (1984), *Equilibrium and Macroeconomics*, Cambridge, Mass.: MIT Press.
Hicks, J.R. (1937), 'Mr. Keynes and the Classics: A Suggested Interpretation', *Econometrica*, **5**, (2), April, pp. 147–59.
Hicks, J.R. (1980–81), 'IS–LM: An Explanation', *Journal of Post Keynesian Economics*, **3**, (2), Winter, pp. 139–54.
Keynes, John Maynard (1936), *The General Theory of Employment, Interest and Money*, London: Macmillan.
Keynes, John M. (1937), 'The General Theory of Employment', *Quarterly Journal of Economics*, **51**, (1), February, pp. 209–33.
Maclachlan, Fiona (1993), *Keynes' General Theory of Interest. A Reconsideration*, London/New York: Routledge.
Moore, Basil (1988), *Horizontalists and Verticalists: The Macroeconomics of Credit Money*, Cambridge: Cambridge University Press.
Robertson, D.H. (1940), *Essays in Monetary Theory*, London: P.S. King and Son.
Rogers, Colin (1989), *Money, Interest and Capital: A Study in the Foundations of Monetary Theory*, Cambridge: Cambridge University Press.
Shackle, G.L.S. (1967), *The Years of High Theory: Invention and Tradition in Economic Thought 1926–1939*, Cambridge: Cambridge University Press.
Shackle, G.L.S (1972), *Epistemics and Economics*, Cambridge: Cambridge University Press.
Wicksell, Knut (1935), *Lectures in Political Economy*, vols I and II, trans. E. Claasen and L. Robbins, London: Routlege.

International Clearing Union

In the autumn of 1941, Keynes was already giving thought to the grave difficulties Britain would face in its external economic dealings after the war. His mood, according to his biographer, was one of 'deep reflection and heart searching' (Harrod, 1951, p. 525). In early September, Keynes retired to his country seat to draft his vision of a postwar monetary order in two papers, 'Post-War Currency Policy' and 'Proposals for an International Currency Union' (*CW*, XXV, pp. 21–40). The latter document soon stimulated widespread comment within the British government, passing through many drafts before emerging as an official Cabinet paper in April 1943. Upon further revision, the 'Proposals for an International Clearing Union' (*CW*, XXV, pp. 168–95) were submitted to the American side for consideration alongside a similar US plan developed by Harry Dexter White. These two plans formed the basis for Anglo-American discussions culminating in the Bretton Woods agreement to establish the International Monetary Fund and the World Bank.

In Keynes's view there had been only two periods in the previous 500 years when the international monetary system had 'worked' – during the long reigns of Queen Elizabeth and Queen Victoria. Outside those eras, the system had been productive of 'impoverishment and social discontent and even of wars and revolutions' (*CW*, pp. 21–2). Continued faith in a system Keynes dubbed 'currency laissez faire' was nothing short of 'doctrinaire delusion'. Neither continued adherence to 'currency laissez faire' nor any of the ad hoc departures from it which nations had embarked upon during the inter-war period promised lasting stability. The gold standard had crumbled. Wartime governments had instituted quotas, barter agreements and a variety of exchange controls.

But the contorted condition of world monetary arrangements presented, to Keynes's eye, an opportunity: 'Things are possible today which would have been impossible if they involved the prior disestablishment of a settled system' (*CW*, XXV, p. 22). He hoped in the war's aftermath to see a more consultative, multilateral approach to international finance, with the International Clearing Union playing a key role. The ICU would stand in relation to national central banks as an individual central bank stands to its own member banks. At this 'clearing bank', member nations would be assigned initial quotas of a monetary unit called 'bancor'. The initial 'quota index', or maximum overdraft limit, of bancor would be proportionate to a nation's average trade volume of the previous five years. National currency values would be fixed in terms of bancor, and bancor itself would be defined in terms of gold. Nations running net trade surpluses with the rest of the world would gain credit balances of bancor, while nations in overall trade deficit would record debit balances. Because all imbalances of commercial payments were to be settled through the clearing bank, central banks would have no further need to hold foreign currencies or gold as reserves.

A distinctive feature of the Keynes plan was its even-handed treatment of debtor and creditor nations. In the theory of the gold standard, nations with persistent balance of payments deficits were expected to defend the external value of their currency by taking steps to deflate their price level, even at the cost of recession and unemployment. Surplus nations, on the other hand, were under no such constraint. They could allow a corrective inflation to take place, or they could choose to have their central banks neutralize the surpluses (in essence, stockpile the gold) and avoid inflation. The burdens of adjustment on debtor and creditor were thus unequal, creating, as Keynes believed, a contractionary pressure on world commerce. Under his ICU plan, a nation with a bancor credit balance that was persistent and exceeded a certain fraction of the country's quota index would be assessed for an interest charge on the excess, just as debtor countries would be charged interest on debit balances that exceeded a certain fraction of their quota index.

For persistent disequilibrium problems, however, Keynes saw the need for some measure of exchange rate flexibility in the new system. Countries that accumulated large enough surpluses or deficits on their bancor accounts were permitted to revalue or devalue their currencies by up to 5 per cent in a year. In extreme cases they might be *required* to do so by the governors of the Clearing Union. The combination of currency revaluations and interest penalties on excessive surpluses and deficits gave substance to Keynes's claim that his ICU plan would feature 'an internal stabilising mechanism, by which pressure is exercised on any country whose balance of payments with the rest of the world is departing from equilibrium in either direction' (*CW*, XXV, p. 169).

The rival plan for a postwar monetary order put forward by the US Treasury Department aimed to achieve the same Keynesian goals of liberalized trade, stable exchange rates and a consultative process for restoring equilibrium. Keynes himself saw the British and American proposals as 'born of the same climate of opinion' and sharing 'identical purposes' (Harris, 1948, p. 366). He and his American counterpart, Harry White, communicated with one another before and, with increasing frequency, after their governments published their respective monetary proposals in 1943. The American plan – less bold and elegant than Keynes's in the judgement of most analysts (including Keynes himself) – envisaged a 'Stabilization Fund' that would function much as Keynes's clearing bank. Nations would contribute an initial 'quota' to this Fund in the form of gold reserves and national currency rather than receiving a maximum overdraft facility at the outset, as Keynes proposed. The total resources to be made available to the Fund were a fraction of those created under Keynes's plan. Details of the settling of balances among nations differed somewhat between the two plans, though both provided mechanisms for dealing with serious imbalances.

Not surprisingly, given the commanding political and economic position of the United States in the mid-1940s, it was the White plan rather than the Keynes plan that prevailed. How much this disappointed Keynes is difficult to know. His friend Roy Harrod was certain that 'it was with a heavy heart that Keynes abandoned his structure' (Harrod, 1951, p. 561), but in public the great economist held his peace. In a speech to the House of Lords he graciously described the incipient International Monetary Fund as 'a considerable improvement on either of its parents'. He went on to declare: 'I like this new plan and I believe that it will work to our advantage' (Harris, 1948, p. 369). At the Bretton Woods conference that summer it was Keynes, heading the British delegation, who moved the acceptance of the American plan.

It is important to note that neither Keynes nor White ever conceived of the international currency-clearing institution as adequate, in itself, to handle all the economic difficulties that the postwar world would face. Both men understood the need for a well capitalized international agency of long-term lending, and both drafted early proposals for such an institution. At Bretton Woods this need was answered by the creation of the International Bank for Reconstruction and Development – the World Bank. Like the IMF, this institution more closely resembled what the Americans had proposed than what the British (that is, Keynes) had proposed, though the similarities were substantial.

GEOFFREY GILBERT

See also:

Bretton Woods; Keynes, John Maynard; Meade, James E.; Robinson, Joan; White, Harry D.

Bibliography

Dillard, Dudley (1948), *The Economics of John Maynard Keynes: The Theory of the Monetary Economy*, New York: Prentice-Hall.

Gardner, Richard N. (1969), *Sterling–Dollar Diplomacy: The Origins and the Prospects of Our International Economic Order*, 2nd edn, New York: McGraw-Hill.

Harris, Seymour (1955), *John Maynard Keynes: Economist and Policy Maker*, New York: Charles Scribner's Sons.

Harris, Seymour and M. Willfort (eds) (1948), *The New Economics: Keynes' Influence on Theory and Public Policy*, New York: Alfred A. Knopf.

Harrod, R.F (1948), 'Keynes and Traditional Theory', in Seymour Harris and M. Willfort (eds), *The New Economics: Keynes' Influence on Theory and Public Policy*, New York: Alfred A. Knopf.

Harrod, R.F. (1951), *The Life of John Maynard Keynes*, New York: Harcourt, Brace and Company.

Moggridge, D.E. (ed.) (1980), *The Collected Writings of John Maynard Keynes*, Vol. XXV: *Activities, 1940–1944: Shaping the Post-War World: The Clearing Union*, New York: Cambridge University Press.

Moggridge, D.E. (1986), 'Keynes and the International Monetary System, 1909–46', in Jon S. Cohen and G.C. Harcourt (eds), *International Monetary Problems and Supply-Side Economics: Essays in Honour of Lorie Tarshis*, New York: St Martin's Press.

Moggridge, D.E. (1992), *Maynard Keynes: An Economist's Biography*, London: Routledge.

Robinson, Joan (1943), 'The International Currency Proposals', *Economic Journal*, **53**, (210), June–September, pp. 161–75.

IS/LM Model and Diagram

The IS/LM model is a multi-market model of simultaneous equilibrium in the goods market and the money market. It was created by John Hicks (although similar models were simultaneously designed by James Meade and Roy Harrod). The goods market equilibrium curve, the IS (investment = savings) curve, is essentially a Keynesian goods market equilibrium curve incorporating an assumed effect of a change in interest rates on investment (and other spending) and the multiplier effect. The money market equilibrium curve, the *LM* (demand for liquidity = supply of money) curve is a money market equilibrium curve incorporating a standard supply and demand for money analysis. Aggregate equilibrium occurs when the money market and the goods market are in equilibrium – when the *IS* curve intersects the *LM* curve. Thus the analysis creates a set of curves for macro that are parallel to the supply demand curves used in micro. For that reason Axel Leijonhufvud has called IS/LM analysis the totem of macro.

Monetary and fiscal policy can be neatly shown in the IS/LM model. Fiscal policy shifts the *IS* curve; monetary policy shifts the *LM* curve. If policy makers are told the interest rate and the income level that the economy is aiming at, they can use some combination of these policies to attain them. The analysis can also be internationalized by adding a *BP* (balance of payments) equilibrium curve.

Initially, and throughout the 1960s, the IS/LM model formed the core of what intermediate students were taught. Keynesians were interpreted as believing the *LM* curve was elastic, and Classicals were interpreted as believing the *LM* curve was inelastic. The problem was that neither side accepted their portion of the curve, and higher-level analysis quickly moved beyond issues that could be discussed meaningfully in such a simple framework. The inflation of the 1970s further complicated the issues since inflation could not be easily amended to the IS/LM model. New Classicals and Post Keynesians have been especially vociferous in their condemnation of the IS/LM model. Nonetheless, it has remained the core model taught to intermediate macro students, albeit with increasing discussion of its limitations.

Another set of criticisms that has been leveled against IS/LM analysis is that it is not a description of what Keynes meant, although this group of critics has had to deal with Keynes's general positive comments about it to Hicks. However Hicks, late in life, rejected it, as did most members of the Cambridge Circus such as Joan Robinson and Richard Kahn. What seems clear is that Keynes meant many things, some of which are consistent with an IS/LM interpretation, and some of which are not.

Despite the criticism, advocates of the IS/LM model are unrepentant. For example, Tobin, even while acknowledging the logical problems with IS/LM analysis, writes: 'I do not think the apparatus is discredited. I still believe that, carefully used and taught, it is a powerful instrument for understanding our economies and the impacts of policies upon them.' Certainly IS/LM's continued use suggests that Tobin's view is not unique to him. For example, Robert Solow concurs and offers an explanation of the phenomenon of IS/LM's use, despite concern about its logical foundations. He argues that IS/LM is useful in 'training our intuition, to give us a handle on the facts'. He says that the IS/LM model has survived because it proves to be a marvelously simple and useful way to recognize and process some of the main macroeconomic facts.

For rough and ready policy analysis, IS/LM serves reasonably well; the problem comes when one looks carefully at the underlying analytics. Because it is carried out in equilibrium space, IS/LM analysis assumes away many of the complex interdependencies that can occur in the dynamics, and makes it seem that determining aggregate equilibrium is a relatively simple job. Modern macroeconomics sees the issues as much more complicated: the dynamic interdependencies must be dealt with if one is to have a foundation for macro. Thus, if IS/LM analysis is to remain the core model in macro, its underlying foundation will have to be changed in the future to fit the new focus on disequilibrium analysis. One way to do that is to not interpret it as a timeless model determining a non-historical equilibrium and instead to interpret it as an historical model in which one is only talking about deviations from historically determined levels.

DAVID COLANDER

See also:

Aggregate Demand – Aggregate Supply Model and Diagram; Crowding Out; Demand Management; Fiscal Policy; Hansen, Alvin H.; Harrod, Sir Roy; Hicks, Sir John R.; Keynes, John Maynard; Keynesian Cross; Liquidity Trap; Meade, James E.; Monetary Policy; Multiplier Effect; Neoclassical Synthesis (Bastard Keynesianism); Real Balance Effect; Samuelson, Paul A.

Bibliography

Hicks, John (1980), 'IS/LM: An Explanation', *Journal of Post Keynesian Economics*, **3**, (2), winter, pp. 139–54.
Solow, Robert (1984), 'Mr Hicks and the Classics', *Oxford Economic Papers*, **36**, Supplement, pp. 13–25.
Tobin, James (1980), *Asset Accumulation and Economic Activity*, Oxford: Basil Blackwell.
Young, Warren (1987), *Interpreting Mr. Keynes*, Boulder, CO: Westview Press.

Johnson, Harry Gordon

Harry Gordon Johnson was one of the most published economists of all economists, living or dead. So formidable is his list of publications that the *Journal of Political Economy* devoted 52 pages to his bibliography (Longawa, 1984). Despite his commitment to advancing the knowledge of economics through his publications, Johnson still found time to serve on the boards of many professional organizations, dominate the conference circuit, educate students and enlighten politicians the world over. Never the first nor the last to speak on a subject, Johnson had the remarkable ability to take new hypotheses, improve them, expand upon them and draw connections between the new and old ideas; between 'real world' and theory.

Johnson was born in 26 May 1923 in Toronto, Ontario. He graduated with honors from the University of Toronto in 1943. He took his first teaching position upon graduation at St Francis Xavier University in Nova Scotia. In 1944, Johnson left academics briefly to serve one year with the Canadian infantry. Remaining in Europe after his service, he earned a second BA at the University of Cambridge in 1946. He earned his first MA from the University of Toronto in 1947 and his second from Harvard in 1948. From 1956 to 1959 he taught at the University of Manchester, while earning a PhD from Harvard in 1958.

From 1959 until his death, Johnson taught at the University of Chicago as a professor of economics. He combined this position with professorships at the London School of Economics (1966–74) and the Graduate Institute for International Studies in Geneva (1976–7). Concurrent with these and his many other teaching positions, Johnson was editor or co-editor of many professional journals, including the *Review of Economic Studies*, *The Manchester School*, *Economica*, the *Journal of Political Economy*, and the *Journal of International Economics*.

Johnson's lectures and lecture notes were world renowned. So organized and explicit were his lectures in macroeconomics that his text, *Macroeconomics and Monetary Theory*, was a compilation of notes from lectures at the London School of Economics in the 1969–70 school year. Jagdish Bhagwati (1977, p. 233) writes of Johnson's succinctness and of how he was 'seduced' into international economics as a lifetime pursuit. Others recount how Johnson generously and cheerfully offered editorial advice to graduate students and researchers.

Johnson's most significant scholarly contributions were in the areas of international trade, macroeconomics and the monetary approach to the balance of payments, but few issues in economics escaped his insight. Johnson first became widely known to the economics profession for his review of James Meade's *The Balance of Payments* (1951). In the review (Johnson, 1951), Johnson complained of the use of qualitative arguments to make quantitative judgements – a recurring theme in his criticism of 'Oxbridge' economics in general. Johnson's first major book was *International Trade and Economic Growth* (1958a), a collection of articles on trade theory, including comparative static analyses of the effects of trade on growth, compiled for his doctorate at Harvard. His work in international trade in the 1950s and early 1960s 'advanced the knowledge by showing that a series of generalizations thought to be true were not in fact true' (Lipsey, 1978, p. S51). He compiled his major contributions to the pure theory of tariffs in *Aspects of the Theory of Tariffs* (1971a).

Johnson complemented international trade literature with his polished views in monetary economics. A significant amount of Johnson's work in monetary economics is reprinted in two books, *Essays in Monetary Economics* (1967) and *Further Essays in Monetary Economics* (1972). The latter contains his time-honored article, 'The Keynesian Revolution and the Monetarist Counter-Revolution', which spells out how to initiate a revolution in economics. While Johnson admired aspects of the works of Keynes, he did not feel that there was need for a new theory (accompanied by a new set of policy prescriptions) from Keynes. He believed Keynes and his followers failed to understand the nature and sources of the Great Depression of the 1930s as a matter of international monetary collapse 'thoroughly reconcilable with the orthodox neo-classical tradition of monetary theory' (Johnson and Johnson, 1978, p. 208). Johnson believed Keynes betrayed the profession by assuming a closed national economy in his models, which essentially ruled out the possibility of such a reconciliation.

Johnson's dual commitments to international trade and monetary economics ultimately led to his devotion to the monetary approach to balance of payments theory in the latter part of his career. He began this line of thinking in 1958, when he distinguished between the elasticities and absorption approaches in an international money context (Johnson, 1958b). He strengthened the idea of a monetary approach when he strongly asserted that changes in the domestic money supply occurred either through changes in domestic credit or through deficits and surpluses on the balance of payments and that international money flows were a consequence of stock disequilibria that were basically transitory and self-correcting (Johnson, 1977). Johnson was also an ardent advocate of flexible exchange rates, promoting the change from fixed to flexible exchange rates prior to the breakdown of Bretton Woods.

Johnson was aggressively pursuing his publishing and conference attending when a stroke in February 1977 abruptly halted his career, followed by a fatal stroke that took his life on 8 May 1977. He averaged about 32 articles a year in the final eight years of his life (during which, in 1974, he endured a stroke which left him mildly disabled).[1] The majority of his 27 books were collections of his prior, published academic papers. In defense of this format, he dared anyone to own every original source of his articles, offering $100 to anyone who could do so (Johnson, 1972, p. 18). He died before receiving his award as a distinguished fellow of the American Economic Association (1977) and with many articles still in line for publication.

CATHERINE CAREY

Note
1   Based on Longawa (1984).

See also:
Balance of Payments: Keynesian and Monetarist Approaches; Bretton Woods; Dornbusch, Rudiger; Friedman, Milton; International Clearing Union; Keynesian Revolution; Meade, James E.; Monetary Policy; Money; Quantity Theory of Money; Viner, Jacob; White, Harry D.

Bibliography
Bhagwati, Jagdish N. (1977), 'Harry G. Johnson', *Journal of International Economics*, **7**, (3), August, pp. 221–9.

Johnson, Harry G. (1951), 'The Taxonomic Approach to Economic Policy', *Economic Journal*, **61**, (244), December, pp. 812–32.

Johnson, Harry G. (ed.) (1958a), *International Trade and Economic Growth*, London: Allen & Unwin.

Johnson, Harry G. (1958b), 'Towards a General Theory of Balance of Payments', in Harry G. Johnson (ed.), *International Trade and Economic Growth*, London: Allen & Unwin.

Johnson, Harry G. (1967), *Essays in Monetary Economics*, London: Allen & Unwin.

Johnson, Harry G. (1971a), *Aspects of the Theory of Tariffs*, London: Allen & Unwin.

Johnson, Harry G. (1971b), *Macroeconomics and Monetary Theory*, London: Gray-Mills.

Johnson, Harry G. (1972), *Further Essays in Monetary Economics*, London: Gray-Mills.

Johnson, Harry G. (1977), *Money, Balance-of-Payments Theory and the International Monetary Problem*, Princeton: Princeton University Press, International Finance Section.

Johnson, Harry G. and Elizabeth S. Johnson (1978), *The Shadow of Keynes, Cambridge and Keynesian Economics*, Chicago: University of Chicago Press.

Lipsey, Richard G. (1978), 'Harry Johnson's Contributions to the Pure Theory of International Trade', *Canadian Journal of Economics*, **11**, (4), Supplement, November, pp. S34–S54.

Longawa, Vicky, M. (1984), 'Harry G. Johnson: A Bibliography', *Journal of Political Economy*, **92**, (4), August, pp. 659–711.

Meade, James E. (1951), *The Balance of Payments*, London: Oxford University Press.

Jorgenson, Dale W.[1]

Dale W. Jorgenson, one of the primary developers of the modern theory of investment expenditures, was born in 1933 in Bozeman, Montana and attended public schools in Helena, Montana. He attended Reed College and Harvard University, receiving his PhD in 1959. From 1959 to 1969 he was on the faculty at the University of California, Berkeley, where he became professor of economics in 1963. In 1969, Jorgenson accepted a position at Harvard University, where he is currently Frank William Taussig Research Professor of Economics.

Jorgenson has authored or co-authored over 190 journal articles, economics books and contributions to books. He has been editor or associate editor of many of the profession's most influential journals. In 1971, he received the prestigious John Bates Clark medal, awarded by the American Economic Association every two years to an economist under 40 for excellence in economic research. Among other honors, he served as president of the Econometrics society during 1987.

Jorgenson is best known for his development and empirical implementation of the (user) cost of capital concept and an accompanying model of capital as a factor of production. The framework has been influential in numerous branches of economics. Its best-known macroeconomic application is Jorgenson's 'neoclassical' theory of investment expenditures (see Jorgenson, 1963, 1965, 1971).

Following Keynes's (1936) emphasis on investment demand as one of the keys to macroeconomic stability, the fast-developing 'Neoclassical Synthesis' of the late 1950s and 1960s (see Snowdon *et al.*, 1994) highlighted the need for improved understanding of investment's determinants. When Jorgenson began work on the problem, little consensus existed about either the determinants of investment or the appropriate means of studying it. Influential statistical studies of the day were based either on 'ad hoc' conceptions (such as a postulated *structural* 'accelerator' relationship between investment and output) or, at most, on informal appeals to neoclassical theory (see reviews by Knox, 1952; Smyth, 1964).

In contrast, neoclassical *methodological* doctrine (then rapidly assuming its present-day form) emphasized that empirical work should be built on rigorous (that is, mathematical) theoretical treatments. Jorgenson accordingly began with an explicit model of the firm's investment decision, in which firms maximize the discounted flow of (expected) profits over time and from this exercise derive their optimal (that is, desired) capital stock. His resulting classic expression for the firm's desired capital stock K^* is (see Jorgenson, 1963, 1965, 1971; Branson, 1989):

$$K^* = \alpha \frac{Py}{C},$$

where α is the share of capital in output and P is the price of the firm's output y. C, the firm's *user cost of capital* (the rental price of capital services) includes terms for the interest rate, depreciation, tax parameters and capital price changes. Jorgenson's approach derives an explicit relationship between capital's price and desired capital (such a role for price variables was lacking in much prior empirical work on investment).

To complete his theory, Jorgenson added distributed ('gestation') lags capturing the evolution over time of desired capital into (net) investment expenditures, and a proportional relationship between the capital stock and replacement investment. Total ('gross') investment I_t then is

$$I_t = \alpha \sum_{j=1}^{J} \beta_{t-j} \left(\frac{P_{t-j} y_{t-j}}{C_{t-j}} \right) + \delta K_{t-1} + u_t$$

where the β_{t-j} are distributed lag coefficients, δ is the (assumed constant) depreciation rate of capital and u_t is a stochastic error term. Jorgenson's lag specification imposes no a priori restrictions on the time structure of the investment process, so that false rejection of the neoclassical theory of K^* due to inappropriate lag structure is not an issue. His theory offers generality, since it encompasses both the flexible accelerator of Chenery and Koyck and the simple accelerator of J.M. Clark as special cases (see Chirinko, 1993). Jorgenson's framework has been a workhorse for empirical studies of investment. The key findings emerging from this work include the following: both accelerator effects of (expected) output on investment and effects of cost-of-capital changes (including interest rate and business tax changes) are important determinants of investment, with accelerator effects dominating cost-of-capital changes; and investment responds to changes in desired capital with lengthy 'gestation' lags (see Jorgenson, 1971; Chirinko, 1993).

Jorgenson's work on investment has not escaped controversy (see Chirinko, 1993, for extensive treatment of criticisms). Three prominent objections to the framework's assumptions are first, aggregation problems are not treated (aggregate investment is taken as a simple 'blow-up' of the firm's decision); second, desired capital does not depend on the time structure of the investment process (more generally, such lags are treated atheoretically); third, a static expectations (perfect foresight) assumption pervades the approach. This last may be most controversial; Keynes, for example, with his vision of radical uncertainty as inseparable from the investment decision process, surely would have been uneasy with this feature of the neoclassical model. Recent literature on 'irreversible' investment decisions made under uncertainty is one attempt to introduce a more 'realistic' treatment of expectations into the general neoclassical framework (see Dixit and Pindyck, 1994).[2]

In recent years the concerns summarized above, plus the influential 'Lucas critique' leveled at pre-rational expectations econometric practice, has produced a shift in the academic literature away from Jorgenson-type frameworks and towards alternative formulations which seek a unified rigorous explanation of K^* and the time structure of the investment process. Building testable, meaningful models on such intricate theoretical foundations has proved a complex, difficult task. Jorgenson's more flexible framework remains influential, especially in policy circles. It still may be the best available compromise between a perceived need for rigorous theoretical microfoundations and the requirement that research strategies be sufficiently tractable to yield useful empirical tests (see Chirinko, 1993). To quote the citation accompanying his John Bates Clark medal in 1971 (see Harvard University, 1994), 'whatever its ultimate lessons,' Jorgenson's work 'will certainly long stand as one of the finest examples in the marriage of theory and practice in economics.'

MICHAEL R. MONTGOMERY

Notes

1   The author acknowledges the assistance of the Harvard University Department of Public Relations in preparing this entry.
2   See Mayer (1995, ch.7) for clarifying discussion of why 'realism' of assumptions matters in empirical economics even on 'instrumentalist' premises.

See also:

Accelerator Principle; Econometric Models, Macroeconomic; Economics of Keynes and of his Revolution, Key Elements of the; Harcourt, Geoff; Lucas Critique; Lundberg, Erik; Neoclassical Synthesis (Bastard Keynesianism); Ricardo Effect; Robinson, Joan; Samuelson, Paul A.; Solow, Robert M.; Sraffa, Piero; Stockholm School of Economics; von Hayek, Friedrich A.; Wicksell, Knut.

Bibliography

Branson, William H. (1989), *Macroeconomic Theory and Policy*, New York: Harper & Row, ch. 13.
Chirinko, Robert S. (1993), 'Business Fixed Investment Spending: Modeling Strategies, Empirical Results, and Policy Implications', *Journal of Economic Literature*, **31**, (4), December, pp. 1875–1911.
Dixit, Avinash K. and Robert S. Pindyck (1994), *Investment under Uncertainty*, Princeton, NJ: Princeton University Press.
Harvard University Department of Public Relations (1994), 'Detailed Biography: Dale W. Jorgenson', mimeo.
Jorgenson, Dale (1963), 'Capital Theory and Investment Behavior', *American Economic Review*, **53**, (2), May, pp. 247–59.
Jorgenson, Dale (1965), 'Anticipations and Investment Behavior', in James S. Duesenberry, G. Fromm, L.R. Klein and E. Kuh (eds), *The Brookings Quarterly Econometric Model of the United States*, Chicago: Rand McNally, pp. 35–92.
Jorgenson, Dale (1971), 'Econometric Studies of Investment Behavior: A Survey', *Journal of Economic Literature*, **9**, (4), December, pp. 1111–47.
Keynes, John Maynard (1936), *The General Theory of Employment, Interest and Money*, London: Macmillan.
Knox, A.D. (1952), 'The Acceleration Principle and the Theory of Investment: A Survey', *Economica*, **19**, (75), August, pp. 269–97.
Mayer, Thomas (1995), *Doing Economic Research*, Aldershot: Edward Elgar.

Smyth, David (1964), 'Empirical Evidence on the Acceleration Principle', *Review of Economic Studies*, **31**, (87), June, pp. 185–202.

Snowdon, Brian, Howard Vane and Peter Wynarczyk (1994), *A Modern Guide to Macroeconomics*, Aldershot: Edward Elgar.

Kahn, Lord Richard F.

Richard Ferdinand Kahn was born in London in 1905, the eldest son of Augustus and Regina Kahn. His father was a schoolmaster. He attended St Paul's school in London and in 1924 won a scholarship to King's College, Cambridge, with which he would be associated for the rest of his life. He read mathematics, earning a first in 1925, then physics, earning a second in 1927. His scholarship allowing him an additional year in Cambridge, Kahn took up the study of economics under the supervision of Gerald Shove and Maynard Keynes, and earned a first in the Economics Tripos Part II in 1928. He had found his calling. Encouraged by Keynes, Shove and Piero Sraffa, who had come to Cambridge in 1927, Kahn decided to write a Fellowship Dissertation for King's on 'The Economics of the Short Period'. In October 1929 he submitted an essay with the same title for the University's Adam Smith Prize, which he won, the essay being rated by Pigou as the best since that submitted by Keynes. Kahn completed his dissertation in record time, less than a year and half, submitting it on 7 December 1929. Thanks to it, he was elected Fellow of King's College in March 1930. His dissertation was eventually published in Italian in 1983 and in English in 1989. He followed up this *tour de force* by publishing an article on the multiplier (Kahn, 1931) by which he became best known to the profession. Several other influential articles followed, including 'Some Notes on Ideal Output' (Kahn, 1935), two on the elasticity of substitution, and one on duopoly (Kahn, 1937) drawn (by memory, not directly) from his dissertation. He also translated into English Wicksell's *Interest and Prices*, which appeared in 1936 and was ranked by Keynes as 'miles above the usual standards of translations' (Moggridge, 1994).

Kahn was a central figure in both the revolutions which economic theory underwent in Cambridge in the 1920s and 1930s: the macroeconomic one which led to the *General Theory* (Keynes, 1936) and the microeconomic one associated with value theory and imperfect competition. The relationship between these revolutions, and Kahn's unique position as catalyst of both, have recently attracted attention (Marris, 1991; Marcuzzo, 1994; Sardoni, 1994). While still working on his dissertation, Kahn had begun his career as Keynes's 'perfect foil', as Moggridge (1978) has characterized him, pointing out errors in the draft of the *Treatise on Money* and assisting with 'the gradual evolution of the book into its final form' (Keynes, 1930, p. xix). Kahn was the principal spokesman to Keynes of the Cambridge Circus, which included James Meade, Joan and Austin Robinson and Sraffa, and met in the academic year 1930–31. They discussed issues arising from controversial passages in the *Treatise* and helped Keynes make the transition from the *Treatise* to the *General Theory* (Kahn, 1984; Harcourt, 1992, 1994). Kahn played an equally important role assisting Joan Robinson with the drafting of her *Economics of Imperfect Competition*. In the Foreword she states that 'the whole technical apparatus was built up with [Kahn's] aid and many of the major problems ... were solved as much by him as by me' (Robinson, 1933, p. v).

Kahn was appointed university lecturer in 1933 and second bursar of his college in 1935, working closely with the first bursar, Keynes, whom he succeeded in that position on Keynes's death in April 1946. Another link between Kahn and Keynes was thus a common interest in the financial administration of their college. After Keynes's death Kahn, along with Geoffrey Keynes, was made a trustee of Keynes's estate, which reverted to the college in 1981 when Lady Keynes died. From December 1939 to September 1946, Kahn forsook the academic life in order to participate in the war effort as a civil servant with the Board of Trade and the Ministries of Production and Supply, spending a year in the Middle East. He displayed great energy and creativity in devising ways to maximize the allocation of resources for military purposes subject to ensuring essential supplies for the civilian population, and rose to the rank of principal assistant secretary. He returned to Cambridge in 1946, where he became professor of economics in 1951, retiring from this position in 1972. In the 1950s and 1960s Kahn served on committees for various international organizations as well as on the (Radcliffe) Committee on the Working of the Monetary System. Previous theoretical work (Kahn, 1954) on extending the concept of liquidity preference influenced the Memorandum of Evidence he submitted to this committee, which formed the basis of its report on the British monetary system. In 1965, Kahn was nominated to the House of Lords as a life peer for his services to the British government, with the title of Baron Kahn of Hampstead, and sat on the cross benches. He died in Cambridge in 1989 at the age of 83.

An accurate assessment of Kahn's place in the history of economic thought is impeded by the inherent difficulty of quantifying the extent of his contributions to the work of other Cambridge economists, notably Maynard Keynes and Joan Robinson, with both of whom he established intense and long-lived intellectual partnerships. Two of his former students (Pasinetti, 1987; Marris, 1992) suggest that Kahn's two most influential publications are, paradoxically, those he wrote at the very beginning of his career: his fellowship dissertation (1929, 1989) and his article on the multiplier (1931). His dissertation, written with encouragement from Gerald Shove and Sraffa, is a remarkably mature work for a 24-year-old whose study of economics had only begun two and a half years earlier (Maneschi, 1988; Marris, 1992; O'Shaughnessy, 1994). Under the influence of a pioneering paper by Sraffa (1926), Kahn explained short-time working in the cotton spinning and coalmining industries via imperfect competition. Using reversed L-shaped prime cost curves and down-ward-sloping demand curves, he showed that prime profit can be earned by firms of varying degrees of efficiency working at less than full capacity. These results 'would turn out relevant in the radical restructuring of the shape of Keynes' own work' (Kahn, 1984, p. 174) by supplying some of the microfoundations for the *General Theory*. Kahn's related discovery of the multiplier (1931), providing a theoretical justification for public works projects in conditions of depression, has been justly celebrated, first and foremost by Keynes himself.

The extent to which Kahn collaborated in the drafting of the *General Theory* is a delicate and difficult question. Opinions vary all the way from Schumpeter's dictum (1954, p. 1172) that his 'share in the historic achieve-ment cannot have fallen very far short of co-authorship' to Kahn's own retort that this 'is clearly absurd' (1984, p. 178) and his self-portrayal as 'Keynes's disciple' (Marcuzzo, 1988). Samuelson (1994) places Pasinetti, Postan and himself on the Schumpeter side of this controversy, and Patinkin, Austin Robinson and Kahn on the other side. What remains beyond doubt is Kahn's vital catalytic role in the process of creation and subsequent propagation of the *General Theory* and his influence in winning intellectual respectability for 'Keynesian' policies to combat the ravages of depression.

ANDREA MANESCHI

See also:

Cambridge Circus; Fiscal Policy; Government Investment Programs (the Socialization of In-vestment); Harrod, Sir Roy; Hicks, Sir John R.; Keynes, John Maynard; Keynesian Revolution; Lerner, Abba, P.; Multiplier Effect; Quantity Theory of Money; Treasury View.

Bibliography

Harcourt, G.C. (1992), 'R.F. Kahn, 1905–89', in C. Sardoni (ed.), *On Political Economists and Modern Political Economy: Selected Essays of G.C. Harcourt*, London: Routledge.
Harcourt, G.C. (1994), 'Kahn and Keynes and the Making of *The General Theory*', *Cambridge Journal of Economics*, **18**, (1), February, pp. 11–23.
Kahn, R.F. (1929), 'The Economics of the Short Period', unpublished Fellowship Dissertation, Cambridge, published 1989 by Macmillan, London.
Kahn, R.F. (1931), 'The Relation of Home Investment to Unemployment', *Economic Journal*, **41**, (162), June, pp. 173–98.
Kahn, R.F. (1935), 'Some Notes on Ideal Output', *Economic Journal*, **45**, (177), March, pp. 1–35.
Kahn, R.F. (1937), 'The Problem of Duopoly', *Economic Journal*, **47**, (185), March, pp. 1–20.
Kahn, R.F. (1954), 'Some Notes on Liquidity Preference', *Manchester School of Economic and Social Studies*, **22**, (3), pp. 229–57.
Kahn, R.F. (1984), *The Making of Keynes' General Theory*, Cambridge: Cambridge University Press.
Keynes, J.M. (1930), *A Treatise on Money*, London: Macmillan.
Keynes, J.M. (1936), *The General Theory of Employment, Interest and Money*, London: Macmillan.

Maneschi, A. (1988), 'The Place of Lord Kahn's "The Economics of the Short Period" in the Theory of Imperfect Competition', *History of Political Economy*, **20**, (2), Summer, pp. 155–71.

Marcuzzo, M.C. (1988), *Richard F. Kahn: Un Discepolo di Keynes*, Milan: Garzanti.

Marcuzzo, M.C. (1994), 'R.F. Kahn and Imperfect Competition', *Cambridge Journal of Economics*, **18**, (1), February, pp. 25–39.

Marris, R.L. (1991), *Reconstructing Keynesian Economics with Imperfect Competition*, Aldershot: Edward Elgar.

Marris, R.L. (1992), 'R.F. Kahn's Fellowship Dissertation: A Missing Link in the History of Economic Thought', *Economic Journal*, **102**, (414), September, pp. 1235–43.

Moggridge, D.E. (1978), 'Cambridge Discussion and Criticism Surrounding the Writing of *The General Theory*: A Chronicler's View', in D. Patinkin and J.C. Leith (eds), *Keynes, Cambridge and* The General Theory, London: Macmillan.

Moggridge, D.E. (1994), 'Richard Kahn as an Historian of Economics', *Cambridge Journal of Economics*, **18**, (1), February, pp. 107–16.

O'Shaughnessy, T.J. (1994), 'Kahn on the Economics of the Short Period', *Cambridge Journal of Economics*, **18**, (1), February, pp. 41–54.

Pasinetti, L.L. (1987), 'Kahn, Richard Ferdinand (born 1905)', in John Eatwell, Murray Milgate and Peter Newman (eds), *The New Palgrave: A Dictionary of Economics*, Vol. 3, New York: Stockton Press.

Robinson, J. (1933), *The Economics of Imperfect Competition*, London: Macmillan.

Samuelson, P.A. (1994), 'Richard Kahn: His Welfare Economics and Lifetime Achievement', *Cambridge Journal of Economics*, **18**, (1), February, pp. 55–72.

Sardoni, C. (1994), '*The General Theory* and the Critique of Decreasing Returns', *Journal of the History of Economic Thought*, **16**, (1), pp. 61–85.

Schumpeter, J.A. (1954), *History of Economic Analysis*, New York: Oxford University Press.

Sraffa, P. (1926), 'The Laws of Returns under Competitive Conditions', *Economic Journal*, **36**, (144), December, pp. 535–50.

Kaldor, Lord Nicholas

Nicholas Kaldor was born in Budapest on 12 May 1908 when Hungary was part of the Austro-Hungarian Empire. His father, Julius Kaldor, was a criminal lawyer who had risen through his own efforts, while his mother, Jean, came from a family of bankers. As the youngest of four children and the only surviving male, Nicholas enjoyed much love and attention during his childhood.

Kaldor attended the Model Gymnasium, a high school famous for its teaching and for its many illustrious alumni. During a family vacation in the German Alps, Kaldor's interest in economics was aroused by witnessing the German hyperinflation. As a result of this experience, Kaldor persuaded his father to permit him to start his studies in political economy at the Humboldt University of Berlin in 1925. In 1927 Nicholas left for the London School of Economics, ostensibly for a term. Once in England, he became involved in journalism and was fascinated by Allyn Young. He stayed on to earn a BSc with first class honours in 1929. His brilliance was noted and Lionel Robbins was to offer him a research scholarship for 1931–2.

Kaldor's merits had received wide academic recognition by the outbreak of World War II. When the LSE was forced to move to Cambridge by the war,

Kaldor was the only member of the LSE faculty who was asked to lecture at Cambridge. He took considerable interest in economic issues raised by the war and contributed an early 'econometric model' to the famous Beveridge report, *Full Employment in a Free Society* (1943).

Kaldor continued at the LSE until 1947, when he left as reader, in order to work for the Economic Commission for Europe. His work as an economic adviser to national and international bodies continued until 1949, when he accepted a fellowship at King's College. It is curious to note that he joined Cambridge as only a lecturer; this was remedied in two years when Kaldor became a reader, but he was not rewarded with a professorship until 1966.

Kaldor belonged to an age when Hungary provided an unusual complement of intellectual brilliance; among the luminaries were the historian Michael Polanyi, the mathematician Theodore von Karman, the physicist Eugene Wigner and the atomic scientists Nicholas Kurti, Leo Szilard and Edward Teller. It is interesting to note that Kaldor met and discussed economics with the legendary mathematician John von Neumann, who contributed heavily to mathematical economics. Of the many Hungarians of his generation, Kaldor's name was most frequently linked with the economist Thomas, later Lord, Balogh. It was said that the difference between the two was that one was Buda, the other Pest. When both of them were elevated to the House of Lords it was rumored that, in order to get a peerage, one had to be Hungarian, Jewish and left-wing!

In academic meetings Kaldor had a colorful and dominating personality, which did not take opposition lightly. He was egocentric, yet ready to give much of himself to friends. He greatly enjoyed family relationships and was fortunate to be surrounded by a doting family, consisting of his wife Clarissa, herself a brilliant student of history, and four daughters.

In 1951, the Chancellor of the Exchequer, Hugh Gaitskell, invited Kaldor to join the Royal Commission on Taxation of Profits and Income. Thus began a period when Kaldor acquired increasing fame as an international tax specialist. It was during his work for the Commission that Kaldor became convinced of the virtues of an expenditure tax and put some of his views into a minority report which raised eyebrows among many Labour Party MPs. Kaldor devoted a year to writing *An Expenditure Tax*, which was published in 1955, to widespread praise. His fame grew rapidly and he was invited to India, China, Chile, Ceylon (Sri Lanka) and many other countries in rapid succession, both to lecture and to give policy advice. In 1961, he was invited to Ghana and to British Guiana to give advice on fiscal and balance of payments crises. Kaldor advocated higher taxes in order to stabilize the budget. His proposals did not sit well with influential sectors of the populace and led to riots, thereby providing wags with a line about the value of economists' advice.

In 1962, Kaldor advocated a progressive land tax for Turkey, which was rejected amidst some heated discussion. His last visits to foreign countries were to Iran in 1966 and to Venezuela in 1976. Further international activity was dampened by the reception given to his tax proposals and by Kaldor's increasing involvement with the Labour government after 1964.

Kaldor was special adviser to three Chancellors of the Exchequer between 1964 and 1976 and his influence during this period has been compared to that exercised by Lord Keynes between 1936 and 1945. Kaldor continued at Cambridge but devoted much of his time to work in London. His advice was concentrated on balance of payments and on taxation, being more heeded in the latter area. Proposals for a capital gains tax and a company tax uniformly on profits were put forward but the most innovative tax, an expenditure tax, did not make headway. In 1979, Kaldor was elevated to the House of Lords as Baron of Newnham, a recognition that gave him great pleasure.

When Edward Heath brought the Conservatives to power during 1970–74, Kaldor became a vocal critic of government policy and developed the thesis that the balance of payments deficit could never be eliminated as long as the national budget was in deficit. With the advent of Margaret Thatcher, Kaldor's opposition became vociferous and even strident. He vehemently criticized the Thatcher government and particularly its monetary policy, an area on which he had already contributed a substantial memorandum to the Radcliffe Committee in 1959.

Throughout the period when Kaldor was so heavily involved in practical economic policy he continued both his teaching and his research, contributing innovative and even radical ideas to the profession, especially in the fields of equilibrium and growth theory. His efforts were honored by many international bodies.

Kaldor began his career as an economist as a supporter of the Austrian School and by implication of free markets. He became a Keynesian late in the 1930s and continued thereafter with consistently socialist goals. His contributions at this time range from his early Austrian papers to his clarifications and extensions of Keynesianism, including a notable paper on 'Speculation and Economic Stability'.

World War II and practical affairs led to a long hiatus, but Kaldor then returned to theoretical issues relating to growth and development. His original theory of income distribution made profits the cause of the expenditure of entrepreneurs. This led to the Pasinetti paradox and subsequently to an extensive debate between the two Cambridges of England and of Massachusetts. Kaldor then summarized the basic facts to be explained in growth theory – the now famous 'stylized facts' – and sought to explain them without recourse to the artificial and exogenous forces used by the neoclassicals. This task led him increasingly to focus upon manufacturing and to increasing returns as fundamental facts of capitalism. The perceived importance of increasing returns also led Kaldor to question and then to object to the stifling role played by equilibrium conditions. Kaldor formulated three 'growth laws' which stress the role of cumulative processes and emphasize how success breeds success.

Kaldor's emphasis upon relevance made him an inspiration to many economists in the 1970s and 1980s. The insistence upon axioms which arise from the facts or are verifiable independently was a salutary reminder that economics must be seen as relevant by policy makers and ordinary people – and not just by the economics profession. Kaldor's second major theoretical contribution actually goes back to his early Austrian sympathies and emphasizes the creative function of markets, as well as complementarity between activities and increasing returns. His sympathies may have been socialist but he always understood and respected the market. It is sad to note that the dull imagination of the Nobel Committee did not see how richly Kaldor deserved the Nobel Prize and how the award would have done credit to the prize itself.

SALIM RASHID

Acknowledgement
I am grateful to John Due and Paul Streeten for their help.

See also:

Kalecki, Michał

Michał Kalecki was born at Lodz in Poland (then part of Russia) of Jewish parents in 1899. After high school, he studied engineering at the Warsaw and Gdansk polytechnics before bankruptcy of his father's business forced him to leave shortly before graduation. Thereafter, during the 1920s, Kalecki earned a living through a variety of casual jobs, eventually moving into economic journalism. In 1929, on the strength of a number of articles analysing particular commodity markets, he was hired as an economist at the Institute of Business Cycles and Prices in Warsaw. At the Institute Kalecki was given the opportunity to develop his macroeconomic theories, as well as making pioneering estimates of Polish national income in association with Ludwik Landau. In what was to be a long and happy union, Kalecki married Ada Sternfeld in 1930.

In 1935, Kalecki received a Rockefeller scholarship to go to Sweden and England to further his theoretical work on business cycles. Resigning his

Institute job in 1936 because of the politically motivated sacking of two of his co-workers, Kalecki remained in Cambridge, impressing Joan Robinson in particular, until 1940, when he moved to the Oxford Institute of Statistics. After World War II and brief interludes with the International Labour Office and a trip back to Poland, Kalecki took work at the United Nations in New York, helping prepare the World Economic Reports. In 1955, McCarthyism within the UN indirectly caused Kalecki to resign and return to Poland, this time, barring trips abroad, for good.

Back in Poland Kalecki was active as an economic planner. In addition he taught and researched on the macroeconomics of capitalism and socialism as well as doing work on developing and mixed economies. In the turmoil of 1968, Kalecki and his Polish school were turned on by the Communist orthodoxy, suffering anti-intellectual and anti-Semitic attacks. For the third time in his career, Kalecki resigned his job in protest. He died in 1970, a deeply disillusioned man. As a result of strongly held moral views, especially regarding capitalism, and considerable and inflexible personal integrity, Kalecki could be difficult. Like many central European intellectuals, he was not, however, without a sharp sense of humour.

Key environmental influences on Kalecki's work were stagnation of the Polish economy during the 1920s, the Great Depression, the rise of Fascism in central Europe and the growth of industrial cartels in Poland during the inter-war years. Intellectually Kalecki was influenced by national income accounting and Marxian economics. However he was not a classical Marxist. He had no time for the labor theory of value. For Kalecki the principal problem of capitalism was not Marxian exploitation but its tendency to mass unemployment, due to a lack of demand, and to monopoly. The class nature of capitalism meant that any solutions to the effective demand problem were themselves problematic.

A Ricardian in method, Kalecki stripped down problems to their essentials by virtue of strong simplifying assumptions. He did not hesitate to draw conclusions regarding the behavior of the world, in combination with a strong intuition and a good feel for the numbers, from models developed from these assumptions. His work also displays a strong liking for the paradoxical. Kalecki made a number of important contributions to mid-twentieth-century macroeconomics. His influence has been felt to different degrees by a number of individuals and schools of thought. The work of Josef Steindl, Paul Baran and Paul Sweezy and Joan Robinson exhibits a strong Kaleckian flavour. A number of Post Keynesians acknowledge Kalecki's inspiration. In addition, there are rarely acknowledged influences. Many of Kalecki's ideas, especially regarding the supply side, were rapidly absorbed in mainstream Keynesianism during the 1950s and have also been a part of New Keynesian developments of the imperfectly competitive microfoundations of macroeconomics.

Taken as a whole, Kalecki's principal contributions to macroeconomics include anticipating and developing, particularly in a dynamic direction, many ideas which became known as part of the Keynesian revolution. However he imbued his contributions with a distinctive Kaleckian flavour, emphasizing non-competitive microfoundations and drawing out what he saw as the contradictions of capitalism. Kalecki's typical starting-point was a Marxian division of the economy into two classes, workers and capitalist, and the assumption that workers spent all their incomes. On this basis he developed the first determinate macroeconomic business cycle model founded on the idea that output variations clear the goods market (the theory of effective demand), where investment both drives effective demand and creates productive capacity (Kalecki, 1933a, 1935). He extended his model into the open economy, presenting the first 'Keynesian' model of effective demand in this setting (Kalecki, 1933b), and analysed the impact of money wage cuts on employment under conditions of quasi-monopoly as well as in an open economy setting (Kalecki, 1939b). In addition he developed a version of the balanced budget multiplier theory (Kalecki, 1937).

Kalecki also developed a short-period model where goods and money market equilibrium was simultaneously determined, showing that, under perfect money wage flexibility, the only possible equilibrium was at full employment. Introducing the first hysteresis-style wage equation into modern macroeconomics, he then assumed that money wage changes depended on employment changes, implying that 'quasi-equilibrium' at less than full employment could result. Changes in capitalists' investment or saving behavior could then raise or lower the quasi-equilibrium level of employment (Kalecki, 1934). Another highly original contribution was Kalecki's theory of the distribution of national income (Kalecki, 1938). Assuming that industrial prices were determined in quasi-monopolistic conditions and that marginal costs were constant, Kalecki showed that the wage share of industrial national income was a function of the 'degree of monopoly' determined by effective competition in the product market, and the ratio of raw materials to wage costs. This theory of pricing and distribution was then linked to his theory of effective demand in a pioneering contribution to macroeconomics with imperfectly competitive microfoundations (Kalecki, 1939a).

Other important contributions include Kalecki's 1943 theory of the political business cycle, like much of his political economy both oversimplified and insightful, and his 1944 analysis of full employment under capitalism. By perhaps 1939, and certainly 1945, Kalecki's most innovative work had been published. From then on, Kalecki refined his theories, particularly his theories of pricing and the determination of investment, but the basic framework remained unaltered.

Since much of Kalecki's early writing was in Polish, because of his politics and, as an autodidact in economics, because of his lack of status within the profession, he did not gain the full recognition that an innovator of his stature deserved.

SIMON CHAPPLE

See also:

Davidson, Paul; Harcourt, Geoff; Incomes Policies; Kahn, Lord Richard F.; Keynes, John Maynard; Keynesian Revolution; Kregel, Jan A.; Post Keynesian School of Economics; Robinson, Joan; Sraffa, Piero; Weintraub, Sidney.

Bibliography

Kalecki, Michał (1933a), *Proba teorii koniunktury*, Warsaw: ISBCP.

Kalecki, Michał (1933b), 'O handlu zagranicznym i "eksporcie wenwnetrznym"', *Ekonomista*, **33**, (3), pp. 27–35.

Kalecki, Michał (1934), 'Trzy uklady', *Ekonomista*, **34**, (3), pp. 54–70.

Kalecki, Michał (1935), 'Essai d'une théorie du mouvement cyclique des affaires', *Revue d'économie politique*, **2**, Mars/Avril, pp. 285–305.

Kalecki, Michał (1937), 'A Theory of Commodity, Income and Capital Taxation', *Economic Journal*, **47**, (187), September, pp. 444–50.

Kalecki, Michał (1938), 'The Determinants of the Distribution of National Income', *Econometrica*, **6**, (2), April, pp. 97–112.

Kalecki, Michał (1939a), *Essays in the Theory of Economic Fluctuations*, London: Allen & Unwin.

Kalecki, Michał (1939b), *Place Nominale i Reale*, Warsaw: ISBCP.

Keynes, John Maynard

John Maynard Keynes, the eldest child of John Neville and Florence Ada Keynes, was born into a professional middle-class English household on 5 June 1883 in Cambridge. There were three children, all gifted and destined to make their own mark, but Maynard Keynes excelled. He was his parents' favorite and modern students of sibling rivalry no doubt could have a field day analysing the consequent impact on his brother, Geoffrey and sister, Margaret. John Neville was a university lecturer in the Moral Science Tripos when Keynes was born (in the year that Karl Marx died). He was to be the author of two 'minor classics', *Studies and Exercises in Formal Logic* (1884) and *The Scope and Method of Political Economy* (1891). He was also a colleague of Alfred Marshall, whose pupil Maynard Keynes became. He subsequently became the Registrary of the University, in 1910.

Maynard Keynes went to Eton, where he excelled intellectually and socially, and then to King's, to read mathematics. He seems to have spent as much time on philosophy as on mathematics and he continued his hectic social and intellectual life. He was elected to the Apostles, spoke at the Union, and made lifelong friends in King's and Trinity. His tripos result –

12th Wrangler – was respectable but disappointing for such a gifted person. He stayed on in Cambridge to read for the civil service examinations in 1906, so having his first contact with economics. He was supervised by Marshall, who quickly realized that he had a genius on his hands. Characteristically, in effect, Marshall said, 'We old men must kill ourselves' – the usual mixture of grudging admiration and envy which characterized this great economist and awful person. Nevertheless Keynes's lowest mark in the civil service examinations was in economics (presumably, he said, because the examiners knew less about the subject than he did) and, as he came second in the examinations as a whole, he had to settle for the India Office rather than his first love, the Treasury. While in the civil service, Keynes started work on a fellowship dissertation for King's (it became *A Treatise on Probability* in 1921). He was elected in 1909, at his second attempt. He had already returned to Cambridge in 1908 to become a lecturer in economics, paid for by Marshall out of his own pocket (here he *was* generous). Keynes was primarily interested in monetary theory and policy, though he lectured on a wide range of topics.

His social life kept on apace, as he was a core member of the Bloomsbury Group and a friend of many of the up and coming artists, theatre people and, subsequently, psychoanalysts – Keynes was vitally interested in the cultural and intellectual developments of his time, especially, of course, the philosophical developments associated with G.E. Moore, Bertrand Russell, Frank Ramsey and Ludwig Wittgenstein.

During World War I, Keynes worked in the Treasury (to the disgust of many of his friends who were pacifists and conscientious objectors). Keynes thought the war was an unspeakable crime but that, if the United Kingdom had to be in it, the war effort should be guided by rational and humane principles provided by intelligent and educated people who accepted 'the presuppositions of Harvey Rd' (Keynes's birth place) as Harrod put it. Keynes was one of Lloyd George's advisors at Versailles; he was so appalled by the vindictive and destructive provisions of the Treaty that in the end he resigned and wrote *The Economic Consequences of the Peace* (1919), which made him world famous. In doing so he changed from being just an extraordinarily clever but often superficially flip and cynical young man into a serious maturity which can only be described as admirable. His beautifully written polemic is still worth reading for its passionate anger, power and application of theory in its best sense to explanation and policy.

Keynes returned to Cambridge in the 1920s, resigning his lectureship but maintaining his fellowship in King's (of which he was now senior bursar) and the editorship of the *Economic Journal* (to which he was first appointed in 1911). He performed an enormous number of roles – speculation, journalism, director of an insurance company, bibliophile, patron of the arts, theatre and ballet (in 1925, he was to marry Lydia Lopokova, the Russian ballerina, a mutually supportive partnership based on love and laughter – all while he 'settled down' in order to write the three books which were to make him an immortal: *A Tract on Monetary Reform* (1923), *A Treatise on Money* (1930) and *The General Theory of Employment, Interest and Money* (1936). (We should also mention *Essays in Persuasion*, 1931 and *Essays in Biography*, 1933.)

Initially Keynes worked on monetary matters within the Marshallian paradigm as he saw it, yet reacting to his teacher by concentrating more and more on happenings in the short run for policy recommendations. His most famous line – 'In the long run we are all dead' – is to be found in a passage where he exhorts economists to live and work and advise on the here and now. But he put the general price level at the centre of what was to be influenced by monetary policy and he had not yet arrived at a coherent theory of an integrated monetary production economy where both the general price level and activity were entwined – *that* was to come with the writing of *The General Theory*.

Keynes's marriage in 1925 marked a major sea change in his personal life. Prior to this Keynes had been actively gay, as Skidelsky tells us in graphic detail in his Volume I (1986), repairing the deliberate omission of this aspect of Keynes's life by Roy Harrod in the first 'official' biography in 1951. The happiness associated with his marriage had, it may be conjectured, a crucial impact on his creativity and understanding, so that his *magnum opus* was both a true work of genius and the work of a contented man, who was therefore all the more passionately angry about a system which brought mass unemployment and poverty to others. Keynes was also supremely confident that he could teach us why these evils happened and what we could – and should – do about them.

In 1937, he had the first of several severe heart attacks and the next two years or so were wiped out – relatively; that is to say, he only did what normally clever people would have done. In particular, though he replied to those he considered the most important of his critics in some important articles, including a summary restatement of his theory in the *Quarterly Journal of Economics* in 1937, he never did write those 'footnotes' to *The General Theory* which he told Ralph Hawtrey in August 1936 he was intending to do. Then came World War II in which (reluctantly at first, because of his health) Keynes became more and more involved. Not only did he 'generalize' *The General Theory* to tackle the inflationary problems of wartime scarcities but he also took a larger and larger role in the actual running of the wartime economy and in the design of institutions to make the postwar world better and more just – Bretton Woods and all that.

Keynes literally killed himself for his country and the world by his efforts. His last major task was to get the British government and people to accept the harsh conditions of the American loan: his speech to the House of Lords on this issue was crucially important for the acceptance of the conditions. Exhausted, he returned to his country home, Tilton, in Sussex (in 1942, he had become Baron Keynes of Tilton) and on Easter Monday 1946 he had his last and this time fatal heart attack, dying far too young, at 62. Yet, as Austin Robinson told us, those whom the Gods love die young – 'a great economist and a very great Englishman', as the *Times* obituarist put it, a man whose life and works provide a resounding 'yes' to the Moorean puzzle with which Keynes and his contemporaries grappled: is it possible both to *be* good and to *do* good?

GEOFF C. HARCOURT

See also:

Bretton Woods; Cambridge Circus; Consumption and the Consumption Function; Depression, The Great; Fiscal Policy; Government Investment Programs (the Socialization of Investment); Harrod, Sir Roy; Hawtrey, Sir Ralph; Hicks, Sir John R.; International Clearing Union; Kahn, Lord Richard F.; Keynes and Probability; Keynes, The Influence of Burke and Moore on; Keynes? What Remains of; Keynesian Revolution; Marshall and Keynes; Meade, James E.; Multiplier Effect; Robertson, Sir Dennis H.; Robinson, Joan; Treasury View.

Bibliography
Skidelsky, Robert (1986), *John Maynard Keynes Hopes Betrayed,, 1883–1920*, London: Macmillan.

Keynes, John N.

John Neville Keynes, logician, political economist and father of John Maynard Keynes, was born in Salisbury on 31 August 1852. He was the only child of John Keynes, a self-made businessman who made his fortune managing nurseries, and Anna Maynard Neville. Keynes was educated at Amersham Hall and University College, London. In 1872, he won a mathematical scholarship to Pembroke College, Cambridge. Once at Cambridge, Keynes switched to the moral sciences, which included philosophy and political economy. In economics he was a student of Alfred Marshall, who had also started his academic career in mathematics. In 1875, Keynes was named Senior Moralist after obtaining a first in the Moral Science Tripos. The following summer, he was awarded a fellowship at Pembroke in addition to an honorary fellowship at University College.

During his fellowship tenure, Keynes decided to specialize in economics and, although he was one of Marshall's most promising students, failed to write anything during this six-year period. When Marshall gave up his Cambridge fellowship in 1877, Keynes began lecturing in logic at several colleges, among them the women's college, Newnham. It was here that he met Florence Ada Brown, daughter of Reverend John Brown and Ada Haydon Ford. They were married once Keynes completed his fellowship at Pembroke. Afterwards Keynes accepted a job in university administration as an assistant secretary of examinations at Cambridge. The rest of his career was spent as an administrator. He later held the position of secretary for local examinations as well as the most important administrative post, the Registrary. John Neville Keynes and Florence Ada Brown were married for 67 years and had three children, the oldest of whom was John Maynard Keynes.

John Neville Keynes's decision to pursue an administrative rather than an academic career disappointed both his wife, who had high ambitions for her husband, and Alfred Marshall, who tried to persuade Keynes to pursue several academic positions. When Keynes died on 15 November 1949 at the age of 97, he had only published two books, both written while he was an administrator at Cambridge, and had submitted a few entries to Ingis Palgrave's *Dictionary of Political Economy*. Both books were based on Keynes's Cambridge lecture notes and both were also used as textbooks. The first, *Studies and Exercises in Formal Logic* was published in 1884. It provided an outline of the method of deductive reasoning. The second book, *The Scope and Method of Political Economy* was published in 1891. It became the standard beginning text in the study of the methodology of political economy.

It is the second book for which Keynes is remembered as an economist. It represents an important contribution to the economics literature because its contents sort out the major methodological controversies that existed between the orthodox classical school and the German historical school. This controversy, called the *Methodenstreit*, is one of the largest methodological debates in political economy. During the late nineteenth century, these debates were based on disagreements over two central issues involving both the scope and the methodology appropriate to the nature of the discipline of political economy. The Classical approach to the study of political economy involved a relatively narrow scope of inquiry. This narrow scope reflected the primary goal of political economy which, according to the Classical economists, was to discover the basic laws that governed the functioning of the economy. Classical economists used a methodology in which basic assumptions were made a priori which abstracted from many circumstances and then, through deduction, conclusions were formed from the initial assumptions. The Classical position was refuted by the German historicists, who felt that the most important goal of political economy was to discover the laws that determined economic growth. Because these economic laws were relative to a particular time and place, their study must involve a realistic deductive approach in which historical material is necessary to understand the current state. Thus their scope of inquiry was much broader than that of the Classical economists.

In his book, Keynes attempted to reconcile this controversy over methodology and argued that abstract deduction and realistic induction were both useful ways to conduct economic analysis. In discussing scope, he distinguished between positive and normative economics. The positive component of economics deals with what is and involves questions that can be verified by use of scientific methods. Answers to positive questions do not involve value judgements. The normative components of economics, on the other hand, deals with questions involving economic policy, answers to which do involve value judgements. Some economists argue that, by the time Keynes's book was published in 1891, the methodological controversy had, for the most part, been resolved. Perhaps, as Marshall once wrote to him, John Neville Keynes's greatest achievement was that he was the father of John Maynard Keynes.

MYRA J. McCRICKARD

See also:

Economics, The Art of; Keynes, John Maynard; Marshall, Alfred; Pigou, Arthur C.

Bibliography
Keynes, John Neville (1884), *Studies and Exercises in Formal Logic*, London: Macmillan.
Keynes, John Neville (1891), *The Scope and Method of Political Economy*, London: Macmillan.

Keynes and Probability

At least three events have precipitated a renewed interest in Keynes: the arguments developed by Leijonhufvud in *On Keynesian Economic and the Economics of Keynes* (1968), the publication of Keynes's *Collected Writings* (1971–89) and the inability of Keynesian economics to propose politically acceptable public policies to combat stagflation. This entry examines one facet of this renewed interest: Keynes's theory of probability. Keynes developed his theory of probability in reaction to G.E. Moore's argument that in certain cases there is a need to follow rules. Using a frequency theory of probability and the concept of expected outcome, Moore argued that rules aid individuals in their pursuit of good. A rule is defined to be the long-run expected outcome of a particular course of action (Moore, 1903).

In *A Treatise on Probability* (1921), Keynes developed a probability theory based on objective degrees of belief. For Keynes, 'probabilities are logical relationships between propositions and the information which supports them and the degree of belief that one has in these relationships' (Bateman, 1990). These logical relationships may be expressed in the following manner: $a/h = p$, where a is the conclusion, h are premises and p is the resulting probability. Keynes articulated three categories of logical propositions: universal induction, propositions that are either true ($a/h = 1$) or false ($a/h = 0$); statistical induction, propositions that are neither true nor false ($0 < a/h < 1$); and uncertainty, propositions where the probabilities are unknown.

Three aspects of this version of Keynes's theory may be highlighted. First, Keynes recognized the importance of the four standard assumptions of statistics: the law of uniform nature, the law of limited independent variety, the law of large numbers and the need for stable statistical frequencies. The first two assumptions provide statisticians with ways for dealing with potential differences in time and space and limiting the characteristics of an event. The last two assumptions permit statisticians to *assume* the existence of a stable pattern in their undifferentiated observations, a position which Keynes found wanting. Keynes argued that the proper procedure was to make careful observations and from these observations *establish* the existence of a pattern which may be stable or unstable. Second, Keynes stressed the importance of proper sampling procedures. Third, Keynes argued that rules are not necessary. Individuals are interested in the next occurrence of an event, not in the long-run expected outcome of an event. Believing that individuals were rational, pursued a single goal – that of maximizing the amount of good in the society – used induction to establish relationships between a and h, and possessed objective degrees of belief in these relationships, Keynes argued that individuals are quite able to decide for themselves what is the best course of action.

This objective theory and its underlying philosophical objection to rules formed the basis of Keynes's attack on the quantity theory of money as a basis for monetary policy. In his attack Keynes distinguished clearly between the equation of exchange and the assumptions which must hold in order to state the long-run conclusions of the quantity theory: namely, that the ratio of cash to deposits and of reserves to deposits, or, in more conventional terminology, velocity, must be constant over time. After carefully examining the information available Keynes established the existence of an unstable pattern in these two ratios. Hence his conclusion that the quantity theory is not a reasonable and practical guide for monetary policy (Keynes, 1924; Schumpeter, 1950). Thus, at this point in his career, Keynes believed that monetary policy should be discretionary and not based on a rule implied by the quantity theory of money.

In response to Ramsey's (1922, 1931) critical review of *A Treatise on Probability*, Keynes began a long journey to escape from his early beliefs. By the time of the *General Theory*, Keynes had developed a subjective theory of probability, dropped the notion of an objective good and concluded that individuals were irrational, pursued many goals, held subjective degrees of belief about a and h that were subject to sudden and violent shifts, and recognized the need to maintain certain conventions and rules (Bateman

1990, 1991, 1995). This subjective theory and its underlying philosophical acceptance of the need for rules and conventions formed the basis of the goal associated with the *General Theory*. This goal was to increase the average level of performance of the economic system. Keynes argued that this goal can only be achieved if the level of gross domestic investment, the sum of gross private and gross public domestic investment, can be increased and then stabilized at this new higher level.

At least two theories of the economics of Keynes and, therefore, the goal of the *General Theory*, are affected by uncertainty. The first theory is Keynes's liquidity preference theory which was developed as part of his attack on the quantity theory of money. One part of this attack was discussed above. Another part of this attack is Keynes's argument that the demand for money should have three components, transactions, precautionary and speculative, and that the speculative demand for money is affected by uncertainty. The second theory is Keynes's investment theory. In his critique of Tinbergen's work on investment activity Keynes argues that a careful examination of the factors that affect gross *private* domestic investment decisions allows one to establish the existence of an unstable pattern in these factors. The primary cause of this unstable pattern is the existence of uncertainty.

In each of these theories, when individuals must make a decision and they are confronted by uncertainty, they fall back on conventions and rules. Embedded in these conventions and rules are expectations and subjective probabilities about the next occurrence of an event. These expectations and subjective probabilities are subject to sudden and violent shifts. Therefore, changes in gross *private* domestic investment, usually accompanied by changes in the speculative demand for money, can be used as a partial explanation of the cyclical movements in employment output and income (Keynes, 1939; Tinbergen, 1939).

To achieve his goal Keynes advocated the adoption of two policies, a policy of low long-term interest rates and a policy of high levels of gross domestic investment. The principal component parts of these two policies are the investment activities of the 'public corporations' which control approximately two-thirds to three-quarters of Britain's capital stock, the division of the government's budget into a current expenditures budget which is always in balance and a capital expenditure budget whose projects are self-liquidating, and the Bank of England which conducts monetary policy so as to maintain low long-term rates of interest. Being unable to control gross *private* domestic investment directly, Keynes sought to influence it indirectly by socializing gross *public* domestic investment. Thus, at the end of his career, Keynes believed that public policy should be based on rules and convention and not on individual discretion (Bateman, 1995).

TOM CATE

See also:

Consumption and the Consumption Function; Demand Management; Economics of Keynes and of his Revolution, Key Elements of the; Expectations, Theories of; Fiscal Policy; Government Investment Programs (The Socialization of Investment); Keynes, John Maynard; Monetary Policy; Quantity Theory of Money.

Bibliography

Bateman, Bradley (1990), 'Keynes induction and econometrics', *History of Political Economy*, **22**, (2), summer, pp. 359–80.

Bateman, Bradley (1991), 'The Rules of the Road: Keynes's Theoretical Rationale for Public Policy', in Bradley W. Bateman and John B. Davis (eds), *Keynes and Philosophy*, Brookfield, VT: Edward Elgar.

Bateman, Bradley (1995), 'Rethinking the Keynesian Revolution', in John B. Davis (ed.), *The State of Interpretation of Keynes*, Boston: Kluwer Academic Publishers.

Keynes, John Maynard (1921), *A Treatise on Probability*, London: Macmillan.

Keynes, John Maynard (1924), *A Tract on Monetary Reform*, London: Macmillan.

Keynes, John Maynard (1936), *The General Theory of Employment, Interest and Money*, London: Macmillan.

Keynes, John Maynard (1939), 'Professor Tinbergen's Method', *Economic Journal*, **49**, (194), September, pp. 558–68.

Leijonhufvud, Axel (1968), *On Keynesian Economics and the Economics of Keynes*, New York: Oxford University Press.

Moore, G.E. (1903), *Principia Ethica*, Cambridge: Cambridge University Press.

Ramsey, Frank P. (1922), 'Mr. Keynes on Probability', *The Cambridge Magazine*, **11**, (1), January, pp. 3–5.

Ramsey, Frank P. (1931), 'Truth and Probability', in R.B. Braithwaite (ed.), *The Foundations of Mathematics*, London: Routledge & Kegan Paul.

Schumpeter, Joseph A. (1950), *History of Economic Analysis*, New York: Oxford University Press.

Tinbergen, Jan (1939), *A Method and Its Application to Investment Activity, Statistical Testing of Business-Cycle Theories*, I, Geneva: League of Nations.

Keynes, The Influence of Burke and Moore on

The publication of Keynes's *Collected Writings* (1971–82; bibliography and index, 1989) as well as the opening to scholars of a mass of unpublished Keynes papers, has provided, for the first time, a proper archival basis for a 'history of thought' approach to Keynes. In particular, his hitherto unknown early writings enable us to reconstruct the chief influences on his thinking before he became a professional economist. These writings have attracted the attention of a growing number of Keynes scholars, not least because they held out the hope of answering three lines of attack on what may be called *General Theory* Keynesianism: the shakiness of its microfoundations, the naivety of its political assumptions and its materialism or consumerism. On all these matters it became apparent that Keynes had much more to say than he included in *The General Theory of Employment, Interest and Money* (*GT*). If the *GT* could be 'framed' by Keynes's ethical, epistemological and political beliefs a much more solid and attractive basis might be established for defending Keynesianism against the assaults of its enemies.

Of the relevant intellectual influences on the young Keynes the names of G.E. Moore and Edmund Burke stand out. Everyone agrees about this. Not only did Keynes directly engage with them as a young man, but *traces* of that engagement are to be found both in his economic theories and in his political assumptions. However beyond this there is little agreement. Three issues stand out: (1) the relative weight of the two influences on Keynes's later thinking; (2) what he actually got from them; (3) the degree to which the influence of either or both persisted. Roderick O'Donnell has given one answer to all these questions. Keynes's philosophical allegiances were established early in life, he did not deviate from them in their essentials subsequently and his theories of economics and politics are practical applications of his early philosophy. Moore suggested to him a general theory of rationality, applying to both ethical beliefs and practical reason, and to the relationship between the two. Burke was attractive to Keynes mainly because his philosophy could be made to fit into his Moore-derived scheme: but he accepted only those parts of Burke consistent with his Moorean allegiance (O'Donnell, 1989, 1991). I have never sought to deny the influence of Moore on Keynes, but have never believed that a political philosophy, or a commitment to economic and social reform, could be extracted from Moore's *Principia Ethica* (*PE*). I therefore see Burke as an independent influence, from whom Keynes derived principles of political action which were not centrally dependent on PE. The two philosophers provided him with separate, partly overlapping frameworks for thinking about private and public duty, respectively (Skidelsky, 1986, pp. 154–7; 1994, pp. 64–6). O'Donnell and I agree that Keynes's *distinctive* philosophy of practical reason – a form of act-consequentialism – was his own invention. It was a serious breach with the rule-consequentialism espoused by both Moore and Burke, being derived from his own logical theory of probability.

Keynes came up to King's College Cambridge from Eton in 1902 to read mathematics. In February 1903, he was elected a member of the Apostles, a secret and highly selective 'conversation' society, consisting of both dons and undergraduates. Its members had for some years been captivated by the personality and ideas of G.E. Moore (1873–1958), a fellow of Trinity College Cambridge from 1898 to 1904, later professor of philosophy at Cambridge. Moore's *Principia Ethica* was published in June 1903. It was concerned with such questions as: What is good? How do we know what is good? How should we behave? Moore was a great figure in twentieth-century philosophy, not just an important influence on Keynes. The arguments started by *PE* and by Moore's way of doing philosophy rumbled on for half a century. Its 'effect on *us*', Keynes recalled of *PE* in 1938, 'dominated, and perhaps still dominate[s], everything else'. By 'us' Keynes meant that Apostles of his generation and their close friends and female relations, later expanded into the Bloomsbury Group. With the Mathematical Tripos out of the way in

1905, Keynes spent much of that summer working through Moore's ideas: he called his notes 'Miscellanea Ethica'. Keynes also recalled that 'the large part played by considerations of probability in [Moore's] theory of right conduct was ... an important contributory cause to my spending all the leisure of many years on the study of that subject: I was writing under the joint influence of Moore's *Principia Ethica* and Russell's *Principia Mathematica*' (Keynes, 1905). The central idea from which grew Keynes's *A Treatise on Probability* (*TP*), published in 1921, but completed before World War I, is already present in a paper he read to the Apostles in January 1904.[1]

Keynes's interest in the Whig conservative philosopher Edmund Burke (1729–97) dates from his time at Eton. But in the summer of 1904 he wrote a 99-page essay on 'The Political Doctrines of Edmund Burke' which is preserved in his papers at King's College, Cambridge. It won the University's English Essay Prize. This was his most extended treatment of the 'theory and methods of politics' which, in 'Miscellanea Ethica', he said should be an integral part of a 'complete ethical treatise'. The issues Burke addressed – the method of reform versus revolution, the justification of elitism and inequality, the limits of individualism and the role of the state were of central concern to the later Keynes, as indeed they were to the twentieth century.

What did Keynes actually get from Moore and Burke? Moore gave Keynes a set of ethical beliefs and a theory of knowledge. 'By far the most valuable things we know or can imagine', Moore wrote in *PE*, 'are certain states of consciousness, which may be roughly described as the pleasures of human intercourse and the enjoyment of beautiful objects'. He went on: 'It is only for the sake of these things – in order that as much as possible of them may at some time exist – that anyone can be justified in performing any public or private duty ... [they] form the rational ultimate end of human action and the sole criterion of progress' (Moore, 1903, pp. 188–9). In his 1938 paper, 'My Early Beliefs', Keynes said: 'I have no reason to shift from the fundamental intuitions of the *Principia Ethica* ... It is still my religion under the surface' (Keynes, 1938). True enough, the list of goods tended to expand: Keynes immediately added 'knowledge' or 'truth' as an ultimate good and he recognized that there were many other valuable states of consciousness which might make claims on conduct proportionate to their value. The possible relevance of Keynes's ethical beliefs to his economics is that economics takes its place with politics as a means to good states of mind, and economic and political states of affairs have to be judged by reference to that criterion.

Keynes also upheld Moore's doctrine of intuition as the foundation of ethical knowledge. Our knowledge of what is good, Moore claimed, is intuitive knowledge: we perceive the quality good in an object just as we perceive that a piece of material is yellow. This suggests that good exists independent of our perception of it. In ethics, Moore was a Platonist, and Keynes followed him. Keynes, however, broke with Moore by arguing that intuition was the foundation of practical knowledge as well. Moore has been called an 'ideal utilitarian' because of his attempt to apply a consequentialist calculus to behavior. Given the ethical goods to be maximized, the question of right action involved an estimate of the likelihood of attaining them. Given that our knowledge of the consequences of our actions is very limited, the best we can do, in most cases, is to follow generally accepted legal and moral rules. Moore, that is, was a rule-utilitarian, though the term did not then exist. Keynes simply said that Moore had the wrong theory of probability. Moore implicitly identified knowledge of probabilities with knowledge of frequencies, whereas probability had to do with what it was rational to believe in the circumstances. Knowledge of probability was intuitive – a form of logical knowledge, not necessarily quantifiable. One 'perceived' a probability relation between the premises (evidence) and conclusion of an argument in exactly the same way as one perceived 'good' as an attribute of objects. This audacious insight, first formulated in 1904, became the basis of Keynes's *TP*. The logical theory of probability was Keynes's own invention, though it reflected the Platonist atmosphere of Cambridge philosophy at the start of the century. Moore and Russell were Platonist as regard truths, empiricist as regards action. Keynes completed the circle of Platonism, sundered by Moore's distinction between ways of knowing values and ways of knowing probabilities. Intuition controlled both.

Keynes added two more criteria for action, which he called 'weight of argument' and 'moral risk'. By the first Keynes meant roughly the *amount* of evidence supporting a probability judgement. A rational belief can be held with greater or lesser confidence, depending on the weight of evidence supporting it. Secondly, in deciding between two different goals of action, it is more rational to aim for a smaller good which seems more probable of attainment than a larger good which seems less so. Other things being equal, therefore, 'a high weight and the absence of risk increase *pro tanto* the desirability of the action to which they refer' (Keynes, 1921, p. 348). It should be noticed that the two principles are equally applicable to empiricist (or frequency) theories of probability, and the second is in Moore's *PE* (Moore, 1903, pp. 166–72). The epistemological basis of Keynes's well-known bias towards risk aversion was laid early in life.

Rational action should be guided by knowledge of what is good, knowledge of probabilities, judgements of weight and judgements of risk. By accepting Moore's 'curious connection between "probable" and "ought"', but by identifying probability with degrees of rational belief rather than with knowledge of frequencies, Keynes believed he had succeeded in setting up individual reason as the ultimate arbiter of what is good and how to behave. Conventions and rules, too, must pass the test of reason.

The possible connection between Keynes's epistemology and his economics might seem to lie in the need for economic theory to believe that agents behave rationally. The apparent dependence of the *GT* on irrational behavior (rigid wages and prices, 'animal spirits' and so on) undermined it as theory and, in the end, undermined the policy prescriptions to which it pointed. Nevertheless the *GT* might be salvaged as economic *theory* if it could be shown that its arguments did not depend on the assumption of irrational behavior, but on an alternative theory of rationality, whose knowledge requirements were less extensive than those implied by classical economics. The *TP* pointed to the existence of such a theory.

From Burke, Keynes got a set of principles of good government. Not surprisingly for the time it was written, his essay (Keynes UA/20) interprets Burke as a liberal–conservative utilitarian – in fact, as the first utilitarian political philosopher. He attributed to him the important discovery that the science of politics is a doctrine of means not of ends; that is, that the forms and duties of government were relative to the purposes for which government exists and could not be decided in the abstract. The primary political question therefore is: What ends do governments exist to achieve? The question: What should governments do? can be answered only in the light of the answer to the first question. Moore opens *PE* with a parallel set of questions and there is no doubt that Keynes credited Burke with doing for politics what Moore did for ethics.

The goods which, according to Burke, government should seek to promote are not Moore's ultimate ethical goods, but the 'happiness of the people', as constrained by the principle of equity, or just dealing ('absence of artificial discrimination') between classes and individuals (which may, of course, also be regarded as a condition of social happiness). The preconditions of happiness were 'physical calm, material comfort, intellectual freedom'. Since these were also amongst the 'great and essential means' to good states of mind, 'a government', Keynes wrote, 'that sets the happiness of the governed before it will serve a good purpose, whatever the ethical theory from which it draws its inspiration' (Keynes UA/20, pp. 17–18). No more than Moore did Burke believe that happiness was the greatest good; but it was what government existed to promote. Thus politically Burke 'may...be described as a utilitarian; but ethically he can in no way be said to have anticipated [Bentham]' (ibid., p. 8).

Turning to the methods of government, Keynes endorses Burke's criterion of 'prudence and practicability'. He writes: 'in the maxims and precepts of the art of government expediency must reign supreme; whatever rights individuals may have, government has and can have no right to do anything which is not for the general advantage' (ibid., p. 36). Thus expediency is a *duty*, not a convenience. Given the slightness of our 'power of prediction' it is 'the paramount duty of governments and of politicians to secure the well-being of the community under the case in the present, and not to run risks overmuch for the future'. A government should aim for smaller goods which can be secured now rather than for larger goods which, being in a further future, are less likely to be achieved. The principle of expediency is closely allied to the principle of 'moral risk' which Keynes, as we have seen, got from Moore and was to develop in the *TP*. But Burke's principle of prudence suggested a further consideration particularly important for statesmanship. The principle of moral risk asserts that the probability of failure needs to be considered in judging the rightness of action. The principle of prudence asserts, in addition, that the benefits of an action must also be weighed against the costs of the transition from the worse to better state. If the loss in welfare over the transition period outweighs the welfare expected over an equivalent future period, the action should not be taken, even if the probability of success is high. These two criteria, but especially the last, will normally rule out war and revolution as a means to welfare. They are also a powerful argument against many forms of protectionism (for example, the infant industry argument).

Keynes criticized Burke, as he did Moore, for his assumption that the best results on the whole are to be got from sticking to generally accepted rules of conduct – the classic liberal critique of conservatism. Burke preferred peace to truth, prejudice to reason, custom to creativity, in part because he 'suspected that the *current* grounds for right action were, in many cases, baseless' (emphasis added). Keynes is not so much attacking Burke here as criticizing the thinness of eighteenth-century rationalism with its abstract ideals divorced from human behavior. His attack on Burke's traditionalist view of governmental duties parallels his criticism of Moore – written eight months before his essay on Burke – for having the 'wrong' theory of probability. If reason were in fact powerless to penetrate the future, it was not wrong to believe that the conduct of rulers should be guided by custom, which could be seen as embodying collective experience. A securer rationalism, rooted in the logical theory of probability, was thus Keynes's answer to both Moore and Burke. Rational reform and creative action based on judgements of probable rightness were open to governments aiming to promote the welfare of the people.

Keynes was generally sympathetic to Burke's view of the agenda or scope of government, though he attacked particular arguments (notably his 'natural order' defence of laissez faire) and thought that, in general, Burke carried good arguments to extremes: he was often, he wrote, as anxious to preserve 'the *outworks* as ... the *central structure* itself' (emphasis added), thus undermining his own principle of expediency. Thus Keynes too favored rule by an elite, but did not think this inconsistent with representative democracy. He also noticed a contradiction between Burke's liberal economics and his social conservatism. Although Keynes did not object strongly to existing inequalities of power and wealth (in England), he thought that questions concerning the scope of democracy, the extent of redistribution and the specific duties of the state should be decided in the light of different and changing circumstances.

Keynes's undergraduate essay can be read as a sympathetic assessment of Burke from the standpoint of late nineteenth-century political liberalism – the hereditary allegiance of Keynes and his parents. There are elements in Keynes's political philosophy – notably his belief in reason as the method for deciding right action – which are alien to conservatism. Also the duties of government in creating the preconditions of goodness were bound to be different in the twentieth century from those in the eighteenth. What he got from Burke was not a set of policies or duties, but an intellectual framework for discussing the purposes and techniques of government.

The question of Burke's influence on Keynes has received far less attention than that of Moore's influence on him. O'Donnell, as we have seen, regards it as 'secondary', mainly because Keynes interpreted Burke in a conceptual framework supplied by Moore. On the other hand, there is nothing in Moore on the 'science of government'. *PE* is about individual, not governmental, duties, with a few background preconditions of good states of mind (such as rules against murder) briefly sketched in. Burke legitimized for Keynes an involvement in public affairs simply by demonstrating how governments might contribute to good states of affairs, and that there were worthy satisfactions to be got from public life. In general it makes more sense to think of Keynes the economist as a Whig reformer than as a Moorean idealist.

Suzanne Helburn holds Burke to believe that it was the duty of a governing class, endowed with the appropriate civic virtues, to promote 'ethical principles', and believes that it was in this sense that Burke influenced Keynes (Helburn, 1991, pp. 30–54). Keynes certainly endorsed Burke's view that people with good characters are more likely to make good rulers than people with bad characters: that is, that the principle of expediency allied to bad character is unlikely to produce good government. But he did not have to go to Burke for this insight: it was a commonplace of Victorian morality. Helburn is wrong to say that Keynes interpreted Burke to say that the duty of government was to promote 'ethical principles': rulers should be moral, something quite different.

Burkean traces abound in Keynes's mature writings. There is little problem of continuity in this case, because World War I and its associated and consequent upheavals made Keynes more, not less, Burkean. He was determined to defend established institutions against revolutionary outbreaks, but was much more flexible than Burke had been in applying the principle of expediency. In his 1938 essay, 'My Early Beliefs', he shreds much of what he took to have been the highly individualist atmosphere of his prewar Cambridge circle:

their irreverence ('we had no respect for traditional wisdom or the restraints of custom'), the 'superficiality' of judgement and feeling which their rationalism produced, their lack of awareness that 'civilisation was a thin and precarious crust' guilefully maintained by laws and conventions. Laws, he playfully suggests, citing Plato, should never be questioned by the young, and only by the old when no young people were present. There were many Burkean sentiments in this essay, dressed up in Moorean language (Keynes, UA/20).

Keynes's conception of the purposes of government did not change from his 1904 essay. The task of economists – and by implication governments – he wrote in 1930 was to solve the economic problem. The solution of the economic problem would disclose mankind's 'permanent problem...how to live wisely and agreeably and well...and cultivate into fuller perfection the art of life' (ibid.). In 1945, he proposed a toast to economists 'who are the trustees, not of civilisation, but of the possibility of civilisation' (Harrod, 1951, p. 194). Material abundance was not a sufficient condition for good states of mind; it might not even be a necessary condition; but without it there would probably be less goodness in the world.

Burke's influence may also be seen in Keynes's habit of justifying radical policies with conservative arguments. (It is a common mistake to identify political arguments with political labels.) The distinction between *outworks* and *central structure* which appears in his essay on Burke, was the pivot of his strategy for defending capitalism and democracy from the revolutionary assaults of central planners and totalitarians, the kernel of his politics of the Middle Way. It emerges most famously in his 'Concluding Notes' to the *GT* (he rightly calls them 'moderately conservative') in which modifications to laissez faire are proposed in order to *preserve* the 'traditional advantages of individualism' – which Keynes identifies as efficiency, freedom and variety – over as wide a field as possible. Keynes's object is not to dispose of the 'Manchester System' but to create an environment in which it can flourish and which can preserve it from the 'authoritarian state systems of to-day' (Keynes, 1936, pp. 379–81). In his political writing he continually emphasizes the need to cede some of the 'outworks' in order to strengthen the 'central structure' of a free society.

Keynes's 1926 essay, 'The End of Laissez-Faire', endorses the Burkean doctrine that the 'agenda' of government must be proportioned to circumstances (Keynes, 1926). Keynes's chief interest was in economic circumstances. He believed that the economic role of twentieth-century government must go beyond supplying a legal framework for private enterprise: the state had to intervene substantively to secure both economic prosperity and equity. The technical demonstration of the need had to wait till the *GT*. But already in the 1920s Keynes was convinced that something had changed in the relationship between economic structures and the conditions of knowledge which made laissez faire unviable as a policy. (What exactly had changed since the nineteenth century is an interesting question in its own right, which cannot be pursued here.)

Keynes's lifelong concern with equity can readily be demonstrated; but the temptation must be resisted as a synonym for equality.[2] (An equal distribution of income may be inequitable, and vice versa.) Keynes typically associates states of inequity or injustice with arbitrary shifts in wealth and incomes caused by avoidable business fluctuations.[3] He believed that the sense of injustice was most strongly aroused by unanticipated disturbances to settled norms, expectations and differentials. In the *GT* he argued that, in their wage bargaining, workers are mainly concerned to defend their *relative* (that is, historically given) positions against other groups, a robust Burkean judgement. Thus Keynes's championship, as an economist, of short-term stabilization policy was linked in his own mind to the duty of government to maintain equity or just treatment between individuals and classes. The one kind of reward he clearly wished to reduce was that accruing to savers or *rentiers*. But this is as an adjunct to the machinery of stabilization, not as a means to an ideal end. In all these discussions Keynes is operating well within the Burkean framework, though he does not always agree with Burke's specifics.

The Burkean maxims of 'prudence and practicability' continually influenced Keynes's own reflections on statesmanship. The following is a very small, but representative, sample from his writings. In 1925/6 he wrote: 'It is fatal for a capitalist government to have principles. It must be opportunistic in the best sense of the word, living by accommodation and good sense' (Keynes, PS/6). He was prepared to carry expediency to the lengths of abrogating the state's contractual obligations to its bond-holders if their fulfillment required excessive deflation: it is 'the absolutists of contract...who are the real parents of revolution'. Finally the principle of risk aversion which Keynes got jointly from Moore and Burke is encapsulated in his most famous remark: 'But this *long run* is a misleading guide to current affairs. *In the long run* we are all dead' (Keynes, 1923, p. 67). Burkean prudence inoculated Keynes against the sacrificial policies of reactionaries and revolutionaries alike.

Keynes's elitism is too well documented to require illustration here. In his writings on politics he simply transforms Burke's virtuous landed aristocracy into a ruling class of Oxbridge graduates. He believed that intellectual authority allied to civic virtue in rulers, backed up by an 'educated bourgeoisie', would be sufficient to offset the irrationality of mass democracy, thus finessing the problem which had caused Burke to repudiate representative democracy.

In sum, Burke provided Keynes with a sufficiently flexible intellectual framework within which to fit, and in terms of which to justify, both the kind of government he wanted and what he wanted government to do in the twentieth century. One could speculate further that the way he thought about government influenced the way he analysed the economic problem.

Tracing the connection between Moore's philosophy and Keynes's economics is more problematic, partly because Moore's ethics does not obviously suggest an economic program, partly because the philosophical situation changed so much in the first half of the twentieth century as to raise a doubt that Keynes brought to the writing of the *GT* philosophic allegiances inherited from before World War I.

O'Donnell believes that the whole of Keynes's political and economic thinking was controlled by Moore's *PE*. From *PE* he derives 'the conception of an ethically rational society as the ultimate end of public action', the view that 'politics was the application of ethical theory to policy questions' and the notion that 'politics was not a direct means to goodness, but, as with economics, a means to the *preconditions* of goodness' (O'Donnell, 1989, p. 276). Moreover the politics thus erected on Moore's ethics '*entailed* quite radical social transformations' (O'Donnell, 1991, pp. 7–8). O'Donnell admits, though, that Keynes had 'remarkably few thoughts to offer' on how Moore's intrinsic goods of personal friendship and aesthetic enjoyment were to be realized through political programmes (ibid., p. 14).

There is no doubt that Moore's ethical ideals influenced Keynes's political aims. But it is important to realize that this was in the face of considerable discouragement from *PE* itself. The most obvious difficulty is that any philosophy which attaches the property good to states of mind rather than to actions is extraordinarily inapt as a philosophy of action. Moore was an unwordly man who produced an ethical philosophy for unwordly people. Keynes was attracted by this philosophy, but his mature life was spent in the public arena, whose purposes and satisfactions could hardly be nourished from the thin ethical soil of *PE*. Two specific difficulties stand out. For reasons connected with his theory of probability, Moore believed private action to secure private goods ('goods affecting [one]self and those in whom [one] has a strong personal interest') is more rational than 'a more extended beneficence', since private goods are more likely to be realized: 'Egoism is undoubtedly superior to Altruism as a doctrine of means' (Moore, 1903, pp. 166–7). O'Donnell acknowledges that Keynes had to 'reconstruct' Moore's theory of probability to put social reform 'back on the main agenda'. Secondly, Moore's ideal utilitarianism offers a pretty flimsy criterion for public action since one has no knowledge of states of mind other than one's own, and therefore there is no certain way of telling whether actions taken by governments to increase material comfort increase or diminish the sum of ethical goodness. This is particularly the case in matters of income distribution. For example, Moore is silent on whether the capacity for friendship and aesthetic enjoyment is equally or unequally distributed. A highly unequal distribution of ethical capacity (in Moore's sense) might sanction a highly unequal distribution of wealth and income. Clive Bell, also a follower of

Moore, concluded that ethical goodness would be maximized by endowing a civilized elite (Bell, 1928).

A *second* reconstruction of *PE* was needed to meet these objections to political reform. In his principle of 'organic unities' Moore offered a bridge between his intrinsic goods and other objects of striving. The chief use of the principle was to limit the power to sum goodness by references to isolated states of consciousness on their own. Thus good states of mind are 'complex organic unities' whose ethical value may be more or less than the sum of their parts. Keynes tried to make the doctrine operational by proposing that only isolated states of mind are good in themselves, but that the goodness of such states could be improved or diminished by the 'fitness' of states of affairs. In 1905, he wrote that practical ethics should concern itself 'with the means of producing (a) good feelings, (b) fit objects' (Keynes, 1905). The second of these two lay within the competence of government. *GT* Keynesianism is concerned purely with the quantity of demand in an economy, but Keynes was also interested in the composition or quality of demand. At various times he proposed grandiose building projects which emphasized beauty as well as use, and was instrumental in setting up a public institution, the Arts Council, to promote demand for the arts.[4]

Keynes's moral disquiet at the effect of money making on character provided him with three ethically based arguments in favor of swift economic progress. First, an increase in material comfort is associated with an increase in 'fit' (that is, aesthetically and intellectually pleasing) objects and is thus conducive to good states of mind. Wealthy homes can afford beautiful pictures and furniture; rich states, beautiful theatres, universities, buildings. Secondly, an increase in material comfort is justifiable if it does not positively decrease the sum of ethical goodness, since a state of affairs in which people are good and happy may reasonably be judged better than one in which they are good and unhappy. In other words, the onus should be on opponents of material progress to show that it decreases the sum of ethical goodness. This is an ethical version of Pareto optimality, which, incidentally, rules out extensive income redistribution. Finally Keynes argued, notably in his essay, 'Economic Possibilities for our Grandchildren' (1930) that the freeing of mankind from pressing economic cares would release time and energy for cultivating good states of mind. Everyone should at least be given the chance to show whether they are capable of ethical goodness.

Keynes's emphasis on maintaining a high level of investment thus serves an ethical as well as an economic purpose. Investment determines income and therefore the standard of living, and through this has a major influence on the value of life, particularly by enlarging the time for leisure. All of these attitudes are consistent with Moore's *PE*, though it must be remembered that there was nothing distinctive in Moore's Ideal. What was distinctive was his method of deriving it.

A final issue to consider is how far Keynes's distinctive theory of rational behavior, which developed out of his engagement with Moore, influenced his interpretation of economic phenomena in the 1930s. All the commentators agree that Keynes's theory of rationality – as set forth in *TP* – differed from the neoclassical theory, in which the rational agent maximizes his utilities under conditions of actuarial certainty. On these assumptions it is hard to see how unemployment can develop, much less persist. In *TP* agents maximize under conditions of uncertainty which cannot, in most cases, be reduced to actuarial risk. They use logical insight into probabilities in order to do the best they can in the circumstances of limited knowledge. When probabilities are unknown, in the sense of being unperceived, 'it will be rational to allow caprice to determine us and to waste no time on the debate' (Keynes, 1921, p. 32). On these suppositions, agents can make large mistakes in trying to realize their aims. In the *GT*, economies misbehave because agents make wrong decisions in conditions of radical uncertainty. But these decisions are not necessarily irrational. So there seems a fairly straight line between the *TP* and the *GT*. The root of the difference between Keynes and the classical economists seems to be epistemological.

There is much to be said for this view, but it is not so clear that the source of the epistemological difference is to be found in the *TP*. The problem is that rational behavior in the *GT* seems to be identified with conventional behavior, whereas in the *TP* rationality is a property of individual judgement: there is little or nothing about rules and conventions. There have been two main (and opposing) strategies for dealing with this apparent lack of continuity. R.M. O'Donnell sees the conventional behavior patterns of the *GT* as 'strategies of weak rationality' adopted by 'informationally deprived agents'. Anna Carabelli reads into the *TP* a Wittgensteinian notion of rationality as 'rooted in human customs and ordinary language' (O'Donnell, 1989, p. 261; Carabelli, 1988, p. 134). Most recently J.B. Davis (1994) has adopted a third strategy. The microfoundations of the *GT* are not neoclassical, but neither can they be found in the *TP*. Keynes abandoned his own earlier theory of rationality under the influence of Ramsey and Wittgenstein, and more generally changes in the philosophical climate, after World War I, and embraced an 'intersubjective' theory of rationality. Thus Keynes's 'argument regarding equilibrium unemployment ultimately turns on his concept of convention' as providing the standard of individual judgement (Bateman, 1994, p. 121). If this is true, it represents a considerable shift of philosophic allegiance. The young Keynes proclaimed the individual's duty to judge society's conventions; the older Keynes, not his duty to conform to them – which would not be so different from what Moore and Burke believed – but his inability to escape them.

Whatever the validity of Wittgenstein's theory of meaning, there is no direct evidence that Keynes subscribed to it. The most that can reasonably be claimed is that Keynes came to believe that herd behavior was much more prevalent than he had believed: not that surprising for someone who had lived through World War I. But this does not mean that he changed his view about the way human beings could, and should, behave: in his own investment behavior he deliberately went against 'common opinion' and claimed it was rational to do so. In other words, Keynes never abandoned the theory of rationality expounded in the *TP*: but it may be doubted whether he found it particularly useful in analysing mass phenomena like booms and slumps. Statesmanship has to deal with the way people do behave, not how they ought to behave. In this department, Burke's intuitions proved more reliable than Moore's.

In the final analysis, Keynes remained more optimistic than either Moore or Burke regarding the power of human reason. That optimism supplied him with reasons for acting. Whether it also furnished him with motives for acting is something which must be left to the psychologists.

ROBERT SKIDELSKY

Notes

1 D.E. Moggridge, *Maynard Keynes: An Economist's Biography*, 1992, pp. 131–6, has queried this dating. Keynes's paper, 'Ethics in Relation to Conduct' (Keynes Papers, UA/19), in which he first develops his distinctive theory of probability by way of a critique of Moore, is unpublished and undated. In *John Maynard Keynes: Hopes Betrayed 1883–1920*, I dated it 23 January 1904 on the basis of evidence supplied to me from the record of meetings of the Apostles by Mr G. Lloyd, then fellow and tutor in classics at King's College, Cambridge. I was under a promise not to reveal the source of this dating. It is now known that the record puts the question Keynes discussed on 23 January 1904 as 'Is there an objective probability?' We also know that he was working on 'probabilities' in connection with the Mathematical Tripos in December 1903. Keynes read many papers to the Apostles, but the record shows that only one, that of 23 January, was about probability. The inference that this was the undated paper is therefore very strong.

2 Both O'Donnell and Helburn sometimes treat the words as synonyms. Thus O'Donnell (1991, p. 20) says that in the *GT* Keynes 'identified the two outstanding faults of capitalism to be employment inefficiency and distributional inequality'. In the reference cited (p. 372 of the *GT*) the phrase Keynes actually uses is '*arbitrary* and *inequitable* distribution of wealth and incomes' [emphasis added]. O'Donnell ignores this coupling, which is quite usual in Keynes, and indicates the connection in his mind between inequity and the business cycle. For Helburn, see Bateman and Davis (1991, p. 40).

3 As when he attributes the 'vast enrichment of individuals out of proportion to any services rendered' mainly to 'the instability in the standard of value' (JMK, *CW*, IX, p. 160).

4 For an example of his grandiose building projects, see JMK, *CW*, IX, p. 139.

See also:

Economics of Keynes and of his Revolution, Key Elements of the; Keynes, John Maynard; Keynes and Probability; Keynesian Revolution.

Bibliography

Bateman, Bradley W. and John B. Davis (eds) (1994), *Keynes's Philosophical Development*, Aldershot: Edward Elgar.

Bell, Clive (1928), *Civilisation*, London: Chatto & Windus.

Carabelli, Anna (1988), *On Keynes's Method*, London: Macmillan.

Harrod, Roy (1951), *The Life of Maynard Keynes*, London: Macmillan.

Helburn, Suzanne (1991), 'Burke and Keynes', in Bradley W. Bateman and John B. Davis (eds), *Keynes and Philosophy*, Brookfield, VT: Edward Elgar.

Keynes, John M. (1905), 'Miscellanea Ethica', Keynes Papers, UA/21.

Keynes, John M. (1921), *A Treatise on Probability*, London: Macmillan.

Keynes, John M. (1923), *A Tract on Monetary Reform*, London: Macmillan.

Keynes, John M. (1926), *The End of Laissez-Faire*, London: Hogarth Press.

Keynes, John M. (1931), 'Economic Possibilities of our Grandchildren', in J.M. Keynes (ed.), *Essays in Persuasion*, London: Macmillan.

Keynes, John M. (1936), *The General Theory of Employment, Interest and Money*, London: Macmillan.

Keynes, John M. (1938), 'My Early Beliefs', in vol. X of *Collected Writings* (1972).

Keynes, John M. (unpublished manuscript), 'The Political Doctrines of Edmund Burke', Keynes Papers, UA/20.

Keynes, John M. (unpublished fragment), PS/6.

Moggridge, Don (1992), *Maynard Keynes: An Economist's Biography*, London: Routledge.

Moore, G.E. (1903), *Principia Ethica*, Cambridge: Cambridge University Press.

O'Donnell, R.M. (1989), *Keynes: Philosophy, Economics and Politics*, London: Macmillan.

O'Donnell, R.M. (1991), 'Keynes's Political Philosophy', in William J. Barber (ed.), *Perspectives on the History of Economic Thought, vol. 6: Themes in Keynesian Criticism and Supplementary Modern Topics*.

Skidelsky, R. (1986), *John Maynard Keynes Hopes Betrayed 1883–1920*, London: Macmillan.

Skidelsky, R. (1994), *John Maynard Keynes The Economist as Saviour 1920–1937*, London: Macmillan.

Keynes? What Remains of

Introduction

This entry deals with the relevance of Keynes in today's world of mass unemployment throughout the developed capitalist world with no foreseeable end. The following kinds of questions are raised and answered. Could the introduction of Keynesian policies lead to a substantial reduction in the unemployment rate? To what extent have structural changes in the capitalist world made his insights incomplete, irrelevant or incorrect? How much of the counterrevolution of neoclassical economics can be accepted and how much should be written off as poor economics or simply political ideology? To summarize the conclusions at the outset, it will be argued that the neoclassical position, which will be referred to as the mainstream view in macroeconomics, is as wrong on the key issues today as when Keynes wrote. It will also be argued that Keynes's position on these same issues remains correct but, and this is a fundamentally different point, under current conditions, Keynes's program must be supplemented.

Two views

A short summary of the basic tenets of the mainstream neoclassical position is a useful starting-point. At its center is the belief that the private sector of a capitalist economy is basically self-regulating, given to steady full employment growth at acceptable rates of inflation in some vaguely-defined long run. To put it differently, in the absence of market imperfections and shocks, including policy mistakes, automatic mechanisms are at work bringing aggregate demand into line with a full employment level of aggregate supply or, at the very least, at the level of output or aggregate supply corresponding to the non-accelerating inflation rate of unemployment, the NAIRU. Discretionary aggregate demand policy measures are unnecessary, inappropriate and most likely to be counterproductive, unless they have been implemented to correct past policy errors. Other than that, 'supply-side' policies may be required to deal with market imperfections.

A summary of Keynes's views is best divided into two parts: his views on the workings of the private sector and his view of the proper role of the state. Keynes's conception of the private sector was one in which employment and output are determined by aggregate demand and not by the real wage. The real wage is determined in the product market. A corollary of this view is that unemployment should not be seen as labour's fault. The system is demand-driven, and in a world of radical uncertainty periods of unemployment will arise from the normal workings of capitalism. There is no automatic tendency for the system to converge to a full employment rate of unemployment.

Keynes's position on state intervention was largely guided by two principles: it could be justified only if the private sector failed to correct a macroeconomic malfunction and then only if the benefits of an intervention were widely spread across the economy. From these principles a limited number of proposals emerged. Most important was that the state must be prepared to guarantee sufficient aggregate demand to achieve full employment even if this entailed deficit spending, as the private sector could not be counted on to fulfil this requirement. Fortunately, from Keynes's perspective, if a stimulation of the economy is needed in order to achieve the full employment target, such policies will act to benefit both capital and labor.

The revolution and the counter revolution

The quarter of a century following World War II is often referred to as the golden age of capitalism. Never before had so many economies grown and transformed themselves so rapidly at low rates of unemployment, and with politically acceptable rates of inflation. This period could just as well have been termed the golden age of Keynesian economics. During these years there developed a growing belief that the success of developed capitalism could be attributed, if not to the actual implementation of Keynesian policies, at least to the belief that the authorities always stood ready to implement them if necessary.

The end of the golden age is usually dated as the early 1970s, although the beginning of the end can be traced to the late 1960s when rates of inflation began to accelerate in most of the OECD economies, the period of the 'Great Inflation'. The early 1970s can also be thought of as the beginning of the end of the dominance of Keynesian economics and the start of the neoclassical counterrevolution. The sequence of events leading from prosperity and growth to mass unemployment and stagnation is fairly easy to document. The accelerating rates of inflation during the late 1960s and early 1970s and payments difficulties in 1973–4 forced the authorities to implement restrictive aggregate demand policies. As a result inflation rates fell somewhat during the second half of the 1970s but remained high compared to their golden age averages. Moreover the cost in terms of unemployment was high: unemployment rates more or less doubled.

To compound the authorities' problems, the oil shock of 1979–80 ignited inflation rates again, leading to the introduction of even more restrictive aggregate demand policies during the early 1980s. This was followed by another short period of falling inflation rates, so that by the mid-1980s inflation rates had fallen back to their golden age rates, but at further cost in terms of higher unemployment. Most economies experienced a recovery in the second half of the 1980s, but even though average unemployment rates were three times their golden age levels, inflation rates accelerated once again. In the recession of the 1990s, unemployment rose, reaching rates experienced in the recession of the early 1980s. This was sufficient finally to bring inflation rates down to their golden age levels. Today the situation can be summed up as one of relatively low rates of inflation and mass unemployment, with little likelihood of any substantial reduction in unemployment rates during this century. On these points there is general agreement; the disagreements arise out of the interpretation of the recent record. In answering the question, 'What remains of Keynes?', attention will be on the actual performance of the advanced capitalist economies over the past 25 years, giving both a mainstream and a Keynesian explanation of the key events.

The mainstream interpretation of events

To many social scientists outside economics, macroeconomic developments of the past 25 years suggest an economic system that has broken down. The long period of high unemployment suggests comparison with the Great Depression, while episodes of accelerating rates of inflation seem to be an added malfunction. To the mainstream neoclassical economist, these social scientists have misread the record. According to the mainstream view, capitalism would have continued to perform in the recent period more or less as it did during the golden age in the absence of shocks, including policy errors of both commission and omission, and certain market imperfections.

A generic interpretation of recent malfunctions would acknowledge that shocks had an adverse effect on the performance of the economy, especially in accounting for the 'Great Inflation', but for the longer period its emphasis is on market imperfections. They are responsible for the upward trend in the unemployment rate. According to this view, under 'normal' circumstances restrictive aggregate demand policies will not only lead to a swift reduction in inflation; they will set in motion automatic mechanisms, such as Pigou and Keynes effects, so that, after only a slight delay, the economy rapidly resumes its natural equilibrium unemployment position. The failure of unemployment rates to decline rapidly to golden age levels (and indeed the slowness with which inflation rates declined) was the result of outward shifts in the long-run vertical Phillips curve, that is, increases in the NAIRU. This made it impossible for unemployment rates to fall to anywhere near their golden age levels without generating accelerating rates of inflation. Given the properties of the NAIRU and a belief in automatic convergence tendencies to this equilibrium unemployment rate, this mainstream interpretation of the widespread secular rise in unemployment rate was simply a natural downward adjustment of aggregate demand to the economy's rising equilibrium unemployment rate.

The rising NAIRU was seen as an indicator of growing market imperfections, especially in the labor market throughout the developed market economies, such as overgenerous unemployment insurance benefits, increased union militancy and mismatches in the labour market. One result of these developments was labor market conditions in which the real wage was too high to employ anything but a diminishing percentage of the labor force. 'Eurosclerosis' was a name given to this situation. The policy prescriptions were to achieve greater market freedom by reducing unemployment insurance benefits, reducing the powers of the trade unions and other so-called 'supply-side' measures. With such changes, aggregate demand would then adjust to the increased supply capabilities and there would be a return to something like the conditions of the golden age.

What is wrong with the neoclassical interpretation and what is right about Keynes's view of events

What about Pigou and Keynes effects?

There are several things wrong with this interpretation of the recent past and, as we outline some of the errors, the correctness of the Keynesian analysis of the same events becomes clearer. The general inappropriateness of mainstream NAIRU analysis in explaining unemployment and inflation developments, especially under mass unemployment conditions, must be emphasized. NAIRU analysis of unemployment and inflation assumes that the economy has strong tendencies for rapid convergence to a unique equilibrium. For such an approach to be a useful method of analysis, at least two conditions must be satisfied: the mechanism adjusting aggregate demand to aggregate supply must be plausible and the underlying assumptions must be internally consistent. NAIRU analysis is an unsatisfactory method of analysis in both these respects, whatever the state of the labor market.

To begin with, there is very little empirical or theoretical support for the position that Keynes effects and Pigou effects are capable of acting as automatic regulators of aggregate demand in the manner assumed by this version of the invisible hand (Tobin, 1993). And without a mechanism adjusting aggregate demand to some exogenous equilibrium aggregate supply, all that remains of the neoclassical theory of unemployment is the concept of a unique equilibrium rate of unemployment, the NAIRU, and associated with it a unique equilibrium level of output or aggregate supply. Their uniqueness and equilibrium properties derive from the fact that, at any other maintained rate of unemployment or level of output, inflation rates accelerate or decelerate without limit. But in the absence of an automatic mechanism adjusting aggregate demand to aggregate supply, such an equilibrium is highly unstable, reminiscent of the Harrod–Domar knife edge in growth theory. An economy would only settle at this output level or unemployment rate by accident. Without a mechanism adjusting aggregate demand to the NAIRU-determined aggregate supply, the NAIRU cannot be considered a useful equilibrium concept.

A basic contradiction

Even if the neoclassical theory of unemployment rate incorporated a plausible mechanism of adjustment, there remains something fundamentally unsound about the mainstream model of unemployment and its interpretation of events. This shortcoming comes out most clearly in the use of NAIRU analysis to explain why unemployment rates have increased so substantially in recent times. Recall that the original formulation of the long-run vertical Phillips curve was based on Friedman's natural rate of unemployment, a very special NAIRU at which all unemployment was voluntary (Friedman, 1968).[2] But as the period of rising unemployment lengthened after the 1970s and more information became available about the importance of layoffs as a cause of being unemployed, about the long duration of unemployment spells and about the importance of the long-term unemployment rate in explaining the rising overall unemployment rate, it became increasingly difficult to interpret unemployment at the NAIRU as voluntary. The empirical evidence too clearly indicated that most of the rising unemployment was an increase in involuntary unemployment.[3]

Oddly this did little to lessen the profession's use of the NAIRU theory of unemployment rate or the long-run vertical Phillips curve. Instead mainstream analysis responded to the facts in one of two ways: either its practitioners and textbook writers glossed over the need to distinguish between the full employment rate of unemployment and the NAIRU, or they allowed that some unemployment at the NAIRU was involuntary but assumed such unemployment to be classical; that is, it could not be reduced by an increase in aggregate demand. Neither of these responses is satisfactory. Consider the confusion of the two unemployment concepts. The defining feature of NAIRU analysis, the view that there is a unique long-run equilibrium rate of unemployment, is derived from the assumption that wage bargaining and settlements are always in real terms. Therefore any recognition of involuntary unemployment at the NAIRU involves a contradiction since, by definition, involuntarily unemployed workers are willing to work at the going real wage or less. Furthermore, if as unemployment rises the proportion of those involuntary unemployed rises, the developments over the last two decades indicate this to be the case, the assumption of real wage bargaining becomes increasingly inappropriate.[4] It then follows that even the long-run Phillips curve must have a negative slope. We are now back in a Keynesian world (which we need never have left) in which stimulative aggregate demand policies can permanently reduce unemployment without a permanent acceleration of inflation rates. In such situations, there are multiple equilibria in the sense that any number of unemployment rates are consistent with a non-accelerating rate of inflation.

It must be noted that these difficulties have been consistently ignored in econometric work; whatever the actual rates of unemployment over the sample period, real wage bargaining has been assumed when deriving estimates of the NAIRU. Typically the estimates are found to be positively correlated with actual rates of unemployment and, from the evidence available, with rates of involuntary unemployment as well (Coe and Gagliardi, 1985, table II; OECD, 1994, table 12). All of this suggests that, during periods of rising unemployment, the difference between the full employment rate of unemployment and estimates of the NAIRU increases. The prevailing failure to distinguish between these two unemployment conditions conceals the high welfare costs that exist even when the economy is at the NAIRU.

Some mainstream economists argue that, even though involuntary unemployment may exist, it still cannot be reduced permanently by stimulative aggregate demand policies because the employed somehow keep real wages too high to justify employers hiring the unemployed; unemployment is involuntary but 'classical'. This argument must also be rejected and here again Keynes is relevant. Money wages are set in the labor market and real wages (given a couple of exceptions) are set in the product market when business decides how much to mark up over costs (Dow, 1990). For example, if, following an expansion of demand and output, profit considerations dictate an increased mark-up over money wages, real wages are automatically reduced, a point stressed in the *General Theory*.

The main implications of this section can be summarized in the following manner. In today's world of mass involuntary unemployment (1) there is no unique long-run equilibrium unemployment rate since any equilibrium depends upon the level of aggregate demand; (2) a sustained increase in aggregate demand will lead to a reduction in unemployment without a permanent acceleration of inflation rates because there is a long-run trade-off between inflation and unemployment rates; (3) much if not most of the pronounced upward trend in unemployment rates since the early 1970s can be explained quite well in terms of a lack of aggregate demand; (4) labor is not to blame for high unemployment; and (5) NAIRU analysis is an inappropriate way to model unemployment and we should dispense with it.

Inflation and its consequences

As just argued, the immediate cause of the increase in unemployment over the past two decades has been a lack of aggregate demand. Had strong stimulative aggregate demand measures been implemented, low unemployment rates would have resulted. The question is: why were the authorities unwilling to provide the necessary aggregate demand for greatly reducing unemployment rates? The simple answer is that, unlike the situation in the golden age period, if the required stimulative policies had been used over the last two decades, politically unacceptable rates of inflation would have resulted. Then as well as now recovery in unemployment is more than simply a matter of aggregate demand stimulation. Policies to control inflation at low unemployment rates are also needed.

What has developed and even intensified since the late 1960s can be described as an increased inflationary bias. In simplest terms, the long-run Phillips curve has shifted outwards. Low rates of unemployment and especially the full employment rate of unemployment have become associated with higher rates of inflation which are politically unacceptable and are met with restrictive policies. It is this increased inflationary bias that so distinguishes the current period from the golden age and from the 1930s.

The emergence of an inflationary bias should not be confused with the mainstream notion of an increased NAIRU, even though each indicates a greater constraint on aggregate demand policies. They are embedded in different theoretical frameworks and, as a result, have a different explanation for movements in the unemployment rate, with different policy implications. Mainstream analysis assumes that there is an automatic adjustment of aggregate demand, bringing it into line with the exogenous level of output corresponding to the NAIRU. Changes in the actual rate of unemployment reflect the extent to which the adjustment mechanisms have moved the economy towards the new NAIRU. In contrast, when a long-run trade-off between inflation and unemployment rates exists, movements in the unemployment rate reflect autonomous changes in aggregate demand, such as the impact of policy.

Second, decreasing the equilibrium unemployment rate in a NAIRU world requires microeconomic measures to shift the NAIRU inward, not a Keynesian stimulation policy. In a Keynesian world of involuntary unemployment and negatively sloped long-run Phillips curves, stimulative policies are a necessary condition for permanently reducing unemployment.

The inflationary bias

The reasons for the increased inflationary bias can only be touched upon. There are three institutional developments worth citing. First, in the second half of the 1960s the majority of the OECD economies experienced a breakdown in what had been successful voluntary incomes policies; these had restrained rates of wage and price inflation during the golden age. Put simply, labor moved from a labor market strategy of money wage restraint in exchange for benefits such as guaranteed jobs and expanded welfare benefits to one of maximum exertion of its market power in wage bargaining (Cornwall, 1994, chs 8 and 9). This marked the beginning of the 'Great Inflation'.

Second, ironically the prolonged period of policy-induced high unemployment generated hysteretic effects that increased this bias. Labor interpreted the restrictive policies introduced in response to the accelerating rates of inflation as efforts to reduce its market power. The resentment this caused, together with the slow growth in real wages that was attributed to the policies, intensified an interest on labor's part in redressing the balance *if and when labor markets again tightened.* Third, following the breakdown of the Bretton Woods agreement and the introduction of greater flexibility in exchange rates, international capital movements were steadily deregulated. International capital flows increasingly shifted from the financing of trade and real investment to financing exchange rate and interest rate speculation. As a result conditions have steadily evolved in which the introduction of strong stimulative aggregate demand policies leads to capital flight, large undesired depreciation of the exchange rate and increased importation of inflation. Taking into account these three institutional changes, any attempt to return unilaterally to low unemployment conditions (for whatever reason) will lead to greater inflationary pressures than during the golden age.

These institutional–structural changes were sufficient to place a constraint on the use of stimulative aggregate demand policies to reduce the unemployment rate to golden age levels; the constraint remains as the economies are caught in a high unemployment equilibrium trap. While some recovery in unemployment might be achieved through stimulative aggregate demand policies, complete recovery in the unemployment rate requires policy-induced changes in beliefs, attitudes, rules and laws to neutralize the institutional changes that now constrain aggregate demand. The required changes include labor's acceptance of a second generation of incomes policies, coordinated fiscal and monetary policies under an international momentary regime more like the Bretton Woods arrangement than the present flexible exchange rate system, and measures to reduce significantly speculative capital flows.

Recovery today and the relevance of Keynes

These are severe conditions and the question must be raised, is a substantial reduction in unemployment rate possible? Certainly in the short run, say over the remainder of the 1990s, there is only a very slight chance of such a recovery. Two reasons are worth citing. First, in spite of periodic announcements by political leaders of the intention to do something about the high unemployment, governments have in fact increasingly adopted the view that 'there is no alternative' to restrictive policies. Inflation must be contained and, if anyone questions the high unemployment costs, the authorities simply deny that the high unemployment rate is due to these policies. Second, and related, alternative programs for changing those institutions responsible for the strong inflationary bias are only now beginning to reach the public. The Tobin tax on international currency speculation is a case in point (Tobin, 1978).

Recovery, then, is only possible in some longer-run sense. But there is no hope even in the longer run that the required policy-induced institutional changes will be made if the political pressure demanding such changes is lacking. And such pressure will not be forthcoming, let alone sustained, unless there is public awareness that there is a program for reducing unemployment rates. As a starting-point we can do no better than to consider further what remains of Keynes.

On the key issues of theory, the policies required for recovery and the main tasks for economists, Keynes had the right answers for his times and they are the right answers for today. His theory of the critical role of aggregate demand and the inability of the private sector to always provide the correct level of aggregate demand holds as true today as it did 60 years ago. Workers are not to be blamed for their unemployment; rather blame can be laid on an economic system that fails to provide sufficient aggregate demand. His critique of the neoclassical view was and still remains true. Capitalism is not a self-regulating system in which aggregate demand adjusts automatically and passively to some exogenously determined aggregate supply. His policy message can also be accepted today. Stimulative aggregate demand policies are a necessary condition for a return to full employment. They are not, however, a sufficient condition and in that sense Keynes's program must be supplemented. Policies must also be introduced to reduce the inflationary bias now plaguing capitalist economies.

Finally, Keynes saw two tasks for the economist during a period of economy-wide market failure: to develop a new research agenda for macroeconomics and to embark on an 'educational' mission. As a prelude to formulating a recovery program, the new research agenda was to determine the changes in the structure of capitalism that led to the breakdown of the 1930s. It would be difficult to think of a more important task than this for economists concerned with today's difficulties. An educational mission was thought necessary by Keynes if he was to get his ideas accepted and implemented. The political leaders as well as the general public had to be convinced that they were being misled by prevailing attitudes about issues such as the role of government and the effects of budgetary deficits. A similar kind of educational mission by economists is needed today. It must be made clear that government must be part of the solution, that past policies advocated by mainstream economists have failed to cure the unemployment problem and that a radically different program is needed for recovery.

JOHN CORNWALL

Notes

1 This work was supported by grants from the Social Sciences and Humanities Research Council of Canada. The title of the entry is intentionally very similar to that of Brittan *et al.* (1994).

2 Friedman's definition of the natural rate of unemployment implies that his analysis deals with a world of market imperfections. However, in his disequilibrium exposition, explaining how the economy converges to the natural rate equilibrium, the explanation is strictly in terms of competitive adjustments.

3 The division of unemployment into voluntary and involuntary categories has fallen into disuse in economics. However, as argued in the text, this is the appropriate distinction for evaluating NAIRU analysis and for measuring the welfare implications of unemployment.

4 For example, data showing the upward trend in unemployment rates and the rising proportion of unemployed in long-term unemployment in the OECD economies are found in OECD, *Employment Outlook*, various issues.

See also:

Business Cycle Theory (I) and (II); Demand Management; Fiscal Policy; Inflation; Keynes, John Maynard; Keynesian Revolution; Lucas Critique; New Classical School of Economics; Real Balance Effect.

Bibliography

Brittan, S. *et al.* (1994), *What is Left of Keynes?*, London: The Social Market Foundation.

Coe, D. and F. Gagliardi (1985), 'Nominal wage determination in ten OECD economies', *Working Papers*, Paris: OECD.

Cornwall, J. (1994), *Economic Breakdown and Recovery: Theory and Policy*, Armonk, New York: M.E. Sharpe.

Dow, Sheila C. (1990), *Financial Markets and Regional Economic Development: The Canadian Experience*, Aldershot: Avebury.

Friedman, M. (1968), 'The role of monetary policy', *American Economic Review*, **58**, (1), March, pp. 1–17.

OECD (1994), *Economic Outlook*, June, Paris: OECD.

Tobin, J. (1978), 'A proposal for international monetary reform', *Eastern Economic Journal*, **4**, (3/4) October/December, pp. 153–9.

Tobin, J. (1993), 'Price flexibility and output stability: an old Keynesian view', *The Journal of Economic Perspectives*, **7**, (1), winter, pp. 45–65.

Keynes's Economics, National Income Accounting and Activism

Gross domestic product, national income and many related measures describing the incomes of those providing inputs into the production process, output levels and expenditures on outputs by various economic sectors are reported by a nation's economic accounting system. National income is the oldest of these measures. *National income accounting* and *national income analysis* remain interchangeable with more modern titles such as *social accounting* and *macroeconomics*.[1] Accounts are often published quarterly to facilitate tracking the economy's interconnected parts. Connections among economic sectors are key aspects of macroeconomics and accounting system designs. Selection of measures, design of presentation tables and descriptions of relationships among accounts serve to enhance understanding of the economy's complete system of flows.

This entry describes the earliest attempts to measure national income as a prelude to its primary discussion of the inspirational role of Keynes and the progenitor roles of Richard Stone and Simon Kuznets during the 1930s and 1940s when British and United States governments institutionalized their national income accounting. Forces which contributed to modern systems development are summarized. Attention is drawn to similar forces now within former Soviet bloc countries and how they may, as many nations have done, adapt the United Nations System of National Accounts (UN/SNA), a design with ancestry to the earliest economists.

National Economic Accounting prior to Keynes

Foundations for modern macroeconomic accounting systems were laid centuries ago.[2] Sir William Petty in Great Britain made the first known estimate of national income in 1665. In *Political Arithmetik*, published posthumously in 1691, Petty chose a definition of national income similar to today's and used a factor income measurement method which summed wages, rent, interest and profit. Gregory King, Petty's immediate intellectual successor, used better data and improved estimation procedures for extrapolating representative micro-level observations of income, production and saving to estimate macro-level statistics. Partly as a reaction against mercantilism, their nationalistic motive was to measure Britain's economic strength and global influence just as families were measured for economic importance in that era. A third

British pioneer, Charles Davenant, attempted political popularization. His *Discourses on the publick revenues and the trade of England* (1698) explained how *political arithmetik* was useful for '(a) formulating effective tax policy, (b) preparing plans for the mobilization of manpower and economic resources in time of war, (c) gauging the economy's resources during war, and (d) formulating a foreign trade policy' (Studenski, 1958, p. 37). Governments did not respond, but the intellectual seeds were sown. Pierre le Pesant Sieur De Boiguillebert's *Détail de France* in 1697 advanced Petty's notions to the Continent. Sixty years later, François Quesnay developed the physiocrats' *tableau économique*, a tabular approach anticipating modern sector accounts, theory's emphasis on circular flows of incomes and products within the entire economy, and the input–output matrix. Analytic macroeconomic modeling began here. Quesnay developed the tableau especially for the French king (ibid., p. 63) and proponents believed alternative nations and policies could be evaluated by changing only a few key pieces of calibrating information. Thus earliest economists moved quickly from accounting to modeling and policy analysis.

Subsequent efforts prior to the era of Keynes were also made by individuals, often with nationalistic reform motives. National income was measured multiple times in multiple ways for multiple nations, tax record and population census statistical methods were improved and truly prodigious improvements were made in economics. But governments remained unmotivated to make frequent routine national income measurements. This was an era of *laissez faire*.

The influence of Keynes

A key aspect of Keynes's theory which encouraged *routine* governmental economic accounting was its emphasis that market equilibration forces could be too meagre during depressions, so that government action was needed in calculated amounts to restore full employment. Particularly influential was Keynes's attack on the notion that an excess supply of lendable funds would exist in a depression to induce interest rate declines that would then stimulate investment and recovery.[3] Prevailing *laissez faire* orthodoxy, ardently held within British and American societies and their communities of economists prior to *The General Theory of Employment, Interest and Money* (1936), maintained that markets were self-correcting and encouraged little demand for economically informed governments. Activism sentiment gained strength amid debate as the Great Depression persisted, worsened and stressed societies. Government national income accounting efforts were initiated to provide large amounts of timely data to many people for consideration in fiscal debates and decisions.[4]

Furthermore, several chapters in *The General Theory* enhanced reader awareness of contemporaneous national income concepts and measurements.

Chapter 6 presented three views of national income consistent with modern definitions. Keynes's rendition of the expenditure approach emphasized consumption and investment, essentially distributing government spending and net exports within these categories. The dichotomy of consumption and investment was appreciated by business cycle analysts long before 1936, but Keynes wanted to change economists' opinions about the economy's cyclical behavior. He also presented the factor income approach. His third context was essentially the modern sum of values added approach which clarified national production contributions across producers and encouraged the complete system thinking his general equilibrium approach required. He also related his definition of national income to that of his teacher Alfred Marshall and discussed gross and net investment relative to A.C. Pigou's national dividend, a measure akin to net national product. Finally, in Chapters 8 and 10, Keynes stressed how the cyclical relation of investment and consumption was revealed in the best available national income account information of the day, citing Colin Clark's *National Income, 1928–31* (1932) and especially Simon Kuznets's *National Bureau of Economic Research Bulletin (No. 52)* (1935). His discussion of the collapse of net investment and the concurrent behavior of national income and consumption displayed vivid understanding of extant data, their frailty and their time series properties.[5]

Contributions of Richard Stone

Keynes later led discussion on how to manage British war production and financing, which provided him with the opportunity to encourage the chancellor of the exchequer to engage James Meade and Richard Stone in a newly formed Central Statistical Office for preparing national income estimates.[6] With detailed advice from Keynes, they published national income and expenditure data in conjunction with the 1941 budget report and an April White Paper, *An analysis of the sources of war finance and an estimate of the national income and expenditure in 1938 and 1940*, which laid the groundwork for future use of their double entry design. This methodology gained international influence. Especially important were the demonstrated fiscal budget connection, the economic supplier–demander transactions character of the double entry approach and a subsequent 1946 White Paper which extended the approach to income and outlay accounts for the four basic sectors in Keynesian macroeconomic models: households, businesses, governments and the rest of the world.

Stone exhibited substantial zeal for this social accounting approach. Within the 1947 *Measurement of National-Income and the Construction of Social Accounts* (with an appendix by Stone) the League of Nations Committee of Statistical Experts formed the basis for accounting systems intended to permit international comparisons, a goal of researchers since the time of Petty.

In 1952 Stone influenced the national income methods of the Organization for European Economic Cooperation. And within the UN/SNA his philosophy and designs have continued since 1953. One design aspect has been his use of arrays which show both grand aggregates and finer details simultaneously and which consistently display the double entry nature of the accounts along the two axes. In this comprehensive way the original inspiration of Quesnay continues to be employed. Angus Deaton has remarked, 'One of the most important features of such "tableaux économiques" is that it is almost impossible to look at them for long without being led into attempts to model the behaviour that they reveal' (Deaton, 1987, p. 510). For such intellectual leadership in economic science and development of economic accounting systems, Stone was knighted in 1978 and made Nobel Laureate in Economics in 1984.

Contributions of Simon Kuznets

Kuznets began national income research before the Great Depression and the economics of Keynes.[7] Completing his PhD in economics in 1926, Kuznets began working at the National Bureau of Economic Research (NBER), an organization created in 1920 by Wesley Clair Mitchell, his mentor at Columbia. Kuznets's work in national income analysis and Mitchell's work with Arthur F. Burns on business cycles became NBER specialty areas. In these early years Kuznets reviewed all known methods of estimating national income, served as NBER consultant to the Department of Commerce and published his influential 'National Income' in the *Encyclopedia of the Social Sciences* (1933). When Congress in 1932 asked the Department of Commerce to prepare national income estimates, Kuznets became project head. His group's *National Income, 1929–32* (1934) provided estimates and methodology sections. At NBER Kuznets refined gross and net investment measurement, publishing *National Income and Capital Formation, 1919–1933* in 1937 and *Commodity Flow and Capital Formation* in 1938, the preliminary findings of which Keynes had cited. In the 1940s, Kuznets demonstrated war production planning uses of national account data. Thereafter he researched modern international economic growth patterns, an endeavor strongly complemented by his global understanding of national income and product accounts. It was for this work that Kuznets became Nobel Laureate in Economics in 1971.

Conclusion

Governments of the world moved *en masse* from sporadic, weak and non-catalytic interest in national income measurement during the eighteenth and nineteenth centuries to total endorsement in the 1930s and 1940s. Refinements have continued among originator nations without apparent loss of enthusiasm. Communist bloc countries advanced their methodology related to Marx's labor theory of value. Capitalist countries pursued various approaches with some convergence towards the United Nations recommendations. Extent of adoption and degree of commitment varied. Dramatic changes in former Communist bloc countries are now unfolding as they explore reliance on market forces. How their statistical and economic institutions will echo these transitions is uncertain.

Many causes influenced development of economic accounting systems, but several have been dominant. Wartime controls and times of prolonged economic crisis have been particularly powerful forces for changes in societies' statistical institutions. The ending of the Cold War and the economic collapse of the Communist bloc are recent examples; chaos and disruption in Europe induced by World War I and the global Great Depression are also twentieth-century examples. People wanted measurements of such big changes in their environments. Improved education and growth in the fields of economics and statistics have been enormously instrumental. People sought causal explanations of patterns revealed in the data. Intellectual motives, as well as nationalism and taxation issues, swayed national income investigations in the 1800s and 1900s. Especially in the 1930s and 1940s, people altered their institutions to attempt greater economic control and prevent repetitions of past catastrophes. *The General Theory* contributed to this transition.

United Nations advocacy of the SNA has been a modern force for convergence and universalization. UNO's *Yearbook of National Accounts Statistics* provides the economic vital signs for the world in a presentation style emanating from the very original definitions of Petty and the tabular arrangements of Quesnay.

John C. Larson

Notes

1   Extensive description of the host of measures presented in the national income and product accounts may be found in most macroeconomics texts. Space constraints disallow such discussion in this entry.

2   This brief section draws from lively, comprehensive histories of national income accounting by Paul Studenski (1958) and John W. Kendrick (1970). Readers interested in nineteenth-century developments in many countries will find a wealth of information in these sources.

3   See Robert L. Heilbroner (1969, pp. 241–50), for a masterful rendition of this Keynesian theme and for the way Keynes evolved towards it.

4   Some may suggest that the broad research agenda prompted by *The General Theory* served as a vital impetus for accounting systems development. Behavioral relations of the Keynesian theory certainly prompted empirical analysis, but such academic interests did not prompt political endorsement any more than in earlier centuries. Kuznets's involvement at the Department of Commerce preceded *The General Theory* by at least several years.

5   It may also be mentioned that Keynes cited Petty and Davenant when discussing early economists in Chapter 23; however their contributions to national income accounting were not mentioned.

6   R.F. Harrod's biography of Keynes (1951, ch.XII, esp. pp. 491–503) elaborates upon this

occasion, and also mentions that Keynes had written an essay on national income analysis for private circulation in 1939–40 as part of his war finance deliberations.
7   This section relies upon Carson (1975), Easterlin (1987) and Kendrick (1970).

See also:
Keynes, John Maynard; Kuznets, Simon; Stone, Sir John Richard N.

Bibliography
Boiguillebert, Pierre le Pesant Sieur De (1697), *Détail de France*, Paris.
Carson, Carol S. (1975), 'The History of the United States National Income and Product Accounts: The Development of an Analytical Tool', *Review of Income and Wealth*, series 21, June, pp. 153–81.
Clark, Colin (1932), *National Income, 1928–31*, London: Macmillan and Co. Ltd.
Davenant, Charles (1698), *Discourses on the publick revenues and the trade of England*, 2 vols, London.
Deaton, Angus (1987), 'Stone, John Richard Nicholas', in John Eatwell, Murray Milgate and Peter Newman (eds), *The New Palgrave: A Dictionary of Economics*, Vol. 4, New York: Stockton Press.
Easterlin, Richard A. (1987), 'Kuznets, Simon', in John Eatwell, Murray Milgate and Peter Newman (eds), *The New Palgrave: A Dictionary of Economics*, Vol. 3, New York: Stockton Press.
Harrod, R.F. (1951), *The Life of John Maynard Keynes*, London: Macmillan.
Heilbroner, Robert L. (1969), *The Worldly Philosophers*, 3rd edn, New York: Simon & Schuster.
Kaldor, N. (1941), 'The White Paper on National Income and Expenditure', *Economic Journal*, **51**, (202–3), June–September, pp. 181–91.
Kendrick, John W. (1970), 'The Historical Development of National-Income Accounts', *History of Political Economy*, **2**, (2), fall, pp. 284–315.
Keynes, John Maynard (1936), *The General Theory of Employment, Interest and Money*, London: Macmillan.
Kuznets, Simon (1933), 'National Income', *Encyclopedia of the Social Sciences*, Vol. 11, New York: National Bureau of Economic Research, pp. 205–24.
Kuznets, Simon (1934), *National Income, 1929–32*, Senate Document 124, 73rd Congress, 2nd session; summarized in *Survey of Current Business*, vol. 14, February, pp. 17–19.
Kuznets, Simon (1935), *National Bureau of Economic Research Bulletin (No. 52)*, New York: National Bureau of Economic Research.
Kuznets, Simon (1937), *National Income and Capital Formation, 1919–1933*, New York: National Bureau of Economic Research.
Kuznets, Simon (1938), *Commodity Flow and Capital Formation*, Vol. 1, New York: National Bureau of Economic Research.
Petty, William (1691), *Political Arithmetik*, reprinted in C.H. Hull (ed.) (1899), *The Economic Writings of Sir William Petty*, vol. I, Cambridge, pp. 108–10.
Stone, J. Richard N. (1947), 'Appendix: Definition and Measurement of the National Income and Related Totals', *Measurement of National-Income and the Construction of Social Accounts*, Studies and Reports on Statistical Methods, No. 7, League of Nations Committee of Statistical Experts, Subcommittee on National Income Statistics, Geneva: United Nations.
Stone, J. Richard N. and James E. Meade (1941), 'The Construction of Tables of National Income, Expenditure, Savings and Investment', *Economic Journal*, **51**, (202–3), June–September, pp. 216–33. White Paper.
Stone, J. Richard N. and James E. Meade (1946), *National Income and Expenditure, 1938 to 1946*, Cmd 7099, London: United Kingdom Central Statistical Office.
Studenski, Paul (1958), *The Income of Nations*, New York: New York University Press.
UNO (annually), *Yearbook of National Accounts Statistics*, New York: United Nations Statistical Office.

Keynesian Cross

No simplified model in economics has proved more controversial than the so-called 'Keynesian Cross'. This appellation most commonly refers to the diagram in which a 45 degree, equilibrium line is interpreted as being an aggregate supply curve. (See Figure 1.) In this model, income (or output) is measured along the horizontal axis and aggregate expenditures are measured along the vertical axis. An aggregate expenditures curve completes the diagram. This

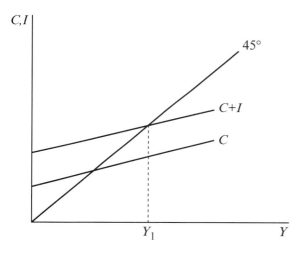

Figure 1   Hansen–Samuelson Keynesian Cross

diagram is the geometric interpretation of a highly condensed version of Keynes's *General Theory*.[1] Total expenditures consist of consumption (*C*), which is a function of income (*Y*) and interest rates (*r*), and investment (*I*), taken to be a function of interest rates alone. In equilibrium,

$$C(Y, r) + I(r) = Y. \qquad (1)$$

Liquidity preference, or the demand for Money, (*L*), is also a function of income and interest rates and in equilibrium must be equal to the exogenously given money supply (*M**).

$$L(Y, r) = M^*. \qquad (2)$$

Assuming linearity, we have a determinate system with two equations and two unknowns.

In Figure 1, equilibrium will occur at income level Y_1, where total expenditures equal income. This equilibrium income level need not correspond to the level of full employment. If Y_1 exceeds the full employment level of output, then an 'inflationary gap' is said to exist. If Y_1 falls short of the full employment level of output, then a 'deflationary Gap' occurs.

Sidney Weintraub (1977, p. 46–7) refers to this Keynesian Cross as 'Hansen–Samuelson 45-degree Keynesianism'. Paul Samuelson (1939) is credited with publishing the first such 45 degree diagram,[2] but an entire generation of American Keynesians honed and extended the underlying model.[3]

Criticisms of this Hansen–Samuelson 45 degree model abound.[4] American Keynesians are prone to interpret the income and expenditure variables on the axes as *nominal* magnitudes.[5] As long as the 45 degree line is depicted solely as an equilibrium line, no *logical* error is committed by conflating changes of real output and the price level. However, once the 45 degree line is interpreted as an aggregate supply curve,[6] the price level must be held constant and income and expenditures on the axes become real magnitudes.[7] Without explicit price levels, the logic of discussing inflationary and deflationary gaps is, at best, suspect.

There is also the question of whether the Hansen–Samuelson version of the Keynesian Cross can be considered an exegetically sound rendering of Keynes's thought.[8] Keynes worked in 'wage units' and deflated nominal magnitudes by the average wage rate. His original aggregate demand and aggregate supply functions (1973, pp. 25–35) were expressed in terms of employment, not output. He never treated inflation and deflation as symmetrical phenomena, amenable to being cured by readily reversible fiscal and monetary policy. Yet such symmetry is precisely what is implied by the Hansen–Samuelson version.[9]

An early version of the Keynesian Cross that is more faithful to the *General Theory* has been attributed to Arthur Burns.[10] But Dudley Dillard (1948, p. 30, fig. 1) published the first such diagram of which we are aware. In these diagrams, employment is measured along the horizontal axis (as a proxy for real output). Along the vertical axis, expected proceeds or receipts are measured in current prices, or in terms of prevailing nominal wages. (See Figure 2.) The aggregate supply curve is upward-sloping and relates the receipts that will *just induce* each level of employment to those alternative levels of employment. The aggregate demand curve is also upward-sloping and represents the proceeds *expected* from selling the output produced by each alternative level of employment. Where the curves intersect, we have the (equilibrium) level of '*effective* demand', where actual and expected receipts are equal, and which again may or may not correspond to full employment.[11]

Given all the controversy surrounding it, just what is the appeal of the Hansen–Samuelson diagram? It is geometrically 'neat' and the underlying

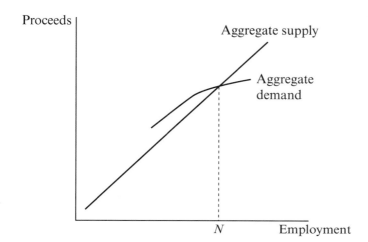

Figure 2 Dillard–Burns Keynesian Cross

equation system is amenable to simplistic algebraic manipulation. This combination is highly compatible with mainstream methodological biases and also permits the drilling and testing of undergraduates in a purely mechanistic manner.

On a more ideological level, the model rationalizes fiscal activism. Overcoming their surprise that the economy did not return to depression conditions after World War II, American Keynesians remained convinced that greater government control of the economy was mandatory. Moreover, at that time, most were also convinced that monetary policy was ineffectual for combating recession, stagnation and unemployment. A generation of undergraduates, drilled in the ways of the Keynesian Cross, were indoctrinated to accept alterations in taxes, transfer payments and government purchases and borrowing as *the* means of maintaining prosperity.

The model has another advantage for rationalizing a program of political activism: it evades any explicit consideration of the distribution (and redistribution) of income. While this is certainly a deficiency from an economist's perspective, veiling the redistributional effects of activism probably improves its political appeal.

WILLIAM GUTHRIE

Notes

1 Elaborate extensions exist of the basic model explored here. See, for example, Bishop (1948), Dillard (1948), Hansen (1949, 1953, esp. pp. 98–107), Klein (1947, esp. pp. 255–74), Samuelson (1948) and Tarshis (1947).
2 Some authorities give priority to the Danish economist, Ivar Jantzen (1935). This conclu-

sion is suspect on two counts: first, Jantzen only depicts a 45 degree, equilibrium line – he includes no Keynesian expenditure curve; second, Jantzen's article appeared several months prior to the publication of the *General Theory*, and there is no evidence that Jantzen saw advance drafts or galleys. See Ambrosi (1981).

3   The more prominent of these are listed in note 1, above. Klein (1947, p. 115) averred, 'This graph represents the building block which forms the entire cornerstone of the Keynesian system.' Samuelson (1948, pp. 134–5) considered the underlying equation system an 'oversimplification' that was, nevertheless, the very 'nucleus of Keynesian reasoning'. Furthermore he compared its importance for the intellectual history of economics as equivalent to the profit-maximization equation and the '"Marshallian-cross" of supply and demand'.

4   Weintraub (1977, pp. 52–3) enumerates the more significant shortcomings.

5   See, for example, Hansen (1949, p. 75, fig.11).

6   Hansen (1953, pp. 29–35) explicitly interprets the 45 degree line not only as an aggregate supply curve, but also *as Keynes's* (1973) [1936] aggregate supply function in Chapter 3 of the *General Theory*. He even employs Keynes's functional notation.

7   Underlying the Hansen–Samuelson version is an assumed functional relationship between output and employment, given the existing capital stock, organization and technology, such that employment and income are uniquely correlated. Logically output and expenditures must, therefore, be real magnitudes and prices must be constant.

8   For a sampling of the literature devoted to this debate, see Amadeo (1989, esp. pp. 90–105), Ambrosi (1981), Davidson (1989), Fusfield (1989) and Patinkin (1989), as well as Weintraub (1977, esp. pp. 46–54).

9   Bishop (1948, p. 318) is explicit on this point: 'Depression and inflation as essentially opposites … . Similarly, anti-inflationary fiscal policies are simply the reverse of those designed to combat depression.'

10   Fusfeld (1985) maintains that Burns formulated this version in 1941, and that Burns claimed that it had the blessing of Keynes himself. In a three-way exchange, Patinkin (1989) takes issue with Fusfeld's 'facts' and with his interpretation of the *General Theory*. Fusfeld (1989) and Davidson (1989) replied that Patinkin's reasoning and his interpretation of the *General Theory* are flawed.

11   The Dillard and 'Fusfeld–Burns' versions differ in that Dillard's aggregate demand curve is concave from below, while Fusfeld–Burns's is convex from below. The implications of these technicalities are beyond the scope of this article.

See also:

Aggregate Demand–Aggregate Supply Model and Diagram; Demand Management; Dillard, Dudley; Hansen, Alvin H.; IS/LM Model and Diagram; Keynesian Revolution; Multiplier Effect; Samuelson, Paul A.

Bibliography

Amadeo, Edward J. (1989), *Keynes's Principle of Effective Demand*, Aldershot: Edward Elgar.
Ambrosi, G.M. (1981), 'Keynes and the 45-degree Cross', *Journal of Post Keynesian Economics*, **3**, (4), summer, pp. 503–9.
Bishop, Robert L. (1948), 'Alternative Expansionist Fiscal Policies: A Diagrammatic Analysis', pp. 317–40 in Lloyd A. Meltzer *et al.*, *Income, Employment and Public Policy: Essays in Honor of Alvin H. Hansen*, New York: W.W. Norton.
Davidson, Paul (1989), 'Patinkin's Interpretation of the Keynes and the Keynesian Cross', *History of Political Economy*, **21**, (4), winter, pp. 737–41 (corrected version of article printed with major typesetting errors in **21**, (3), fall 1989, pp. 549–53).
Dillard, Dudley (1948), *The Economics of John Maynard Keynes*, New York: Prentice-Hall.
Fusfeld, Daniel (1985), 'Keynes and the Keynesian Cross: a Note', *History of Political Economy*, **17**, (3), fall, pp. 385–9.
Fusfeld, Daniel (1989), 'Keynes and the Keynesian Cross: Reply to Don Patinkin', *History of Political Economy*, **21**, (3), fall, pp. 545–7.

Hansen, Alvin H. (1949), *Monetary Theory and Fiscal Policy*, New York: McGraw-Hill.
Hansen, Alvin H. (1953), *A Guide to Keynes*, New York: McGraw-Hill.
Jantzen, Ivar (1935), 'On the Theory of a Planned Economy', *Norkisk Tidcskrift for Teknisk Okonomi*, cited in *Selected Contributions to Methods of Quantitative Analysis*, np, nd.
Keynes, John Maynard (1936), *The General Theory of Employment, Interest and Money*, New York: Macmillan.
Klein, Lawrence K. (1947), *The Keynesian Revolution*, New York: Macmillan.
Patinkin, Don (1989), 'Keynes and the Keynesian Cross: A Further Note', *History of Political Economy*, **21**, (3), fall, pp. 537–44.
Samuelson, Paul A. (1939), 'A Synthesis of the Principle of Acceleration and the Multiplier', *Journal of Political Economy*, **47**, (6), December, pp. 786–97.
Samuelson, Paul A. (1948), 'The Simple Mathematics of Income Determination', pp. 133–55 in Lloyd A. Meltzer *et al.*, *Income, Employment and Public Policy: Essays in Honor of Alvin H. Hansen*, New York: W.W. Norton.
Tarshis, Lorie (1947), *The Elements of Economics: An Introduction to the Theory of Prices and Employment*, Boston: Houghton Mifflin.
Weintraub, Sidney (ed.) (1977), *Modern Economic Thought*, Philadelphia: University of Pennsylvania Press.

Keynesian Economics, Deficit Finance in

Deficit finance refers to a sovereign government spending more than it collects in explicit tax revenue over a given time frame. In the absence of previous surpluses, such activity must imply government borrowing, usually through the issue of new government bonds. Deficit finance, therefore, has potential implications for the levels of public spending and overall economic activity, as well as private investment decisions and the interest rate.

An alternative to bond finance is to finance government deficits through the issue of new money. This is often considered as an independent topic warranting separate treatment. However deficit finance and monetary policy can be inextricably linked if the fiscal and monetary authority have the same identity, or if the monetary authority willingly accommodates a fiscal deficit pro forma, or if deficit finance triggers a change in monetary policy.

The idea of intentionally running a budget deficit is a relatively recent phenomenon traced back to the ascendency of Keynesian macroeconomics. Before Keynes, public finance scholars uniformly held a balanced budget as a normative goal (see Buchanan and Wagner, 1977). Although it has been contended that Keynes never directly argued for a government budget deficit as a policy option, the *General Theory* makes clear that deficient aggregate demand was the source of economic maladies of the Great Depression. Moreover Keynes explicitly illustrates the multiplier effect using a public spending example, concluding: 'Thus public works even of doubtful utility may pay for themselves over and over again in times of severe unemployment' (Keynes, 1936, p. 326).

As early as 1938, Alvin Hansen, clearly aware of the implications of the *General Theory*, referred to the 'income stimulating expenditures of the federal government' (p. 121) as a primary cause of the recovery of 1935 and blamed the 1937 recession on increased Social Security taxes. Keynesians such as Abba Lerner actively proposed countercyclical fiscal policy as a tool for attaining macroeconomic growth and stabilization goals in 1943. By the 1950s, the dullest of economics students could dutifully show the hypothetical benefits of deficit finance in the standard $C + I + G$ macroeconomic exposition.

In a Keynesian macro model aggregate demand determines the level of real income. Variations in aggregate demand lead to variations in national income and are, consequently, the cause of the business cycle. Government deficits and surpluses become an ideal tool for fine-tuning the economy. Increasing public spending or reducing taxes when autonomous components of private spending decline prevents an economy from sliding into recession. Correspondingly, decreasing public spending or increasing taxes when autonomous components of spending rise excessively put the brakes on an inflationary expansion. A wisely managed fiscal policy avoids the boom–bust cycle of market economies, much to the benefit of society.

Several criticisms and complications, however, make such a vision of macroeconomic management less than straightforward. Two of the critiques, the *knowledge and lag problems* associated with the operation of fiscal policy and the well-known phenomena of *crowding out*, are essentially independent of the political process. Two other critiques, *influence on monetary policy* and *public choice* analysis, argue that deficit finance coupled with the political process is doomed to failure.

The technical management of a countercyclical fiscal policy is problematic. This is so if for no other reason than knowledge problems. If policy makers forecast changes in private demands incorrectly and adjust fiscal policy according to those incorrect forecasts, fiscal policy amplifies the business cycle rather than moderates it. Moreover simple lags in the executive and legislative implementation of correct policy advice undermine the applicability of the framework. Add in anticipation effects of policy changes, as is common in the *rational expectations* literature, and fiscal policy is at very best ineffective.

A second pervasive criticism of Keynesian macromanagement centers on the possibility of crowding out. Although there are many versions of this theme, the essence is that government debt issue reduces private spending. The reduction in private spending offsets the stimulative effect of new public spending. At the very least this makes fiscal policy less effective than it would otherwise be, or in the extreme case renders it completely sterile. A standard version of this argues that rising interest rates occurring with debt finance crowd out private investment spending. The evidence of such crowding out is less than definitive, at least as seen through the lens of deficits influencing interest rates.

Robert Barro's famous 1974 paper argues for complete crowding out from another perspective. If agents are infinitely long-lived or have sufficiently interdependent utility with future generations, tax finance and debt finance are equivalent. Debt is, in Barro's world, nothing more than future tax obligations. In the presence of capital markets, individuals who wish to avoid future taxes opt to buy bonds. Debt finance cannot have any net stimulus above what a tax-financed increase in public spending would, because of offsetting private adjustments, namely increased private savings implying reduced private consumption.

That budget deficits are inflationary is a widely held perception. From a strict monetarist perspective there is little reason to worry about the inflation implications of increased government spending per se. As long as the money supply is held constant and demand for money is sufficiently inelastic (precluding significant changes in velocity in $Mv = pQ$) deficits do not exert inflationary pressures. However, if monetary policy is influenced by deficit finance, such assurances no longer holds. Central bank accommodation of treasury bond issues makes deficit finance an almost precise equivalent to pure inflation finance, although in this case the government issue of new money is 'laundered' through the central bank buying up the newly issued government bonds. Early on, Keynesian critics saw a potential inflationary implication for the *General Theory*. In 1937, Jacob Viner argued: 'In a world organized with Keynes' specification there would be a constant race between the printing press and the business agent of trade unions' (p. 49).

Finally public choice critiques of deficit finance have focused on the practical political implications of such a policy option. Buchanan and Wagner (1977) argue that Keynesian economic thinking did undermine an informal but powerful constraint against government deficits. Given the tendency for government officials to find it politically advantageous to expand spending or cut taxes, but politically difficult to reduce spending or raise taxes, the fiscal authority will likely follow a countercyclical policy in bust times, but ignore it in booms. This implies that a Keynesian macroeconomic policy will simply increase government spending and public debt. The philosophy of deficit spending, therefore, is purported to make government spending larger than it would otherwise be, and certainly more than is optimal.

Deficit finance is certainly at the top of the public policy agenda in the late 1990s. Popular sentiment for reducing the budget deficits seems to transcend party and ideological lines, at least in the United States. The simple and clear vision of countercyclical fiscal policy is held by few, and seems to hold little weight in popular policy discussions. Only time will tell, however, whether the Keynesian doctrine of fiscal management will be politically resurrected or relegated to a footnote in policy history.

CECIL E. BOHANON

See also:
Crowding Out; Depression, The Great; Fiscal Policy; Functional Finance; Hansen, Alvin H.; Keynes, John Maynard; Keynesian Revolution; Lerner, Abba P.; Lucas Critique; Pigou, Arthur C.; Ricardian Equivalence; Robbins, Lord Lionel; Viner, Jacob.

Bibliography
Barro, Robert (1974), 'Are Government Bonds Net Wealth?', *Journal of Political Economy*, **82**, (6), (November/December), pp. 1097–1117.
Buchanan, James and Richard Wagner (1977), *Democracy in Deficit*, New York: Academic Press.
Hansen, Alvin (1938), *Full Recovery or Stagnation*, New York: Norton and Norton.
Keynes, John Maynard (1936), *The General Theory of Employment, Interest and Money*, London: Macmillan.
Lerner, Abba (1943), 'Functional Finance and the Federal Debt', *Social Research*, **10**, (1), February, pp. 38–50.
Lerner, Abba (1951), *The Economics of Employment*, New York, McGraw-Hill.
Viner, Jacob (1937), 'Mr. Keynes on the Causes of Unemployment'; reprinted in Henry Hazlitt (ed.), *Critics of Keynesian Economics*, New York, D. Van Nostrand, 1960.

Keynesian Indicators

To speak of 'Keynesian' indicators is to presume that at least some statistical indicators of current or future economic activity are purely Keynesian in nature, or at least strongly influenced by the contributions of Lord Keynes. That we can even speak in these terms is yet another tribute to the legacy of the Keynesian revolution, given the fact that business cycle research was relatively well developed by the time the *General Theory* was published in 1936. In fact, with the possible exception of econometric model building, the contributions of Keynes were so dramatically different from the traditional approach to business cycle research that they are best examined from a historical perspective.

The business cycle literature is so rich that it is not possible to give it full justice here. Even so, three observations are relevant. First, the study of business cycles has a very long history. For example, the American economist Willard Phillips (*Manual of Political Economy*, 1828) and the English journalist John Wade (*History of the Middle and Working Classes*, 1833) were among the earliest writers to recognize the recurrent periods of expansion and contraction that characterize the business cycle (Hansen, 1951). Second, the study was truly international in nature. Contributors included Jevons and Kitchin (Britain), Juglar (France), Kondratieff (Russia), Schumpeter (Austria) and Mitchell (United States) to name just a few. Third, and perhaps most important, everyone had a common problem – that of finding sources of reliable and continuous data that could be used to document their particular theories or view of the cycle. Out of convenience, if not necessity, most writers used whatever series were available, with most coming from specific industries that took care to preserve records of their activities.

By 1930, a substantial variety of sophisticated statistical series was available in the United Kingdom. A.C. Pigou's *Industrial Fluctuations* provides one such example and includes series such as unemployment rates (overall as well as by occupation), aggregate money wages (in both nominal and real terms), consumption of industrial materials (such as pig iron), consumption of consumer products (including beer and meat per capita), indices of various kinds (covering everything from manufactured imports, agricultural products, industrial products and the cost of living to general price levels in Germany, the United Kingdom and the United States), bank credit (in both the United Kingdom and the United States) and various interest rates (Pigou, 1929).

In the United States, the study of business cycles was especially intense. Wesley Mitchell published his immensely influential *Business Cycles* in 1913 and, by 1920, had founded the National Bureau of Economic Research (NBER). Arthur F. Burns rose to prominence at the NBER, and in 1939 Geoffrey H. Moore joined the senior research staff, where he eventually went on to become the Director of Research and one of the most distinguished American business cycle researchers. According to Philip A. Klein, the NBER 'played no small part in the creation of a reliable statistical data base for the United States, one which surpasses that of any other country in the world' (Klein, 1990). Eventually the prestige of the NBER was such that the US Department of Commerce agreed to sponsor a monthly publication – originally titled *Business Cycle Developments* and later renamed *Business Conditions Digest* – which chronicled the status of the leading, lagging and coincident indicators that were developed by Moore and others at the NBER.[1]

The methodology employed by the NBER was to collect as many economic series as possible, and then examine each to see how the series behaved in relation to movements of the broader economy. By as early as 1942, 1277 series had been collected, with 970 pertaining to the United States and the remainder covering Great Britain, Germany and France (Burns and Mitchell, 1946). From this database the NBER then identified a much smaller group of indicators by creating a type of 'average' or 'reference' cycle that was plotted against a background of expanding and contracting economic activity.[2] The timing of the reference cycle's peaks and troughs with respect to the peaks and troughs of the overall economy determined the leading, lagging or coincident indicator status of the series. Using this approach, Burns and Mitchell developed their first list of business cycle indicators in 1938 (Klein, 1990).

This methodology was sound from a descriptive point of view, but it was roundly criticized because it was also devoid of hypothesis which could be used to explain the apparent recurrent nature of the business cycle. According to Metzler, 'the procedure followed in *Measuring Business Cycles* consists in *first* setting up a statistical measure and *later* using this measure to test certain generalizations by other economists' (Metzler, 1947). In fact, and even though it was written ten years after the Keynesian revolution, *Measuring Business Cycles* contains only one dismissive sentence in a footnote concerning Keynes.[3]

The approach of the *General Theory* could not have been more different from that of the empiricists at the NBER. Whereas the efforts of economists at the NBER were devoted to testing thousands of individual series, Keynes focused on the relationship between a small number of aggregate variables that included income, investment, savings and consumption. The approach at the NBER was highly disaggregated and descriptive in nature, whereas the approach introduced by Keynes was highly aggregated and conceptual. In short, Keynes and the business cycle economists at the NBER had very little in common during the early years of the Keynesian revolution.

Another difference between Keynes and business cycle theorists of the period was the concept of macroeconomic equilibrium. Prior to the 1930s, according to Robert Gordon, the non-NBER 'business-cycle theorists concerned themselves with why the economy naturally generated fluctuations in employment and output,' while the rest of the profession 'continued to operate on the assumption that full employment was the natural, equilibrium position for the economy' (Gordon, 1952). The issue for Keynes was quite different, however, because he was concerned with how the economy might find itself stuck in a different type of equilibrium, or a condition of 'underemployment equilibrium'. In short, Keynes explained how a given level of savings and investment could determine a given level of employment, but he did not address the issue of why the economy would tend to expand and contract in recurrent phases over time. As a result, J.R. Hicks concluded that 'Keynesian economics, in spite of all that it has done for our understanding of business fluctuations, has beyond all doubt left at least one major thing quite unexplained; and that thing is nothing less than the business cycle itself' (Hicks, 1950).

Eventually Keynes found favor with an emerging group of theorists – econometricians – who were attracted to the elegant simplicity of the Keynesian framework and its focus on aggregate demand, multipliers and accelerators. While significant pioneering work was done by Tinbergen (1939), the power of the Keynesian equations soon became evident when Samuelson (1939) demonstrated that the stability of national income in an econometric model could be determined by the relative magnitudes of the multiplier and the accelerator. Later work took on even more of a Keynesian flavor, the classic example being the macroeconomic model developed by Lawrence R. Klein and A.S. Goldberger (1955). By the 1950s, according to Victor Zarnowitz, 'the models for the United States as well as for the other countries, generally utilize[d] the structure of national income accounts and [were] for the most part of Keynesian persuasion' (Zarnowitz, 1992).

The creation of the national income and product accounts (NIPA) was a parallel development that had it roots in the early work done at the NBER – specifically the pioneering efforts of Simon Kuznets, who worked on the concept of national income in the early 1930s.[4] Today's NIPA is distinctly Keynesian, of course, but it added three dimensions to the field of business cycle research not present prior to the Keynesian revolution. First, and already mentioned above, the NIPA provided a structure for many of the econometric models that were to appear in the 1940s and 1950s. Second, the NIPA provide a comprehensive estimate of the *size* of the overall economy, something that allows us to determine the *magnitude* of the changes that take place both at and between the turning points. This is an improvement over the early work at the NBER which focused primarily on the *timing* of the turning points and generally neglected the magnitude of the changes. Finally the many individual accounts that make up the NIPA – including not only the aggregate series such as GDP and GNP, but lesser ones as well – provided a wealth of new data which could be examined to see if they exhibited the characteristics of leading, lagging or coincident economic indicators.

Table 1 shows the NIPA with the familiar GDP 'expenditures approach' used by the US Department of Commerce. The individual accounts appear in the left side of the table, while 19 individual cyclical indicators appear in the middle. Finally the cyclical indicator status of each series, as determined by the Bureau of Economic Analysis, is listed in the last column.[5] The seven series in bold type are subcategories directly from the NIPA, while the remaining 12 series relate to a respective NIPA category, but do not define it.[6] Even other NIPA categories such as net exports of goods and services, as well as government purchases, simply have no cyclical indicator counterpart.[7]

A similar table showing the 'income' side of the NIPA would be even more abbreviated. Specifically the only other statistical series with cyclical indicator status reported in the *Survey of Current Business* is series 52, personal income in constant dollars, which has a coincident indicator status for both peaks and troughs. So, despite the enormous volume of data collected and maintained by the US Department of Commerce, the short list of boldface series in Table 1, plus the series on personal income, are the only published NIPA series that have cyclical indicator status as determined by the US Department of Commerce.

Table 1 Cyclical indicators and the NIPA

Gross domestic product	**55. Gross domestic product in constant dollars**	[C,C,C]
Gross national product	**50. Gross national product in constant dollars**	[C,C,C]
Personal consumption expenditures		
Goods	75. Index of industrial production: consumer goods	[C,L,C]
Durable goods	73. Index of industrial production: durable manufacturers	[C,C,C]
Non-durable goods	74. Index of industrial production: non-durable manufacturers	[C,L,L]
Services		
Gross private domestic investment		
Fixed investment	27. Manufacturers' new orders in constant dollars, non-defense capital goods industries	[L,L,L]
Non-residential	**86. Gross private non-residential fixed investment in constant dollars**	[C,Lg,C]
Structures	**87. Gross private non-residential fixed investment in constant dollars, structures**	**[Lg,Lg,Lg]**
	9. Construction contracts awarded for commercial and industrial buildings	[L,C,U]
Producers' durable equipment	**88. Gross private non-residential fixed investment, const. dollars, producers' durable equipment**	[C,Lg,C]
	20. Contracts and orders for plant and equipment in constant dollars	[L,L,L]
	100. New plant and equipment expenditures by businesses in constant dollars	[C,Lg,Lg]
	69. Manufacturers' machinery and equipment sales and business construction expenditures	[C,Lg,Lg]

Residential	76. Industrial production, business equipment	[C,Lg,U]
	89. Gross private residential fixed investment in constant dollars	**[L,L,L]**
	29. New private housing units authorized by local building permits (index: 1967=100)	[L,L,L]
	28. New private housing units started (annual rate, millions)	[L,L,L]
Change in business inventories		
Non-farm	**30. Change in business inventories in constant dollars**	**[L,L,L]**
Farm	31. Change in manufacturing and trade inventories (ann. rate, current dollars, moving average)	[L,L,L]
Net exports of goods and services		
Exports		
Imports		
Government purchases		
Federal		
National defense		
Non-defense		
State and local		

Source: Cyclical indicators and their leading (L), lagging (Lg) or coincident (C) status are from the *Survey of Current Business*, US Department of Commerce, GDP categories from file NIPA.BEA on the Economic Bulletin Board, US Department of Commerce.

Interestingly enough, the NIPA and its macro measures of GDP and GNP did not supplant the exhaustive search for series that mark the turning points in aggregate economic activity. Out of respect for the pioneering work of the NBER, the US Department of Commerce has long deferred to that group when it comes to identifying the *official* business cycle turning points. The timing decisions, even today, are made by a seven-member business cycle dating committee that examines a number of individual series before declaring that a trough or peak in economic activity has occurred.[8]

In conclusion, the statistical series that can truly by called 'Keynesian' are few in number, although they are immensely important in practice. The most Keynesian of these indicators are the seven boldfaced series in Table 1 plus series 52, personal income in constant dollars. The most aggregate series (GDP and GNP) have a coincident classification, whereas the three non-residential fixed investment series (86, 87 and 88) tend to exhibit more of a lagging status. The remaining series, residential fixed investment and the change in business inventories (series 89 and 30) behave as leading indicators. Other series in Table 1 match up well with other NIPA categories and provide further evidence of the lasting influence of the Keynesian revolution.

GARY E. CLAYTON

Notes

1   *Business Conditions Digest* was discontinued as a separate publication in March 1990. Several hundred key cyclical indicators (in both tabular and graphic formats) were then moved to the 'buff', or yellow, pages of the *Survey of Current Business*. The 'buff' pages were discontinued in January 1996 when responsibility for maintaining the leading, coincident and lagging economic indicators was transferred to the Conference Board.

2   See L.A. Metzler (1947) for an excellent description, complete with a short numerical example, of a reference cycle in his review of Burns and Mitchell's *Measuring Business Cycles*.

3   The single sentence devoted to Keynes states that 'It may be noted parenthetically that this evidence, so far as it goes, gives no support to J.M. Keynes' thesis that the substitution of a downward for an upward tendency often takes place suddenly and violently, whereas there is, as a rule, no such sharp turning-point when an upward is substituted for a downward tendency' (Burns and Mitchell, 1946, p. 83).

4   See *National Income, 1929–32* (written mainly by Simon Kuznets), Senate Document 124, 72nd Congress, 2nd Session, Government Printing Office, Washington, DC, 261 pp. Earlier volumes dealing with income in the United States were published at the NBER by W.C. Mitchell, W.I. King, F.R. Macaulay and O.W. Knauth.

5   The list was obtained from the buff or 'C' pages in the January 1995 edition of the *Survey of Current Business*, US Department of Commerce.

6   The word 'relate' is used in the broadest possible sense. Some of the series are indices of production in an area, whereas others report on the dollar amount of a portion of production in the category. Even then we make a leap of faith when we assume that production is the same as consumption, especially when we do not know the specific inventory adjustments that would apply to the series.

7   The Department of Commerce keeps detailed records of expenditures in these areas. However none of these series exhibits the type of recurrent behavior over time that would allow them to be classified as cyclical indicators.

8   This can produce occasionally odd results namely that turning points in aggregate economic activity as measured by NIPA do not always coincide with the turning points identified by

the NBER. In fact, three of the last six NBER turning points took place in a different (but adjacent) quarter than would be indicated by the level of real GDP on a quarterly basis. In 1990, for example, real GDP reached its peak in the second quarter, whereas the NBER ascertained that the actual turning point took place in the month of July.

See also:

Burns, Arthur F.; Business Cycle Theory (I) and (II); Hansen, Alvin H.; Keynesian Revolution; Kuznets, Simon; Samuelson, Paul A.; Stone, Sir John Richard N.

Bibliography

Burns, Arthur F. and Wesley C. Mitchell, (1946), *Measuring Business Cycles*, New York: National Bureau of Economic Research.
Gordon, Robert A. (1952), *Business Fluctuations*, New York: Harper & Brothers.
Hansen, Alvin H. (1951), *Business Cycles and National Income*, New York: Norton.
Hicks, J.R. (1950), *A Contribution to the Theory of the Trade Cycle*, London: Oxford University Press.
Klein, Lawrence R. and A.S. Goldberger (1955), *An Econometric Model of the United States*, New York: Wiley.
Klein, Philip A. (1990), 'Geoffrey H. Moore and His Impact on Modern Business Cycle Research', *Analyzing Modern Business Cycles: Essays Honoring Geoffrey H. Moore*, Armonk, New York: M.E. Sharpe.
Metzler, Lloyd (1947), 'Review of Burns and Mitchell, *Measuring Business Cycles*', *Social Research*, **14**, (4), September, pp. 370–77.
Pigou, A.C. (1929), *Industrial Fluctuations*, London: Macmillan.
Samuelson, Paul A. (1939), 'Interactions Between the Multiplier Analysis and the Principle of Acceleration', *Review of Economic Statistics*, **21**, (2), May, pp. 75–8.
Tinbergen, J. (1939), *Statistical Testing of Business-Cycle Theories: I. A. Method and Its Application to Investment Activity; II. Business Cycles in the United States of America, 1919–1932*, Geneva: League of Nations.
Zarnowitz, Victor (1992), *Business Cycles: Theory, History, Indicators and Forecasting*, Chicago: University of Chicago Press.

Keynesian Revolution

On Thursday, 26 December 1935, Keynes informed his mother that 'I finished my book on Tuesday – it has been five years – ... it ought to be published at the beginning of February' (*CW*, 1973, XIII, p. 653).[1] The book of course was *The General Theory of Employment, Interest and Money*, (Keynes, 1936), about which on New Year's Day 1935, in an oft-quoted letter to George Bernard Shaw basically concerned with other issues, he opined his belief that the book would 'revolutionize ... the way the work thinks about economic problems' (*CW*, 1973, XIII, p. 492). He was not wrong. But was it a revolution? One approach is to define formally the notion of revolution. A shortcoming of concentration on definitions, however, is that it may evolve into an end in itself. Another shortcoming is that the search for and application of the definition may result in a semantic game.

That Keynes indeed spawned a revolution is clear from three interrelated considerations. First, there is the weight of professional opinion, as evidenced by the subsequent frequent prefacing of and reference to the 'Keynesian revolution', a term introduced to many by Lawrence Klein (Klein, 1944) in a book based on his MIT dissertation of two years earlier. Nowadays it is common to hear the term, and not just from those sympathetic to the framework and analysis encapsulated in *The General Theory*. The principal exception is Harry G. Johnson, who in the quarter-century after its publication often referred to the revolution but then increasingly hedged this appraisal.

Not only is there a dominance of professional opinion that there indeed was a Keynesian revolution, there also is the Kuhnian hypothesis (Kuhn, 1970) of paradigm, normal science and revolution. This hypothesis cannot be rejected when applied to *The General Theory*, in which Keynes set forth an alternative paradigm to the then prevailing activity of normal science, one that he believed contained fundamental flaws. The question was not so much whether the classical paradigm was completely incapable of dealing with the problems with which Keynes was concerned. Rather the point of departure was that Keynes offered an alternative structure for aggregative analysis, one that was to dominate the profession for decades in terms of terminology, outlook, framework for analysis and empirical considerations.

And it is these that are the lasting legacy of the revolution. Today, when the fires of the Keynesian controversies have died, much of the edifice built along his prescription remains. For one, the national income accounts reflect his organizing principles; interest rate movements are viewed by economists largely in his terms, that is, as reflecting changes in the excess demand for money. Then there is the notion of macroeconomics as a distinct subdiscipline in the profession, an essentially unknown area of specialization before *The General Theory*. Most importantly he brought to a central place the analysis of real output and influences thereon, an issue central to policy making in society.

Of what did the revolution consist? Meade argues that there were 'in fact two distinct, though closely related, Keynesian Revolutions: first, the theoretical revolution in economic analysis; and second, the practical revolution in governmental policies' (1975, p. 82). The revolution in theoretical analysis is of course the thing for which the Keynesian revolution has the most meaning because, without the theoretical discovery, the notion of a Keynesian policy revolution would be meaningless. In asserting this, it should be clear that his central discovery was not the rationalization of deficit spending. After all, political agents have a considerable history of the at least short-term economic, hence political, benefits of such policies.

The common root from which the revolution can be traced was the continued high level of British unemployment in the 1920s, which for many was associated with the 1925 return of gold at the prewar parity. The particular difficulties of British unemployment were exacerbated when mass unemployment became a worldwide issue in the 1930s. The research program thus became one of developing, that is, discovering, an analytically satisfactory model of aggregate output, specifically one of understanding output levels other than at full employment, an endeavor easier said than done.

Lorie Tarshis, then a first-year graduate student at Cambridge, dates the start of the revolution as Keynes's announcement on 10 October 1932 at the beginning of his eight Michaelmas term lectures: 'Gentlemen, the change in the title of these lectures is significant' (Tarshis, 1987, p. 47), the change being from 'The Pure Theory of Money' – the title of the first volume of the *Treatise*, published just two years earlier – to 'The Monetary Theory of Production', the tentative title he assigned to his projected new book (*CW*, 1979, XXIX, pp. 49–50). And so, through these and the three subsequent years' autumn lectures, the struggle to develop such a theory was pursued.

Keynes's thinking at the time can be seen in a virtually identically titled article written in late 1932 for the Arthur Spiethof *Festschrift*. Though no specifics were given, some general observations that were important to *The General Theory* were presented. A monetary theory of production is one

in which money plays a part of its own and affects motives and decisions and is, in short, one of the operative factors in the situation....

The divergence between real-exchange economics [that is, those in which money is neutral] and my desired monetary economics is...perhaps most important when we come to the discussion of the rate of interest and to the relation between the volume of output and the amount of expenditure....

I am saying that booms and depressions are phenomena peculiar to an economy in which...money is not neutral. (*CW*, 1973, XIII, pp. 408–11)

To that end at any rate, 'work[ing] out in some detail a monetary theory of production...is the task on which I am now occupying myself, in some confidence that I am not wasting my time' (1973, XIII, p. 411). What is truly remarkable is that Keynes, having so recently completed the *Treatise on Money*, a major monetary work and one properly regarded by him and the profession at the time as his *magnum opus*, did not rest on his laurels. He not only perceived that there was more of consequence to say but he also intuited the path of pursuit. Though the direction was indicated, the particular roads were full of detours and misleading markers. In contrast to the solitary activity leading to the *Treatise*, it was a journey that was best undertaken with the most able assistance available, those integral to his Loxbridge World – London, Oxford and Cambridge – particularly his coterie of junior colleagues principally at Cambridge, but also including some at Oxford.

Moggridge in his recent in-depth biography (1992, pp. 551–3) makes much of the role of intuition in Keynes's work, noting in particular that he invariably thought through the structure of his arguments before committing to paper any details. The well traveled trail from the *Treatise* to the *General Theory* by subsequent scholars reveals ample signs of this. Two of the best maps of the trail are Patinkin (1976, esp. chs 7–9), where the emphasis is on theoretical development, and Dimand (1988, esp. chs 4 and 5) which adds the professional milieu to the theoretical development.

Keynes completed the *Treatise* in mid-September 1930 and it was published at the end of the following month. Its principal theoretical innovation was the development in Chapter 10 of the fundamental equations, ones that were intended as a substitute for the quantity theory as a means of understanding movements of the price level. Central to those equations was the relation that an excess of investment over saving, each defined in the manner peculiar to the *Treatise*, gave rise to, in fact was identical with, business profits that in turn served to push the price level higher. That book has 'strange and forbidding formulas, and even stranger concepts' (Patinkin, 1976, p. 33).

In a three-lecture talk, 'An Economic Analysis of Unemployment', presented in June 1931 at the Harris Foundation Conference at the University of Chicago dealing with 'Unemployment as a World Problem', Keynes analysed the worldwide depression from the vantage point of the fundamental equations, laying particular stress on the decline of investment relative to savings:

> Looking back, it is now clear that the decline of investment began early in 1929, that it preceded (and according to my theory, was the cause of) the decline in business profits, and that it gathered considerable momentum prior to the Wall Street slump in the autumn of 1929.... it is easy on my theory of the causation of these things to see why a severe decline in the volume of investment should have produced the results that we see around us in the world today. (*CW*, 1973, XIII, pp. 349–52)

The interplay of investment relative to savings, hence the effect on profits and the price level, was the 'secret, the clue to the scientific explanation of booms and slumps ... which I offer you' (*CW*, 1973, XIII, p. 354). The intuition that somehow output variations could be linked to saving–investment actions was made clearer in his further analysis where he attempted to establish that a given decline in investment had associated with it a new equilibrium level of output: 'Now there is a reason for expecting an equilibrium point of decline to be reached. A given deficiency of investment causes a given decline of profit [and output]. ' Unless the fall in investment is constantly *increasing*, 'there is eventually reached, therefore, a sufficiently low level of output which represents a kind of spurious equilibrium' (*CW*, 1973, XIII, pp. 355–6). However, he did not have a model capable of demonstrating a movement to a new equilibrium that he intuited.

The motivating element behind Keynes's explicit consideration of an output equilibrium, though a 'spurious' one, may well have been the searching discussions of the 'Cambridge Circus': the arguing out of the *Treatise* in the academic year in which it appeared. Here the famous analogy with the widow's jar – which was exogenously replenished with oil no matter how much used – from I Kings 17: 7–16 is of consequence. Recall the quote: 'Thus profits, as a source of capital increment for entrepreneurs, are a *widow's cruse* which remains undepleted however much of them may be devoted to riotous living' (*CW*, 1971, V, p. 125, emphasis added). In the 'Circus,' it was pointed out that the widow's cruse analogy was dependent on a fixed output assumption with prices bearing the entire brunt of adjustment. Austin Robinson first saw this implicit assumption and the contradiction with the *Treatise*'s general assumption of profits inducing greater output. He is thus credited with naming it the 'widow's cruse fallacy' (*CW*, 1973, XIII, p. 340, n. 1). Robertson's (1931) *Economic Journal* review of the *Treatise* similarly noted the fixed output assumption, for which James Meade, a member of the 'Circus', was thanked for indicating the several passages in which full employment was assumed.

Whether the demonstration that the widow's cruse analogy was fallacious was fundamental to Keynes's thinking, we do not know. What is clear, however, is that discussions of employment in connection with savings–investment considerations were of sufficient consequence that Keynes specifically concerned himself with such in the aforementioned Harris Foundation lectures immediately following the discussions in the 'Circus'. Mention must also be made of the role of Ralph G. Hawtrey, a Treasury official whose professional monetary writings in the inter-war period rivaled Keynes's and Robertson's. His detailed comments on the *Treatise*'s page proofs, the substance of which appeared in Hawtrey (1962, pp. 332–411), particularly those where he also criticized Keynes's implicit assumption of fixed output (*CW*, 1973, XIII, pp. 152, 165–7), added further impetus to moving the focus of attention from the behavior of the price level to output adjustment. This bombardment of criticism regarding full employment was thus a major incentive to develop the central core of the *General Theory*, the theory of effective demand with its less than full employment equilibrium result.

For this, as well as for the many other areas of criticism to which the *Treatise* was subjected by Hawtrey, Hayek and Robertson in correspondence and print, Keynes continued revising his thinking. His initial plan, as noted in the April 1932 Japanese edition of the *Treatise*, was 'to publish a short book of a purely theoretical character, extending and correcting the theoretical basis of my views as set forth in [the *Treatise*]' (*CW*, 1971, V, p. xxxvii).

In the public policy arena (that is, in his non-professional writings) he was advocating a program of public works spending as an effective way of reducing unemployment, with his *Essays in Persuasion* monograph written in May 1929 with Hubert Henderson, *Can Lloyd George Do It?* (*CW*, 1971, IX, pp. 86–127) being a prime example. The difficulty with exhortations for increased governmental spending, however, was that there was no satisfactory framework to support such proposals. In fact, arrayed against proposals for a deficit-financed public works program was the intellectual edifice of the 'Treasury View', this holding that, with a fixed pool of savings, the funds necessary to finance a public works program would have to come from those that would have financed private investment projects; consequently there would be no net effect on employment and output – crowding out in the extreme. For Meade, this was the classical notion that the dog called savings wagged the tail called investment, a mind-set that the Keynesian revolution reversed so that it would be the dog called investment that would wag the tail called savings (Meade, 1975, p. 82).

The *Treatise* was no help in this, nor in providing a model for rationalizing a public works program. In fact, it was a barrier because its savings–investment nexus was conditioned on marginal spending propensities of unity. This can be most clearly seen in the fabled 'banana plantation' parable (*CW*, 1971, V, pp. 158–60). Here a 'thrift campaign' – an exogenous increase in saving – causes the economy to spiral downwards continuously. No new equilibrium is reached. Output and employment go to zero, unless there is either a *deus ex machina* decrease in saving or increase in investment, Keynes's other possibilities.

The crucial innovation linking expenditure decisions to employment and output effects was the 'fundamental psychological law' of consumption in which the marginal propensity to consume 'is positive and less than unity' (Keynes, 1936, p. 96). But this did not come directly. Rather it was in the context of the multiplier analysis in R.F. Kahn's famous 1931 *Economic Journal* article, 'The Relation of Home Investment to Unemployment' that the overriding importance of the marginal propensity to consume came to be realized. The multiplier, Kahn's ratio of secondary, that is, induced, employment to primary employment, of which Keynes was acutely aware, both because Kahn was his favorite pupil and, in effect, his closest collaborator and in his role as editor of the *Economic Journal*, was important for two reasons. First, it established analytically that there were secondary income and, as Kahn stressed, employment effects associated with an increase in public spending, something that heretofore was suspected but for which there was no satisfactory theory until Kahn's work (Patinkin, 1976, p. 131, n.15). Given that, the problem then became one of trying to understand why those effects were not infinite: that is, why the induced spending and employment effects did not continue indefinitely, as had been the case in the banana plantation parable. And that was the second proposition Kahn demonstrated. The principal insight for understanding that the multiplier was not infinite was 'Mr Meade's relation', which was that the leakages from the induced spending stream come to equal the increases in initial spending (*CW*, 1973, XIII, p. 341).

As is normal in science, the discovery of the multiplier was a multiple discovery. Hawtrey, for instance, in the comments on the *Treatise* he sent to Keynes, derived it along with the algebraic expression that it was the reciprocal of the marginal propensity to save, though his saving propensity related to savings being transformed in the classical manner to investment (Hawtrey, 1962, p. 351). With the multiplier, the development of the theory of effective demand was under way, but it would be several years before it would come to fruition. By mid-1934, Keynes drafted a table of contents in which the full title, *The General Theory of Employment, Interest and Money*, was used for the first time and in which the theory of effective demand was set in place (*CW*, 1973, XIII, p. 423). And it is that theory – The Principle of Effective Demand, Chapter 3 in *The General Theory* – that is the central discovery of the Keynesian revolution.

That theory has been so well accepted that it is now standard fare for beginning students and is most conveniently summarized in the output equals expenditure, $Y = C + I$, two-dimensional graph of elementary economics. Effective demand is aggregate demand as reflected in the expenditure schedule, the sum of consumption, itself a function of income via the 'fundamental psychological law' of consumption, and investment. If there is excess aggregate supply, the resulting adjustment is not that the price level declines; rather it is the critical role of the decline in output, hence income, that leads to a new, less than full, employment equilibrium, because the adjustment process has output declining by more than income, hence aggregate expenditure, this because the marginal propensity to consume is less than unity.

That is, it is changes in output that are the equilibrating force bringing the economy to a new equilibrium. Keynes, of course, does not formally employ a graph; his development of the theory reads nonetheless as though he was thinking in such terms:

> Thus the volume of employment is given by the point of intersection between the aggregate demand function $[D = f(N)]$ and the aggregate supply function; [adding incorrectly] for it is at this point that the entrepreneurs' expectation of profit will be maximised. The value of D at the point of the aggregate demand function, where it is intersected by the aggregate supply function, will be called *the effective demand*. (Keynes, 1936, p. 25)

Furthermore the equilibrium is both unique and stable, unique in that 'given the propensity to consume and the rate of new investment, there will be only one level of employment consistent with equilibrium' (Keynes, 1936, p. 28). The emphasis on stability is due, not to Keynes, but to Patinkin, who argues that Keynes not only solved 'the equilibrium equation $F(Y)=Y$' but also demonstrated 'the stability of this equilibrium as determined by the dynamic adjustment equation $dY/dt = \Phi[F(Y) - Y]$, where $\Phi' > 0'$ (Patinkin, 1982, p. 10). In fact, Patinkin argues that this is the distinguishing feature of *The General Theory*, namely the emphasis on output as the equilibrating variable.

Keynes was quite aware of the importance of the analysis of effective demand. He saw that it was central to his work. In the preface, for instance, he maintains that, in the *Treatise*, 'I failed to deal thoroughly with the effects of *changes* in the level of output' and that consequently *The General Theory* 'has evolved into what is primarily a study of the forces which determine changes in the scale of output and employment as a whole' (Keynes, 1936, p. xxii). And it was not only there that he indicated the centrality of the theory of effective demand. His correspondence similarly stressed that he was quite clear in his own mind that the theory of effective demand was the core discovery.

It was precisely Keynes's theory of effective demand that Patinkin emphasized in his study of others who, it was alleged, developed 'Keynesian economics' before Keynes; in other words, was the Keynesian revolution misnamed? Specifically both the Swedish economists of the Stockholm School – Ohlin, Myrdal, Wicksell and Lindahl – with their Investment–Saving apparatus and Michał Kalecki with his emphasis on investment generating profits, hence savings, have advocates who argued that the Keynesian revolution was anticipated by them. Patinkin took the theory of effective demand as the 'central message' of Keynes. With that as a measure, he compared the respective 'central messages' of both the Stockholm School and Kalecki with Keynes's, and concluded that the Swedish theory was one of prices, as indeed was the *Treatise*, with its investment–savings discrepancies resulting in price level movements (Patinkin, 1982, pp. 36–57). As for Kalecki, his principal theme had to do with explaining the cyclical behavior of investment and not with formulating a theory of unemployment equilibrium (ibid., pp. 58–78). Subsequently Simon Chapple (1991) uncovered an article, written in 1933, that appeared in the Polish journal *Ekonomista* and was subsequently translated into English, in which Kalecki developed the theory of effective demand.

There were, of course, other important innovations in *The General Theory*, among them the liquidity preference theory of interest and the marginal efficiency of capital and its associated theory of investment. These, along with the principle of effective demand, were what Keynes considered the three major innovations of the *General Theory*. In addition, he attempted to refute classical economics in his assertion that labor bargains for wages in nominal terms, with the consequent vigorous denial that labor bargained in terms of the real wage; that underlies the extensive appendix to Chapter 19 in which Keynes addressed *The Theory of Unemployment* by Pigou – 'the Prof' in the correspondence among Keynes and his followers. Subsequent research has either dismissed this position or argued for nominal wage rigidity in other terms.

The marginal efficiency of capital, a key ingredient in the theory of investment, was the last important ingredient of *The General Theory* to be developed. Though it was discovered independently of Irving Fisher's rate of return over cost (1930, 155–9), Keynes realized that in its final state the marginal efficiency of capital was the same as the rate of return over cost (Keynes, 1936, pp. 140–41), though he was slow in coming to that realization. Some claim that the process of developing his theory of investment began in the *Treatise*, but the evidence from his correspondence in volumes XIII and XXIX of the *CW* indicates that, if such was the case, Keynes certainly was oblivious to it.

The theory of liquidity preference did, however, have its origins in the *Treatise* (*CW*, 1971, V, pp. 127–9), although the role of expectations was not nearly so pronounced. The argument in *The General Theory*, however, was much more contentious, with its sharply drawn challenge about the determination of the interest rate. Here Keynes argued that the classical theory's saving–investment model was unsatisfactory because it did not yield a determinate rate of interest. To establish that, he argued on the basis of a graph, suggested by Roy Harrod, and the only graph in the book, that increases in investment raise income, which increases saving, thereby leading to the indeterminacy in that the 'diagram does not contain enough *data* to tell us what [the new income, Y] value will be; and therefore, not knowing which is the new appropriate Y-curve, we do not know at what point the new investment demand-schedule will cut' the new saving curve (Keynes, 1936, p. 181). The Marshallian basis for this is clear: a shift in, say, a demand curve cannot cause the supply curve to shift; otherwise the result is indeterminate, and that was Keynes's position. Thus he threw out the classical interest determination model and substituted the liquidity preference theory, believing that he had resolved the indeterminacy issue because an increase in the demand for money would not affect the exogenous supply. He did not realize that the indeterminacy argument he leveled against the classical model was just as applicable to his. An increase in the money supply would raise income through the lowered interest rate and multiplier; but, to paraphrase his argument, 'not knowing which is the new appropriate Y-curve, we do not know at what point the new [money] demand-schedule will cut' the money supply curve. Robertson, for one, strongly objected to Keynes's insistence that the rate of interest reflected money demand and money supply consideration alone; he argued that the interest rate was essentially a general equilibrium phenomenon and thus was influenced by saving, liquidity preference and the productivity of capital. Keynes, however, did not yield. In fact, in the enormous post-publication literature spawned by his *magnum opus*, he made no substantive modifications. That reflects as much as anything his confidence in it as a result of the continued interaction with and feedback from his junior colleagues in its preparation, which stands in marked contrast to the *Treatise*.

On 4 February 1936, the book appeared, priced to make it accessible to students, students who carried the revolution through the next several decades.

FRANK G. STEINDL

Notes

1 References to Keynes's writings are to the *Collected Writings of John Maynard Keynes*, hence the *CW* notation. Volumes XIII and XXIX of the *CW* trace the evolution of his thinking, including extensive notes between him and his colleagues, friendly and adversarial, from the *Tract* to the *Treatise* and especially from there to *The General Theory*.

See also:

Cambridge Circus; Consumption and the Consumption Function; Crowding Out; Currie, Lauchlin; Demand Management; Depression, The Great; Dillard, Dudley; Fiscal Policy; Government Investment Programs (the Socialization of Investment); Hansen, Alvin H.; Harrod, Sir Roy; Hicks, Sir John R.; Kahn, Lord Richard F.; Kalecki, Michał; Keynes, John Maynard; Keynes?, What Remains of; Keynesianism in America; Kuznets, Simon; Lerner, Abba P.; Meade, James E.; Multiplier Effect; Robertson, Sir Dennis H.; Robinson, Joan; Samuelson, Paul A.; Stone, Sir John Richard N.; Tarshis, Lorie.

Bibliography

Chapple, Simon (1991), 'Did Kalecki Get There First? The Race for the General Theory', *History of Political Economy*, **23**, (2), summer, pp. 243–61.

Dimand, Robert W. (1988), *The Origins of the Keynesian Revolution*, Aldershot: Edward Elgar.

Fisher, Irving (1930), *The Theory of Interest*, New York: The Macmillan Company.

Hawtrey, Ralph G. (1962), *The Art of Central Banking*, 2nd edn, New York: Augustus M. Kelley.

Keynes, John Maynard (1930), *A Treatise on Money*, London: Macmillan; Keynes (1971), *Collected Writings*, Volumes V and VI.

Keynes, John Maynard (1936), *The General Theory of Employment, Interest and Money*, London: Macmillan; Keynes (1971), *Collected Writings*, Volume VII.

Keynes, John Maynard (1973), *The General Theory and After: Part I. Preparation*, ed. Donald Moggridge, London: Macmillan; *Collected Writings*, Volume XIII.

Keynes, John Maynard (1979), *The General Theory and After: A Supplement*, ed. Donald Moggridge, London: Macmillan; *Collected Writings*, Volume XXIX.

Klein, Lawrence R. (1944), *The Keynesian Revolution*, New York: Macmillan.

Kuhn, Thomas S. (1970), *The Structure of Scientific Revolutions*, 2nd enlarged edn, Chicago: University of Chicago Press.

Meade, James (1975), 'The Keynesian Revolution', in Milo Keynes, *Essays on John Maynard Keynes*, Cambridge: Cambridge University Press, pp. 82–8.

Moggridge, D.E. (1992), *Maynard Keynes: An Economist's Biography*, London: Routledge.

Patinkin, Don (1976), *Keynes' Monetary Thought*, Durham: Duke University Press.

Patinkin, Don (1982), *Anticipations of the General Theory?*, Chicago: University of Chicago Press.

Tarshis, Lorie (1987), 'Keynesian Revolution', in John Eatwell, Murray Milgate and Peter Newman (eds), *The New Palgrave: A Dictionary of Economics*, Vol. 3, New York: Stockton Press.

Keynesianism in America

Since historians of economic thought have only recently begun to analyse the mechanisms by which economic ideas enlarge themselves and gain dominance, any total grasp of the phenomenon that came to be American Keynesianism must necessarily elude us. Nevertheless such excitement attended the advent of this economic revolution that many of its details came to be etched on the memories of its American founders and ultimately bequeathed by them to posterity. Appearing in two distinct forms, as theory and as policy, early Keynesianism was transmitted by word of mouth, professional journals and textbooks, as well as by Keynes's own articulation of it in his *General Theory*, published in 1936. Three intertwined aspects of the Keynesian revolution and the Keynesianization of America are notable: (1) the introduction of a new set of theoretical tools that helped to pave the way for a significant widening of the scope of economics; (2) a modification and expansion of government's role in the economy entailing a rejection of Say's Law and admission of the macro instability of market economies; (3) an argument for compensatory fiscal policies founded on a new appraisal of possible consequences of government budgets.

This simple listing belies the complexity of the history at hand, since these three aspects of the Keynesian revolution, though related, grew independently of one another, each seeming to follow its own program, as did the theoretical revolution and policy revolution, which often seemed totally disjointed in relation to one another, with each experiencing separate and contrasting peaks and troughs in any given period. The theoretical revolution, for example, had died by the early 1960s, just as the policy revolution reached its peak and the demise of the policy revolution in the 1990s coincided with a second coming of the theoretical revolution. Additionally one may consider the introduction and the spread of Keynesian thought in America as entailing not only revolutions in theory and policy but also a pedagogical revolution eventually reaching its broadest diffusion with the introduction of macroeconomic models into economics textbooks. This class of macroeconomic Keynesian thought first unfolded in the lectures, scholarly writing and textbooks of academics already living in America, and in those of a significant group of immigrant future Americans. The spread of Keynesianism must be examined, therefore, within the context of the broader political, social and intellectual forces beginning shortly after World War I that brought these scholars to the New World and shaped their ideas once they had arrived, including the rise of Communism in Russia and Fascism in Germany and Italy and the massive, unprecedented depression of the 1930s. These events combined to raise doubts, in some minds, as to the viability of market societies and to precipitate a movement of intellectual capital out of Western Europe to England and the United States. Keynes's ideas came to the

United States, to some extent, in the baggage of these future Americans from Canada, Germany, Hungary, Italy and Russia.

While ethnically diverse, the new Keynesians almost without exception shared one characteristic: their youth. These untenured young professors, many foreign-born, with typical youthful enthusiasm and vitality, soon became dedicated disciples ready to proselytize on behalf of their new-found economic faith. Alvin Hansen (1887–1975) became, at this stage, the rare exception of an over-40 professor succumbing to the new Keynesian ideas.

Cambridge, England
One parcel of this narrative of international beginnings opens in Cambridge, England, in 1932 with two young Canadians, Lorie Tarshis (1911–1990) and Robert Bryce (born 1910), attending both Keynes's lectures and the meetings of the Keynes Club, a group of students that, along with some faculty, assembled weekly with Keynes in his quarters at Cambridge. Others involved in the English genesis of American Keynesianism included Walter Salant (born 1911), who attended Keynes's lectures in 1933, and Paul Sweezy (born 1910) and Abba Lerner (1903–82), then enrolled at the London School of Economics. Bryce, Tarshis, Salant and Sweezy later moved to Cambridge, Massachusetts, where Tarshis secured a teaching position at Tufts, while the others enrolled in the graduate economics program at Harvard.

The first key figure of this group, Robert Bryce, would almost certainly not have been a player at all if he had not decided to switch his major from engineering, which he had been studying in Canada, to economics when he went to England in 1932. As it happened, he played a unique role in bringing Keynesianism to America. Quickly recognizing that Keynes's new ideas could be simplified, he wrote a paper in 1935 summarizing what he regarded to be the essential points in Keynes's lectures and, before the publication of *The General Theory*, read it to a seminar of F.A. Hayek's at the London School of Economics. Thereafter he became an ardent advocate, attempting to convert all non-believers, whom he called 'the heathens'.

Keynes's book still had not been published by the time Bryce, Tarshis, Salant and Sweezy had abandoned Cambridge, England, for Cambridge, Massachusetts, where they eagerly began to sow the seeds of the new economics. Thus an historically novel situation arose in which three graduate students and a new assistant professor initiated a process of trying to wean all who would listen from the neoclassical concept of the macro functioning of market economies. Joseph Schumpeter, tolerant of others' views but generally preferring his own version, epitomized Bryce's role when he declared that Keynes was Allah and Bryce his prophet.

Other Americans-to-be, passing through England on their way to academic positions in the United States, also played key roles in the dissemination of

Keynesian thought throughout America: Abba Lerner, born in Romania, Tibor Scitovsky, born 1910 in Hungary, Evsey Domar, born 1914 in Lodz, Russia (now Poland), Richard Musgrave, born 1910 in Germany, and John Kenneth Galbraith, born 1908 in Canada. The young Keynesians at Cambridge, Massachusetts, found an ally, too, in the newly appointed (1937) first Littauer Professor at Harvard, Alvin Hansen. On the one hand, Hansen appears to have been an unlikely propagator of Keynesian ideas: his principles book had been basically neoclassical and his early reviews of *The General Theory* critical. On the other hand, he had received his PhD from Wisconsin, whose institutional posture favoring government involvement in solving deficiencies of the market economy would seem to have rendered it more amenable to Keynesian ideas than those of conventional universities. The administration of the progressive governor of Wisconsin, Robert Marion LaFollette and John R. Commons had worked out a close relationship between government and academy, and Wisconsin had passed legislation influencing the control of public utilities, industrial safety, workmen's compensation, child labor, minimum wages for women and unemployment compensation, before Keynes's *General Theory* and the New Deal. The concept of a cooperative relationship between government and academia would be institutionalized at Harvard in 1936, with the opening of the Littauer School of Public Administration. Hansen, with John H. Williams, eventually established a fiscal policy seminar at Harvard that became a fertile medium for the development of new theoretical policy approaches to the macro economy as well as a Harvard–Washington, DC nexus that helped propagate Keynesian thought within the federal government and Federal Reserve System.

The intellectual setting before the *General Theory*

Anyone seeking a crystallization of pre-Keynesian thinking in the early 1930s in the United States would do well to read *The Economics of the Recovery Program* (1934), written by a group of young Harvard professors including Douglass Brown, E.H. Chamberlin, Seymour Harris, Wassily Leontief and Edward Mason, along with Joseph Schumpeter. The younger men analysed and criticized various New Deal programs and Schumpeter discussed business-cycle theory and the depression. O.H. Taylor added a broad concluding essay on some of the economic, political and ethical issues raised by the New Deal. Of the younger authors, only Seymour Harris moved into the Keynesian camp. The intellectually more exciting issues addressed by economists in the early 1930s centered on anomalies in Alfred Marshall's microeconomic theory and reactions to it embodied in Joan Robinson's *Economics of Imperfect Competition* and E.H. Chamberlin's *Theory of Monopolistic Competition*, both published in 1933, and not on macroeconomic theory and policy.

Keynes's *Treatise on Money* (1930) was being intensively and enthusiastically examined in a Cambridge, England, seminar including Richard Kahn, James Meade, Piero Sraffa and Joan and Austin Robinson, but was received less favorably by Ralph Hawtrey, Dennis Robertson and F.A. Hayek. Dennis Robertson had been applying a sequential equilibria approach to some of the same issues Keynes had addressed and Allyn Young, two of whose students, Alvin Hansen and Lauchlin Currie, helped bring Keynes to America, had been applying monetary analysis to similar problems. Many of these pre-Keynesian and non-Keynesian approaches, however, were much more complex and sophisticated than *The General Theory* and, therefore, required a relatively advanced understanding of classical monetary theory. Many of the young Keynesians, unencumbered by this deeper understanding of the complex core of the classical model, understandably preferred the simplicity of Keynesian theory, which doubtless was a factor in its more widespread acceptance by the young than by more experienced economists.

Keynes comes to America

Few of the world's great economic theorists have been able to attract a such phalanx of fervid disciples as Keynes did to proclaim their message to the intelligentsia and eventually to the populace at large: Adam Smith, David Ricardo, J.S. Mill, Alfred Marshall and Thorstein Veblen all had their votaries, but only Marshall and Veblen attracted such numerous and dedicated followings. The theorists who most closely approached Keynes's popularity in the history of economic thought may well have been the physiocrats – though their movement lasted a mere three decades – and Karl Marx. To borrow Keynes's own remark about Ricardo, Keynes conquered America as completely as the Inquisition conquered Spain. How did it happen? Again we have to say it was the enthusiasm of so many young intellectuals who, having readily devoured the new ideas, proceeded vigorously to advance them by working out all of their theoretical and policy implications and nuances in seminars, professional journals and textbooks.

Keynes's innovations meshed with some methodological aspects of contemporary economic theory. Long before *The General Theory*, notable changes had been occurring in the methodological bent of American and European economics. The spread of Keynesian thought in America must be viewed, therefore, in the context of an increased mathematization and quantification of economics begun nearly one hundred years earlier and maintained in a more or less continuous line from Cournot's *Researches* (1838) through the works of Walras, Pareto, Jevons, Edgeworth, Fisher and Newcomb. And though Keynes himself, like Marshall, remained somewhat ambivalently outside this line, the form of both his *Treatise on Money* and *General Theory*, with their concepts of aggregate demand, separate preference functions for consumption, investment and liquidity; multipliers and accelerators; and implicit national income accounts demanded further formalization and specification to render them empirically testable. Quantification of *macroeconomic* variables, likewise, had appeared as far back as William Petty (1690) and reappeared and persisted in the works of W.S. Jevons, Henry L. Moore, Irving Fisher, Wesley Clair Mitchell, Ragnar Frisch and Jan Tinbergen.

That Keynes's theory invited similar empirical work was central to the spread of its policy and theoretical revolutions. The empirical implementation of Keynes's theory, moreover, invested it with an aura of scientific objectivity and definitiveness that smoothed the way for those seeking widespread policy applications of the model, and the young Keynesians, with none of Keynes's ambivalence, aggressively pursued the required methodology. Keynesian theory, Keynesian policy, more abstract mathematical models and increased quantification simultaneously created incentives and opportunities for the recently trained to publish their research, and at the same time destroyed – or at least set aside for a considerable time – the massive investments in intellectual capital of their seniors. Mathematics, statistics and econometrics typically replaced economic history, history of economic thought and foreign languages in PhD curricula. Paul Samuelson (born 1915), of signal importance in the theoretical, policy *and* textbook revolutions, has remarked, 'Bliss it was in that dawn to be alive, but to be young was very heaven!' (Samuleson, 1946, p. 187).

The resistance to Keynesian ideas
All professions tend to resist change, particularly in those broad sets of beliefs that ensure continuity and stability in the performance of everyday professional tasks, but the structure of the academy in particular provides sets of institutions and procedures designed to perpetuate and propagate what some now call 'paradigms' and others regard as 'the hard core of theory': senior professors at PhD-granting institutions, with their courses, syllabi, and research programs, instruct the fledgling academics in the accepted matter of each discipline, the newly minted PhDs then carry the favored message to their students and advance it in their publications, and thus a network persists from age to age to disseminate and perpetuate the 'truth'. But against these institutions designed to preserve the old in academia stands another that richly rewards those able convincingly to advance new ideas to replace the old. Thus, although most academic research consists of what has been called 'normal science' – probing and testing the implications of the prevailing paradigm – more innovative research bold and capable enough to seriously question prevailing views or to point to anomalies in them may be generously repaid. The academic response to Keynesianism was strong resistance by the

older tenured professors and evangelical conversion by the newly minted PhDs.

Keynes's ideas met strong resistance in government and industry, not because of their theoretical content but because their implementation demanded procedures that clashed with long-held views of the role of government in society and with sound principles of fiscal responsibilities. Deficits, for example, had been considered on general principles unacceptable for government as well as individual budgets, but resistance to Keynes was colored by certain very specific, even unique, circumstances of the times and must, therefore, be viewed within the broader framework of the political ferment in America in the 1930s, 1940s and early 1950s. During the 1930s a depression longer and more severe than any previous threatened the economy and the basic fabric of society. Consequently various philosophical, social and political alternatives appeared, including Marxism, which was gaining increasing numbers of recruits. Germany, Italy and Russia, moreover, were already implementing political alternatives frightening to many Americans, and although Keynes argued in Chapter 24 of *The General Theory* that he was suggesting an alternative between the old policy of laissez faire and those advocating Marxist abolition of private property, many non-academics who rejected Keynesianism along with Marxism did so because they found it difficult to differentiate between the two. This is one reason for Keynesian ideas encountering strong and determined political resistance and for its foes attempting to remove Keynesians and Keynesian ideas from government and colleges.

In an attempt to gain wider audience for the new economics, a group of young Keynesians in Cambridge, Massachusetts, published in 1938 *An Economic Program for American Democracy*. Three of its authors, because of their government jobs, chose not to be listed as such. Lorie Tarshis, apparently feeling more secure in his academic ivory tower at Tufts, allowed his name to be affixed to the document and consequently found himself blamed for alumni financial support's being withdrawn from the school. In 1947, Tarshis published an introductory textbook in which Keynesian theory and policy appeared for the first time in an American undergraduate principles text. The book was successful, especially at better colleges, but this success immediately met an organized effort directed towards college trustees to remove the book from classrooms. Resistance continued into the 1950s: William F. Buckley's *God and Man At Yale* (1951), for example, included an extended criticism of the spread of Keynesianism at Yale. Keynesian ideas, therefore, faced not only the usual resistance to new ideas but also, because of contemporaneous political and economic situations, elicited significant political resistance.

The Keynesian theoretical revolution

Economic theory has a complex core and a simpler surface structure. The Keynesian theoretical revolution during the 1930s, 1940s and most of the 1950s dealt almost exclusively with the surface of theory, never really engaging the complex core of neoclassical economics. This becomes clear upon examination of one theoretical issue: did Keynes ever succeed in demonstrating that, given the neoclassical assumptions, particularly of flexible wages and prices, a unique equilibrium at less than the full employment level of income would be likely? The early Keynesians did not pursue such issues, focusing rather on surface aspects of theory, or what might be termed 'theoretical policy'. A pure theoretical revolution did not occur, as issues centering on the multiplicity of aggregate equilibria and the possibility of dynamic forces being strong enough to effect a unique, desirable equilibrium were skirted. Only after the various opponents to Keynesianism raised these more fundamental and complex theoretical issues did Keynesians attempt to complete the theoretical revolution begun earlier.

Even at the limited level of theoretical policy, many Keynesians did not want to dig very deep. Keynes had tried to create the illusion that previous economists, all of whom he lumped together as 'the classicals', shared a single view encompassing economic theory *and* policy. But there were, in fact, orthodox neoclassical theorists on both sides of the Atlantic who, before the publication of *The General Theory*, had advocated deficits to counteract the depression. It was not easy to get Keynesians to accept the full implications of their theory even at the level of theoretical policy. And, curiously, Keynes himself did not immediately want to accept these implications. Abba Lerner in 1941 had pushed one aspect of Keynesian theoretical policy to its logical conclusion with the metaphor of an economic steering wheel used by government to follow the tenets of *functional* finance as contrasted with laissez-faire policy and sound conventional finance. When aggregate demand is not sufficient to provide full employment, the government should increase spending and/or reduce taxes. If aggregate demand is excessive, the government should prevent inflation by operating at a surplus. Proper monetary policy, according to Lerner, aims to produce an interest rate that yields optimum levels of investment by means of either government borrowing or repayment of debt. The government, according to this model, should focus on the consequences of its fiscal and monetary actions on the level of income and employment and ignore the inconsequential side-effects on the size of the national debt and the money supply. Many Keynesians, however, including Keynes, did not publicly accept Lerner's conclusions. But even though the theoretical revolution left mostly unexamined many purely theoretical core questions and hesitated to commit itself fully to the logical implications of the theoretical policy revolution, it was still fundamental in that it provided a new vision of the workings of the macroeconomy.

The Keynesian policy revolution

The most controversial aspect of the new Keynesianism was, undoubtedly, its policy conclusions, which at one point at least owed a considerable debt to Alvin Hansen. The influential Harvard thrust to the Keynesian movement derived from the interests and proclivities of Hansen, who was policy-oriented in general and, at the theoretical level, theoretically policy-oriented. Since multiplier accelerator interaction, balanced budget and foreign trade multiplier, and policy all interested him, he focused on explaining and extending Keynes's policy ideas in these directions, rather than on pure theory. Keynesianism, like mercantilism, calls for greater government intervention and that, along with its recognition of the income-stimulation impacts of foreign trade surpluses, has led some to characterize the Keynesians as neomercantilists. More fundamentally, the two groups shared a vision of the economy that formally acknowledged the possibility of abstractly analysing the emerging economy and of attaining a grasp of the economy sufficiently comprehensive to allow governments successfully to prescribe policies aimed at accomplishing certain goals, particularly increasing the wealth of a nation. The mercantilists used the analogy of the doctor diagnosing the disease and prescribing the needed medicine in reference to government manipulation of the economy; the Keynesians, being farther along in the machine age, preferred the steering wheel image.

As a result of this sanguine disposition, Keynesians metamorphosed over time from the somewhat bewildered young men of the early 1930s to presumptuous 'experts' who had all the answers and could solve all economic problems if they could just take that wheel. This new-found confidence that economics as a discipline had progressed so rapidly in its understanding of the economy and could lead society to the promised land of full employment, stable prices and high rates of growth conferred new and much appreciated stature on the economics profession for a time and made teaching undergraduates during this period more rewarding, since they finally could be shown just how to fine-tune the economy, if only on the blackboard.

The pedagogical revolution

The spread of Keynesian theoretical and policy ideas across America proceeded on a broad pedagogical front. A new conception of the scope of economics developed with major changes in the content of both graduate and undergraduate education. Professors began to identify themselves as macroeconomists, and courses in macroeconomics, national income accounting and economic development appeared more and more frequently in the curriculum. The content of previously existing courses changed significantly:

money and banking as a field of study became heavily dependent upon Keynesian models. The last year that Hansen taught at Harvard in the mid-1950s, the graduate course in macroeconomics he taught was still called money and banking. He devoted the first term to Keynesian theory and John H. Williams and the second to the former content of the money and banking course. Econometricians now came in two colors – micro and macro. Professional journals, monographs and books reflected the increasing interest in the new areas of macroeconomic theory and policy.

The bulk of society gets its understanding of new ideas and information from formal education, and those professional economists who took off their 'research hats', often for only part of the day, and put on their 'teaching hats' played important roles in bringing Keynes to citizens, businesspersons and politicians. The most important carrier of Keynesianism, however, was the college-level introductory economics textbook.

The first course in any discipline plays a crucial role in transmitting ideas. The simplification of the material in such a course allows for clearer, less cluttered exposition of the key theoretical and applied concepts, but the models used may tend to frame issues in such a way as to constrain the students' creative and critical exploration of the ideas involved and block consideration of alternatives. It was by such a process that the new Keynesian textbooks with their helpful models came to assume a life of their own differing from anything in *The General Theory*, while being unequivocally identified by their authors and the teachers using them as Keynesian. And so today what many who have not read *The General Theory* regard as Keynesian is really Keynes as modified and presented by the revolutionists.

Robert Bryce realized before the publication of *The General Theory* that these intellectually complicated new ideas being taught by Keynes could more effectively be conveyed to a broader audience if simplified so as to elucidate their major theoretical and policy implications. Abba Lerner picked up his pen in 1936 and Joan Robinson hers in 1937 to explain *The General Theory* to economists and the interested public (Lerner, 1936; Robinson, 1937). James Meade was one of the first (Meade, 1936) to use Keynesian theory in an introductory textbook, but since his book was published and distributed mostly in England, it had little or no direct influence in America. The pedagogical revolution in its textbook dimension, therefore, was not brought to birth in America until the appearance of the textbooks of Lorie Tarshis, Paul A. Samuelson, Dudley Dillard and Alvin Hansen, all of whom recognized that Keynes's ideas could be simplified for undergraduate consumption, if one was willing to ignore some of the theoretical intricacies so that policy implications could more forcefully be drawn. Of these 'retailers' of Keynesian ideas, Samuelson and Hansen become the most important at the textbook level and Lerner at the non-economist general public level.

Keynesian theory in these works was presented in a form which permitted a clear and simple understanding of the role of fiscal and monetary policy in bringing about a full utilization of economic resources. The approach and models used in the textbooks were readily accepted by the young professors and their younger students and endorsed by liberal businesspersons, whose views appeared, for example, in the publications of the Committee for Economic Development.

Lorie Tarshis seized the opportunity and devoted himself full time to writing the first American introductory textbook to incorporate the new Keynesian ideas (Tarshis, 1947). It was immediately successful beyond his dreams – but then came the nightmare. Colleges began dropping the book as those who found Keynesian ideas too radical found means of applying political pressure. Paul Samuelson was asked by his dean at MIT to write an introductory book to use for students there and published his *Economics* one year after Tarshis's (Samuelson, 1948). Although Samuelson's book also encountered political headwinds, he was able to surmount them, and his introductory book contributed significantly to the spread of Keynesianism, selling over three million copies and, one might estimate, with a used-book multiplier of 2.5, probably being read by least eight million. It was a crucial element in the way Keynes's ideas came to be understood. The organization of introductory economics books and courses was changed, particularly when the new area called macroeconomics gained added thrust by being presented before microeconomics.

It is not often that economists instrumental in developing a new discipline at its pure theoretical level also directly influence the student masses taking their first, and generally their only, economics course. Samuelson, in playing this dual role, contributed much to the spread of Keynes from Harvard, to Stanford, to Peoria. His success, moreover, was not merely fortuitous. He had purposefully decided to devote time and energy to a textbook in order to influence not just pure theory but people and events. He commented, 'I don't care who writes a nation's laws – or crafts its advanced treaties – if I can write its economics textbooks' (Samuelson, 1990, p. ix). And being aware of the controversial nature of his material, he had taken special care not to offend but rather to appear legitimate. Samuelson escaped Tarshis's fate partly by formalizing his material by an extensive use of graphs – which Keynes had not done – and he introduced a Keynesian Cross which complemented the Marshallian supply and demand totem of microeconomics. Translated into 30 languages, Samuelson's book has played a worldwide role in the spread of Keynesianism.

Dudley Dillard's *The Economics of John Maynard Keynes* (1948) and Alvin Hansen's *Guide to Keynes* (1953) helped transmit the new ideas above the introductory textbook level. Both were used extensively by students and professors trying to master this new theory and its policy implications. The pedagogical revolution was completed before 1960, 12 years after Samuelson's first edition, when Campbell R. McConnell brought out what became the most printed American introductory economics textbook. It closely followed Samuelson and the legions of clones that followed it consolidated the theoretical, policy and pedagogical revolutions begun when that first group of young economists moved from Cambridge, England, to Cambridge, Massachusetts.

HARRY LANDRETH
DONNA LANDRETH

See also:

Currie, Lauchlin; Dillard, Dudley; Employment Act of 1946; Galbraith, John K.; Hansen, Alvin H.; Heller, Walter W.; Keynesian Cross; Keyserling, Leon; Kuznets, Simon; Metzler, Lloyd A.; Neoclassical Synthesis (Bastard Keynesianism); Samuelson, Paul A.; Tarshis, Lorie; White, Harry D.

Bibliography

Colander, David C. and Harry Landreth (1995), *The Coming of Keynesianism to America*, Brookfield, VT: Edward Elgar.
Davis, J. Ronnie (1971), *The New Economics and the Old Economists*, Ames: Iowa State University Press.
Dillard, Dudley (1948), *The Economics of John Maynard Keynes*, New York: Prentice-Hall.
Dimand, Robert W. (1990), 'The New Economics and American Economists in the 1930s Reconsidered', *Atlantic Economic Journal*, **18**, (4), December, pp. 42–7.
Galbraith, John Kenneth (1971), 'How the Keynesian Revolution Came to the United States', *Economics, Peace and Laughter*, Boston: Houghton Mifflin.
Hansen, Alvin (1953), *Guide to Keynes*, New York: McGraw-Hill.
Lerner, Abba (1936), 'Mr Keynes' *General Theory of Employment, Interest and Money*', *Internatinal Labour Review*, **34**, pp. 435–54.
Lerner, Abba (1941), 'The Economic Steering Wheel', *The University Review*, June, pp. 2–5.
Meade, James (1936), 'A Simplified Model of Mr Keynes' System', *Review of Economic Studies*, **4**, pp. 98–107.
Robinson, Joan (1937), *Essays in the Theory of Employment*, London: Macmillan.
Salant, Walter S. (1989), 'The Spread of Keynesian Doctrines and Practices in the United States', in Peter A. Hall (ed.), *The Political Power of Economic Ideas*, Princeton: Princeton University Press, p. 27–51.
Samuelson, Paul A. (1946), 'Lord Keynes and the General Theory', *Econometrica*, **14**, (3), July, pp. 187–200.
Samuelson, Paul A. (1948), *Economics: An Introductory Analysis*, New York: McGraw-Hill.
Samuelson, Paul A. (1990), 'Foreword', in Philip Saunders and William B. Walstad (eds), *The Principles of Economics Course*, New York: McGraw-Hill.
Tarshis, Lorie (1947), *The Elements of Economics*, Boston: Houghton Mifflin.

Keyserling, Leon

Leon Keyserling is chiefly remembered as President Truman's last chairman of the Council of Economic Advisers. Although he was involved in the drafting of the Employment Act of 1946 – containing parts of Keyserling's second prize-winning Pabst Blue Ribbon essay of 1944 – which created the Council of Economic Advisers, he was only deputy director under Edwin Nourse in the early Truman years. Nourse favored an apolitical CEA, while Keyserling considered it appropriate for the CEA to be an advocate for the administration in power.

During the late 1940s, Nourse was more concerned about the inflation problem, which involved double digit inflation until 1948. Keyserling was more worried about the slack in the system and opposed a tax increase which had been called for by Nourse. The 1949 recession proved Keyserling right and Nourse resigned.

Keyserling was at first only acting chairman and there was considerable opposition within the economics profession over the appointment of a non-PhD in economics to head the CEA. Keyserling had first obtained an undergraduate degree at Columbia University before transferring to Harvard for a law degree. He returned to Columbia for graduate work in economics under Rexford Tugwell, but failed to complete a dissertation before following Tugwell to Washington, where the latter was in the Department of Agriculture.

In Washington, Keyserling played a major role, as legislative assistant to Senator Robert F. Wagner of New York (1933–7), in the creation of various New Deal legislation: the National Industrial Recovery Act (1934), National Housing Act (1934–5) and the US Housing Act (1937).

Keyserling's reaction to the 1949 recession was to remember the experience of the United States economy during World War II when increased aggregate demand (largely through military spending) produced full employment with unemployment rates of between 1 and 2 per cent. He initially drew up a plan for increased government non-military spending to end the 1949 recession. Eventually, in early 1950, Paul Nitze got wind of the Keyserling plan and together they drew up National Security Council secret memorandum 68, calling for a threefold increase in military spending which became the basis for the military Keynesianism that affected the economic policies of succeeding presidents, principally Kennedy, Johnson and Reagan.

Although political scientists frequently give full credit to Paul Nitze for NSC-68, it was clearly based on Keyserling's economic paradigm. Interestingly Keyserling claimed to be neither a Keynesian nor a Post-Keynesian, but rather a 'pragmatist'. When asked in 1983 whether he was the architect of NSC-68 – which had been declassified by Henry Kissinger towards the end of the Ford administration – he claimed that it was that part of his life's work of which he was most proud. It also helps explain why he was typically hawkish on communism and the Vietnam War. It would eventually result in his dropping out of the Americans for Democratic Action (ADA) in the early 1970s.

While Keyserling was chairman of the CEA he refused to go along with the Treasury Accord of March 1951. Until this time, monetary policy had been 'neutral' since 1942 and interest rates were pegged at 2 per cent despite the double digit inflation of the postwar years. The Accord represented the liberation of the Federal Reserve Board and recognition of the usefulness of monetary policy in fighting inflation which had broken out in the fall of 1950 as a result of speculation in materials associated with the Korean conflict. Despite Keyserling's opposition, the stars of the economics profession such as Paul Samuelson supported the move at a post-Accord conference at Princeton.

With the election of General Eisenhower as President in 1952, the CEA was threatened with extinction, since the Republicans favored markets with minimal government planning. Eventually Eisenhower appointed the monetarist, Arthur Burns, to head the CEA and thereby supported Keyserling's view that the CEA should reflect the administration in power rather than maintain its neutrality, as Nourse had advocated.

After retiring from government service, Keyserling established and directed the Conference on Economic Progress, a tax-exempt non-profit foundation dealing with United States economic developments and policies from 1954 to 1971. In various publications and in many public appearances he advocated more emphasis on growth and less attention to the inflation problem. He reasoned that interest rates should be as low as possible and, as fixed costs, should be spread over as many units as possible. During the Kennedy years, when the 'New Economics' prevailed, Keyserling criticized the CEA for being too cautious in stimulating the economy.

His last influence on legislation was the Balanced Growth Act of 1978, usually referred to as Humphrey–Hawkins, which was intended as a tribute to the dying Senator Hubert Humphrey. The Act called for a calculation by the CEA of the year when full employment (defined as 3 per cent unemployment) would be achieved. The CEA complied for a number of years, but during the Reagan era it ceased to publish estimates of the target year when the achievement of 3 per cent unemployment was projected into the next century. The acceptance of a 'natural' rate of unemployment which is greater than 3 per cent has in effect repealed the Humphrey–Hawkins legislation.

LYNN TURGEON

See also:

Ackley, Gardner; Burns, Arthur F.; Currie, Lauchlin; Demand Management; Employment Act of 1946; Fiscal Policy; Hansen, Alvin H.; Heller, Walter W.; Keynesian Revolution; Keynesianism in America; Okun, Arthur M.; Samuelson, Paul A.

Klein, Lawrence R.

Lawrence Klein was born in Omaha, Nebraska in 1920. After work at the University of California, Berkeley, he received his doctoral degree from MIT in 1944. He served on the faculties of the University of Chicago, University of Michigan and Oxford University before joining in 1958 the University of Pennsylvania, where he taught for 33 years and is now Benjamin Franklin Professor, emeritus. He is the author and co-author of 21 books and over 200 major papers. His most well known works are *The Keynesian Revolution* (1949), *Economic Fluctuations in the United States* (1950) and *An Econometric Model of the United States, 1929–1952* (1955, in association with Arthur Goldberger).

Lawrence Klein published writings include many on economic theory, statistical work and macroeconometric modeling, but this summary focuses solely on his pioneering role in development of econometric model building. He was awarded the Nobel Prize in Economics in 1980 for his many and varied contributions to econometric model building and applied econometrics.

Klein's early interest in model building started at Chicago's Cowles Commission immediately after his graduation from MIT, with his inter-war model of the US economy. But the famous Klein–Goldberger model that has served as the paradigm for much macroeconomic model building since its development was initiated at the Survey Research Center at the University of Michigan. It consisted of 20 equations, explaining endogenous variables, and exogenous variables of the model were labor force characteristics and 'noneconomic political decision' variables. The statistical technique of limited information maximum likelihood was used. It also included Koyck distributed lags, time trend and cumulated investment to make the model dynamic.

Since annual models could not predict business cycles on many occasions, Klein (1964) used quarterly data in modeling of the United States economy in early 1960s in 'A Postwar Quarterly Model'. This was a direct descendant of the Klein–Goldberger model, but it was less aggregative and became a predecessor of the quarterly Wharton model. The purpose of the development of this model was to provide an empirically supported understanding of the present-day economic system. Additionally it could be used to test the effects of alternative economic policies.

At the same time Michael Evans had developed a quarterly model of the US economy in his PhD dissertation submitted at Brown University. After Evans joined the faculty of the University of Pennsylvania at the time of founding of the Econometrics and Forecasting Unit at that university, Evans's and Klein's postwar quarterly models were merged to combine the best features of each. This Evans–Klein version of the Wharton model (Wharton models were originated, maintained and operated by Wharton Econometric Forecasting Associates) consisted of 80 equations and approximately 40 endogenous variables. The Wharton models also had a much greater degree of disaggregation relative to the earlier, smaller models. The major application of the Wharton models since their inception in 1963 has been in forecasting. Many of the Latin American students and colleagues of Professor Klein have generated Wharton models, some of which have become continuous.

Although Klein was not the first econometrician to construct several statistical macro models, there is little doubt that his contributions in model building has influenced model builders worldwide. As the founder and one of the principal investigators at Wharton Econometric Forecasting Unit at the University of Pennsylvania, he gathered many talented econometricians and, by extending his model building to the other economies with special attention to their specific institutional characteristics, he set an example for many other investigators. Klein and his associates founded Project LINK in 1968 and various versions of this model have been developed since then. Project LINK essentially combines models from countries throughout the world for studying various international economic issues. Project LINK is an effective way to link national economic models. This global multi-country model estimates the world trade and the associated domestic activity levels in each country by using realistic policy simulations. The US economy is represented by the Wharton model in Project LINK.

The basic economic framework of Professor Klein is an essentially Keynesian view of national account analysis. His Keynesian view is evident from the title of one of his papers published in 1974, 'The Wharton Mark II Model – A Modern IS–LM Construct'. Klein's approach is to interpret the features of Keynesian view in terms of mathematical model building and empirical forecasting techniques. Thus the challenge to his theoretical efforts has often come from the monetarists, the rational expectationists and the supply-siders who believe either that the role of money has not been adequately reflected in his models or that the supply side has not been explicit.

Klein has consistently emphasized the public policy analysis of model building and scientific prediction as its ultimate objective. His analyses of the effects of the shift from defense spending after the Vietnam War and the oil crisis of the 1970s are prime examples of his concerns. Additionally his role in coordinating Jimmy Carter's successful campaign for the presidency of the United States in 1976 is noteworthy.

Klein's contribution to economics is broad and distributed across a wide professional spectrum. His contributions to economic theory, especially in interpreting the Keynesian system, and applied statistics, especially the bringing together of the least squares, two-stage least squares and limited information method of estimation, are as impressive as his role in development of model building.

MOSTAFA MEHDIZADEH

See also:

Business Cycle Theory (I) and (II); Clark, Colin; Econometric Models, Macroeconomic; Frisch, Ragnar; Haavelmo, Trygve; Keynesian Indicators; Keynesian Revolution; Kuznets, Simon; Stone, Sir John Richard N.

Bibliography

Blaug, Mark (1985), *Great Economists Since Keynes*, Totowa, NJ: Barnes & Noble Books.
Bodkin, Ronald G., Lawrence R. Klein and Kanta Marwah (1991), *A History of Macroeconometric Model-Building*, Aldershot: Edward Elgar.
Evans, Michael and Lawrence R. Klein (1967), *The Wharton Econometric Forecasting Model*, Philadelphia: Graphic Printing Associates.
Klein, Lawrence (1949), *The Keynesian Revolution*, New York: Macmillan.
Klein, Lawrence (1950), *Economic Fluctuations in the United States*, New York: Wiley.
Klein, Lawrence R. (1961), 'An Econometric Analysis of the Postwar Relationship between Inventory Fluctuations and Changes in Aggregate Economic Activity', in *Inventory Fluctuation and Economic Stabilization*, Part III of Study of Inventory Fluctuations and Economic Instability, Joint Economic Committee of the 87th US Congress, First Session, Washington, DC: US Government Printing Office, pp. 69–89.
Klein, Lawrence (1964), 'A Postwar Quarterly Model', *Models of Income Determination*, vol. 28 of National Bureau of Economic Research.
Klein, Lawrence and A.S. Goldberger (1955), *An Economic Model of the United States, 1929–1952*, Amsterdam, North Holland.
Spiegel, Henry W. and Warren J. Samuels (eds) (1984), *Contemporary Economists in Perspective*, Volume 1, Part A, Greenwich, Conn.: JAI Press.

Kregel, Jan A.

Jan Allen Kregel, born in Dallas, Texas in 1944, is currently professor of political economy in the political science faculty of the University of Bologna. He received his PhD from Rutgers University in 1970 (P. Davidson was the dissertation committee chairman), and also studied under the supervision of N. Kaldor and J. Robinson at the University of Cambridge. His past appointments have included lecturer in Economics, University of Bristol, UK (1969–72), lecturer and senior lecturer in economics, University of Southampton (1973–9), professor of economics at Livingston College, Rutgers University (1977–81), professor of monetary theory at Rijksuniversiteit, Groningen, Netherlands (1980–85) and professor of international economics at The Johns Hopkins University School of Advanced International Studies, Bologna Center (1985–90). In addition, he has held a number of part-time visiting and honorary appointments, including those at Université Catholique de Louvain, Belgium; New School for Social Research; University of Tennessee; Universität Bremen; Università di Firenze; Università degli Studi di Roma, La Sapienza; Università di Pavia; Université d'Orléans, France; Libera Università Internazionale degli Studi Sociali, Roma; Université de Nice, France; and Universidad Nacional Autonoma de Mexico. In addition, he was one of the organizers of the Trieste International School which met for a number of years for two weeks of lectures, seminars and discussion on Post Keynesianism.

Kregel's publications can be divided into four categories: early (until the mid-1970s), middle (until the mid-1980s), and late research (to the present) as well as policy and institutionally oriented writings. In his early work, he was concerned with synthesis, integration and delineation of a Post Keynesian methodology and paradigm. The earliest research was related to concerns of the 'Cambridge' (England) branch of Post Keynesianism: growth theory (1971, 1972, 1980b), profits and income distribution (1971, 1978) and the capital debates (1976a). He was quite interested in integrating Keynes's theory of monetary production with this approach, influenced by the views of Robinson and Sraffa and informed by the Classical approach (1973, 1976a, 1976c, 1980a, 1980b). Something of a synthesis emerged in his *Reconstruction* (1973), which might be considered the first attempt to present a Post Keynesian *general* theory. With A.S. Eichner, Kregel co-authored the influential *Journal of Economic Literature* article (1975) which proclaimed a new paradigm in economics. Finally he explored the differences between the methodology of Keynes and that of the bastard Keynesians, arguing that, unlike the orthodox approaches, the Keynesian methodology was one of shifting equilibrium, required when one models expectation formation under conditions of uncertainty (1983b).

In his middle period, Kregel moved away from the Cambridge–Sraffian–Classical approaches and concentrated on analysis of decision making under uncertainty (1976b, 1977, 1980d, 1983b), on formation of asset prices and Keynes's analysis of Chapter 17 of the *General Theory* (1988a, 1988b, 1992c) and on theories of effective demand (1983a, 1984–5, 1986b, 1987). This culminated in an interesting piece (1988a) demonstrating that Keynes's multiplier theory and own rate analysis were actually equivalent expressions of his theory of effective demand. During this period, Kregel became more critical of heterodox approaches that neglected Keynes's insights regarding expectation formation, variously criticizing the Cambridge approach, the French Circuit approach, those who interpret Keynes's analysis as 'long run' and the Sraffian approach (1985, 1986a). Finally, he wrote several pieces on the determinants of investment and on the investment–saving relation, defending the Keynesian position against both orthodox and purported Kaleckian attacks (1984–5, 1986b).

The work on Keynes's own rate analysis generated Kregel's most recent research – that on price formation and market structure – which appears both to provide a powerful critique of neoclassical price theory and to point to a Keynesian alternative. He has shown that price formation in a Walrasian general equilibrium model is based on a particular market form – the call market – which, while it has existed, is actually rare. Furthermore, as the size and complexity of the market increased, the call market form became increasingly cumbersome and costly and was replaced by the dealer market form (1995).

The implication of Kregel's analysis is that the 'general' equilibrium model is institutionally specific and cannot claim generality, nor can existence proofs and the like be carried over straight to dealer markets. Furthermore the price formation process will depend critically on institutions, technology, trading rules and government constraints (1980c, 1982, 1988c, 1990). In contrast to general equilibrium theory, Kregel's analysis follows from Keynes's methodology in which decisions are made in the presence of uncertainty, in which expectations of the future go into current price determination and in which institutional arrangements undergird the process of price formation.

The final category of publications concerns policy and institutional analysis. Most recently, Kregel has written a number of articles and co-edited a book on the transition to market economies in eastern Europe (1992 with E. Matzner and G. Grabher; 1994a). He is quite critical of the 'market shock' approach, arguing that orthodox proposals neither take account of existing institutions nor adequately define what constitutes a market, a position that follows directly from his research on market form (1992). In a similar vein, he has analysed the evolution of the stock market, international financial institutions and the international monetary system (1988c, 1992a, 1992b, 1994a, 1994b). He has been critical of almost universal tight money policy and the orthodox belief that budget deficits must be fought through high interest rate policy. He sees much of the instability in international financial markets as well as the innovations (such as the explosion of derivatives) as a response of markets to instability brought on by inappropriate monetary policy. In addition, he has criticized the view that Keynesianism dominated early postwar economic policy and that it failed, arguing rather that much of the aggregate fiscal policy was essentially based on supply-side arguments similar to those advanced in the 1980s; as Keynesianism was not tried, it certainly could not have failed (Kregel, 1994–5).

L. RANDALL WRAY

See also:
Davidson Paul; Kaldor, Lord Nicholas; Kalecki, Michał; Keynesian Revolution; Leijonhufvud, Axel; Lerner, Abba P.; Minsky, Hyman P.; Post Keynesian School of Economics; Robinson, Joan; Sraffa, Piero; Weintraub, Sidney.

Bibliography
Kregel, J.A. (1971), *Rate of Profit, Distribution and Growth: Two Views*, London: Macmillan/ Chicago, Aldine.
Kregel, J.A. (1972), *The Theory of Economic Growth*, London: Macmillan.
Kregel, J.A. (1973), *The Reconstruction of Political Economy*, London: Macmillan.
Kregel, J.A. (1976a), *The Theory of Capital*, London: Macmillan.
Kregel, J.A. (1976b), 'Economic Methodology in the Face of Uncertainty: The Modelling Methods of Keynes and the Post-Keynesians', *Economic Journal*, **86**, (346), June, pp. 209–25.
Kregel, J.A. (1976c), 'Sraffa et Keynes: le taux d'intérêt et le taux de profit', *Cahiers d'Economie Politique*, **3**, pp. 135–63.

Kregel, J.A. (1977), 'On the Existence of Expectations in English Neoclassical Economics', *Journal of Economic Literature*, **15**, (2), June, pp. 495–500.

Kregel, J.A. (1978), 'Post-Keynesian Theory: Income Distribution', *Challenge*, **22**, (4), September–October, pp. 37–43.

Kregel, J.A. (1980a), 'Marx, Keynes and Social Change: Is Post-Keynesian Theory Neo-Marxist?', in E.J. Nell (ed.), *Growth, Profits and Property*, New York: Cambridge University Press.

Kregel, J.A. (1980b), 'Economic Dynamics and the Theory of Steady Growth: An Historical Essay on Harrod's Knife Edge', *History of Political Economy*, **12**, (1), spring, pp. 97–123.

Kregel, J.A. (1980c), 'Markets and Institutions as Features of a Capitalistic Production System', *Journal of Post Keynesian Economics*, **3**, (1), fall, pp. 32–48.

Kregel, J.A. (1980d), 'The Theoretical Consequences of Economic Methodology: Samuelson's Foundations', *Metroeconomica*, **32**, (1), February, pp. 25–38.

Kregel, J.A. (1982), 'Microfoundations and Hicksian Monetary Theory', *de Economist*, **130**, (4), pp. 465–92.

Kregel, J.A. (1983a), 'Effective Demand: Origins and Development of the Notion', in *Distribution, Effective Demand and International Economic Relations*, London: Macmillan, pp. 50–68.

Kregel, J.A. (1983b), 'The Microfoundations of the "Generalisation of the General Theory" and "Bastard Keynesianism": Keynes' Theory of Employment in the Long and the Short Period', *Cambridge Journal of Economics*, **7**, (3/4), September–December, pp. 343–61.

Kregel, J.A. (1984–5), 'Constraints on the Expansion of Output and Employment', *Journal of Post Keynesian Economics*, **7** (2), pp. 139–52.

Kregel, J.A. (1985), 'Hamlet Without the Prince: Cambridge Macroeconomics Without Money', *American Economic Review*, **75**, (2), May, pp. 133–9.

Kregel, J.A. (1986a), 'Shylock and Hamlet: Are There Bulls and Bears in the Circuit?', *Economies et Sociétés*, série MP 3, pp. 11–22.

Kregel, J.A. (1986b), 'A Note on Finance', *Journal of Post Keynesian Economics*, **9**, (2), fall, pp. 91–100.

Kregel, J.A. (1987), 'The Effective Demand Approach to Employment and Inflation Analysis', *Journal of Post Keynesian Economics*, **10**, (2), fall, pp. 133–45.

Kregel, J.A. (1988a), 'The Multiplier and Liquidity Preference: Two Sides of the Theory of Effective Demand', in A. Barrère (ed.), *The Foundations of Keynesian Analysis*, London: Macmillan.

Kregel, J.A. (1988b), 'Irving Fisher, Great-grandparent of the General Theory', *Cahiers d'Economie Politique*, **14–15**, pp. 59–68.

Kregel, J.A. (1988c), 'Financial Innovation and the Organisation of Stock Market Trading', *Banca Nazionale del Lavoro Quarterly Review*, **40**, (167), December, pp. 367–86.

Kregel, J.A. (1990), 'The Formation of Fix and Flex Prices and Monetary Theory: An Assessment of John Hicks' A Market Theory of Money', *Banca Nazionale del Lavoro Quarterly Review*, **42**, (175), December, pp. 475–86.

Kregel, J.A. (1992a), 'Some Considerations on the Causes of Structural Change In Financial Markets', *Journal of Economic Issues*, **26**, (3), September, pp. 733–47.

Kregel, J.A. (1992b), 'Universal Banking, US Banking Reform and Financial Competition in the EEC', *Banca Nazionale del Lavoro Quarterly Review*, **44**, (182), September, pp. 231–54.

Kregel, J.A. (1992c), 'Minsky's "Two Price" Theory of Financial Instability and Monetary Policy: Discounting vs. Open Market Intervention', in S. Fazzari and D. Papadimitriou (eds), *Financial Conditions and Macroeconomic Performance: Essays in Honor of Hyman P. Minsky*, Armonk, NY: M.E. Sharpe.

Kregel, J.A. (1994a), 'Currency Speculation and the Summer 1993 Crisis in the ERM: Irrational Expectations and Imperfect Information', *Economies et Sociétés*, Série MP 9, Janvier–Février, pp. 301–14.

Kregel, J.A. (1994b), 'Global Portfolio Allocation, Hedging and September 1992 in the European Monetary System', in *Growth, Employment and Finance – Economic Reality and Economic Theory*, P. Davidson and J.A. Kregel (eds), Aldershot: Edward Elgar, pp. 168–83.

Kregel, J.A. (1994–5), 'The viability of economic policy and the priorities of economic policy', *Journal of Post Keynesian Economics*, winter, **17**, (2), pp. 261–77.

Kregel, J.A. (1995), 'Neoclassical Price Theory, Institutions and the Evolution of Securities Market Organisation', *Economic Journal*, **105**, (429), March, pp. 459–70.

Kregel, J.A. and A.S. Eichner (1975), 'Post-Keynesian Economic Theory: A New Paradigm in Economics?' *Journal of Economic Literature*, **13**, (4), December, pp. 1293–1314.

Kregel, J.A., E. Matzner and G. Grabher (1992), *Market Shock: An Agenda for the Economic and Social Reconstruction of Central and Eastern Europe*, Ann Arbor: University of Michigan Press.

Kuznets, Simon

Simon Kuznets, second American Nobel Laureate in economics, was born in Pinsk, Russia, on 30 April 1901, and died in Cambridge, Massachusetts, on 9 July 1985. When he emigrated to the United States in 1922, he came, in his own words, 'with a peculiar equipment: formal training in a scientific *gymnasium*, a fair amount of experience with statistical research in economics, a fair amount of reading (I knew Schumpeter's work well before I came here), and a liking for orderly quantitative procedures applied to socially oriented topics'.[1] His predispositions were strengthened by his association with Wesley C. Mitchell at Columbia University, where Kuznets took his BA (1923), MA (1924) and PhD (1926). Mitchell was critical of the deductive direction economic theory had taken; he believed that theory must be thoroughly grounded in empirical work. Kuznets held the same view. His life's work was empirical, but it was directed by large theoretical concerns and was thoroughly analytical.

In 1927, Kuznets joined the National Bureau of Economic Research (NBER), a connection he maintained until 1961. The Bureau is an independent, non-partisan research group concerned chiefly 'to ascertain and to present to the public important economic facts and their interpretation in a scientific and impartial manner'.[2] Kuznets was initially put in charge of the Bureau's project to build estimates of the national accounts. There were no official GNP series at that time, and Kuznets had the opportunity to lay out a theoretical structure for these accounts and to devise methods by which they could be estimated. He was subsequently brought into the US Department of Commerce to design the official accounts.

At the heart of Kuznets's work in this area is the idea that the measure of the national product should reflect human material welfare. He was well aware of the theoretical and empirical problems that stood in the way of the implementation of this idea, but believed that to settle for anything else would be a serious mistake. Opposition grew within the Department of Commerce and, although much of the basic structure of the official national accounts reflected, and still reflects, his work, important details changed, particularly the handling of government. The Department abandoned the notion that the national product was permeated by welfare significance.

Kuznets's achievements with the national accounts coincided with a shift in emphasis in economic theory from micro to macro concerns and, within the macro field, a redirection of interests by the theoretical ideas of John Maynard Keynes. There was a nice fit between the results of Kuznets's empirical research and Keynes's theory. The timing of the work of the two could hardly have been better: the Great Depression was on, and the contributions of the two scholars were seized upon to reorient public policy towards the business cycle.

During World War II, Kuznets was associate director (1942–4) of the Bureau of Planning and Statistics of the US War Production Board. His prior activities with NBER and the Department of Commerce had prepared him well for his new tasks. He believed that American productive capacity was so underutilized that the volume of war materials produced could be quickly and massively increased, and military plans speeded up. His position finally prevailed, despite opposition from some elements of the military.

In the postwar years, Kuznets began a new major body of research with the study of modern economic growth. His contributions in this area were many. He developed a theoretical account and description of the epoch of modern growth, from the mid-eighteenth century to the present. He constructed long-term measurements of the pace and structure of economic growth in the United States, organized and found finance for the building up of similar measurements for many other countries, and wrote major interpretations of modern growth based on the results of this research. He made a particularly close study of the 15–25-year-long fluctuations that are observed in the history of many economies, but especially in the American, and that have been given the name, Kuznets cycles, in recognition of his contributions. Also in the postwar years, honors came his way. In 1949, he was elected president of the American Statistical Association; in 1954, president of the American Economic Association; and, in 1971, he was awarded the Nobel Prize in Economics for his work on economic development.

Kuznets joined the faculty of the University of Pennsylvania in 1930 and remained there until 1954, when he moved to the Johns Hopkins University. In 1960, he left Hopkins for Harvard. He retired from Harvard in 1971, although he continued with his research. In the period after 1971, he returned to a subject that he had addressed in his presidential talk to the American Economic Association in 1954, the distribution of income. His last book, published four years after his death, is devoted chiefly to this topic.[3] It also contains a foreword and an afterword by two of his students, Richard A. Easterlin and Robert W. Fogel. Easterlin has also published a biographical essay in the *New Palgrave*; Fogel, who has since won a Nobel Prize, is preparing a biographical memoir.

Kuznets was not known as a spellbinding public speaker. His soft voice did not fill a room. But he was an exciting teacher, not because of his pedagogical style, but because of his erudition and because he conveyed to his students his commitment to scholarship – to the study of large questions that have important social dimensions. His students knew they were in the presence of a great man. In personal situations, Kuznets was warm, gentle and kindly. He was well-read in many subjects, held interesting opinions and was a charming companion.

ROBERT E. GALLMAN

Notes

1 Simon Kuznets, *Economic Development, the Family and Income Distribution: Selected Essays*, Cambridge: Cambridge University Press, 1989, p. 435; a transcription of remarks made at a conference held in Cambridge in 1981 in honor of his eightieth birthday.
2 The statement is part of a resolution adopted on 25 October 1926; the resolution is printed in Bureau publications.
3 Cf. note 1. The book also contains a comprehensive bibliography. It includes 31 books written or edited, 120 essays, notes, forewords and so on, and 49 reviews.

See also:

Business Cycle Theory (I) and (II); Clark Colin; Domar, Evsey D.; Harrod, Sir Roy; Hicks, Sir John R.; Keynesian Indicators; Keynesian Revolution; Keynesianism in America; Stone, Sir John Richard N.

Lausanne, The School of

The school of Lausanne, active during the latter part of the nineteenth century and the first third of the twentieth, took its name from Lausanne in Switzerland, where its founders and most creative and eminent members, Léon Walras (1834–1910) and subsequently Vilfredo Pareto (1848–1920), were professors of economics at the University of Lausanne. In order to bring out its distinguishing characteristics, the school can be contrasted with the work of Alfred Marshall. Whereas Marshall concentrated upon the analysis of an industry, a market, a consumer or a firm on the assumption that it is analytically temporarily independent of the rest of the economy, and thereby developed particular equilibrium analysis, the members of the school of Lausanne believed that it is necessary to consider simultaneously the interaction of all parts of the economy in order to understand the behavior that transpires in any part of it, and for that reason developed general equilibrium analysis. Whereas Marshall contended that mathematics is an instrument that helps with the resolution of the details of economic problems and that enables a theorist to work out conclusions that would otherwise be reached only more laboriously by a process of verbal reasoning, the school of Lausanne thought that economics is essentially a mathematical discipline and that without the use of mathematics it is impossible to frame the questions of general equilibrium analysis and impossible to solve them. Whereas Marshall believed that it is essential to refer continuously to economic facts in the elaboration of economic theory and to interpenetrate the theory with empirical considerations, the school of Lausanne argued that the structure of economic theory should be constructed on the basis of assumptions drawn from reality and that only at the end of the elaboration of the model should it be confronted by facts. Whereas Marshall was prepared to recognize some foibles and vagaries in the behavior of consumers and firms, the school of Lausanne assumed that consumers, service suppliers and entrepreneurs proceed strictly rationally to consider all available information and their preferences in order to maximise their utility.

Walras was the first economist to develop a comprehensive purely competitive model of general equilibrium that includes all commodities, capital formation, credit and money (1874, 1877). He developed the approach of specifying its parameters, asserting that equilibrium exists, describing the static equilibrium properties of the model, trying to establish that it has dynamic properties which will lead it to converge to equilibrium, giving some consideration to the uniqueness of equilibrium and varying the parameters in order to study comparative statics. He elaborated the marginal utility theory of consumer demand. He developed a model in which entrepreneurs are the agents who undertake economic change by moving resources from activities that are unprofitable into those which are profitable. Walras thus expounded the notion of consumer sovereignty, showing that in his model the structure of production reflects the structure of consumer preferences and spending decisions. He also showed how entrepreneurs link input and output markets by hiring services and paying incomes, on the one hand, and by producing outputs and selling them in output markets, on the other; he constructed a theory of saving, investment and interests; he developed the cash balances approach to understanding the use of money and its value; and he developed propositions in welfare economics to the effect that a competitive system tends to produce a relative maximum of utility for its participants.

Pareto (1896–7, 1909, 1911) built upon Walras's models in four basic ways. First, he developed a theory of demand on the basis of the assumption of ordinally measurable utility and with the use of indifference curves. Second, to Walras's assumption of fixed factor proportions he added the assumption that they are variable. Third, he extended Walras's model of the entrepreneur by treating the case of an entrepreneur who is a monopolist. Fourth, he extended Walras's work on welfare economics, developing certain models and propositions which became the foundation of the new welfare economics.

Walras and Pareto were greatly interested in applications of economic theory to practical problems and Walras was interested in normative economics; that is, in the formulation of propositions regarding desirable conditions and courses of action in economic life. It cannot be said, however, that their ideas in those regards were adopted by others sufficiently to constitute a body of shared policy attitudes or belief. The school of Lausanne was a school of theoretical and methodological thought.

Many of those who expounded and elaborated upon the ideas of Walras and Pareto were Italian. Among them was Enrico Barone, who developed fundamental aspects of the theory of marginal productivity that was adopted by Walras and Pareto (1896), contributed to the theory of public finance and applied general equilibrium theory in a model of a socialist economy (1908). Maffeo Pantaleoni can also be included, not so much for contributions to general equilibrium theory, although he certainly adhered to its tenets, but because his book (1889) on economics persuaded Pareto that Walras's work was worthy of being studied. Pasquale Boninsegni, who taught at the University of Lausanne after Pareto's departure, made contributions to the theory of general equilibrium from the beginning of this century until the 1930s (see Walras, 1965, vol. 3, pp. 364, 368–9). In France, Walras did not have many followers during his lifetime, with the notable exceptions of Albert Aupetit, who attempted to elaborate the theory of money in a general equilibrium setting (1901) and made other contributions to Walrasian economics (1914), Etienne Antonelli (1939), who delivered lectures on Walras's theories in France (1914), and Hermann Laurent (1902), Władysław Zawadzki (1914), and Jacques Moret (1915), who gave expositions of mathematical economics and general equilibrium theory. There were a few non-Continental adherents of the school of Lausanne. Arthur Bowley (1924) was the first important English academic who supported its central tenets. The American economist Henry Ludwell Moore (1929) undertook empirical tests of general equilibrium models, added to general equilibrium theory by introducing imperfectly competitive market structures into a model of dynamically growing economy and began studying business cycles in a Walrasian model. With respect to much of his work, Irving Fisher (1892, 1896) adopted methods and an outlook that mark him as a member of the school.

A complication in the history of the school of Lausanne is that Pareto was thought by a number of economists to have founded a school of his own (Schumpeter, 1954, pp. 829, 855, 858). They were inspired directly by him, so to them the 'school of Lausanne' meant the 'Paretian school' rather than the Walras–Pareto school. Writers of that persuasion included Luigi Amoroso (1921), Alfonso de Pietri-Tonelli (1927), Antonio Osorio, whose book (1913) was introduced by Pareto, and economists of the generation after Pareto such as Constantino Bresciani-Turroni, Gustavo Del Vecchio, Umberto Ricci, Luigi Einaudi and Marco Fanno. Arthur W. Marget observed that 'extravagant praise has been bestowed on the monetary theory of Pareto by members of the Lausanne school who have had no such words of praise for the monetary theory of Walras' (Marget, 1935, p. 152) and Guido Sensini (1929, p. 215) stated that everything that is true regarding the theory of money is found in Pareto's work. Among the French, François Divisia (1928) believed that Pareto had formulated the true theory of price determination and Georges-Henri Bousquet (1928b) and Roberto A. Murray (1920) also ignored some of Walras's main contributions to economic theory and praised Pareto's. Nevertheless, although Pareto developed some of his contributions along his own lines, they were, as stated above, mainly based upon Walras's work.

A second generation of economists subscribed to the tenets of the school of Lausanne even though they were subject to other influences and had diverse interests. Knut Wicksell (1898) wrote to Walras: 'It is always your general method of treating the problem in question that I employ... My debt of gratitude to you is thus very great' (Wicksell to Walras, 6 November 1893, in Walras, 1965, vol. 2, letter 1168, p. 596). Wicksell analysed the impact of money and the natural and market rates of interest upon the real part of a general equilibrium model, introduced the Austrian notion of a period of production and the consideration of time into the treatment of capital and interest in the model, and contributed to the marginal productivity theory of distribution. Gustav Cassel (1899, 1918), who wrote on general equilibrium theory without acknowledging Walras's influence, developed a growth model in which capital and labor increase at uniform rates, and analysed its equilibrium path; Karl Schlesinger (1914) formulated propositions about money in a general equilibrium setting; and the historians of economic thought François Bompaire (1931) and Gaëtan Pirou (1934) promoted the ideas of the school of Lausanne. After about 1930, the major general equilibrium theoreticians cannot be considered members of the school, because their work became significantly different in method and content from that of Walras and Pareto. The modern theoreticians were contributors to the mainstream of general equilibrium theory which sprang from the school of Lausanne.

DONALD A. WALKER

See also:
Arrow, Kenneth J.; Hahn, Frank H.; Lucas Critique; Marshall, Alfred; New Classical School of Economics; New Keynesian Macroeconomics; Robbins, Lord Lionel; Wicksell, Knut.

Bibliography
Amoroso, Luigi (1921), *Lezioni di economia mathematica*, Bologna: N. Zanichelli.
Antonelli, Etienne (1914), *Principes d'économie pure*, Paris: Librairie des sciences politiques et sociales.
Antonelli, Etienne (1939), *L'Economie pure du capitalisme*, Paris: Guillaumin et Cie.
Aupetit, Albert (1901), *Essai sur la théorie générale de la monnaie*, Paris: Guillaumin et Cie.
Aupetit, Albert (1914), *Principes d'économie pure*, Paris: Guillaumin et Cie.
Barone, Enrico (1896), 'Studi sulla distribuzione', *Giornale degli Economisti*, **12**, Series 2, February, pp. 107–252.
Barone, Enrico (1908), 'Il Ministro della produzione nello stato collettivista', *Giornale degli Economisti*, **37**, September, pp. 267–93.
Bompaire, François (1931), *Du principe de liberté économique dans l'œuvre de Cournot et dans celle de l'école de Lausanne (Walras, Pareto)*, Paris: Recueil Sirey.
Bousquet, Georges-Henri (1927), *Essai sur l'évolution de la pensée économique*, Paris: M. Giard.
Bousquet, Georges-Henri (1928a), *Cours d'économie pure*, Paris: Librairie des sciences politiques et sociales.
Bousquet, Georges-Henri (1928b), *Vilfredo Pareto. Sa vie et son œuvre*, Paris: Payot.
Bowley, Arthur L. (1924), *The Mathemetical Groundwork of Economics; An Introductory Treatise*, Oxford: The Clarendon Press.
Cassel, Karl Gustav (1899), 'Grundriss einer elementaren Preislehre', *Zeitschrift für die gesamte Staatswissenschaft*, **55**, (3), pp. 395–458.
Cassel, Karl Gustav (1918), *Theoretische Socialökonomie*, Leipzig: C.F. Winter; 4th edn, revised, 1927.
Divisia, François (1928), *Economique rationelle*, Paris: G. Doin.
Fisher, Irving (1892), 'Mathematical Investigations in the Theory of Value and Prices', *Transactions of the Connecticut Academy of Arts and Sciences*, **9**, July.
Fisher, Irving (1896), *Appreciation and Interest*, publications of the American Economic Association, third series, **11**, (4), August, New York: Macmillan Company.
Laurent, Hermann (1902), *Petit traité d'économie politique mathématique, rédigé conformément aux préceptes de l'école de Lausanne*, Paris: C. Schmid.
Marget, Arthur W. (1931), 'Léon Walras and the "Cash-Balance Approach" to the Problem of the Value of Money', *Journal of Political Economy*, **39**, (5), March, pp. 569–600.

Marget, Arthur W. (1935), 'The Monetary Aspects of the Walrasian System', *Journal of Political Economy*, **43**, (2), April, pp. 145–86.

Moore, Henry Ludwell (1929), *Synthetic Economics*, New York: Macmillan.

Moret, Jacques (1915), *L'Emploi des mathématiques en économie politique*, Paris: M. Giard et E. Brière.

Murray, Roberto A. (1920), *Leçons d'économie politique suivant la doctrine de l'école de Lausanne*, Paris: Payot and Cie.

Osorio, Antonio (1913), *Théorie mathématique de l'échange*, Paris: M. Giard et E. Brière.

Pantaleoni, Maffeo (1889), *Principii di economia pura*, Florence: Barberà.

Pareto, Vilfredo (1896–7), *Cours d'économie politique*, 2 vols, Lausanne: F. Rouge; reprint edited by G.-H. Bousquet and G. Busino, Geneva: Librairie Droz, 1964.

Pareto, Vilfredo (1909), *Manuel d'économie politique*, Paris: V. Giard et E. Brière.

Pareto, Vilfredo (1911), 'Economia Diméssa', *La Libertà Economica*, **10**, (17–18).

Pietri-Tonelli, Alfonso de (1927), *Traité d'économie rationnelle*, 3d edn, Paris: M. Giard.

Pirou, Gaëtan (1925), *Les Doctrines économiques en France depuis 1870*, Paris: A. Colin.

Pirou, Gaëtan (1934), *Les Théories de l'équilibre économique: L. Walras et V. Pareto*, Paris: Les Editions Domat-Montchrestien.

Schlesinger, Karl (1914), *Theorie der Geld- und Kreditwirtschaft*, Munich/Leipzig: Dunker und Humblot.

Schumpeter, Joseph A. (1954), *History of Economic Analysis*, New York: Oxford University Press.

Sensini, Guido (1929), 'Vilfredo Pareto e la teoria della moneta', in *Studi di scienze sociali*, 1932.

Walras, Léon (1874, 1877), *Eléments d'économie politique pure*, 1st and 2nd parts, Lausanne: L. Corbas/Paris: Guillaumin/Bâle: H. Georg; 5th edn, 1926, trans. William Jaffé as *Elements of Pure Economics*, Homewood, Ill.: Irwin, 1954.

Walras, Léon (1965), *Correspondence of Léon Walras and Related Papers*, 3 vols, ed. William Jaffé, Amsterdam: North-Holland.

Walras, Léon (1988), *Eléments d'économie politique pure*, comparative edition, prepared by Claude Mouchot, vol. 8 of Auguste et Léon Walras, *Œuvres économiques complètes*, Paris: Economica.

Zawadzki, Władysław (1914), *Les mathématiques appliquées à l'économie politique*, Paris: M. Rivière.

Leijonhufvud, Axel

Axel Leijonhufvud is one of the leading figures in modern disequilibrium macroeconomics. His interpretation of Keynes is considered to be a breakthrough in explaining the linkages and differences between the *General Theory* and Keynesian economics as entombed in income–expenditures models.

Axel Leijonhufvud was born in Stockholm in 1933 and was educated at the Universities of Stockholm and Lund, receiving a fil. kand (BA) at Lund in 1960, before leaving on a one-year fellowship for the United States at the age of 27. Inspired by US academic economics, he began graduate studies, obtaining a MA at Pittsburgh in 1961 and a PhD at Northwestern University in 1967. He went to UCLA in 1964, still working on his PhD, although he had no intention of staying. However he did stay, became full professor and made a distinguished career at UCLA until his retirement in 1994, serving as department chairman for many years. Leijonhufvud holds honorary degrees from the University of Lund (1983) and the University of Nice, Sophia Antipolis (1995).

In his PhD dissertation Leijonhufvud focused on the coordination of the activities of firms and households over time and between markets. To him this was the central problem of macroeconomic theory. His dissertation sought to shift theoretical attention away from price rigidities as the explanation of coordination failures to the pattern of information flows in the market network characteristic of a monetary economy. This theme was elaborated in his magnus opus, *On Keynesian Economics and the Economics of Keynes: A Study of Monetary Theory*, published in 1968. This monumental study was highly acclaimed. It has been translated into half a dozen languages.

Leijonhufvud was inspired by his UCLA colleagues Armen Alchian and Robert Clower: Alchian's work on incomplete information and transactions costs and Clower's on notional versus effective demands. Leijonhufvud argued that, viewed from the standpoint of Walrasian general equilibrium theory (already dominant in the 1960s), Keynes's *General Theory* should be understood as dealing with systems in which trade does not necessarily take place only at equilibrium prices. In the market adjustment process postulated by Walras, in contrast, no trade takes place until market-clearing prices have been established. The Walrasian auctioneer – an anthropomorphic version of tâtonnement that gained widespread acceptance through Leijonhufvud's use – performed a crucial role as information coordinator, a role for which no institutional counterpart exists in actual economies.

According to Leijonhufvud, Keynes struggled to explain how coordination failures could develop in economies lacking the auctioneer. Leijonhufvud discussed at great length the problems that might arise in coordinating individual economic activities when agents are not just costlessly and inexplicably provided with all the information given by the general equilibrium price vector. Chapter 2, which analysed the 'income-constrained process' resulting from trade at non-equilibrium prices, became the starting-point for much of the subsequent literature. According to Leijonhufvud, the message of the *General Theory* was quite different from the subsequent Keynesian tradition based on the income–expenditure approach. Leijonhufvud disparaged much of the Keynesian heritage. His interpretation of Keynes's work became the subject of an intense debate. As a consequence of Leijonhufvud's interpretation, disequilibrium analysis became a central element of macroeconomics prior to the Lucasian revolution. By focusing on the information-disseminating role of the price mechanism and seeking to base the explanation of central macroeconomic problems on the limitations of what a realistic version of the price mechanism can achieve, Leijonhufvud also contributed to the revival of interest in Friedrich von Hayek's work.

Leijonhufvud returned to many of the themes of *On Keynesian Economics and the Economics of Keynes* in a collection of essays published as *Information and Coordination* in 1981. This collection includes the 'Life Among the

Econ', a satirical piece that has become a minor classic by itself. Over his career he has contributed to methodology, economic philosophy and history of economic thought as well. Recently his research has focused on the experience of high inflation and monetary regimes, summarized in *High Inflation*, written jointly with Daniel Heyman. Leijonhufvud's interest in far-from-equilibrium processes has also led him to work most recently on the socialist transformation problem. In 1993, Leijonhufvud founded the Center for Computable Economics at UCLA, of which he is director.

Leijonhufvud's approach to economics is a verbal and inductive one, preoccupied with conceptual foundations and seldom reaching the level of policy-oriented modeling. The processes driven by the inconsistent beliefs of heterogeneous agents, which have been the focus of his interest, lend themselves less readily to modeling with traditional mathematical tools than do, for example, representative agent equilibrium models. Thus Leijonhufvud's stock in trade stands in stark contrast to the mathematical formalism characteristic of modern economics. Indeed, at one stage in the 1970s, macroeconomics was at a crossroads – the choice between the Clower–Leijonhufvud disequilibrium analysis and the Lucas equilibrium approach. The Lucas route became the preferred one, being easier to formalize and to subject to econometric testing.

MICHAEL D. BORDO
LARS JONUNG

See also:

Clower, Robert W.; Dual Decision Hypothesis; Economics of Keynes and of his Revolution, Key Elements of the; Lausanne, The School of; Lucas, Jr., Robert E.; New Classical School of Economics; Post Keynesian School of Economics.

Bibliography

Bordo, M. and L. Jonung (1996), 'Monetary Regimes, Inflation and Monetary Reform: An Essay in Honour of Axel Leijonhufvud', in D.E. Vaz and K. Velupillai (eds). (This work summarizes Axel Leijonhufvud's work on monetary regimes and subjects it to empirical testing.)

Heyman, D. and A. Leijonhufvud (1995), *High Inflation*, Oxford: Oxford University Press.

Howitt, P. (1990), *The Keynesian Recovery and Other Essays*, New York: Philip Allan. (This volume contains a review of central parts of Axel Leijonhufvud's work.)

Leijonhufvud, A. (1968), *On Keynesian Economics and the Economics of Keynes: A Study of Monetary Theory*, Oxford: Oxford University Press.

Leijonhufvud, A. (1981), *Information and Coordination. Essays in Macroeconomic Theory*, Oxford: Oxford University Press.

Vaz, D.E. and K. Velupillai (eds) (1996), *Inflation, Institutions and Information*, essays in honour of Axel Leijonhufvud, London: Macmillan. (This is the Festschrift to Leijonhufvud on his sixtieth birthday, partly illustrating the spread of his approach to economics.)

Leontief, Wassily W.

Wassily W. Leontief was born on 5 August 1906 in Saint Petersburg, Russia, where he spent his youth. His father was a professor of economics. Events of the early Russian Revolution and the country's deep mourning for the death of the beloved Leo Tolstoy left indelible impressions on him. He married a poet, Estelle Marks, in 1932 and became a Nobel Laureate in economics in 1973. Leontief's daughter and only child, Svetlana Alpers, carried on the family's academic traditions. She is a professor of the history of art at the University of California at Berkeley.

At the age of 15, Leontief entered the University of Leningrad and studied philosophy, sociology and economics. In 1925, he received the degree of Learned Economist. Leontief entered the University of Berlin where he studied under Werner Sombart and Ladislaus Bortiewicz, receiving his PhD in 1928. His dissertation, 'Wirtschaft als Kreislauf' was a theoretical disquisition concerning business cycles. He worked from 1927 to 1930 at the Institute for World Economics at the University of Kiel, where the focus of his research was the statistical derivation of demand and supply curves. In 1931, he moved to the National Bureau of Economic Research in New York. He joined the faculty at Harvard University in 1932 and became professor of economics in 1946. Two years later, he established the Harvard Economic Research Project, serving as its director until 1973.

Among the dozens of honorary degrees and other prestigious awards that Professor Leontief has received for his work in economics are the Bernard-Harms Prize in Economics in West Germany, 1970, Doctor Honoris Causa from the University of Paris (Sorbonne) in 1972 and his election as a foreign member to the Union of Soviet Socialist Republics Academy of Sciences in 1988.

The practical side of Professor Leontief's work is exhibited by his service as advisor to the governments of several countries, including the United States, Italy, Japan and China, and as consultant to various agencies of the United Nations. His involvement with professional associations is evident through membership and service to numerous organizations, including the Royal Statistical Society, American Philosophical Society and the American Association for the Advancement of Science. He served as president of the Econometric Society in 1954 and as president of the American Economic Association in 1970.

Little of importance in the discipline has escaped Leontief's attention. He has contributed to the theory of international trade, wage determination, composite commodities and index numbers, economic growth and grants economics. However, input–output analysis is the contribution which is most closely associated with his name. Preoccupied by the theory of business cycles and having arrived at the conclusion that the partial equilibrium analysis cannot provide a broad basis for analysing the structure of the economy, Leontief formulated a general equilibrium theory that can be empirically estimated. The input–output approach to understanding the structure and operation of economic systems was first introduced in his article, 'Quantitative Input–Output Relations in the Economic System of the United States', published in the *Review of Economics and Statistics* in August 1936. This work was closely followed by his first book on the subject, *The Structure of the American Economy, 1919–1929* published by Oxford University Press in 1941. Several other books based on the input–output paradigm were subsequently published by Professor Leontief, including *Studies in the Structure of the American Economy* (Oxford University Press, 1953), *Input–Output Economics* (Oxford University Press, 1966) and *The Future of the World Economy*, (Oxford University Press, 1977).

Leontief's input–output model represents the sectors of an economy in terms of their input requirements (for example, capital, labor, energy, raw materials and various outputs from other sectors) per unit of their respective output. Each of the economy's sectors is integrated into a comprehensive and consistent system of linear equations. The simultaneous solution of these equations yields quantitative estimates of direct and indirect requirements that must be produced by each sector for any given level of consumption, investment, government expenditures and foreign trade. Input–output analysis assumes final demand for the economy as a given. It is possible to vary the level of final demand and then calculate the input and output of each sector required to satisfy the target demand. Thus the analysis has proved very useful to policy makers and has become one of two primary methodological tools (the other being econometric models) used for policy evaluation, economic planning and forecasting by both the developed and developing nations.

Input–output analysis has been used to analyse and formulate policy on such diverse topics as disarmament in the United States after World War II, economic growth in developing countries, and changes in consumer tastes and preferences in industrialized nations and the long-term economic consequences of pollution and its abatement. Leontief's input–output analysis has been influential. Today input–output tables with nearly 90 sectors are published annually in the United States. Larger tables are published periodically for the United States that include as many as 450 sectors. Tables are also routinely prepared and published for about 120 countries, including most industrial and the majority of developing countries.

Among the important books Professor Leontief published that are not focused exclusively on input–output analysis are his two volumes of collected scientific works, *Essays in Economics: Theories and Theorizing* (Oxford University Press, 1966) and *Essays in Economics: Theories, Facts and Poli-*

cies, Volume Two (Oxford University Press, 1977). The work in these volumes ranges from specific applications of input–output analysis to macroeconomic measurement problems to the implications of Marxian economics for modern economic theory. Even though Leontief is primarily known for his contributions to the empirical aspects of economic analysis, he has contributed much to the philosophy and institutional understanding of economics.

It is not by chance that Wassily Leontief received one of the first Nobel Prizes awarded in Economic Sciences. His many contributions to the discipline have done much to shape modern economic analysis. His seminal work on input–output analysis provided the analytical basis for policy that has done much to improve the economic conditions of people around the world.

HEDAYEH SAMAVATI

See also:

Business Cycle Theory (I and (II); Econometric Models, Macroeconomic; Frisch, Ragnar; Haavelmo, Trygve; Multiplier Effect.

Bibliography

Greenwood, Douglas (1994), *The McGraw-Hill Encyclopedia of Economics*, 2nd edn, New York: McGraw-Hill.
Lindbeck, Assar (ed.) (1981), *Economic Sciences, 1969–1980*, Stockholm: Bank of Sweden.
Miernyk, William H. (1965), *The Elements of Input–Output Analysis*, New York: Random House.

Lerner, Abba P.

Abba Lerner was born in Russia; his parents immigrated to the East End of London, England, when Abba was very young. In his youth he worked in a variety of jobs, such as capmaker, and also dabbled in socialist ideas. That dabbling led him to an interest in economics. He entered the London School of Economics in the early 1930s and soon became known as one of the leading students there.

His early work focused on geometric treatments of what are now standard concepts in economics such as marginal revenue and elasticity. Throughout his life he maintained an ability to translate difficult relationships into two-dimensional graphs. In 1932, he and other students at LSE founded the *Review of Economic Studies*. Then, in 1934, he won a scholarship which his advisers meant for him to use to go to Manchester to learn to do statistical work. He never made it to Manchester; on the way there he stopped at Cambridge to clear up the confusion of students about the workings of the aggregate economy. He wanted to convert them back to the Classical truth. Instead he himself was converted to Keynesian economics, and thereafter he argued for it with the passion of a true convert. He was one of the most important early expositors of Keynes's *General Theory* and he wrote one of the earliest 'approved by Keynes' translations of it (Lerner, 1936). That was the first of many articles interpreting and extending Keynesian economics.

Lerner went to the United States in 1937 under a Rockefeller Fellowship and was an itinerant scholar for a number of years. (Centres of learning at which he taught in his career include Columbia University, the University of Virginia, Kansas City University, Amherst College, The New School for Social Research, Roosevelt University, Johns Hopkins University, Michigan State University, the University of California at Berkeley, City College of the City of New York and Florida State University.) His moving around so much was due in part to his Bohemian nature, his Jewishness, and his proclivity for saying whatever he thought without regard for the consequences.

In 1944, while at Kansas City, he wrote *The Economics of Control* (1944a), the first part of which spelled out the general equilibrium principles for the market economy and of welfare economics, and the second the rules of functional finance – of Keynesian economics. Combined, the two parts of the book gave the rules which could be applied by policy makers to improve the economic efficiency of the economy. This book was well received and it became the text in many graduate school courses. With its success, Lerner's star rose and his functional finance interpretation of Keynesian economics, which focused Keynesian policy on fiscal and monetary policy, became the central focus of textbook treatments of Keynesian economics in the 1960s. Besides his work on functional finance Lerner also played important roles in interpreting a number of other aspects of the Keynesian revolution. His work cleared up confusion about interest theory (Lerner, 1938, 1944b) and on the ambiguity of the marginal efficiency of capital concept (it should instead be the marginal efficiency of investment: Lerner, 1953).

Lerner was one of the most micro-oriented of the early Keynesians, and his interpretation of Keynes's theory and of Keynesian policy always had a micro flavor to it. He was continually worried about the way in which macroeconomics fitted microeconomics and he maintained a macro externality explanation of the relationship (Lerner, 1960) in which the role for macro policy comes about because of what might be called macro externalities: individuals did not consider the extended consequences of their spending and saving decisions. Functional finance was a way to internalize that externality. From early on, his interpretation also emphasized the role of money in the economy.

In 1951, Lerner wrote *The Economics of Employment*, which further developed his ideas of functional finance. This work also first showed his interest in inflation and anti-inflation policy – an interest that was his central focus through much of his career from that point on. The reason for this was the problem that inflation posed for Lerner's proposed policies. Functional finance was designed to achieve a low level of unemployment (3 per cent) *and* a stable price level. If accelerating inflation began before that point, the policy was not useful. As time when on, it became more and more apparent that, long before this 3 per cent level of unemployment was reached, inflation would begin and accelerate. This led Lerner to distinguish between a high level of unemployment – achievable under existing institutions – and a low level of unemployment – achievable under alternative institutions. The policy problem was to find what those alternative institutions were and how they could be made to be politically acceptable.

For Lerner inflation that occurred before 3 per cent unemployment was a product of faulty institutions; it was not a problem inherent in markets. Thus he refused to accept that we should raise the target level of unemployment to whatever level it took to stop inflation. Instead he argued that we should redesign institutions so that inflation did not occur. From the 1970s until his death his research interest was in large part designed to find such desirable institutions. One such institution was his market anti-inflation plan (Lerner and Colander, 1980) under which rights in value added prices would be tradable, so that any firm wanting to change its nominal price would have to make a trade with another firm that wanted to change its nominal price in the opposite direction. Thus by law the average price level would be constant, but relative prices would be free to change.

DAVID COLANDER

See also:
Demand Management; Functional Finance; Incomes Policies; Inflation; Interest, Theories of; Keynesian Revolution; Post Keynesian School of Economics; Robinson, Joan.

Bibliography
Lerner, Abba (1936), 'Mr Keynes' "General Theory of Employment, Interest and Money"', *International Labour Review*, **34**, (4), October, pp. 435–54.
Lerner, Abba (1938), 'Alternative Formulations of the Theory of Interest', *Economic Journal*, **48**, (190), June, pp. 211–30.
Lerner, Abba (1944a), *The Economics of Control*, New York: Macmillan.
Lerner, Abba (1944b), 'Interest Theory – Supply and Demand for Loans or Supply and Demand for Cash', *The Review of Economics and Statistics*, **26**, (2), May, pp. 88–91.
Lerner, Abba (1947), 'Money as a Creature of the State', *American Economic Review*, **37**, (2), May, pp. 312–17.
Lerner, Abba (1951), *The Economics of Employment*, New York: McGraw-Hill.
Lerner, Abba (1953), 'On the Marginal Product of Capital and the Marginal Efficiency of Investment', *Journal of Political Economy*, **61**, (1), February, pp. 1–14.
Lerner, Abba (1960), 'On Generalizing the General Theory', *American Economic Review*, **50**, (1), March, pp. 121–43.
Lerner, Abba and David Colander (1980), *MAP: A Market Anti-Inflation Plan*, New York: Harcourt Brace Jovanovich.

Life Cycle Hypothesis

Keynes's (1936) analysis of the consumption function led him to surmise that consumption was a function of current income only. Classical economists believed that the interest rate influenced consumption: at higher interest rates people saved more and therefore consumed less, as demonstrated by Irving Fisher's (1930) analysis of intertemporal choice. Keynes further surmised that the marginal propensity to consume (MPC), the amount of an additional dollar of income spent on consumption, was between zero and one. Keynes believed that, as a person's income increased, the person spent more on consumption, but not as much more as the increase in income. He also surmised that the average propensity to consume (APC), consumption divided by income, declined as income increased.

The third relationship that Keynes surmised was the focus of much attention. In cross-section data, the APC was found to decline as income increased, as Keynes surmised. In time series data, however, Simon Kuznets (1946) found that, over decades, the APC was constant or relatively stable over a narrow range, even though income increased. This finding, the so-called Kuznets paradox, led to modifications of Keynes's consumption function. Write Keynes's consumption function as

$$C = c_0 + \beta Y$$

C is the annual level of consumption expenditures and Y is the annual income. The constant term is c_0 and β is the marginal propensity to consume or the amount C changes when Y increases by one unit. Dividing both sides by Y gives the APC or $C/Y = c_0/Y + \beta$. Since c_0 is a constant term or intercept and β is the slope, an increase in Y implies a decline in APC, as Keynes surmised. But this decline in APC as Y increases contradicts Kuznets's empirical findings.

Franco Modigliani and his collaborators Albert Ando and Richard Brumberg wrote a series of articles in the 1950s designed to reconcile Keynes's consumption function with the Kuznets paradox. They looked at Irving Fisher's intertemporal choice model which says that consumers face an intertemporal budget constraint. They noted that Fisher's theory implies that consumption expenditures depend on the consumer's expected lifetime resources, not on current income only. Modigliani and his collaborators emphasize that consumers can move income from times in life when income is high to times in life when income is low. By saving a larger part of income when income is high the consumer can provide resources for retirement years when income is low. This saving when income is high enables the consumer to smooth consumption over the consumer's lifetime: hence the name 'life cycle hypothesis of consumption' (LCH).

The LCH did reconcile the consumption data with the Kuznets paradox. Mankiw (1994) gives a clear illustration why that is so. Assume that the consumer lives T more years, works R more years of those, has initial wealth W and earns Y per year when he works. Lifetime resources $(W + RY)$ consist of initial wealth W and lifetime earnings R times Y. Assume that the interest rate is zero. Assume that the consumer wants to maintain a smooth level of consumption over life. Yearly consumption would be:

$$C = (W + RY)/T$$

Dividing each term by T we can write:

$$C = (1/T)W + (R/T)Y$$

Let the marginal propensity to consume out of W be α or $(1/T)$ and let the marginal propensity to consume out of income be β or (R/T). In this formulation, consumption depends on wealth and on income.

$$C = \alpha W + \beta Y$$

Divide both sides by Y to obtain the APC which is $C/Y = ((\alpha W)/Y + \beta)$. If W is constant in cross-section data the APC falls as Y rises. Recall that in Keynes's consumption function the APC falls as Y increases. If in time series data W rises with Y then, in the LCH, $((\alpha W)/Y + \beta)$ or the APC will be constant as Y rises. This property of the LCH reconciles the consumption function data with the Kuznets paradox. Keynes's consumption function does not explain this property of the time series data.

Two other theories of consumption were proposed at approximately the same time as the LCH. Duesenberry's (1949) relative income hypothesis assumes that, when income falls, people save less and consume more to maintain past consumption, but when income rises people increase their spending but not by as much as the income increased. The asymmetric ratchet effect provides an explanation of the Kuznets paradox, but makes empirical testing problematic. Friedman's (1957) permanent income hypothesis is based on Fisher's model of intertemporal choice, as is the LCH. It assumes that consumption is a function of lifetime resources. Friedman's model divides lifetime resources into transitory and permanent income instead of the initial wealth and lifetime earnings in LCH. Friedman's model assumes that income has two components, one permanent and one transitory, but that consumption is a function only of the permanent component. Friedman's model assumes an infinite lifetime instead of the finite lifetime assumed in LCH. Friedman's model assumes that income varies over a person's lifetime in a random way instead of the predictable way assumed in LCH.

One implication of the LCH has received much attention. Although the LCH implies that the elderly will dissave, studies indicate that the elderly do not dissave as much as the LCH predicts. Incorporating both uncertainty over length of life and a bequest motive may account for such results (Hurd, 1990). Other implications, as well as the origin, of the LCH are described eloquently by Modigliani (1986) in his Nobel Prize address. First, the LCH implies an additional channel through which monetary policy can alter aggregate demand, namely wealth. Second, the LCH implies that transitory income tax changes do not alter consumption because consumption is a function of lifetime resources, not current income only. Third, the LCH implies that consumption rather than current income should be taxed progressively. Fourth, the LCH implies that budget deficits financed by borrowing are paid for by future generations, not by the current generation.

CHRISTINE AMSLER

See also:

Absolute Income Hypothesis; Consumption and Consumption Function; Modigliani, Franco; Permanent Income Hypothesis; Relative Income Hypothesis

Bibliography

Duesenberry, J. (1949), *Income, Saving and Theory of Consumer Behavior*, Cambridge, Mass.: Harvard University Press.

Fisher, I. (1930), *The Theory of Interest*, New York: Macmillan.

Friedman, M. (1957), *A Theory of the Consumption Function*, Princeton: Princeton University Press.

Hurd, M. (1990), 'Research on the Elderly: Economic Status, Retirement, and Consumption and Saving', *Journal of Economic Literature*, **28**, (2), June, pp. 565–637.

Keynes, J.M. (1936), *The General Theory of Employment, Interest and Money*, London: Macmillan.

Kuznets, S. (1946), *National Income: A Summary of Findings*, NBER, New York: Arno Press.

Mankiw, G. (1994), *Macroeconomics*, New York: Worth Publishers.

Modigliani, F. (1986), 'Life Cycle, Individual Thrift and the Wealth of Nations', *American Economic Review*, **76**, (3), June, pp. 297–313.

Lipsey, Richard G.

Richard G. Lipsey, PhD, is currently professor of economics at Simon Fraser University in Vancouver, British Columbia and fellow of the Economic Growth and Policy Program, Canadian Institute for Advanced Research. He was born in Victoria, British Columbia, on 28 August 1928. He did his undergraduate work at Victoria College and the University of British Columbia. He graduated from the latter in 1951 with a BA and first class honors. He got his MA from the University of Toronto in 1953 and his PhD from the University of

London at the London School of Economics in 1957. He started his professional career at the London School of Economics. He then moved to the University of Essex as the chairman, in 1964. In 1970, he became the Sir Edward Peacock professor of economics at Queens University in Kingston, Ontario, and in 1989 he took up his current position. While he was at the London school, he was also the editor of the *Review of Economic Studies*, from 1962 to 1964. His PhD dissertation in 1957 was on the theory of customs unions; this was summarized as an article in the *Economic Journal* of September 1960 and it appeared as a book in 1973.

Lipsey is most widely known for his introductory textbook, *Economics* (1966), in the United States and Canada, originally co-authored with P. Steiner and more recently co-authored with P. Courant and D. Purvis. It has gone through ten editions and is widely used throughout the world. Another interesting book written with G.C. Archibald is *An Introduction to a Mathematical Treatment of Economics* (1967). This is a more advanced textbook and is used in upper division (third and fourth year undergraduate students) economics classes throughout the world.

Lipsey's main research interest in the early phase of his career was theoretical microeconomics, but he has also done good work in many specialized fields of economics, the most important of which are welfare, mathematical economics, the micro foundations of unemployment and inflation, the macro foundations of inflation, location and spatial economics, international trade and monetary policy. Lipsey's most famous article (written with K. Lancaster) is 'The General Theory of Second Best' (1956). This article may be summarized by a quotation from page 11: 'if one of the Pareto optimum conditions cannot be fulfilled, then an optimum situation can be achieved only by departing from all the other Paretian conditions'. This is an important theorem in welfare economics and it can be applied in different ways. One of the more interesting applications and the one used by Lipsey is related to one of his other early interests: the theory of customs unions. The result of this paper confirms Professor Viner's conclusion that 'the discriminatory reduction of tariffs among members of a customs union may reduce, rather than raise, the efficiency of world production' (Viner, 1950). The main proposition proved in this article shows that the adoption of free trade policy by only one country may actually hurt the growth of real income, not only in that country, but in the rest of the world. This type of result is still used by authors in the theory of international trade.

'The Relation Between Unemployment and the Rate of Change of Money Wage Rates in the UK, 1862–1957' (1960a) used A.W. Phillips's famous 1958 discussion of the relation between unemployment and inflation and generalized it by adding new results. The most important section of the paper is devoted to the construction of a theoretical model which accounts for the relations between unemployment and inflation. This was something that was left out of the Phillips original. M. Blaug, in *Great Economists Since Keynes* (1985), states that: 'Lipsey managed to provide a microeconomic explanation for the macroeconomic relationship between unemployment and wage inflation which Phillips had earlier discovered, and in so doing was perhaps more responsible than anyone else in publicizing the Phillips curve' (p. 144).

'Monetary and Value Theory: A Critique of Lange and Patinkin' (written with G.C. Archibald, 1958) discussed the famous 'real balance effect' that Patinkin made a vital part of his book, *Money, Interest and Prices* (1956). Patinkin had regarded the classical dichotimization of the economy as being a serious problem. He argued that it could be eliminated by the real balance effect, which provided the needed link between the real and money sectors of the economy. But Lipsey and his co-author found that the real balance effect is irrelevant to this process. It only provides an explanation of 'how the system behaves in disequilibrium'. Also they found the unexpected result that the classical model has a consistent equilibrium solution which does not depend on the real balance effect. Therefore the dichotomy between the real and monetary sectors of the economy is no longer a problem.

'The Understanding and Control of Inflation: Is There a Crisis in Macro-economics?' (1981) was originally written as a speech given as the Presidential Address to the annual meeting of the Canadian Economics Association in May 1981. It contains an analysis of one of Lipsey's favorite topics: the theory of inflation. But, contrary to some of his other articles on this subject, it approaches inflation from the macro rather than the micro viewpoint. In this article, Lipsey analyses the 'neo-Keynesian' model and finds that from 'the last 50 years of evidence' it has done a 'surprisingly good' job of prediction (p. 545). This is because the 'asymmetry' (p. 548) inherent in the Keynesian model is an important factor in helping to make accurate predic-tions of what would happen to inflation when aggregate demand changed. If the economy were close to full capacity and demand increased, this would increase inflation; if demand decreased, mainly real output would fall, but this need not lower the inflation rate. Lipsey wishes to get across the fact that an up-to-date version of the Keynesian paradigm would stand in very good stead as a predictor of modern inflation as well as real movements in the economy. The reason that Keynesian theory, as interpreted by modern econo-mists, has not been able to control inflation is the fault of 'policy instruments' rather than the theory itself. This is why the last part of the article is devoted to describing policy instruments not normally associated with the Keynesian model, such as monetarism, which could be used to control inflation.

Much of Lipsey's current research is on trade policy. He has written on many topics such as NAFTA, multinational plant location in a regional trad-ing area and the political economy of inflation control. Several of his articles have been on the relation between Canada and the United States, especially as regards the free trade agreement implicit in NAFTA. He has also written recently on problems of developing countries.

MICHAEL J. GOOTZEIT

See also:

Economics, The Art of Inflation; Lausanne, The School of; Microfoundations of Macroeconomics; Phillips Curve, The; Real Balance Effect; Viner, Jacob.

Bibliography

Blaug, Mark (1985), *Great Economists Since Keynes, An Introduction to the World of One Hundred Modern Economists*, Iotowa, NJ: Barnes & Noble Books.

Lipsey, Richard G. (1960a), 'The Relation Between Unemployment and the Rate of Change of Money Wage Rates in the UK, 1862–1957', *Economica*, **27**, (105), February, pp. 1–31.

Lipsey, Richard G. (1960b), 'The Theory of Customs Unions: A General Survey', *Economic Journal*, **70**, (279), September, pp. 496–513.

Lipsey, Richard G. (1973), *The Theory of Customs Unions*, London: Weidenfeld & Nicolson.

Lipsey, Richard G. (1981), 'The Understanding and Control of Inflation: Is There a Crisis in Macroeconomics?', *Canadian Journal of Economics*, **14**, (4), November, pp. 545–76.

Lipsey, Richard G. and G.C. Archibald (1958), 'Monetary and Value Theory: A Critique of Lange and Patinkin', *Review of Economic Studies*, **26**, (69), October, pp. 1–22.

Lipsey, Richard G. and G.C. Archibald (1967), *An Introduction to a Mathematical Treatment of Economics*, London: Weidenfeld & Nicolson.

Lipsey, Richard G. and Kevin Lancaster (1956), 'The General Theory of Second Best', *Review of Economic Studies*, **24**, (63), October, pp. 11–32.

Lipsey, Richard G. and P. Steiner (1966), *Economics*, New York: Harper & Row.

Patinkin, Don (1956), *Money, Interest and Prices*, New York: Harper & Row.

Viner, Jacob (1950), *The Customs Union Issue*, New York: Carnegie Endowment for International Peace.

Liquidity Trap

The liquidity trap occurs in a portion of the money demand (or liquidity preference) function where the demand for money becomes perfectly interest elastic. This possible shape for the money demand curve follows from a liquidity preference model in which individuals hold either money or bonds (debt). At some low level of the interest rate, everyone in the economy may expect interest rates to rise in the future and, consequently, individuals will then wish to hold all speculative balances as money, and will then be unwilling to hold bonds. According to Keynes,

> There is the possibility, for reasons discussed above, that, after the interest rate has fallen to a certain level, liquidity preference may become virtually absolute in the sense that almost everyone prefers to hold cash to debt which yields such a low rate of interest. (Keynes, 1936, p. 207)

Keynes does not discuss the liquidity trap in much detail. It has been raised into a key Keynesian position more by Keynes's commentators than by Keynes himself (Hicks, 1937; Hansen, 1953, pp. 132–3).

The consequences of such a region in the money demand curve are very interesting. If this region exists, the LM curve will be horizontal at that low interest rate. It follows that, in that area of money demand, increases in the real money supply, due either to increases in nominal money or to falls in the price level, will not lower the interest rate, and will not result in an increase in aggregate demand, so that in this area, the aggregate demand curve becomes perfectly price inelastic. If the economy is then below full employment, a falling price level will not restore output to the full employment level. (If real money balances influence spending levels then, as prices fall, spending will increase and aggregate demand will rise, even if the interest rate does not fall. Thus a falling price will cause the *IS* curve to shift to the right, crossing the horizontal *LM* curve at a higher level of output.)

Not surprisingly, because of the important policy implications of the liquidity trap, there have been several empirical attempts to test for its existence. Laidler (1966), using the years 1892–1960, divides the data into two groups: one group of observations with interest rates above average and one with interest rates below average. Using long-term and short-term interest rates, he finds no evidence of a higher interest elasticity for the below average interest rate groups. Pifer (1969) estimates a log-linear money demand function of the form:

$$\frac{M^d}{P} = kX^{\beta_1}(r - r^{\min})^{\beta_2}E$$

Pifer argues that, if this equation fits better with a non-zero $r^{\min}$ than a zero $r^{\min}$, this would provide evidence of a liquidity trap. Using data for the United States from 1900–1958, he found no evidence of a liquidity trap. Barth and Kraft (1976), using spline functions find no evidence that the interest elasticity of money increases as interest rates fall using short-term and long-term interest rates.

Karl Brunner argues that there is no evidence of a liquidity trap. According to him, a liquidity trap implies 'an excess of marginal transactions costs over benefits for any level of transactions'. Brunner (1978) notes that the liquidity trap would imply no activity or transactions in a financial market: 'This condition held in the 1930s only in the Federal Funds Market. Transactions continued in all other financial markets and thus assured the transmission of monetary impulses to economic activity and the price level.'

The liquidity trap seems to be an interesting footnote in the development of macroeconomics. While it was an interesting topic in intermediate macroeconomics textbooks for a certain period of time, its importance in intermediate macroeconomics is beginning to decline. Many new intermediate macroeconomics books do not even mention it. Keynes himself was apparently not very sure of the existence of a liquidity trap, writing: 'But whilst this limiting condition might have become of some practical importance in the future, I know of no example hitherto' (Keynes, 1936, p. 207).

NICHOLAS R. NOBLE

See also:
Economics of Keynes and of his Revolution, Key Elements of the; Interest, Theories of; IS/LM Model and Diagram; Monetary Policy; Money.

Bibliography
Barth, James and Arthur Kraft (1976), 'Estimation of the Liquidity Trap Using Spline Functions', *Review of Economics and Statistics*, **58**, (2), May, pp. 218–22.
Brunner, Karl (1978), 'Issues in Post-Keynesian Monetary Analysis', in Thomas Mayer (ed.), *The Structure of Monetarism*, New York: W.W. Norton.
Hansen, Alvin H. (1953), *A Guide to Keynes*, New York: McGraw-Hill.
Hicks, J.R. (1937), 'Mr Keynes and the Classics: A Suggested Interpretation', *Econometrica*, **5**, (2), April, pp. 147–59.
Keynes, John M. (1936), *The General Theory of Employment Interest and Money*, London: Macmillan.
Laidler, David (1966), 'The Rate of Interest and the Demand for Money: Some Empirical Evidence', *Journal of Political Economy*, **74**, (6), December, pp. 545–55.
Pifer, H.A. (1969), 'A Nonlinear Maximum Likelihood Estimate of the Liquidity Trap', *Econometrica*, **37**, (2), April, pp. 324–32.

Lucas, Jr., Robert E.

Robert Lucas is without doubt one of the leading figures in modern macroeconomics. He was born in Yakima, Washington in 1937. He grew up in a family of four children and his parents were New Deal Democrats. They owned a restaurant, the Lucas Ice Creamery, which went bankrupt shortly after his birth. His father worked as a steamfitter and later owned a refrigeration business.

Lucas earned his BA in history from the University of Chicago in 1959, and began graduate school in history at the University of California at Berkeley. He soon turned to economics, however, and returned to the University of Chicago to earn his PhD in 1964. His dissertation work, on capital/labor substitutability, was supervised by Al Harberger. After graduate school, Lucas taught at Carnegie Mellon University from 1963–1974. He returned to the University of Chicago in 1975, is currently John Dewey Distinguished Service Professor, and was awarded the Nobel Prize in Economics in 1995.

Lucas states that two of the most important influences on him were Milton Friedman and Paul Samuelson. Friedman taught price theory and in addition provided the intellectual background to much of Lucas's later work. Lucas claims to have read everything Friedman has ever written, and that he prefers to view himself as a monetarist rather than as a new classicalist. As for Paul Samuelson, Lucas admired the way *Foundations of Economic Analysis* (1947) showed the profession how to formalize questions that had previously been endlessly debated, and how this formalization provided answers that just ended the debate.

Robert Lucas is one of the originators (some would say *the* originator) of the new classical macroeconomics, and his views on macro and monetary economics have influenced a legion of modern economists. His views on the importance of equilibrium modeling – of modeling economies as experiencing continuous market clearing – continue to influence the profession in the real business cycle school, a school that began as an offshoot of the new classical macroeconomics and has quickly grown to surpass the new classical school in terms of current practitioners. Ironically Lucas has expressed admiration for the modeling principles espoused by the real business cycle school while doubting its eventual success at modeling business cycles as non-monetary phenomenon.

In more recent years Lucas has turned his attention to the microfoundations of monetary theory and most recently to studying economic growth. In his contributions to what is called the 'new monetary economics', Lucas has worked on the foundations of monetary economics and on asset pricing in a monetary economy. Most recently Lucas has turned his attention to economic growth and he has had a large influence on the resurgence of growth theory in general and on the development of endogenous growth theory in particular. In encouraging research along these lines, he has espoused the view that the rate of economic growth has a much stronger influence on the well-being of individuals in a society than any choices a society makes in dealing with business cycle fluctuations.

Lucas's contributions to business cycle research are many. His work places a strong emphasis on equilibrium business cycle theories. In this work, individual preferences, technology and the rules of the game (such as price-taking behavior) are made explicit. The economy is generally modeled as being in a stationary state except that it is always being affected by stochastic disturbances. The key approach is how to model such an economy while maintaining the ability to derive results that accord with the widely believed empirical regularities that characterize real world business cycles.

In many ways Lucas's answers to these questions define the new classical economics. They contain several well known features. First is the so-called Lucas supply curve, which resulted from work published with Leonard Rapping. The Lucas supply curve specifies that aggregate output is at the natural rate, except that it changes in response to changes in the price level from some expected value. Expectations are rational and, in one version of the Lucas supply curve, the price response is generated by an intertemporal substitution effect. If prices today are higher than they are expected to be in the future, agents will supply more today to take advantage of the temporarily high current prices.

An alternative form of the Lucas supply curve has the price response generated by noisy price signals. In this approach, agents observe a market price and have to disentangle the information contained in that observation. The market price consists of two components, an aggregate price level component and a market-specific component, and each component is subject to stochastic shocks. When the market price rises, it may be because the aggregate price level has risen, in which case the rising market price does not signal a relative price change and suppliers would not want to respond to the price change. Alternatively the market price rise could be due to a relative price change, in which case suppliers would want to increase supply. If suppliers observe only the market price and not the aggregate price level, they are faced with a signal extraction problem, a problem of determining what part of any market price change reflects a relative price change.

A second feature of Lucas's business cycle work is the reliance on the assumption of rational expectations. The idea of rational expectations comes from work by John Muth and can be stated in a weak form as requiring agents to make the most efficient use of all publicly available information when forming expectations. One way to look at this assumption is that it restricts the choices available to economists when modeling the economy, in that it disallows models in which agents are assumed to forecast inefficiently. The widespread acceptance of the assumption of rational expectations has been one of the most lasting contributions of the new classical macroeconomics. While originally quite controversial, the assumption of rational expectations is now very commonplace, even among New Keynesian models and other competing schools of thought. Criticisms of rational expectations today generally focus on rational expectations as one possible end result of agents learning about the economy, and ask whether various learning procedures will result in agents knowing enough about the economy to form rational expectations.

A third feature of Lucas's business cycle work is the emphasis, even the insistence, on equilibrium modeling. The assumption of continuous market clearing follows in the Walrasian tradition. At each instant of time the price level adjusts instantaneously to clear the market. This assumption is still quite controversial. It survives and thrives in real business cycle models, but it is questioned by Keynesian and New Keynesian proponents, and does not completely accord with the views of the original monetarists.

In the course of developing his work on business cycles, Lucas expounded what has become widely known as the Lucas critique, a criticism of many policy evaluation exercises. The main idea of this critique is that policy evaluation is often done with econometric models that include parameters that may themselves change with changes in policy. One example is the Phillips curve, the relationship between inflation rates and unemployment. Higher inflation rates are generally associated with lower unemployment rates. However this relationship need not be structural, or invariant to policy actions. In fact, in new classical models an increase in the variance of the inflation rate will lead to noisier price signals and less of an employment response to inflation, making the Phillips curve steeper. Thus attempts to use an estimated Phillips curve in policy evaluation would be misleading if the policy under consideration would lead to a change in the variance of inflation.

DENNIS W. JANSEN

See also:

Business Cycle Theory (I) and (II); Demand Management; Econometric Models, Macroeconomic; Expectations, Theories of; Fiscal Policy; Lausanne, The School of; Lucas Critique; Microfoundations of Macroeconomics; Monetary Policy; New Classical School of Economics; Treasury View.

Bibliography

Lucas, Robert E. Jr. (1972), 'Expectations and the Neutrality of Money', *Journal of Economic Theory*, **4**, (2), April, pp. 103–24.
Lucas, Robert E. Jr. (1973), 'Some International Evidence on Output–Inflation Tradeoffs', *American Economic Review*, **63**, (3), June, pp. 326–34.
Lucas, Robert E. Jr. (1975), 'An Equilibrium Model of the Business Cycle', *Journal of Political Economy*, **83**, (6), December, pp. 1113–44.
Lucas, Robert E. Jr. (1976), 'Econometric Policy Evaluation: A Critique', in K. Brunner and A.H. Meltzer (eds), *The Phillips Curve and Labor Markets*, Carnegie–Rochester Conference Series on Public Policy, Amsterdam: North-Holland.
Lucas, Robert E. Jr. (1978), 'Asset Prices in an Exchange Economy', *Econometrica*, **46**, (6), November, pp. 1429–45.
Lucas, Robert E. Jr. (1988), 'On the Mechanics of Economic Development', *Journal of Monetary Economics*, **21**, (3), July, pp. 3–42.
Lucas, Robert E. Jr. (1993), 'Making a Miracle', *Econometrica*, **61**, (2), March, pp. 251–72.
Lucas, Robert E. Jr. and Edward C. Prescott (1971), 'Investment Under Uncertainty', *Econometrica*, **39**, (5), September, pp. 659–81.
Lucas, Robert E. Jr. and Leonard A. Rapping (1969), 'Real Wages, Employment and Inflation', *Journal of Political Economy*, **77**, (5), September/October, pp. 721–54.
Lucas, Robert E. Jr. and Nancy L. Stokey (1987), 'Money and Interest in a Cash-in-Advance Economy', *Econometrica*, **55**, (3), May, pp. 491–513.
Samuelson, Paul A. (1947), *Foundations of Economic Analysis*, Cambridge, Mass.: Harvard University Press.
Stokey, Nancy L. and Robert E. Lucas Jr. (1989), *Recursive Methods in Economic Dynamics*, Cambridge, Mass.: Harvard University Press.

Lucas Critique

The Lucas (1976) critique is often described as a contribution and character-istic feature of the new classical school, but this misconstrues its proper place within (macro)econometrics. On the one hand, the critique is better under-stood as part of the (much older) literature on what Haavelmo (1943) and Marschak (1953) two of its founders, called the 'autonomy' of structural econometric equations, the extent to which particular specifications were robust with respect to possible régime shifts. On the other, its particular identification as an element in the broader new classical critique of Keynesian economics, an identification that is perhaps essential to neither, conflates several distinct theoretical and methodological controversies.

Savin (1987) reminds us that the principle that 'outcomes' and 'expecta-tions' are often bicausal has been understood (in broad terms, at least) for decades: current outcomes are a function (perhaps correspondence) of expec-tations over future outcomes but expectations are themselves functions of current outcomes. Under some conditions, then, there exists a well-behaved 'map' from outcomes to expectations and back, fixed points of which (there are often several, and sometimes none) constitute 'expectations-consistent' equilibria. (Savin, 1987, calls these 'rational expectations equilibria', but this connotes the presence of additional structure.) If the parameters of the map and therefore its fixed points are estimable, robust or autonomous, calcula-tions of the consequences of (for example) alternative macroeconomic policies become feasible. In effect, the Lucas critique asserts that the 'structural' equations of (in particular) Keynesian macroeconometric models are not autonomous because of their failure to incorporate the parametric restrictions that are embodied in maps of this kind: in Lucas's (1972) own benchmark model, for example, the correlation between output and inflation varies with the extent to which individual firms can or should expect price movements to be relative or absolute.

To provide a more concrete illustration, consider a simple model of income determination in which C_t is assumed to be a linear function (with random error) of permanent income Y_t^P, defined here for the sake of convenience as a linear combination of current income Y_t and expected income next period $E_t Y_{t+1}$:

$$C_t = \alpha + \beta Y_t^P + u_t \tag{1}$$

$$Y_t^P = \theta Y_t + (1-\theta) E_t Y_{t+1} \tag{2}$$

The equilibrium condition $Y_t = AE_t = C_t + A_t$, where A_t is current 'autonomous expenditure', becomes:

$$Y_t = \frac{\alpha}{1-\beta\theta} + \frac{\beta(1-\theta)}{1-\beta\theta}E_t Y_{t+1} + \frac{1}{1-\beta\theta}A_t + u_t \tag{3}$$

This is not an estimable reduced form, however: $E_t Y_{t+1}$ is not observable and, even if it were, its dependence on Y_t and therefore, A_t complicates matters. The second problem is resolved once (3) is transformed into:

$$Y_t = \frac{\alpha}{1-\beta} + \left(\frac{\beta(1-\theta)}{1-\beta\theta}\right)^m Y_{t+m} + \sum_{j=0}^{m-1} \frac{\beta^j(1-\theta)^j}{(1-\beta\theta)^{j+1}} E_t A_{t+j} + u_t \tag{4}$$

(Because (3) also implies that $E_t Y_{t+1}$ is a linear function of $E_t E_{t+1} Y_{t+2}$ and $E_t A_{t+1}$, and so on (4) is the result of repeated substitution and application of the so-called 'law of iterated expectations'.) If each series is measured in terms of deviations from its respective trend, the second term vanishes in the limit, so that:

$$Y_t = \frac{\alpha}{1-\beta} + \sum_{j=0}^{\infty} \frac{\beta^j(1-\theta)^j}{(1-\beta\theta)^{j+1}} E_t A_{t+j} + u_t \tag{5}$$

The first problem is exacerbated, however: next period's expected income has been 'replaced' by expectations over an infinite stream of autonomous expenditures A_{t+j}. Suppose, however, that 'laws of motion' that characterize the evolution of A_t are known to both outside and inside observers:

$$A_t = \mu A_{t-1} + e_t \tag{6}$$

where e_t is an error term that is uncorrelated with u_t. (The belief that the evolution of A_t, part of which reflects the 'animal spirits' of investors, is both simple and predictable in a probabilistic sense is problematic, of course, but the difficulties are not specific to this model.) This implies that $E_t A_{t+j} = \mu^j A_t$ so that (5) collapses into:

$$Y_t = \frac{\alpha}{1-\beta} + \frac{1}{(1-\beta\theta)-\mu\beta(1-\theta)} A_t + u_t \tag{7}$$

The researcher who estimates the reduced form $Y_t = \pi_0 + \pi_1 A_t + u_t$ in order to calculate the multiplier effects of alternative fiscal policies must therefore realize that π_1 is itself a function of μ: the reduced form parameters are not autonomous with respect to regime shifts and therefore cannot be used to simulate the effects of these shifts.

As the illustration hints, awareness of the Lucas critique is not (and need not be) limited to new classical models: Tobin's (1980) claim that Keynesian models could (in principle) incorporate 'rational' expectations implies, for example, that earlier econometric models should be revised, not abandoned. The oft-cited maxim that the cross-equation restrictions (between (6) and (7) in this case) embodied in critique-sensitive models are the 'hallmark of the rational expectations' revolution (Sargent, 1979) must therefore be understood in its narrowest sense. In fact, it seems reasonable to ask whether rational expectations, in whatever context, are themselves essential: models in which households and firms 'learn' about their complicated (perhaps even non-stochastic) economic environments, for example, will also impose cross-equation restrictions.

Because the specification of autonomous structures is difficult and the estimation of its so-called 'deep parameters' vulnerable to underidentification problems (Sargent, 1976), recent efforts to articulate an 'atheoretical macroeconometrics' (Sims, 1980) based on unrestricted (but low-dimensional) vector autoregressions (VARs) have drawn considerable attention both within and outside the new classical movement. In fact, both VARs and, Fair (1987) concludes, more conventional macroeconometric models have performed well relative to critique-sensitive ones, a reflection, some believe, of their (modified Walrasian) structure.

PETER HANS MATTHEWS

See also:

Demand Management: Econometric Models, Macroeconomic; Expectations, Theories of; Fiscal Policy; Friedman, Milton; Lucas, Jr., Robert E.; Monetary Policy; New Classical School of Economics.

Bibliography

Fair, Ray C. (1987), 'Macroeconometric Models', in John Eatwell, Murray Milgate and Peter Newman (eds), *The New Palgrave: A Dictionary of Economics*, Vol. 3, New York: Stockton Press.
Haavelmo, T. (1943), 'The Statistical Implications of a System of Simultaneous Equations', *Econometrica*, **11**, (1), January, pp. 1–12.
Haavelmo, T. (1944), 'The Probability Approach in Econometrics', *Econometrica*, **12**, Supplement, July, pp. 1–115.
Lucas, Robert (1972), 'Expectations and the Neutrality of Money', *Journal of Economic Theory*, **4**, (2), April, pp. 103–24.
Lucas, Robert (1976), 'Econometric Policy Evaluation: A Critique', in Karl Brunner and Allan Meltzer (eds), *The Phillips Curve and Labor Markets*, Amsterdam: North-Holland.
Marschak, Jacob (1953), 'Economic Measurements for Policy and Prediction', in William Hood and Tjalling Koopmans (eds), *Studies in Econometric Method*, New York: Wiley.
Sargent, Thoms J. (1976), 'The Observational Equivalence of Natural and Unnatural Rate Theories of Macroeconomics', *Journal of Political Economy*, **84**, (3), June, pp. 631–40.
Sargent, Thomas J. (1979), *Macroeconomic Theory*, New York: Academic Press.
Savin, N. Eugene (1987), 'Rational Expectations: Econometric Implications', in John Eatwell, Murray Milgate and Peter Newman (eds), *The New Palgrave: A Dictionary of Economics*, Vol. 4, New York: Stockton Press.
Sims, Christopher A. (1980), 'Macroeconomics and Reality', *Econometrica*, **48**, (1), January, pp. 1–48.
Tobin, James (1980), *Asset Accumulation and Economic Activity*, Chicago: University of Chicago Press.

Lundberg, Erik

Erik Lundberg (1907–1987), a member of the internationally renowned Stockholm School, was born to a family with long academic and intellectual traditions. After matriculating from Saltsjöbaden's gymnasium in 1925, he entered Stockholm University, where he received a fil. kand. (BA) in 1928, and a fil. lic. (MA) in 1931. He thereafter spent two years in the United States as a Rockefeller Foundation stipendiate. Here Lundberg specialized in theoretical and statistical business cycle research, trying to deepen Keynes's theory as formulated in *A Treatise on Money*, by reconciling Böhm-Bawerk's and Wicksell's capital theories with more traditional sequential business cycle theories. In the United States he made contact with, among others, W.C. Mitchell, F. Knight, J. Viner and S. Kuznets. After returning to Sweden, he worked for Sweden's Central Bank (1934–5) and as advisor to the government of Iceland.

In 1937, Lundberg became a docent at Stockholm University, having successfully defended his PhD thesis, 'Studies in the Theory of Economic Expansion', through which he became recognized as a theoretician representing the dynamic modeling approach in the sequence tradition of the Stockholm School. Lundberg was soon appointed to initiate and lead the Swedish National Institute of Economic Research (Konjunkturinstitutet), where he stayed until 1955, when he resigned and assumed a full-time professorship at Stockholm University. At the Institute he made pioneering attempts to measure deflationary/inflationary gaps and the degree of instability of the economy. In 1965, he succeeded Bertil Ohlin as professor at the Stockholm School of Economics, a position he held until retirement in 1974. Lundberg was president of the Royal (Swedish) Academy of Science, 1973–6, and also chairman of its committee for the 'Nobel prize' in economics, 1975–9. Politically and ideologically he belonged to the leading circle of Sweden's liberal party, long led by Ohlin.

In the formative years around 1930, Lundberg was mainly involved with work on writing a 600-page volume on wages in Sweden between 1860 and 1930, and a paper submitted for the licentiate degree, on the concept of economic equilibrium. The wages book is most representative of Lundberg's later work, which was mainly empirical. Among his published works, writings on policy questions and analyses of current developments dominate. Lundberg himself considered this his prime professional domain, although the licentiate paper especially and the doctoral thesis were more analytical and theoretical.

Lundberg's main contribution to economic theory was his 1937 dissertation, which was 'an attempt to apply the methods developed by Wicksell and his followers to the system of explanation formulated by Keynes' (Lundberg,

1937, p. 3). Lundberg wanted to describe the sequence resulting when equilibrium conditions are not fulfilled or are disrupted. To do this the whole equilibrium construction has to be abandoned. The analysis must take into consideration more fundamentally the element of time. By doing this it will be possible to analyse the changes taking place in a time sequence, as in Wicksell's cumulative processes. Lundberg considered Keynes's (business cycle) theory undynamic and unrealistic, mainly because it took many important factors as given, instead of endogenously explaining their changes. Schumpeter (1954, pp. 1173–4) later acknowledged Lundberg's methodological superiority to Keynes, although Lundberg never derived his macroeconomic equations from microeconomic analysis, as, for example, Lindahl and Myrdal did.

Lundberg's central point in the analysis of business cycles was that there were two different kinds of setbacks from a boom to a depression. In the first kind, it was the lack of capital and savings that brought the boom to an end. In the second kind, it was rather a disproportionate expansion of some sectors that led to an apparent savings surplus and underconsumption. Lundberg now wanted to analyse the ensuing crises, using Cassel's assumption of a continuous balanced growth in the economy, with attention paid to the relationship between investments and savings during the expansion phase of the cycle.

Lundberg's contribution to the analysis of the Stockholm School was mainly in accentuating the dual role investments played, both on the demand and supply side. A certain level of investments was necessary to keep aggregate effective demand up. Wicksell's capital theory entered the analysis where one had to take into account the impact investments had on the supply side (production capacity, structure and productivity). The different models Lundberg set up demonstrate that this dual role of investments could precipitate an imbalanced growth with a surplus or deficit in effective demand. Lundberg also shows, with the famous Wicksellian 'rocking horse' examples, how cycles could be created within a Keynesian frame formulated in a dynamic sequential model. He extends Wicksell's analysis by also studying what happens to the sequence when the nominal (and not only the real) rate of interest changes.

Among Lundberg's many other works, a few deserve mention. *Business Cycles and Economic Policy* (1957) contains an interesting discussion on how to measure ex ante inflation and deflation gaps by way of excess demand/supply in the goods and labor market. *Produktivitet och räntabilitet* (Productivity and profitability, 1961) was Lundberg's major empirical work on economic growth. He emphasizes the importance of a microeconomic perspective for understanding the driving forces behind the process of growth, the role played by differences in profitability between firms, and the kind of economic growth that is connected with technological improvement rather than capital investments. The study became known mostly for its discussion of the so called 'Horndal effect', a concept denoting disembodied productivity increase without new investments. In *Instability and Economic Growth* (1968) he compares the business cycles and stabilization policies in a number of countries during the postwar era of growth. Lundberg here poses the question whether, in many cases, governmental stabilization measures may have actually been destabilizing. In *Ekonomiska kriser förr och nu* (Past and present economic crises, 1983) and *Kriserna och ekonomerna* (The crises and the economists, 1984) Lundberg explores the crisis of the 1970s and compares it with earlier ones, paying special attention to his own and other Swedish economists' role in the economic policy debates in the inter-war and post-war periods.

LARS PÅLSSON SYLL

See also:

Business Cycle Theory (I) and (II); Frisch, Ragnar; Haavelmo, Trygve; Interest, Theories of; Keynes, John Maynard; Kuznets, Simon; Myrdal, Gunnar; Ohlin, Bertil; Stockholm School of Economics; Wicksell, Knut.

Bibliography

Bagge, Gösta, Erik Lundberg and Ingvar Svennilson (1933), 'Wages in Sweden, 1860–1930. Part One', *Stockholm Economic Studies*, No 3a, London: P.S. King & Son.

Lundberg, Erik (1930), 'Om ekonomisk jämvikt' (Translated as 'On the Concept of Economic Equilibrium', in Lundberg, 1995), *Ekonomisk Tidskrift*, **32**, pp. 130–60.

Lundberg, Erik (1937), 'Studies in the Theory of Economic Expansion', *Stockholm Economic Studies*, **6**, London: P.S. King & Son.

Lundberg, Erik (1957), *Business Cycles and Economic Policy*, London: Allen & Unwin.

Lundberg, Erik (1961), *Produktivitet och räntabilitet* (Productivity and profitability), Stockholm: SNS.

Lundberg, Erik (1968), *Instability and Economic Growth*, New Haven, Conn.: Yale University Press.

Lundberg, Erik (1983), *Ekonomiska kriser förr och nu* (Past and present economic crises), Stockholm: SNS.

Lundberg, Erik (1984), *Kriserna och ekonomerna* (The crises and the economists), Malmö: Liber.

Lundberg, Erik (1995), *Studies in Economic Instability and Change* (selected writings from the 1930s to the 1980s), Stockholm: SNS.

Schumpeter, Joseph (1954), *A History of Economic Analysis*, London: Allen & Unwin.

Machlup, Fritz

Born in 1902, in Wiener Neustadt, Austria, Fritz Machlup received the degree of Doctor Rerum Politicarum from the University of Vienna in 1923. Because of his connection with Schumpeter, Machlup was one of many scholars from abroad who visited Harvard on Rockefeller fellowships during the second half of the 1930s. In 1935 he became professor of economics at the University of Buffalo, where he remained until 1947. From 1947 to 1960 he was the Hutzler Professor of Political Economy at Johns Hopkins University. In 1960, he moved to Princeton University as the Walker Professor of Economics, remaining until 1971 when, after retiring from Princeton, he began teaching at New York University. Fritz Machlup died in January 1983.

Possessing an extremely sharp intellect, he not only wrote more than two dozen books and over 200 articles but he significantly affected the lives and careers of many students who later became prominent economists. Robert Fogel, Nobel Laureate, who encountered Fritz Machlup at Johns Hopkins in the late 1950s, has indicated that Professor Machlup had a significant impact on his intellectual development (private conversation, December 1980). Many other former students have indicated as much (see chapters by Robert Eisner and Burton Malkiel in Jacob S. Dreyer, 1978).

Machlup's writing spanned a wide range of topics in economics as well as other related areas. In microeconomics, *The Economics of Sellers' Competition* (1952) provides one of the best discussions of duopoly theory as well as other aspects of the conduct of sellers. Machlup's 1955 work is a tutorial on how to determine the presence and extent of monopoly power. He defended the use of marginal analysis by economists when attempting to explain business behavior, even when the empirical evidence indicated that businesses did not pay attention to or understand marginal analysis.

In his presidential address to the American Economic Association in December 1966, Machlup returned to the debate concerning the correctness of using marginalism as the basis of a theory of firm behavior. Using the 'theoretical automobile driver' as a metaphor, Machlup noted that the marginalist theory of firm behavior did not always predict firm behavior accurately. Actual firm behavior, as indicated in the results of a survey of firms, support Machlup's contention. This debate was to continue in the profession for at least another decade.

His work on methodological issues is best captured in *Methodology of Economics and Other Social Sciences*, which is a collection of his articles that he published in 1978. That this volume was published as part of the Academic

Press's *Economic Theory, Econometrics and Mathematical Economics* series is a testament to the rigor maintained by Machlup while at the same time he remained true to the non-mathematical format of the Austrian School. Students of economics as well as other fields could benefit from reading these essays.

The Production and Distribution of Knowledge in the United States (1962) and *Education and Economic Growth* (1970a) are representative of Machlup's work in the economics of education. In the latter he describes the prospects of the rising cost of higher education. His forecast of an increase of 50 per cent between 1970 and 1980 was not far from the mark. Greater numbers of educated workers allow economies to grow, but the faster an economy grows the greater the cost of the educated worker. He argues that the technology of teaching will necessarily have to change by the year 2000 (Machlup, 1970, pp. 98–100).

During the international monetary crisis of the 1960s, Machlup wrote extensively on the distinction between the use of reserves and credit availability as mechanisms for providing international liquidity. In a series of articles that appeared in the *Banca Nazionale del Lavoro Quarterly Review* Machlup first argued for the necessity for reserves to grow with the volume of foreign trade, and for these reserves to be permanent. International provision of liquidity was necessary in light of the fact that the international gold stock was not growing steadily. This debate was settled with the creation of Special Drawing Rights (SDRs) by the International Monetary Fund in 1970. SDRs satisfied the dual criteria that Machlup discussed in his 1967 paper: newly created reserves were to be permanent and it would be desirable for them to be in the form of credit, to avoid the issues involved with deciding who receives the seigniorage. SDRs are open lines of credit that are allocated to the member countries on the basis of their quota. If used by a country, they must be paid back with interest: they are permanent and no seigniorage is created.

Throughout his life Machlup was a staunch defender of the individual's right of free speech, no matter what the point of view or topic. Robert Eisner's recounting of his days at Johns Hopkins as a Machlup student (Dreyer, 1978, p. 3) and Paul Samuelson's statement that 'Alone among the members of the Mt. Pelerin Society the name of Fritz Machlup stood out as one willing to incur personal cost to speak up for John Stuart Mill values' (Szenberg, 1992, p. 239) are testaments to the value Machlup attached to personal freedom and freedom of speech in particular. This statement is reiterated in a 1970 article in which Machlup indulged in another of his favorite topics, semantics. He says that 'There should be freedom of speech, even freedom of vague and ambiguous speech', when he is discussing the topic of exchange rate adjustment.

WILLIAM K. HUTCHINSON

See also:

Austrian School of Economics, The; Balance of Payments: Keynesian and Monetarist Approaches; Chicago School of Economics; Friedman, Milton; Schumpeter, Joseph A.; Viner, Jacob; von Hayek, Friedrich A.

Bibliography

Bitros, George (1976), *Selected Economic Writings of Fritz Machlup*, New York: New York University Press.

Dreyer, Jacob S. (ed.) (1978), *Breadth and Depth in Economics: Fritz Machlup – The Man and His Ideas*, Lexington, Mass.: D.C. Heath and Company.

Eisner, Robert (1978), 'Machlup on Academic Freedom', in Jacob S. Dreyer (ed.), *Breadth and Depth in Economics*, Lexington, Mass.: D.C. Heath and Company.

Machlup, Fritz (1952), *The Economics of Sellers' Competition*, Baltimore: The Johns Hopkins Press.

Machlup, Fritz (1955), *The Political Economy of Monopoly*, Baltimore: The Johns Hopkins Press.

Machlup, Fritz (1962), *The Production and Distribution of Knowledge in the United States*, Princeton: Princeton University Press.

Machlup, Fritz (1966), 'The Need for Moentary Reserves', *Banca Nazionale del Lavoro Quarterly Review*, **19**, (78), September, pp. 175–220.

Machlup, Fritz (1967), 'Credit Facilities or Reserve Allotments?', *Banca Nazionale del Lavoro Quarterly Review*, **20**, (81), June, pp. 135–56.

Machlup, Fritz (1970a), *Education and Economic Growth*, Lincoln: The University of Nebraska Press.

Machlup, Fritz (1970b), 'On Term, Concepts, Theories and Strategies in the Discussion of Greter Flexibility of Exchange Rates', *Banca Nazionale del Lavoro Quarterly Review*, **23**, 92, March, pp. 3–22.

Machlup, Fritz (1978), *Methodology of Economics and Other Social Sciences*, New York: Academic Press.

Szenberg, Michael (1992), *Eminent Economists: Their Life Philosophy*, Cambridge: Cambridge University Press.

Malinvaud, Edmond

Edmond Camille Malinvaud was born in 1923 in Limoges, France. He received his Diplôme Ecole Polytechnique and Diplôme Ecole Nat. de la Stat. et de l'Admin. Econ. in 1946 and 1948. While much of his career has been spent at the Institut National de la Statistique et des Etudes Economiques (INSEE) in Paris, where he became the director general in 1974, he has also held visiting and temporary posts in international administration and academia in French institutions, the University of California, Berkeley, and United Nations headquarters in Geneva.

Edmond Malinvaud has been an extremely influential economist, both in France and among economists in general. He has shown great mastery of the wide expanse of economics subject matter, writing many important papers in economic theory and widely used though advanced textbooks in microeconomics (*Lectures on Microeconomic Theory*, 1969) and in econometrics (*Statistical Methods of Econometrics*, 1980). Additionally he is an expert on the French economy (cf. *French Economic Growth*, 1972). His greatest contributions to economic thought, however, may well be judged by the profession to lie in his continuing study of the causes of unemployment. In this area he has increasingly turned to consideration of the phenomenon of 'mass unemployment', which has plagued both developed and developing countries even as industrialization has raised living standards.

In his frequently cited *The Theory of Unemployment Reconsidered* (1977), Malinvaud develops a theoretical rationing model which allows for general macroeconomic equilibrium with involuntary unemployment. He considers this a fixed-price equilibrium model rather than a disequilibrium model and is careful to separate his thinking on the question of persistent involuntary unemployment from that stemming from Barro and Grossman's 1971 disequilibrium model. Malinvaud distinguishes between three types of unemployment: frictional – the difference between registered labor force and effective labor supply; Keynesian – the share of unemployment attributable to deficient demand for goods; and classical – the balance of unemployment, which is therefore only indirectly linked with rationing; he believes it more precise to identify classical unemployment with the lack of productive capacity.

In his 1980 article, 'Macroeconomic Rationing of Unemployment', Malinvaud builds upon his 1977 book by trying to show 'why some recent theoretical developments provide a new vision of the major and essential contribution of J.M. Keynes: analysis of involuntary unemployment should first concentrate on the aggregate demand for goods' (p. 188). In this paper he attempts to bolster the Keynesian view that a 'theory of the short-term general equilibrium was needed and that Keynes had presented such a theory' (ibid.). He also argues that disaggregation is critical in identifying how different economic sectors face different disequilibrium constraints and therefore respond differently to macroeconomic policies. An economy can therefore be both Keynesian and classical simultaneously, both across sectors and clearly, therefore, in the labor market as a whole.

Malinvaud's next major work in this area, *Mass Unemployment* (1984), first continues his critique of the classical tradition in economics which essentially assumes away the phenomenon of involuntary unemployment. The book goes on to extend his earlier discussions of the distinction between Keynesian and classical unemployment and considers the role of profitability in economic growth, arguing that unemployment is often associated with profitability in both the short and the long term. This line of reasoning represents a significant departure from the Keynesian view that insufficient aggregate demand is the main cause of mass unemployment. Malinvaud argues instead that rising costs and decreased profitability cause insufficient capital formation and therefore mass unemployment is possible even when capacity utilization is high.

Malinvaud's most recent book in this subject area, *Diagnosing Unemployment* (1994; as with the first two books, written in 1977 and 1984, this book is a compiled set of lectures he was invited to give), considers the questions of how policy makers can identify what type of unemployment they are dealing with in an economy at a point in time – in this case, western European economies in the 1980s – and, once they have analysed unemployment, what policies are appropriate countermeasures. He argues that Keynes himself was highly pragmatic and case-oriented in his policy-making roles during the inter-war years, diagnosing and analysing each policy issue afresh as it arose, rather than attempting to fit all phenomena neatly into 'Keynesian theory' (Malinvaud, 1994, p. 6). In Chapter 5 of this book, Malinvaud discusses explicitly the various institutional factors in these economies that could cause both workers' lack of mobility and reduced economic incentives for taking a job or leaving the labor force, including changes in structural diversity and search duration. He concludes this chapter by expressing dissatisfaction about attributing increased unemployment to these two causes. In the final chapter, he turns to consideration of real wage inflexibility as the main cause of increased unemployment and again points out our lack of knowledge regarding the full set of causes of this apparent inflexibility. Malinvaud returns to his theme from the preceding book that understanding how the real wage 'reacts on the demand for goods and on both the volume and composition of the capital equipment' (ibid., p. 132) is critical for understanding real wage movements (or lack thereof) and laments the difficulty of understanding these relationships given existing data.

Judging by the large number of citations from this body of work, it is already clear that Malinvaud has had a significant effect on the direction research has taken within macroeconomics. Additionally, in this set of writings from the mid-1970s to the mid-1990s, Malinvaud has created a consistent and compelling research agenda which presents a challenge for the next generation of macroeconomists.

JOYCE P. JACOBSEN

See also:

Coordination Failures and Keynesian Economics; Economics of Keynes and of his Revolution, Key Elements of the; Grossman, Herschel, I., Microfoundations of Macroeconomics; New Classical School of Economics; New Keynesian Macroeconomics.

Bibliography

Barro, Robert J. and Herschel I. Grossman (1971), 'A General Disequilibrium Model of Income and Employment', *American Economic Review*, **61**, (1), March, pp. 82–93.

Carré, Jean-Jacques, Paul Dubois and Edmond Malinvaud (1972), *La Croissance Française: Un Essai D'Analyse Économique Causale de L'Après-Guerre* (trans. (1975) as *French Economic Growth*), Paris: Senil.

Champsaur, Paul (ed.) (1990), *Essays in Honor of Edmond Malinvaud*, three vols, Cambridge, Mass.: MIT Press.

Malinvaud, Edmond (1969), *Leçons de Théorie Microéconomique* (trans. (1972) as *Lectures on Microeconomic Theory*), Amsterdam: North-Holland.

Malinvaud, Edmond (1977), *The Theory of Unemployment Reconsidered*, New York: Wiley.

Malinvaud, Edmond (1980a), 'Macroeconomic Rationing of Unemployment', in Edmond Malinvaud and Jean-Paul Fitoussi (eds), *Unemployment in Western Countries*, New York: St Martin's Press.

Malinvaud, Edmond (1980b), *Statistical Methods of Econometrics*, 3rd rev. edn, trans. A. Silvey, Amsterdam: North-Holland.

Malinvaud, Edmond (1984), *Mass Unemployment*, New York: Basil Blackwell.

Malinvaud, Edmond (1994), *Diagnosing Unemployment*, New York: Cambridge University Press.

Markowitz, Harry M.

Harry M. Markowitz, the son of Morris and Mildred (Groben) Markowitz, was born in Chicago on 24 August 1927. He attended the University of Chicago, where he earned his BPh (1947), MA (1950) and PhD (1954). During the defense of his dissertation Friedman remarked that Markowitz should not be granted his degree because no matter how erudite and scholarly the dissertation the topic was not part of the discipline of economics. The committee chose to ignore Friedman's advice. In 1990, Markowitz was awarded the Nobel Prize in Economics for his work in the area of portfolio theory and, through the efforts of Baumol (1952), Tobin (1958) and Sharpe (1964), portfolio theory has become integrated into economics and finance courses throughout the world.

When he was 11, Markowitz read Darwin's *The Origin of Species* (1859) and was intrigued by the way that Darwin marshaled the facts to make his point about evolution. This led Markowitz to read other books – pieces of scientific literature and philosophy usually read by individuals who were older. After reading a piece by David Hume, Markowitz made Hume 'his' philosopher. As was the case with Darwin, Markowitz was struck by Hume's line of reasoning. In particular, Markowitz took to heart the idea that 'what is fact should be viewed as hypothesis' (Markowitz, 1993). No matter how many times an 'experiment' is performed, there is no guarantee that the next iteration will yield the same results. We live in a world which cannot be known with certainty.

From that statement, it is but a short step to Markowitz's innovation in the area of portfolio theory. While waiting to see one of his professors about the choice of a dissertation topic, Markowitz had a conversation with a businessperson about stock prices. His interest piqued, Markowitz began his investigations of portfolio theory. He began with John Burr Williams, who argued that the value of a stock is equal to the present value of the future dividend stream yielded by the stock (Williams, 1938). Because there is a time lag between when the decision to produce is made and when the output of the production process is sold, the price at the time of the sale may differ from the price which the producer had in mind when the decision to produce was made. To take into account the uncertainty associated with the sales price, Markowitz argued that the concept of expected value must be introduced into Williams's argument for computing the value of a stock. From Savage (1954) came two ideas: that 'a rational agent acting under uncertainty would act according to "probability beliefs" where no objective probabilities are known' (Markowitz, 1991); and that 'degrees of belief should be formalized in terms of the actions of a rational decision maker, i.e., a decision maker who is not omniscient, but makes no mistakes in logic or arithmetic' (Markowitz, 1993). Thus, when computing the value of a stock, one must be aware of at least two variables: the stock's expected rate of return and the stock's risk factor. From common practice comes the idea that if the future is certain then the optimal portfolio will contain a single asset. But since the future is uncertain investors diversify their holdings and have a diverse collection of assets whose rates of return and degrees of riskiness vary.

Markowitz set out to answer two questions: what are the characteristics of an optimal portfolio; and can a procedure be developed to identify such a portfolio? The constrained quadratic programming problem developed by Markowitz answered these two questions. Markowitz's solution revealed that there exists a set of portfolios which satisfy the constraint, and that a portfolio's rate of return is affected both by the variance and covariance of a given stock's rate of return relative to the individual rates of return of all stocks in the portfolio. Markowitz's approach to portfolio theory is different from Arrow's approach. Arrow preferred to develop a precise and general solution to this problem, whereas Markowitz 'wanted as good an approximation as could be implemented' (Arrow, 1963; Markowitz, 1991).

Two other aspects of Markowitz's economic activities must be noted. First, portfolio theory is not the only area of economics in which he has worked. Dynamic programming and its application to business is an area of great interest for Markowitz. Developing and providing practical solutions to business problems is an important niche for economists to fill. Second, since one should practice what one preaches, Markowitz has spent a great deal of his professional life working in the business sector.

A brief final comment on some of the differences in the ways Markowitz and Keynes define and use the terms 'risk' and 'uncertainty' is in order. In the three versions of the *Theory of Probability* (1907, 1908, 1921) Keynes devised a probability theory based on objective degrees of belief. For Keynes, 'probabilities are logical relationships between propositions and the information which support them and the degree of belief that one has in these relationships' (Bateman, 1990). These logical relationships may be expressed in the following manner: *a/h* = p, where *a* is the conclusion, *h* is premises and *p* is the resulting probability. Keynes articulated three categories of logical propositions: propositions that are either true (*a/h* = 1) or false (*a/h* = 0), propositions that are neither true nor false (0 < *a/h* < 1) and propositions where the probabilities are unknown. These categories are universal induction, statistical induction and uncertainty, respectively.

Keynes distinguished clearly between the concept of risk and the concept of uncertainty. He argued that the riskiness of an event implies that the individual has or can obtain information about *h*, and is able to induce a degree of belief about *a/h*. Thus when 0 < *a/h* < 1 there is risk associated with an event. Uncertainty, on the other hand, implies that the individual does not possess and cannot obtain information about *h* and therefore cannot induce a degree of belief about *a/h*. An example of uncertainty is: what is the likelihood of a war between Chile and the Republic of Palau in 1997. When confronted with uncertainty, individuals fall back on conventions (Keynes, 1936). This distinction between risk and uncertainty is not always clear in Markowitz or in Baumol (1952), Tobin (1958) and Sharpe (1964). Indeed there is a tendency to use the two terms interchangeably.

TOM CATE

See also:
Keynes and Probability; Sharpe, William F.

Bibliography
Arrow, Kenneth J. (1963), *Aspects of the Theory of Risk-Bearing*; reprinted 1971, Chicago: Markham Publishing Co.
Bateman, Bradley (1990), 'Keynes, induction and econometrics', *History of Political Economy*, **22**, (2), summer, pp. 359–80.
Baumol, William J. (1952), 'The Transactions Demand for Cash: An Inventory Theoretical Approach', *Quarterly Journal of Economics*, **66**, (4), November, pp. 545–56.
Darwin, Charles (1859), *The Origin of Species*; reprinted 1897, New York: D. Appleton and Company.
Keynes, John Maynard (1921), *Theory of Probability*, London: Macmillan.
Keynes, John M. (1936), *The General Theory of Employment, Interest and Money*, London: Macmillan.
Keynes, John Maynard (1983), *The Collected Writings of John Maynard Keynes*, ed. Donald Moggridge, vol. XII, *Economic Activities and Correspondence: Investment and Editorials*, New York: Cambridge University Press for the Royal Economic Society.
Markowitz, Harry M. (1952a), 'Portfolio Selection', *Journal of Finance*, **7**, (1), March, pp. 77–91.
Markowitz, Harry M. (1952b), 'The Utility of Wealth', *Journal of Political Economy*, **60**, (2), April, pp. 151–80.
Markowitz, Harry M. (1956), 'The Optimization of a Quadratic Function Subject to Linear Constraints', *Naval Research Logistics Quarterly*, **3**, (1), March, pp. 111–34.
Markowitz, Harry M. (1959), *Portfolio Selection: Efficient Diversification of Investment*, New York: Wiley and Sons.

Markowitz, Harry M. (1991), 'Foundations of Portfolio Theory', *Journal of Finance*, **42**, (2), June, pp. 469–77.

Markowitz, Harry M. (1993), 'Trains of Thought', *American Economist*, **37**, (1), spring, pp. 2–9.

Savage, L.J. (1954), *Foundations of Statistics*, New York: Wiley.

Sharpe, William F. (1964), 'Capital Asset Prices: A Theory of Market Equilibrium under Conditions of Risk', *Journal of Finance*, **19**, (3), September, pp. 425–42.

Tobin, James (1958), 'Liquidity Preference as Behaviour toward Risk', *Review of Economic Studies*, **25**, (2), February, pp. 65–86.

Varian, Hal (1993), 'A Portfolio of Nobel Laureates: Markowitz, Miller, Sharpe', *Journal of Economic Perspectives*, **7**, (1), winter, pp. 159–69.

Williams, John Burr (1938), *The Theory of Investment Value*, Cambridge, Mass.: Harvard University Press.

Marshall, Alfred

Marshall was the founder of the Cambridge School of Economics, which rose to world eminence in the inter-war years, and the teacher of two of its leading figures, A.C. Pigou and J.M. Keynes. He was born at Bermondsey, a London suburb, on 26 July 1842, the second son of William Marshall (1812–1901), a clerk at the Bank of England. The family resided in the pleasanter suburb of Clapham during most of Marshall's youth and his early education was completed at the venerable Merchant Taylors' School, where he revealed a talent for mathematics. Entering St John's College, Cambridge, in 1862, he prepared for Cambridge University's highly competitive Mathematical Tripos, emerging in 1865 in the distinguished position of 'second wrangler' and being made a fellow of his college. His interests having turned to the philosophical and psychological bases of human behavior and social organization, his college made him a lecturer in moral science in 1868. His teaching responsibilities for the Moral Science Tripos included political economy, for which he soon displayed a marked aptitude. By 1870, he had adopted this subject as his life's work, convinced that schemes for social amelioration and reform must be based upon a firm grasp of economic consequences and constraints.

During the early 1870s, Marshall clearly established his authority as the leading teacher of his subject in Cambridge, but published little. Marriage in 1877 to his one-time unofficial student, Mary Paley (1850–1944) required Marshall to resign his fellowship. Exile in Bristol, where administrative duties at the new University College proved irksome, and ill-health limited his activities, brought him to the attention of Benjamin Jowett, the redoubtable Master of Balliol, and Marshall moved to Balliol College, Oxford, in 1883. But in January 1885, he returned to Cambridge as professor of political economy, Henry Fawcett the incumbent having died unexpectedly. Marshall held this chair until his voluntary retirement in 1908. His tenure was marked by a persistent and sometimes undiplomatic struggle to increase the scope and resources for teaching his subject and attracting able students to it. His success was limited. Even when he succeeded in 1903 in gaining establishment of a specialized Economics Tripos, resources and students remained meagre. But his efforts sowed the seeds from which the Cambridge School blossomed after his retirement. Despite his frequent complaints about the paucity of able students, Marshall did attract to economics some distinguished followers, including H.S. Foxwell and J.N. Keynes (father of J.M.) from the 1870s and A.W. Flux, A.L. Bowley, S.J. Chapman, J.H. Clapham, D.H. Macgregor, A.C. Pigou, J.M. Keynes, C.R. Fay and W.T. Layton from the later period.

Marshall's retirement years were spent laboring to complete long-delayed literary plans, an ambition only partly realized. He died at Balliol Croft, his Cambridge home of many years, on 13 July 1924. His devoted wife, who had co-authored Marshall's first book, *Economics of Industry* (1879), survived him by 20 years, blossoming anew in widowhood as 'tutelary goddess' of Cambridge's Marshall Library of Economics. She had taught economics at Bristol, and subsequently for many years at Newnham College, Cambridge, but any literary ambitions she may have had were sacrificed to shielding her hypersensitive husband from domestic vexations and serving as his editorial assistant.

Marshall's characteristic ideas on economics had been well developed in the early 1870s, but relatively little was in print until the appearance of *Principles of Economics* in 1890. This work was widely acclaimed and cemented Marshall's international reputation. The book introduced or popularized many familiar and still-invoked concepts: partial equilibrium, period analysis, consumer surplus, demand elasticity, derived demand, and so on, but such a list hardly exhausts the many strands woven into this complex, challenging and still stimulating work. The book was extensively revised through eight editions, the last in 1920, but plans to add a second volume never materialized. Britain's tariff controversy turned Marshall in 1903 to questions of international competition and industrial structure, a project only half completed in his *Industry and Trade* (1919). His unsatisfactory last book, *Money Credit and Commerce* (1923) attempted to rescue some of his earlier and never published work on money and international trade.

Maynard Keynes attended Marshall's lectures in 1905–6, while preparing for the civil service examination, but his return to lecture in Cambridge occurred only upon Marshall's retirement in 1908, although Marshall had certainly encouraged him and had formed a high opinion of his potential as an economist. The two remained in fairly frequent contact until Marshall's last days and were closely allied in a 1909–10 controversy about the effects of parents' alcoholism on their offspring, Karl Pearson being the main opponent. Keynes wrote his splendid memoir of Marshall within a few weeks of the latter's death and a charming later one on Mary Marshall.

Keynes must have been quite familiar with the ideas of the *Principles*, while his early monetary work doubtless owed much to the Marshallian monetary tradition, partly oral. (Eshag, 1963, supplies useful background.) Besides *Money Credit and Commerce*, Marshall's important monetary publications were his 1887 essay, 'Remedies for Fluctuations of General Prices' (reprinted, with other occasional writings, in Pigou, 1925) and his oral evidence of 1887–8 and 1899 to government enquiries into currency matters (reprinted, with other official contributions, in Keynes, 1926).

Marshall's biography is covered in detail in Groenewegen (1995) and his correspondence (including all extant correspondence with Maynard Keynes) in Whitaker (1996). Whitaker (1975) reproduces Marshall's early manuscripts and the privately printed 'Pure Theory' chapters of 1879. A virtually comprehensive list of Marshall's publications is appended to Pigou (1925).

JOHN WHITAKER

See also:

Classical Economics; Keynes, John Maynard; Keynes, John N.; Marshall and Keynes; Pigou, Arthur C.; Quantity Theory of Money.

Bibliography

Eshag, Eprime (1963), *From Marshall to Keynes: An Essay on the Monetary Theory of the Cambridge School*, Oxford: Basil Blackwell.

Groenewegen, Peter D. (1995), *A Soaring Eagle: Alfred Marshall 1842–1924*, Aldershot: Edward Elgar.

Guillebaud, Claude W. (ed.) (1961), *Alfred Marshall's Principles of Economics: Ninth (Variorum) Edition*, London: Macmillan.

Keynes, John M. (1924), 'Alfred Marshall, 1842–1924', *Economic Journal*, **34**, (135), September, pp. 311–72 (reprinted with minor changes in Pigou (1925) and in the various editions of Keynes's *Essays in Biography*).

Keynes, John M. (ed.) (1926), *Official Papers of Alfred Marshall*, London: Macmillan.

Keynes, John M. (1944), 'Mary Paley Marshall (1850–1944)', *Economic Journal*, **54**, (214), June–September, pp. 268–84.

Marshall, Alfred (1890), *Principles of Economics*, London: Macmillan.

Marshall, Alfred (1919), *Industry and Trade*, London: Macmillan.

Marshall, Alfred (1923), *Money Credit and Commerce*, London: Macmillan.

Marshall, Alfred and Mary P. Marshall (1879), *Economics of Industry*, London: Macmillan.

Pigou, Arthur C. (ed.) (1925), *Memorials of Alfred Marshall*, London: Macmillan.

Whitaker, John K. (ed.) (1975), *Early Economic Writings of Alfred Marshall, 1869–1890*, London: Macmillan.

Whitaker, John K. (ed.) (1996), *The Correspondence of Alfred Marshall, Economist*, Cambridge: Cambridge University Press.

Marshall and Keynes

Keynes's Marshallian heritage has been emphasized in many rehabilitations of Keynes's economics (Leijonhufvud, 1968; Clower, 1989). The nature and extent of the heritage has, however, been less satisfactorily documented, with important consequences for Keynes scholarship. Examples include Joan Robinson's (1962, p. 79) claim that Keynes had never mastered the theory of value (a story derived from Shove and already rebutted by Keynes's official biographer, Harrod, 1951, pp. 323–5) and recent biographical studies of Keynes (Moggridge, 1992; Skidelsky, 1983, 1992) which inadequately portray the depth of the Marshall–Keynes relationship. Its chronology, an indispensable foundation for assessing the intellectual links between Keynes's and Marshall's work, draws on the preserved record, not least of which are the 50 letters between the two which survive (41 from Marshall and 9 from Keynes).

When Keynes first met Marshall is not known. The young Maynard would have seen Marshall from an early age as a visitor to Harvey Road when Marshall called on his father, John Neville Keynes, to discuss university and faculty business (Groenewegen, 1995, pp. 682–6). Maynard Keynes himself recalled attending dinner parties at Balliol Croft, the Marshalls' residence, which can be dated from 1904 or not long after he had turned 21 years of age. From the time Keynes graduated as 'twelfth wrangler' until Marshall's death, the considerable contact between the two Cambridge men falls into three phases. The first covers the 12 months from June 1905 to mid-1906, when Marshall tried to lure Keynes to attempt the second part of his Economics Tripos. The second covers the period from 1908 to 1914, when Keynes was an economics lecturer at Cambridge. The years of World War I form a third period, when contact was largely by letter. There is also a fourth period of contact. It lasted for the two years from May 1924 when Keynes visited Marshall at the start of Marshall's 'final illness', so lovingly described in a letter to Lydia (Hill and Keynes, 1989, p. 195). He then wrote his obituary memoir of Marshall (Keynes, 1972), assisted Pigou in editing the *Memorials* (Pigou, 1925) and edited Marshall's *Official Papers* for the Royal Economic Society (Marshall, 1926, p. v). This posthumous contact is particularly important since it enabled Keynes to acquaint himself with the whole of Marshall's *œuvre*.

Keynes enrolled formally in Marshall's economics classes in October 1905. His enrolment card, prepared in accordance with Marshall's long-standing practice (reproduced in facsimile in Groenewegen, 1988, p. 667), shows his intention to attempt Part II of the Economics Tripos and the amount of economics reading he by then claimed to have accomplished. Keynes's idea of attempting the tripos was not abandoned until well into December 1905, that is, after completing Marshall's October term classes, including essays which Marshall set as a regular part of his teaching. Keynes also took Marshall's advanced lectures and, on his own account (Keynes, 1972, p. 216), Marshall's Lent Term lectures on money. Together, these elements provided a solid introduction to the subject, and one sufficient, according to Marshall (letter to Keynes, 2 May 1906, in *Collected Writings of John Maynard Keynes*,

XV, p. 2) for him to get 'probably' a first class result, if he sat the examination. Marshall's comments on Keynes's essays (many of which are preserved among the Keynes papers) show how highly Marshall thought of his new pupil and that he repeatedly tried to get Keynes to become an economist, preferably by joining the small, enthusiastic band of Cambridge economics teachers. Successful completion of Part II of the tripos would have given Keynes formal qualifications similar to those of Pigou. Hence it is incorrect to suggest that Keynes never received formal training in economics. Furthermore Keynes's essays, together with the scope and contents of Marshall's 1905–6 lectures as disclosed by Layton's lecture notes (preserved in Trinity College, Cambridge) show that Keynes had a very thorough introduction to all the principles of economics. This enabled him to cooperate with Pigou on bargaining diagrams which formed the appendix to Pigou's 1905 book, *Industrial Peace*, and which Collard (1981, p. 107) has described as 'an astonishing early collaboration'.

The second stage in the Marshall–Keynes relationship covers Keynes's initial period as an economics lecturer at Cambridge (1908–14). This period produced the bulk of the surviving Marshall–Keynes correspondence, much of it generated by the Pearson controversy in which Marshall and Keynes were actively involved for much of the second half of 1910 (Skidelsky, 1983, pp. 223–6; Moggridge, 1992, pp. 205–7; Groenewegen, 1995, pp. 479–82). Marshall's nurturing role during Keynes's early teaching experience can be mentioned first. Keynes's lecturing included teaching general economic principles and his preserved papers indicate that for his first set of lectures in 1909 he drew extensively on the notes he had taken from Marshall's classes three years previously. The controversy with Karl Pearson over the effects of alcoholic parents on their offspring is the best documented case of Marshall's influence, but correspondence offers additional insights on why Keynes later claimed that Marshall, rather than Pigou, had made him into an economist (cf. Vaizey, 1976, for an assessment of the significance of this). Correspondence indicates Marshall's intention of transferring some of his books at this stage to Keynes's custody, on behalf of the Economics Board (the original name for the Faculty) and for Keynes's own use (Marshall to Maynard Keynes, 26 February, 30 May and 4 December 1909). Another letter mentions Marshall's extended loan to Keynes of his copy of Rau (with its supply and demand curves), an occasion used by Marshall to provide Keynes with anecdotes about Marshall's associations with Jenkin. A subsequent letter discusses Cunynghame's hyperbola drawing machine presented to the Cambridge Philosophical Society in 1873 with a paper on its usefulness by Marshall (Marshall to Keynes, 12 December 1910). The correspondence also reveals the growing intimacy between the two men. Examples are congratulatory postcards and letters from Marshall on Keynes's appointment to the Girdlers' lectureship and to the Indian Currency Commission (Marshall to Keynes, 14 June 1910, 12 April 1913) and his pleasure at the role Keynes was playing in the local Eugenics Society (Marshall to Keynes, 18 May 1911). The letters reveal the range and intensity of the Marshall–Keynes connection during this stage of Keynes's academic career.

Marshall's contact with Keynes during World War I and its aftermath marks the third phase in their relationship. More than a dozen letters from Marshall to Keynes are preserved for this period, some reprinted in the *Memorials* (Pigou, 1925, pp. 481–3). They deal with aspects of war finance through increased taxation, through overseas borrowings in the United States and its implications, and through the sale of requisitioned United Kingdom-owned United States investments. They also contain a compulsory savings plan to tap the high earnings of young male workers, a proposal inspired 'by a message from Lavington sent thro' Pigou' (Marshall to Keynes, 14 October, 25 October and 15 November 1915). Most interesting is a letter from Marshall outlining a scheme of punitive taxation for those unwilling to go to the front though not domestically employed in occupations essential to the war effort (Marshall to Keynes, 29 December 1915). What Keynes thought of this proposal has not been recorded. However its thrust would have sat uneasily with the actions of several of his Bloomsbury friends who avoided the war by escaping to light agricultural duties in the countryside. The war correspondence ends with letters (9 and 12 June 1917) congratulating Keynes on his award of the CB and exhorting him to continue with his administrative work, made so valuable to the country by Keynes's economic skills. Letters in 1920 (29 January) and 1923 belatedly thanked Keynes for sending Marshall his *Economic Consequences of the Peace* and *Tract on Monetary Reform*. The 1923 letter also hinted at Marshall's imminent death: 'I am soon to go away, but if I have the opportunity I shall ask newcomers to the celestial region, whether you have succeeded in finding a remedy for currency maladies' (Marshall to Keynes, 19 December 1923). On 13 July 1924, Marshall died, Keynes having paid his last visit to his teacher the previous May.

The two years after Marshall's death, busy though they were for Keynes with other activities, nevertheless involved him to a considerable extent in matters relating to Marshall. First came Marshall's obituary memoir for the *Economic Journal*, completed in two months and assisted by meetings with, and written recollections from, Mary Paley Marshall and examination of the Marshall papers. How thoroughly Keynes studied these can only be inferred partly from the Memoir's actual contents. Whether, for example, it covered study of Marshall's research notes on stock exchange speculation would be interesting to know, given their recent scrutiny by Dardi and Gallegati (1992). The memoir also drew on Keynes's knowledge of Cambridge University history, his father's diaries, his own correspondence and personal friendship with Marshall, other friends of Marshall such as Edgeworth and inquiries he himself initiated to shed light on aspects of Marshall's life.

Keynes's role in Pigou's editing task of the *Memorials* cannot be identified beyond Pigou's general acknowledgement in its preface that Keynes 'shared ... the more general work of making this tribute to our Master' (Pigou, 1925, p. v). Keynes's cooperation certainly involved him in revising his *Memoir* (which opened the volume) to accommodate comments he had received from its readers acquainted with Marshall. If Keynes assisted in reading proofs, he would have reviewed most of Marshall's published essays. Keynes's more significant editorial was editing Marshall's *Official Papers* for the Royal Economic Society. This coincided with the start on *Treatise on Money*, undoubtedly refreshing memories about Marshall's rich evidence to Royal Commissions. Keynes had savoured this first as a student, and praised its great originality in the Marshall *Memoir* (Keynes, 1972, pp. 189–95). The *Treatise* cited *Official Papers* on five occasions, all concerned with the market rate of interest. The *General Theory*, as Robertson (1936, p. 178, n.1) explicitly noted in his review of the book, failed to mention the evidence from *Official Papers*, 'for so many years in Cambridge the basis of exposition on this subject'.

Grasping the nature of the Marshall–Keynes relationship more fully allows a better appreciation of the Marshallian content in Keynes's own work, including the *General Theory*. It also enables assessment of the ramifications of Marshall's thinking into Keynes's wider social and political thought. Some illustrations follow. These draw on Keynes's *General Theory* and focus briefly on visible Marshallian content in Keynes's outlines for planned works which he never had time to start (O'Donnell, 1992). Similarities in methodological outlook apparent in Keynes's Marshall *Memoir* (Keynes, 1972) are noted first.

The general characteristics of Marshall's economics highlighted by Keynes are its practical nature: 'the whole point lies in applying the bare bones of economic theory to the interpretation of current economic life' (Keynes, 1972, p. 196). This quality also gives economics its transitory nature, because the 'profound knowledge of actual facts of industry and trade' are constantly and rapidly changing (ibid., p. 196), as was so strikingly illustrated in Marshall's own *Industry and Trade* (ibid., p. 228). Economics was therefore 'far from a settled affair – like grammar or algebra – which had to be learnt, not criticised', to use Sanger's words, which Keynes approvingly quoted (ibid., p. 223). This implied the importance of developing an engine of analysis rather than a body of settled principles. Such an engine had to be capable of organizing and selecting relevant facts and assisting the discovery of solutions to actual problems. It should be emphasized in the quite different world of economics in the 1990s that this meant that determinate solutions to theoretical problems had relatively little importance in Marshall's foundations of economics. He was interested in comprehending an actual economic situation in order to try to grasp the economic and social mechanisms by which certain desirable social and economic consequences over the longer period could be achieved. Facts went hand-in-hand with theory. Application was as essential as explanation. The final chapter of Book I of the *Principles* illustrates Marshall's economic philosophy to perfection.

The engine that Marshall built in those *Principles* enabled him to deal with the particular in terms of the general; to explain a wide range of economic issues by the sophisticated analytical armoury that he brought into action under the rubric of the theory of value or, more broadly, the theory of supply and demand. In this context, Marshall's theory of supply and demand should not be narrowly conceived in terms of stable functions of price. These were only a minor part of the analytical apparatus, despite the attention lavished on their detail by some of his early pupils. Marshall used supply and demand as shorthand for the major forces in economic and social life: wants and activities, production and consumption, to use his terminology for variously titling Books III and IV. These categories were capable of assisting in explanations of the theory of relative prices and the theory of factor prices, the theory of output and the theory of employment, the theory of money and the theory of crises, the theory of taxes and the theory of trade. They were to be seen as drawer labels in the filing cabinet for storing and classifying relevant detail. They had to be handled with the greatest of care because they needed *ceteris paribus* clauses with respect to time, interdependence, space and institutions; for a person is a poor economist, Marshall remarked (1920, p. 368), who claims to find the theory of value easy. In building his apparatus for the mind, Marshall was searching for the holy grail of the ability to discover temporary, relevant truths. He never looked for timeless, universal, equilibrium positions, useful though these could be in devising preliminary and exploratory strategies for analysis. Economics was a way of thinking, not a fund of ready-made conclusions and propositions.

Keynes's sympathy with his program is clear from the introduction he wrote for the *Cambridge Economic Handbooks*, whose publication commenced in the early 1920s (Keynes, 1922, pp. v–vi). Although this paid homage to both Marshall and Pigou as the persons who have 'chiefly influenced Cambridge thought for the past fifty years', it was Marshall's influence which stayed dominant so far as Keynes was concerned. Keynes's emphasis on the virtue of economics' relative imprecision contrasts sharply with the formal mathematization in which Pigou liked to indulge when writing theory and in presenting those parts of Marshall's system which were left purposefully untidy and allusive in a way which made them unambiguous, precise, clear and, often enough, banal (Vaizey, 1976). This difference in style was already apparent in Marshall's and Pigou's lectures when Layton and Keynes attended them. Moreover Pigou's attempts at tidying Marshall's theory by simplification annoyed Marshall personally on several recorded occasions (Marshall to Pigou, 12 April 1916, in Pigou, 1925, pp. 43–4; Bharadwaj, 1972). The difference creates a substantial wedge between Marshall and the Marshallians, particularly those who developed Pigou's neat theorems, whose actual foundations in the volumes of Marshall's principles and applied economics were invariably qualified in the way Marshall himself had left them to his students. Pigou never absorbed Marshall's message on method, conceptualization, the nature of abstraction, style and vision: parts of Marshall's economic legacy which Keynes found attractive and emphasized, not only in his tribute to Marshall, but in the practice of his own work. Keynes tentatively acknowledged this in his preface to the Japanese edition of the *General Theory*. It clearly differentiated Marshall from his immediate followers on the subject of the need to construct a theory of output and consumption as a whole (Keynes, 1936, 1973a, p. xxix).

This Marshallian methodological legacy is visible in the *General Theory*, which uses important parts of Marshall's analytical engine. One of these is Marshall's limited emphasis on the virtues of market clearing as compared with Pigou, and his hesitancy in applying the supply and demand apparatus to labor and capital markets. Secondly, Marshall's analysis was far more aware of the monetary nature of economic life, despite the explicit intention to omit such monetary considerations from his *Principles*. However Marshall drew attention to the dangers from this omission in matters like the rate of interest (Marshall, 1920, pp. 593–5) while his concluding paragraph in the *Principles* alerted readers to the provisional nature of its contents. The first volume was unable to reach 'practical conclusions', because 'nearly every economic issues depends, more or less directly, on some complex actions and reactions of credit, of foreign trade, and of modern developments of combination and monopoly' (ibid., p. 722).

It can also be argued that Marshall's main engine of analysis, broadly presented as the theory of supply and demand, played a major part in the conceptual apparatus of the *General Theory*. After all, its key elements were aggregate supply and demand, with the supply analysis totally Marshallian in its conception. Supply and demand as broadly conceived are also embodied in many of the key variables of the analysis, even though sometimes in startlingly new dress (for example, in the theory of interest). Moreover, given Marshall's feelings about the transitory nature of economic principles and his acceptance of the fact that texts like his *Principles* had the inevitable fate of becoming 'waste paper' (Marshall to Fay, 23 February 1915, in Pigou, 1925, pp. 489–90), it is doubtful whether he would have been as upset about Keynes's treatment of part of his theory as some of his indirect pupils were. Marshall may in fact even have welcomed Keynes's treatment as a solution to the conundrum of his implicit supply and demand analysis of the capital market, with its ambiguities in labeling the horizontal axis and his doubts about portraying saving as a simple increasing function of the rate of interest.

Marshall's critical perspective on mathematical economics was fully captured in Keynes's (1972, pp. 185–8), which also recognized Marshall's claim to being 'the founder of modern diagrammatic economics'. Keynes's account drew on the preface to the first edition of the *Principles* (Marshall, 1920, pp. x–xi) where Marshall suggested such criticisms and expressed a qualified preference for diagrams if they were used for illustrative purposes or for self-clarification. Ten years previously, Marshall had made this point to Edgeworth, arguing that 'curves' were to be preferred to algebra because 'they bear more obviously on the science of statistics' (Marshall to Edgeworth, 28 March 1880). Keynes's reluctance to use diagrams in the *General Theory* is well known; the one diagram in that book was 'suggested' to him by Harrod after prolonged debate (Keynes, 1936, 1973a, p. 180 n.1; Keynes, 1973b, p. 558). Even then, as a loyal Marshall pupil, Keynes told Harrod that such a diagram could never constitute a theory of interest.

Keynes's criticism of econometrics in correspondence with Harrod and Tinbergen has been frequently elaborated. However its association with Marshall deserves some discussion. Their joint assault on Pearson had been highly critical of the regression techniques which Pearson was employing on social data, and had induced Marshall to tell Keynes about similar methodological criticisms which he had heard Todhunter make. Marshall expanded on such criticisms in correspondence with H.L. Moore. His random dips into Moore's *Laws of Wages* told him that

> no important economic chain of events seems likely to be associated with any one cause so predominantly that a study of the concomitant variations of the two can be made as well by mathematics, as by a comparison of a curve representing these two elements with a large number of other curves representing their operative causes: the '*caeteris paribus*' clause – though formally adequate seems to me impracticable. [Secondly] nearly a half of the whole operative economic causes have refused as yet to be tabulated statistically.

Over long periods of time, results from this method were particularly dangerous. Marshall later wrote Moore (15 December 1921) that he had tried to solve issues of interrelating many variables during the 1870s by means of statistical data recorded in his Red Book. This contained, on an annual basis for both the nineteenth and earlier centuries, consecutive statistics of basic economic variables, political and other events, and by this means he had tried to obtain '*a posteriori* results by the method of concomitant variations ... The result was that I found the depth of my ignorance as to the relations between the development of different economic phenomena to be even greater than I had supposed, and that is saying much.'

The methodological empathy between Marshall and Keynes, far greater than that existing between Keynes and Pigou, undoubtedly owed much to their close relationship over the last two decades of Marshall's life. As Keynes wrote in the context of Pigou's Marshall memorial lecture (Hill and Keynes, 1989, p. 241), Pigou had failed to grasp this strong side of Marshall's methodological work, an aspect which Keynes had highlighted in his own appreciation of Marshall. Keynes of course went much beyond Marshall's position, but he shared Marshall's strong distrust of theory for theory's sake, his love for facts and his aim of the practical nature of economic science.

Keynes's treatment of Marshall in the *General Theory* provides further illustrations of the empathy existing between the two which rarely seems to have existed between Keynes and Pigou (Keynes's brief cooperation with Pigou in 1905 on *Principles and Methods of Industrial Peace* is an interesting exception). This is not to say that Marshall escaped criticism in the *General Theory*. From his general perspective, Keynes correctly ranked Marshall with his 'classical' economists (Keynes, 1936, 1973a, p. 3, n.), criticized Marshall for his fundamental adherence to Say's Law (ibid., pp. 19–21), condemned him for excessive emphasis on the virtues of thrift (ibid., p. 242) and, perhaps less justifiably, criticized Marshall's view on the equilibrating role of the rate of interest in the capital market (ibid., pp. 175–6, 186–8). This was mild criticism compared to that given to Pigou. Despite this, Keynes's treatment of Marshall greatly pained Robertson (1935, pp. 504–6 offers a splendid example) as an unwarranted attack, a statement reiterated by Pigou (1953, esp. pp. 33–5). Keynes's critique of Marshall's interest theory is undoubtedly the weakest part of the *General Theory* condemnation of the 'master'. However, even in this context, Keynes was invariably careful to note the ambiguities and complexities in Marshall's treatment, pointing out that the mature Marshall was far too clever to be pinned down on specific fallacies and logical errors (Keynes, 1936, 1973a, p. 20, n.1). Examples include a remark (ibid., pp. 186–8) where attention is drawn to Marshall's implicit assumption that income cannot be held constant when discussing issues of capital theory including the rate of interest and that, in Marshall's treatment of the capital market, interest is only associated with 'free capital' or liquid resources. Moreover Keynes also drew attention to his agreement with Marshall on quasi-rent and efficiency earnings (ibid., p. 139) while he fully acknowledged that the mature Alfred Marshall could never be caught on simple statements of belief in Say's Law (ibid., pp. 191–21). For Keynes of course, the mature Marshall was somebody whom he had personally encountered; which was not the case for more dogmatic 'defenders of Marshall' such as Robertson.

There is much real praise of Marshall in the *General Theory* on significant points. Although Marshall and Pigou are bracketed at one stage in critical comments on their definition of national dividend (Keynes, 1936, 1973a, pp. 37–8), only Pigou is cited by direct reference on the subject. Twenty pages later Marshall is effectively exonerated: Keynes's 'definition of *net income* comes very close to Marshall's definition of *income*, when he decided to take refuge in the practice of the Income Tax Commissioners' (ibid., p. 59), as the realistic Marshall of course generally tended to do. Keynes also saw closer similarities between his use of supplementary cost and Marshall's conception as compared with that of Pigou (ibid., p. 56) while on 'user cost' Marshall's admittedly incomplete treatment is also, albeit implicitly, favorably compared with Pigou's (ibid., p. 72). Keynes (ibid., p. 139) saw his definition of marginal efficiency of capital as 'fairly close to what Marshall intended to mean by the term' and Marshall's treatment of quasi-rent provided many of the essentials for Keynes's analysis. On another capital-theoretic issue, Marshall is favorably quoted in Keynes's criticism of the 'Böhm-Bawerk proposition that roundabout processes are always "physically efficient"' (ibid., p. 214 and n.1). Even on mercantilism, Marshall's statement is considered 'not altogether unsympathetic', as can be seen from Marshall's treatment of the subject in *Industry and Trade* (1919, pp. 719–48). However Marshall remained sufficiently 'classical' (in Keynes's sense of the word) to deny that protection could lower unemployment, as explicitly stated in his *Fiscal Policy of International Trade*, which Keynes had edited for inclusion in *Official Papers* (Marshall, 1926; for example, pp. 389–91).

The penultimate paragraph of Keynes's Marshall *Memoir* (1972, p. 231) drew attention to the fact that Marshall's last two years were partly devoted to an attempt at constructing a final volume dealing 'with the possibility of social advance'. At one time, Marshall had described this intention to his wife as writing a twentieth-century Plato's *Republic*, a sketch of an Utopia, in which the ideal was to be blended with the realities that made achievement difficult. Marshall's sharply declining powers of concentration and memory from 1922 onwards meant that the task effectively got no further than a bundle of scrappy notes. These contained various outlines, sketches for some of the chapters, and various reflections on the characteristics of 'utopias'. Whether Keynes gleaned the information about this project from Mary Paley Marshall, the preface of *Money, Credit and Commerce* (Marshall, 1923, p. vi) or from a perusal of these notes in the Marshall papers during the months after Marshall's death is not clear. What is clear is that some time during the early 1920s Keynes himself was sketching an outline of essays on the 'Economic Future of the World', a project to which his mind was probably turned by the pessimistic outlook for humanity during the aftermath of World War I (O'Donnell, 1992, pp. 778–81, 806).

Marshall's interests in this type of topic had been long-standing. As Keynes had argued in his *Memoir* (Keynes, 1972, pp. 170–71), Marshall's need to understand the economic constraints on the possibilities for social progress had driven him initially to study political economy in the second half of the 1860s. Marshall's enduring loyalty to this basic aim in economic study is visible from at least part of the opening chapter of the *Principles*, concerned as it is with alleviating, and ultimately removing, the human degradation involved in poverty. Moreover the high theme of progress, an almost inevitable consequence of human evolution, permeates substantial sections of the book.

'Aims for the future' was suggested as a separate book for the second volume of the *Principles* as projected to Macmillan in 1887 (Whitaker, 1990, p. 195); and one which, although omitted from the 1903 outline of that volume (ibid., p. 201), resurfaced when the final volumes actually started to take shape. By his eightieth year, Marshall transformed a separate volume on the future into the more realistic project of reprinting earlier essays dealing with functions of government and possibilities for social advance. However the nature of this abandoned volume remains visible. Preserved outlines give a clear indication of the form it was intended to take (see Whitaker, 1990, p. 217, for an example).

Fragments held in the Marshall Library give more vividly the flavor of Marshall's ideas on progress which he wished to include in the final volume. Examples of his ideals include 'work for all intelligent but not carried to the length to exhaust the nervous energies'; and 'true human progress', described as 'an advance in capacity for feeling and for thought', needed sustenance from 'vigorous enterprise and energy'. Risk taking was crucial to all human progress, a problem for socialism when risk taking was a quality difficult to achieve in nationalized industries with bureaucratic management. Hence government enterprise is only supportable 'when it can make a strong prima facie case for efficiency and economy' (for a larger sample, see Groenewegen, 1995, pp. 726–30).

Marshall's brief and varied hints on future economic progress and ideals compare interestingly with Keynes's projected essay on the 'Economic Future of the World' (reproduced in O'Donnell, 1992, p. 806) even if much of this outline can be traced to Keynes's own work immediately before, and after, World War I (ibid., pp. 779–80). Its segments on population, the Malthusian specter and eugenics derive from recurring themes in Keynes's writing of the early 1920s, and from 1912 lecture notes dealing with factors influencing labor supply. The last have a strong Marshallian flavor, given the attention Marshall had lavished on the topic in Books IV and VI of the *Principles*. The same can be said about parts of Keynes's outline dealing with equality and inequality in progress broadly conceived, the need to curtail great fortunes, the psychology of reward and incentives and the need to examine a theoretical socialist framework in order to preserve its good, humanistic values while at the same time not eliminating those of the values of capitalism so essential to economic progress. Such sentiments are very visible in Marshall's extant notes on economic progress and ideals, just as earlier, but in a more restrained way, they had been published in his 'Social Possibilities of Economic Chivalry' (1907).

Marshallian sentiments from these sources are likewise replicated in the projects Keynes was developing in the mid-1920s in his outlines for 'Prolegomena to a New Socialism' and a 'Critical Examination of Capitalism' (O'Donnell, 1992, pp. 781–93, 806–12). The thrust of Keynes's new socialism lay in the end of laissez faire, the theme on which Keynes published a famous essay in 1926 (Keynes, 1931, pp. 312–22), one of the few major outcomes in print from these projects. It associated the individualism of laissez faire with the 'technical superiority of small units in certain cases', possessive 'instincts of risk-taking … [and] of avarice and hoarding' and a 'criterion of profit' for which any new system should 'preserve opportunities'. These qualities gave it superiority over the state. However, such 'alleged disadvantages of the State [became] equally disadvantages of the large scale entrepreneur using other people's money' under the joint stock system which separated ownership from control and developed general bureaucratic tendencies (cf. ibid., pp. 314–15). The 'large' this brought with it for business organization appeared to both Keynes and Marshall as not necessarily beautiful and efficient. Marshall, after all, had adopted such notions to deal with his so-called 'Cournot problem', or the possibility of increasing returns destroying effective business competition.

In the prolegomena's subsequent two parts, Keynes intended to develop the philosophical foundations to explore the role of 'benevolence', the public good and, more particularly, the means thereto in 'economic well-being'. It then planned to address the chief preoccupation of the state under six different heads: population, including eugenics; money; enterprise issues lumped together as 'adequacy of saving, investment of fixed capital, public utilities'; labor matters lumped together including 'wage levels, [employment and social] insurance, industrial disputes'; 'natural resources'; and ; 'defence, peace' (O'Donnell, 1992, p. 807). Much of this proposed content reflected Keynes's own interests at the time. Monetary reform and the need for 'a drastic remedy for unemployment' with its explicit rejection of 'the old principle of laissez faire' as *passé* both for the labor and the capital market (see Harrod, 1951, pp. 345–9) are clear examples. However these arguments fit equally some of Marshall's published and unpublished pronouncements on the matter (summarized in Groenewegen, 1995, ch. 16, pp. 592–8, 608–12). Of special relevance are Marshall's thoughts about the impact of developments in joint stock companies on the case against public enterprise and, more generally, the 'master's' recognized emphasis on the transitory nature of economic phenomena. Developments in joint stock companies divorcing management from ownership were a striking example of this transitional quality, as was the general demise of laissez faire in its traditional, late Victorian meaning. Moreover there was little in this list of proposed government responsibilities that Marshall could not have endorsed.

The first outline for a critical examination of capitalism, which O'Donnell (1992, pp. 785–6) provisionally dates at November 1924, followed closely on Marshall's death and, in particular, Keynes's October visit to Mary Paley, when he went through 'papers and things'. This may explain the structure of 'ideal, actual and practicable' as a model for organizing Keynes's thoughts on the subject equally well as the appeal to Moore's ethical foundations made by O'Donnell (ibid., p. 788). Justice in distribution with critical remarks on inheritance, and more pertinently observations on the structure and purpose of an ideal society (utopias), were important aspects of Marshall's outlines for his projected final volume which Keynes, when looking through Marshall's papers, could hardly have missed. Many of the themes to be raised by Keynes under the possible had likewise gained the attention of Marshall in his prognostications on potential postwar developments in his *Industry and Trade*. These included reflections on state saving, alternative social organizations based on state socialism, guild socialism and co-partnership, and the necessity of devising regulatory mechanisms for controlling public utilities and trusts. Keynes's project to examine critically the contemporary operations of capitalism seems therefore to have a strong Marshall pedigree, since this was part and parcel of the research program which Marshall had laid out for himself in his study of economics, and which in fact he had partially achieved in his *Industry and Trade* (cf. Keynes, 1972, p. 228).

Hence, in developing his own brand of liberal socialism, Keynes probably drew on similar ideas about this subject which the 'master' had left to his 'pupils' and of which he himself was clearly aware (Keynes, 1972, p. 214). The perspectives on politics by the two Cambridge economists resemble each other in some of their approaches to specific questions, and insofar as those of one is concerned, formed a substantial part of the roots of the other, even though, equally characteristic of the two men, their level of political involvement was very different.

Studying Marshall's potential influences on the system of thought developed by his most outstanding pupil considerably benefits the evaluation of Keynes's thought. For settling interpretative debates about the *General Theory* and Keynes's economics before that book, this is a well-recognized procedure. Fully appreciating the nature of the relationship between the two men aids this process, particularly when it recognizes the posthumous contact with Marshall's views which Keynes imposed on himself in the two years following Marshall's death. Misunderstanding the extent of Marshall's influence on Keynes owes much to inadequate grasp of this biographical aspect; it also arises from inadequate perception of the thrust and objectives of Marshall's own enormous, albeit incomplete, opus. The *Principles, Money Credit and Commerce*, and especially the monetary evidence, have received the major focus in assessing the Marshall–Keynes relationship. This may not be enough, given the extent of the relationship suggested by the evidence.

PETER GROENEWEGEN

See also:

Keynes, John Maynard; Keynes, The Influence of Burke and Moore on; Marshall, Alfred.

Bibliography

Bharadwaj, Krishna (1972), 'Marshall on Pigou's Wealth and Welfare', *Economica*, N.S., **39**, (153), pp. 32–46.

Clower, R.W. (1989), 'Keynes' General Theory: the Marshall Connection', in R.A. Walker (ed.), *Perspectives on the History of Economic Thought*, Aldershot: Elgar.

Collard, David (1981), 'A.C. Pigou 1877–1959', in D.P. O'Brien and J.R. Presley (eds), *Pioneers of Modern Economics in Britain*, London: Macmillan.

Dardi, Marco and Mauro Gallegati (1992), 'Alfred Marshall on Speculation', *History of Political Economy*, **24**, (3), fall, pp. 571–94.

Groenewegen, Peter (1988), 'Alfred Marshall and the Establishment of the Cambridge Economics Tripos', *History of Political Economy*, **20**, (4), winter, pp. 627–67.

Groenewegen, Peter (1995), *A Soaring Eagle: Alfred Marshall 1842–1924*, Aldershot: Edward Elgar.

Harrod, R.F. (1951), *The Life of John Maynard Keynes*, London: Macmillan.

Hill, P. and R. Keynes (eds) (1989), *Lydia and Maynard*, London: André Deutsch.

Keynes, J.M. (1922), Introduction to D.H. Robertson, *Money*, Cambridge Economic Handbook, London: Nesbitt and Company.

Keynes, J.M. (1931), *Essays in Persuasion*, London: Rupert-Hart Davis: reissued 1951.

Keynes, J.M. (1972), 'Alfred Marshall 1842–1924', in *Essays in Biography, The Collected Writings of John Maynard Keynes*, Vol. X, London: Macmillan.

Keynes, J.M. (1973a) [1936], *General Theory of Employment, Interest and Money*, in *Collected Writings of John Maynard Keynes*, Vol. VII, London: Macmillan.

Keynes, J.M. (1973b), 'The General Theory and After. Part I: Preparation', in *Collected Writings of John Maynard Keynes*, Vol. XIII, London: Macmillan.

Leijonhufvud, A. (1968), *On Keynesian Economics and the Economics of Keynes*, London: Oxford University Press.

Marshall, Alfred (1907), 'The Social Possibilities of Economic Chivalry', *Ecohnomic Journal*, **17**, (65), March, pp. 7–29.

Marshall, Alfred (1919), *Industry and Trade*, London: Macmillan.

Marshall, Alfred (1920), *Principles of Economics*, 8th edn, London: Macmillan.

Marshall, Alfred (1923), *Money, Credit and Commerce*, London: Macmillan.

Marshall, Alfred (1926), *Official Papers*, ed. J.M. Keynes, London: Macmillan for The Royal Economic Society.

Moggridge, D. (1992), *Maynard Keynes. An Economist's Biography*, London: Routledge.

O'Donnell, R.M. (1992), 'The Unwritten Books and Papers by Keynes', *History of Political Economy*, **24**, (4), pp. 767–817.

Pigou, A.C. (ed.) (1925), *Memorials of Alfred Marshall*, London: Macmillan.

Pigou, A.C. (1953), *Alfred Marshall and Current Thought*, London: Macmillan.

Robertson, D.H. (1935), 'Letter to Keynes', 3 February, in *Collected Writings of John Maynard Keynes*, Vol. XIII, London: Macmillan.

Robertson, D.H. (1936), 'Some Notes on Mr. Keynes's General Theory of Employment', *Quarterly Journal of Economics*, **521**, (1), November, pp. 168–91.

Robinson, Joan (1962), *Economic Philosophy*, The New Thinkers Library, London: C.A. Watts & Co.

Skidelsky, Robert (1983), *John Maynard Keynes   Hopes Betrayed 1883–1920*, London: Macmillan.

Skidelsky, Robert (1992), *John Maynard Keynes   The Economist as Saviour 1920–37*, London: Macmillan.

Vaizey, John (1976), 'Keynes and the Cambridge Tradition', *Spectator*, 19 May, pp. 20–21.

Whitaker, John (1990), 'What Happened to the Second Volume of the Principles? The Thorny Path to Marshall's last Books', in John Whitaker (ed.), *Centenary Essays on Alfred Marshall*, Cambridge: Cambridge University Press, pp. 193–222.

Meade, James E.

James Edward Meade was born on 23 June 1907 in Swanage, Dorset and educated at Malvern College and Oriel College, Oxford. Upon graduation in 1930, he was elected a fellow of Hertford College, Oxford, and appointed to a lectureship in economics. He assumed that position in 1931, however, after spending a year on graduate work at Trinity College, Cambridge, where he became a member of the 'Circus' around Keynes.

His published work includes more than 40 books and pamphlets and numerous scientific papers (a complete bibliography of Meade's work until 1977 can be found in Johnson, 1978; Vines, 1987, lists selected works). In 1977, he was awarded the Nobel Prize in Economics (jointly with Bertil Ohlin) for his work on international economics as presented mainly in the two volumes of his treatise *The Theory of International Economic Policy* (1951–5): Volume 1, *The Balance of Payments* (1951) and Volume 2, *Trade and Welfare* (1955a). Given that his work on international economics has been presented critically elsewhere (Johnson, 1978; Corden and Atkinson, 1979), this entry presents a rather incomplete summary of his principal contributions in economics.

Meade's early contributions include his *Introduction to Economic Analysis and Policy* (1936), published almost simultaneously with Keynes's *General Theory*, which synthesized the ideas of the Keynesian revolution, emphasized the importance of imperfect competition and examined international problems emanating from a poor coordination of macroeconomic policies, and his paper, 'A Simplified Model of Mr Keynes' System', in the *Review of Economic Studies* in 1937, which presented an earlier form of Hicks's IS/LM model.

After spending three years in Geneva as an economist for the League of Nations, he returned to London in 1940 to serve as director to the Economic

Section of the British Cabinet Office. In an attempt to estimate funds available for the war, he worked with Richard Stone and David Champernowne on what resulted in the first 'double-entry' national accounts. Although these were not the first national accounts,[1] the double-entry bookkeeping format was pathbreaking in that it ensured consistency, since every income item on one side of the balance sheet had to be matched by an expenditure item on the other side.[2]

Meade returned to academic life in 1947 as professor of commerce at LSE, where his Nobel Prize-winning work on international economics was done. *The Balance of Payments* (1951) attempted, first, to synthesize the Keynesian macroeconomic theory with the Hicksian general equilibrium framework and, second, to analyse the relationship between a country's targets, on the one hand, and instruments, on the other. The attempt was successful on both counts. With regard to the first objective, by presenting a Keynesian two-country model, Meade raised the level of sophistication at which international macroeconomic theory was conceived and liberated it from the Marshallian partial equilibrium analysis. With regard to the second objective, he demonstrated the then revolutionary idea that, if two targets are to be achieved (internal and external balance), then two instruments ought to be used (aggregate demand management and exchange rate change).[3] The second volume of *The Theory of International Economic Policy*, published four years later, made a series of theoretical contributions on, among other things, the relationship between optimal population and optimal savings, the 'theory of the second best', and welfare economics. Other significant work, published while Meade was at LSE, includes *Geometry of International Trade* (1952a), which presented a formal derivation of 'offer curves' in the presence of factor allocation changes, *The Theory of Customs Unions* (1955b), which extended Viner's work on customs unions and introduced the so-called 'consumption effect' of trade creation, and his article in the *Economic Journal* in 1952, 'External Economies and Diseconomies in a Competitive Situation', the first rigorous analysis of externalities.

In 1957, Meade became professor of political economy at the University of Cambridge, where he studied issues of economic growth. His book, *A Neo-Classical Theory of Growth* (1961), though it failed to resolve the 'Cambridge controversies', 'covers a number of aspects (such as the presence of the fixed factor land) usually omitted in more high powered mathematical treatments, and presents in detail the mathematics of a two sector growth model' (Johnson, 1978, p. 79). The latter constituted the starting-point for the work by Uzawa, Srinivasan and other growth theorists in 1960s.

Meade retired in 1969, in order to concentrate on writing, and was a senior research fellow of Christ's College, Cambridge, until his death, on 22 December 1995. He has played a pivotal role in the discussion on economic policy in England, advocating that aggregate demand management should be exercised for the cure of inflation, while income policies should be used to promote employment. Above all, however, Meade was an economist who tried to make the world a better place. On the way to Thomas More's *Utopia* (No place), he discovered the island of *Agathotopia* (Good place), where there exists a labor–capital partnership, while competitive mechanisms and special fiscal arrangements promote efficiency and equity. In the introduction of his *Liberty, Equality and Efficiency* (1991), he wrote:

> I am saddened that so many of my professional colleagues seem at present to be so exclusively engaged in discussing how best to design fiscal, monetary, foreign exchange and wage-setting policies and institutions so as to get the best pay-off between inflation and employment, given the present combination of distributional and efficiency objectives in setting rates of pay. This work is very important and very valuable. But I appeal to some of them to divert some of their attention away from making the best of the present bad job and onto the design of a better job. They may not accept Agathotopia as the best possible model for this purpose, in which case I challenge them to produce a better one.

THEODORE PALIVOS

Notes

1   Simon Kuznets had already constructed national accounts for the United States.
2   Richard Stone received the Nobel Prize in Economics for his work on national accounting in 1984.
3   This principle, regarding the instruments and targets problem, at a more general level was developed simultaneously but independently by Jan Tinbergen.

See also:

Balance of Payments: Keynesian and Monetarist Approaches; Bretton Woods; Cambridge Circus; Demand Management; Dornbusch, Rudiger; Fiscal Policy; Incomes Policies; International Clearing Union; Keynesian Revolution; Metzler, Lloyd A.; Mundell–Fleming Model; Ohlin, Bertil; Robinson, Joan; Samuelson, Paul A.; Solow, Robert M.; Swan, Trevor W.; Viner, Jacob; White, Harry D.

Bibliography

Blaug, M. (1985), *Great Economists Since Keynes, An Introduction to the Work of One Hundred Modern Economists*, Totowa, NJ: Barnes & Noble Books.
Corden, W.M. and A.B. Atkinson (1979), 'Meade, James E.' in D.L. Sill (ed.), *International Encyclopedia of the Social Sciences*, Vol. 18, New York: Free Press/London: Macmillan.
Johnson, H.J. (1978), 'James Meade's Contribution to Economics', *Scandinavian Journal of Economics*, **80**, pp. 64–85.
Meade, James (1936), *Introduction to Economic Analysis and Policy*, London: Oxford University Press.
Meade, James (1937), 'A Simplified Model of Mr Keynes' System', *Review of Economic Studies*, **4**, pp. 98–107.
Meade, James (1951), *The Theory of International Economic Policy, vol. 1, The Balance of Payments*, London: Oxford University Press.
Meade, James (1952a), *Geometry of International Trade*, London: Allen & Unwin.

Meade, James (1952b), 'External Economies and Diseconomies in a Competitive Situation', *Economic Journal*, **62**, (245), March, pp. 54–67.

Meade, James (1955a), *The Theory of International Economic Policy, vol. 2, Trade and Welfare*, London: Oxford University Press.

Meade, James (1955b), *The Theory of Customs Unions*, Amsterdam: North-Holland.

Meade, James (1961), *A Neo-Classical Theory of Growth*, London: Allen & Unwin.

Meade, James (1991), *Liberty, Equality and Efficiency*, New York: New York University Press.

Vines, D. (1987), 'Meade, James E.', in John Eatwell, Murray Milgate and Peter Newman (eds), *The New Palgrave: A Dictionary of Economics*, Vol. 2, New York: Stockton Press.

Meltzer, Allan H.

Born on 6 February 1928 in Boston, Massachusetts, Allan Meltzer is the son of George B. and Minerva I. (Simmons) Meltzer. He attended Duke University, where he earned his AB in 1948. After graduation Meltzer went to Los Angeles where he worked in the family business. In 1953, he enrolled in UCLA's graduate program where he earned his MA (1955) and PhD (1958). Here also he met Karl Brunner, who, at the time Meltzer entered the program, was an assistant professor. Meltzer felt a great loss when his co-author, colleague and lifelong friend died in 1989.

In addition to the classes, seminars and 'over coffee' discussions with Brunner, Meltzer took classes from William Allen, Warren Scoville and Armen Alchian. Upon completion of his formal course work, Meltzer wanted to go to France but Brunner wanted him to stay at UCLA to work on a thesis in the area of monetary theory. The awarding of a Fulbright Scholarship and a Social Science Research Council grant resolved the issue. The topic for the thesis would be the determinants of France's stock of money during World War II and the inflation which occurred in the immediate postwar period. The research would be conducted in France. The principal results of the thesis were published as 'The Behavior of the French Money Supply 1938–1954' (Meltzer, 1959).

Upon his return from France, Meltzer joined the University of Pennsylvania's economics faculty. Here he worked on revising his thesis and, because he became dissatisfied with the working environment at Penn, spent time looking for another place to work. In Carnegie Mellon, Meltzer found a good match and he has been there since 1957. While in France Meltzer's faith in the role of the government had begun to unravel Meltzer's faith in the role of the government came from his grandmother, a F.D.Roosevelt democrat who viewed government as a benevolent force within the society. According to this view the government is charged with the responsibility of helping people with problems, improving the overall performance of society and increasing justice. Given this perspective, Meltzer saw the Marshall Plan as an attempt on the part of the American government to improve the welfare of Europe and was attracted to economics because economics seeks ways to improve the welfare of society. This stance led to Meltzer's break with the Progressive Party, whose North Carolina branch he had helped organized during his undergraduate days at Duke.

The more he studied economics the more Meltzer became aware of, and interested in, the gap which existed between theory and practice, objectives and outcomes, and in the role which institutions play in the development and implementation of economic policy. Four forces – discussions and observations which he had and made about religion, conclusions which he drew about the way the French government attacked the problem of inflation, arguments which he read in Hayek's *Constitution of Liberty* (1960) and Popper's *The Open Society and Its Enemies* (1950), and observations which he made while working on two studies commissioned by Wright Patman, a study of the dealer market and a study of the Fed's method of conducting monetary policy – have slowly moved Meltzer to the position that discretionary policies decrease the stability and welfare of the economic system. Meltzer now believes that government policy should be based on 'rules' and not on forecasting models, a position not unlike the Lucas critique (Lucas, 1976). The impact of this shift may be seen in his subsequent work in economics.

In his attack on discretionary monetary policy Meltzer, like Friedman and Schwartz (1963), is a harsh critic of the Federal Reserve (Fed). He believes that the Fed has relied on, and continues to rely on, unreliable control procedures and has made no attempt to improve those control procedures. Because the Fed's monetary policy is not based on a thorough examination of what happens when the assumptions of the formal models are relaxed and when institutions are introduced into these models, the Fed was a major contributor to the Great Depression of the 1930s and the 'Great Inflation' of the 1970s. As Meltzer sees the problem, the Fed uses discretionary policy in an attempt to improve the average level of performance of the economy, but the result is that discretionary monetary policy decreases the stability and welfare of the economy. The Fed must avoid the use of discretionary policy and become more aware of the way institutions affect policy decisions, a position which is consistent with his attack on discretionary fiscal policy.

Meltzer argues that Keynes did not advocate the use of discretionary fiscal policy in the *General Theory* because he (Keynes) believed that the goals of reducing the uncertainty associated with the investment process and increasing the average performance of the English economy could not be attained with it. Meltzer's reading of the *General Theory* suggests that these goals can only be achieved through the use of rules. An example of one such rule is a growth rule for the rate of growth of the money supply. This particular interpretation of the *General Theory* is subject to the criticism that the investigation's frame of reference is the theory of rational expectations. A different approach, one that is more consistent with Keynes's philosophy, is to examine the *General Theory* from the perspective of Keynes's theory of probability. The policy goal of the *General Theory* is to increase the average level of performance of the economic system. This goal follows from the theory of probability which he used at this time. According to this theory, individuals are irrational, pursue many goals, possess subjective degrees of belief about the next occurrence of an event which are subject to sudden and violent shifts and, in the face of uncertainty and sudden shifts in their degrees of belief, tend to fall back on conventions and rules.

Keynes argues that gross domestic investment is the sum of gross private and gross public domestic investment. In his critique of Tinbergen's analysis of investment activity Keynes states that, from a careful examination of the factors that affect gross private domestic investment, one is able to induce an unstable pattern which can be traced to business confidence and uncertainty (Keynes, 1939: Tinbergen, 1939). Keynes realizes that one cannot influence gross private domestic investment directly, so he proposes to do so indirectly by socializing gross public domestic investment. The purpose of the socialization of gross public domestic investment is to establish or maintain conventions or rules which are acceptable to the business community (Bateman, 1990, 1991). To do this, and to achieve the goal of the *General Theory*, Keynes advocates the adoption and implementation of two policies, a policy of low long-run rates of interest and a policy of high gross domestic investment. These two policies rely on the Bank of England's monetary policy, the division of the government's budget into two sub-budgets, a current expenditures budget which is always in balance and a capital expenditures budget whose projects are self-liquidating, and 'public corporations' which control two-thirds to three-quarters of the nation's capital stock. Thus, by the time of the *General Theory*, Keynes had moved from the position that monetary policy should be left to individuals' discretion to the position that public policy should be based on rules and conventions acceptable to the business community. The term 'rules and conventions', as used by Keynes, lies somewhere between individuals' discretion and the interpretation given to it by Meltzer. Meltzer tries to place Keynes in the New Classical School of macroeconomics and he just does not fit (Bateman, 1995).

TOM CATE

See also:

Brunner, Karl; Cagan, Philip; Demand Management; Economics of Keynes and of his Revolution, Key Elements of the; Economics, The Art of; Fiscal Policy; Friedman, Milton; Lucas Critique; Monetarist School of Economics; Monetary Policy; Money; New Classical School of Economics; Quantity Theory of Money; Schwartz, Anna J.

Bibliography

Bateman, Bradley (1990), 'Keynes, induction and econometrics', *History of Political Economy*, **22**, (2), summer, pp. 359–80.

Bateman, Bradley (1991), 'The Rules of the Road: Keynes's Theoretical Rationale for Public Policy', in Bradley W. Bateman and John B. Davis (eds), *Keynes and Philosophy*, Brookfield, VT: Edward Elgar.

Bateman, Bradley (1995), 'Rethinking the Keynesian Revolution', in John B. Davis (ed.), *The State of Interpretation of Keynes*, Boston: Kluwer Academic Publishers.

Bernanke, Ben (1983), 'Non-Monetary Effects of the Financial Crisis in the Propagation of the Great Depression', *American Economic Review*, **73**, (3), June, pp. 257–76.

Friedman, Milton and Anna Schwartz (1963), *A Monetary History of the United States 1967–1960*, Princeton, NJ: Princeton University Press for the National Bureau of Economic Research.

Keynes, John Maynard (1939), 'Professor Tinbergen's Method', *Economic Journal*, **49**, (194), September, pp. 558–68.

Lucas, Jr., Robert (1976), 'Econometric Policy Evaluation: A Critique', in K. Brunner and A.H. Meltzer (eds), *The Phillips Curve and Labour Markets*, Carnegie–Rochester Series on Public Policy, Amsterdam: North-Holland.

Meltzer, Allan H. (1959), 'The Behavior of the French Money Supply 1938–1954', *Journal of Political Economy*, **67**, (3), June, pp. 275–96.

Meltzer, Allan H. (1963), 'The Demand for Money: The Evidence from Time Series', *Journal of Political Economy*, **71**, (3), June, pp. 219–46.

Meltzer, Allan H. (1969), 'On Efficiency and Regulation of the Securities Industry', in Henry G. Manne (ed.), *Economic Policy in the Regulation of Corporate Securities*, Washington, DC: American Enterprise Institute.

Meltzer, Allan H. (1976), 'Monetary and Other Explanations of the Start of the Great Depression', *Journal of Monetary Economics*, **2**, (4), November, pp. 455–76.

Meltzer, Allan H. (1980), 'Monetarism and the Crisis in Economics', *The Public Interest*, Special Issue, pp. 35–45.

Meltzer, Allan H. (1983), 'Monetary Reform in an Uncertain Environment', *Cato Journal*, **3**, (1), spring, pp. 93–112.

Meltzer, Allan H. (1988), 'Money and Credit in the Monetary Transmission Process', *American Economic Review, Papers and Proceedings*, **78**, (2), May, pp. 446–51.

Tinbergen, Jan (1939), *A Method and Its Application to Investment Activity, Statistical Testing of Business-Cycle Theories, I*, Geneva: League of Nations.

Metzler, Lloyd A.

Lloyd A. Metzler was born in Lost Springs, Kansas, in 1913. He earned a BS in 1935 and an MBA in 1938 from the University of Kansas. He did his doctoral studies at Harvard, where he earned his Masters in 1941 and PhD in 1942 in economics. His dissertation, 'Interregional Income Generation', was awarded the Wells Prize for 1944–5. During the next four years he held a variety of governmental posts: staff economist at the Office of Strategic Services (1943–4) and at the Federal Reserve System's Board of Governors (1944–6), consultant to the House of Representatives (1945) and member of the Mission to Germany on Currency Reform (1946). From 1946 to 1947 he taught at Yale, and in 1947 he joined the department of economics at the University of Chicago, where he was to remain until his death in 1980. Poor health severely restricted his professional activity over the last three decades of his life.

Metzler's published work includes some 20 papers, covering four broad fields: international economics; business cycles and economic fluctuations; money, interest and prices; and mathematical economics and statistics. His *Collected Papers* were published in 1973, and his career was honored in the volume edited by Horwich and Samuelson, *Trade, Stability and Macroeconomics* (1974). Much of Metzler's work was concerned with the application of ideas from Keynes's *General Theory* to the open economy. In his doctoral dissertation he worked out the essential properties of the foreign trade multiplier in a two-country model with unemployment, published as 'Underemployment Equilibrium and International Trade' (1942a). While his approach was similar to that used by Machlup (1943), Metzler went farther in considering the stability properties of the model.

His best-known contributions to international economics fall into three areas: the transfer problem, tariff theory and the effects of terms-of-trade changes. He first studied the transfer problem in the second chapter of his dissertation, published as 'The Transfer Problem Reconsidered' (1942b). He departed from classical analyses by using a Keynesian framework of fixed prices and demand-determined output, and focused on the endogenous adjustment of expenditure and income. Under the assumption that both the paying and receiving countries are stable (that is, their marginal propensities to spend are less than unity), Metzler showed that the transfer would always leave the paying country's trade balance in deficit, and that the final effect on both countries' income levels would depend on their respective fiscal policies.

Regarding tariff theory, Metzler showed in two papers (1949a, 1949b) that an import tariff (or, equivalently, an export tax) could lead to an improvement in the country's terms of trade so large as to cause a decline in the *domestic* relative price of the importable – a result known as 'Metzler's paradox', which requires that the foreign offer curve be sufficiently inelastic. In such case, the tariff fails to be protective, and lowers the real income of the factor used intensively in the production of importables rather than raising it, contrary to the prediction of the Stolper–Samuelson theorem, which was the original concern of Metzler's work.

In a joint paper with Svend Laursen (1950), Metzler examined the insulation from external disturbances provided by flexible exchange rates. Their work highlighted a link between devaluation and aggregate expenditure (or, equivalently, saving): devaluation brings about a terms-of-trade deterioration that Laursen and Metzler argued would lead to increased expenditure (or reduced saving) at given income. This has come to be known as the 'Laursen–Metzler effect', sometimes with the addition of the name of Harberger, who had arrived independently at similar results. Over the last two decades, this finding has been extensively scrutinized under varying assumptions with the help of formal intertemporal models, with results that depend on model specification and on the nature of the terms-of-trade disturbance.

A final paper on open economy macroeconomics worth mentioning, written with Triffin and Haberler, is 'Exchange Rates and the International Monetary Fund' (1947), where the authors examined the problems of applying the purchasing power parity hypothesis as a guideline for setting exchange rates in the immediate postwar period. Metzler argued that this procedure would result in overvaluation of some currencies and undervaluation of others, and related these exchange rate misalignments to the internal and external balances of the nations involved, anticipating some of the difficulties that later plagued the Bretton Woods system.

Metzler's work on business cycles and economic fluctuations centered on the integration of inventory behavior into the Keynesian multiplier/accelerator mechanism. His classic paper, 'The Nature and Stability of Inventory Cycles' (1941) laid the groundwork for much of the subsequent investigation on inventory fluctuations. It showed that any disturbance tended to produce cyclical fluctuations around the equilibrium level of income. Further, if anticipated sales vary with actual sales and desired inventories depend on anticipated sales, the adjustment process could be unstable. In 'Factors Governing the Length of Inventory Cycles' (1947), Metzler showed that the length of the cycle varies positively with the marginal propensity to consume and the inventory accelerator, and negatively with the elasticity of expected changes in sales with respect to their actual value.

Metzler's imprint on monetary theory stems from an influential paper, 'Wealth, Saving and the Rate of Interest' (1951), whose ideas were already anticipated in the third chapter of his dissertation. The paper addressed the question of whether a change in the money supply would affect the real side of the economy, a possibility questioned by the neoclassical view. While Keynes's critics had underscored the positive relation between real balances and total expenditure (the 'Pigou effect') as an equilibrating macroeconomic mechanism, Metzler argued that such a relation should apply to a broader concept of wealth, including both real balances and financial claims on the capital stock. In such conditions, an open market purchase of securities, that reduces the private sector's total wealth through price level increases, would encourage savings and thereby reduce the equilibrium rate of interest.

In the field of mathematical economics, Metzler's work centered on the conditions for stability of multiple markets, motivated by his research on the comparative statics properties of multi-country models. His brilliant, classic paper, 'Stability of Multiple Markets: the Hicks Conditions' (1945) made two important contributions: it clarified the conditions for (static) Hicksian perfect stability and the relationship of the latter with Samuelson's dynamic stability. Metzler showed that, although these two concepts are different in general, they are equivalent under gross substitutability. He also noted that the criterion of Hicksian perfect stability could be viewed as an implication of the requirement that dynamic stability should hold independently of adjustment speed – what is known as 'total stability'. To derive these results, Metzler focused on the properties of the matrix of partial derivatives of market excess demands with respect to prices. Under gross substitutability, for example, the negative of this matrix has positive diagonal elements and negative off-diagonal elements. This sign pattern defines what is termed a 'Metzler matrix', a type of matrix that has played an important role in subsequent research on the stability of market equilibrium.

LUIS SERVEN

See also:

Balance of Payments: Keynesian and Monetarist Approaches; Business Cycle Theory (I) and (II); Demand Management; Frisch, Ragner; Haavelmo, Trygve; Interest, Theories of; Keynesian Revolution; Machlup, Fritz; Money; Multiplier Effect; Mundell-Fleming Model; Myrdal, Gunnar; Ohlin, Bertil; Viner, Jacob.

Bibliography

Harberger, Arnold C. (1950), 'Currency Depreciation, Income and the Balance of Trade', *Journal of Political Economy*, **58**, (1), pp. 47–60.

Horwich, George and Paul A. Samuelson (1974), *Trade, Stability and Macroeconomics: Essays in Honor of Lloyd A. Metzler*, New York: Academic Press.

Laursen, Svend and Lloyd A. Metzler (1950), 'Flexible Exchange Rates and the Theory of Employment', *Review of Economics and Statistics*, **32**, (4), November, pp. 281–99.

Machlup, Fritz (1943), *International Trade and the National Income Multiplier*, Philadelphia: Blakiston.

Metzler, Lloyd A. (1941), 'The Nature and Stability of Inventory Cycles', *Review of Economics and Statistics*, **23**, (3), August, pp. 113–29.

Metzler, Lloyd A. (1942a), 'Underemployment Equilibrium in International Trade', *Econometrica*, **10**, (2), April, pp. 97–112.

Metzler, Lloyd A. (1942b), 'The Transfer Problem Reconsidered', *Journal of Political Economy*, **50**, (3), June, pp. 397–414.

Metzler, Lloyd A. (1945), 'Stability of Multiple Markets: the Hicks Conditions', *Econometrica*, **13**, (4), October, pp. 277–92.

Metzler, Lloyd A. (1947), 'Factors Governing the Length of Inventory Cycles', *Review of Economics and Statistics*, **29**, (1), February, pp. 1–15.

Metzler, Lloyd A. (1949a), 'Tariffs, the Terms of Trade and the Distribution of National Income', *Journal of Political Economy*, **57**, February, pp. 1–29.

Metzler, Lloyd A. (1949b), 'Tariffs, International Demand and Domestic Prices', *Journal of Political Economy*, **57**, August, pp. 345–51.

Metzler, Lloyd A. (1951), 'Wealth, Saving and the Rate of Interest', *Journal of Political Economy*, **59**, (2), April, pp. 93–116.

Metzler, Lloyd A. (1973), *Collected Papers*, Cambridge, Mass.: Harvard University Press.

Metzler, Lloyd A., Robert Triffin and Gottfried Haberler (1947), 'Exchange Rates and the International Monetary Fund', in *International Monetary Policies*, Postwar Economic Studies, no. 7, Washington: Board of Governors of the Federal Reserve System.

Microfoundations of Macroeconomics

Introduction

It is important to define microeconomics and macroeconomics before the issue of microfoundations is discussed. In this entry, microeconomics is viewed as a way of studying the economy in which (1) the behavior of individual agents is considered to be rational and modeled as the outcome of some form of a constrained optimization problem and (2) the actions of individual agents are supposed to form an equilibrium. (For some alternative definitions, see the overview in Janssen, 1993.) A historically important part of microeconomics is general equilibrium analysis (GEA) according to which fully flexible prices bring about an equilibrium between demand and supply in perfectly competitive markets. Macroeconomics, on the other hand, is viewed in one of two ways. The term 'macroeconomic phenomena' is meant to describe a set of (stylized) observations about aggregate variables such as fluctuations in the level of unemployment. The term 'macroeconomic theory' is used for an interrelated set of concepts (such as effective demand and involuntary unemployment) that are not (yet) based on microeconomics. The quest for microfoundations of macroeconomics can thus be understood either as an investigation into the possibilities of employing the microeconomic method in the study of macroeconomic phenomena or as an investigation into the possibilites of making macroeconomic theory compatible with microeconomics.

Historical background

Theoretical curiosity with respect to the relation between microeconomics and macroeconomic theory has existed from the beginning of modern macroeconomics (see, for example, Hicks's 1937 interpretation of Keynes, 1936). One of the main concerns was the apparent conflict between the GEA conception of the economy and the Keynesian view focusing on the underutilization of resources in general and on unemployment in particular. As the result of work by Patinkin (1956), among others, a synthesis was created in which Keynesian analysis was thought to be concerned with short-run market imperfections. Consequently involuntary unemployment was regarded as a temporary phenomenon itself being a consequence of short-run rigidities in nominal (money) wages.

From a theoretical point of view this state of affairs was unsatisfactory, however. As the imposition of a fixed money wage (or, more generally, fixed prices) affects the structure of the theory of supply and demand, one cannot simply attribute unemployment to sticky money wages while leaving the theoretical structure of GEA intact (Clower, 1965; Leijonhufvud, 1968). This view culminated in a variety of fixprice models. These models have microfoundations in the sense that they are based on rational individual behavior and a notion of equilibrium, the cornerstones of microeconomics. Several types of fixprice equilibria were proposed in which an equilibrium was brought about by quantity constraints (Bénassy, 1975; Drèze, 1975). Moreover it turned out that the fixprice models capture a number of ideas associated with Keynesian macroeconomic theory. Involuntary unemployment could be regarded as an equilibrium phenomenon in which optimizing households face a quantity constraint on the amount of labor they can supply. Also the Keynesian concepts of effective demand and the multiplier were reformulated within the new models. An overview of this literature is provided by Weintraub (1979).

New classical economics

New classical economics (NCE) attempts to explain macroeconomic phenomena such as unemployment in terms of GEA. Involuntary unemployment is regarded as a theoretical construct that is not a necessary part of an explanation of unemployment (Lucas, 1978). NCE criticizes fixprice explanations of unemployment for the fact that the explanation is incomplete insofar as no account is given to explain why prices are fixed. In particular, it is not clear why rational agents do not change prices once they find out that this is in their own interest. In fact, NCE regards many equilibrium notions, apart from the competitive one, as being incompatible with microfoundations.

New classical business cycle models provide an answer to the question how to reconcile fluctuations in the level of employment with the GEA notion of competitive equilibrium. The early models regard incomplete information about the aggregate money supply as the major cause of the cycle (see, for example, Lucas and Rapping, 1969; Lucas, 1972). Insofar as monetarist macroeconomic theory and these early NCE models both consider the variability of the money supply the main cause of business cycles, these early models provide microfoundations for monetarism.

Real business cycle models (see, for example, Kydland and Prescott, 1982) regard the business cycle as the optimal response of the economy to exogenous shocks in real variables such as technology and preferences. Nominal variables such as the money stock are assumed to have no role in explaining the business cycle. The real business cycle approach is closer to GEA, the paradigm of microeconomics, because it does not rely, as the monetary imperfect information models do, on some sort of failure in the market for information.

New Keynesian economics

New Keynesian economics (NKE) can be regarded as a family of models that take the new classical critique on the fixprice assumption seriously. The family is probably best circumscribed by the belief that market imperfections (such as asymmetric information, imperfect competition and sticky prices) are crucial for an understanding of the functioning of the economy. Two family branches will be distinguished here: (1) studies that supplement the fixprice models with an explanation why rational individuals might choose to set prices at levels that differ from the competitive equilibrium values, and (2) studies that build models with relative prices determined 'by the market' and individuals behaving rationally.

Within NKE there are at least two types of models explaining why prices may differ from competitive equilibrium prices. First, in the basic efficiency wage model, production does not only depend on the number of workers employed, but also on the productivity per worker. Unemployed workers would strictly prefer to work at the going wage rate or even at a lower wage rate, but firms do not lower wages because this would reduce the productivity of all workers. Second, the small menu costs approach shows that *even if* menu costs are small, profit-maximizing firms may choose not to change prices, which in turn may cause large fluctuations in output. Mankiw and Romer (1991) provide an anthology of important papers in each of the above two directions.

The diversity of the second branch of studies within NKE distinguished above can be illustrated by briefly presenting the arguments of three key papers. Hart (1982) studies a general equilibrium model with oligopolistic competition that exhibits underemployment equilibria. The concept of under-employment is used to indicate that the equilibrium level of employment is lower than in the corresponding competitive equilibrium. In the Nash equilibrium of the model, firms individually choose not to increase their production level, because the consequent fall in prices is such that the firm's revenue will decrease. Weitzman (1982) argues that increasing returns to scale is a necessary condition for Keynesian economics in general and for involuntary unemployment in particular. His basic argument is that with non-increasing returns to scale the unemployed can produce goods at least as efficiently as the employed can, so that they can 'produce themselves out of unemployment'. Finally Cooper and John (1988) point out that the concept of coordination failure is a key concept in NKE. A coordination failure arises when there are multiple Pareto-ranked equilibria and when the economy finds itself in a 'bad' equilibrium.

All models in NKE have microfoundations in the sense that individual agents are supposed to behave rationally and that the individual behaviors are in equilibrium. The models depart, however, in one way or the other from GEA, the paradigmatic example of microeconomics.

Policy implications

The policy implications of NKE are not univocal. It is even not always clear what the Keynesian element of NKE is: in many models unemployment is *not* a consequence of deficiencies in aggregate demand and the desirability of monetary and/or fiscal policy is not universally subscribed to either. As outlined above, there are many different approaches and what they have in common is the understanding that markets do not function perfectly. This does not imply, however, that the NKE models with microfoundations provide a rationale for government intervention in the market.

MAARTEN C.W. JANSSEN

See also:

Business Cycle Theory (I) and (II); Clower, Robert W.; Coordination Failures and Keynesian Economics; Leijonhufvud, Axel; Lucas, Jr., Robert E.; Lucas Critique; New Classical School of Economics; New Keynesian Macroeconomics.

Bibliography

Bénassy, J.-P. (1975), 'Neo-Keynesian Disequilibrium Theory in a Monetary Economy', *Review of Economic Studies*, **42**, (132), October, pp. 502–23.

Clower, R.W. (1965), 'The Keynesian Counterrevolution: A Theoretical Appraisal', in F. Hahn and F. Brechling (eds), *The Theory of Interest Rates*, London: Macmillan.

Cooper, R. and A. John (1988), 'Coordinating Coordination Failures in Keynesian Models', *Quarterly Journal of Economics*, **103**, (3), August, pp. 441–63.

Drèze, J. (1975), 'Existence of an Equilibrium with Price Rigidity and Quantity Rationing', *International Economic Review*, **16**, (2), June, pp. 301–20.

Hart, O. (1982), 'A Model of Imperfect Competition with Keynesian Features', *Quarterly Journal of Economics*, **97**, (1), February, pp. 109–38.

Hicks, J. (1937), 'Mr. Keynes and the Classics: A Suggested Interpretation', *Econometrica*, **5**, (2), April, pp. 147–59.

Janssen, M. (1993), *Microfoundations*, London: Routledge.

Keynes, J.M. (1936), *The General Theory of Employment, Interest and Money*, London: Macmillan.

Kydland, F. and E. Prescott (1982), 'Time to Build and Aggregate Fluctuations', *Econometrica*, **50**, (6), November, pp. 1345–70.

Leijonhufvud, A. (1968), *On Keynesian Economics and the Economics of Keynes*, New York: Oxford University Press.

Lucas, R. (1972), 'Expectations and the Neutrality of Money', *Journal of Economic Theory*, **4**, (2), April, pp. 103–24.

Lucas, R. (1978), 'Unemployment Policy', *American Economic Review*, **68**, (2), May, pp. 353–7.

Lucas, R. and L. Rapping (1969), 'Real Wages, Employment and Inflation', *Journal of Political Economy*, **77**, (5), September/October, pp. 721–54.

Mankiw, N. and P. Romer (eds) (1991), *New Keynesian Economics Vols 1 and 2*, Cambridge: MIT Press.

Patinkin, D. (1956), *Money, Interest and Prices*, New York: Harper & Row.

Weintraub, E.R. (1979), *Microfoundations*, Cambridge: Cambridge University Press.

Weitzman, M. (1982), 'Increasing Returns and the Foundations of Unemployment', *Economic Journal*, **92**, (368), December, pp. 787–904.

Minsky, Hyman P.

Hyman Minsky was born in Chicago in 1919. Educated in the public schools of Lima, Ohio, New York City and Chicago, Minsky received his bachelor's degree from the University of Chicago in 1941. Although he majored in mathematics, it appears that the lectures on economics he attended as part of the University of Chicago's integrated social science course catalyzed an incipient interest in economics that was a product of his family's involvement in the American socialist movement. His graduate work, interrupted by a period in the US Army during the mid-1940s, was taken at Harvard, where he earned a master's of public administration in 1947 and his PhD in 1954. The dissertation, directed by Schumpeter until his death in 1950 and then by Leontief, was on the relationship among banking, industrial organization and business cycles.

Minsky taught at Brown from 1949 to 1958 at the University of California at Berkeley from 1956 to 1965 and for the next 25 years at Washington University of St Louis. From 1980, he was also on the faculty at the Center for Advanced Economic Study in Trieste, Italy. Following his retirement from Washington University, he was a Distinguished Scholar at the Jerome Levy Economics Institute at Bard College in Annandale-on-Hudson, New York until his death in 1996.

As pointed out in the useful review of Minsky's work by Dymski and Pollin (1992), his work can best be viewed as an integrated view of the workings of a modern capitalist macroeconomy, rather than as a set of separate insights into pieces of the system. Minsky's essential contribution is the argument that there are financial forces inherent in a private capitalist economy creating the preconditions for business cycles. While these threats can be offset by monetary and fiscal policy in the short and medium term, the application of stabilization policy runs the danger in the longer term of creating inflationary problems and of intensifying the risks of even greater deflationary crises. Like Keynes, Minsky proposes that the prime mover of economic fluctuations is fluctuations in investment demand. The immediate source of those fluctuations, as hypothesized by Keynes in the *General Theory* (1936, p. 151) and re-emphasized by Tobin (1974) is changes in the relative price of producing new capital assets compared to the price of buying existing capital assets. The point is that, when the relative price of new assets compared to existing assets is low, firms will choose to expand by building new physical capital rather than purchasing existing capital either through equity markets or direct markets for physical capital. This will then lead to high rates of investment in plant and equipment. On the other hand, if the relative price of new assets to existing assets is low, investment will be retarded, since it is then cheaper for firms to expand by buying existing assets. What Minsky offers that adds to Keynes and Tobin is an explanation why in market economies this ratio will systematically change over time in a way that propagates traditional business cycles.

Minsky's explanation begins with the observation that, in a trough, most firms have sound balance sheets, in large part due to the bankruptcy of insolvent firms in the previous contraction. Business expansion is slow at first, the prior contraction having created pessimistic memories and low existing asset values, but then, slowly, the expansion creates profits that exceed expectations and euphoria of investors develops. The euphoria affects financial institutions which rapidly expand the supply of credit, driving up existing asset prices and making investment by businesses more attractive. This expansion continues beyond potential GDP because the expansion of credit continues beyond this point, as do the euphoric expectations of business. Since this expansion is largely financed by credit to firms, it leads their balance sheets to become increasingly fragile as the ratio of liabilities to net worth increases. To describe firm balance sheets, Minsky uses the terms 'hedge', 'speculative' or 'Ponzi', connoting progressively more speculative behavior. Using these terms, Minsky would say that the expansion leads to a gradual change in the typical firm's financing from 'hedge' to 'Ponzi'.

In a market economy without an active stabilization policy, the expansion continues beyond potential output, for two reasons. First, businesses are in part guided by non-rational animal spirits to expand, and in part by the observation that their more speculative competitors have been more successful than they have. Second, the supply of credit to non-financial firms rises as the result of innovations in financial institution liabilities such as Eurodollars or money market funds. While these factors lead to expansion beyond potential, they sow the seeds that threaten collapse. The balance sheets of both non-financial and financial firms become more risky, increasing the danger of bankruptcy. This contributes to the deflation of the value of existing assets, including the value of loans to these firms. In turn the value of financial firms' loans and investments is reduced, threatening them with insolvency and, with that, a collapse of economic activity owing to an inability of financial institutions to continue to provide credit.

This threat of contraction is temporarily obviated by a stabilization policy in modern capitalist economies. Through monetary policy, particularly the central bank acting as lender of last resort, bank asset prices can be supported. Through fiscal policy, particularly running large government deficits in recessions, business cash flow can be maintained. (This results from both the stimulation of aggregate demand and the fact that a government deficit tends to create greater surpluses of saving over investment in other sectors, including business.) However, unless undertaken cautiously, these policies lead to even more speculative finance by firms because of the developing confidence that public policy will not allow firms to fail. They also lead to inflation by creating added aggregate demand and adding to labor's bargaining power by providing it with confidence that public policy will act to prevent contractionary crises. Hence these policies create greater inflationary pressure over time and, by turning firm balance sheets more speculative and Ponzi-financed, threaten contractionary crises which will be still more severe.

DAVID WEINBERG

See also:

Business Cycle Theory (I) and (II); Demand Management; Economics of Keynes and of his Revolution, Key Elements of the; Post Keynesian School of Economics.

Bibliography

Dymski, Gary and Robert Pollin (1992), 'Hyman Minsky as Hedgehog: The Power of the Wall Street Paradigm', in Steven Fazzari and Dimitri Papadimitriou (eds), *Financial Conditions and Macroeconomic Performance: Essays in Honor of Hyman Minsky*, New York and London: ME Sharpe.

Keynes, John Maynard (1936), *The General Theory of Employment, Interest and Money*, London: Macmillan.

Minsky, Hyman (1975), *John Maynard Keynes*, New York: Columbia University Press.

Minsky, Hyman (1982), *Can 'It' Happen Again?*, Armonk, NY: M.E. Sharpe.

Minsky, Hyman (1986), *Stabilizing an Unstable Economy*, New Haven, Conn.: Yale University Press.

Papadimitriou, Dimitri B. (1992), 'Minsky on Himself', in Steven Fazzari and Dimitri Papadimitriou (eds), *Financial Conditions and Macroeconomic Performance: Essays in Honor of Hyman Minsky*, New York and London: M.E. Sharpe.

Tobin, James (1974), 'Monetary Policy in 1974 and Beyond', *Brookings Papers on Economic Activity*, **1**, pp. 219–32.

Modigliani, Franco

Franco Modigliani was born in Rome on 18 June 1918. As a child, he attended one of Italy's outstanding high schools in Rome. He decided to skip the last year of high school in order to enter the University of Rome ahead of the normal schedule. He was accepted and he enrolled in the Faculty of Law. He was asked to translate some German articles into Italian for one of the trade associations and thus began his exposure to economic problems. After winning an essay competition in economics (on price controls) he began to think of himself as an economist.

Because of the political situation in Italy, where laws had been passed by the Fascist regime discriminating against Jews, he left Italy for France. In 1939, he returned to Italy to defend his thesis, and thus complete his doctorate degree in jurisprudence, whereupon he departed for the United States in August 1939. In the United States he obtained a scholarship at the New School for Social Research, from which he received his doctoral degree in 1944. His academic appointments were as follows: New Jersey College for

Women, 1942; Bard College (Columbia), 1942–4; New School for Social Research, 1943–4, 1946–8; Cowles Commission, 1949–54; University of Illinois, 1949, 1950–52; Carnegie Institute of Technology, 1952–60; Northwestern University, 1960–62; Massachusetts Institute of Technology, 1962 to the present.

Modigliani's article, 'Liquidity Preference and the Theory of Interest and Money' (1944) contributed greatly to his recognition as an economist, and later to his election as a fellow in the Econometric Society in 1949. In this paper he argued that the main stabilization device deriving from the Keynesian system was monetary policy, not fiscal policy, the latter being more suitable for *special* circumstances under which the mechanism breaks down, such as the Great Depression. During this period he also became concerned with the study of savings, an interest which continued throughout his career. Although his early work was similar to that of Duesenberry, so that the resulting theory is now known as the Duesenberry–Modigliani hypothesis, as well as the relative income hypothesis, his work with Richard Brumberg, while at Carnegie, completed his contribution on the life cycle hypothesis. This was similar to Friedman's permanent income hypothesis, except that the life cycle hypothesis depends on life being finite and differentiated – dependency, maturity and retirement. The main result of this work was to demonstrate that the main determinant of national savings is not income, but growth (Modigliani, 1954).

Another early research interest which later culminated in several articles while Modigliani was at Carnegie was to explain the role of expectations in business planning and how they affect the stability of the economy. Later, while at Carnegie, he collaborated with Simon, Holt and Muth on a book about production scheduling (Holt *et al.*, 1960) together with several articles in this area. Also while at Carnegie-Mellon, he returned to his 1949 monetary theory article and presented a fairly definitive form of his views on money (Modigliani, 1963). In addition, in 1959, he and Merton Miller produced two papers, containing the so-called 'Modigliani–Miller theorems', which represented an important contribution to the field of finance. The first paper offered the proposition that the financial structure (debt–equity ratio) of a firm in a perfect capital market has no effect on its market valuation; the second paper posed the argument that, in a perfect capital market and with no taxes, dividend policy makes no difference on the market value of this firm.

Two other articles written while Modigliani was at Carnegie deserve mention. One is a contribution to oligopoly theory ('New Developments on the Oligopoly Front', 1958) and the other, written with Emile Grunberg, is a methodological one which argues that accurate forecasts are possible even when agents react to them ('The Predictability of Social Events', 1954).

Modigliani's period at MIT can be divided into two parts: the period 1962–74 and the period since. The first period corresponds to the 'golden age of Keynesianism', exemplified by Solow, Samuelson, Tobin and Heller. During this period a Keynesian-type model for forecasting and policy analysis was built in collaboration with Albert Ando, in which money was very important because of the interaction between the consumption function and monetary policy. The model was later modified to account for inflation in the late 1960s.

The second period represented a head-on collision with the monetarists, the first shot being fired during Modigliani's presidential address to the American Economic Association in 1977. The basic theme of the address was that the differences between the monetarists and non-monetarists are basically philosophical and political and not about the workings of the economy or monetary versus fiscal policy. He also voiced disagreement with the idea that national debt makes no difference to the economy, and finally attacked the rational expectations paradigm, an attack whose foundation rests on his earlier analysis regarding the forecasting of social events.

In summary, the one unifying thread throughout Modigliani's many diverse contributions to economics is the propensity to challenge the self-evident orthodoxies in fashion at the time in a proficient and convincing manner. For his contributions to economics, Modigliani was awarded the Nobel Prize in 1985.

VINCENT J. TARASCIO

See also:

Economics of Keynes and of his Revolution, Key Elements of; Friedman, Milton; Interest, Theories of; Life Cycle Hypothesis; Monetarist School of Economics; Monetary Policy; Permanent Income Hypothesis.

Bibliography

Grunberg, Emile and Franco Modigliani (1954), 'The Predictability of Social Events', *Journal of Political Economy*, **62**, (6), December, pp. 465–78.

Holt, Charles C., Franco Modigliani, John F. Muth and Herbert A. Simon (1960), *Planning Production, Inventories and Work Forces*, Englewood Cliffs, NJ: Prentice-Hall.

Miller, Merton H. and Franco Modigliani (1961), 'Dividend Policy, Growth, and the Valuation of Shares', *Journal of Business*, **34**, (4), October, pp. 411–33.

Modigliani, Franco (1944), 'Liquidity Preference and the Theory of Interest and Money', *Econometrica*, **12**, (1), January, pp. 45–88.

Modigliani, Franco (1949), 'Fluctuations in the Saving–Income Ratio: A Problem in Economic Forecasting', *Studies in Income and Wealth*, New York: National Bureau of Economic Research.

Modigliani, Franco (1954), 'Utility Analysis and the Consumption Function: An Interpretation of Cross-Section Data', in K.K. Kurihara (ed.), *Post-Keynesian Economics*, London: George Allen & Unwin.

Modigliani, Franco (1958), 'New Developments on the Oligopoly Front', *Journal of Political Economy*, **66**, (3), June, pp. 215–32.

Modigliani, Franco (1963), 'The Monetary Mechanism and Its Intersection with Real Phenomena', *Review of Economics and Statistics*, **45**, (1, Part 2), February, Supplement, pp. 79–110.

Modigliani, Franco (1977), 'The Monetarist Controversy or, Should We Forsake Stabilization Policies?', *American Economic Review*, **67**, (2), March, pp. 1–19.

Modigliani, Franco and Merton Miller (1958), 'The Cost of Capital, Corporation Finance and the Theory of Investment', *American Economic Review*, **48**, (3), June, pp. 261–97.

Monetarist School of Economics

The monetarist school of economics may be traced back to rudiments of the quantity theory of money, on the one hand, or it may be viewed as coming about in the post-World War II years. The 'monetarism' label first appears in July 1970 in Lord Nicholas Kaldor's 'The New Monetarism', in which, in the *Lloyds Bank Review*, he addresses a Milton Friedman-led flow of influence from the United States to London. In the 1970 article Kaldor said 'the new monetarism' is a 'Friedman Revolution' more truly than Keynes was the sole fount of the 'Keynesian Revolution'.

To be sure, a 'school' reflects a body of thought rather than a location, but in the postwar period the ideas were coming to Britain from across the Atlantic. Although many players may be associated with the school in its beginning, the more visible Americans were primarily Friedman and his immediate students, and secondarily Karl Brunner, a Swiss national who came to the United States, and his co-worker Alan Meltzer (Frazer, 1995). The principal Friedman/monetarist-connected institutions were the National Bureau of Economic Research (NBER), the Federal Reserve Bank of St Louis, and Friedman's Chicago during his tenure there.

The 'Friedman revolution' was a revolution in ideas, not unlike the revolution fostered by J.M. Keynes. Both had considerable impact on events and the implementation of political change in the United States and the United Kingdom, as well as elsewhere. Hence the title, *Power and Ideas*, is a reference to influence on government through persuasion. The words in the sub-title *The Big U-Turn*, were added to deal with ideas as they appear through political actions, beginning mainly with Margaret Thatcher's government in the United Kingdom and Ronald Reagan's presidency in the United States. Even so, the Friedman/monetarist influence was quite widespread, extending to Chile and selected central banks around the world. Key features of the Reagan era reappear in the Newt Gingrich-led 104th Congress. The use of the label 'monetarism' was more diluted in the United States than in the United Kingdom in the 1970s and 1980s. This was the case because in the former 'monetarism' competed with the label 'supply-side economics' for use in economics, while in the latter 'supply-side economics' was subsumed under the label of 'monetarism'.

Early in the Friedman revolution there were efforts to list the main tenets of monetarism. Some concluded that doing so was arbitrary, possibly because of the diversity of beliefs among interested parties and because of the depth, breadth and complexity of Friedman's work and influence. Friedman's student, Richard Selden, spread his net in 1976 to include as monetarists those who believed (1) that 'money matters' and (2) that monetary changes can be controlled by central banks. Continuing, Selden noted that, 20 years earlier few economists held these beliefs while many economists now shared them.

Friedman himself did not like the term 'monetarism'. He preferred the label 'the new quantity theory of money'. However, I regard Friedman as offering a philosophically based, total, overall analytical system where even some key features of the system were not widely shared as the system emerged (Frazer 1988, 1994a). Consequently, in narrowing the scope of the investigation, I list and annotate seventeen tenets. Some of this list may be restated.

1. *Friedman's law*: inflation is everywhere and in every place a monetary phenomenon. For most of the 1867–1975 period for which Friedman and Schwartz (1982) analysed data, causation runs from the time rate of change in the money stock to business conditions (or income) with some feedback. However, in the presence of fiscal policy (viewed as a deficit) with monetary accommodation, Kaldor causation enters: it is from the time rate of change in income to the money stock ($\dot{Y} \rightarrow \dot{M}$). Nevertheless the inflation still follows from the monetary accommodation and not from fiscal policy itself. There is a government budget constraint (tenet 3).

2. *Friedman's rule*: for relatively stable, non-inflationary growth in income, money stock growth takes place at the sustainable rate of growth in real output. This includes allowance for secular trend changes in the velocity ratio. The inverse of velocity is the Cambridge k as found in the cash balance, quantity-theoretic expression $[M = k(...)Y]$ where the factor k is a variable factor in Keynes's 1923 work and in Friedman's work.

3. *The government budget constraint*: in the law and rule context above, all fiscal policy as a deficit (surplus) can do is to drive the private sector out of (into) the total spending on the output of goods and services.

4. *Identification of the money demand function*: the central bank controls the nominal money stock while households control the real stock. They do so through the demand for money viewed as velocity (or its inverse). Indeed, via this route Friedman dealt with the technical problem of identification.

5. *An alternative system*: the Friedman system is an alternative to an interest rate orientation with fiscal policy (à la Kaldor and the Bank of England) for controlling income and/or for stabilizing business condi-

tions. Attempts to combine the alternative M and i systems are futile, even with reliance on heavy doses of *ceteris paribus*, because the key variables are not in fact independent of one another and because monetary and fiscal policy appear as substitutes. Inflationary expectations enter into the long-bond rate to make it uncontrollable by the direct means of the central bank, and money stock growth is not in fact independent of the inflation rate (tenet 1 above).

6. *Time frames and inflation*: following practices initiated by Wesley Mitchell's NBER, turning points in business conditions are dated. Time series lead, coincide with or lag these conditions. Trends are fitted in reference to averages of data points between peaks and troughs and deviations in the series from the trends are transitory or cyclical components of the series. Viewing these deviations in inflationary and decelerated inflation terms there may be an illusion (albeit rational in personalistic probability terms) on the part of agents about the inflationary moves. These moves are such that the agents do not fully sense them and build them into anticipated changes along the Bayesian/personalistic probability lines. However Friedman and Schwartz observed (1982, pp. 569–73) a change in the structure underlying the formation of inflationary expectations in the mid-1960s.

7. *The money illusion*: expectations of inflation on the part of agents adjust to the fundamentals with less lag in the mid-1960s; hence a reduction in money illusion. The change in structure (tenet 6) held considerable importance for Friedman and Schwartz, in view of the search for a stable statistical relation, especially between money growth, income and interest rates. This is because simple lead and lag relationships are complicated by the greater sensitivity of agents, in the formation of personalistically weighted, inflationary expectations ($Pb[\dot{P}^e]\dot{P}^e$).

8. *Long-bond rates, a surrogate for monetary policy*: in the light of greater sensitivity in the formation of expectations (tenets 6 and 7) and in the presence of predominating data errors and related data problems in relating to the short-run control over the money stock (M) and its velocity (V), some interest rate phenomena are encapsulated in concepts such as 'New York's revenge' and 'the Bundesbank effect'. In this money aggregates/errors/sensitivity context, the long-term bond rate is viewed as a surrogate for monetary policy considered in terms of accommodation, neutrality and discipline. In the context, bond traders adjust prices of the bellwether bonds and the 'trading books' are elevated in importance in the short and medium term in relation to the concept of a portfolio of securities.

9. *Psychological time*: agents respond to a current episode and look backward to prior analogous situations in forming views about the outcome

of the impact from the current episode. Time is not simply a calendar time, lagged distribution of the recent past but a looking backward to analogous events which may occur in a more or less distant time interval. After it had first been mentioned by Maurice Allais, Friedman put psychological time into the economic analysis.

Turning to the diversity of those who may be called monetarists, even Karl Brunner and Allan Meltzer would share only six of the seventeen tenets (Frazer, 1997). Monetarism was Friedman's show.

WILLIAM FRAZER

See also:

Aggregate Demand–Aggregate Supply Model Diagram; Brunner, Karl; Business Cycle Theory (I) and (II); Cagan, Philip; Demand Management; Expectations, Theories of; Friedman, Milton; Inflation; Keynesian Revolution; Lucas Critique; Meltzer, Allan H.; Monetary Policy; Money; Neutrality of Money: The Keynesian Challenge; Quantity Theory of Money; Schwartz, Anna J.

Bibliography
Frazer, William (1988), *Power and Ideas: Milton Friedman and the Big U-Turn*, Gainesville, FL: Gulf/Atlantic Publishing Company.
Frazer, William (1994a), *The Legacy of Keynes and Friedman*, Westport Conn.: Praeger Publishers.
Frazer, William (1994b), *The Central Banks*, Westport, Conn.: Praeger Publishers.
Frazer, William (1997), 'Tenets of Monetarism: A Friedman Variation', in William Frazer, *The Friedman System: Economic Analysis of Time Series*, Westport, Conn.: Praeger.
Friedman, Milton and Anna J. Schwartz (1963), *A Monetary History of the United States, 1867–1960*, Princeton: Princeton University Press.
Friedman, Milton and Anna J. Schwartz (1982), *Monetary Trends in the United States and the United Kingdom*, Chicago: University of Chicago Press.
Kaldor, Nicholas (1970), 'The New Monetarism', *Lloyds Bank Review*, **22**, (97), July, pp. 1–18.
Keynes, John M. (1923), *Tract on Monetary Reform*, London: Macmillan.
Selden, Richard (1976), 'Monetarism', in Sidney Weintraub (ed.), *Modern Economic Thought*, Philadelphia: University of Pennsylvannia Press.

Monetary Policy

Central banks affect the level of economic activity by influencing the size of a nation's money supply or the level of nominal interest rates. Through their ability to issue high-powered money by purchasing securities in the open market or by lending to banks, central banks influence both the quantity of money created by banks and the interest rate on loans. Monetary policy refers to the use of central bank policy tools to achieve macroeconomic or financial goals.

The choice of an appropriate policy goal depends on the structure of the economy. The viewpoint held by a large majority of economists before the appearance of Keynes's *General Theory* in 1936 was that monetarily induced changes in aggregate demand have only temporary effects on output and the unemployment rate but have lasting effects on prices. The popularity of Keynesian economics and the empirical finding of a trade-off between wage inflation and the unemployment rate by A.W.H. Phillips combined in the 1950s and 1960s to persuade many that higher inflation could be exchanged for permanently lower unemployment. In the late 1960s, however, Milton Friedman and Edmund Phelps reasserted the view that no long-run trade-off exists. Friedman and Phelps argued that the unemployment rate tends toward a 'natural rate' determined by real factors, such as the size and quality of the labor force, the size of the capital stock, the state of technology and the economy's tax, welfare and regulatory structure. Events of the 1970s converted most economists to this viewpoint. The current majority view maintains that monetary policy affects output and the unemployment rate only temporarily but affects the price level permanently.

Such a view naturally leads central bankers to give high priority to price level stability, since the long-run behavior of the price level depends on the growth of aggregate demand relative to the trend growth of aggregate output. Most debate since the early 1970s has centered on the way central banks should attempt to achieve price level stability and whether they should attempt simultaneously to achieve any subsidiary goals. In practice, most central banks attempt to protect the liquidity of their nations' financial systems, and many attempt to dampen output fluctuations around the trend growth path, while retaining price stability as their primary goal.

The optimal strategy for achieving monetary policy goals has been debated for more than 150 years. Economists are divided over two issues. First, should central bankers be constrained to follow explicit policy rules, or should they be permitted to use discretion in determining the course of policy? Second, should monetary policy focus on the quantity of money (however defined) or on interest rates? Both issues arise from the fact that monetary policy affects aggregate demand indirectly.

Proponents of policy rules, a group that includes members of the British 'currency school' of the 1840s as well as modern monetarists and new classical economists, argue that rules are valuable for a number of reasons. First, a rule prevents monetary policy from being used for short-term political purposes. Second, a rule prevents central bankers from attempting to 'fine-tune' the economy. Monetarists claim that aggressive efforts to offset the business cycle contributed to the inflationary policies pursued by some central banks in the 1970s. Third, proponents of rules argue that monetary policy is less disruptive to the economy when policy actions are anticipated correctly by producers and consumers. Without a rule to constrain them, policy makers have the incentive to change policies suddenly to produce short-term economic gains. Any commitment to a stable-price policy is not credible unless enforced by a rule, a proposition known as the time-inconsistency problem.

Opponents of rules, from the British 'banking school' of the 1840s to Keynesian and other modern economists representing a variety of viewpoints, typically argue that the fragility of the financial system and the complexity of the monetary policy process make rules inferior to discretionary policy. Steadfastly following rules limits the ability of the central bank to respond to liquidity problems in the financial sector, making financial crises more probable. Rules that constrain the quantity of high-powered money the central bank can make available to the the economy tend to increase the variability of interest rates, which may have negative effects on economic activity.

Beyond the financial problems that may follow from rigid adherence to rules, opponents argue that rules presume that the structure of the economy does not change over time. If the economic structure changes significantly, the results from following a rule will also change. For example suppose the central bank is following a monetary aggregate growth rule in an attempt to maintain zero inflation. The equation of exchange, expressed in terms of growth rates, is $m + v = \pi + y$, where m is the growth rate of a monetary aggregate, v is the growth rate of the corresponding velocity, π is the inflation rate, and y is the growth rate of real output. By controlling m, policy makers can hold inflation to zero on average over the course of business cycles only if the trend rate of output growth (y) and the trend behavior of velocity growth (v) remain constant. Cyclical fluctuations in output would cause inflation to deviate from zero, although constant money growth might stabilize output growth to some extent. However procyclical velocity behavior would exacerbate cyclical fluctuations in aggregate spending ($\pi + y$). Regardless of the cyclical consequences, changes in the trend rates of growth of v or π would defeat the purpose of the rule: to maintain zero inflation.

Not all opponents of policy rules reject the idea that central banks should be required by law to pursue particular policy goals. The relatively low inflation rates maintained by (West) Germany and Switzerland during the 1970s and 1980s are testimony to the importance attached to price stability by the German and Swiss governments. Even the banking school, which opposed using a rule constraining the quantity of high-powered bank notes the Bank of England could issue, regarded the maintenance of gold convertibility, a legislated policy goal, as their highest priority. How best to ensure continued convertibility of Bank of England notes was the question.

The second issue, whether to concentrate on a monetary aggregate or an interest rate (or some set of related interest rates), also continues to be debated. Advocates of money growth targets cite the historical relationship between money growth and inflation. Although various factors affect the price level over relatively short time periods, extended and severe inflation has always been accompanied by relatively high money growth rates. The policy implication drawn from this fact, and from the quantity theory of money that purports to explain it, is that the central bank must control money growth if it is to control inflation.

A further argument in favor of a monetary aggregate target is that utilizing a pure interest rate target leads to procyclical monetary policy. During a cyclical expansion, the demand for money increases, as shown in Figure 1. To maintain the interest rate at its target level, policy makers must allow the quantity of money to increase to accommodate the increased demand for money. The increased stock of money, in turn, encourages even more rapid spending growth. During a recession, the opposite occurs.

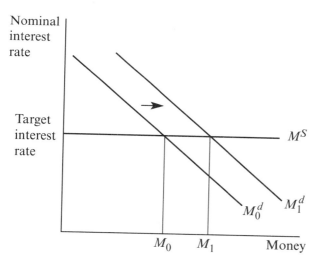

Figure 1

Not all proponents of interest rate targets reject these arguments. Many economists – and central bankers – argue that policy makers should use an interest rate to control a monetary aggregate or should consider information on money growth when setting an interest rate target. In the first case, the relationship between high-powered money and a particular monetary aggregate (the money multiplier) may be unstable. It may prove easier to control the quantity of money by using interest rates to affect the quantity of money demanded than by rigidly controlling the quantity of high-powered money. However such a strategy works only if the target monetary aggregate is related to aggregate demand in a stable manner.

Many economists and policy makers believe that the effects of monetary policy are transmitted primarily through interest rates and that the quantity of money is determined endogenously by a variety of real and financial factors. If this is so, policy makers should use the information gleaned from a variety of policy 'indicators' in setting interest rate targets. On this view, money growth is not a policy variable, but an information variable. Using information on the growth rates of various monetary aggregates in conjunction with output and price data, central bankers can adjust interest rate targets to avoid contributing to inflationary or recessionary movements in the economy. Such a strategy calls for raising interest rate targets when inflationary conditions emerge and reducing interest rates when the economy appears to be weakening.

NEIL T. SKAGGS

See also:
Adjustment Mechanisms of the Basic Classical and Keynesian Models; Aggregate Demand–Aggregate Supply Model and Diagram; Clower, Robert W. Davidson, Paul; Friedman, Milton; IS/LM Model and Diagram; Keynes and Probability; Keynesian Revolution; Leijonhufvud, Axel; Lucas Critique; Meltzer, Allan H.; Minsky, Hyman P.; Monetarist School of Economics.

Bibliography
Friedman, Milton (1968), 'The Role of Monetary Policy', *American Economic Review*, **58**, (1), March, pp. 1–17.
Fuhrer, Jeffrey (ed.) (1994), *Goals, Guidelines, and Constraints Facing Monetary Policymakers*, Federal Reserve Bank of Boston Conference Series No. 38.
Taylor, John B. (1993), 'Discretion versus Policy Rules in Practice', Carnegie-Rochester Conference Series on Public Policy, vol. 39, New York: North-Holland.

Monetizing the (Federal) Debt

Debt monetization is a process which involves federal government debt (bonds) being used as an instrument to create new money.

How does the process of debt monetization operate?
In the United States context, debt monetization occurs when the Treasury sells bonds to the Federal Reserve, a process which involves the creation of new reserves in the banking system and, subsequently, an increase in the money supply. The Treasury selling bonds to the central bank is equivalent to printing money and is a modern method of creating new money. Monetary expansion occurs whether the new bonds sold by the Treasury to the Fed are to replace old bonds held by the public or are to finance a current budget deficit. Debt monetization may also occur by the Treasury selling securities to the public, while the Fed simultaneously buys securities from the public

(in open market operations), so that the government securities held by the public remain constant. The Fed thus lends to the Treasury indirectly. The effect is the same in either case: an increase in bank reserves and the money supply.

Debt monetization is different from the Treasury's routine debt management. Debt management involves the refinancing of the national debt by selling new bonds directly to the public either to repay other maturing bonds or to finance current budget deficits. Debt management as just described does not create money, whereas debt monetization (selling bonds to the Federal Reserve) does create money.

Some policy implications of debt monetization

The implications of debt monetization are related to the new money created by the process and how this increase in the money supply will affect the economy. Much depends upon the state of the economy. Debt monetization could be an appropriate policy action under some circumstances, but in other situations it could be inappropriate and could destabilize the economy by causing inflation.

In the circumstances of widespread and persistent unemployment and deflationary pressure, as existed in the 1930s (and which inspired John Maynard Keynes to write the *General Theory of Employment, Interest and Money*), debt monetization could be a part of an expansionary government policy aimed at increasing employment and economic activity. In this instance current government budget deficits might be financed by monetizing debt, which would provide a monetary stimulus to accompany the fiscal stimulus. There would be monetary 'accommodation' to the fiscal stimulus. At issue would be the relative amounts of debt to be monetized to provide a suitable stimulus to the economy. In this instance the issuance of new government debt is merely a modern way of printing money and increasing the money supply. Monetizing (some/all of) a budget deficit in the unemployment/deflationary context would be more stimulative than a policy of selling equivalent bonds to the public. In the first case, the money supply expands; in the second case, it does not.

Most governments have substantial national debts, so the fraction of an existing debt which might be appropriate to monetize as part of an expansionary policy would remain very small. The fraction of a *current budget deficit* which might be monetized would be larger. In the circumstances of full employment and upward pressures on the price level, debt monetization would be destabilizing. The resulting increase in the money supply would increase inflationary pressures. In this case selling debt to the public would be preferable because such sales would not increase the money supply. Care must be taken in judging the appropriateness of debt monetization.

Debt monetization, war finance and interest rate pegs

Debt monetization is an important aspect of wartime deficit financing and inflation. In war or in other circumstances, monetization may occur as a result of an official commitment to stabilize (peg) interest rates at low levels relative to market conditions. The US experience with World War II financing and the policy of the Federal Reserve supporting the government bond market during and after the war is illustrative.

During World War II and until March 1951 the Fed was committed to supporting the price of government bonds at the low nominal interest rates inherited from the 1930s depression. The Fed's commitment was necessary to stabilize the interest rates paid on government bonds. Supporting the government bond market was seen as part of the national war effort. Continued support after the war was aimed at holding down the interest cost of the greatly expanded national debt. During this period the Federal Reserve was, in effect, subordinated to the Treasury.

The Fed's ability to control the money supply and inflation was compromised by its support of the government bond market. Bond prices and interest rates vary inversely, so maintaining a high price on government bonds was necessary to keep the interest rates low. Thus the Fed stood ready to purchase all government bonds which the private market would not buy at the supported price/interest rate. The Fed's purchase of bonds monetized debt and created inflationary pressures. In purchasing the 'surplus' bonds in the market the Fed was releasing new money into the economy. Had the Fed not purchased the excess bonds, bond prices would have fallen and driven up interest rates.

The inflationary effect of debt monetization was partially concealed during the war by price controls and rationing. The price level rose somewhat when price controls and rationing ended after the war, but the Federal Reserve policy of supporting the government bond market continued. The bond purchases necessary to support the market limited the Fed's freedom to control the money supply and pursue an independent policy. An effort to tighten monetary policy would tend to increase interest rates and depress the bond prices, which meant the Fed had to purchase whatever bonds the private market did not buy, and thus monetize part of the debt. Interest rates and the money supply could not *both* be controlled.

The Fed regained its ability to pursue an independent monetary policy as a result of the Federal Reserve–Treasury Accord of March 1951, which released the Fed from its obligation to support the price of government securities. The Accord was prompted by the inflationary potential associated with the outbreak of the Korean War in June 1950. The US experience during World War II and up to March 1951 demonstrated the inflationary potential of debt monetization. In that instance, however, much of the new debt was sold to the public and was not monetized. The inflation could have been worse.

Debt monetization is common in wartime but is also seen in some inflation-prone countries. Where a country has a weak fiscal system, is unable to collect adequate taxes for routine governmental functions and consequently runs large deficits, debt monetization is a significant cause of inflation. In such circumstances a relationship between budget deficits and persistent inflation may be evident. However the association between deficits and inflation may be largely absent where both old debt and moderate amounts of new debt are sold to the public, rather than to the central bank. Care must be exercised in making generalizations regarding the relationship of government budget deficits and inflation. There may be little relationship where debt monetization does not occur, but a strong relationship where substantial monetization takes place.

Retiring the national debt via monetization

Debt monetization is one approach to retiring the national debt. Gradual debt monetization (over several decades) would be a way to provide for the necessary expansion of the money supply and would also reduce the interest costs of the debt. Publicly held debt would be reduced, while debt held by the Federal Reserve would increase. (Most of the interest paid to the Fed is returned to the Treasury.) The process would have to be very gradual to avoid destabilizing the economy. An effort to pay off the debt by monetizing it over a period of just a few years would result in a massive increase in the money supply, hyperinflation and a corresponding decline in the international value of the dollar. (The dollar price of foreign currency would increase.) Paying off the debt by rapid monetization would be very close to repudiation. The debt would be repaid in dollars seriously depreciated by inflation. Holders of bonds and cash balances would suffer serious losses of purchasing power.

WILLIAM E. LAIRD

See also:

Deficits: Cyclical and Structural; Demand Management of; Economics of Keynes and of his Revolution, Key Elements of the; Fiscal Policy; Functional Finance; Keynesian Revolution; Monetary Policy.

Bibliography

Levy, Mickey D. (1981), 'Factors Affecting Monetary Policy in an Era of Inflation', *Journal of Monetary Economics*, **8**, (3), November, pp. 351–73.

Money[1]

Throughout history, the range of objects used as money has varied widely. Such different media as blankets, cows, stones, bushels of wheat and cigarettes have served as embodiments of money at different times.[2] A central focus of economic inquiry has long been to determine the definition of money and to analyse the forces that give rise to the emergence of a monetary economy.

Since at least the publication of Keynes's *General Theory* (1936), the issue of defining money has been pursued in terms of delineating the essential properties of money (for example, Hicks, 1967, p. 1). The functions of money as a medium of exchange, standard of value and store of wealth are widely acknowledged as generic to the phenomenon of money. This tripartite characterization of money is, however, inadequate in capturing the essence of the monetary phenomenon. In particular, the listing of the essential properties of an object does not constitute a definition of that object.

In order to demonstrate this proposition, consider first the store of wealth function of money. It has long been observed that this function is shared by a wide variety of goods and services in a monetary economy. Moreover any durable good can be accumulated as wealth in a barter economy. Thus the accumulation of wealth in the form of different physical objects is feasible within a barter-exchange economy. Next, consider the medium of exchange and unit of account functions of money. Since at least the time of the classical writers, it has been commonplace to assign primacy to the medium of exchange function of money (Chick, 1978, p. 144; Laidler, 1991). In fact it is the unit of account, or numeraire, function of money that is essential for the emergence of a monetary economy. The primacy of the numeraire can be conveyed both in terms of monetary history and in terms of the development of monetary theory. With regard to the former, there have been a number of historical episodes during which the unit of account function of money existed without money also serving as a medium of exchange. For example, in ancient Sparta, the government outlawed the use of money as a medium of exchange; trade was conducted by the direct exchange of goods. Yet, to facilitate such transactions, the government created (and held) huge coins – too heavy to be carried about – which served only as units of account. In turn, during the thousand-year span from the reign of Charlemagne to the French Revolution, the unit of account and the medium of exchange were separate phenomena (see Aschheim and Park, 1976; Guggenheim, 1989, pp. 9–16).[3]

With regard to the development of monetary doctrine, at least since Walras, a major strand of monetary economics imparts primacy to the capacity of money to serve as a numeraire. Specifically, in his classic work, *The Elements of Pure Political Economy* (1889), Walras's formulation of a general equilibrium model demonstrates the primacy of money's role as a unit of account. It is Walras's inclusion of the numeraire quality of money that imparts to his model the clear-cut character of a money-exchange as contrasted to a barter-exchange framework. In particular, in his general equilibrium model, Walras incorporates the numeraire as an integral part of his system of equations. Each of his market-clearing equations is denominated in the numeraire. The existence of a numeraire allows market clearing to occur, through a continuous groping for prices. Prices emerge at the point of equation of the quantity supplied with the quantity demanded in individual markets. Yet this process of tâtonnement takes place without money having changed hands (means of payment) and without money having been saved (store of value). Consequently it is the existence of money solely as a numeraire that allows the distinction to be made between a money-exchange system and a barter-exchange system. The introduction of a numeraire involves a switch of regimes from a barter-exchange economy to a money-exchange economy (Aschheim and Tavlas, 1994). The contraction in transaction costs (for example, calculation, information or search) imparts a non-neutrality character to money. It is Walras's grasp of the numeraire role of money as essential for the economic calculus at the core of a money-exchange economy that has permeated the subsequent development of general equilibrium and capital theory. It is for this reason that Aschheim and Tavlas (forthcoming) have advanced the primacy of the unit of account as the theory of the core of the nature of money – what the authors have named 'embryonic money'.

The primacy of the unit of account was articulated by Keynes in his *Treatise on Money* (1930), in which the distinction is made between money-of-account and 'money in itself'. Keynes observed: 'Now if the same thing answered to the same description, the description would have no practical interest. But if the thing can change, while the description remains the same, then the distinction can be highly significant' (1930, vol. I, pp. 3–4). More recently Hicks (1989) has also focused on the primacy of the unit-of-account function of money, whereby the numeraire quality emerges as crucial to both the calculation of economic value and the denomination of debt obligations.[4]

The regime switch non-neutrality involved in the transition from a barter to a monetary economy is differentiable from the non-neutrality principles which apply after a money economy has been established. The basis for comparison of these additional non-neutrality principles is Say's Law of Markets, whereby the supply of goods creates its own demand; money is neutral both in the short run and in the long run, so that money can make no difference to either the level or the growth rate of the trend path of real output (Lucas, 1994, p. 6). A literal interpretation of such a generalization is tantamount to the proposition that aggregate demand, as separable from demand at the micro-unit level, is non-existent. The absence of aggregate demand is conceivable only within the context of a barter-exchange economy. In a barter system, wherein by definition generalized purchasing power does not exist, there can be borrowing and lending of goods and services alongside the change of ownership involved with outright purchase and sale transactions. Therefore the barter-exchange economy can include credit; but the scope for credit under barter rules out financial markets. The emergence of financial claims presupposes the presence of a numeraire and, once a numeraire surfaces, the barter-exchange system will be transmuted into a money-exchange system.

In this vein, adherence to the prevalence of Say's Law abstracts from the distinctiveness that embryonic money injects into the performance of exchange transactions. Such abstraction logically necessitates the double coincidence of wants, the roundaboutness of the search process for trading partners and the heightening of transaction costs in effecting credit links, as well as outright purchases and sales. Thus the heuristic device of injecting Say's Law into the conceptualization of a macroeconomy is equivalent to short-circuiting not only the totality of financial markets but the entire process of speculation in such markets and the role of changes in relative prices as a signalling mechanism for changes in demand and supply.

The view that money is non-neutral in the sense that the existence of money invalidates Say's Law of Markets has been a predominant theme of the Post Keynesian literature. Such writers as Davidson (1972, 1978), Minsky (1982), Dow (1985), Arestis (1992) and Rousseas (1992) stress the themes of uncertainty, historical time and the importance of money demand contracts. In particular this approach has sought to expand upon Keynes's argument in the *General Theory* that 'the importance of money essentially flows from its being a link between present and the future' (1936, p. 293). In a world of uncertainty, when production takes time, there is a gap between the capitalist's initial purchases of means of production and the realization of sales revenue. The existence of money contracts permits the sharing of the burdens of uncertainty. Accordingly, in order to enter into long-term contracts, economic agents must have confidence that the value of money will be stable (Davidson, 1972, pp. 869–71; 1978, p. 148). Uncertainty with regard to the price level interferes with the smooth functioning of the monetary economy, since economic agents will be reluctant to enter into monetary debt contracts, and imparts a clear-cut non-neutrality character to money.

In reaching this conclusion, Post Keynesians draw a distinction between logical time and historical time. Logical time can be illustrated by way of the Walrasian system. Specifically the time-consuming process of establishing prices, during which there could be uncertainty, is eliminated by assuming that the Walrasian auctioneer establishes prices through the process of tâtonnement. As Dow (1985, p. 15) put it: 'The short run and long run do not have a time dimension in the historical sense; it is a logical distinction between consecutive events.' In contrast, for Post Keynesians, it is the uncertainty inherent in historical time which is both the necessary and the sufficient condition for the existence of money (Arestis, 1992, p. 93). The prices of goods and services in the present do not contain enough information to be able to form precise predictions about prices in the future. Unlike the concept of risk (in the Knightian sense), which is confined to objective probability and therefore amenable to probability statements, uncertainty includes subjective probabilities and is not measurable. Accordingly money is needed to bridge the uncertainty gap that characterizes the real world (Davidson, 1972, p. 872). Although post-Keynesians recognize that other liquid assets can fulfill this function, as Chick (1992, p. 141) has argued, 'money retains distinctiveness ... in being the asset acceptable as final means of payment'.

It is interesting to compare the above Post Keynesian view with the non-neutrality propositions set forth by monetarist and new classical writers. With regard to monetarism, Friedman (1968) has described a short-run Phillips curve process whereby changes in the money supply lead to changes in prices and, with wages slow to adjust because of the inertia of expectations (that is, expectations are adaptive), profits and output are both affected, rendering money non-neutral. With regard to new classical economics, Lucas (1972) has emphasized the signal extraction problem associated with unexpected changes in the money supply; under rational expectations, the inability of economic agents to decompose the resulting price changes into variations due to the absolute level of prices and changes attributable to relative prices produces non-neutralities in the short run. Note the underlying similarity between the Post Keynesian non-neutrality proposition and the non-neutrality propositions articulated by Friedman and Lucas, respectively. Uncertainty, in one guise or another, is at the core of all three non-neutrality propositions.

Nevertheless there is a fundamental difference between the monetarist and new classical monetary theories, on the one hand, and the Post Keynesian analysis on the other. This difference concerns the issue of exogeneity versus endogeneity of money. Monetarists and new classical writers typically assume that the demand for money is stable (Friedman, 1987; Lucas, 1988) and that the supply of money is subject to the control of the monetary authorities. Open market operations, for example, can be used to set the supply of money at a predetermined level, provided that interest rates are allowed to vary. Accordingly, if the monetary authorities desire to do so, they can control the money supply and therefore achieve price level stability, eliminating short-run non-neutralities associated with money.

For Post Keynesian writers, however, the money supply process is considered to be endogenous. This view flows logically from the crucial roles assigned in Post Keynesian analysis to the production process and the historical-time dimension of a modern economy. As pointed out by Arestis (1992, p. 93), the emphasis on the contractual relationship involved in the production process leads to the proposition that money is credit-driven and demand-determined. Credit is demanded by businesses because the production process takes time; since production costs are incurred and paid before revenues from sales materialize, the need arises to bridge this gap. Such financing is met by bank borrowing (in addition to the use of any internally generated funds). Thus the supply of money responds primarily to the demand-driven behavior of the private economic agents rather than to the exogenous behavior of the monetary authorities (Arestis, 1992, p. 109). Moreover such writers as Kaldor (1986), Moore (1983) and Rousseas (1985) have argued that direct control over the monetary base would conflict with the monetary authorities' commitment to preserve the liquidity of the system. In the limit, the supply of money function becomes a horizontal line at the policy-determined short-term nominal interest rate (Kaldor, 1986; Moore, 1988; Smithin, 1994). Should the central bank refuse to supply the needed reserves, it would risk financial disaster (Cottrell, 1994, p. 597). Indeed, according to Minsky (1982), the risk of a financial disaster is endemic to the capitalistic system, as the emergence of a speculative bubble is apt to induce the monetary authorities to raise interest rates. Such action by the authorities not only discourages productive investment but is likely to trigger cash flow problems that render highly geared financial structures more fragile and vulnerable to collapse (Minsky, 1982, pp. 90–116).

Thus the controversial concept of money supply endogeneity looms large in Post Keynesian monetary theory. Another controversial concept that also looms large in the reformulation of Keynes's analysis as a consequence of Post Keynesian monetary theory is the inherent instability of capitalism. This instability is an inevitable by-product of the modern financial sector that the existence of money engenders. Fundamentally it is the negation of Say's Law that accounts for money supply endogeneity and capitalism's instability. Keynes was consistent and persistent in denying Say's Law.

JOSEPH ASCHHEIM
GEORGE S. TAVLAS

Notes

1 The views expressed below are those of the authors and are not to be interpreted as those of the International Monetary Fund.
2 Tobin (1992, p. 771) has argued that 'the variety of choice defies generalization about the intensive properties of money'. We take issue with this view below.
3 The numeraire function of money also determines, to a large extent, the choice of currencies that are used internationally. Specifically, once a contract is denominated in a certain currency, payment is typically made in that currency. For an elaboration of this argument, see Tavlas (1991).
4 Most writers, however, do not recognize the importance of the numeraire function in giving

rise to a money economy. For example, in his survey of post-Keynesian monetary economics, Cottrell (1994, p. 590) states that 'one can analyse a modern economy as if it were ultimately equivalent to a barter system, in which all decisions are made in terms of "real" goods, with money supervening as a veil – *a mere numeraire*' (emphasis added).

See also:

Clower, Robert W.; Davidson, Paul; Economics of Keynes and of his Revolution, Key Elements of the; Friedman, Milton; Keynesian Revolution; Lausanne, The School of; Meltzer, Allan H.; Monetarist School of Economics; Quantity Theory of Money; Say's Law.

Bibliography

Arestis, P. (1992), *The Post-Keynesian Approach to Economics*, Aldershot: Edward Elgar.

Aschheim, J. and Y.S. Park (1976), *Artificial Currency Units: The Formation of Functional Currency Areas*, Essays in International Finance, No.114, Princeton, NJ: Princeton University Press.

Aschheim, J. and G.S. Tavlas (1994), 'Nominal Anchors for Monetary Policy: A Doctrinal Approach', *Banca Nazionale del Lavoro Quarterly Review*, **46**, (191), December, pp. 469–94.

Aschheim, J. and G.S. Tavlas (1995), 'Monetary Economics in Doctrinal Perspective: A Comparative Study on Embryonic Money', *Journal of Money, Credit and Banking*.

Chick, V. (1978), 'Unresolved Questions in Monetary Theory: A Critical Review', *De Economist*, **126**, (1), pp. 37–60.

Chick, V. (1992), 'Money', *On Money, Method and Keynes*, London: Macmillan, pp. 141–2.

Cottrell, A. (1994), 'Post-Keynesian Monetary Economics', *Cambridge Journal of Economics*, **18**, (6), December, pp. 587–605.

Davidson, P. (1972), 'A Keynesian View of Friedman's Theoretical Framework for Monetary Analysis', *Journal of Political Economy*, **80**, (5), September/October, pp. 864–82.

Davidson, P. (1978), *Money and the Real World*, 2nd edn, New York: John Wiley.

Dow, S. (1985), *Macroeconomic Thought*, Oxford: Basil Blackwell.

Friedman, M. (1968), 'The Role of Monetary Policy', *American Economic Review*, **58**, (1), March, pp. 1–17.

Friedman, M. (1987), 'Quantity Theory of Money', in John Eatwell, Murray Milgate and Peter Newman (eds), *The New Palgrave: A Dictionary of Economics*, Vol. 4, New York: Stockton Press.

Guggenheim, T. (1989), *Preclassical Monetary Theories*, London: Printer Publishers.

Hicks, J.R. (1967), *Critical Essays in Monetary Theory*, Oxford: Oxford University Press.

Hicks, J.R. (1989), *A Market Theory of Money*, Oxford: Clarendon Press.

Kaldor, N. (1986), *The Scourge of Monetarism*, 2nd edn, Oxford: Oxford University Press.

Keynes, J.M. (1930), *A Treatise on Money*, London: Macmillan.

Keynes, J.M. (1936), *The General Theory of Employment, Interest and Money*, London: Macmillan.

Laidler, David (1991), *The Golden Age of the Quantity Theory*, Princeton: Princeton University Press.

Lucas, R.E. (1972), 'Expectations and the Neutrality of Money', *Journal of Economic Theory*, **4**, (2), April, pp. 103–24.

Lucas, R.E. (1988), 'Money Demand in the United States: A Quantitative Review', *Carnegie Conference Series on Public Policy*, Autumn, pp. 137–67.

Lucas, R.E. (1994), 'Review of Milton Friedman and Anna J. Schwartz's *A Monetary History of the United States, 1867–1960*', *Journal of Monetary Economics*, **34**, (1), August, pp. 5–16.

Minsky, H. (1982), *Can 'It' Happen Again? Essays on Instability and Finance*, Armonk, NY: M.E. Sharpe.

Moore, B. (1983), 'Unpacking the Post Keynesian Black Box: Bank Lending and the Money Supply', *Journal of Post Keynesian Economics*, **5**, (4), Summer, pp. 537–56.

Moore, B. (1988), *Horizontalists and Verticalists: The Macroeconomics of Credit Money*, Cambridge: Cambridge University Press.

Rousseas, S. (1985), 'Financial Innovation and the Control of the Money Supply: The Radcliffe Report Revisited', in M. Jarsulic (ed.), *Money and Macro Policy*, Dordrecht: Kluwer.

Rousseas, S. (1992), *Post Keynesian Monetary Economics*, 2nd edn, Armonk, NY: M.E. Sharpe.

Smithin, J.N. (1994), *Controversies in Monetary Economics*, Aldershot: Edward Elgar.

Tavlas, G.S. (1991), *On the International Use of Currencies: The Case of the Deutsche Mark*, Essays in International Finance, No. 181, Princeton, NJ: Princeton University Press.

Tobin, J. (1992), 'Money', in P. Newman, M. Milgate and J. Eatwell (eds), *The New Palgrave Dictionary of Money and Finance*, Vol. 2, New York: Stockton Press.

Walras, L. (1889), *The Elements of Pure Political Economy*, 2nd edn, Lausanne: Stockton Press.

Multiplier Effect

The multiplier concept first appeared in an unpublished memorandum from Richard F. Kahn to England's Economic Advisory Council in the summer of 1930, and shortly thereafter in Kahn's (1931) *Economic Journal* article, 'The Relation of Home Investment to Unemployment'. These writings implicitly discuss an *employment multiplier* – the number of jobs ultimately created as the result of one new position. The idea behind the multiplier is that new employment leads to new spending which leads to more new employment. The process continues until leakages from this cycle cause successive rounds of spending to fall to zero, at which time the initial injection of income will have entirely dissipated into savings, taxes, imports and the like. The underlying notion of secondary employment (employment created by employment) was also discussed in earlier writings by Colin G. Clark (1938), Hubert Henderson and John Maynard Keynes (1929), among others.

In an 11 June 1934 article in *The Times*, Keynes described his related version of the multiplier as 'the cumulative effect of increased additional individual incomes (volume of income rather than merely of money) because the expenditure of these incomes improves the incomes of a further set of recipients and so on' (Keynes, 1973, vol. 21, p. 326). Although the seminal increase could be in any component of aggregate demand, Keynes referred to shifts in investment demand. More formally, his *investment multiplier*, k, is the ratio of an increase in real income to the autonomous increment in aggregate investment that caused it. (An autonomous increase in one determined outside the system rather than by changes in income.)

As an example, consider a simple economy with no taxes and with net exports that do not depend on income. Suppose the marginal propensity to consume for individuals in this economy, denoted by m, is 0.75. If the government uses an otherwise idle $100 to have a double yellow line painted down the center of Main Street, income for the painter will increase by $100. Given his marginal propensity to consume of 0.75, the painter will save $25, and spend $75 on, say, a set of books. The bookstore will use the money to pay its employees' incomes and to order replacements for the books that were purchased. Again, since we are assuming that $m = 0.75$, $18.75 of the income earned by the employees of the bookstore and the book publishers will be saved, and the balance, $56.25, will be spent and transformed into additional income. In these three rounds of spending, the $100 expenditure has resulted in $100.00 plus $75.00 plus $56.25 or $231.25 of new income. This succession of ever-diminishing expenditures and income increments ends when the entire $100 is consumed by savings, at which time it will have generated $400 of new income. In this simplified case, the formula for the multiplier (proved below) turns out to be $k = 1/(1 - m)$; every dollar of autonomous expenditure results in a total of $1/(1 - 0.75) = 2$ dollars of new income.

Keynes used the multiplier effect to explain the cyclical nature of business transactions. He argued that business cycles result from fluctuations in business investment which yield magnified fluctuations in income and output due to the multiplier. To explain the changes in investment levels that feed the multiplier, Keynes spoke of 'animal spirits' meaning spontaneous shifts in business optimism or pessimism that alter perceptions of the marginal product of capital. In *The General Theory*, Keynes writes: 'Most, probably, of our decisions to do something positive, the full consequences of which will be drawn out over many days to come, can only be taken as a result of animal spirits – of a spontaneous urge to action rather than inaction, and not as the outcome of a weighted average of quantitative benefits multiplied by quantitative probabilities (Keynes, 1973, vol. 12, p. 161).

The Keynesian model assumes an excess supply of goods, meaning that output is determined solely by demand. This was often the case during the Great Depression, when the multiplier was conceived. A prominent alternative view is embodied in the classical market-clearing model, in which the multiplier effect for an increase in aggregate demand is replaced by the dampening effect of higher interest rates. In the classical model, an increase in aggregate demand results in an increased demand for money, which in turn drives interest rates upward. Consumers respond to the higher interest rates by saving more and shifting parts of their consumption expenditure into future periods. The ultimate increase in real income is thus *less* than the initial increase in demand. For a *decrease* in aggregate demand in the classical model, interest rates fall, leading consumers to decrease current expenditures by an increment less than the initial decrease in demand.

Following the work of Kahn and Keynes, myriad applications for the multiplier concept surfaced. Some scholars applied the term to entirely different cases of repercussions exacerbating primary effects; for example, Jeong J. Rhee and John A. Miranowski (1984) describe a *pollution control multiplier* that depicts the relationship between excess pollution and pollution control activity levels. Others have expressed concepts similar to the Keynesian multiplier, replacing investment and real income with similar measures more relevant to particular inquiries.

Shortly after the publication of the *General Theory*, Colin M. Clark (1938) described a *money income multiplier* that was essentially Keynes's investment multiplier in nominal rather than real terms. Keynes responded on 31 May 1938 in comments on Clark's forthcoming article, saying 'It saves very little trouble, and the marginal propensity to consume is likely to be much more stable in terms of real income than of money income whenever prices and wages are suffering significant changes in terms of money' (Keynes, 1973, vol. 12, pp. 804–5).

The *tax multiplier* is the ratio of a change in real income to an autonomous change in net taxes. Since an autonomous change in net taxes results in a change in consumption of m ($-\Delta tx$), the tax multiplier is $-mk$. For example, with a marginal propensity to consume of 0.75 and an autonomous spending multiplier of 4.0, each one-dollar increase in taxes will decrease consumption by 75 cents and thus decrease income and output by $0.75 \cdot 4 = 3$, the value of the tax multiplier.

The *balanced-budget multiplier* measures the effect on equilibrium income and output of equal changes in taxes and government spending. When taxes are exogenous, the balanced-budget multiplier is one, because each dollar that is taxed and spent increases income and output by k due to the spending and $-mk$ due to the taxes. The combined effect is $k - mk = k\,(1 - m) = [1/(1 - m)]\,(1 - m) = 1$. When taxes are endogenous (depend on income), the tax multiplier is decreased owing to the additional leakages from income going to taxes rather than spending as income increases. The balanced-budget multiplier will thus be less than one.

The *autonomous spending multiplier* generalizes Keynes's investment multiplier to include a broader range of injections. Any exogenous change in expenditure results in a final change in (short-run equilibrium) income and output that amounts to the multiplier times the initial change. An exogenous change in spending could result from a change in autonomous consumption, government spending, net exports or investment.

The *foreign trade multiplier* is another name for the Keynesian multiplier when the change in aggregate demand is in the form of net exports. By means of this multiplier, the health of one country's economy is inflicted upon that of its trading partners. If there is a recession abroad, net exports to the affected countries will decrease, leading to a succession of decreased domestic income and employment.

The *government spending multiplier* is the ratio of the change in real income to the change in government purchases. With this application of the multiplier in mind, Keynes advocated adjustments in government spending to temper overheated economies or bring ailing economies out of recession.

The *money multiplier* is the amount of total bank deposits created from a new deposit of one dollar. If all excess reserves are loaned out, the money multiplier will equal $1/r$ where r is the required reserve ratio – the fraction of each dollar of deposits that must be held in reserves by the bank. The mathematical derivation of the multiplier formula is as follows. The initial increment of investment, ΔI, leads to an increase in consumption of $m\Delta I$. The second round of income boosts consumption by $m (m\Delta I)$. Similarly, the ith round of income boosts consumption by $m^i\Delta I$. The ultimate change in income and output, ΔO, is thus the series:

$$\Delta O = \Delta I + m\Delta I + m^2\Delta I + m^3\Delta I + \dots + m^n\Delta I, \tag{1}$$

where n is the number of the last round that produces a non-zero income increment. Multiplying both sides of equation (1) by $-m$ yields

$$-m\Delta O = -m\Delta I - m^2\Delta I - m^3\Delta I - m^4\Delta I - \dots - m^{n+1}\Delta I. \tag{2}$$

Adding equations (1) and (2), and noting that $m^{n+1} \Delta I = 0$, yields

$$(1 - m)\Delta O = \Delta I \tag{3}$$

or equivalently

$$\Delta O = \frac{\Delta I}{(1-m)}. \tag{4}$$

DAVID A. ANDERSON

See also:

Accelerator Principle; Demand Management; Economics of Keynes and of his Revolution, Key Elements of the; Fiscal Policy; Functional Finance; Kahn, Lord Richard F.; Keynes, John Maynard; Keynesian Cross, The; Lerner, Abba P.

Bibliography

Clark, Colin M. (1938), 'Determination of the Multiplier from National Income Statistics', *Economic Journal*, **48**, (191), pp. 435–48.

Kahn, R. (1931), 'The Relation of Home Investment to Unemployment,' *Economic Journal*, **41**, (162), pp. 173–98.

Keynes, John M. and Hubert Henderson (1929), *Can Lloyd George Do It?*, London: Hogarth Press.

Rhee, Jeong J. and John A. Miranowksi (1984), 'Determination of Income, Production and Employment Under Pollution Control: An Input–Output Approach', *The Review of Economics and Statistics*, **66**, (1), February, pp. 146–50.

Mundell, Robert A.

In international macroeconomics, Robert A. Mundell has been the most prolific influence in the second half of the twentieth century. Building on the work of Keynes and Meade, Mundell developed an elegant and formal model of the open macroeconomy which is still in use decades later; he explored the policy implications and limitations of alternative exchange rate regimes; he challenged a very Keynesian approach with hard-core monetarism and upset a demand-oriented profession with a provocative dose of supply-side economics.

Born in Canada in 1932, Robert Mundell did his undergraduate work at the University of British Columbia and holds an MA from the University of Washington. His graduate studies took him to the London School of Economics and MIT, where he received a PhD in 1956, part of that prolific group who grew up under the stewardship of Charles Kindleberger and Paul Samuelson. His thesis dealt with 'International Capital Mobility', a key theme for much of his pathbreaking research. An important part of his influence and research interest stems from a stay in 1961–3 at the IMF's research department, then directed by Marcus Fleming. In his influential teaching career he has held professorships, among others, at the University of Chicago and now at Columbia University.

Mundell's main contributions are collected in two fine books, *International Economics* and *Monetary Theory*. Mundell's earliest contributions were on trade, in particular his work on transport costs in trade theory, highly original research on the equivalence of trade and factor mobility and a definitive survey of the pure theory of trade. That interest in trade-oriented microeconomics would come back later in his influential role as a supply-sider.

His pathbreaking work in open economy macroeconomics starts with the notion of a policy mix: how to combine internal balance and external balance – balance of payments equilibrium and full employment in a world of mobile capital but fixed prices and currency rates? Mundell's answer involves the assignment of fiscal policy to create demand and monetary policy to finance any resulting external imbalances. With a high degree of capital mobility that assignment, relying on dynamic stability or the 'principle of effective market classification', as he called it, is stable. It means that countries with unemployment should run budget deficits and finance themselves by using high interest rates which attract the external capital flows that finance the budget and the current account.

This research direction continues in a series of important papers on what has been called the 'Fleming–Mundell Model' – a two-country IS/LM model of a world integrated in goods and capital markets. The central finding of this research is that the effectiveness of monetary and fiscal policy depends on the exchange rate regime: in small countries, fiscal policy is effective with fixed rates and monetary policy when rates are flexible. More specifically the work highlights the endogeneity of money under fixed rates.

While most international economic research of the 1950s and 1960s was starkly fixprice Keynesian, Mundell very early paid attention to price flexibility and its incorporation in modeling. In particular the inclusion of inflationary expectations in real interest rates – now commonly called the 'Mundell effect' – was the topic of two short papers.

Mundell's years at the University of Chicago marked a very special time both in his career and in Chicago's economics department. Those were golden years of debate and creativity for all: Milton Friedman was there, and the prolific Harry G. Johnson, as well as Arnold Harberger; among the students and younger faculty were Arthur Laffer and Stan Fischer, Michael Mussa, Jacob Frenkel and many more. Mundell's influence was pervasive: in Socratic style in the classroom, in the workshops and as editor of the *Journal of Political Economy*. With the apparent demise of the dollar standard, Mundell became a leader in thinking about exchange rate regimes and the world monetary system. Global monetarism was in the making. He opened a discussion (along with Robert Triffin) on how to restructure the world monetary system to address the three key questions at the time: confidence, liquidity and adjustment. The themes were connected around the role of the US dollar in the world monetary system: if the United States issued too little there would be a shortage of world liquidity and if it issued too much there would be a world glut and hence a crisis of confidence; any amount the United States issued would give it seigniorage, a point increasingly questioned by Europe at the time. A 1973 blueprint, 'Toward a Better International Monetary System' is an important part of Mundell's contribution to the debate. Mundell's skepticism about existing monetary arrangements, and the apparent deficiency evidenced in rising world inflation at the time, led him increasingly to hard money ideas, including even gold-based systems. It is hard to know just how serious he was about this; he always had an undeniable streak of the *enfant terrible*.

Yet another phase of decisive influence started in the 1970s and was devoted to supply-side economics. Mundell has always favored tax cuts; here we see the reflection of his early work on the pure theory of trade where taxes distort allocation and suppress efficiency. His immensely controversial *The Dollar and the Policy Mix* (1971a) started the zest for tax cuts. Although there is no direct writing of his to credit here, the important public policy impact came from his involvement with the discussion group of the *Wall Street Journal* op ed page. Anderson (1988) and Bailey (1988) report the central role Mundell played in creating intellectual support and raw enthusiasm for supply-side economics. In more than 50 articles over the past 20 years,

Mundell has stuck to these two themes: how to organize sound money and how to promote growth via supply side-friendly policies.

Mundell's interests outside the broad field of international economics and political economy are twofold. He is an enthusiastic and accomplished painter. His other passion is the rebuilding of a twelfth-century castle, Santa Colomba, near Monteregione, Italy – a hobby he has been at for a quarter of a century already.

RUDIGER DORNBUSCH

See also:
Balance of Payments: Keynesian and Monetarist Approaches; Dornbusch, Rudiger; Friedman, Milton; Johnson, Harry Gordon; Monetary Policy; Money; Mundell–Fleming Model; Samuelson, Paul A.

Bibliography
Anderson, Martin (1988), *Revolution*, San Diego: Harcourt Brace Jovanovich.
Bailey, Robert (1988), *The Seven Fat Years*, New York: Free Press.
Mundell, Robert A. (1968), *International Economics*, London/New York: Macmillan.
Mundell, Robert A. (1971a), *Monetary Theory Interest, Inflation and Growth in the World Economy*, Pacific Palisades, CA: Goodyear.
Mundell, Robert A. (1971b), *The Dollar and the Policy Mix*, Essays in International Finance, No. 85, Princeton, NJ: Princeton University Press.
Mundell, Robert A. (1972), 'Toward a Better International Financial System' in Acheson, Chant and Prachowny (eds), *Bretton Woods Revisited*, Toronto: University of Toronto Press.

Mundell–Fleming Model

The Mundell–Fleming model is the name often used to describe the open economy version of the standard IS/LM macroeconomic framework, especially when capital is assumed to be perfectly mobile internationally. In separate papers, J. Marcus Fleming (1962) and Robert Mundell (1960, 1963) showed that international capital mobility can either reinforce or undercut the effectiveness of macroeconomic stabilization policies, depending on whether the exchange rate is fixed or floating and whether monetary or fiscal policy is employed.

The key insight in the Mundell–Fleming analysis is that, when domestic macroeconomic policy raises aggregate spending, it affects the balance of payments through two distinct channels. With a fiscal stimulus (higher government spending and/or lower taxes), higher aggregate expenditure is associated with higher imports, thus pushing the current account toward deficit. In the absence of monetary accommodation, higher aggregate expenditure also tends to raise the domestic interest rate, thus pushing the capital account toward surplus. The relative size of these opposing effects depends on the marginal propensity to import and the degree of capital mobility. The net impact on the overall balance of payments or the exchange rate is therefore ambiguous.

Assuming sufficient capital mobility eliminates the ambiguity; the capital account effect then necessarily dominates. Under these conditions, a market-determined floating rate must appreciate in order to restore equilibrium. However the higher currency value shifts demand towards foreign goods, thereby undercutting the effect of the fiscal stimulus. To maintain a fixed exchange rate rather than allowing the rate to float, the central bank must buy foreign exchange. Unless intervention is 'sterilized' through domestic open market bond sales, the domestic money supply will rise, thereby reinforcing the fiscal stimulus. By this reasoning, fiscal policy is ineffective when rates are floating but effective when rates are fixed, given that capital is highly mobile internationally.

These alternative scenarios are illustrated in Figure 1, adapted from Mundell (1963). In addition to the usual *IS* and *LM* curves, the diagram includes a *BP* schedule. The *BP* curve indicates pairs (Y, i) consistent with overall balance of payments equilibrium. The *BP* schedule is typically shown to have a positive slope; a higher value of Y is associated with higher imports and a lower current-account balance, which must be offset by a higher capital-account balance induced by a higher value of the domestic interest rate i. A higher degree of capital mobility causes the *BP* curve to be flatter.

In Figure 1, the assumption of perfect capital mobility is captured by a *BP* curve that is horizontal at the world interest rate. The economy is initially in equilibrium at *A*. Fiscal expansion, shown by a rightward shift of the *IS* curve

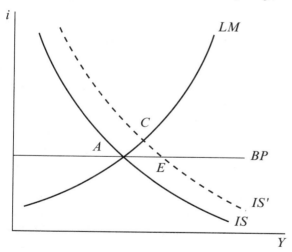

Figure 1　Fiscal policy with perfect capital mobility

to *IS'*, pushes the interest rate above the world rate, thus moving the balance of payments into a potential surplus position at *C*. With a flexible exchange rate, the resulting appreciation will continue until the *IS* curve returns to its initial position, that is until appreciation completely offsets the fiscal stimulus. With a fixed rate, the economy can remain at *C* through sterilized intervention, accumulating international reserves. With unsterilized intervention, the domestic money supply rises to accommodate the new, higher expenditure level; the resulting equilibrium is at *E*.

The assumed high degree of capital mobility is essential to the conclusion that fiscal policy is effective under fixed rates but not under floating rates. At the opposite extreme of no international capital mobility (a vertical *BP* curve), expansionary fiscal policy under a fixed exchange rate leads to deterioration of the current account and necessarily also of the overall balance of payments. The resulting loss of international reserves and, in the absence of sterilization, the associated monetary contraction at home undercut the fiscal stimulus. Sterilized intervention prevents the monetary contraction but does nothing to stem the loss of reserves. Accordingly the fiscal authority will be forced sooner or later to abandon the fiscal stimulus. In contrast, restoration of equilibrium through induced depreciation of a floating rate reinforces the fiscal stimulus by shifting demand towards domestic goods. By this reasoning, with immobile capital the associated loss of reserves limits the use of fiscal policy under fixed rates, while under floating rates the associated exchange rate depreciation strengthens its effectiveness.

A similar analysis can be made for the case of monetary policy. Regardless of the extent of capital mobility, expansionary monetary policy always causes the country's balance of payments position to deteriorate. Under a flexible exchange rate, the initial monetary stimulus is reinforced by a market-determined currency depreciation. In contrast, the monetary stimulus is undercut by maintenance of a fixed rate unless intervention is sterilized through open market bond purchases to prevent the money supply from falling back towards its previous level. Again viability of the fiscal stimulus with a fixed rate is limited by the associated loss of reserves.

In a related earlier analysis, Mundell (1960) explored what has subsequently been called the assignment problem: the best use of monetary *and* fiscal policy to achieve simultaneous 'internal balance' (full employment) and 'external balance' (a desired balance of payments position with a given fixed exchange rate). Noting that fiscal policy has an ambiguous effect on the overall balance of payments, depending on the extent of capital mobility, while monetary policy affects both components in the same direction, Mundell argued that fiscal policy should be assigned the task of achieving internal balance and monetary policy the task of achieving external balance.

The classic papers by Mundell and Fleming were likely inspired by the experience of the 1950s, when many countries gradually reduced their use of capital controls and international capital flows began to grow in importance relative to trade flows. Canada, perhaps the best real-world example of the 'small open economy' of macroeconomic theory, maintained a floating exchange rate from 1950 until 1961 and experienced a high degree of capital mobility, particularly to and from the United States.

Parts of a large subsequent literature elaborating on the Mundell–Fleming model are surveyed in Frenkel and Razin (1987). However the model in its unembellished form enjoyed a revival in the 1980s. It provided a simple yet persuasive explanation of the spectacular rise in the international value of the US dollar during the period when the Reagan administration cut taxes while the US Federal Reserve maintained tight money.

RACHEL MCCULLOCH

See also:

Bretton Woods; Dornbusch, Rudiger; Fiscal Policy; International Clearing Union; IS/LM Model and Diagram; Keynes, John Maynard; Meade, James E.; Metzler, Lloyd A.; Monetary Policy; Mundell, Robert A.; White, Harry D.

Bibliography

Fleming, J. Marcus (1962), 'Domestic Financial Policies Under Fixed and Floating Exchange Rates', *International Monetary Fund Staff Papers*, **9**, (3), November, pp. 369–79.
Frenkel, Jacob A. and Assaf Razin (1987), 'The Mundell–Fleming Model a Quarter Century Later: A Unified Exposition', *International Monetary Fund Staff Papers*, **34**, (4), December, pp. 567–620.
Mundell, Robert A. (1960), 'The Monetary Dynamics of International Adjustment Under Fixed and Floating Rates', *Quarterly Journal of Economics*, **4**, (2), May, pp. 227–57. Also in Mundell (1968).
Mundell, Robert A. (1963), 'Capital Mobility and Stabilization Policy Under Fixed and Flexible Exchange Rates', *Canadian Journal of Economics and Political Science*, **29**, (4), November, pp. 475–85. Also in Mundell (1968).
Mundell, Robert A. (1968), *International Economics*, New York: Macmillan.

Myrdal, Gunnar

Gunnar Myrdal died on 17 May 1987, on the anniversary of the *Brown* v. *Board of Education* decision, one of several civil rights advances of the twentieth century that were influenced by this great social architect. Gunnar Myrdal was born in rural Sweden in 1898 and settled in Stockholm when he was an adolescent. As a student at the University of Stockholm, he was exposed to the teachings of economists Karl Gustav Cassel, Eli Heckscher and Knut Wicksell, and received his doctorate in 1927. His formal education was completed by a few additional years of graduate study, as a Rockefeller

Foundation Fellow, in the United States. He held a professorship in economics at the University of Stockholm from 1933 to 1965.

Influenced by his lifelong (they met in 1919) collaborator and wife Alva Reimer Myrdal's passion for social equality and justice and by progressive social scientists like John Dewey, he soon became known as a social architect who saw economics not as the technical toolkit of neoclassicism that was to become the stronghold of economics in the United States, but as essentially an interdisciplinary course of study. In Sweden, Myrdal became a leading member of the Stockholm School of Economics, as well as an economic adviser to the government and a member of parliament. He greatly influenced the formation of the Swedish welfare state. In the decade following the end of World War II, he helped plan the economic reconstruction of Europe, and then turned his energy to issues of poverty and inequality in the developing as well as the affluent nations. During his appointment as Minister of Commerce, he negotiated a highly criticized treaty with the Soviet Union, putting into effect the early view that economic collaboration with the Soviets should be selected above Cold War détente.

Myrdal's published works, spanning almost half a century, are milestones recording the emphasis he gave to social issues during his academic and political careers. The monumental *An American Dilemma: The Negro Problem and Modern Democracy* (1944) was an eye-opening study, begun in 1938 under sponsorship of the Carnegie Corporation, on the effect of white racism on the lives of Afro-Americans. The civil rights movement's anti-racism campaigns have often relied on this text to formulate arguments against racial discrimination, and it was cited by Chief Justice Earl Warren in the historical Supreme Court decision in the case of *Brown* v. *Board of Education of Topeka*. In this book, Myrdal exhibited a typical demonstration of what was to become his trademark: he could lay his finger on the cause of social problems and provide his critique, value judgement and proposed solution all in one. Thus the book makes clear that the 'Negro problem' in the United States could be solved if the real problem, namely white racism, was recognized.

Issues of world poverty were addressed in a series of works, notably *Rich Lands and Poor; The Road to World Prosperity* (1957), *Challenge to Affluence* (1963), *Beyond the Welfare State; Economic Planning and Its International Implications* (1966), the three volumes of *Asian Drama; An Inquiry Into the Poverty of Nations* (1968) and *The Challenge of World Poverty; A World Anti-Poverty Program in Outline* (1970). In addressing world poverty, Myrdal stressed the need of a two-part solution for world poverty, the first part of which requires a much greater concern and substantial sacrifices for the common good on the part of the rich nations, as well as the willingness of developing nations to enact radical economic and social reforms. While substantial progress has been made in the second area, the first requirement has yet to be fulfilled. In *Challenge to Affluence* (1963), a counterpoint to J.K. Galbraith's *Affluent Society* (1958), he demonstrated that affluence in the US economy ignored the growth of a substantial class of poor and destitute Americans, and that this poverty problem would worsen (as it did) unless global human need became the primary focus of economic policy makers and policies focusing on education and welfare and training programs were put in place. Although Myrdal was shocked by the setbacks to equity and the war against poverty experienced during the Reagan years, he believed that the era would constitute a relatively minor step backward in America's social development. He would have been appalled by the persistent new conservatism expressed by the American Congress in the mid-1990s.

Myrdal was one of the early recipients of the Nobel Prize in Economics, which he was awarded in 1974, sharing it with Friedrich Hayek. Alva Reimer Myrdal, whose career as diplomat and feminist rivaled that of Gunnar, would receive the Nobel Peace Prize in 1982 for her work on disarmament. The Myrdals thus became the only married couple to be awarded separate Nobel Prizes for achievements in different fields.

Myrdal's practice of combining academic work and social engineering also reflects his deep conviction that normative and positive economics cannot and should not be separated. In *Value in Social Theory; A Selection of Essays on Methodology* (1958), *Objectivity in Social Research* (1969) and *Against the Stream: Critical Essays on Economics* (1974), his criticism of traditional and mostly neoclassical economic theory, with its positive approach, its focus on equilibrium and its reluctance to recognize social and political realities, and his central message that economists must admit that there are implicit value judgements in their so-called 'objective approaches' are laid out. Thus Gunnar Myrdal has become an early champion of radical economics as well as feminist economics, which has as the central premise that orthodox economic theory is based implicitly on values, judgements and achievements that are especially relevant for white males. In his world travels and his experience as an architect of social change, Myrdal had essentially come to a similar methodological conclusion.

Although Gunnar Myrdal remained active as a writer and thinker into old age, a gradual deterioration in his health, and his wife's passing in 1986, contributed to his own death. He was survived by two daughters, Sissela Bok and Kay Fölster, and two grandsons.

BRIGITTE BECHTOLD

See also:
Keynes, John Maynard; Stockholm School of Economics.

Bibliography
Galbraith, J.K. (1958), *The Affluent Society*, Boston: Houghton Mifflin.
Jackson, Walter A. (1990), *Gunnar Myrdal and America's Conscience; Social Engineering and Racial Liberalism, 1937–1987*, Chapel Hill, NC: University of North Carolina Press.
Lundberg, E. and L.G. Reynolds (1984), 'Gunnar Myrdal's Contributions to Economics', in H.W. Spiegel and W.J. Samuels (eds), *Contemporary Economists in Perspective*, Conn. and London: JAI Press.
Myrdal, Gunnar (1944), *An American Dilemma; The Negro Problem and Modern Democracy*, New York: Harper and Brothers.
Myrdal, Gunnar (1957), *Rich Lands and Poor: The Road to World Poverty*, New York: Harper and Brothers.
Myrdal, Gunnar (1958), *Value in Social Theory: A Selection of Essays on Methodology*, New York: Harper and Brothers.
Myrdal, Gunnar (1963), *Challenge to Affluence*, New York: Pantheon Books.
Myrdal, Gunnar (1966), *Beyond the Welfare State: Economic Planning and Its International Implications*, New Haven: Yale University Press.
Myrdal, Gunnar (1968), *Asian Drama: An Inquiry Into the Poverty of Nations*, Twentieth Century Fund.
Myrdal, Gunnar (1969), *Objectivity in Social Research*, New York: Pantheon Books.
Myrdal, Gunnar (1970), *The Challenge of World Poverty: A World Anti-Poverty Program in Outline*, New York: Pantheon Books.
Myrdal, Gunnar (1974), *Against the Stream: Critical Essays on Economics*, New York: Random House.

Neoclassical Synthesis (Bastard Keynesianism)

With the publication of Keynes's *General Theory*, economists began what was to be a long and arduous attempt to understand and interpret Keynes's message. One particularly influential interpretation, especially in the United States during the 25-year period following World War II, is known as the neoclassical synthesis. Based on the works of Hicks (1937), Modigliani (1948), Samuelson (1966), Solow (1978) and Tobin (1958, 1972), the central message of the synthesis is the view that long-term equilibrium is determined by the supply side and may be understood through the analysis provided by classical economics, whereas short-term departures from equilibrium are the result of demand fluctuations and market imperfections, in particular the sluggish movement of wages and prices in response to changes in demand. The major effort of economists who worked to develop the neoclassical synthesis was directed towards an understanding of these short-run demand fluctuations in order to develop effective policy measures. The major theoretical tool developed for these purposes was IS/LM analysis, originally formulated by Hicks.

IS/LM analysts look at the interaction of the output and money markets in developing a theory of aggregate demand.[1] The theory can be represented by the following equilibrium conditions:

$$\frac{\overline{M}}{\overline{P}} = L(r, Y), \tag{1}$$

where $\overline{M}$ is fixed money supply, $\overline{P}$ is fixed price level, r is rate of interest and Y is level of output; and

$$I(r) = S(Y), \tag{2}$$

where I is investment and S is savings.

Condition (1), the equilibrium condition for the money market, arises from the following theory of the demand for money, L. The demand for money consists of two elements, the transaction demand, which is positively related to the level of income, and the speculative demand, which varies inversely with the rate of interest. For a given money supply, an increase in the rate of interest lowers the speculative demand for money. To maintain equilibrium, the transaction demand for money must increase. This will occur if Y increases. Thus is derived a direct relation between r and Y, for a given money supply, which illustrates all combinations of the interest rate and the level of income yielding equilibrium in the money market, a relation known as the *LM* curve.

Condition (2), the equilibrium condition in the output market, is based on the theory that investment is inversely related to the interest rate, while saving is directly related to the level of income. Since equilibrium requires equality between saving and investment, an increase in *Y* which raises saving must be matched by a reduction in *r*, if investment is to increase to match the change in saving. Thus is derived a positive relation between *r* and *Y*, known as the *IS* curve, which reveals all possible combinations of the interest rate and the level of income yielding equilibrium in the output market. Overall equilibrium requires the simultaneous occurrence of equilibrium in both markets, which occurs at the intersection of the *IS/LM* curves, as shown in Figure 1.

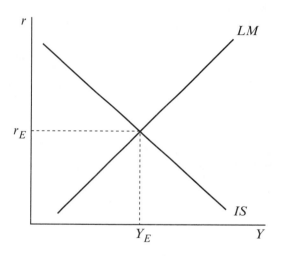

Figure 1   The IS/LM model

Will the equilibrium level of income portrayed in Figure 1 necessarily be the full employment level of income? Not necessarily, in the view of neoclassical economists, for reasons having to do with the elasticities of the *IS/LM* curves and/or with the sluggishness of price movements. One situation is where, in Hicks's words, 'there are conditions in which the interest-mechanism will not work. The special form in which this appears in the *General Theory* is the doctrine of a floor to the rate of interest – the [liquidity trap] as Sir Dennis Robertson has called it' (Hicks, 1957, p. 287). In such a case, the *LM* curve becomes horizontal and the intersection with *IS* may occur at a level of income below that required for full employment. A second situation wherein unemployment might result is the case in which the interest elasticity of investment is close to (or equal to) zero. In such a case, the *IS* curve will be (nearly) vertical, again presenting the possibility of an intersection with *LM* at a level of income less than that required for full employment. These cases are illustrated in Figures 2 and 3.

However, both these cases were viewed by most neoclassical economists as extreme cases. More typically, neoclassical economists depicted the *IS/LM*

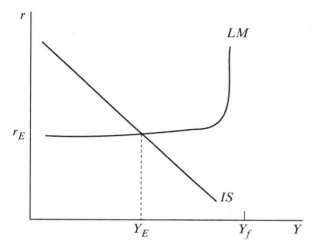

Figure 2   The liquidity trap

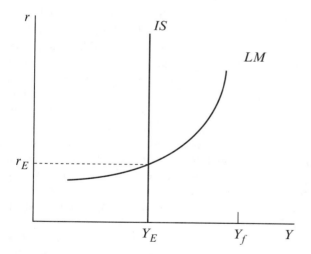

Figure 3   Inelastic investment

curves as in Figure 1, and relied on the sluggishness of prices to explain why the resulting, short-term level of income might be less than the full employment level. It is important to note that neoclassical economists stressed the sluggishness, not the rigidity of prices (Tobin, 1972, p. 855). Short-term sluggishness of prices was required however; for if prices were completely flexible, the real supply of money could also change instantaneously, shifting the *LM* curve until full employment was reached.[2] Neoclassical economists did not, however, put much effort into explaining the reasons for such sluggishness, because, in Tobin's words, 'its authors and practitioners were too busy with pragmatic macroeconomics to develop formally the several sources of market failure described by Keynes' (Tobin, 1985, p. 114). In particular neoclassical practitioners devoted great effort to the development of a theory of fiscal and monetary policy capable of maintaining the economy at full employment. In principle government spending and tax policy could be used to shift the *IS* curve to any desired position, while changes in monetary policy could accomplish the same with respect to the *LM* curve. In practice, this required a detailed knowledge of the empirical magnitudes of the various elasticities of the important macroeconomic variables. Difficulties in obtaining these values led to a continuing controversy as to the relative potency of fiscal policy vis-à-vis monetary policy and to the allocation of ever greater resources to the building of large-scale econometric models which, it was hoped, would provide answers to the empirical questions.

The failure to devote greater attention to the issue of market imperfections or, more generally, the microfoundations of macroeconomics would, however, prove a serious problem for the neoclassical synthesis with the return of inflation as a serious issue in the 1960s. At first the problem of inflation seemed to pose no special problem. Indeed the work of Phillips, and Samuelson and Solow led to the Phillips curve, which purported to provide policy makers with a new tool for making decisions concerning the trade-off between inflation and unemployment (Phillips, 1958; Samuelson, 1966, pp. 1346–51; Solow, 1978). The explanation provided by neoclassical economists for this trade-off, more aggressive wage demands as the economy moved closer to full employment, became less and less persuasive as evidence mounted of a serious deterioration in this relationship during the 1970s. The difficulty neoclassicals encountered in explaining this deterioration opened the doors, not only for the monetarist and new classical views, which play down the significances of market imperfections, but also for the new Keynesian school, which attempts to provide those explanations for market imperfections which the economists of the neoclassical synthesis failed to provide.

While the neoclassical synthesis has been the dominant view of Keynes, particularly in the United States, many economists have challenged whether it accurately captures the essence of Keynes's message (Davidson, 1980). Of particular importance is the fact, as Hicks himself has noted, that IS/LM analysis is static in nature (Hicks, 1977, p. 148). As a result, neoclassical analysis essentially eliminates the concept of time. Keynes, however, believed that real, historical time introduces complexities which are at the heart of his explanation of unemployment. For Keynes, the existence of time implies the possibility of a future which may differ from today in ways which are unknowable at the present moment. Thus time introduces true uncertainty: a situation wherein one does not know all the possible future outcomes or their associated probabilities. This type of uncertainty is alien to the neoclassical synthesis, which assumes known and unchanging probability distributions over time. Tobin's article (1958) is an excellent example.

This difference in the notion of uncertainty leads to a fundamentally different understanding of the decision to invest in real capital goods. Since investment commits real resources to an unknown future, investors will need to find ways to reduce their vulnerability to unexpected events. One way to accomplish this is to stipulate in advance, through contractual arrangements, the monetary commitments which a firm will be required to make. As Davidson has noted, such an attempt will succeed only if investors have confidence in the stickiness of the money wage (Davidson, 1978, p. 98). Thus, unlike neoclassical economists who see sluggishness as a market imperfection, Keynes saw wage stickiness as necessary for the successful undertaking of investment decisions. The necessity of maintaining sticky wages means that Keynes may well have viewed policies such as tax-based income policies in a far more favorable light than do neoclassical economists, for whom such policies are of marginal significance.

A second method of reducing vulnerability to uncertainty is to create a mechanism which makes it possible not to commit real resources during times of great uncertainty. Money, of course, is such a mechanism, and the failure of neoclassicals to adopt the same concept of uncertainty as did Keynes perhaps also explains their lack of interest in Keynes's precautionary and financial motives for holding money, as well as their lack of attention to the detailed attributes of financial institutions.

Finally it should be noted that the neoclassical economists' adoption of classical theory of supply tied Keynesian thought to a theory wholly at variance with that advanced by Keynes himself, in Chapter 3 of the *General Theory*. Had neoclassicals not done this, it is unlikely that they would have neglected the issue of price formation. And, given the nature of Keynes's theory, it is certain that the issue of income distribution would have assumed far greater prominence than it has in the neoclassical synthesis.

Edward J. McKenna
Diane C. Zannoni

Notes

1 Note that Hicks takes the wage, rather than the price level, as fixed.
2 Brief mention should be made of a second issue related to price changes, the real balance effect developed by Pigou and Patinkin. If consumption depends on real wealth, a change in the price level, by changing real wealth, can shift consumption and, hence, the *IS* curve. Most neoclassicals believed the empirical magnitude of the real balance effect to be small, but the issue did raise interesting questions concerning the constitution of wealth in what was known as the inside–outside money debate. See Patinkin (1965) and Gurley and Shaw (1960).

See also:

Economics of Keynes and of his Revolution, Key Elements of the; Friedman, Milton; Hansen, Alvin H.; Hicks, Sir John R.; IS/LM Model and Diagram; Keynesian Revolution; Modigliani, Franco; Monetarist School of Economics; New Classical School of Economics; New Keynesian Macroeconomics; Phillips Curve; Post Keynesian School of Economics; Robinson, Joan; Samuelson, Paul A.; Solow, Robert M.

Bibliography

Davidson, Paul (1978), *Money and the Real World*, New York: Halsted Press.
Davidson, Paul (1980), 'Post Keynesian Economics', *Public Interest*, special edition, pp. 151–73.
Gurley, J.G. and E.S. Shaw (1960), *Money in a Theory of Finance*, Washington, DC: Brookings Institution.
Hicks, J.R. (1937), 'Mr. Keynes and the "Classics", A Suggested Interpretation', *Econometrica*, **5**, (2), April, pp. 147–59.
Hicks, J.R. (1957), 'A Rehabilitation of "Classical" Economics?', *Economic Journal*, **67**, (266), June, pp. 279–89.
Hicks, J.R. (1977), *Economic Perspectives*, Oxford: Clarendon Press.
Keynes, J.M. (1936), *The General Theory of Employment Interest and Money*, London: Macmillan.
Modigliani, F. (1944), 'Liquidity Preference and the Theory of Interest and Money', *Econometrica*, **12**, (1), January, pp. 45–88.
Patinkin, Don (1965), *Money, Interest and Prices*, 2nd edn, London: Harper & Row.
Phillips, A.W. (1958), 'The Relation between Unemployment and the Rate of Change of Money Wage Rates in the United Kingdom, 1861–1957', *Economica*, N.S., **25**, (100), November, pp. 283–99.
Samuelson, P.A. (1966), *The Collected Scientific Papers of Paul A. Samuelson*, Vol. 2, ed. Joseph E. Stiglitz, Cambridge, Mass.: MIT Press.
Solow, R.M. (1978), 'What We Know and Don't Know About Inflation', *Technology Review*, **81**, (3), pp. 2–18.
Tobin, J. (1958), 'Liquidity Preference as Behaviour Towards Risk', *Review of Economic Studies*, **25**, (67), February, pp. 65–86.
Tobin, J. (1972), 'Friedman's Theoretical Framework', *Journal of Political Economy*, **80**, (5), September–October, pp. 852–63.
Tobin, J. (1985), 'Theoretical Issues in Macroeconomics', in George R. Feiwel (ed.), *Issues in Contemporary Macroeconomics*, Albany: State University of New York Press.

Neo-Keynesianism

John Maynard Keynes struggled mightily to avoid comparison of the *General Theory* with his earlier literary efforts such as *The Economic Consequences of the Peace*. In the struggle, Keynes succeeded marvelously, but at the cost of clarity and the begetting of a host of interpretations, one of which has been labeled 'neo-Keynesian', an aging term initially attached to the generation of American economists growing up during the Great Depression and, then, emerging from the fire and smoke of World War II. The basic issue is whether there are market failures of a macroeconomic nature in a market economy and whether government demand management can keep the economy close to its equilibrium track; neo-Keynesians think there are and that it can, whereas the monetarists and the new classicals think not. The neo-Keynesian tree itself has two branches – fiscal Keynesians and neoclassical Keynesians.

Most of these men learned about Keynes at Harvard. James Tobin returned from war to graduate. A very young Paul A. Samuelson and a slightly older John Kenneth Galbraith were already there, as well as the much older Alvin H. Hansen. Robert Solow, who had remembered from his childhood the unpleasantness of the Great Depression for his family and others, came to Harvard in 1940. When the war came, he joined the army, only to return in 1945 to study economics. Tied together by friendship, the neo-Keynesians were to dominate economic policy during the two postwar decades.

Keynes's most important recruit in the later 1930s was Hansen. As he was a prestigious figure, the establishment could ignore neither his tardy endorsement of Keynes nor the views of his students, among whom was Samuelson. A mathematical paper he wrote for Hansen in 1939, depicting a capitalistic system inherently cyclical but not wildly unstable, brought Samuelson worldwide fame. After the war, Samuelson's textbook, *Economics: An Introductory Analysis* (1948), aroused a storm of dissent for its devotion to Keynesianism. Ultimately the text made Keynes an accepted part of American economic thought. Samuelson's *Economics* popularized the idea that unemployment could be ended by the intentional creation of governmental deficits. Samuelson advised President John F. Kennedy during the early 1960s, at high tide for US Keynesianism. Kennedy had appointed a gifted Council of Economic Advisers, one member of which was Tobin, with Solow on its staff.

Samuelson's 1948 version of Keynes's thought became associated with the 'Keynesian Cross', the intersection of Keynes's aggregate demand function and a 45° line. The Keynesian Cross, alternatively 'the 45° model', shows that, as national income rises, the dollar value of goods and services potentially supplied rises by the same amount. This is virtually a 'Keynes Law' wherein 'demand creates its own supply'. In national income equilibrium, expenditures must exactly equal the dollar value of goods and services. If the dollar value of goods and services supplied were in excess of the total demanded at a particular national income level, *a deflationary gap would exist*. True to Keynes's idea that an insufficiency in aggregate demand caused unemployment, government expenditures could close the deflationary gap and induce full employment. The Keynesian multiplier would guarantee that the amount of the necessary government stimulus would be much less than 100 per cent of the required national income increment. So, having suffered the despair of the Great Depression, policy makers clung to the old Keynesian Cross.

In 'normal' times, however, when national income is stimulated by fiscal policy, part of the increase comes from rising prices. The cross diagram cannot distinguish these rising prices and real output. Samuelson and the fiscal Keynesians ignored this limitation and proceeded to use the diagram to explain a purely inflationary condition with the *inflationary gap* wherein the total dollar demand at a particular national income is *greater* than the total dollar value of supply. In fiscal Keynesianism, there is not supposed to be a trade-off between inflation and unemployment, but there was, in a drawing by A.W. Phillips, the anomalous Phillips curve. An excess demand for labor can drive up wages, which translates into a higher product inflation rate. At such times the unemployment rate falls. An excess supply of labor characterizes a slump. These disequilibria in labor markets became an accepted part of neo-Keynesianism during the 1960s whereby policy makers were given the Hobson's choice of more inflation or more unemployment.

Samuelson's stature and style – mostly derived from his arcane *Foundations of Economic Analysis* (1947) – were also to influence neoclassical Keynesianism. *Foundations* mesmerized the Keynesians and provided the microfoundations of neoclassical Keynesianism. Even so, Samuelson did not embrace neoclassical Keynesianism at its conception. The *General Theory* was barely in the hands of the public when John R. Hicks, an English economist, recast its message. In Marshallian economics, Keynes had noted, investment and savings alone were inadequate to account for the interest rate, but they could join with the interest rate to predict the level of income, or with the level of income to predict the interest rate. As Keynes's explanation of the interest rate was at best incomplete and at worst muddled, Hicks merged Marshall with Keynes, devising what became the IS/LM model. The economy was reduced to only two curves crossing at a single point, telling the world the value of the interest rate *and* the national income.

Hicks's *LM* curve traces out all the possible national income and interest rate combinations at which a fixed money supply just equals the preference for liquidity (demand for money). The upward-sloping *LM* curve shows how increases in national income come at the expense of rising interest rates in the money market. The *IS* curve traces out all those combinations of national income and interest rates at which saving equals investment, and it is downward-sloping. If the interest rate fell, investment would rise; saving and investment would still be equal in a Keynesian national income equilibrium, though at higher and higher levels of national income. The greatest excitement occurs where the *IS* and *LM* curves cross; at that point – almost magically – general equilibrium exists.

This little apparatus is important for monetary and fiscal policy. An increase in the money supply (shifting the *LM* curve to the right) produces a lower equilibrium interest rate and, predictably, more national income. A larger federal budget deficit (shifting the *IS* curve to the right) increases national income but not without a rise in the interest rate. There is a 'crowding out' of some investment at higher debt-inspired interest rates. This latter effect, a dampening in the Keynesian multiplier as interest rates rise, is the most important new characteristic for Keynesianism.

At the time, Keynes and Hicks disagreed. Keynes, in a letter to Hicks dated 31 March 1937, contended that investment would not necessarily be limited by a rising interest rate. The use of current national income in the IS/LM model disguised the critical importance of expectations in determining business investment. Moreover the model makes no judgement regarding labor market conditions. Hicks at the time missed Keynes's main point, namely, how expectations and uncertainty outweighed the interest rate in the investment decision and in individuals' preferences for liquidity – for cash.

It seemed for a time that the American Keynesians would be spared Hicks's reinterpretation altogether, even though Hansen prominently displayed Hicks's smooth curves in a new book in 1953. But his former student, Samuelson, apparently read it on the road to Damascus and was converted. Universal equilibrium was apparently irresistible. Samuelson incorporated the Hicksian system into his famous textbook, in the 1961 edition jubilantly referring to the rapprochement as the 'grand neoclassical synthesis'. The ensuing debate bore little resemblance to the Epistles, however. Increasingly the difference between Keynes and the original neoclassicals was described merely as a debate about the exact shape and importance of 'various curves'. Judicious fiscal policy, the new gyroscope for the economy, made simultaneous equilibria in all markets possible. As to the product markets, Keynes's system had left them in whatever state of competition the reader preferred, and the neoclassicals naturally chose perfect competition. Of course, to the extent that perfect competition assures low inflation rates, the belief in equilibrium and economic stability fit reality.

Some 37 years after Sir John Hicks unwittingly began the counter-reformation, he recanted, admitting to a deeper meaning in Keynes's view of money, investment and uncertainty, but, at the time, there was little reason for economists to notice. Inflation and high interest rates were not problems during the 1950s and much of the 1960s. When inflation became the central problem during the 1970s, fiscal Keynesianism and neoclassical Keynesianism seemed less relevant. Fiscal Keynesianism had a brief policy rebirth during President Reagan's second term after a blend of monetarism and supply-side economics had created the greatest downturn since the Great Depression. Meanwhile a more complete total demand and total supply picture from Keynes was seized on by the self-proclaimed legitimate heirs of Keynes, the Post Keynesians. This, they believed, would save the theory during periods of inflation.

Keynes's early interpreters had made good use of his antidepression nostrums. Nonetheless the neo-Keynesians' version of what Keynes meant did not work well when turned against inflation, and IS/LM displayed fatal weaknesses in its premises of perfect competition in product markets. Keynes's theories were taken out of historical time because the past, present and future are indistinguishable in equilibrium. The newer generation of neo-Keynesians represented by Solow's former student, Alan Blinder, generally view Keynesian economics as the economics of nominal rigidities everywhere. All Keynesians still carrying the label reject the idea that labor and other markets clear under conditions of completely flexible prices.

E. RAY CANTERBERY

See also:

Galbraith, John K.; Hansen, Alvin H.; Hicks, Sir John R.; Neoclassical Synthesis (Bastard Keynesianism); Samuelson, Paul A.; Solow, Robert M.; Tobin, James.

Bibliography

Canterbery, E.R. (1968), *Economics on a New Frontier*, Belmont, CA: Wadsworth.
Canterbery, E.R. (1995), *The Literate Economist: A Brief History of Economics*, New York: HarperCollins, chs 11–16.
Hansen, A. (1953), *A Guide to Keynes*, New York: McGraw-Hill, pp. 140–53.
Hicks, J.R. (1937), 'Mr. Keynes and the "Classics", A Suggested Interpretation', *Econometrica*, **5**, (2), April, pp. 147–59.
Hicks, J.R. (1974), *The Crisis in Keynesian Economics*, New York: Basic Books.
Johnson, E. and D. Moggridge (eds) (1971), *The Collected Writings of John Maynard Keynes*, Volume XIV, London: Macmillan, pp. 79–81.
Keynes, J.M. (1937), 'The General Theory of Employment', *Quarterly Journal of Economics*, **51**, pp. 209–223.
Samuelson, P. (1939), 'Interactions Between the Multiplier Analysis and the Principle of Acceleration', *Review of Economics and Statistics*, **21**, (2), pp. 75–8.
Samuelson, P. (1947), *Foundations of Economic Analysis*, Cambridge, Mass.: Harvard University Press.
Samuelson, P. (1948), *Economics*, New York: McGraw-Hill.

Neutrality of Money: The Keynesian Challenge

The idea of the neutrality of money is a basic axiom in classical and neoclassical economics. Keynes's challenge to this axiom forms an essential pillar of Keynesian economics.

A definition

The term 'neutrality of money' means that money is neutral: it has no effect in the functioning of the economy. It means that the size of the money supply and changes in the size of the money supply have no influence on the real macroeconomic variables: employment, output, income or economic growth.

The classical–neoclassical argument for the neutrality of money

The argument for the neutrality of money rests on two basic propositions of classical economics: Say's Law and the quantity theory of money. Say's Law tells us that the economy's rate of output is determined by supply, and supply is determined by the economy's ability to produce: by the quantity and quality of the available inputs.

The quantity theory of money assumes that the velocity of circulation of money is fixed and, given that assumption, total spending depends entirely on the quantity of money in the economy. Since output is determined by the economy's ability to produce, a change in spending can only influence the price level – not the actual quantity of output. So an increase in the size of the money supply will bring an increase in total spending and the only effect of that will be an increase in the price level. The size of the real output will not change.

The equation of exchange

In terms of the equation of exchange:

$$MV = PQ,$$

where M is the money supply, V is the velocity of circulation of money, P is the price level, Q is the aggregate quantity of output, and both V and Q are assumed to be fixed so that any increase in M will only influence P.

The real value of the money supply is the nominal value of the money supply (M) divided by the price level (P). According to the quantity theory of money, all changes in the size of the nominal money supply generate identical changes in the price level, so that the real money supply (M/P) remains unchanged. Given these conditions, money is completely neutral.

When the nominal money supply increases, the increased nominal money automatically 'self-destructs': it is 'washed out' by increases in the price level. Since there is no change in the *real* money supply, changes in the nominal money supply have no effect on the economy. Money is neutral.

In the classical–neoclassical theory, real conditions in the economy are determined by supply-side factors (the available inputs and their productivity). The economy's real output and income are not influenced at all by the demand side – by changes in the size of the money supply and total spending.

Classical theory requires a stable demand for money
The accuracy of the quantity theory rests on the assumption of a stable demand for money. The theory assumes that the quantity of money the public will want to hold is determined entirely by the total transactions people want to undertake. And that is determined entirely by the size of nominal national income. So the quantity of money demanded in the economy is a function of national income. Since the only reason for wanting to hold money is for transactions, the quantity of money demanded by the public is a fixed percentage of total spending (national income).

The Keynesian challenge to the quantity theory: the speculative demand for money
The attack by Keynes on the 'neutrality of money' axiom centered on the neoclassical assumption that velocity is fixed – does not change as M changes. Keynes constructed a theory explaining that, and explaining why, velocity does indeed change as M changes. Keynes introduced the speculative demand for money – the desire to hold money, not for transactions, but as a preferred portfolio asset. When people hold money as a portfolio asset, they will increase or decrease the size of their money balances, according to their outlook.

People have the choice of holding their assets in the form of money, or goods, or other non-money financial assets. Keynes referred to the choice between holding money or holding bonds. When bond prices are expected to rise, people reduce their money balances and shift their assets into bonds. As money balances shrink, velocity increases. When bond prices are expected to fall, people shift their assets out of bonds and into money. As money balances increase, velocity slows. Once we admit an 'asset demand' for holding money, no longer do we have the invariable link between the size of the money supply and total spending. The amount of money being held as a 'preferred asset' can increase or decrease. The direct link between the size of the money supply and total spending no longer exists.

A money supply change forces interest rates to change
In Keynesian theory, when the money supply increases, people find themselves holding more of their assets in money than they wish to. So they shift some of their assets out of money and into bonds to earn a higher return. As they do this, bond prices are forced upward and interest yields are forced downward. This continues to the point where interest rates (return on bonds) are low enough for people to be content to forgo bonds and hold the larger quantity of money.

With speculative (asset) demand, money is no longer neutral

In the Keynesian model, the initial effect of an increase in the money supply is to push the public's holdings of money above the level of their desired holdings. The next step is when people begin trying to get rid of their surplus money balances by buying bonds. The increased demand for bonds pushes up bond prices and pushes down yields. Interest rates fall throughout the economy. Rates continue to fall until the speculative demand to hold money balances increases to where people are satisfied to hold the larger money balances which they find themselves holding.

Lower interest rates induce greater investment spending and speed the economy

In this Keynesian scenario, money is definitely not neutral. As interest rates fall, more investment projects become profitable. The rate of investment spending increases. If there is unemployment in the economy, the increased investment spending will bring real increases in employment, output and income. When we recognize the fact that people do have an asset demand for money balances, both the stability of velocity and the neutrality of money fade away. Keynes rejected the idea of the neutrality of money in the following words:

> The theory which I desiderate would deal ... with an economy in which money plays a part of its own and affects motives and decisions and is, in short, one of the operative factors in the situation, so that the course of events can not be predicted either in the long period or in the short, without a knowledge of the behaviour of money .... And it is this which we ought to mean when we speak of a monetary economy .... Booms and depressions are peculiar to an economy in which ... money is not neutral. (Moggridge, 1973, p. 409)

The idea of the non-neutrality of money is a key element, right at the heart of Keynesian macroeconomics.

Policy implications

If the role of money in the economy is neutral in the real functioning of the economy, as is assumed in the classical/neoclassical model, any attempt to use any kind of monetary policy to influence the economy will be doomed to failure. Activist monetary policy to try to achieve macroeconomic objectives would not only fail to achieve those objectives, but would be destabilizing to the naturally self-stabilizing economy described in the neoclassical model. But with money playing a causal role, activist monetary policy can be used to influence real conditions in the macroeconomy.

ELBERT V. BOWDEN

See also:

Classical Economics; Friedman, Milton; Hawtrey, Sir Ralph; Kahn, Lord Richard F.; Keynesian Revolution; Lucas Critique; Marshall, Alfred; Monetarist School of Economics; Money; New Classical School of Economics; New Keynesian Macroeconomics; Pigou, Arthur C.; Post Keynesian School of Economics; Quantity Theory of Money; Say's Law; Schumpeter, Joseph A.; Stockholm School of Economics; Treasury View; Wicksell Knut.

Bibliography

Moggridge, Don (ed.) (1973), *The Collected Writings of John Maynard Keynes, vol. XIII, The General Theory and After: Part I Preparation*, London: Macmillan.

New Classical School of Economics

The new classical school of economics came into prominence during the 1970s as a response to criticisms of Keynesian macroeconomic models on both theoretical and empirical grounds. Large-scale Keynesian structural models, widely used during the 1960s for macroeconomic forecasting and policy analysis, were based on an output–inflation trade-off that implied policy makers could actively manage the economy through the use of discretionary fiscal and monetary policy. Questioning the theoretical basis for such a trade-off, Friedman (1968) and Phelps (1970) were the first to posit a 'natural rate hypothesis' that illustrated that such trade-offs could not be permanently exploited. In addition, Keynesian structural models forecast poorly in the early 1970s, with the unpredicted combination of high inflation *and* high unemployment rates suggesting fundamental problems with the underlying Keynesian macroeconomic model.

During this period many economists were growing progressively dissatisfied with the theoretical underpinnings of Keynesian macroeconometric models, in particular with the Keynesian treatment of expectations. The output–inflation trade-off inherent in Keynesian models was based largely on *adaptive expectations*, the idea that future economic activity could be predicted solely by observing past activity. Increasingly, however, economists embraced the notion of *rational expectations*, which recognizes that optimizing individuals use *all* available information when making predictions of future economic events, information which may include expected *future* economic policy as well as past economic behavior. In addition, economists criticized the ad hoc assumptions that Keynesians used in identifying their models, assumptions which were inconsistent with microeconomic theory. In response, new classical economists sought to develop general-equilibrium models based on internally consistent microeconomic principles. The twin assumptions that markets clear and individuals employ rational expectations in their economic decision making are at the heart of the new classical school of economics and are responsible for the policy conclusions for which this school of thought has become known.

Robert Lucas at the University of Chicago is responsible for initiating the research program that evolved during the 1970s into the new classical school of macroeconomics.[1] In addition, economists at the Minneapolis Federal Reserve Bank and the University of Minnesota played a key role in the development of this school of thought. Over the last 25 years many of the leading proponents of the new classical school have been associated with these institutions, including Thomas Sargent, Neil Wallace and Ed Prescott.[2]

Monetary neutrality

Lucas (1972, 1973) was the first to incorporate the assumptions of rational expectations, optimizing behavior and market clearing in a simple general-equilibrium macroeconomic model. The conclusions from Lucas's papers are clear: while monetary shocks are capable of producing a negative relationship between unemployment and inflation rates, policy makers cannot systematically exploit this trade-off. Under the dual assumptions of market clearing and rational expectations, monetary policy has positive effects on output only when it is *unanticipated*; only then will individuals misinterpret aggregate price level changes as relative price movements and modify their labor supply and production decisions. Anticipated monetary policy affects only the aggregate price level and consequently has no effect on employment or output, even in the short run.

Lucas's results had a dramatic impact on the development of macroeconomic theory, as they challenged current views of the role of macroeconomic policy. In particular the new classical results overthrew the Keynesian claim that policy makers could *systematically* move the economy to full employment through discretionary aggregate demand policies. While yielding similar policy recommendations as the monetarists, Lucas's 'policy ineffectiveness' results implied that systematic monetary policy was incapable of affecting output and employment even in the short run, a conclusion the monetarists did not share. The policy ineffectiveness result is most closely associated with classical economic theory. However, while classical models assume perfect foresight, in new classical models agents form *expectations* of future economic activity based on imperfect information. In such an environment, monetary policy can have real consequences, but only if it is unanticipated.

Initial econometric tests by Barro (1977, 1978) of the rational expectations hypothesis underlying Lucas's model provided empirical support for the new classical school's doctrines. Barro's results indicated that only unanticipated monetary policy affected output. Later work by Mishkin (1983), however, suggested that *both* unanticipated and anticipated monetary policy affect output, leaving the issues of rational expectations and policy ineffectiveness undecided.

The Lucas critique

Lucas's (1972, 1973) research emphasized that changes in monetary policy affect the supply responses of individuals in the economy. The implication that economic behavior may change when economic policy changes provides perhaps the most important and long-lasting economic contribution of the new classical school and is the central focus of Lucas's (1976) econometric policy evaluation critique. In that paper, Lucas argued on theoretical grounds that Keynesian models were 'fundamentally flawed' in their ability to evaluate the outcomes of alternative economic policies. In-sample behavior provides little guidance to policy makers in predicting the effects of changes in economic policy. Changes in policy are likely to change the underlying structure of large 'structural' econometric models as individuals adjust their behavior in response to the policy changes, leading to invalid inferences about the effects of alternative economic policies.

One of the implications of the 'Lucas critique' was that policy makers could no longer treat policy making as a series of unrelated actions but rather should view it as a choice among 'feasible rules of the game'. Recognizing that individuals' actions depend on these rules in a way that current models could not capture provided a serious criticism of Keynesian macroeconomic models and dramatically changed the focus of macroeconomic research.

Real business cycles

In addition to uncovering theoretical problems with the Keynesian model, new classical economists shifted attention away from questions of maintaining full employment and back towards the pre-Keynesian focus on *business cycle* behavior. In particular, Lucas and Sargent (1979) argued for the development of theoretical models of business cycle behavior based on rational, optimizing individuals that could overcome many of the theoretical shortcomings of the Keynesian models and yet account for observed data. By the early 1980s, Kydland and Prescott (1982) had developed a fully articulated general-equilibrium business cycle model that was capable of mimicking the behavior of the US economy, initiating a research program that has become the centerpiece of new classical macroeconomics. The resulting *real business cycle* models replaced earlier new classical monetary misperception models and emphasize supply (productivity) shocks rather than demand shocks as the primary source of economic fluctuations.

By focusing on stochastic supply shocks and selecting theoretically plausible parameter estimates for the model's underlying theoretical structure, Kydland and Prescott were able to generate simulated macroeconomic time series with business cycle properties that broadly matched those of US macroeconomic aggregates, a significant finding given the Keynesian focus on aggregate demand shocks as the major source of cyclical fluctuations. Kydland

and Prescott's analysis provided important empirical support for the real business cycle class of models and signaled an important change in the way macroeconomic models are evaluated. Rather than emphasizing the estimation and testing of structural parameters, as Keynesians had, Kydland and Prescott focused attention on the ability of their artificial economy to replicate the time series behavior of an actual economy. Testing the adequacy of business cycle models by determining their ability to mimic real economies has since become the standard by which business cycle models are judged.

The fact that a general-equilibrium model without money could broadly account for the pattern of business cycle behavior observed in the United States was viewed at the time as a dramatic achievement in support of the new classical school, which holds that monetary policy plays a minimal role in driving the real economy. Since then numerous extensions to Kydland and Prescott's basic real business cycle model have been developed to address a variety of criticisms by Keynesians.[3] Despite these criticisms, real business cycle models remain the central focus of new classical macroeconomics, primarily because of their internal logical consistency and focus on microeconomic foundations.

Summary

New classical macroeconomics has posed a serious challenge to Keynesian views of macroeconomic theory and policy. Lucas's policy ineffectiveness result and critique of Keynesian econometric policy evaluation were the primary forces that led to the emergence of the new classical school of macroeconomics. However these were merely opening volleys in a battle of competing paradigms that has permanently changed the face of macroeconomics. One of the most significant changes has come in returning the focus of macroeconomics to the observation and explanation of the business cycle, a topic that was actively researched prior to the 'Keynesian revolution' but has only recently enjoyed renewed interest.

New classical assumptions and policy conclusions (such as rational expectations and policy ineffectiveness) have been challenged by Keynesians, but the lasting impact of the new classical school is illustrated by the modern emphasis on building internally consistent general-equilibrium macroeconomic models of the economy. New Keynesians fail to embrace the market-clearing assumption of the new classical school, yet they are continually challenged to provide microeconomic justification for market disequilibrium rather than simply relying on observed economic behavior. Whether this emphasis on maximizing behavior will lead to a synthesis of classical and Keynesian ideas in macroeconomics remains to be seen, but the emergence of the new classical school has helped to sharpen the focus of the debate.

SCOTT SIMKINS

Notes

1 The development of the new classical school of macroeconomics is traced in two volumes of collected works. Lucas (1981) contains 14 of Robert Lucas's papers, a number of which were pioneering contributions to the developing new classical school of macroeconomics. In addition, Lucas and Sargent (1981) provide a comprehensive summary of the role of rational expectations in the development of new classical macroeconomics and its dramatic implications for policy making and econometric analysis.
2 A survey of the contributions to the new classical school made by Minneapolis Federal Reserve Bank economists is contained in Miller (1994).
3 See Miler (1994), in particular Chapter 15, for a summary of Keynesian criticisms of the real business cycle approach in macroeconomics.

See also:

Business Cycle Theory (I) and (II); Coordination Failures and Keynesian Economics Demand Management; Expectations, Theories of; Keynesian Revolution; Lucas, Jr., Robert E.; Lucas Critique; Phillips Curve.

Bibliography

Barro, Robert J. (1977), 'Unanticipated Money Growth and Unemployment in the United States', *American Economic Review*, **67**, (1), March, pp. 101–15.

Barro, Robert J. (1978), 'Unanticipated Money, Output and the Price Level in the United States', *Journal of Political Economy*, **86**, (4), August, pp. 549–80.

Friedman, Milton (1968), 'The Role of Monetary Policy', *American Economic Review*, **58**, (1), March, pp. 1–17.

Kydland, Finn E. and Edward C. Prescott (1982), 'Time to Build and Aggregate Fluctuations', *Econometrica*, **50**, (6), November, pp. 1345–70.

Lucas, Jr., Robert E. (1972), 'Expectations and the Neutrality of Money', *Journal of Economic Theory*, **4**, (2), April, pp. 103–24.

Lucas, Jr., Robert E. (1973), 'Some International Evidence on Output–Inflation Tradeoffs', *American Economic Review*, **63**, (3), June, pp. 326–34.

Lucas, Jr., Robert E. (1976), 'Econometric Policy Evaluation: A Critique', in Karl Brunner and Allan H. Meltzer (eds), *The Phillips Curve and Labor Markets*, Carnegie–Rochester Conference Series on Public Policy 1, Amsterdam: North-Holland.

Lucas, Jr., Robert E. (1981), *Studies in Business-Cycle Theory*, Cambridge, Mass.: MIT Press.

Lucas, Jr., Robert E. and Thomas J. Sargent (1979), 'After Keynesian Macroeconomics', *Federal Reserve Bank of Minneapolis Quarterly Review*, **3**, (2), Spring, pp. 1–16.

Lucas, Jr., Robert E. and Thomas J. Sargent (eds) (1981), *Rational Expectations and Econometric Practice*, Minneapolis, Minn.: University of Minnesota Press.

Miller, Preston J. (1994), *The Rational Expectations Revolution: Readings from the Front Line*, Cambridge, Mass.: MIT Press.

Mishkin, Frederic S. (1983), *A Rational Expectations Approach to Macroeconometrics: Testing Policy Ineffectiveness and Efficient-market Models*, Chicago: University of Chicago Press/ National Bureau of Economic Research.

Phelps, E.S. (ed.) (1970), *Microeconomic Foundations of Employment and Inflation Theory*, New York: W.W. Norton.

New Keynesian Macroeconomics

This perspective focuses on a representative agent's reactions to changes in nominal variables through output, capital and labor markets. In this way it seeks a distinctively microeconomic foundation to what have previously been accepted as *Keynesian* macroeconomic conclusions. Weak new Keynesian economics, as defined by Rosser (1996), implies that fluctuations in output and employment in the aggregate are seen to be caused by market failures or coordination problems, uniquely focused on the supply side, which either cause wages and prices to be relatively sticky in a downward direction or which settle at suboptimal equilibria in response to aggregate demand shocks. Strong new Keynesian economics lays greater emphasis on questions of interdependencies, spillovers and strategic complementarities (see Cooper and John, 1988) in the context of such coordination failures of the market.

New Keynesian macroeconomists by and large support the belief that, in the long period, one would expect sufficient wage and price flexibility to cause any random exogenous nominal shock to be totally borne by other nominal, rather than real, variables. In the short period, however, there are small costs perceived by firms which inhibit them from lowering prices in the face of nominal demand shifts which, new Keynesian economists contend, have large external aggregate effects on output and welfare loss (see Mankiw, 1985; Akerlof and Yellen, 1985). In the labor market, this perspective seeks explanations as to why nominal as well as real wages do not fall in the light of fluctuations in demand for output and therefore for labor. Plausible interpretations can be found in the theories of shirking, implicit contracts (Azariadis and Stiglitz, 1983), efficiency wages (Yellen, 1984) and hysteresis (Lindbeck and Snower, 1987). In the capital market, nominal and real interest rates are sticky downwards, preventing market clearing caused by credit rationing, as a result of asymmetric information between lenders and borrowers about the prospective yields on capital assets (Stiglitz and Weiss, 1981).

Since there is no Walrasian auctioneer to orchestrate the internalization of these externalities, fluctuations in nominal variables will be disproportionately borne by fluctuations in real output and employment, rather than in nominal prices and wages. Thus the classical dichotomy is violated as nominal changes affect real outcomes and the economy experiences so-called 'Keynesian features', that is secondary effects on employment and output (a form of multiplier mechanism) and 'Keynesian type' involuntary unemployment as these secondary falls in demand for output, coupled with firms' unwillingness to offer lower wages in response to these demand failures, cause the full impact to be borne by unemployment rather than by downward real wage flexibility.

New Keynesian models that rely on questions of spillover (actions affecting others' payoffs) and strategic complementarities (actions affecting others' strategies) indicate that multiple symmetric Nash equilibria may occur which are suboptimal but stable, in the sense that a series of individual actions will cause outcomes which do not necessarily improve Pareto optimality. Low-level equilibria can occur because no individual has the incentive to lower their price or change output. However any change in output benefits consumers through a spillover effect or demand externality which, in turn, allows for strategic complementarities and movements to higher-level equilibria through multiplier effects (Cooper and John, 1988). The potential richness of this approach is reflected in the extent to which multiplier effects brought about by strategic complementarities cause *income* to change, affecting the underlying data facing each individual.

In fact critiques from Post Keynesian circles (Davidson, 1992, 1996; Rotheim, 1996) address just those aspects of the new Keynesian perspective where interdependencies cause income to change. In such cases, economies should be depicted, not as closed or ergodic, a prerequisite for any theory attempting to address macroeconomic activity from aggregate labor and capital markets, but rather as open or non-ergodic. In these latter instances, economies should be understood as path-dependent, vitiating the presumed dichotomy between real and nominal variables.

Roy J. Rotheim

See also:
Business Cycle Theory (I) and (II); Coordination Failures and Keynesian Economics; Davidson, Paul; Lausanne, The School of; Lucas Critique, The; Microfoundations of Macroeconomics; New Classical School of Economics; Say's Law.

Bibliography
Akerlof, George and Janet Yellen (1985), 'A Near-Rational Model of the Business Cycle, with Wage and Price Inertia', *Quarterly Journal of Economics*, **100**, (Supplement), pp. 823–38.
Azariadis, Costas and Joseph Stiglitz (1983), 'Implicit Contracts and Fixed-Price Equilibria', *Quarterly Journal of Economics*, **98**, (3), (Supplement), pp. 1–22.
Cooper, Russell and Andrew John (1988), 'Coordinating Coordination Failures in Keynesian Models', *Quarterly Journal of Economics*, **103**, (3), August, pp. 441–63.
Davidson, Paul (1992), 'Would Keynes be a New Keynesian?', *Eastern Economic Journal*, **18**, (4), fall, pp. 449–64.
Davidson, Paul (1996), 'Setting the Record Straight', in R.J. Rotheim (ed.), *New Keynesian Economics/Post Keynesian Alternatives*, Aldershot: Edward Elgar.
Lindbeck, Assar and Dennis Snower (1987), 'Union Activity, Unemployment Persistence and Wage Employment Ratchets', *European Economic Review*, **31**, (1/2), February/March, pp. 157–67.
Mankiw, N. Gregory (1985), 'Small Menu Costs and Large Business Cycles: A Macroeconomic Model of Monopoly', *Quarterly Journal of Economics*, **100**, (2), May, pp. 529–37.
Mankiw, N. Gregory and David Romer (eds) (1990), *New Keynesian Economics*, 2 vols, Cambridge, Mass.: MIT.
Rosser, Barkley (1996), 'A Complex Systems Dynamics Perspective on New Keynesian and Post Keynesian Economics', in R.J. Rotheim (ed.), *New Keynesian Economics/Post Keynesian Alternatives*, Aldershot: Edward Elgar.
Rotheim, R.J. (ed.), (1996), *New Keynesian Economics/Post Keynesian Alternatives*, Aldershot: Edward Elgar.
Stiglitz, Joseph and Andrew Weiss (1981), 'Credit Rationing in Markets with Imperfect Information', *American Economic Review*, **71**, pp. 393–410.
Yellen, Janet (1984), 'Efficiency Wage Models of Unemployment', *American Economic Review*, **74**, (2), May, pp. 200–205.

Niemeyer, Sir Otto E.

Sir Otto Ernst Niemeyer (1883–1971) was one of the leading Treasury mandarins in the 1920s. A graduate in classics of Balliol College, Oxford, he joined the Treasury in 1906 after winning first place in the civil service examination of that year. He rose rapidly in the pecking order of the office, and by 1922 was appointed Controller of Finance – one of the three leading officials of the Treasury who reported directly to the Chancellor of the Exchequer. He was thus intimately involved in the formation and presentation of the 'Treasury View' on the main economic issues of the day during a crucial period of English and European history: the aftermath of World War I and most of the 1920s.

The term 'Treasury View' surfaced only in the late 1920s in Churchill's well-known budget speech (of April 1929) in which he referred to 'orthodox treasury dogma' in the context of the debate on public works, but though by that time Niemeyer had left the Treasury for the Bank of England, the phrase coined by Churchill represented by and large the 'sound money' axiom which, according to Niemeyer's vision, had an operational meaning in those years: the return to England to the gold standard at the pre-World War I gold parity, as decreed by the Cunliffe committee (in 1918). The pursuance of that target, which meant the re-establishment of the prewar dollar/sterling (stable) exchange rate, was of course the creed of all the leading lights of the Treasury and, inevitably, of the Bank of England personified by Montagu Norman.

Niemeyer's contribution to the formation and implementation of that policy and the doggedness with which it was pursued, and defended after implementation in 1925, was highly significant. The long years of service at the Treasury of its top civil servants, in contrast to the revolving door of political personalities serving as Chancellor, gave significant weight to the views of the former on the strategic issues of the day which required resolution. The six Chancellors of the Exchequer who were in charge of the Treasury between the end of the war and the return of England to the gold standard in April 1925 thus had no alternative but to rely on the knowledge, opinion and advice of a small group of civil servants, who occupied the top positions of the office, on the major issue of the day: the exchange rate regime and specifically the setting of the rate of exchange.

This undoubtedly applied to Churchill, who had to make up his mind on the feasibility – the cost and benefits – of the restoration of the gold standard at the 1914 par vis-à-vis the dollar within six months of assuming office. He thus relied heavily on the advice of Niemeyer, his controller of finance, who had been studying and deliberating on that issue for several years. Like almost anyone involved in those deliberations, he identified restoration of a *stable exchange rate* regime with a *specific* gold, thus dollar, par at which it would be implemented as the only relevant option. If anything, his membership of the small Chamberlain–Bradbury committee, which had been taking evidence since its appointment in May 1924 and had recommended an 'immediate' restoration of the gold standard early in February 1925, meant that his opinion on that matter was of special weight. Thus he was one of the four addressees of 'Churchill's Exercise' – a memorandum prepared by the Chancellor in which its recipients were challenged to respond to a number of queries, all of which, by implication, poured cold water on the proposal of an immediate return to the gold standard at the 1914 gold parity.

Niemeyer's response to that challenge on the restoration issue, a decision which he described as 'probably the most important financial decision of the present decade', was presented in two memos, one responding to each of the six points raised in the 'Exercise', the other a review of the domestic and international economic scene, within the specific historical context. In the latter he argued that 'experience' had proved that the gold standard is the monetary regime which is 'the best for trade'. Thus, though admitting that restoration would require sacrifice in the short run (that is, deflation and its consequences), this highly sophisticated and closely argued piece concluded that it would be highly beneficial in the long run. In view of the proximity of the actual rate to the 1914 par, and the expected lapse of the law which prevented gold exports at the end of 1925, Niemeyer claimed that immediate restoration of the gold standard was the only relevant option open to the government of Great Britain in the 'present [1925] circumstances'.

Niemeyer's position in the pecking order of the Treasury and the group of officials around the Chancellor of the Exchequer was in those days underlined by his participation in the well known dinner party of six (on 17 March 1925), set up by Churchill. On this occasion he and Bradbury of the Treasury were to argue out the case for restoration with Keynes and McKenna, who were highly skeptical on the *timing*, though not on the principle, of return to the gold standard at prewar parity, with Churchill himself acting as the referee. This was the second direct confrontation of Niemeyer and Keynes. In the first, in 1906, he beat Keynes into second place in the civil service examination, which gained him an immediate posting to the Treasury. With McKenna weakening in his opposition to restoration during that meeting, Niemeyer beat Keynes for the second time: Churchill was convinced that the Treasury people won the argument. The weakening of McKenna's opposition to the move may have been crucial. The formal decision to return to the gold standard was taken three days after that event.

The resolution of the gold standard issues proved soon to be the zenith of Niemeyer's service at the Treasury. With England's economy in the doldrums from 1921 onwards, the defence of the newly established gold standard required a highly restrictive monetary policy. The ensuing deflation, and the

1926 General Strike in its wake, soon suggested to many, including Church-ill, that it was Keynes and not Niemeyer and Montagu Norman who was after all right in that debate. The change in the Chancellor's attitude to the policy which Niemeyer recommended both publicly and privately to Churchill was undoubtedly a major consideration, in Niemeyer's decision to leave the Treas-ury in 1927 and accept Montagu Norman's long-standing proposal to join the Bank of England, in the capacity of an adviser first, and from 1938 to 1952 as an executive director.

The recession in Britain, and later the world economic crisis from late 1929 onwards, did not shatter Niemeyer's belief in the old time religion of sound money, or his view on the proper macroeconomic policy. In 1930, as the world economic crisis was deepening, he headed a British economic mission to Australia to discuss the deep recession there. His advice was that Australia should stick to the sterling (thus to the gold) parity of the Australian dollar, though maintenance of that exchange rate would require deflation. In a mission to India in 1936, he made proposals similar in vein to those he had made six years before in Australia. If anything, the inflation (and sometimes hyperinflation) in several European countries in the wake of two world wars strengthened his view on the crucial relevance of sound money and the importance of the city of London as the dominant European money and capital market.

Niemeyer's work at the Bank, in close contact with Montagu Norman with whom he agreed on all important matters, changed focus. In the late 1920s and early 1930s, he was intimately involved in the reconstruction of the monetary and fiscal systems of the small Baltic and Balkan states. His activ-ity in the realm of international finance began, indeed, early in 1922 when he joined the Financial Committee of the League of Nations, of which he became chairman in 1927. This set the pattern of his activity on the fiscal and financial issues of the small European powers during the next four decades. As director of the newly established Bank of International Settlements (BIS), set up to help to implement the German reparation payments and settle, on a long-term basis, the inter (Western) allied debts created during World War I, he sat on the board from 1932. He was chairman of the board in 1937–9 and its vice-chairman from 1940 until 1964. Niemeyer's experience in the reset-ting of the finances of the small European powers in the 1930s was tapped again in the wake of World War II. As a board member of BIS he was deeply involved in the restoration of the monetary and fiscal regimes during the outstandingly successful economic reconstruction on the Continent in the decades following World War II.

HAIM BARKAI

See also:

Classical Economics; Crowding Out; Economics of Keynes and of his Revolution, Key Elements of the; Government Investment Programs (The Socialization of Investment); Hawtrey, Sir Ralph; Kahn, Lord Richard F.; Keynesian Revolution; Multiplier Effect; Pigou, Arthur C.; Robertson, Sir Dennis H.

Bibliography

Black, L. and C.S. Nichols (eds) (1986), *Dictionary of National Biography 1971–1980*, Oxford: Oxford University Press.

Boyle, A. (1967), *Montagu Norman*, London: Cassell.

Howson, S. (1975), *Domestic Monetary Management in Britain 1919–1938*, Cambridge: Cambridge University Press.

Kindleberger, C.P. (1973), *The World in Depression 1929–1939*, London: Alan Lane, The Penguin Press.

Moggridge, D.E. (1969), *The Return to Gold, 1925*, Cambridge: Cambridge University Press.

Moggridge, D.E. (1981), *The Collected Writings of John Maynard Keynes, vol. XIX, Activities 1922–1929: The Return to Gold and Industrial Policy* I, London: Macmillan.

Moggridge, D.E. (1993), 'From Theory to Policy: The Keynesian Revolution in Britain', in H. Barkai, S. Fisher and N. Liviatan (eds), *Monetary Theory and Thought*, London: Macmillan.

Ohlin, Bertil

Bertil Ohlin was born on 24 April 1899. He attended a private school in Halsingborg where he excelled in mathematics. Agreeing with his parents' assessment of his abilities he entered the University of Lund, where he studied economics, mathematics and statistics. At the end of two years of study (1915–17) he earned the degree of fil. kand (BA). In 1917, he entered the Stockholm School of Economics and Business where, in addition to French and Russian, he studied economics under the direction of Eli Heckscher. In 1918, he became a member of the Political Economy Club whose membership at that time included Heckscher, Davidson, Wicksell and Cassel.

In 1919, he moved on to the philosophy faculty at the University of Stockholm, where his main professors were Gustav Cassel and Gosta Bagge. In 1921, upon the successful defense of his thesis, which was completed under the supervision of Cassel, Ohlin was awarded his 'licentiatus philosophiae'. After earning his degree he served in the navy for one year and then spent a few months in Grenoble, France.

In 1922, Ohlin received a grant from the Swedish American Foundation which permitted him to spend the 1922–3 academic year at Harvard, where he studied under Frank Taussig, John H. Williams, Thomas Carver and Allyn Young. During the return trip Ohlin spent a few months at the University of Cambridge. The result of this study abroad program was his dissertation, 'The Theory of Trade', for which he was awarded his doctorate in May 1924. In 1925, he took a position at the University of Copenhagen. He stayed there until 1930, when he returned to the Stockholm School of Economics and Business to assume the chair in economics vacated by Heckscher. Ohlin remained at the Stockholm School until his retirement in 1970.

Ohlin's work in economics was concentrated in two areas: international trade and macroeconomics. Cassel's *The Theory of Social Economy* (1918) examined a closed economy in which the principles of Walrasian general equilibrium were investigated. Ohlin's dissertation used a general equilibrium model to investigate the impact of interregional trade on Cassel's model and international trade on an open economy. Ohlin considered this aspect of his work to be his most significant contribution to economic theory. His line of inquiry assumed that commodities moved without cost between regions and nations, that factors of production were immobile and that trade occurred because of the difference in relative scarcity of the factors of production. Ohlin's principal conclusion was that interregional and international trade resulted in the equalization of commodity prices and, to some extent, factor prices. This conclusion was similar to the one developed by Heckscher (1919). Hence the 'Heckscher–Ohlin theory of trade'. Ohlin's conclusion has been examined, extended and criticized by Stolper and Samuelson (1941), Samuelson (1948, 1949), Johnson (1957), Robinson (1964) and Trefler (1995).

In *Interregional and International Trade* (1933b), the work cited by the Nobel Committee as being his principal contribution to economic theory, Ohlin developed a more sophisticated version of his trade model. Three aspects of this work are worthy of mention. First, one of the implications of this model is that the United States should export capital-intensive commodities and import labour-intensive commodities. Leontief (1953, 1956), in what has become known as the 'Leontief paradox', examined and criticized this aspect of Ohlin's model. Second, Ohlin concluded that, if the underlying assumptions of his model were relaxed, large-scale economies became a principal factor in determining trade. From this conclusion it is but a short step to the new theory of international trade as articulated by Krugman (1979, 1980), Dixit (1984) and Dixit and Kyle (1985).

Third, Ohlin investigated the effect of changes in income on trade. This aspect of his model forms the basis of Ohlin's position on the German transfer problem. In this debate Keynes's argument refers to movements along a given demand curve: Germany could not make the reparation payments demanded of her by the Allies because low price elasticities of demand for imports and exports prevented Germany from reducing its real wages to the extent necessary to create a balance of trade surplus. Ohlin's argument refers to shifts in the entire demand schedule: if Germany used monetary and fiscal policies to reduce her level of income, she could create a balance of trade surplus out of which reparations could be paid. Later in life, Ohlin suggested that this disagreement between himself and Keynes could have been avoided if Keynes had taken the time to read and understand the argument which he (Ohlin) had developed in a paper which was rejected by Keynes in his role as the editor of the *Economic Journal*.

Macroeconomics was the second area of economic theory where Ohlin made significant contributions. His work was based on the analysis developed by Myrdal in *Monetary Equilibrium* (1931). Myrdal's ex ante–ex post analysis focused on total monetary demand relative to total monetary supply. In *Get Production Going* (1927) and in 'To the Question of the Structure of Monetary Theory' (1933a) Ohlin developed all of the essential elements of the *General Theory*. Thus, when the *General Theory* came to Sweden, the Stockholm School could not see what all the fuss was about: the members of this school had been thinking along these lines for quite some time. Ohlin tried to communicate this to the English-speaking world in his 1937 article, 'Some Notes on the Stockholm Theory of Savings and Investment'. While some students of the history of economic thought would delve deeply into the question of priority of discovery, a different approach would focus on the parallel development of countercyclical fiscal policy in two different nations which had one thing in common: the impact of the Great Depression on their respective economies.

In addition to his work in economics, for which he was awarded the Nobel Prize in Economics in 1977, Ohlin was very active in politics. From 1934 to 1939 he was chairman of The Liberal Youth Federation. He was the long-time leader of the Liberal Party, serving as the Minister of Trade from 1944 to 1945. Ohlin also contributed articles about current economic events to newspapers on a regular basis. He died on 3 August 1979.

End note

In an interesting sidelight to the German transfer problem, since the reunification of Germany the German government has earmarked at least $167 million for the redemption of the bonds associated with four specific loans: the German External Loan of 1924 (the Dawes Plan), the German International Loan of 1930 and the 1926 and 1927 External Sinking Fund Dollar Bonds of the State of Prussia. Efforts were initiated by the German government in January 1995 to locate the owners of these bonds and to begin the redemption process.

Tom Cate

See also:

Cassel, Karl G.; Demand Management; Economics of Keynes and of his Revolution, Key Elements of the; Fiscal Policy; Keynes, John Maynard; Keynesian Revolution; Leontief, Wassily W.; Meade, James E.; Myrdal, Gunnar; Robinson, Joan; Samuelson, Paul A.; Stockholm, School of Economics; Wicksell, Knut.

Bibliography

Cassel, Gustav (1918), *The Theory of Social Economy*; reprinted 1967, New York: Augustus M. Kelley.

Dixit, Avinash (1984), 'International Trade Policy for Oligopolistic Industries', *Economic Journal*, **94**, supplement, pp. 1–16.

Dixit, Avinash and Albert S. Kyle (1985), 'The Use of Protection and Subsidies for Entry Promotion and Deterrence', *American Economic Review*, **75**, (1), March, pp. 139–52.

Heckscher, Eli (1919), 'The Effect of Foreign Trade on the Distribution of Income', *Ekonomisk Tidskrift*, **21**, pp. 497–512; reprinted 1991 in Harry Flam and M. June Flanders (eds), *Heckscher–Ohlin Trade Theory*, Cambridge, Mass.: MIT Press.

Johnson, Harry G. (1957), 'Factor Endowments, International Trade and Factor Prices', *The Manchester School of Economic and Social Studies*, **25**, (3), September, pp. 270–83.

Keynes, John Maynard (1929a), 'The German Transfer Problem', *Economic Journal*, **39**, (153), March, pp. 1–7.

Keynes, John Maynard (1929b), 'The Reparation Problem: A Rejoinder', *Economic Journal*, **39**, (154), June, pp. 179–82.

Keynes, John Maynard (1929c), 'Mr. Keynes' Views on the Transfer Problem', *Economic Journal*, **39**, (155), September, pp. 388–99.

Krugman, Paul (1979), 'Increasing Returns, Monopolistic Competition and International Trade', *Journal of International Economics*, **9**, (4), November, pp. 469–79.

Krugman, Paul (1980), 'Scale Economies, Product Differentiation and the Pattern of Trade', *American Economic Review*, **70**, (5), December, pp. 950–59.

Leontief, W.W. (1953), 'Domestic Production and Foreign Trade: The American Capital Position Re-examined', *Economica Internazionale*, **7**, (1), February, pp. 9–38.

Leontief, W.W. (1956), 'Factor Proportions of the Structure of American Trade: Further Theoretical and Empirical Analysis', *Review of Economics and Statistics*, **38**, (4), November, pp. 386–407.

Myrdal, Gunnar (1931), *Monetary Equilibrium*; reprinted in 1965, New York: Augustus M. Kelley.

Ohlin, Bertil (1927), *Get Production Going*, Copenhagen: Aschenhoug.

Ohlin, Bertil (1929a), 'The Reparation Problem: A Discussion', *Economic Journal*, **39**, (154), June, pp. 172–8.

Ohlin, Bertil (1929b), 'Mr. Keynes' Views on the Transfer Problem: A Rejoinder', *Economic Journal*, **39**, (155), September, pp. 400–404.

Ohlin, Bertil (1933a), 'To The Question of the Structure of Monetary Theory', *Ekonomisk Tidskrift*, **35**, (1), March, pp. 45–81.

Ohlin, Bertil (1933b), *Interregional and International Trade*, Cambridge, Mass.: Harvard University Press.

Ohlin, Bertil (1937), 'Some Notes on the Stockholm Theory of Savings and Investment: I and II', *Economic Journal*, **47**, (185), March, pp. 53–69; (186), June, pp. 221–40.

Robinson, Joan (1964), 'Factor Prices not Equalized', *Quarterly Journal of Economics*, **78**, (2), May, pp. 202–7.

Samuelson, Paul A. (1948), 'International Trade and Equalization of Factor Prices', *Economic Journal*, **58**, (230), June, pp. 163–84.

Samuelson, Paul A. (1949), 'International Factor-Price Equalization Once Again', *Economic Journal*, **59**, (234), June, pp. 181–97.

Samuelson, Paul A. (1982), 'Bertil Ohlin, 1899–1979', *Journal of International Economics*, supplement, January, pp. 31–49.

Stolper, Wolfgang and Paul A. Samuelson (1941), 'Protection and Real Wages', *Review of Economic Studies*, **9**, (1), November, pp. 58–73.

Trefler, Daniel (1995), 'The Case of the Missing Trade and Other Mysteries', *American Economic Review*, **85**, (5), December, pp. 1029–46.

Okun, Arthur M.

Arthur Melvin Okun was born 28 November 1928 in Jersey City, New Jersey to Louis and Rose (Cantor) Okun. He married Suzanne Grossman on 1 July 1951 and subsequently had three boys. Okun is best known for his work with the Council of Economic Advisors in forecasting and his ability to integrate his academic interests with his policy interests. Okun was masterful in his ability to write for the non-academic public and he was widely quoted in major national newspapers. He died of a heart attack at the age of 51 in Washington, DC.

Okun earned his BA in economics from Columbia College of Columbia University in 1949. As an undergraduate he edited the student newspaper and won the Albert Asher Green Prize for the highest scholastic record. He subsequently entered the doctoral program in economics at Columbia University and graduated in 1957 with the doctorate of philosophy in economics. His dissertation was titled 'The Effect of Open Inflation on Aggregate Consumer Demand'.

Hired as an instructor of economics at Yale University in 1952, he advanced to an assistant professorship in 1956 and to the associate level in 1960. In 1963, he was assigned to direct the graduate program in economics at Yale and was promoted to the position of full professor. At the urging of James Tobin, Okun took a leave of absence from the university in 1961–2 to serve President Kennedy on his Council of Economic Advisors as a staff economist, becoming known for the accuracy of his macroeconomic forecasts. His forecasting was not based upon large-scale econometric models but rather a combination of keen analytical insight and artful judgement. Okun was appointed as a member of the Council of Economic Advisors in 1964 and served in that capacity until 1968, when he became chairman.

During his service as a Council staff member, Okun developed what subsequently became known as 'Okun's Law'. According to his empirical analysis there existed a tractable and consistent relationship between unemployment and the long-run rate of growth of productivity. For every one per cent increase in the gap between real GNP and potential GNP (the long-run growth rate of real GNP), Okun posited that unemployment would drop by one-third of one per cent. According to the law, this relationship holds during both the expansion and contraction phases of the business cycle. For a number of years Okun's Law held very well. With the advent of stagflation in the late 1970s, however, the relationship weakened.

After the 1968 presidential election Okun left government service to take a position at the Brookings Institution as a senior fellow. In 1972, he co-founded with George Perry the *Brookings Papers on Economic Activity* and served as co-editor of the journal until his death.

Okun's collected writings include ten books and monographs and over 50 professional articles. He was known primarily for his work on the macroeconomy. Inflation was, for Okun, a harmful entity that, left unchecked, threatened to destabilize the US economy. Stagflation presented a particularly intractable policy problem and his experience with it caused him to reject at least some tenets of Keynesian policy in his later years. To reduce inflationary pressures in the macroeconomy, Okun proposed the use of wage–price policies combined with a reduction of infrastructure costs to firms resulting from excessive regulation and taxation. Okun was also influential in the area of labor economics. According to Okun, labor and firms establish an implicit contract with one another which is marked by longevity. Firms hire workers on a long-term basis as an efficiency device designed to reduce search and training costs. These agreements reduce the downward flexibility of wages. This institutionalized wage rigidity helps to explain the initial ineffectiveness of countercyclical fiscal and monetary policies. This implicit contract between employer and employee became known as the 'invisible handshake'.

In the area of fiscal and monetary policy, Okun was convinced that activist policies were needed and, on the whole, successful. He spent much of his time on empirical research designed to better the timing of the major policy tools. He wrote in a number of areas relating directly to policy, including inflation, taxation, poverty, forecasting and the political aspects of policy advising. Okun was firmly convinced that the role economists play in policy decisions was important and influential. As an economic advisor he believed that it was his duty to support the decisions of policy makers once they were made, unless there was broad and substantial disagreement with the decision within the professional economics community. Arthur Okun was also interested in the social effects of economic policy. In *Equality and Efficiency: The Big Trade-Off* (1975) he lays out the basic tensions between the economists' quest for efficiency and the egalitarians' quest for fairness in a capitalist economy.

BRADLEY K. HOBBS

See also:
Ackley, Gardner; Business Cycle Theory (I) and (II); Demand Management; Incomes Policies; Inflation; Keynesian Indicators; Keynesian Revolution; Okun's Law; Phillips Curve; Tobin, James.

Bibliography
Arthur Okun, 51, Dies in Capital; Led Council of Economic Advisors, New York Times, Obituary Section, section II:9, 24 March 1982.
Fadool, Cynthia R. (ed.) (1978), *Contemporary Authors*, Detroit: Gale Research Company.
Moritz, Charles (ed.) (1970), *Current Biography Yearbook: 1970*, New York: The H.W. Wilson Company.
Okun, Arthur M. (1975), *Equality and Efficiency: The Big Tradeoff*, Washington, DC: The Brooking Institution.
Pechman, Joseph A. (ed.) (1983), *Economics for Policymaking: Selected Essays of Arthur M. Okun*, Cambridge, Mass.: MIT Press.

Okun's Law

'Okun's Law' is a rule-of-thumb forecasting tool developed by Arthur M. Okun which relates changes in the rate of unemployment to changes in gross national product (GNP). Based upon his forecasting work, it was developed by Okun in 1961, while he was a staff member of the Council of Economic Advisors and an associate professor at Yale University.

Arthur Okun's empirical forecasting work revealed a tractable and consistent relationship between unemployment and the spread between actual GNP and potential or trend GNP. Potential GNP is the long-run, sustainable growth rate of real GNP which can be expected given a country's resource levels, productivity growth patterns and full employment. According to Okun's Law, the rate of unemployment can be expected to drop (rise) by one-third of one per cent for each positive (negative) one per cent by which actual GNP exceeds potential GNP. The law was posited to hold during both the expansion and contraction phases of the business cycle.

Okun realized that the unemployment rate was essentially capturing a number of underlying structural components of the economy which occur over the business cycle, particularly with respect to the productivity of labor, changes in the average working week and the rate of labor force participation. For instance, Okun posited that, during the recovery phase of the business cycle, businesses will be cautious in expanding the structural level of employment within the firm. As a result, in the early stages of recovery, unemployment recedes in stages: employed workers will be pushed to increase the number of hours they work, then cyclically unemployed workers will be hired back into the firm and, eventually, if business optimism is sustained, additional workers will be hired. Okun maintained that these factors combined to make unemployment particularly difficult to deal with other than through real gains in the productive capacity of the nation.

For a number of years Okun's Law held very well. With the advent of stagflation in the late 1970s, however, the relationship weakened. Okun recognized that the law might not hold, particularly if structural change was introduced in the economy. In the *New York Times* in 1975, he was quoted as follows: 'The law is operating right on the button now...[but] that doesn't mean the law always was on the button or that it always will be.' Subsequent analysis by real business cycle theorists and economists studying sectoral unemployment have challenged macroeconomists' commitment to Okun's Law. Some Keynesian economists have suggested that Okun's Law continues to hold, though at a 2 to 1, rather than a 3 to 1 ratio.

BRADLEY K. HOBBS

See also:

Business Cycle Theory (I) and (II); Inflation; Keynes's Economics, National Income Accounting Activism and; Okun, Arthur M.

Bibliography

Holloway, Thomas M. (1989), 'An Updated Look at Okun's Law', *Social Science Quarterly*, **70**, (2), June, pp. 497–504.

Okun, Arthur M. (1962), 'Potential GNP: Its Measurement and Significance', *Proceedings of the Business and Economics Statistics Section*, Washington, DC: American Statistical Association.

Okun Law on the Jobless Seems to Prevail, New York Times, 2 July 1975, p. 43.

Pechman, Joseph A. (ed.) (1983), *Economics for Policymaking: Selected Essays of Arthur M. Okun*, Cambridge, Mass.: MIT Press.

Permanent Income Hypothesis

Milton Friedman (1957) proposed the permanent income hypothesis as a means to reconcile the observed disparity between the short-run and long-run average propensity to consume estimates. Short-run annual time series and cross-sectional family budget studies tended to support the Keynesian absolute income hypothesis in the existence of a nonproportional relationship between consumption and income. On the other hand, long run time series studies supported a proportional relationship between consumption and income. Both the permanent income hypothesis and the life cycle hypothesis set forth by Ando and Modigliani (1963) focus on the role of long-term income as the primary determinant of consumption expenditures. According to Friedman's permanent income hypothesis, consumption is proportional to permanent income where permanent income is simply the expected average long-term income from both human and non-human wealth. Human wealth is the expected return from human capital, namely, labor income, whereas non-human wealth represents the expected returns associated with asset holdings.

Friedman decomposes current income into two parts: permanent and transitory. The transitory component of income can be either positive or negative, causing reported income to be above or below permanent income. Thus the permanent component of income only influences current consumption while transitory income does not affect current consumption. The empirical issue underlying the permanent income hypothesis is how individuals formulate their long-term expectations with respect to their income stream. Friedman suggests that, in each period, individuals adjust their estimates of permanent income to be a portion of the difference between actual income in the current period and the prior period's estimate of permanent income. If actual income exceeds the permanent income then the permanent income level is revised upward. On the other hand, if the actual income is below the permanent income then the permanent income level is revised downward. Permanent income is an exponentially weighted average of current and past measured income levels with the weights summing to unity. Empirically, permanent income follows a distributed lag function. Using annual real per capita data for the United States over the period 1905–51, Friedman estimates the marginal propensity to consume associated with permanent income to be 0.88, and the marginal propensity to consume from current income to be 0.29.

The permanent income hypothesis resolves some of the earlier disparities between the long-run and short-tun average propensities to consume. In the long run, income growth is influenced by changes in permanent income with transitory changes in income canceling each other, hence the proportional long-run consumption function yields a constant average propensity to consume. However, in the short run, periods of high income due to positive transitory income decrease the average propensity to consume since consumption increases only in response to increases in permanent income. During periods of low income caused by negative transitory income, the average propensity to consume increases since consumption decreases only in response to decreases in permanent income. Thus the short-run non-proportional consumption function appears.

The policy implications of the permanent income hypothesis parallel those of the life cycle hypothesis in many ways. First, the effectiveness of tax policy to control aggregate demand is questioned. Temporary tax changes will only affect transitory income, not consumption. On the other hand, permanent tax changes will affect permanent income insofar as individuals adjust their estimates of permanent income. If estimates of permanent income are not very responsive to changes in current income then tax changes will not induce large changes in consumption. On the other hand, if estimates of permanent income are highly responsive to changes in current income then tax changes will induce changes in consumption.

Research by Robert Hall (1978) has extended the permanent income hypothesis by replacing the assumption of backward-looking expectations in the formulation of permanent income with forward-looking (rational) expectations. Under the assumption of rational expectations, all available information prior to the current period would have been incorporated in the estimate of permanent income. Thus changes in consumption result from unanticipated income changes which induce changes in permanent income. The empirical results of the rational expectations permanent income hypothesis have been mixed.

JAMES E. PAYNE

See also:

Absolute Income Hypothesis; Consumption and the Consumption Function; Economics of Keynes of his Revolution, Key Elements of the; Friedman, Milton; Life Cycle Hypothesis; Modigliani, Franco; Relative Income Hypothesis.

Bibliography

Ando, Albert and Franco Modigliani (1963), 'The Life Cycle Hypothesis of Saving: (I) Aggregate Implications and Tests', *American Economic Review*, **53**, (1), March, pp. 55–84.

Friedman, Milton (1957), *A Theory of the Consumption Function*, Princeton, NJ: Princeton University Press.

Hall, Robert (1978), 'Stochastic Implications of the Life Cycle–Permanent Income Hypothesis: Theory and Evidence', *Journal of Political Economy*, **86**, (6), December, pp. 971–87.

Phillips, A.W.H.

Few economists in the postwar period have made such a lasting impression on macroeconomic policy as Alban William Housego ('Bill') Phillips. The empirical curve, with which he is most often associated, examined wage inflation and unemployment data for the United Kingdom for 1861–1957, with a view to gauging the size of the equilibrant forces that would be necessary to reduce the swing of the business cycle 'pendulum'. The idea of an inflation–unemployment 'trade-off', derived by others from his curve, was 'snatched at' first by American Keynesians (for example, Samuelson and Solow, 1960) and, in an extraordinarily brief period of time, it became the cornerstone of applied macroeconomics. In the process, much of the subtlety of Phillips's analysis was replaced by wishful thinking about the potency of macroeconomic manipulation. Phillips's zero inflation advocacy was likewise replaced by the belief that continuing inflation would purchase sustainable reductions in unemployment. Keynesian advocates, in their moment of apparent triumph, gave a hostage to fortune which Milton Friedman, and others, brilliantly exploited, thus facilitating the monetarist counterrevolution.

Phillips was born on 18 November 1914, at Te Rehunga, Dannevirke in Southern Hawke's Bay in the North Island of New Zealand. He matriculated in December 1929 (shortly after his fifteenth birthday), but the onset of the Depression curtailed his education. For a decade he 'wandered': running a cinema in Tuai; carrying his swag – and his violin – across Australia; earning a living by shooting crocodiles; travelling to Britain, via China and Russia (where he was unable to obtain a job in the mines because of the plentiful supply of political prisoners); graduating at the Institute of Electrical Engineers, in November 1938, following several years of correspondence study.

Phillips was commissioned into the RAF in August 1940, and was appointed munitions officer at Kallany Aerodrome, Singapore. He was evacuated from Singapore on *The Empire Star*, and operated a machine gun for three and a half hours during an attempt by the Japanese to sink the ship. Shortly afterwards he volunteered for further action at Java, and was shot down by Japanese aircraft. He and two colleagues attempted to make a discarded bus seaworthy in preparation for the voyage to Australia but they were betrayed by some local villagers and captured.

Thus began three and a half years of incarceration in prisoner-of-war camps. Phillips's heroic role in making and operating a secret radio which kept the prisoners in touch with the war has been documented by Laurens van der Post (1985) and Edward 'Weary' Dunlop (1990) and summarized in Leeson (1994a). At great risk to himself – he would have been tortured to death had the radio been discovered by the Japanese – Phillips played a truly remarkable role in maintaining morale amongst the prisoners, under some of the most unfavorable conditions that human beings could face. These qualities of selflessness, endurance and fearlessness enabled him to survive his ordeal, although he weighed only seven stone by the time of liberation. He possessed quite outstanding characteristics; in a profession where jealousy and resentment of the fame of others are not altogether unknown, he was universally admired by all economists who knew him, regardless of their political or policy allegiances.

Phillips was awarded an MBE (Military Division) for a variety of contributions, including fearlessness in the face of the enemy. He completed an undergraduate degree in sociology in 1949, a PhD in economics in 1953, and rose to the rank of Tooke Professor of Economics in 1958 – all at the London School of Economics. He accepted a chair at the Australian National University in 1967; after his first stroke he taught a course on 'The Development of the Chinese Economy since 1949' at the University of Auckland.

Had World War II not intervened, Phillips would, in all likelihood, have been a brilliant, but largely anonymous, electrical engineer. As it was, his wartime experiences persuaded him to retrain as a social scientist. As a consequence of his incarceration, he had just over a decade (1950–1961) to make his contribution to the formulation of macroeconomic policies which aimed at preventing the type of dislocation which had led to the war. In the 1960s, he became dogged by ill-health, and at age 54 he suffered a crippling stroke. He suffered a fatal stroke on 4 March 1975. It is highly likely that his ill-health and premature death were in part caused by the malnourishment and maltreatment inflicted upon him during his wartime incarceration.

Phillips left three eponymous legacies. The first was the Phillips machine, which he constructed while still an undergraduate (Phillips, 1950; Meade, 1951; Newlyn, 1950; Barr, 1988). It was a brilliantly original 7 feet by 5 feet by 3 feet representation of the macroeconomy, one model of which is now displayed near Babbage's machine in the Science Museum, in South Kensington, London. Oriented around monetary stocks and flows – represented by colored water flowing around plastic pipes – this machine, or Moniac, offered the opportunity of policy simulation exercises. When demonstrated at an American Economic Association meeting in 1950, it caused a minor sensation, lending an almost magical aura to any relationship which bore the prefix Phillips. This may help to explain why the curve which was named after him so rapidly conquered policy thinking in the 1960s.

He also developed (1968a) the Phillips critique, which was subsequently named after Robert Lucas (Leeson, 1994a; Blyth, 1989). But his most famous contribution was his curve. First developed at a theoretical level (1953, 1954) and subsequently fleshed out with empirical analysis (1958a, 1959a), Phillips intended to offer an analysis both of the business cycle and of the perilous nature of naive countercyclical policies. His empirical work was designed to illustrate the magnitude of the equilibrant forces necessary to reduce the deviations of the macroeconomy from the position of zero inflation. Although Phillips had no tolerance for the idea that continuing inflation would purchase sustainable reductions in the level of unemployment, this trade-off proposition, which came to be named after him, was rapidly thrust into operation as a supposedly reliable basis for macroeconomic policy manipulation.

Phillips's life and work were models of scholarship, integrity and service. But in the competition for influence in the political market-place, other values became dominant. The posturing and promising of the 1960s and 1970s were ill-suited to a modest and unassuming scholar, such as Phillips. Consequently, the subtlety and wisdom of Phillips's stabilization exercises were largely overlooked as monetarists and Phillips curve Keynesians battled it out for policy influence. Both invoked Phillips's name – the monetarists worked with a concept called the Natural-Rate Expectations Augmented Phillips (N-REAP) curve model. Much of this disputation invoked the 'Manichean fallacy of two species' (Leeson, 1994a, p. 614), which inevitably resulted in the tendency to characterize policy opponents as 'stage villains'. Phillips found all of this profoundly distasteful and depressing, and gradually abandoned macroeconomics for Chinese economic studies.

The Phillips curve episode serves as a reminder that it was nearly fatal for Keynesian economics to become associated with the proposition that continuing inflation would purchase sustainable reductions in levels of unemployment – a proposition that both Keynes and Phillips cautioned against. It also serves as a reminder that we neglect at our peril the sociology of knowledge in the economics profession. If more attention were paid to the ways in which ideas are picked up, simplified (and sometimes distorted) and transmitted to policy makers, then perhaps there would be a much wider appreciation of the unbridgeable gap between Phillips's contributions to dynamic stabilization policy and the trade-off misinterpretation of that work.

ROBERT LEESON

See also:
Lucas Critique; Phillips Curve; Samuelson, Paul A.; Solow, Robert M.

Bibliography
Barr, N. (1988), 'The Phillips Machine', *LSE Quarterly*, **2**, (4), winter, pp. 305–47.
Bergstrom, A.R., A.J.L. Catt, M.H. Peston and B.D.J. Silverstone (eds) (1978), *Stability and Inflation: A Volume of Essays to Honour the Memory of A.W.H. Phillips*, New York: John Wiley and Sons.
Blyth, C.A. (1975), 'A.W.H. Phillips', *The Economic Record*, **51**, (135), September, pp. 303–7.
Blyth, C.A. (1989), 'Alban William Housego Phillips', in John Eatwell, Murray Milgate and

Peter Newman (eds), *The New Palgrave Dictionary of Economics*, Vol. 3, New York: Stockton Press.

Dunlop, E.E. (1990), *The War Diaries of Weary Dunlop*, London: Penguin.

Leeson, R. (1994a), 'A.W.H. Phillips, M.B.E. (Military Division)', *Economic Journal*, **104**, (424), May, pp. 605–18.

Leeson, R. (1994b), 'A.W.H. Phillips, Inflationary Expectations and the Operating Characteristics of the Macroeconomy', *Economic Journal*, **104**, (427), November, pp. 140–21.

Leeson, R. (1994c), 'The Phillips Curve Paradox and the Smallest Probability in the History of Economic Research', *History of Economics Review*, summer, pp. 22–3.

Leeson, R. (1994d), 'The Rise and Fall and Rise *and Fall* of Keynesian Economics?', *Economic Record*, **70**, (210), September, pp. 262–6.

Leeson, R. (1994e), 'Some Misunderstandings Concerning the Contribution Made by A.W.H. Phillips and R.G. Lipsey to the Inflation–Unemployment Literature', *History of Economics Review*, **22**, summer, pp. 70–82.

Leeson, R. (1996), 'The Trade-Off Interpretation of Phillips' Dynamic Stabilisation Exercise', *Economica*, **63**.

Leeson, R. (1997a), 'The Political Economy of the Inflation–Unemployment Trade-Off', *History of Political Economy*.

Leeson, R. (ed.) (1997b), *The Collected Works of A.W.H. Phillips*, Cambridge: Cambridge University Press.

Meade, J.E. (1951), 'That's the Way the Money Goes', *London School of Economics Society Magazine*, January, pp. 10–11.

Newlyn, W. (195), 'The Phillips/Newlyn Hydraulic Model', *Yorkshire Bulletin of Economic and Social Research*, **2**, September, pp. 111–27.

Newlyn, W. (1992), 'A Back of the Garage Job', *Royal Economic Society Newsletter*, **77**, April, pp. 12–13.

Phillips, A.W.H. (1950), 'Mechanical Models in Economic Dynamics', *Economica*, **17**, (67), August, pp. 283–305.

Phillips, A.W.H. (1953), 'Dynamic Models in Economics', PhD thesis, University of London.

Phillips, A.W.H. (1954), 'Stabilisation Policy in a Closed Economy', *Economic Journal*, **64**, (254), June, pp. 290–323.

Phillips, A.W.H. (1956), 'Some Notes on the Estimation of Time-Forms of Reactions in Interdependent Dynamic Systems', *Economica*, **23**, (90), May, pp. 99–113.

Phillips, A.W.H. (1957), 'Stabilisation Policy and the Time Form of Lagged Response', *Economic Journal*, **67**, (266), June, pp. 265–77.

Phillips, A.W.H. (1958a), 'The Relation Between Unemployment and the Rate of Change of Money Wage Rates in the United Kingdom, 1861–1957', *Economica*, **25**, (100), November, pp. 283–99.

Phillips, A.W.H. (1958b), 'La Cybernétique et le Contrôle des Systèmes Economiques', *Etudes Sur la Cybernétique et l'Economie*, **21**, pp. 41–50.

Phillips, A.W.H. (1959a), 'Wage Changes and Unemployment in Australia 1947–58', *Economics Monograph No. 219*, Economic Society of Australia and New Zealand, New South Wales Branch.

Phillips, A.W.H. (1959b), 'The Estimation of Parameters in Systems of Stochastic Differential Equations', *Biometrika*, **46**, pp. 67–76.

Phillips, A.W.H. (1961), 'Employment, Money and Prices in a Growing Economy', *Economica*, **28**, (112), November, pp. 360–70.

Phillips, A.W. H. (1962a), 'Employment, Inflation and Growth', *Economica*, **29**, (113), February, pp. 1–16.

Phillips, A.W.H. (1962b), 'Estimation in Continuous Time Series Models with Autocorrelated Disturbances', mimeo, in Phillips's private papers, available at the London School of Economics Library.

Phillips, A.W.H. (1967), 'Analysis of the Operation of a Buffer Stock for Cocoa', mimeo, in Phillips's private papers, available at the London School of Economics Library.

Phillips, A.W.H. (1968a), 'Models for the Control of Economic Fluctuations', in *Mathematical Model Building in Economics and Industry*, New York: Hafner Publishing Co.

Phillips, A.W.H. (1968b), 'Economic Policy and Development', mimeo, in Phillips's private papers, available at the London School of Economics Library.

Phillips, A.W.H. (1978), 'Estimation of Systems of Difference Equations with Moving Average Disturbances', 1966 Walras-Bowley Lecture, San Francisco, in A.R. Bergstrom, A.J.L. Catt, M.H. Preston and B.D.J. Silverstone (eds), *Essays in Honor of A.W.H. Phillips*, New York: John Wiley and Sons.

Phillips, A.W. and M.H. Quenouille (1960), 'Estimation, Regulation and Prediction in Interdependent Dynamic Systems', *Bulletin de l'Institut International Statistique*, pp. 335–43.

Samuelson, P. and R. Solow (1960), 'Analytical Aspects of Anti-Inflation Policy', *American Economic Review*, **50**, May, (2), pp. 177–94.

van der Post, L. (1985), *The Night of the New Moon*, London: Chatto & Windus.

Phillips Curve

From the early 1960s, macroeconomics became organized around the Phillips curve trade-offs between inflation and unemployment; from the mid-1970s, the Natural-Rate Expectations Augmented Phillips (N-REAP) curve model has dominated policy thinking. The N-REAP model is anti-Keynesian, in that it suggests that increasing unemployment is an appropriate method of reducing inflation, thus allowing the unemployment rate to fall back to its 'natural' level, at a lower rate of inflation. The Phillips curve trade-off was pseudo-Keynesian, in that it suggested that continuing inflation would purchase sustainable reductions in unemployment. Neither model bears much resemblance to the work of A.W.H. Phillips.

The term 'Phillips curve' is loosely used to describe equations, or diagrams, which attempt to relate either wage or price inflation to unemployment. Phillips's curve made a theoretical appearance in his PhD, in 1953, and in an *Economic Journal* article in 1954. This was followed by empirical illustrations for UK data (1958), for Australian data (1959) and for US data (1962, p. 15). Most of the rest of Phillips's work is related to this dynamic stabilization exercise. In his first empirical curve (for the United Kingdom) Phillips considered the periods 1861–1913, 1913–48 and 1948–57 separately (see Figure 1). His curve was derived from his analysis of pre-World War I data, which he divided into six groups (each represented by a cross), corresponding to values of the rate of change of money wage rates, and percentage unemployment, in those years in which unemployment lay between 1 and 2, 2 and 3, 3 and 4, 5 and 7, and 7 and 11 per cent, respectively (1958, p. 290). There appeared to be some systematic anti-clockwise loops around this curve, corresponding to the various business cycles. The 1861–1913 curve – derived from these six crosses – was then presented, together with data from 1914–48 (1958, pp. 293–5) and 1948–57 (1958, pp. 295–9). Phillips discussed his data sources and offered some explanations for the observations not repeating their pre-1914 pattern.

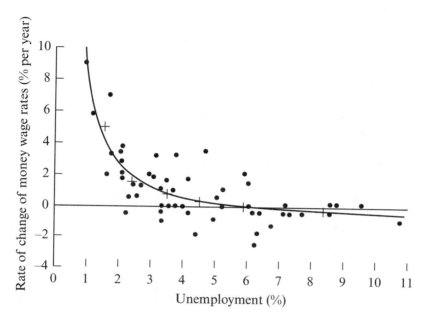

Figure 1   Phillips curve 1861–1913

The inter-war period clearly did not fit the pre-war curve at all well, and Phillips's innocence with respect to data analysis led him to gear, without adjustment, postwar and prewar unemployment data, although they were measured in different ways. Thus the 1948–57 data should have been located well to the right of his 1861–1913 curve. Phillips had located an interesting nineteenth-century relationship; his haste – he had a boat to Melbourne to catch – led him to extrapolate this relationship into the twentieth century, without the rigorous self-scrutiny which was typical of the rest of his work.

Phillips's policy conclusion had been unambiguous (1958, p. 299). He stated in his inaugural professorial lecture:

> employment has been maintained at an extremely high level ... The average rate of rise of the retail price index between 1948 and 1960 was 3.7 per cent per annum. There would be a fairly general agreement that this rate of inflation is undesirable [1962, p. 1]; one of the main problems in western countries today is whether it is possible to prevent continually rising prices of consumer goods while maintaining high levels of economic activity [1959, p. 1]; the problem therefore reduces to whether it is possible to prevent the price of labour services, that is average money earnings per man-hour, from rising at more than about 2 per cent per year ... one of the main purposes of this analysis is to consider what levels of

demand for labour the monetary and fiscal authorities should seek to maintain in their attempt to reconcile the two main policy objectives of high levels of activity and stable prices. I would question whether it is really in the interests of workers that the average level of hourly earnings should increase more rapidly than the average rate of productivity, say about 2 per cent per year. [1959, pp. 3–4]

Phillips sought to emphasize the alarming inflationary consequences of holding demand at higher levels than this (1959, p. 4). A depreciation of the currency 'would offset any initial benefits derived from inflation' (ibid.). The consequent rise in the price of imports would constitute an adverse shock to aggregate supply, leading to stagflation. Fiscal and monetary authorities might be forced to step in 'to restrain the general demand for goods ... and increase the level of unemployment' (ibid., pp. 4–5; see also 1968b, pp. 3–5). He also investigated the theoretical conditions for achieving both a constant price level and 'normal capacity output' (1961, p. 366). If these warnings were ignored, and demand was raised too far, 'the rate of growth [might] be retarded rather than increased, as a result of general shortages and inefficient operation' (1968b, p. 7).

Like Keynes, Phillips saw in economic stabilization the 'extremely intricate' mechanism which might, if successfully pursued, facilitate the survival of democracy and of the free enterprise system (1957, p. 275; 1968a, p. 159). He was also concerned that inappropriate policy 'had often caused, in the past, unnecessary and harmful fluctuations in economic activity' (1962, p. 2; 1957, p. 276). Phillips also recognized that the 'rational process of decision making' with respect to this stabilization exercise was likely to be subverted or thwarted by policy makers who were 'reluctant to engage in the intellectually difficult and politically hazardous task of actually specifying quantitative objectives and a criterion of performance' (1968a, p. 161). Prophetically, as Blyth (1989) has pointed out, Phillips also outlined the critique of macroeconomic policy which was subsequently named after Robert Lucas (Leeson, 1994a, pp. 612–13). Phillips's approach to policy was one of extreme caution: policy might well induce instability (1954, p. 299); disastrous policy could result from insufficient analysis of the evidence (1958, pp. 294–5); potential corrective action should be based on actual observations 'rather than on forecasts which are themselves largely derived, perhaps by dubious processes, from those observations' (1962, p. 7); premature application to policy would be unjustified (1957, pp. 275–7; 1958, p. 299; 1961, p. 369). Phillips saw his work as an aid to 'organise one's thoughts on economic conditions and policies' (1961, p. 369) although 'the knowledge and understanding which have so far been gained are fare from being adequate for a firm and detailed appraisal of economic policy' (1962, p. 3). In spite of this, Phillips's work came to be confidently misinterpreted as a series of trade-off equilibrium points, a 'menu of choice' from which policy makers could choose.

Samuelson and Solow (1960) were the first to offer the trade-off interpretation of Phillips's work. It rapidly became part of 'Keynesian' received wisdom, combined with points of tangency with community indifference curves (Reuber, 1964). But in the late 1960s and early 1970s, when continuing inflation increased rather than decreased unemployment, this facilitated the anti-Keynesian revival. Phillips's stabilization model had been based on an extensive monetary section (1950; 1954, p. 315; 1961) and, in 1952, he pioneered the introduction of inflationary expectations into this type of analysis (Leeson, 1994b). But Milton Friedman (1966, 1968) and others were able to accuse the Phillips curve Keynesians of neglecting both money and inflationary expectations. Thus the monetarists resurrected the old wisdom of the economics profession, that continuing inflation would produce and not reduce unemployment, but in modern N-REAP language. Measured unemployment (U) was different from its 'natural' level (U^N) only because of expectationary disequilibrium, (that is, inflationary expectations, ΔP^e, were not equal to actual inflation, ΔP). Thus any 'unnatural' (U^{UN}) divergence of U from U^N was a function of the speed of adjustment (α) of incorrect inflationary expectations. Thus, in the N-REAP model:

$$U = U^N + U^{UN} \tag{1}$$

$$U^{UN} = f[\alpha(\Delta P^e - \Delta P)] \tag{2}$$

While U^N could be reduced by microeconomic manipulation (improving labor market flexibility and so on), macroeconomic policy could effect disinflation only by increasing U above U^N; the speed of reduction of ΔP, and therefore U^{UN}, would depend on α: the delusion variable. But macroeconomic policy could not sustainably reduce U below U^N without incurring the cost of accelerating inflation.

However, for the N-REAP model to be able to describe adequately the macroeconomy in the disinflationary zone, a number of other criteria must be met.

1. The short-run Phillips curve must not become horizontal, otherwise increasing unemployment will not create a divergence between actual and expected inflation. But Phillips (1958), Lipsey (1960) and many others all found that the curve approximated a wage change floor at higher levels of unemployment.
2. The short-run Phillips curve must be a tight, reliable and exploitable relationship. But this was, and is, extremely doubtful for twentieth-century data, even for periods when inflationary expectations were relatively constant.

3. The 'natural rate' must exist and be invariant with respect to the loss of human capital and so on associated with increases in unemployment. But the 'natural rate' is non-observable: almost, indeed, a metaphysical concept.
4. Full adjustment must also be reasonably rapid, much shorter than the 'couple of decades' which Milton Friedman (1968, p. 11) thought would be necessary.

The Phillips curve, in both its original and its N-REAP form, has proved to be an inadequate guide to policy. It is a profound injustice to the memory of Bill Phillips that his name should be associated with either of these policy failures.

ROBERT LEESON

See also:

Business Cycle Theory (I) and (II); Expectations, Theories of; Friedman, Milton; Lucas Critique; Neoclassical Synthesis (Bastard Keynesianism); Samuelson, Paul A.; Solow, Robert M.

Bibliography

Blyth, C.A. (1975), 'A.W.H. Phillips', *The Economic Record*, **51**, (135), September, pp. 303–7.
Blyth, C.A. (1989), 'Alban William Housego Phillips', in John Eatwell, Murray Milgate and Peter Newman (eds), *The New Palgrave: A Dictionary of Economics*, Vol. 3, New York: Stockton Press.
Friedman, M. (1966), 'Comments', in G.P. Schultz and R.Z. Aliber (eds), *Guidelines, Informal Controls and the Market Place*, Chicago: University of Chicago Press.
Friedman, M. (1968), 'The Role of Monetary Policy', *American Economic Review*, **58**, (1), March, pp. 1–17.
Leeson, R. (1991), 'The Validity of the Expectations-Augmented Phillips Curve Model', *Economic Papers*, **10**, (2), June, pp. 94–6.
Leeson, R. (1994a), 'A.W.H. Phillips M.B.E. (Military Division)', *Economic Journal*, **104**, (424), May, pp. 605–18.
Leeson, R. (1994b), 'A.W.H. Phillips, Inflationary Expectations and the Operating Characteristics of the Macroeconomy', *Economic Journal*, **104**, (427), November, pp. 1420–21.
Leeson, R. (1994c), 'The Phillips Curve Paradox and the Smallest Probability in the History of Economic Research', *History of Economics Review*, summer, pp. 22–3.
Leeson, R. (1994d), 'The Rise and Fall and Rise *and Fall* of Keynesian Economics?', *Economic Record*, **70**, (210), September, pp. 262–6.
Leeson, R. (1994e), 'Some Misunderstandings Concerning the Contribution Made by A.W.H. Phillips and R.G. Lipsey to the Inflation–Unemployment Literature', *History of Economics Review*, **22**, summer, pp. 70–82.
Leeson, R. (1996a), 'The Trade-Off Interpretation of Phillips' Dynamic Stabilisation Exercise', *Economica*, **63**.
Leeson, R. (1996b), 'Does the Expectations Trap Render the Natural-Rate Model Invalid in the Disinflationary Zone?', *Cambridge Journal of Economics*.
Leeson, R. (1997a), 'The Political Economy of the Inflation–Unemployment Trade-Off', *History of Political Economy*.
Leeson, R. (ed.) (1997b), *The Collected Works of A.W.H. Phillips*, Cambridge: Cambridge University Press.
Lipsey, R.G. (1960), 'The Relation Between Unemployment and the Rate of Change of Money Wage Rates in the United Kingdom 1862–1957: A Further Analysis', *Economica*, **27**, (105), February, pp. 1–32.
Phillips, A.W.H. (1950), 'Mechanical Models in Economic Dynamics', *Economica*, **17**, (67), August, pp. 283–305.

Phillips, A.W.H. (1953), 'Dynamic Models in Economics', PhD thesis, University of London.

Phillips, A.W.H. (1954), 'Stabilisation Policy in Closed Economy', *Economic Journal*, **64**, (254), June, pp. 290–323.

Phillips, A.W.H. (1956), 'Some Notes on the Estimation of Time-Forms of Reactions in Interdependent Dynamic Systems', *Economica*, **23**, (90), May, pp. 99–113.

Phillips, A.W.H. (1957), 'Stabilisation Policy and the Time Form of Lagged Response', *Economic Journal*, **67**, (266), June, pp. 265–77.

Phillips, A.W.H. (1958), 'The Relation Between Unemployment and the Rate of Change of Money Wage Rates in the United Kingdom, 1861–1957', *Economica*, **25**, (100), November, pp. 283–99.

Phillips, A.W.H. (1959), 'Wage Changes and Unemployment in Australia 1947–58', *Economics Monograph No. 219*, Economic Society of Australia and New Zealand, New South Wales Branch.

Phillips, A.W.H. (1961), 'Employment, Money and Prices in a Growing Economy', *Economica*, **28**, (112), November, pp. 360–70.

Phillips, A.W.H. (1962), 'Employment, Inflation and Growth', *Economica*, **29**, (113), February, pp. 1–16.

Phillips, A.W.H. (1968a), 'Models for the Control of Economic Fluctuations', in Scientific Growth Systems, *Mathematical Model Building in Economics and Industry*, New York: Hafner Publishing Co.

Phillips, A.W.H. (1968b), 'Economic Policy and Development', mimeo, in Phillips's private papers, available at the London School of Economics Library.

Reuber, G. (1964), 'The Objectives of Canadian Monetary Policy, 1949–1961: Empirical "Trade-Offs" and the Reaction Function of the Authorities', *Journal of Political Economy*, **72**, (2), April, pp. 109–32.

Samuelson, P. and R. Solow (1960), 'Analytical Aspects of Anti-Inflation Policy', *American Economic Review*, **50**, (2), May, pp. 177–204.

Santomero, A. and J. Seater (1978), 'The Inflation Unemployment Trade Off: A Critique of the Literature', *Journal of Economic Literature*, **16**, (2), June, pp. 499–544.

Shultz, G.P. and R.Z. Aliber (eds) (1966), *Guidelines: Informal Controls and the Market Place*, Chicago: University of Chicago Press.

Pigou, Arthur C.

Arthur Cecil Pigou was born on 18 November 1877. He attended Harrow, where Winston Churchill was one of his contemporaries. In 1897, he entered King's College, Cambridge, where he excelled in a variety of academic areas. He earned a first in history, a first in part II of the Moral Tripos, and won the Chancellor's Burney Prize, the Cobden Prize and the Adam Smith Prize.

In 1901, he began his teaching career at King's College. In 1908, when Marshall retired from teaching, Pigou, with Marshall's blessing and backing, succeeded him in the chair of political economy. At this time, some considered Pigou's appointment to be controversial because of his relatively young age (he was 31) and his lack of statute within the profession. With the publication of *Wealth and Welfare* (1912), the second objection fell by the wayside. He occupied the chair until 1943.

When World War I came, Pigou did not enlist in the armed forces, but instead, during his summer vacations, he chose to do voluntary ambulance work with a unit organized by the Society of Friends. The horrors of war which he experienced during those vacations profoundly affected Pigou, to the extent that his natural shyness increased. Gradually he withdrew from the university community and was open only to a very small circle of acquaintances. Outside of economics he did have one passion, and that was mountain climbing. Each year he would set aside time to go to the Continent to do some climbing and, on occasion, would be in the company of world-class climbers. Even at the age of 80, he was still climbing, albeit at a much more stately pace.

Pigou was arguably the most prominent economic theorist in England between 1824 and 1936, when he was eclipsed by John Maynard Keynes. He stood as the link between Marshall and Keynes, having been Marshall's favorite pupil and Keynes's teacher. As a result of his position between the two great economic thinkers of the century between 1850 and 1950, much of the debate in economic thought which resulted from the depression is reflected in Pigou's work and in Keynes's reaction to Pigou. It was during his time in the chair of political economy that Pigou, following Marshall's example of personally financing promising young lecturers, brought Keynes into his first lectureship at Cambridge.

Keynes set up Pigou as the bogeyman in opposition to the principles laid out in his *General Theory*. While they were in fundamental opposition to one another, with Pigou as the defender of Marshall's classical thought and Keynes as the proponent of the new economics, much of Keynes's work flows from Pigou, departing on only a few key issues. For example, where Keynes stressed the link between income and expenditure in the aggregate, Pigou stressed the importance of wealth in the determination of income. This led to what has come to be called the 'Pigou', or 'real balances' effect, which Pigou used quite effectively to criticize Keynes (Pigou, 1950). On the other hand, Pigou supported Keynes in attacking Ricardo's notion that public expenditure merely diverts funds from productive private use and can have no real impact on aggregate income. This is what Keynes refers to as the 'Treasury view'. Additionally, Pigou's unsuccessful attempt to complete Bagehot's development of an income multiplier (Bagehot, 1873) (which was eventually completed by Richard Kahn in 1931 and made famous by Keynes) must have influenced Keynes's thought on the functioning of an economic system. Pigou's primary contributions to economic thought, however, lie in his development of welfare economics, not in his conflict or communality with Keynes.

In the tradition of Smith and Ricardo, Pigou concentrated on England's 'social problem' – expanding wealth in the face of poverty-ridden masses. To Pigou the important questions were those relating to the source and size of national income, questions which had lain fallow as attention was focused on the allocation of an income of fixed size. National income arises from – and is measured by – public and private wealth as expressed through prices.

Pigou devoted much of his work to interpreting and establishing methods to correct the divergence of public and private wealth, evidenced in England's 'social problem'.

Pigou's approach to welfare economics dominated the profession until the rise of the public choice school led by Buchanan and Tullock (1962) and the recognition of the powerful implications of the Coase theorem (1960). Whereas Pigou gave birth to the idea that under certain conditions market failures could emerge and articulated a set of policies for dealing with those market failures, Buchanan argued that the public sector could fail to perform its assigned duties. Public choice theory articulates a set of policies for dealing with public-sector failure. The Coase theorem – when parties can bargain without cost and to their mutual advantage, the resulting outcome will be efficient, regardless of how the property rights are specified – provides another way of dealing with market failures, one that does not advocate an activist role for the government.

Following the lead which James Maitland, eighth Earl of Lauderdale, set forth in *Inquiry into the Nature and Origin of Public Wealth* (1804), Pigou defined public wealth as arising from that which is useful, while private riches consist of goods which have value. This divergence forms the central focus of Pigou's welfare, concentrating on the possibility of divergence between marginal social and marginal private net product. It is from the work of Pigou that much of our standard approach to externalities springs. While the use of taxes and subsidies to rectify any imbalance between public wealth and private income does not have its origin in Pigou's work, he brought the previous work together to form a coherent whole. In Pigou's most important work, *The Economics of Welfare* (1920), continuing work begun in *Wealth and Welfare* (1912), as in most of his work, he points to a future which is better than the present and prescribes an active policy role for the attainment of improved social well-being. The idealism evident in the work of Pigou and others of the Cambridge School flows directly from John Hobson's beginnings of welfare economics through Henry Sidgwick's system of ethics. Sidgwick (1883) put forward a system of rational utilitarianism, guided by an innate moral sense as the test of the good. This approach, profoundly Kantian in its roots, provides the base for Pigou and the Cambridge School.

Pigou's work and place in the history of economics is well established. In his life he published nearly 30 books and over 100 pamphlets and articles. His crowning achievements are in welfare economics, but he made valuable contributions in unemployment, public finance and especially in the theory of business cycles, which he saw as primarily psychological in nature. An excellent chronology of Pigou's work appears in Spiegel (1991, pp. 806–7).

Pigou was a wide-ranging thinker, having written early in his life on both theism and the works of Robert Browning. His fundamental concern with humanity and the human condition shows through in all his work. Driving his work seems to be a conscience which pushes him to analyse, not for the sake of analysis, but for the good of humanity. What good may have come directly from his work is open to debate, but, to use an astronomical metaphor, his importance as the gravitational object around which Keynes gained the momentum to fly free of the conventional wisdom is profound. However much he contributed directly to economics, it may be that the most important role Pigou played was to serve as the stone against which Keynes's blade was sharpened.

After a long and distinguished career at Cambridge, Pigou relinquished the chair of political economy to Dennis Robertson. He died on 7 March 1959, but the system of economic thought developed by Marshall and expanded by Pigou still lives on in its influence on policy.

JAMES BARBOUR

See also:

Classical Economics; Keynes, John Maynard; Keynes? What Remains of; Keynesian Revolution; Marshall, Alfred; Real Balance Effect; Treasury View.

Bibliography

Bagehot, Walter (1873), *Lombard Street*, London.
Buchanan, James M. and Gordon Tullock (1962), *The Calculus of Consent: Logical Foundations of Constitutional Democracy*, Ann Arbor: University of Michigan Press.
Coase, Ronald (1960), 'The Problem of Social Cost', *Journal of Law and Economics*, **3**, October, pp. 1–44.
Haney, Lewis H. (1949), *History of Economic Thought*, 4th edn, New York: Macmillan and Co.
Houseman, Daniel M. (ed.) (1984), *The Philosophy of Economics: An Anthology*, Cambridge: Cambridge University Press.
Maitland, James, Earl of Lauderdale (1804), *Inquiry into the Nature and Origin of Public Wealth and into the Means and Causes of it's Increase*, Edinburgh.
Pigou, Arthur C. (1912) *Wealth and Welfare*, London: Macmillan and Co.
Pigou, Arthur C. (1920), *The Economics of Welfare*, London: Macmillan and Co.
Pigou, Arthur C. (1950), *Keynes General Theory*, London: Macmillan and Co.
Pribram, Karl (1983), *A History of Economic Reasoning*, Baltimore: Johns Hopkins University Press.
Sidgwick, Henry (1883), *Principles of Political Economy*, London: Macmillan and Co.
Spiegel, Henry W. (1991), *The Growth of Economic Thought*, 3rd edn, Durham: Duke University Press.

Post Keynesian School of Economics

The Post Keynesian school of economics officially became a school in the 1970s when American economists Sidney Weintraub and Paul Davidson joined hands with British economists Joan Robinson and John Eatwell in response to the neo-Keynesian model developed by such economists as Samuelson,

Hicks, Patinkin, Modigliani, Solow and Friedman. Post Keynesian economics is not characterized by a single, complete body of theory. Nevertheless there are particular features of the school that make it easily distinguishable from other schools of economic thought, even though these features have been developed in different ways by various Post Keynesian writers.

Post Keynesians have traditionally been divided into two camps. The first camp has been called the European Post Keynesians. Mostly based in Cambridge, England, the major figures on this side of the Atlantic are Joan Robinson, Richard Kahn, Nicholas Kaldor, Piero Sraffa and, from Poland, Michał Kalecki. The primary contribution of the European Post Keynesians is their direct attack upon neoclassical income distribution theory. Strongly influenced by the works of Piero Sraffa and Michał Kalecki, they maintain that income allotments are not determined by the neoclassical theory of marginal productivity of factor inputs, but by macroeconomic aggregates and social and political forces. By developing a theory of income distribution where distributive allotments are logically prior and independent of determining value, the European Post Keynesians have returned to the classical model of Ricardo and this explains why they are called 'neo-Ricardians'.

An important influence on the European Post Keynesians is the general equilibrium model developed by Piero Sraffa (1960). Assuming perfect competition, Sraffa's model starts out with n commodity outputs, which are known, with n unknown prices. Output is produced by fixed units of homogeneous labor and capital receiving an unknown average rate of return as either wages for labor or gross profits to capital. The inputs and outputs of the model are joined by technologically and socially determined production coefficients that give us n equations relating each output to its input. This gives us an equation where the sum of outputs consumed is equal to national income. The model also establishes constant wage and profit rates that are set as the equilibrium condition. What is unique about Sraffa's model is that the gross profit rate is knowable only if the wage rate is given. Sraffa's model returns us to Ricardo's description of production and provides an alternative to the neoclassical theory of income distribution based on marginal productivity analysis. Profits are no longer a return to capital because the profit rate varies with the wage rate, showing that prices change because of income distribution and technology and not changes in demand.

Starting with Sraffa's model, the European Post Keynesians turned to the work of Polish economist Michał Kalecki to extend their theory of income distribution. It has been said that Kalecki's theory of income determination and distribution can be summed up in his statement: 'The workers spend what they earn and capitalists earn what they spend.' The essence of Kalecki's model is that, if workers spend all their earnings on consumption goods, the rest of national income must be profits for capitalists. If capitalists spend all of their profits on consumption or investment goods then total demand is equal to production and total output and profits will be high. If the 'animal spirits' of capitalists change so that they become uncertain about the future, they will cut back on their expenditures to save and total demand and production will fall along with profits. Kalecki's model is based on the following assumptions: (1) even if capitalists spent all of their income from profits on consumption goods their income from profits would not decrease, because increases in the purchases of goods and services lead to a higher level of production; (2) all of labor's wages will be spent on consumption goods, meaning that there is no saving by labor. The consequence of these two assumptions is that capitalists determine their own well-being. If they spend all their profits on consumption and investment goods, demand will be equal to output and profits will be high. If they cut back on spending, profits will suffer, unemployment will be up and output down. Kalecki's model is similar to Sraffa's in that it is macroeconomic aggregates and not marginal theory that determine the level and distribution of income.

Another major contributor to the European Post Keynesians is Joan Robinson. Robinson's contribution include the theories of imperfect competition and capital accumulation. Building on Sraffa's attack on the neoclassical theory of the firm, she developed a theory of imperfect competition where producers have an element of monopoly power created by product differentiation. Also working from the writings of Keynes, Harrod and Ricardo, she developed a theory of capital accumulation which provides an alternative to traditional neoclassical growth theory. She also used the insights of her capital accumulation theory to critique the meaning of capital during the capital controversy of the 1950s and 1960s. Robinson's writings fit well with the major contributions of the European Post Keynesians in their attack on the neoclassical theory of income distribution based on marginal productivity.

The second camp can be called the American Post Keynesians. Major contributors to this camp include Sidney Weintraub, Paul Davidson, Hyman Minsky, Edward Nell and Jan Kregel. What stands out about the American Post Keynesians is their strong belief that Keynes's *Treatise* and *General Theory* provided the groundwork for an intellectual revolution in economics and that revolution was aborted and replaced by what has been called the 'grand neoclassical synthesis' by such economists as Samuelson, Solow, Tobin and Modigliani. By questioning some basic classical assumptions regarding the way labor and capital markets work, and by bringing money and financial markets into the determination of real output and employment, Keynes posed a serious challenge to the classical model that is still relevant today, according to the American Post Keynesians. Keynes's revolution in economics will occur, according to this camp, when the classical model of real exchange is replaced by a monetary production economic model.

An essential element in the American Post Keynesian model is the importance of uncertainty: From Chapter 12 of Keynes's *General Theory*, they argue that situations of uncertainty cannot be adequately modeled in terms of probability distributions and because of this a difference needs to be made between uncertainty and risk. The real world economic system that entrepreneurs and consumers face is not a system that can be statistically controlled by probability theory or predicted by future outcomes of variables determined by some present value formula. Recognizing the importance of non-probabilistic uncertainty in economic decision making also brings up the importance of looking at the economy as moving through historical time. Rather than looking at time as a symmetric variable where in the long run economic agents never make mistakes, American Post Keynesians argue that the economy moves through real historical time where economic decisions are made in a world that has a future that is unknowable, influenced by one's past. Within this context we can see the importance of institutions and how they affect the way the economy works. In an economy where the future is unknown, contractual agreements through institutional arrangements are needed to incur the factor inputs necessary for efficient production through historical time. Such contractual agreements require money and liquidity, so that entrepreneurs are able to meet their contractual liabilities before production takes place. This leads us to the importance of monetary and financial institutions or the role of money in an entrepreneurial money exchange economy.

Keynes, according to the American Post Keynesians, rejected the neoclassical theory of loanable funds where the interest rate is determined by the supply of savings and demand for investments in the capital market. Coming up with a theory of liquidity preference where the interest rate is determined by portfolio allocations under uncertainty, Keynes was able to provide an alternative theory of investment which relies on the behavior of the financial sector of the economy and the institutional structure of the banking and monetary systems. The demand for money for liquidity leads to another important tenet of American Post Keynesians, which is that the money supply is endogenously determined.

Moving beyond the neoclassical assumption that the money supply is simply exogenously determined by the central bank, American Post Keynesians argue that, when large financial institutions and corporations demand credit for liquidity purposes to expand production, the central bank needs to accommodate that demand, which means that the money supply is not something that is given but an endogenous variable determined by economic outcome. For American Post Keynesians it is economic agents through their animal spirits that influence the rise and fall of the money supply. This has led to Hyman Minsky's financial instability theory of cyclical fluctuations caused by the interaction between real and monetary factors. When entrepreneurs, corporations and banks have their animal spirits up and demand credit this can lead to speculative or even Ponzi finance positions as banks and businesses take on more uncertain prospects for profits. This can put the economy in a position of instability when an event occurs to end the flow of credit, causing a chain of bankruptcies.

In conclusion the Post Keynesian school of economics provides two wide camps, with the European Post Keynesians emphasizing more concern with the nature and behavior of the real economy, while the American Post Keynesians seem more concerned with uncertainty and monetary and financial influences. But such perspectives are more a matter of emphasis of different approaches than an inconsistency between these two camps regarding how the economy works in an entrepreneurial monetary production economy.

RICHARD P.F. HOLT

See also:

Davidson, Paul; Harcourt, Geoff; Kalecki, Michał; Keynes, John Maynard; Minsky, Hyman P.; Neoclassical Synthesis (Bastard Keynesianism); Robinson, Joan; Sraffa, Piero; Weintraub, Sidney.

Bibliography

Davidson, Paul (1972), *Money and the Real World*, 2nd edn, New York: Macmillan.
Davidson, Paul (1980), 'Post Keynesian Economics', *The Public Interest*, special edition, pp. 151–73.
Davidson, Paul (1982), *International Money and the Real World*, New York: Halsted Press.
Davidson, Paul (1994), *Post Keynesian Macroeconomic Theory*, Aldershot: Edward Elgar.
Davis, J.B. (1987), 'Three Principles of Post Keynesian Methodology', *Journal of Post Keynesian Economics*, **9**, (4), summer, pp. 552–64.
Eichner, Alfred I. and J.A. Kregel (1985), 'An Essay on Post-Keynesian Theory: A New Paradigm in Economics', *Journal of Economic Literature*, **14**, (4), December, pp. 1293–1314.
Harcourt, G.C. (1972), *Some Cambridge Controversies in the Theory of Capital*, Cambridge: Cambridge University Press.
Harcourt, G.C. (1987), 'Post-Keynesian Economics', in John Eatwell, Murray Milgate and Peter Newman (eds), *The New Palgrave: A Dictionary of Economics*, Vol. 3, New York: Stockton Press.
Johnson, L.E. (1980), 'A Neo-Paradigmatic Model for Studying the Development of Economic Reasoning', *Atlantic Economic Journal*, **8**, (4), December, pp. 52–61.
Johnson, L.E. (1983), 'Economic Paradigm: A Mission Dimension', *Journal of Economic Issues*, **17**, (4) December, pp. 1097–1111.
Johnson, L.E. (1984), 'Ricardo's Labour Theory of the Determinant of Value', *Atlantic Economic Journal*, **21**, (1) March, pp. 50–59.
Johnson, L.E. (1988), 'The Legacy of Ricardo: A Review Article', *Rivista Internazionale di Scienze Economiche e Commerciali*, **35**, (8), August, pp. 781–96.
Johnson, L.E. and Robert D. Ley (1988), *Origins of Modern Economics: A Paradigmatic Approach*, Lexington, Mass.: Ginn Press.
Johnson, L.E., Warren S. Gramm and David J. Hoaas (1989), 'Marx's Law of Profit: The Current State of the Controversy', *Atlantic Economic Journal*, **17**, (4) December, pp. 55–62.
Johnson, L.E., Warren S. Gramm and David J. Hoaas (1991), 'The Falling Rate of Profit Debate

in Marx: Alternative Lines of Interpretation', in Giovanni A. Caravale (ed.), *Marx and Modern Economic Analysis*, Vol. II, Aldershot: Edward Elgar.

Kahn, R.F. (1929), *The Economics of the Short Period*; reprinted 1989, New York: St Martin's Press.

Kahn, Richard F. (1954), 'Some Notes in Liquidity Preference', *Manchester School of Economic and Social Studies*, **22**, (3), September, pp. 229–57.

Kalecki, Michał (1966), *Studies in the Theory of Business Cycles 1933–1939*, New York, Augustus M. Kelley.

Kalecki, Michał (1971), *Selected Essays on the Dynamics of the Capitalist Economy*, Cambridge: Cambridge University Press.

Keynes, John M. (1936), *The General Theory of Employment, Interest and Money*, London: Macmillan.

Keynes, John M. (1980), *Collected Writings of John Maynard Keynes*, Vol. XXVII, *Activities 1940–1946: Shaping the Post-War World Employment*, New York: Cambridge University Press.

Keynes, John M. (1981), *Collected Writings of John Maynard Keynes*, Vol. XIX, *Activities 1922–1929: The Return to Gold and Industrial Policy*, New York: Cambridge University Press.

Keynes, John M. (1983), *Collected Writings of John Maynard Keynes*, Vol. XII, *Economic Articles and Correspondence: Investment and Editorial*, New York: Cambridge University Press.

Kregel, Jan A. (1971), *Rate of Profit, Distribution and Growth: Two Views*, Chicago: Aldine.

Kregel, Jan A. (1973), *The Reconstruction of Political Economy*, New York: Halsted Press.

Minsky, Hyman P. (1975), *John Maynard Keynes*, New York: Columbia University Press.

Minsky, Hyman P. (1977), 'An "Economics of Keynes" Perspective on Money', in Sidney Weintraub (ed.), *Modern Economic Thought*, Philadelphia: University of Pennsylvania Press.

Minsky, Hyman P. (1982), *Can 'It' Happen Again?*, New York: M.E. Sharpe.

Nell, Edward (1988), *Prosperity and Public Spending: Transformational Growth and the Role of Government*, Boston: Unwin Hyman.

Robinson, Joan (1933), *The Economics of Imperfect Competition*, London: Macmillan.

Robinson, Joan (1953–4), 'The Production Function and the Theory of Capital', *Review of Economic Studies*, **21**, (55), pp. 81–106.

Robinson, Joan (1962), *Essays in the Theory of Economic Growth*, London: Macmillan.

Robinson, Joan (1974), *History versus Equilibrium*, London: Thames Polytechnic.

Sraffa, Piero (1926), 'The Laws of Return Under Competitive Conditions', *Economic Journal*, **36**, (144), December, pp. 535–60.

Sraffa, Piero (1960), *The Production of Commodities by Means of Commodities*, Cambridge: Cambridge University Press.

Weintraub, Sidney (1978), *Capitalism's Inflation and Unemployment Crisis*, Reading, Mass.: Addison-Wesley.

Post Walrasian Economics

'Post Walrasian economics' is the name used by some economists to describe the coordination failure interpretation of macroeconomics. The post Walrasian vision of the macro economy is of a functionally complex economy, by which is meant that the economy is assumed to have complex dynamics and multiple equilibria that are caused by those complex dynamics. One of the implications of this assumption is that a unique rational expectation for individuals cannot be derived since such derivation is beyond the modeling capabilities of individuals.

In a functionally complex economy extra market coordination mechanisms are necessary; some unspecified 'market' cannot be assumed to fully coordinate individuals' actions. How is this extra market coordination accomplished? In the post Walrasian vision that coordination is accomplished via institutions which place constraints on individuals which limit their range of choice, thereby reducing the set of achievable equilibria. Given institutions, there may be a unique equilibrium, but that equilibrium can only be understood in reference to the institutions that play a central role in determining it. In order to have a full analytic model, one must (1) model the institutions within which individuals interact; (2) explain how those institutions are compatible with the assumptions of individual rationality that one has assumed, and (3) explain how those institutions play a role in determining the equilibrium of the economy.

In modeling those institutions, post Walrasians argue that a sequential modeling approach is the most reasonable. All questions cannot be addressed simultaneously and, at any moment in time, most individuals simply accept large numbers of institutions, and the constraints those institutions place on them, in order to reduce the complexity of decision making to a manageable level.

In the absence of sequentially determined institutions, the complexity of interactions would lead one to expect that aggregate results would fluctuate wildly. That does not happen to anywhere near the degree that the complexity of the interactions would lead one to predict. Walrasians interpret that lack of fluctuation as an indication that their unique equilibrium approach is the correct one. Post Walrasians interpret that lack of fluctuations differently; they see it as an indication of the central role of institutions limiting the interactions in the economy to manageable proportions for individuals, and thereby creating a surface stability over a core of chaos. Thus the post Walrasian view is that the economy processes information in a quite different way than is assumed in the Walrasian view. In post Walrasian economics much of the information processing is built into existing institutions and is not fully understood by the participants. Specialists may understand parts of it and they may be working on changing institutions to take advantage of that understanding, but the complexity of the economy precludes a full understanding and complete reliance on the results of their analysis. Post Walrasian rationality has local, institutionally based, characteristics; it is bounded, not global rationality.

An analogy to a computer may shed some light on this post Walrasian view of the role of institutions. A computer has a general design, an operating system, software built around that operating system, and sub software built around that software. In using the computer most individuals take the existing software for granted, much as they take institutions for grated. They operate within the limitations of that software, and their rationality is defined by that software. Thus, when someone asks, 'Why hit *Control Z* when the computer isn't responding?', one responds: 'That's what one does.' Implicit in this response is the acceptance of a DOS environment. In a MAC environment hitting *Control Z* is meaningless. Other aspects of rationality carry over between two environments – double clicking with a mouse, for example, to open a file.

The same thing happens with institutions; individuals accept the constraints imposed by institutions on their actions as necessary constraints to operate in a complex environment. In the United States, when asked why one drives on the right-hand side of the street, one responds, 'That's what one does.' Similarly, when asked why one displays the degree of honesty that one does, one does not respond, 'I have analysed the situation and determined that, given the costs and benefits, that is the optimal degree of honesty to reflect', as a Walrasian homo economicus would. Instead a post Walrasian individual would state, 'It's what is right.' Now this does not mean that post Walrasian homo economicus is honest, or that he or she does not take costs and benefits of being honest into account. Instead it simply means that there is a large non-linear cost to determining optimal actions and, in many areas, the rational decision is to follow rules, learn what is, and is not, institutionally acceptable and generally follow those institutional rules. Post Walrasians follow what Herbert Simon calls 'process rationality'.

This sequential choice view of the way the economy operates also dictates the modeling strategy used. To have a full model one must have a set of multiple nested systems – one explaining why institutions are adopted and why sub-institutions are adopted. Most models will not concern such grand theories: instead they will accept existing institutions as given, and incorporate the constraints – like knowing about double clicking or *Control Z* – of those institutions into the analysis. One of the most important considerations for individuals will be limiting the nature of the decision they are making: efficiently reducing the amount of information processing they can do. Thus the macro constraints on micro behavior will be a central part of any but the grandest of models. They certainly play a central role in all short-run analysis; they place constrains on the type of behaviour that can reasonably be assumed.

This computer analogy also sheds light on the multiple equilibria aspect of post Walrasian macro, how it pictures institutions leading people to choose among those equilibria and the approach to policy it suggests. In the grandest of models, there are many operating systems, and the choice of one of them will exclude others. Most policy issues are addressed given an operating system and hence it is difficult to make any global statements about optimality from short-run models. Policy can influence not only decisions within operating systems, but also the choice of sub-operating systems, and one must take all dimensions of the operating system into account when one is analysing a problem. That is why, in post Walrasian macro, policy analysis is an art rather than a science, because formal models do not take into account all the dimensions of policy that must be considered and thus are suggestive, rather than deterministic.

DAVID COLANDER

See also:

Coordination Failures and Keynesian Economics; Dual Decision Hypothesis; Lausanne, The School of.

Bibliography

Colander, David (ed.) (1996), *Beyond Microfoundations: Post Walrasian Macroeconomics*, Cambridge: Cambridge University Press.

Quantity Theory of Money

General equation of exchange

The alternative versions of the quantity theory of money are embodied in that well-known identity relation, the equation of exchange. The general equation of exchange may be written:

$$M_S V \equiv P_L Y^*. \tag{1}$$

Here M_S represents the nation's stock or supply of money. M_S is the total monetary units in private circulation, and has been traditionally taken to include all private cash balances and checkable deposits held at a point in time. V stands for the velocity of circulation, which can be defined in general terms as the number of times the stock of money must circulate (that is, be spent) through the economy to purchase the monetary value of national product. P_L is the general price level, an average, of the market prices of final goods and services. Y^* is the economist's approximation of real income or output.

The equation of exchange is an identity or tautology, which says that the monetary value of final output sold equals the monetary value of the final goods and services purchased. That is, the equation of exchange simply says that, ex post, national income as a flow of expenditures will always be equal to national income as a flow of receipts. This is so because of the definition of V, where:

$$V \equiv \frac{P_L Y^*}{M_S}. \tag{2}$$

The basic quantity theory of money

The quantity theory of money in its basic form states that the supply of money is the main determinant of the general price level, hence the value of a unit of currency. More specifically the basic quantity theory of money postulates that any change in the money supply will cause an equal proportional change in the general price level. This conclusion emerges once we give content to the equation of exchange by making behavioral assumptions about the variables involved. First, pre-Keynesians assumed that V is determined independently of M_S, P_L, and Y^*. The value of V is determined by individual spending habits and credit practices of financial institutions. Both of these can be presumed to change only slowly over time; hence V can be taken as constant at a given point in time. Second, it is assumed that Y^* depends on the level of employment and can also be taken as constant at a given point in time. The resulting equilibrium condition postulates the direct proportional relation between the supply of money and the general price level.

$$M_S\overline{V} = P_L\overline{Y}^*. \tag{3}$$

The underlying premise of the basic quantity theory is that no rational person holds money idle, for it produces nothing and yields no satisfaction. Thus people demand money only for transaction purposes. With the basic quantity theory, people use all the cash they receive from the sale of goods or services to buy other goods and services prior to their next receipt of income. How rapidly this occurs is dependent on how the production process is organized, how frequently incomes are paid, and other institutional considerations which are independent of the supply of money or the general price level.

The direct proportionate relationship between M_S and P_L in the basic quantity theory can be expressed by rewriting equation (3) in a functional form where P_L is the dependent variable and M_S is the independent variable, with V and Y^* held constant:

$$P_L = \frac{M_S\overline{V}}{\overline{Y}^*}. \tag{4}$$

The basic quantity theory shows how the money supply determines the general price level in a fashion that will not affect relative market prices as long as there is a 'neutral' distribution of extra cash in proportion to individual holdings, thus leaving relative demands for products unaffected. Thus the fundamental relationship of the basic quantity theory can be seen by using supply and demand analysis in an economy with two goods: money and a single composite product. If the supply of the product increases, its price will fall and, when supply decreases, its price rises. However, if the supply of money increases, its price falls and, since its price is the inverse of the price of the product, this is equivalent to a proportional increase in the product's price. Moreover the basic quantity theory is itself an extension of supply and demand analysis to money since it implies a theory of the supply and demand for money.

The basic version of the quantity theory of money can be expressed in two alternative forms. In its transactions form it may be written:

$$M_S\overline{V}_T = P_T\overline{T}. \tag{5}$$

Here V_T represents transactions velocity. Transactions velocity refers to the average number of times per year that units of money are used in purchase–sale transactions. Individual units of money may vary in turnover, but on average a unit changes hands V_T times per year. P_T is a price index reflecting the average prices at which transactions occur, appropriately weighted. T then represents the physical volume of transactions. In the transactions version of the basic quantity theory, V_T and T are assumed constant. V_T is constant at its maximum level, since no one holds idle balances, and depends on the spending habits of consumers and the lending habits of banks. If P_T is perfectly flexible, T will always be constant at its maximum level, given the level of technology and the willingness of the labor force to work. As such, P_T must be directly proportional to M_S. The transactions version of the basic quantity theory is not commonly employed today by quantity theorists since there exists no acceptable measurement of the physical volume of transactions, or average prices at which transactions occur.

The basic quantity theory in its income form may be written:

$$M_S \overline{V}_Y = P_Y \overline{Y}^*. \tag{6}$$

Here V_Y represents income velocity and refers to the average number of times a year that units of money are used to buy final output. Since there are intermediate goods, income velocity will be less than transactions velocity. However it is typically assumed that the ratio of transactions to income is nearly constant, so that the two velocities are directly related. P_Y represents the national income deflator, and Y^* is real income or output. With V_Y and Y^* constant, P_Y is again directly proportional to M_S.

The origins and early quantity theorists

The origins of the basic quantity can be found in the work of Copernicus, Navarrus and Bodin, all of whom sought an explanation of inflation other than the debasement of coinage. The three wrote at a time when the money supply was coin, ignored velocity, ignored the impact of monetary changes on relative prices and seemed to discuss the quantity theory in its income form. Before Europe's sixteenth-century inflation, Copernicus (*Monetae Cudendae Ratio*, 1526) presented the fundamental conclusions of the basic quantity theory. However he expressed the impact of a change in the money supply in terms of the value of a unit of currency rather than the general price level. His example involved silver money and the price of silver bars. He did not extend his analysis to all goods and the general price level.

Navarrus (*Comentario Resolutorio de Usuras*, 1556) also discussed the basic quantity theory in the context of his evaluation of the morality of usury and foreign exchange transactions. He stated that increases in the money supply reduce the value of money proportionally and increase the general price level. Consequently, he argued that differences in the values of different currencies were based on differences in purchasing power, resulting from differences in the national money supplies. In addition some claim that Navarrus and other members of the School of Salamanca came close to a supply and demand theory of money, later developed in a rigorous form at Cambridge by Marshall and Pigou (Dempsey, 1935; Grice-Hutchinson, 1952; Monroe, 1923; Spiegel, 1971).

Bodin (*Reply to the Paradoxes of Monsieur de Malesstroit*, 1568) is most commonly given credit for discovering the basic quantity theory. He argued that changes in the money supply would result in a proportionate change in the price level. While Bodin believed that inflation could be caused by monopoly power, debasement, exportation and the conspicuous consumption of the nobility, he argued that the sixteenth century inflation in France was a result of an increased money supply resulting from the inflow of specie from the New World.

Mun (*England's Treasure by Foreign Trade*, posthumously, 1664) discussed the basic quantity theory in its income form. While he did not explain velocity, he implicitly assumed income velocity and output to be constant, making the price level proportionate to the money supply. Locke (*Some Considerations of the Consequences of the Lowering of Interest and Raising the Values of Money*, 1692) presented the most sophisticated version of the basic quantity theory to date at a time when paper currency was becoming important. He anticipated Newcome and Fisher by presenting the basic quantity theory in its transactions form. Moreover Locke defined the role of velocity, recognized the motives for holding cash balances and saw that the volume of trade depended on both the money supply and velocity. Finally he argued that velocity was determined by the payment habits of individuals and the practices of lenders.

The most refined pre-classical treatment of the basic quantity theory is found in Cantillon and Hume. Cantillon (*Essai sur la Nature en Général*, 1755) focused on the importance of velocity and made it clear that the effect of an increase in velocity is equivalent to an increase in the supply of money. He was the first to recognize that the effect of a change in the money supply would in part depend on how cash is injected into the economy. He showed that the structure of prices as well as the general price level will change with the money supply unless there is 'neutral' injection of cash to individual holdings, leaving relative demands for goods unaffected. Hume (*Treatise of Human Nature*, 1739–40) also understood the role of velocity and that an injection of cash could effect relative prices as well as the general price level. Moreover he articulated in a rigorous fashion an extension of the basic quantity theory to the monetary effects of deficits and surpluses in the trade balance via the specie-flow mechanism. This mechanism describes the tendency for market forces to allocate the world's money supply so as to equate national trade balances. The specie-flow mechanism had been hinted at by Mun and was discussed by Cantillon, but Hume was the first to put it in modern form.

The basic quantity theory in classical political economy

Classical political economists agreed with Cantillon and Hume that changes in the money supply could affect both relative prices and the general price level, though in most instances they made little of this result. Moreover these writers presented the quantity theory in its income form. Most political economists adhered to what may be termed the 'direct effect' (Blaug, 1966) of linking the changes in the money supply to the general price level through its impact on aggregate demand. Real income was assumed constant in the classical view (with the exception of Malthus and Marx) since unemployment was viewed as either voluntary or frictional. The economy, then, always tended towards full employment. The classicals also assumed that velocity was constant so that the product of the money supply and velocity, that is nominal income, was also constant. Consequently the real income–general price level relation is a rectangular hyperbola. Given the stability of real income, changes in the money supply and aggregate demand cause proportionate changes in the price level. The classical theory of aggregate demand based on the quantity theory is consistent with the full employment results of Say's identity.

Beginning with Thornton (*The Nature of Paper Credit of Great Britain*, 1802), Ricardo (*The High Price of Bullion*, 1810; *The Principles of Political Economy and Taxation*, 1821) and J.S. Mill (*Principles of Political Economy*, 1848), monetary changes were also linked to changes in the price level via the money rate of interest, the 'indirect effect'. These writers saw that equilibrium in an economy with non-monetary assets will exist only when the money rate of interest equals the rate of return on capital. Here an increase in the money supply results in an injection into the loanable funds market causing the money rate of interest to fall below the rate of return on capital. The demand for loanable funds will then rise, bringing the money rate into equality with the return on capital. The general price level will increase, but the money rate and rate of return on capital will be equal at their former levels. Thus the rate of interest is independent of the supply of money in circulation. This argument was later articulated in Wicksell's discussion (*Interest and Prices*, 1898) of the natural versus market rate of interest.

Origins of basic quantity theory of money equations
The basic equiproportionate relationship between changes in the money supply and the general price level was presented first in mathematical form by Briscoe (*Discourse on the Late Funds*, 1694), although he expressed the relationship in terms of the stock of specie and the value of goods exchanged. Later Lloyd (*Essay on the Theory of Money*, 1771) also presented the conclusions of the quantity theory in equational form. Neither of these writers, however, incorporated velocity into their formulations. It was not until Kroncke (*Das Steuerwesen nach seiner Natur und seinen Wirkungen untersucht*, 1804), Lang (*Grundlinien der politischen Arithmetik*, 1811), Cagnazzi (*Elementi di Economia Politica*, 1813) and Turner (*Letter Addressed to the Right Hon. Robert Peel*, 1819) that velocity entered the equation. Lubbock (*On Currency*, 1840) offered the most refined version of these formulations since he not only included velocity, but also recognized differences in velocity owing to different elements of the money supply, thereby, admitting alternative definitions of money. It was not until the work of Rau (*Lehrbuch der politischen ökonomie*, 1826–37) that the basic quantity theory equation was expressed in a more modern income form (Humphrey, 1984; Milgate, 1991).

The neoclassical versions of the basic quantity theory of money
The neoclassical quantity theory took two basic forms. The first originated in Locke's treatment, presenting quantity theory in its transactions form. The second was the Cambridge version, which we may term the demand for money formulation. The transactions version of the quantity theory was articulated as in equation (5) by Newcome (*Principles of Political Economy*, 1885). It was elaborated and extended by Fisher (*The Purchasing Power of Money*, 1911). Fisher distinguished between what he termed 'the supply of money' (M_S), which included coin and bank notes issued by private banks, on the one hand, and what he termed 'deposit currency' ($M_{S'}$), which included checkable deposits, on the other. Fisher's equation can then be written:

$$M_S \overline{V}_T + M_{S'} \overline{V}_{T'} = P_T \overline{T}. \tag{7}$$

Fisher also attempted to verify empirically the conclusion that monetary changes would result in proportionate changes in the general price level. However he also recognized that involuntary unemployment could occur in disequilibrium and treated investment as a function of the real rate of interest. As such, changes in the money supply could affect T as well as P_T when the economy was at less than full employment, since a change in P_T would alter the real rate of interest, investment, output and T.

Picking up on the implications of discussions of Navarrus and other members of the School of Salamanca, Marshall (*Principles of Economics*, 1890;

Money, Credit and Commerce, 1923) and Pigou ('The Value of Money', 1917) developed the demand for money formulation of the basic quantity theory in the Cambridge equation:

$$M_S = k(P_L Y^*). \tag{8}$$

Here k is the constant fraction of nominal income which businesses and consumers wish to hold for transactions purposes in the form of cash balances; it is the reciprocal of V_Y in the income formulation of the quantity theory in (6) above. The right-hand side of (8) represents the transactions demand for money and the value of k depends on the factors which influence people's desire to hold cash for transaction purposes. These writers thought the main determinants of velocity, hence k, were the ratio of cash to deposits and the ratio of reserves to deposits. The Cambridge quantity theory then expresses an equilibrium condition in the money market, which would exist when the supply and demand for money are equal. The supply of money represents the ex post supply of money, while the demand for money defines the ex ante transactions demand for money. When the supply and demand for money are equal, actual cash balances equal desired cash balances and the market clears. In the Cambridge formulation, V_Y, hence k, is constant. Since these writers took full employment to be the norm in equilibrium, real output was taken as given. Thus changes in the supply of money cause direct proportionate changes in the general price level, where the price level is determined by the supply and demand for money. However Cambridge economists were perfectly willing to admit that involuntary unemployment was possible in disequilibrium. In this case, changes in the money supply would affect real output as well as the price level.

Monetarism and the modified quantity theory of money

The modified version of the quantity theory is usually associated with Friedman *et al.* (*Studies in the Quantity Theory of Money*, 1956; 'The Demand for Money: Some Theoretical and Empirical Results', 1959); and Friedman and Schwartz (*A Monetary History of the United States, 1867–1960*, 1963; 'The Role of Monetary Policy', 1968). Some aspects of Friedman's work, especially those which view economic fluctuations as monetary phenomena, were anticipated by some of the later mercantilists (Law, *Money and Trade Considered*, 1705; Vanderlint, *Money Answers all Things*, 1734; Berkeley, *Querist*, 1737) who expounded a 'money stimulates trade' doctrine, in the form of a theory of 'beneficial inflation', or of a 'forced savings' doctrine (Holtrop, 1929).

Modern quantity theorists for a long time committed themselves methodologically to Friedman's version of positivism, which holds that the quality of a theory is to be judged only by its predictive power. This was the basis for their adopting an alternative measure of the money supply. Monetarists favored M2 over M1 because of the former's superior ability to explain changes in national income. Arguing for a broader definition of money, one which includes some non-transactions deposits as well as cash and checkable deposits, would have been perfectly consistent with Keynes's argument that money is an asset as well as a medium of exchange but, because of their methodological predictions, Friedman, Schwartz and their followers chose to base their definition on empirical rather than theoretical grounds.

The monetarist version of the quantity theory equation is significantly different from that of earlier quantity theorists and it is expressed in terms of income rather that transactions. There is an explicit rejection of the idea that the money supply is tied to nominal income or either of its components. Instead it is the rate of change in these series which is believed to be correlated. Thus

$$\%\Delta M_S + \%\Delta V_Y = \%\Delta P_Y + \%\Delta Y^*. \tag{9}$$

Velocity in this formulation is explicitly treated as a variable. This is not surprising, since the monetarist view of the demand for money is as part of a broader problem of portfolio choice, where cash and deposits are but two of a range of real and financial assets. Although the functional relationship between velocity and causal variables including wealth, the returns in other assets and inflation may be stable over time, short-run fluctuations in velocity are seen as being sufficiently volatile to prevent the central bank from using its control over monetary growth to fine tune the growth path of nominal income.

How the economy responds to a change in monetary growth depends very much on the time frame involved, according to the monetarist perspective. In the long run, a change in the rate of monetary growth will lead to change in the inflation rate in the same direction. These changes, moreover, will tend to be equal. Given the monetarist belief in a natural (as opposed to full employment) level of output to which the system returns over time, real asset returns, growth in the real demand for money and the trend in velocity will all be stable at long-run equilibrium. In the short run however, changes in monetary growth can affect real variables. Beginning at long-run equilibrium, a monetary surprise will change the inflation rate, but for informational or institutional reasons, wage growth does not respond immediately. As a result, the real wage is knocked out of equilibrium, leading to changes in output and employment which persist until workers succeed in accelerating wage increases sufficiently to restore the equilibrium real wage. Such 'fooling models' of the Friedman/ Phelps variety may be viewed as unsatisfactory (1) because of their requirement that the real wage move countercyclically and (2) because many observers doubt that imperfections in price information are persistent enough to account for departures from equilibrium that last as long as a typical business cycle. Nevertheless the approach is important in the history of economic doctrines as beginning a line of research which was perceived at the time as an alternative to Keynesian expectation and demand-driven models of the cycle.

In the area of policy it would be easy to exaggerate the differences between the Keynesian and monetarist positions. The latter is certainly consistent with the notion that monetary policy could be used to hasten the economy's return to long-run equilibrium. Fiscal policy might also be effective if, via interest rate effects, it led to predictable changes in velocity. However, in general, the notion of policy ineffectiveness as elaborated and expanded over the past 30 years by Friedman and others may represent the monetarists' greatest challenge to the Keynesian heritage. For good or ill, it is an opinion which has come to enjoy considerable support. Moreover, whether monetarism and the modified quantity theory represents a theory of money at all, or a monetary theory of trade and the business cycle, is an open question, one that in part depends on one's macroeconomic perspective, of which there are certainly a number in fashion.

Keynes and the quantity theory of money

Keynes (*The General Theory of Employment, Interest and Money*, 1936) rejected the basic quantity theory he had inherited from the Cambridge theorists, to which he himself had contributed (*A Treatise on Money*, 1930). His attack on the Cambridge quantity theory was two-pronged. First, Keynes's theory of probability, which shaped his views regarding the nature of expectations and uncertainty, led him to conclude that the ratios of cash to deposits and reserves to deposits which determined velocity could not be treated as constants as they were in the Cambridge quantity theory. Consequently monetary policy would be better based on the discretion of the central bank than on some maxim derived from the quantity theory. Second, Keynes attacked the fundamental premise of the basic quantity theory that no rational person holds money idle; that is, people demand money only for transaction purposes. Emphasizing the store of value function of money, he argued that the demand for money must also include precautionary and speculative components. With his liquidity preference theory of the demand for money, Keynes argues that the rate of interest is determined in the money market, rather than the market for loanable funds as postulated by the British neoclassical orthodoxy. From this perspective, discretionary monetary policy became central to his views regarding stabilization.

L.E. JOHNSON
ROBERT D. LEY
TOM CATE

See also:

Brunner, Karl; Business Cycle Theory (I) and (II); Cagan, Philip; Chicago School of Economics; Classical Economics; Depression, The Great; Friedman, Milton; Hawtrey, Sir Ralph; Inflation; Keynes, John Maynard; Marshall, Alfred; Meltzer, Allan H.; Monetarist School of Economics; Monetary Policy; Money; New Classical School of Economics; Real Balance Effect; Say's Law; Schwartz, Anna J.; Wicksell, Knut.

Bibliography

Blaug, M. (1966), *Economic Theory in Retrospect*, Homewood, Ill.: Richard D. Irwin.

Dempsey, B.W. (1935), 'The Historical Emergence of the Quantity Theory', *Quarterly Journal of Economics*, **50**, (1), November, pp. 174–84.

Grice-Hutchinson, M. (1952), *The School of Salamanca: Readings in Spanish Monetary Theory, 1544–1605*, London: Clarendon Press.

Holtrop, M.W. (1929), 'Theories of Velocity of Circulation of Money in Earlier Economic Literature', *Economic History*, January, pp. 503–24.

Humphrey, T.M. (1984), 'Algebraic Quantity Equations Before Fisher', *Economic Review*, Federal Reserve Bank of Richmond, **70**, (5), pp. 13–22.

Milgate, M. (1991), 'The Quantity Equations: Early History', in John Eatwell, Murray Milgate and Peter Newman (eds), *The New Palgrave: A Dictionary of Economics*, Vol. 4, New York: Stockton Press.

Monroe, A.E. (1923), *Monetary Theory Before Adam Smith*, reprinted in 1966, New York: A.M. Kelley.

Spiegel, H.W. (1971), *The Growth of Economic Thought*, Englewood Cliffs, New Jersey: Prentice-Hall.

Real Balance Effect

Patinkin defines the real balance effect as the sum of the Pigou effect and the Keynes effect (Patinkin, 1965). The Pigou effect is the name given to that author's explanation of the way the price level affects aggregate expenditure, where saving is inversely related to the wealth/income ratio (Pigou, 1943, 1947; Hansen, 1941). As defined by Patinkin, the real balance effect depends on: (1) the inclusion of wealth in the representative consumer's demand function for commodities, and (2) the inclusion of money balances as part of wealth (Patinkin, 1965). A change in the price level will then change the real value of the stock of money held, leading to a different flow demand for commodities. Patinkin reports that the real balance effect is identical with the 'Pigou effect', as he defined it in his 1948 paper, and that the 'Keynes effect' may be viewed as the operation of the same mechanism in the bond market. By that reasoning, we may take the real balance effect to include both the Keynes and the Pigou effects. (This approach may not be one that Pigou would be comfortable with, but it has become widely accepted. It is at least not inconsistent with Pigou's own work, although the range of assets included in most contemporary discussion of this effect is wider than considered by Pigou.)

The real balance effect as described can be evoked in support of the neoclassical doctrine of a self-correcting economy. Suppose that the economy is not operating at its potential level of output, Y_P in Figure 1, but at some lower level, such as Y_A. According to the Pigou effect, a decrease in wages and prices will decrease real saving, increasing real consumption expenditures, shown in Figure 1(a) as the shift to the right of the IS curve, IS_1 to IS_2. This change may be reinforced by the Keynes effect. Here a lower price level induces individuals to reduce their holding of cash, which results in a rightward shift in the LM curve, from LM_1 to LM_2 (Figure 1(b)) and a stimulus to real investment as a consequence of the lower equilibrium interest rate. Whether the IS or LM curve is more responsive to changes in the price level is an empirical question, but the economy will eventually return to Y_P, as long as deflation causes one or both of the curves to shift. Government intervention is not required for stability here, although it may still have the practical advantage of operating more quickly than deflation.

The operation of the Pigou effect depends on the type of money used in the economy. If the price level decreases and the net wealth of the economic system increases, the money being used can be classified as 'outside' money. Examples of outside money are gold, government bonds (assuming no

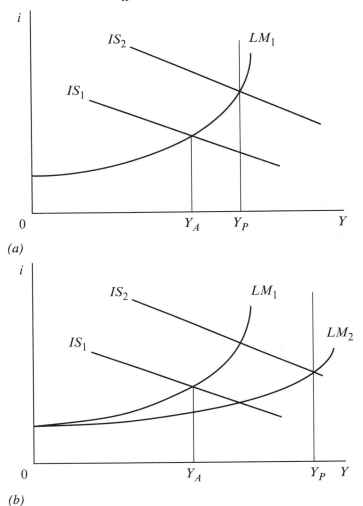

Figure 1

bequests so as to rule out Barro's point about the Ricardian equivalence theorem) and fiat paper money. If, on the other hand, the price level decreases and the net wealth of the economic system does not change, the money involved is classified as 'inside' money. Checking deposits are an example of inside money. The Pigou effect assumes the existence of outside money. Its impact is greater the larger the ratio of outside to inside money.

This point was first raised by Kalecki (1949), who argued that bank deposits are not net wealth, since any change in their value which benefits their holders will be offset by a corresponding loss in the real wealth of bank debtors. Consequently the real balances effect would apply only to the monetary base. This idea was extended and formalized by Gurley and Shaw (1960), a view which was criticized by Pesek and Saving (1967). Empirical tests of the real balance effect are obviously sensitive to assumptions made concerning the range of assets to which it applies. The basic point is that only outside money – money assets against which there is no corresponding private debt – will be subject to the real balance effect.

Similar concerns can be raised with respect to whether or not government debt represents net wealth. Traditionally the fixed maturity values of these instruments, plus the fact that they are not liabilities of the private sector, led to the conclusion that such debt should also be subject to a real balance effect. On the other hand, were Ricardo–Barro equivalence to apply, government debt would not be a component of private net wealth, and would therefore not be subject to a real balance effect.

At first blush the real balance effect appears to disprove a central message of the *General Theory*, namely that an inequality between savings and planned investment at the economy's potential output was possible and could prevent that potential from being realized. Mayer (1959) suggests that this may not be the case. A perusal of the literature reveals two distinct versions of the real balance effect. One interpretation is found in Pigou's 1947 paper. Given infinite price flexibility, this argument asserts that there exists some degree of price changes which will keep the economic system operating at its potential level of output without government intervention. That Pigou's discussion abstracted from time, so that price flexibility assures stability at potential output only in some undefined long run, undermines the practical appeal of this argument, however elegant. When this version of the real balance effect is combined with the theoretical model of the *General Theory*, the result, according to Hicks, is to reduce Keynes's model to a special case of neoclassical macroeconomics, one which hinges on the seemingly arbitrary assumption of wage/price rigidity. The principal problem with this version of the real balance effect is the lack of historical evidence to support the notion that prices are infinitely flexible. A second version of the real balances effect, associated with the monetarist tradition, argues that price changes operate as an automatic stabilizer: changes in wages and prices can keep the economic system operating at its potential level of output in the long run without the assistance of discretionary policy. Friedman mentions the real value of government bonds held by the public as being subject to a real balance effect as well as the real value of cash holdings (Friedman, 1948). Presumably the larger the share of wealth subject to this effect, the more powerfully it will operate.

Unfortunately this version of the real balances effect, which imagines an institutional framework in which the economy will be stable if left on automatic pilot, begs at least four questions. First, what is the time frame of the analysis? The Great Depression began in England in 1919, the *General Theory* was published in 1936, and in the intervening 17 years the economic system had never approached its potential level of output. To say that the individuals who were unemployed during that time period had voluntarily chosen to withdraw their services from the market seems mean spirited, if not bizarre, and is completely at odds with British policy discussions concerned with combating 'excess unemployment' during the 1920s (Skidelsky, 1992). Second, even if the real balances effect operates as described, it is not certain that the decrease in the price level will enrich the community. With debts fixed in nominal terms, lower prices and smaller income streams will lead to defaults and bankruptcies. Even if defaults do not reduce net private wealth, bankruptcies disturb production and reduce real income while reorganization is proceeding. Third, by how much must wages and prices decline to restore the economic system to its potential level of output? The Great Depression precipitated declines in wages and prices of at least 20 per cent to 30 per cent without appreciably stimulating recovery. Moreover the distributional consequences of deflation make it extremely likely that there will be strong political opposition to substantial reductions in the price level, while legal and other institutional rigidities, the most obvious of which is the minimum wage, make it an open question as to how downwardly flexible wages and prices are within a time period corresponding to a 'typical' business cycle. Fourth, to support the case that the *General Theory*'s theoretical model is a special case of neoclassical macroeconomics would require empirical validation of the real balance effect. What are the empirical results? Although Tanner (1970) found the real balance effect to be statistically significant in Canada, the consensus of those who have studied the matter (Lerner, 1952; Archibald and Lipsey, 1958; Mayer, 1959; Okun, 1972) is that, while the real balance effect has important theoretical implications, its practical value is quite limited.

An application of the real balances insight has been to provide a framework through which discretionary monetary policy might influence the macroeconomy (Freidman, 1970, 1972). Thus assume a portfolio which is initially allocated over a range of valued assets including debt, equities, consumer durables and real balances. An increase in the public's cash holdings will disturb the initial equilibrium, both by increasing total wealth and by increasing the share represented by real balances. Portfolio adjustments to re-establish an optional portfolio will then raise the demand for real and financial assets, boosting real private demand both directly and indirectly. In this connection, a relevant issue is how wide is the range of assets having significant cross-elasticities vis-à-vis real balances. Where Keynes's liquidity preference model had assumed debt instruments to be the only substitutes for cash, equities and real assets were also included in monetarist portfolios by the late 1960s. One may admit the prospect of long and variable lags being associated with the portfolio adjustment process and still recognize that the effects of discretionary policy may be more prompt and more predictable than the automatic workings of the real balance effect via Pigou.

In our judgement, the use of the expression 'real balance effect' is unfortunate. The differences between what that term means when associated with the monetarist tradition (that is, an automatic stabilizer) and in its association with Pigou's argument that there is some price level at which the economy will operate at capacity are important enough to make one wish that the same name were not applied to both. The central issue is probably which assets should be included in the portfolio. Here Pigou stayed closer to Keynes's money model, where those in the monetarist tradition have worked with a broader portfolio, including various real and financial assets.

Two conclusions follow from this discussion. First, the economic system is not self-correcting through the operation of the real balance effect. Second, the real balance effect will not be a factor when practical policy options are under discussion. Both of these conclusions are consistent with the notion that public policy can play a potentially important role in hastening the economy's return to its potential level of output following a negative demand shock. For Keynesian economists, practical policy options include monetary and fiscal policy. If the economic system is operating at less than its potential output and if the private sector is unwilling or is unable to increase its portion of aggregate expenditures, monetary and fiscal policy should be used to move the economy to its potential level of output. For Keynes, practical policy involves 'monetary policy in conjunction with the stabilization of investment by means of a permanent rise in the proportion of income spent by governments' (Blaug, 1994). If the central message of the *General Theory* is that government plays a critical role in stabilizing the macroeconomy, that message is not seriously compromised by the real balance effect in any of its versions.

ROBERT D. LEY
TOM CATE

See also:

Classical Economics; Demand Management; Fiscal Policy; Pigou, Arthur C.; Quantity Theory of Money; Ricardian Equivalence.

Bibliography

Archibald, G.C. and R.G. Lipsey (1958), 'Monetary and Value Theory: A Critique of Lange and Patinkin', *Review of Economic Studies*, **26**, (69), October, pp. 1–22.
Barro, Robert (1974), 'Are Government Bonds Net Worth?', *Journal of Political Economy*, **82**, (6), November/December, pp. 1095–1117.
Blaug, Mark (1994), 'Recent Biographies of Keynes', *Journal of Economic Literature*, **32**, (3), September, pp. 1204–15.

Fellner, William (1957), 'What Is Surviving?', *American Economic Review*, **47**, (2), May, pp. 67–76.

Friedman, Milton (1948), 'A Monetary and Fiscal Framework for Economic Stability', *American Economic Review*, **38**, (2), June, pp. 245–64.

Friedman, Milton (1970), 'A Theoretical Framework for Monetary Analysis', *Journal of Political Economy*, **78**, (2), March–April, pp. 198–238.

Friedman, Milton (1972), 'Comments to the Critics', *Journal of Political Economy*, **80**, (5), September–October, pp. 30–80.

Gurley, J.G. and E.S. Shaw (1960), *Money in a Theory of Finance*, Washington: Brookings.

Haberler, G. (1941), *Prosperity and Depression: A Theoretical Analysis of Cyclical Movements*, Geneva: League of Nations.

Haberler, G. (1952), 'The Pigou Effect Once More', *Journal of Political Economy*, **60**, (3), April, pp. 240–46.

Hansen, Alvin (1941), *Fiscal Policy and Business Cycles*, New York: W.W. Norton.

Hicks, John (1937), 'Mr. Keynes and The "Classics": a suggested interpretation', *Econometrica*, **5**, (2), April, pp. 147–59.

Johnson, Harry G. (1969), 'Inside Money, Outside Money, Income, Wealth and Welfare in Monetary Theory', *Journal of Money, Banking and Credit*, **1**, (1), February, pp. 30–45.

Kalecki, M. (1949), 'A New Approach to the Problems of Business Cycles', *Review of Economic Studies*, **16**, (40), pp. 57–64.

Keynes, J.M. (1936), *The General Theory of Employment, Interest and Money*, London: Macmillan.

Lerner, Abba (1952), 'The Essential Properties of Interest and Money,' *Quarterly Journal of Economics*, **62**, (2), May, pp. 172–93.

Mayer, Thomas (1959), 'The Empirical Significance of the Real Balance Effect', *Quarterly Journal of Economics*, **73**, (2), May, pp. 275–91.

Melitz, Jacques (1967), 'Pigou and the "Pigou Effect": Rendez-vous with the Author', *Southern Economic Journal*, **43**, (2), October, pp. 268–79.

Modigliani, F. (1944), 'Liquidity preference and the theory of interest and money', *Econometrica*, **12**, (1), January, pp. 45–88.

Okun, Arthur (1972), 'Fiscal–Monetary Activism: Some Analytical Issues', *Brookings Papers on Economic Activity*, **3**, (1), pp. 123–63.

Patinkin, Don (1948), 'Price Flexibility and Full Employment', *American Economic Review*, **38**, (4), September, pp. 543–64.

Patinkin, Don (1965), *Money, Interest and Prices*, 2nd edn, New York: Harper & Row.

Pesek, B.P. and T.R. Saving (1967), *Money, Wealth and Economic Theory*, New York: Macmillan.

Pigou, A.C. (1943), 'The Classical Stationary State', *Economic Journal*, **53**, (211), December, pp. 343–51.

Pigou, A.C. (1947), 'Economic progress in a stable environment', *Economica*, **14**, (54), August, pp. 180–88.

Presley, John R. (1986), 'J.M. Keynes and the Real Balance Effect', *Manchester School of Economic and Social Studies*, **54**, (1), March, pp. 22–30.

Scitovsky, T. (1941), 'Capital accumulation, employment and price rigidity', *Review of Economic Studies*, **8**, (2), February, pp. 69–88.

Skidelsky, R. (1992), *John Maynard Keynes: The Economist as Savior, 1920–1937*, New York: Penguin Books.

Tanner, J.E. (1970), 'Empirical evidence on the short-run real balance effect in Canada', *Journal of Money, Credit and Banking*, **2**, (4), November, pp. 473–85.

Relative Income Hypothesis

James Duesenberry formulated his relative income hypothesis to address the shortcomings of the consumption function which described the key relationship in Keynes's income–expenditure approach to national income determination (Keynes, 1936). Keynes's theory of consumption behavior – sometimes also labeled 'the absolute income hypothesis' – predicted that households will tend to spend a decreasing proportion of their income as their level of income increases. This prediction was intuitive; it seemed logical that in periods of declining income consumers would reduce their savings efforts in order to maintain the standard of living to which they had become accustomed. It was also supported by cross-sectional data. Time series data, however, showed something different. In his long-term study of savings behavior and national income, Simon Kuznets established a constant long-run savings–income ratio (Kuznets, 1952). In addition, events following World War II showed that consumption behavior is influenced not only by income but also by wealth, an aspect that was ignored altogether by Keynes's simple consumption theory.

Among the first economists to look for ways to improve on Keynes's theory was Duesenberry. He tried to address the following, seemingly contradictory, empirical evidence: cross-sectional budget studies and short-run studies (over the duration of a business cycle) showed that the average propensity to consume (APC = C/Y) was larger than the marginal propensity to consume (MPC = $\Delta C/\Delta Y$) and that the average propensity to consume declined as the level of income increased. On the other hand, the long-run APC was thought to be fairly constant and equal to the long-run MPC.

Duesenberry based his critique of Keynes's consumption function on two different ideas, using social and psychological arguments to explain the consumption behavior of households (Duesenberry, 1949). His first hypothesis argued that households are less concerned with their own absolute level of spending than with their spending level relative to other households. His second hypothesis claimed that, while households tend to adapt easily to higher living standards as their income increases, they find it more difficult to adapt to lower living standards and reduce their spending when their income declines. While Duesenberry's theory was insightful and initially embraced by economists, it has since been overshadowed by two other, more elegant, theories of consumption behavior, namely Friedman's permanent income hypothesis and Modigliani's life cycle hypothesis.

These latter approaches rely on intertemporal maximization models in which consumers try to maximize their own personal utility subject to a lifetime budget constraint. Duesenberry, on the other hand, based his theory on a utility function in which household consumption levels are weighted by the consumption level of the rest of the population. Therefore a household's level of utility only increases if its consumption level rises relative to that of the average household. This approach asserts that households care about their relative position in the overall income distribution. Consumers in the lower-income brackets are assumed to spend a higher proportion of their income in an effort to afford lifestyles similar to those of higher-income groups – in other words, they try 'to keep up with the Joneses'. But consumers in the higher-income brackets, who *are* the 'Joneses' – can afford to save a much larger proportion of their income while still maintaining their high living standard. Duesenberry called this the 'demonstration effect' and used it to explain why cross-sectional household budget studies show variations in the APC of households with different incomes. At the same time, he used this demonstration effect to show that the APC can be stable in the long run as long as a country's income distribution does not change significantly as national income increases. The nation's aggregate APC, which is the average APC for all income classes, will not change over time, since all households will try to maintain their relative position in terms of their consumption patterns.

Duesenberry used another idea, the so-called 'ratchet effect', to explain why the APC fluctuates in the short run, but remains fairly constant in the long run. Combining both long-run and short-run consumption behavior, he argued that a household's current level of consumption is not determined solely by the current absolute and relative income level but also by the previous peak income level. As long as household income rises along a trend, the prior year's income will always be the previous peak income level. Since households easily adjust their level of consumption if their income level increases, the APC will remain constant over the long run since consumption and income will grow at the same rate. However the more household income declines below the previous peak, the higher the APC will get, since households are not willing to reduce their expenditures proportionally to lower income. In other words, households with declining incomes will lower their savings in an attempt to maintain their previous standard of living.

By using a linear consumption function (which is slightly different from the non-linear approach used in Duesenberry's book) this can easily be demonstrated. Assume consumption is defined as follows: $C_t = c_1 Y_t + c_2 Y^*$, where Y^* is the peak income level. As long as income Y_t increases steadily, we can calculate $apc_1 = C_t/Y_t = c_1 + c_2$, since $Y_t = Y^*$. However, when income starts to decline, we get $apc_2 = c_1 + c_2*(Y^*/Y_t)$, with $apc_2 > apc_1$ and apc_2 increasing as income decreases, since $Y_t < Y^*$.

Unfortunately Duesenberry was unable to formulate a meaningful budget constraint that incorporated his 'ratchet effect'. How, for example, could households imitate the rich and live beyond their means for several years in spite of declining incomes? His theory also ignored the influence of wealth on consumption. This is particularly interesting, since Duesenberry's own research (showing that white families save a lower proportion of their income relative to families of color with the same income), seems to have been the impetus for Friedman's and Tobin's later exploration of this issue.

While Duesenberry relied on social and psychological arguments to describe the strong dislike that many rational consumers feel about giving up consumption as their income declines, the major share of research by other economists in this area has focused on microfoundations. In such studies households do not look at their neighbors' behavior but instead look towards the future when determining their current level of consumption. Hall even applied the methodology of rational expectations to the theory of consumption behavior, by implying that consumption may be a 'random walk'. Hall's study supported the permanent income hypothesis by suggesting that lagged consumption is the most significant factor in determining future consumption (Hall, 1978). Using the relative income approach, however, one could probably instead interpret Hall's results as an indication that households are indeed reluctant to lower their living standards as their incomes fall.

Unfortunately most economists seem too stuck on the simple utility maximization approach to accept the notion that interdependence should be introduced into utility functions. Economists are notoriously unwilling to accept so-called 'irrational' behavior. Since the relative income hypothesis is based more on amateur psychology than rigorous economic theory, it is not surprising that little conclusive empirical evidence has been produced that strongly supports its implications. On the other hand, most other theories of consumption behavior fail to give adequate attention to the role of the distribution of income or the importance of cross-sectional analysis.

Complete consensus among economists on any issue is hard to find, and views in regard to consumption behavior are no exception. The theories of Friedman and Modigliani are now more widely accepted than Duesenberry's relative income approach, but even the life cycle hypothesis, while most widely used, has had its share of criticism. First, it had to be amended to account for bequest motives and liquidity constraints, and just recently it was found that so-called 'inter vivos' transfers (gifts throughout a person's lifetime to children or grandchildren) are, like bequests, actually intended and are an important savings motive (Gale and Scholz, 1994). This constitutes a clear departure from the life cycle hypothesis. One cannot dismiss the possibility that, as more studies are undertaken and more empirical evidence surfaces, future research may further validate Duesenberry's ideas.

Despite its obvious shortcomings, Duesenberry's relative income approach cannot be entirely dismissed. It remains an important contribution to the theory of consumption behavior, most certainly as an example of advancements in macroeconomic theory relating to consumption behavior in conjunction with the permanent income and life cycle hypotheses. It is unfortunate that many modern macroeconomics textbooks almost ignore Duesenberry's theories and contributions.

JUERGEN FLECK

See also:
Absolute Income Hypothesis; Consumption and the Consumption Function; Friedman, Milton; Life Cycle Hypothesis; Modigliani, Franco; Permanent Income Hypothesis.

Bibliography
Ando, A. and F. Modigliani (1963), 'The "Life Cycle" Hypothesis of Saving: Aggregate Implications and Tests', *American Economic Review*, **53**,(1), March, pp. 55–84.
Duesenberry, J.S. (1949), *Income, Saving and the Theory of Consumption Behavior*, Cambridge, Mass.: Harvard University Press.
Friedman, M. (1957), *A Theory of the Consumption Function*, Princeton, NJ: Princeton, University Press.
Gale, W.G. and J.K. Scholz (1994), 'Intergenerational Transfers and the Accumulation of Wealth', *Journal of Economic Perspectives*, **8**, (4), fall, pp. 145–60.
Hall, R.E. (1978), 'Stochastic Implications of the Life Cycle–Permanent Income Hypothesis: Theory and Evidence', *Journal of Political Economy*, **86**, (6), December, pp. 971–88.
Keynes, John M. (1936), *The General Theory of Employment, Interest and Money*, London: Macmillan.
Kuznets, S. (1946), *National Product Since 1869*, New York: National Bureau of Economic Research.
Kuznets S. (1952), 'Proportion of Capital Formation to National Product', *American Economic Review*, **42**, (2), May, pp. 507–26.
Modigliani, F. and R. Brumberg (1954), 'Utility Analysis and the Consumption Function: An Interpretation of Cross-Section Data', in K.K. Kurihara (ed.), *Post-Keynesian Economics*, New Brunswick, NJ: Rutgers University Press.
Tobin, J. (1951), 'Relative Income, Absolute Income and Savings', in H.L. Waitman (ed.), *Money, Trade and Economic Growth, in Honor of John Henry Williams*, New York: Macmillan.

Ricardian Equivalence

'Ricardian equivalence' asserts that the behavior of rational economic agents is unaffected by the choice of funding a given amount of government spending by lump sum taxes or by government borrowing. In the case of a debt-financed tax cut, a rational agent would recognize that the present discounted value of the future taxes implied by borrowing is equal in amount to the current tax cut. Thus the agent would not change his consumption, but would simply save his extra disposable income to meet his future tax liability. This occurs regardless of whether the debt is held domestically or by foreign investors. In the latter case, the initial purchase of bonds involves an inflow of wealth from abroad that equals the present value of the future outflow of tax revenues. As Ricardian equivalence predicts that a debt-financed tax cut will have no effect on the level of consumption, saving, investment or output in the economy, it stands in direct contrast to the standard analysis in the context of the Keynesian model. The latter approach predicts that an increase in public debt provides a short-run stimulus by making agents appear wealthier, but has harmful long-term growth effects as government borrowing raises interest rates and crowds out private investment.

Consider a simple two-period numerical example. In period 1 there is a reduction in lump sum taxes of $1000, financed by a $1000 issue of one-year bonds yielding a 10 per cent return. One year later, taxes must be raised by $1100 in order to finance the payment of interest and the repayment of the principal of the bonds. If we assume that agents have perfect foresight, they would increase their saving in period 1 by $1000, in anticipation of an $1100 tax payment in period 2. Thus overall consumption would be unaffected by the bond issue. This reasoning can easily be applied to an *n*-period model.

The Ricardian equivalence proposition has its origins in the work of classical economist David Ricardo (1817). The idea owes its prominence in the modern debate over public debt to its restatement by Barro (1974). Buchanan (1976) subsequently chided Barro for ignoring the existing literature on the subject and generously paid tribute to the originator of the concept by coining its present appellation. However, as has been shown by O'Driscoll (1977), this label is misleading, for although Ricardo did indeed anticipate Barro's theoretical reasoning, he did not reach a similar conclusion as to its applicability to the real world.

For Ricardian equivalence to hold, it is necessary that economic agents base their consumption decisions not merely on their current income but on some notion of wealth. That this is so has come to be widely acknowledged with the development of the permanent income and life cycle hypotheses as a framework for the analysis of consumption decisions. Ricardian equivalence also requires that economic agents are fully informed and make their consumption decisions rationally. Ricardo himself was the first to recognize that taxpayers might suffer from 'fiscal illusion'. He argued that myopic taxpayers do not recognize the full weight of future taxation implied by a substitution of debt for tax finance, and thus improperly perceive such a substitution as an increase in their net worth, and increase their current consumption accordingly. Among the modern writers who considered this problem was Patinkin (1965), who suggested that in modelling this issue, some fraction 'k' of the stock of outstanding government bonds should be treated as wealth: the less the degree of fiscal illusion, the lower the value of k; Ricardian equivalence would be represented by $k = 0$. The possibility that $k = 0$ is supported by the theory of rational expectations.

The argument has been made that a purely self-interested agent might consider public debt issue an increase in real wealth if it is anticipated that full debt retirement will not occur prior to his death. However Barro (1974) showed that Ricardian equivalence holds in a finite horizon model if altruistic agents regard their heirs as extensions of themselves and thus include the consumption of their descendants in their own utility function. In a model involving intergenerational bequests, parents would use the increase in their disposable incomes resulting from the substitution of debt for current taxes to augment their children's inheritances by an amount large enough to allow them to pay the resulting future taxes. One interesting issue which arises in consideration of a model such as this is the possibility that the issuance of public debt may increase intertemporal efficiency by allowing for the possibility of negative bequests (Drazen, 1978).

Uncertainty may also lead to the violation of Ricardian equivalence. If an agent faces uncertainty regarding future income (this may result from uncertain income or from an uncertain life span), he is unable to determine with certainty the amount of the bequest for which to provide. Thus the agent will not be indifferent between a dollar of income today, its value known with certainty, and an uncertain future payment to his heir which can only be estimated to have the present value of a dollar. Uncertainty experienced by an agent as to future tax liabilities implies similar problems. Two opposing effects have been described. The first is that confused cost signals may lead to an underestimation of future tax payments, raising net wealth and leading to increased consumption (Buchanan and Wagner, 1977). The second is that risk-averse agents facing uncertainty may overestimate their future tax liabilities, leading to precautionary saving and reducing consumption (Barro, 1974).

The Ricardian equivalence argument is also predicated on the assumption that the future tax burden to service a given issue of debt is borne by those who benefit from the initial tax cut. If this is not the case, a transfer of income will result, and if consumption patterns differ across economic agents, aggregate consumption may be altered. For example, if the marginal propensity to consume of the recipients is high relative to that of the taxpayers, aggregate consumption will increase and Ricardian equivalence will be violated. The situation is further complicated if the assumption of lump sum taxes is lifted. In an economy in which the tax structure is known and unchanging, equivalence will obtain, but if changes in the tax structure which would shift the tax burden between different groups are anticipated, the issuance of debt may have real effects.

Capital market imperfections may also lead to violation of Ricardian equivalence. If an economic agent is unable in the existing credit environment to borrow against his future income, the possibility provided by the existence of public debt for a reduction of current in favor of future taxes may prove to be attractive. Likewise benefits may result if the government faces a lower borrowing rate than some or all economic agents. The existence of public debt means that liquidity-constrained agents or agents facing higher interest rates can receive loans from other agents with the government acting as an intermediary, effectively guaranteeing loan repayment by means of its powers of tax collection. Debt issue will thus increase net wealth if the government is more efficient than the private market in carrying out the loan process (Barro, 1974).

It has been suggested by Feldstein (1976) that under certain circumstances a public debt may never be redeemed. Feldstein took issue with Barro's simplifying assumptions of constant population and zero economic growth, pointing out that the growth rate plays a crucial role in determining whether a current tax cut necessarily implies a future tax increase. If the growth rate exceeds the rate of interest, the government can roll over the principal and interest on the debt forever, a situation of dynamic inefficiency known as a 'Ponzi game'. In such a case, the issuance of debt would raise net wealth. Barro (1976) responded to this argument by questioning the likelihood of a situation where the growth rate would exceed the interest rate.

Despite the many questions that have been raised as to its realism, Ricardian equivalence has attracted a great deal of attention in recent years. The theorem has many testable implications, and these have been explored in an attempt to determine whether it is an adequate approximation to reality. The methodology and results of empirical studies are comprehensively surveyed and assessed by Seater (1993), who concludes that Ricardian equivalence or approximate Ricardian equivalence is more strongly supported by the data than are the predictions of the traditional model.

NANCY CHURCHMAN

See also:

Demand Management; Expectations, Theories of; Keynesian Revolution; Life Cycle Hypothesis; Lucas Critique; Neoclassical Economics (Bastard Keynesianism); New Classical School of Economics; Permanent Income Hypothesis.

Bibliography

Barro, Robert J. (1974), 'Are Government Bonds Net Wealth?', *Journal of Political Economy*, **82**, (6), pp. 1095–1117.

Barro, Robert J. (1976), 'Reply to Feldstein and Buchanan,' *Journal of Political Economy*, **84**, (2), 343–9.

Barro, Robert J. (1979), 'On the Determination of the Public Debt', *Journal of Political Economy*, **87**, (5), pp. 940–71.

Buchanan, James M. (1976), 'Barro on the Ricardian Equivalence Theorem', *Journal of Political Economy*, **84**, (2), 337–42.

Buchanan, James M. and R.E. Wagner (1977), *Democracy in Deficit: The Political Legacy of Lord Keynes*, New York: Academic Press.

Drazen, A. (1978), 'Government Debt, Human Capital and Bequests in a Lifecycle Model', *Journal of Political Economy*, **86**, (3), June, pp. 505–16.

Feldstein, Martin (1976), 'Perceived Wealth in Bonds and Social Security: A Comment', *Journal of Political Economy*, **84**, (2), April, pp. 331–6.

O'Driscoll, Gerald P. (1977), 'The Ricardian Nonequivalence Theorem', *Journal of Political Economy*, **85**, (1), February, pp. 207-10.

Patinkin, D. (1965), *Money, Interest and Prices*, 2nd edn, New York: Harper & Row.

Ricardo, David (1817), *Principles of Political Economy*; 1951 edn, ed. Piero Sraffa, Cambridge: Cambridge University Press.

Seater, John J. (1993), 'Ricardian Equivalence', *Journal of Economic Literature*, **31**, (1), March, pp. 142–90.

Ricardo Effect

The Ricardo effect (RE) is a particular sequence of price changes that *may* occur during the boom phased of a nineteenth century-style business cycle. According to its champion, Friedrich A. Hayek, it occurs during a *prolonged* expansion of the economy when that expansion has been artificially financed by the easy money and credit policies of the monetary authorities (Hayek, 1931, 1939, 1942, 1969). The RE puts an end to this extravagant investment boom, heralding the onslaught of depression, crisis and economic readjustment. Towards the end of the boom the prices of consumer goods rise more quickly and 'ahead of' the rise in money wages, and that triggers the crisis (Haberler, 1947). On the microeconomic level, the production manager, who is at all times trying to keep costs down, is induced by the comparatively lower cost of labor to switch to less capital-intensive, more labor-intensive methods of production. On the macroeconomic level, the separate and distinct actions of many production managers adding labor and cutting back on capital goods leads to a general collapse in the overall market demand for investment goods (Moss and Vaughn, 1986). Distress in the capital goods sector leads to layoffs, and the sinking of investment goods prices causes additional dislocations and further declines in employment (Lachmann, 1940). The depression is the necessary adjustment of the real structure of production of the economy to the excesses of the previous boom (Hayek, 1931; Rothbard, 1963).

In a nutshell, the RE guarantees that, if a boom financed by credit expansion does not end for any other reason, it must end when consumer goods prices race upwards ahead of money wages. Consumer goods and intermediate product prices must race upwards ahead of money wages when the financial sector succeeds in diverting more and more resources to investment projects beyond what the voluntary net savings of households and corporations allow. According to the Mises–Hayek wing of the modern Austrian School, had the expansion of the economy been financed by the voluntary net savings of households and firms prudently channeled through the financial sector, the boom-like conditions would have persisted and the subsequent collapse would not have been required (Rothbard, 1963). Savings-fed expansions produce a genuine ratcheting up in living standards. Credit-fed booms end in crisis and despair.

The political economy of the Ricardo effect
The RE does not have to accompany each and every credit expansion business cycle. Indeed the attempt to 'fool' investors into thinking that more real net savings are available than would in fact be made accessibile by acting agents involved what the modern Austrian School termed a lowering of the interest rate below the natural rate. Knut Wicksell's notion of a 'cumulative expansion' implied as much (Wicksell, 1936; Pivetti, 1987). In most historical situations,

the credit expansion boom ends because the modern fractional reserve banking system is continuously losing reserves either through international capital outflows (the external drain) or through a steady rise in the cash holdings of former but now less trustful depositors (the internal drain). At some point the banking authorities, fearing collapse of the banking system, tighten credit and raise nominal interest rates, thereby making many investment projects unprofitable and sparking the financial collapse and subsequent business depression (Wicksell, 1936; von Mises, 1934). In these cases the boom ends before the Ricardo effect proves decisive in triggering the business collapse.

In 1939, Hayek modified his version of the Austrian trade cycle theory to rebut the rapidly emerging Keynesian school and especially the so-called 'acceleration principle of investment demand' (Hayek, 1939; Haberler, 1947). Hayek set out to show that, even if the interest rate could be held permanently below the natural rate, and even if unemployed labor were available, a prolonged credit expansion boom would still come to a crashing halt. The end would come because of a particular sequence of price changes, which he called the Ricardo effect.

Hayek also insisted that, if the monetary authorities tried to offset the incentives produced by the Ricardo effect, by lowering interest rates and expanding credit further and/or increasing the rate of growth of money and credit, the Ricardo effect would become more pronounced and increasingly more difficult to overcome.[1] In his later writings, Hayek characterized the twentieth-century industrial world as enjoying an 'inflation-borne prosperity which depends for its continuation on continued inflation' (Hayek, 1972, p. 112). His metaphor of an inflation-driven economy behaving like some unfortunate soul trying to hold onto a tiger by the tail is best presented in his own words:

> it has taken 25 years [from the end of World War II] to reach the stage where to slow down inflation produces a recession. We now have a tiger by the tail; how long can this inflation continue? If the tiger (of inflation) is freed he will eat us up; yet if he runs faster and faster while we desperately hold on, we are *still* finished! (Ibid.)

What motivates the authorities to bring about this miserable situation? According to Hayek (and Mises also), the monetary authorities are motivated to create the boom because they choose to cater to the short-run demands of labor union officials and others for the immediate creation of jobs and profits (Hayek, 1972, p. 119; von Mises, 1980, pp. 150–61). Rather than face up to the needed structural changes that would permanently expand economic activity, the political leaders encourage the monetary authorities simply to expand money and credit, thereby ignoring the longer-run consequences of choosing this method of increasing production.

For Hayek and subsequent generations of modern Austrians, John Maynard Keynes in his *The General Theory of Employment, Interest and Money* per-

sonified the economist willing to service the short-run demands of dema-
gogues and union leaders while ignoring the long-run readjustments that such
quick-fix palliatives necessarily require (Hayek, 1941, pp. 353–410). Quite
expectedly, neither Keynes nor his students took kindly to this characterization, and thus began one of the most bitter of the twentieth-century debates
about macroeconomic theory and policy. The Keynesian school versus Austrian School drama unfolded during the 1930s and 1940s, especially among
the graduate students and faculty at the London School of Economics, where
Hayek taught (Lerner, 1983, pp. 563–83).

Nicholas Kaldor's attempt to demonstrate the 'non-existence' of the RE

In a series of well-crafted journal articles, Nicholas Kaldor, who was in those
years a young faculty member at the London School, set out to prove that
Hayek's conceptual understanding of markets was deeply flawed (Kaldor, 1942,
pp. 148–76). Kaldor argued that, even if Hayek were partially correct and that
during an investment boom real wages fell and plant managers did substitute
labor for capital, the *aggregate* demand for investment goods would not therefore trigger any crisis. So long as credit market conditions were not tightened
and unemployed labor remained readily available, the economy would expand
and absorb any displaced investment goods (Haberler, 1947, pp. 481–91; Kaldor,
1942; Tsiang, 1947, pp. 119–53). Kaldor calculated that the decline in the
demand for particular capital goods in individual production processes – the
substitution effect – would be more than offset by an expansion in the number
of production processes in play during the course of the boom: the expansion
effect. Hence, according to Kaldor, there are logical reasons for believing that
the expansion effect will outweigh the labor substitution effect to produce a net
expansion of the economy and more jobs. In short, Kaldor proved that the RE
is inconsistent with comparative–static reasoning in economics (Moss and
Vaughn, 1986, pp. 560–61).

Despite the formidable challenge Hayek faced from Kaldor and other critics,
he steadfastly held to his basic 1939 position that the RE was something that
would end a credit-financed investment boom if that boom did not end for any
of the usual reasons; furthermore the RE would operate even if the economy
did not reach full employment of resources (labor). At full employment, some
versions of Keynesian economics would permit Austrian analysis to have some
relevance. It is basic Austrian macroeconomics that any artificial rise in consumption expenditure must sooner or later lead to a fall in investment; this
premise, as Harald Hagemann and Hans-Michael Trautwein have explained, is
'strongly anti-Keynesian in spirit' (Hagemann and Trautwein, 1995).

According to Moss and Vaughn, Kaldor may have criticized Hayek for the
wrong reasons (Moss and Vaughn, 1986, pp. 560–61). Hayek was trying to
explain how, from the initial conditions of macroeconomic equilibrium, it

would be impossible for an economy to find a trajectory adequate to restore macroeconomic balance when the original departure from coordinated equilibrium is financed by bank credit rather than real net savings. The RE is a *disequilibrium* phenomenon, and as such it cannot be detected in the manner Kaldor supposed by using tradition comparative–static analysis. Declaring that the economy is always 'in equilibrium' assumes away the specific problem of a Wicksellian-style cumulative process that fascinated Hayek and other modern Austrians (ibid.; Steele, 1988). And so all that Kaldor proved was that during an investment boom, if the economy was always in equilibrium, it would always be in equilibrium. Clearly Kaldor had not made much progress beyond the definitions he employed.

Statistical evidence
During the 1940s, one of Hayek's students at the London School, Sho-Chieh Tsiang, included in his dissertation research an empirical test to see how often real wages did in fact decline during the boom phase of recorded business cycles (Tsiang, 1947). Did real-world actual cycles ever end in the manner Hayek described? Did the real wage of labor fall towards the end of the cycle, even when measured in the output of the industry in which that labor was employed? Tsiang concluded that the historical record was at least to some extent consistent with Hayek's view that during booms real wages fall while output and employment rise (Haberler, 1947, pp. 490–91; Tsiang, 1947, p. 117). Tsiang qualified his empirical findings by pointing out that he could find no theoretical reason for believing that wages and product prices had to move in the manner Hayek specified. Tsiang's theoretical reasoning bore the mark of Kaldor's theoretical views about which some observations have been offered above (Tsiang, 1947, pp. 119–53). Surprisingly neither Hayek nor the subsequent commentators on Hayek refer to Tsiang's statistical work on the RE. That is because at the time it was published, in 1947, the profession appears to have lost interest in Hayek and his economics: Keynesian economics had become the dominant method of analysis and would remain so until the 1970s, when there was a rebirth of interest in Austrian economics and related themes (Vaughn, 1994, pp. 1–11).

Ricardo effect as a logical theorem
The RE is only an ultimate check on even the most clever set of political machinations designed to insulate the economy and banking system from the dangers of paper money or bank credit expansion. When the RE finally ends the boom, then and only then will the RE be a matter of public record and perhaps be detectable in the economic time series statistics. The fact that the RE was not statistically measurable during any particular historical episode does not prove that the RE is not *real* or *does not exist*. Ontologically

speaking, the RE can be inherent in the logic of the situation and become manifest only when circumstances warrant. This realist-style claim that a RE is deeply situated within the structure of a capital goods-using market system is probably what has caused so much confusion, since the economists of Hayek's day (and Hayek himself!) were deeply anti-realist in their approach to economic analysis (Maki, 1990).

Like other ideas and concepts presented by the modern Austrian School, the RE may be more firmly ingrained in logic than in time series data. According to Hayek and others, the RE is a principled response to the Keynesian claim that an expansion in aggregate demand will permanently cure unemployment by causing investment demand to expand also. The Keynesian argument is that, as long as unemployed resources exist, any expansion in aggregate demand fueled by an increase in either actual consumption or investment (even if that increase were 'artificially' financed by bank credit!) will have a positive multiplier effect on income. Income will increase enough to generate sufficient voluntary net savings to equal the previous increase in planned spending. This in a nutshell is an important line of argument which all students of modern economics are expected to master. It constitutes one great legacy of Keynesian economics to the modern economics curriculum and is often used in the textbook literature to explain why market systems are unstable (Haberler, 1947, pp. 94–105; Junakar, 1987; Samuelson and Nordhaus, 1995, pp. 198, 897).

According to Hayek, unless the net saving has been provided for *in advance* and reflects a prior change in the habits and routines of the community (that is, the community's implied willingness to substitute future consumption goods for present consumption goods), the artificially propped-up rise in spending will not last.[2] The expansion in aggregate demand even in the face of unemployed resources will set in motion the RE mechanism and guarantee only a subsequent depression in investment spending. The inevitability of the RE during prolonged credit-financed booms was, according to Hayek and his students, almost a logical proposition. It had to happen because the banking authorities were trying to bring about a permanent reallocation of resources between present and future consumption that was out of line with the subjective time preferences of the public (Hayek, 1941, pp. 392–3; 1972, p. 63; Rothbard, 1963, pp. 11–38). This point has always seemed to be fundamental to modern Austrian writers, despite their several other disagreements with each other about the details of the inflationary process.

The historians' attack on the Ricardo effect

Hayek first described the essential pattern of events known as the 'Ricardo effect' in his controversial *Prices and Production* (1931). For the next decade or so, he expounded on themes presented in that early work while holding the distinguished Tooke Chair at the London School of Economics. In 1939, Hayek crystallized his thoughts about how prolonged booms would end despite the desperate efforts of government officials and union leaders and first called the sequence of price changes the 'Ricardo effect' (O'Driscoll, 1977). During the 1940s, Hayek pointed out that there were two places in David Ricardo's *Principles of Political Economy* where the RE could be found (Hayek, 1949, p. 220n). A 1969 article repeated his arguments about the RE, although this time in a more explicitly comparative–static framework (Hayek, 1969).

A number of scholars have strenuously objected to Hayek's interpretation of Ricardo's *Principles* and, therefore, to his use of Ricardo's name. Stefano Zamagni (1987), Ferdinando Meacci (1995), Harald Hagemann and Hans-Michael Trautwein (1995) have separately questioned the accuracy of Hayek's reading of Ricardo's *Principles of Political Economy*. What is not disputed is that Hayek referred to Chapters 1 and 31 of Ricardo's *Principles* for evidence of the RE mechanism. A careful reading of Ricardo's Chapter 1, however, demonstrates that Ricardo's description of a rise in money wages that dispro-portionately affects relative commodity prices depending on the capital–labor ratio was an application of comparative–static reasoning. Unlike Ricardo, Hayek was mostly interested in the transition between stages of equilibrium. Because of this difference in focus, the RE critics maintain that, whatever resemblance there might be between Ricardo's discussion of a rise in money wages and Hayek's discussion of the lagged adjustment of money wages behind rising consumer goods prices is more superficial than real (Meacci, 1995). Furthermore, in Chapter 31 of the *Principles*, where Hayek claimed that he also found traces of his price sequence, Ricardo dealt with a sudden switch in the composition of capital from circulating to fixed capital followed by a displacement of labor and a decline in real wages. The decline in real wages is the *consequence* of a sudden switch in the choice of what technique of production will be used. In Hayek's version of the RE, the decline in real wages is what *induces* the switch in the choice of techniques. Again the resemblance between Ricardo's and Hayek's respective arguments is more apparent than real (Zamagni, 1987).

Hayek's critics therefore requested that the phenomenon be renamed 'the Hayek effect' because, whatever its analytic roots, they are not in Ricardo's *Principles*. This particular line of attack about the name Hayek chose for his idea seems at best picky and perhaps mean-spirited. Indeed we have it on Hayek's own authority that he was inspired to recognize the Ricardo effect after reading Ricardo (Hayek, 1949, p. 220n).[3] This means that Ricardo's pattern of argument probably was at least a catalyst in the development of Hayek's ideas.

Future research

The RE mechanism comes into operation because either the government or the banking system is forcing resources into channels other than those in which the private market would have invested. The benchmark against which the credit expansion boom must be compared is not some final state of equilibrium but what sequence of events would otherwise have occurred. What would have otherwise occurred is that community savings would have been channeled through financial institutions into selected investment projects evaluated at interest rates that reflect the deep-seated time preferences of the investment public (Rothbard, 1987). The future of the RE remains with those post-Hayekians who must spell out in more detail the linkages between time preferences, financial intermediation and capital markets. Subsequent generations of Austrian writers seem to have moved away from these developments and lost interest in the Austrian School's capital theory, with its sequential description of capitalist production as a series of stages in historical time.[4] The RE seems threatened with neglect, and the prospect of its being forgotten entirely now seems a realistic possibility. The substantive problem is whether or not the RE is logically implied by what we understand to be the market mechanism. The ultimate questions raised by Keynes and his students remains: Can investment spending be expanded beyond the limits set by voluntary net savings. And will any such expansion prove to be durable? At this stage in the debate, the burden of denying the possibility remains with the modern Austrian school.

LAURENCE S. MOSS

Notes

1 Strictly speaking, the claim that the duration and intensity of the subsequent depression is a function of the duration and intensity of the previous boom is not part of the Ricardo effect, in the sense that it can be logically deduced from the RE as it has been described so far. With additional assumptions about the nature of the investment process itself, Hayek's writings sometimes imply that there is such a connection between booms and depressions but the actual logic is left undiscussed. (See Hayek, 1969 and 1972.)

2 Rothbard's account in *America's Great Depression* is based on Hayek's earliest accounts of the business cycle and is able to tell the story of the 1930s crisis without much reference to Hayek's favorite effect (see pp. 11–38). According to Rothbard (and Hayek, circa 1931), 'The proper monetary policy, even after a depression is underway, is to deflate or at the least to refrain from further inflation' (*America's Great Depression*, p. 148). The terms 'inflation' and 'deflation' do not mean what they mean in neoclassical economics (that is, general changes in prices); rather the terms refer to decreases or increases in the money supply broadly defined to include time deposits. Hayek and, especially, Rothbard are interpreted here as supporting a general monetary contraction as the proper remedy for an artificially created boom.

3 Despite the importance of the Ricardo effect in Hayek's economics the debate is not discussed in Friedrich A. Hayek, *Hayek on Hayek*, ed. Stephen Kresge and Leif Wenar, Chicago: University of Chicago, 1994.

4 In *Austrian Economics in America*, Vaughn does not discuss the Austrian theory of production in any detail, suggesting (incorrectly) that active research on this subject has stopped. An important exception is Mark Skousen (1990), where the subject is reviewed with much insight.

See also:

Austrian School of Economics; Business Cycle Theory (I) and (II); Interest, Theories of; Kaldor, Lord Nicholas; Keynes, John Maynard; Keynesian Revolution; Monetary Policy; von Hayek, Friedrich A.; Wicksell, Knut.

Bibliography

Haberler, Gottfried (1947), *Prosperity and Depression*, Geneva: League of Nations.

Hagemann, Harold and Hans-Michael Trautwein (1995), 'Cantillon and Ricardo Effects: Hayek's Contributions to Business Cycle Theory', Amsterdam: Conference on Austrian Economics at the Tinbergen Institute.

Hayek, F.A. (1931), *Prices and Production*, London: Routledge & Sons.

Hayek, F.A. (1939), *Profits, Interest and Investment*, London: Routledge & Sons.

Hayek, F.A. (1941), *Pure Theory of Capital*, Chicago: University of Chicago Press.

Hayek, F.A. (1942), 'A Comment', *Economica*, **9**, (36), November, pp. 383–5.

Hayek, F.A. (1949), 'The Ricardo Effect', in F.A. Hayek (ed.), *Individualism and Economic Order*, London: Routledge.

Hayek, F.A. (1969), 'Three Elucidations of the Ricardo Effect', *Journal of Political Economy*, **77**, (2), March/April, pp. 274–85.

Hayek, F.A. (1972), *A Tiger by the Tail*, London: Institute for Economic Affairs.

Junakar, P.N. (1987), 'Acceleration Principle', in John Eatwell, Murray Milgate and Peter Newman (eds), *The New Palgrave: A Dictionary of Economics*, vol. 1, New York: Stockton Press.

Kaldor, Nicholas (1942), 'Professor Hayek and the Concertina-effect', *Economica*, November.

Lachmann, Ludwig M. (1940), 'A Reconsideration of the Austrian Theory of Industrial Fluctuations', *Economica*, **7**, (26), May, pp. 179–96.

Lerner, Abba P. (1983), 'A Keynesian on Hayek', in David Colander (ed.), *Selected Economic Writings of Abba P. Lerner*, New York: New York University Press.

Maki, Uskali (1990), 'Scientific Realism and Austrian Explanation', *Review of Political Economy*, **2**, pp. 31–44.

Meacci, Ferdinando (1995), 'Hayek and the Deepening of Capital', in M. Colonna, H. Hagemann and O.F. Hamouda (eds), *Capitalism, Socialism and Knowledge: The Economics of F.A. Hayek*, Vol. II, Aldershot: Edward Elgar.

Moss, Laurence S. and Karen I. Vaughn (1986), 'Hayek's Ricardo Effect: A Second Look', *History of Political Economy*, **18**, (4), Winter, pp. 545–65.

O'Driscoll, G.P. (1977), *Economics as a Coordination Problem: The Contribution of Friedrich A. Hayek*, Kansas City: Sheed, Andrews and McMeel.

Pivetti, Massimo (1987), 'Wicksell's Theory of Capital', in John Eatwell, Murray Milgate and Peter Newman (eds), *The New Palgrave: A Dictionary of Economics*, vol. 4, New York: Stockton Press.

Rothbard, Murray N. (1963), *America's Great Depression*, Princeton: D. Van Nostrand.

Rothbard, Murray (1987), 'Time Preference', in John Eatwell, Murray Milgate and Peter Newman (eds), *The New Palgrave: A Dictionary of Economics*, vol. 3, New York: Stockton Press.

Samuelson, Paul A. and William D. Nordhaus (1995), *Economics*, New York: McGraw-Hill.

Skousen, Mark (1990), *The Structure of Production*, New York: New York University Press.

Steele, G.R. (1988), 'Hayek's Ricardo Effect', *History of Political Economy*, **20**, (4), winter, pp. 669–72.

Tsiang, Sho-Chieh (1947), *The Variations of Real Wages and Profit Margins in Relation to the Trade Cycle*, London: Sir Isaac Pitman.

Vaughn, Karen I. (1994), *Austrian Economics in America: The Migration of a Tradition*, Cambridge: Cambridge University Press.

von Mises, Ludwig (1934), *The Theory of Money and Credit*, New Haven: Yale University Press.

von Mises, Ludwig (1980), *Planning for Freedom and Sixteen Other Essays and Addresses*, South Holland, Ill.: Libertarian Press.

Wicksell, Knut (1936), 'Interest and Prices', London: Macmillan.
Zamagni, Stefano (1984), 'Ricardo and Hayek Effects in a Fixed Model of Traverse', *Oxford Economic Papers*, **36**, November (supplement), pp. 135–51.
Zamagni, Stefano (1987), 'Ricardo–Hayek Effect', in John Eatwell, Murray Milgate and Peter Newman (eds), *The New Palgrave: A Dictionary of Economics*, vol. 3, New York: Stockton Press.

Robbins, Lord Lionel

Lionel Robbins was born in 1898 at Sipson Farm, west of London. His father, Rowland Robbins, was a progressive leader in agricultural and community affairs who served as president of the Farmers' Union and High Sheriff of Middlesex.

Robbins volunteered for military service during World War I and was wounded in action in France. In 1920, he entered the London School of Economics, where he came under the influence of a group of important economic thinkers including Edwin Cannan and Hugh Dalton. After receiving his BSc degree in 1923, he taught at New College, Oxford and at the London School of Economics, where his association spanned a period of over 50 years.

Robbins made a major contribution to the methodology of economics in his *An Essay on the Nature and Significance of Economic Science* (1932) in which he defended the theoretical and deductive approach in economics and established what has become one of the best-known definitions of the nature of the field: 'Economics is the science which studies human behaviour as a relationship between ends and scarce means which have alternative uses.'

> From the point of view of the economist, the conditions of human existence exhibit four fundamental characteristics. The ends are various. The time and the means for achieving these ends are limited and capable of alternative application. At the same time the ends have different importance. ... But when time and the means for achieving ends are limited and capable of alternative application, and the ends are capable of being distinguished in order of importance, then behaviour necessarily assumes the form of choice. Every act which involves time and scarce means for the achievement of one end involves the relinquishment of their use in the achievement of another. It has an economic aspect. (2nd edn, pp. 12–14)

Robbins's position represented a sharp break from the tradition of the classical economists who defined the ends of economic activity as improvements in material welfare and the means as real costs. Robbins followed the ideas of Menger and the Austrians who emphasized alternative cost, considered both material and non-material benefits and costs in their analysis of economic actions, and included time among the important constraints on choice.

In his *Essay*, Robbins argued that scientific economics was comprised of positive as opposed to normative propositions (or as 'is' v. 'ought'). This followed the reasoning of earlier writers such as Hume and Weber who, like Robbins, sought to distinguish value judgements from positive economics. Robbins questioned the validity of welfare economics of the type advanced by Pigou because its conclusions were largely based on interpersonal comparisons of utility.

Robbins was criticized by defenders of the Cambridge school for attempting to narrow the scope of economics, for recommending a stance of ethical neutrality among economists and for implying that the role of economists in policy making should be more limited than was then widely accepted. Robbins always denied that he wanted economists to avoid giving policy advice but he insisted that they should make their value judgements explicit and not attempt to mask them under the rubric of economic science. He returned to the subject of the *Essay* in one of his last public lectures:

> It is sometimes questioned whether in the discussion of any social or economic relationships this quality of what the Germans call *Wertfreiheit* is attainable. No less an authority than Gunnar Myrdal has devoted a whole book to the argument that, explicitly or implicitly, all propositions of economic theory…must involve judgments of value. I do not agree with this position. I don't think that the proposition that, if the market is free and demand exceeds supply, prices will tend to rise, has any ethical content whatever. Nor do I concede that recognition of the consequences on investment of disparities between rates of interest and rates of return depends in the least on the political preposessions of the economist who perceives it. (Robbins 1981, p. 4)

Robbins had a major role as an economic policy advisor in Britain during and after World War II. He was director of the Economic Section of the War Cabinet and after the war he worked with Keynes in designing the International Monetary Fund and the World Bank. Like Keynes, Robbins made important contributions to the arts as chairman of the National Gallery, director of the Royal Opera House, president of the British Academy and trustee of the Tate Gallery. He was also chairman of the *Financial Times* and of a national committee (known as the 'Robbins Committee') which redesigned higher education in Britain to make it more democratic and widely available. He received a life peerage in 1959, adopting the title 'Lord Robbins of Clare Market' in recognition of his academic home, the London School of Economics.

Robbins was a noted historian of economic thought and for many years gave one of the most popular lecture series at the LSE. He had a deep understanding of and appreciation for the classical economists and sought to rescue them from the popular view that they were doctrinaire defenders of laissez faire. He considered his book, *Robert Torrens and the Evolution of Classical Economics* (1958) to be the work 'by which I would most wish to be judged as a scholar'.

Robbins's relationship with Keynes was a complicated one. He was appointed by Keynes to the Committee of Economists of the Economic Advisory Council in 1930 in the depths of the Great Depression, but resigned from the committee in protest over the protectionism and economic interventionism recommended under Keynes's leadership. He elaborated his criticism of these policies in his *The Great Depression* (1934) but later expressed regret at having written the book and called his dispute with Keynes 'the greatest mistake of my professional career'. Despite this apology, he maintained throughout his life a position nearer to the classical school than to Keynes on the issue of the proper role of government in the economy. His personal admiration for Keynes was very great, however. In a review celebrating the publication of Keynes's *Essays in Biography*, Robbins wrote:

> It is in such papers...that the reader, who did not know Keynes, can get some idea of the more intimate characteristics of the man himself. There is the same expository force and depth of perception and the same felicity of phrase and cadence as elsewhere. But...there is a wider background of the author's values and wisdom – with all his worldly success, his devotion to Cambridge and its tradition of high thinking and plain living. ...As one reads one can hear him speaking and get some notion of how infinitely outstanding and rare a personality he was.

Robbins died in 1984, having never recovered from a severe stroke suffered two years earlier. Among the many tributes to his life and work was one published in the *Financial Times* which called him 'the true Renaissance man'.

PHILIP E. SORENSEN

See also:
Austrian School of Economics; Classical Economics; Depression, The Great; Economics, The Art of; Keynes, John Maynard; Marshall, Alfred; Pigou, Arthur C.

Bibliography
Kirzner, Israel (1960), *The Economic Point of View*, Menlo Park, CA: Institute for Humane Studies, ch. 6, pp. 108–45.
O'Brien, D.P. (1988), *Lionel Robbins*, London: Macmillan.
Robbins, Lionel (1932, 2nd edn 1935), *An Essay on the Nature and Significance of Economic Science*, London: Macmillan.
Robbins, Lionel (1934), *The Great Depression*, London: Macmillan.
Robbins, Lionel (1958), *Robert Torrens and the Evolution of Classical Economics*, London: Macmillan.
Robbins, Lionel (1970), *The Evolution of Modern Economic Theory*, London: Macmillan.
Robbins, Lionel (1971), *Autobiography of an Economist*, London: Macmillan.
Robbins, Lionel (1973), 'Review of J.M. Keynes, *Essays in Biography. Collected Works, vol. X*', *Economic Journal*, **83**, pp. 530–31.
Robbins, Lionel (1981), 'Economics and Political Economy', *American Economic Review*, **71**, (2), May, pp. 1–10.

Robertson, Sir Dennis H.

Dennis Robertson was born, the youngest of four boys in a family of six, at Lowestoft, Suffolk on 23 May 1890. His father was James Robertson, one of a long line of Scots teachers and clerics; his mother Constance Elizabeth Wilson. His father had been a fellow in classics of Jesus College, Cambridge before taking up schoolmastering at Rugby, at Harrow and eventually, as headmaster, at Haileybury. From 1890, when he resigned from Haileybury on a matter of principle, James was vicar of Whittlesford, a village just south of Cambridge, where he also devoted himself to the education of his children.

Dennis was educated at home until he went to Eton as second King's Scholar in 1902. He then proceeded to Trinity College, Cambridge in 1908 as a classical scholar but, after achieving a first in Part I of the Classical Tripos in 1910, he switched to economics and got another first in Part II of the Economics Tripos in 1912. His director of studies and principal supervisor was a young King's don, J.M. Keynes. After his tripos, Robertson stayed on as a research student, preparing a fellowship dissertation for Trinity. As so often happens, the first version was unsuccessful (although it won the university's Cobden Prize) but the second won him a prize fellowship in 1914. The dissertation was published unrevised in 1915 as *A Study of Industrial Fluctuation*.

The outbreak of war prevented revisions. Robertson joined up on 4 August 1914. He spent much of the war in the Middle East. Although his war was generally a quiet one, he did win a Military Cross in 1917 and took part in the campaign in Palestine and the occupation of Constantinople. He did not return to Cambridge and his Trinity fellowship until the autumn of 1919.

At Cambridge, he was a university lecturer in economics from 1924 to 1928; Girdlers' lecturer in economics, 1928–30 and reader in economics, 1930–38. During his years in Cambridge he also served (or began to serve) with A.L. Bowley in an examination of the statistical and other information on economic conditions in India and on means of improving them (1934), as a consultant to the League of Nations project on business cycles financed by the Rockefeller Foundation (1936–9) and as a member of the Committee on Economic Information of the Economic Advisory Council (1936–9). In October 1938, he accepted the Cassel Professorship of Economics with special reference to money and banking at LSE, but he taught at the School for only two terms before the outbreak of World War II took him into the Treasury as an adviser on overseas finance. In October 1944, he returned to Cambridge to succeed A.C. Pigou as professor of political economy, a post which he held until his retirement in 1957. In 1944–6, he was a member of the Royal Commission on Equal Pay and, throughout the Cambridge period, he continued to give advice, mostly on an informal basis, to the Bank of England and the Treasury. In the first year of his retirement he served as one of the three 'wise men' on the Council on Prices, Productivity and Incomes. Thereafter his life was centered on Cambridge, where he died on 21 April 1963. His honors included a fellowship of the British Academy (1932), a string of honorary degrees, including Harvard (1936) and Columbia (1954), a CMG (1944) and a knighthood (1953).

Robertson is best known as a monetary economist. However his fellowship dissertation might be regarded as an early example of real business cycle theory, with money not making an appearance until the book was four-fifths over (Goodhart, in Presley (ed.) 1992). His Cambridge Economic Handbook, *Money* (1922, rev. edns 1924, 1928; new edn 1948) marked his entry into the monetary field. He consolidated his position with *Banking Policy and the Price-Level* (1926) and a steady stream of theoretical articles and commentaries, many of which were eventually collected together in five volumes published in his lifetime. These contributions could be regarded as putting monetary flesh on his original cyclical notions. But he continued to make contributions to trade-cycle theory right up to the 1950s. He also involved himself in questions of industrial structure with another Cambridge Handbook, *The Control of Industry* (1923, rev. edn, 1928; new edn, with S.R. Dennison, 1960). But if one wanted to cover the full range and richness of Robertson's contributions, particularly in his contributions to the 'empty economic boxes' debate, to the representative firm discussions of the later 1920s and to utility theory, not to mention his highly polished *Lectures on Economic Principles* (1957–9) and *Britain in the World Economy* (1953), one would also need to add micreconomics and international economics to his areas of interest and strength.

Much of Robertson's contribution to monetary theory reflected interaction with the evolving ideas of J.M. Keynes or, later, his disciples. Not only did Keynes teach him and 'supervise' his dissertation, but Keynes also commissioned *Money* from, the then unknown Robertson in 1920. Robertson's *Banking Policy* and the 1928 edition of *Money* also bear strong very marks of collaboration, as does Keynes's *Treatise on Money* (1930). Indeed the interaction was such that Keynes would later acknowledge Robertson in the *Economic Journal* as 'my parent in the paths of errancy' (Moggridge, 1973, *CW*, Vol. XIV, p. 202, n. 2). After the publication of the *Treatise*, reaction began to dominate – a change made clear with their break over the *General Theory* (1936). After the break, as Paul Samuelson remarked, 'a new note enters into Robertson's writing ... a querulous note of protest over the pretension and correctness of so-called new ideas and a somewhat repetitive defense of earlier wisdom' (1963, p. 520). The break with Keynes did not prevent effective, if occasionally prickly, collaboration, in the construction of the post-1945 international monetary order that emerged at Bretton Woods. But the disputes with Keynes's Cambridge disciples, in part a result of his self-acknowledged, long-standing inability to get on with Joan Robinson, continued, with greater intensity, after Keynes's death, poisoning the intellectual life of the faculty, with results that still color Cambridge economics.

The difficulties of the break were exacerbated by how much Keynes and Robertson had in common: they 'were both Marshallians, using terminologies that sprang from the same roots, and looked alike' (Hicks, 1966, p. 17). Both of them had abandoned certain pieces of traditional theory such as Say's Law and found it illuminating to cast their theories in savings–investment terms. As some sympathetic observers have noted, for all their differences, Robertson and Keynes (but not necessarily Keynes's disciples) were often more alike than Keynes or, more particularly, Robertson was prepared to admit (Wilson, 1953; in Presley (ed.) 1992). But when directly challenged by Tom Wilson to prepare, as Robertson put it, 'a full length synthetic theory of Money or Fluctuations', he replied:

> I am too old and too lazy! But even if I were younger and less lazy, I think history had made it impossible. I believe that, once Keynes had made up his mind to go the way he did, it was my particular function to go for the 'damned [jessant] dots'[1] and to go on pegging away at them (as is still necessary). It will not be easy for *anyone* for another twenty years to produce a positive and constructive work which isn't in large measure a commentary on Keynes – that is the measure of his triumph. For me it would be psychologically impossible, and the attempt is not worth making. (Robinson to Wilson, 31 October 1953)

D.E. Moggridge

Note

1 See Wilson's introduction to his article (p. 98):

> Professor Hicks once said of Keynes that he was 'the most impressionist' of all great economists, and went on to observe that Professor Robertson's criticisms 'sometimes remind me of a man examining a Seurat with a microscope and denouncing the shape of the individual dots'. There may be an element of truth in this remark about some of Professor Robertson's comments; but it would scarcely apply to all of them.

The reference is to J.R. Hicks (1942), 'The Monetary Theory of D.H. Robertson', *Economica*, **9**, (39), February, pp. 54–7.

See also:

Business Cycle Theory (I) and (II); Government Investment Programs (the Socialization of Investment); Keynes, John Maynard; Keynesian Revolution; Marshall, Alfred; Monetary Policy; Money; Pigou, Arthur C.; Treasury View.

Bibliography

Dennison, S.R. and J.R. Presley (eds) (1992), *Robertson on Economic Policy*, London: Macmillan.
Hicks, J.R. (1966), 'A Memoir: Dennis Holme Robertson, 1890–1963', in J.R. Hicks (ed.), *D.H. Robertson, Essays in Money and Interest*, London: Fontana.

Johnson, E.S. and H.G. Johnson (1978), *The Shadow of Keynes: Understanding Keynes, Cambridge and Keynesian Economics*, Chicago: University of Chicago Press.

Keynes, John M. (1930), *A Treatise on Money*, London: Macmillan.

Moggridge, D.E. (ed.) (1973), *The Collected Writings of John Maynard Keynes*, Vol. XIV, *The General Theory and After: Defence and Development*, London: Macmillan.

Presley, J.R. (1978), *Robertsonian Economics: An Examination of the Work of Sir D.H. Robertson on Industrial Fluctuation*, London: Macmillan.

Presley, J.R. (ed.) (1992), *Essays on Robertsonian Economics*, London: Macmillan.

Robertson, D.H. (1915), *A Study of Industrial Fluctuation*, London: P.S. King & Son Ltd.

Robertson, D.H. (1922), *Money*, London: Nisbet & Co. Ltd., rev. edns 1924, 1928; new edn; with two additional chapters, 1948.

Robertson, D.H. (1923), *The Control of Industry*, rev. edn 1928; new edn (with S.R. Dennison) 1960.

Robertson, D.H. (1926), *Banking Policy and the Price-Level*, London: P.S. King & Son Ltd., reprinted with corrections 1932.

Robertson, D.H. (1931), *Economic Fragments*, London: P.S. King & Son Ltd.

Robertson, D.H. (1934), *A Scheme for an Economic Census of India: Report by A.L. Bowley and D.H. Robertson*, New Delhi: Government of India Press.

Robertson, D.H. (1940), *Essays in Monetary Theory*, London: P.S. King & Son Ltd.

Robertson, D.H. (1952), *Utility and All That*, London: George Allen & Unwin.

Robertson, D.H. (1953), *Britain in the World Economy*, London: George Allen & Unwin.

Robertson, D.H. (1956), *Economic Commentaries*, London: Staples Press.

Robertson, D.H. (1957–9), *Lectures on Economic Principles*, 3 vols, London: Staples Press.

Robertson, D.H. (1960), *Growth, Wages, Money*, Cambridge: Cambridge University Press.

Robertson, D.H. (1963), *Memorandum to the Canadian Royal Commission on Banking and Finance 1962*, International Finance Section, Princeton University, *Essays in International Finance*, No. 42, May.

Robertson, D.H. (1966), *Essays in Money and Interest* (ed. J.R. Hicks), London: Fontana.

Robertson, D.H. and A.C. Pigou (1931), *Economic Essays and Addresses*, London: P.S. King & Son Ltd.

Samuelson, P.A. (1963), 'D.H. Robertson, 1890–1963', *Quarterly Journal of Economics*, **77**, (4), November, pp. 517–36.

Wilson, T. (1953), 'Professor Robertson on Effective Demand and the Trade Cycle', *Economic Journal*, **63**, (251), September, pp. 553–78.

Robinson, Joan

Joan Violet Robinson (née Maurice) was born at Camberley, Surrey, on 31 October 1903. She studied at the University of Cambridge, graduating in 1925 and, after a few years abroad, returned with her husband and economist E.A.G. Robinson to Cambridge, where she was based for the rest of her life. She started her formal career as a junior assistant lecturer in 1931 and retired as a professor in 1971, although she remained intellectually active after that. She died in Cambridge on 5 August 1983.

Robinson's published work spans almost every area of economic theory and also deals with economic policy and broader political economic issues. A bibliography of her writings (Marcuzzo, 1991) lists 378 distinct publications (books and articles) between 1930 and 1985. Areas to which she made significant contributions include imperfect competition, international trade and payments, theory of employment, development economics, growth theory, Marxian economics, inflation, technical change, monetary theory, capital theory and methodological issues (especially concerning equilibrium and time). Keynes was the major influence on her economic work and views, although she was also influenced by other economists, including Ricardo, Marx, Marshall, Wicksell, Luxemburg, Harrod, Kalecki and Sraffa. This entry focuses on her work directly related to Keynesian economics; for more comprehensive, brief discussions, see Harcourt (1979), Gram and Walsh (1983) and Pasinetti (1987).

In the 1930s, when Keynes worked on *The General Theory*, Robinson was an important member of the group of young economists called the 'Cambridge Circus' (which additionally included Harrod, Kahn, Meade, Austin Robinson and Sraffa) which regularly met with Keynes to discuss his work, and which arguably played a key role in the evolution of the book. During this time she wrote two books (1937a, 1937b) attempting to clarify and popularize Keynes's theory of employment. Robinson at this time also extended Keynes's work to open economies (being one of the first to do so), developing in this context the notion of 'beggar-thy-neighbour' policies.

On the theory of unemployment, following Keynes's Marshallian method, Robinson focused on the problem of decision making (especially regarding investment by firms) between 'an irrevocable past and an uncertain future', and stressed the importance of business expectations in determining the level of employment. She argued that a fall in wages and prices is likely to reduce investment owing to its adverse effects on expected profits, and thus to exacerbate the problem of unemployment, *pace* the neoclassical Keynesian approach which implies that downward wage flexibility results in full employment. Dismissing this approach, she instead espoused that of Kalecki (whose work she regarded as being 'more robust than Keynes''), because of his emphasis on imperfect competition and on the differential savings behavior of wage earners and profit recipients (see Robinson, 1951–80, Vol. V, pp. 184–96).

Robinsons's most original contributions to Keynesian economics are in growth theory, in which she has extended Keynes's short-period analysis (in the Marshallian sense) to the long period. Her most ambitious work in this vein is Robinson (1956), where she developed a two-sector model with a finite number of techniques to examine the interaction of distribution, accumulation, technical change, entrepreneurial expectations and competition. She used the concept of 'Golden Ages', in which the economy is on a steady-state growth path with full employment, and provided a taxonomy of other growth regimes for examining the difficulties of attaining such a path. Her subsequent writing (Robinson, 1951–80, 1962) clarified and extended her analysis in various ways. Her rich analysis incorporates the roles of technical conditions, investment policy (which depends on expectations), savings by firms and rentiers, the state of competition, the behavior of money wages and financial conditions. To summarize parts of her analysis she introduced a diagram to depict the two-sided relationship between capital accumulation and the profit rate: higher (expected) profitability results in higher (desired) accumulation, while higher (realized) profitability makes higher (actual) accumulation possible. This analysis, which shows that the growth of output and employment depends mainly on capital accumulation, which is in turn determined primarily by business expectations (and which may not ensure full employment growth) has become the centerpiece of neo-Keynesian growth theory.

In the realm of methodology, Robinson raised important issues concerning the concepts of equilibrium (distinguishing between two notions of equilibrium, one as an outcome of a process and the other as a notional device to examine long-run tendencies in which expectations are realized) and time (distinguishing between logical and historical time) in economics. She criticized neoclassical economics for its tendency to interpret equilibrium as the outcome of a process and its use of the mechanical concept of logical time, dubbing the neoclassical synthesis Keynesian approach (as exemplified, for instance, by the IS/LM model) 'bastard Keynesianism' (Robinson, 1951–80, Vol. III, pp. 53–69, Vol. V, pp. 127–8). She also criticized the neoclassical notion of capital and its theory of distribution, and participated vociferously in the Cambridge controversies in capital theory (see Robinson, 1951–80, Vol. II). But, while she used the Sraffian framework in her criticism of neoclassical theory, she was unwilling to follow the neo-Ricardians in accepting a classical long-period equilibrium interpretation of Keynes's theory of unemployment in which expectational factors are excluded from consideration.

Robinson can justifiably be seen as one of the leading critics of orthodox economic theory and perhaps the foremost bearer of Keynes's theoretical mantle. She has gained the attention and respect of the mainstream of the profession (see Feiwell, 1989) and her work remains a major inspiration of Post Keynesian economists who are concerned with understanding and overcoming the problems of unemployment and inequality in capitalist economies.

AMITAVA KRISHNA DUTT

See also:

Cambridge Circus; Harrod, Sir Roy; Interest, Theories of; Kahn, Lord Richard F.; Kalecki, Michał; Keynes, John Maynard; Keynesian Revolution; Marshall, Alfred; Meade, James E.; Post Keynesian School of Economics; Samuelson, Paul A.; Solow, Robert M.; Sraffa, Piero; Wicksell, Knut.

Bibliography

Feiwell, George R. (ed.) (1989), *Joan Robinson and Modern Economic Theory*, New York: New York University Press.

Gram, Harvey and Vivian Walsh (1983), 'Joan Robinson's Economics in Retrospect', *Journal of Economic Literature*, **21**, (2) June, pp. 518–50.

Harcourt, Geoff C. (1979), 'Robinson, Joan', in D.L. Sills (ed.), *International Encyclopedia of the Social Sciences, Biographical Supplement*, New York: Free Press.

Marcuzzo, Maria Cristina (1991), 'Bibliography: The Writings of Joan Robinson', in I. Rima (ed.), *The Joan Robinson Legacy*, Armonk, NY: M.E. Sharpe.

Pasinetti, Luigi L. (1987), 'Robinson, Joan Violet', in John Eatwell, Murray Milgate and Peter Newman (eds), *The New Palgrave: A Dictionary of Economics*, vol. 3, London: Macmillan.

Robinson, Joan V. (1937a), *Essays in the Theory of Employment*, London: Macmillan.

Robinson, Joan V. (1937b), *Introduction to the Theory of Employment*, London: Macmillan.

Robinson, Joan V. (1951–80), *Collected Economic Papers*, Vol. I, 1951, Vol. II, 1960, Vol. III, 1965, Vol. IV, 1973, Vol. V, 1980, Oxford: Basil Blackwell.

Robinson, Joan V. (1956), *The Accumulation of Capital*, London: Macmillan.

Robinson, Joan V. (1962), *Essays in the Theory of Economic Growth*, London: Macmillan.

Rothschild, Kurt W.

Kurt W. Rothschild, one of the most famous and prominent of a long list of modern Austrian economists, was born on 21 October 1914. He attended the University of Vienna where, in 1938, he earned his law degree. Upon completion of his studies he emigrated to the United Kingdom for the purpose of studying economics at the University of Glasgow in Scotland. After he completed his studies Rothschild was appointed a lecturer in economics at the University of Glasgow, a position which he held for the next seven years (1940–47). In 1947, Rothschild returned to his native land. From 1947 to 1966, he was employed as a senior research fellow by the prestigious Austrian Institute of Economic Research. From 1966 until his retirement in 1985, he was professor of economics at the University of Linz. He was an inspiring teacher and some of his former students have become prominent economists in their own right. Ewald Nowotny and Egon Matzner, known for their work in the areas of macroeconomic aspects of taxation and full employment policies, respectively, come to mind. Since his retirement Rothschild has returned to the Austrian Institute, where he is retained as a consultant. His work in economics has earned him an international reputation, as is evidenced by his honorary degrees from Bremen (1984), Aachen (1987), Augsburg (1990) and Leicester (1995) and by his visiting professorships at Vienna, Glasgow and Minneapolis.

Rothschild is a gifted theoretician and an outstanding empirical researcher. He is a prolific writer, being the author, co-author and editor of 140 book reviews, 117 journal articles, 113 articles in edited volumes and 25 books. In this outpouring of work Rothschild makes every effort to link the pure theory of economics to practical considerations of the day: the development of policy proposals which would be considered seriously by politicians is an important aspect of his writings. While Rothschild must be considered a leading proponent of Keynesian economics in Austria, his writings can be divided into six major areas of exploration: price theory, labor economics, the theory of income distribution and growth, economic policy and political economy. In his 1947 paper, 'Price theory and oligopoly', Rothschild criticized neoclassical economics for its inadequate discussion of the problem of uncertainty. In this article he focused on the very important point that profit maximization is very difficult to achieve in the case of oligopolies and under uncertainty. Rothschild (1947, p. 450) concludes that, 'since uncertainty is pervasive, the desire for secure profits is every bit as important as optimisation, and cannot be reduced to a species of long-run maximisation'.

Three aspects of his work in the area of labor economics can be identified. First, he uses marginal productivity theory to analyse the firm's demand curve for labor. Second, he states that imperfect, not perfect, competition is the norm in the labor market. Third, in his 1971 survey of the Phillips curve literature, Rothschild argues that the existence of a negatively sloped Phillips curve is evidence of the bargaining power of unions and the resultant wage push effects on the unemployment–inflation trade-off. In the area of growth theory Rothschild has taken a position that is quite different from that of Kahn. In his 1959 paper, Kahn examines the assumptions of the 'Golden Age'. Rothschild, on the other hand, takes individuals to task for ignoring the impact of historical, institutional and social data which affect the operation of the invisible hand. Thus, in his work on growth theory, he addresses the question of what happens exactly when the heroic assumptions of the Golden Age are relaxed. This point of view is well established in his writings on political economy: there are no hard and fast rules, only informed judgement. Economic policy making is an art, not a science.

In the area of economic policy Rothschild may be placed in the category of a moderate Austro-Keynesian. That is to say, when advocating economic policies he favored the use of demand-side policies which encouraged investment by reducing uncertainty. Those policies should be combined with supply-side policies designed to control the rate of inflation. Such policies included the use of interest rate subsidies, generous depreciation allowances, incomes policies and a fixed exchange rate system which tied the Austrian currency to the German mark.

Kurt W. Rothschild's scientific work is challenging everybody who wants to see what type of research has been done out- and inside mainstream economics. He was always challenging traditional neoclassical economics, but in most cases he asked the important questions on a wide range of issues. Criticism of the traditional economics was a major challenge for him and quite often he pointed out weaknesses of neoclassical theory. He also asked relevant policy questions and developed practical answers to these questions. He was always an extremely friendly and stimulating researcher. He could be quite critical, but his criticism was always positive and inspiring.

FRIEDRICH SCHNEIDER

See also:

Demand Management; Domar, Evsey D; Harcourt, Geoff; Harrod, Sir Roy; Kahn, Lord Richard F.; Phillips Curve; Solow, Robert M.

Bibliography

Kahn, R.F. (1959), 'Exercises in the Analysis of Growth', *Oxford Economic Papers*, NS, **11**, (1), June, pp. 146–63.

Rothschild, Kurt W. (1942), 'A note on advertising', *Economic Journal*, **52**, (1), April, pp. 112–21.

Rothschild, Kurt W. (1944), 'The small nation and world trade', *Economic Journal*, **54**, (1), April, pp. 26–40.

Rothschild, Kurt W. (1947), 'Price theory and oligopoly', *Economic Journal*, **57**, (2), September, pp. 299–320.

Rothschild, Kurt W. (1954), *The Theory of Wages*, Oxford: Blackwell.

Rothschild, Kurt W. (1965), 'Illusions about Money Illusion?', *Journal of Political Economy*, **70**, (3), June, pp. 456–71.

Rothschild, Kurt W. (1971), 'The Phillips curve and all that', *Scottish Journal of Political Economy*, **18**, (2), August, pp. 245–80.

Rothschild, Kurt W. (1978), 'Is There Such a Thing as Unemployment?', *Kyklos*, **31**, (1), March, pp. 21–35.

Samuelson, Paul A.

Paul Anthony Samuelson was born in 1915 in Gary, Indiana. After attending 14 schools in Indiana, Florida and Chicago, he entered the University of Chicago in 1932. His graduate work in economics was completed at Harvard (1935–40). After three years as a Harvard junior fellow, he did not receive the anticipated assistant professorship and accepted a position at MIT, where he remained. 'Economics in a Golden Age: A Personal Memoir' (*Collected Scientific Papers*, Vol. IV, 1977, p. 278) presents useful biographical insights. Samuelson's posterity as a leading world economist is assured, with contributions to all major branches of economic theory. He led revolutionary shifts in the organization and content of formal economics. Mathematically conditioned economics displaced fact-related, historical, institutionally focused social and political economics. Strategically located at Harvard in the late 1930s, he combined his Chicago-initiated affinity for neoclassicism with the new Keynesianism. His widely used principles text presented the new division of economic study and analysis into micro- and macroeconomic sections, supplanting the preceding convention of production, consumption, exchange and distribution.

He has received all of economics' top professional honors: the first John Bates Clark medal (1947), president of the Econometric Society (1951), the American Economic Association (1961) and the International Economic Association (1965–8) and he was the first United States economist to win the Nobel Memorial Prize in Economics (1970). His professional position was established with his first book, *Foundations* (1947), based on his 1940 doctoral dissertation. His extensive contributions are assembled in five volumes of collected papers (1966–86). The last two volumes include policy-oriented pieces in non-academic publications, excluding his *Newsweek* column (1973–81). Continuing commentary on Samuelson's economics is represented in Feiwel (1982) and Brown and Solow (1983). Fischer's detailed essay (1987) emphasizes Samuelson's theoretical contributions, noting the problem of evaluating such a range of diverse works.

Samuelson's fundamental positions on method and theory were established at the outset of his career. While commonly associated with the rise of aggregative economics, from the beginning, his major interest was Walrasian micro-equilibrium relationships. In the *Foundations* his mathematically grounded, positivist analytic vision was focused on an empirically meaningful comparative equilibrium schema, based on two general principles. First, in contrast to the behavioral assumption of orthodox equilibrium analytics, his maximization argument holds that mathematical properties indicate the comparative-static properties of the analytic system. Second, Samuelson's theory of revealed preference (1938) was oriented towards elimination of the idea of an individual utility function. He developed significant linkages between revealed preference, demand theory, index numbers and welfare principles. He accepted a Bergsonian social welfare function and Pareto optimum as bases for social welfare analysis. The operational econometric content of revealed preference for demand and welfare theory remains debatable. His contributions to growth, production and capital theory present a functional link between analytical method and content. Linked to the 'two-Cambridge' reswitching, capital controversy, they illustrate problems inherent in wedding mathematical modeling to the requisites of science. Committed to neoclassicism, to the marginal productivity theory, he rejected as the 'classicists' [that is, Smith–Ricardo] delusion', the idea that there are significant conceptual differences between labor and capital. Both are analytically reducible to infinitely divisible, marginal monetary units. Within the pseudo-surrogate production function, capital is reduced to putty clay, an early anticipation of 'virtual reality'. His voluminous research and writing did not lead to a Samuelsonian system or school.

Samuelson's formal analyses and asides on economic thought reinforced his conservative political economy. In his equilibrium-dominated neoclassical value and production theory he eschewed such non-compatible concepts as economic surplus (Marshallian or Marxian) and increasing returns. His interpretations of Smith and Marx derogated or played down their grounding on realities of human behavior and technology, especially their principles of labor value and cognizance of capitalist power relationships. For example, 'Adam Smith held a labor theory of value for about as long as it takes a grown man to turn two pages of his book' (*Collected Scientific Papers*, Vol. III, 1972, p. 271). Arguably Smith still held it 250 pages later in identifying a functional relationship between profits and the value-added (surplus) increments of productive labor. Samuelson's contributions to macro theory (for example, the multiplier–accelerator relationships) were extended to the possibility of fine-tuned macroeconomic policy. His neoclassical synthesis embodied reincarnation of Say's Law, reinforcing both the aura of general equilibrium and a truncated, reactionary, 'bastard' Keynesianism.

Samuelson recognized the truism that his posterity would reflect changes in the worlds of ideas and 'reality'. Perhaps his contributions to both theory and policy will evoke Aquinas rather than Einstein. His analytical tensions are noted in continuing criticism: theory is pre-eminent, yet actual economic performance remains most important; logic is central, but factual disproof should be dominant. Still, his Popperian falsificationism contrasts with the assertion that 'It takes a theory to kill a theory, facts can only dent the theorist's hide.' Mathematics is the scientific economist's only effective language, yet he was a master of often caustic rhetoric. He both denied and recognized a methodological, metaphorical association of economics with physics (Mirowski, 1989, pp. 182–3).

With the reality of stagflation, macroeconomic policy in the United States has become moribund. Keynesian fiscal policy, incorporating a cyclically balanced budget, reduction of inequalities and social priority planning, was still-born. As Samuelson foresaw, exclusive reliance on high interest rate counterinflationary monetary policy conduces to long-term stagnation. More important are changes in analysis, the interrelated demise of Samuelson's methodological base, his grounding in positivism, modernism and foundationalism. Mathematical analysis became extended beyond what he saw as its useful bounds. Successful formulation of an equilibrium-based 'general theory of economic theories' (*Foundations*, 1983, p. xxvi) is now widely regarded as neoclassical–imperialist fantasy.

WARREN S. GRAMM

See also:

Demand Management; Hansen, Alvin H.; Harcourt, Geoff; Hicks, Sir John R.; IS/LM Model and Diagram; Keynes, John Maynard; Keynesian Revolution; Keynesianism in America; Lausanne, The School of; Neoclassical Synthesis (Bastard Keynesianism); Robinson, Joan; Say's Law; Solow, Robert M.; Swan, Trevor W.

Bibliography

Brown, E. Cary and Robert M. Solow (1983), *Paul Samuelson and Modern Economic Theory*, New York: McGraw-Hill.

Feiwel, George R. (ed.) (1982), *Samuelson and Neoclassical Economics*, Boston: Kluwer Nijhoff.

Fischer, Stanley (1987), 'Samuelson, Paul Anthony', in John Eatwell, Murray Milgate and Peter Newman (eds), *The New Palgrave: A Dictionary of Economics*, Vol. 4, New York: Stockton Press.

Mirowski, Philip (1989), 'How Not to do Things with Metaphors: Paul Samuelson and the Science of Neoclassical Economics', *Studies in History and Philosophy of Science*, **20**, (2), June, pp. 175–91.

Samuelson, Paul A. (1947), *Foundations of Economic Analysis*, enlarged edn, 1983, Cambridge, Mass.: Harvard University Press.

Samuelson, Paul A. (1948), *Economics, an Introductory Analysis*, New York: McGraw-Hill.

Samuelson, Paul A. (1966–86), *The Collected Scientific Papers of Paul A. Samuelson*, Cambridge, Mass.: MIT Press; vol. 1 (1966) ed. Joseph Stiglitz; vol. 2 (1966) ed. Joseph Stiglitz; vol. 3 (1972) ed. Robert C. Merton; vol. 4 (1977) ed. Hiroaki Nagatani and Kate Crowley; vol. 5 (1986) ed. Kate Crowley.

Samuelson, Paul A., R. Dorfman and R.M. Solow (1958), *Linear Programming and Economic Analysis*, New York: McGraw-Hill.

Say's Law

Jean Baptiste Say (1767–1832) was a French economist who did much to popularize the ideas of Adam Smith on the continent of Europe. In his *A Treatise On Political Economy*, published originally in 1803, and in his letters to Thomas Malthus relating to 'general gluts' in the economy, he elaborated a principle which has been referred to as Say's Law of Markets, and is stated simply as 'products are paid for by products'. Say was not very precise in his development of the idea that the process of supplying commodities creates purchasing power sufficient to buy them. This imprecision resulted in several variations or versions of the principle.

Say's identity

In a barter economy it is asserted that suppliers produce in order to consume; to consume more, suppliers produce more. In such a case, supply equals demand ($S = D$) and Say's Law is perceived as simply an identity – each sale is a purchase. This continues to be true when money enters the picture if it is assumed that people hold money only for exchange rather than as a store of value. Then, when the money market is in equilibrium, that is $Ms = Md$, people again supply goods only to use the money received to buy goods immediately; in which case, again $S = D$, which is Say's identity. Blaug (1978, p. 159) says that statements like 'money is only a medium of exchange, that money is a veil because relative prices are exclusively determined by real forces, that supply automatically creates its own demand irrespective of what happens to the quantity of money – are all expressions of Say's Identity'.

Say's equality

This expression implies something more than Say's identity. It captures the idea that a free enterprise competitive economy always tends towards equilibrium at full employment; that is, that the equilibrium between S and D will occur at full employment levels of production. It amounts to asserting that an excess supply of goods or an excess demand for money will be self-correcting by virtue of prices changing to clear markets and interest rates changing to equilibrate savings and investment.

Keynes's version

Many scholars have argued that Keynes misrepresented what Say meant (Sowell, 1972, p. 211); nevertheless the version of Keynes is what is normally understood today as Say's Law. In the *General Theory*, Keynes described Say's Law as 'supply creates its own demand', although Say never used that phrase. Keynes took as the bases of this depiction of Say's Law not only

Say's writing, but also some strategically selected quotes of John Stuart Mill and Alfred Marshall. What is implied by the phrase 'S creates its own D' is the notion that the very process of producing anything generates sufficient income within the economy to buy what is produced; that is, the payments for supplies, labor, land and capital will sum to an amount equal to the value of all things produced. Thus there can be no lack of purchasing power within the economy in general. Hardly anything to debate, so far, but economists after Say had explained how savings on the part of consumers would be put back into the economy in the form of investment, so that whatever income was generated would be spent (savings would be equal to investment because of the equating forces of interest rates). As Keynes said (1936, p. 26), classical economists saw no inherent limits to demand; demand could always be increased by increasing supply. Classical writers (which also included neo-classical writers, since Keynes lumped them all together) accepted that there could be overproduction or excess supply of a commodity, but that would mean that an alternative good(s) would be in short supply and experiencing rising prices, whereas the overproduced good(s) would find prices weakening and losses occurring for its producers. Resources made redundant in the industry of the overproduced good(s) would find employment in the industry of the good(s) in short supply. The flexibility of wages and prices would ensure that the equilibrating market adjustment, as driven by the self-interest of workers and the profit-maximizing behavior of producers, would occur. So, as Keynes said, classical doctrine, based on Say's Law, offered no obstacle to full employment.

Keynes's attack

The implication of classical doctrine for the role of government when an economy was faced with a condition of underconsumption was clear: government should take no policy action to interfere with an adjusting economy. Keynes was convinced that this policy prescription was inappropriate and must be replaced with a proactive fiscal policy, but, to persuade others, he had to deny the validity of the bases for the classical position. This meant that he had to a certain extent to create a straw man by attributing to Say a principle that in its simplest form was uncontroversial. This he did by citing evidence of classical writings which denied the possibility of a permanent underconsumption condition and claimed that such writings were the essence of Say's Law. As is often said, 'the rest is history'.

CLAIR E. MORRIS

See also:

Adjustment Mechanisms of the Basic Classical and Keynesian Models; Classical Economics; Keynes, John Maynard; Liquidity Trap; New Classical School of Economics.

Bibliography

Blaug, Mark (1978), *Economic Theory in Retrospect*, 3rd edn, Cambridge: Cambridge University Press.
Keynes, John Maynard (1936), *The General Theory of Employment, Interest and Money*, London: Macmillan.
Sowell, Thomas (1972), *Say's Law*, Princeton: Princeton University Press.

Schumpeter, Joseph A.

Joseph Alois Schumpeter (1883–1950) is regarded as one of the greatest economists of the twentieth century, ranking with John Maynard Keynes, who was born in the same year. Schumpeter was born in Triesch, Moravia (now the Czech Republic). His father, a textile manufacturer, died when Schumpeter was four. Owing to his mother's remarriage to a high-ranking army officer, Schumpeter was able to enter the high society of the Austro-Hungarian Empire and was educated at the Theresianum in Vienna and at the University of Vienna.

Schumpeter studied law, history and economics and soon made his debut as an *enfant terrible* in the field of abstract economic theory. Although his major teachers were Eugen von Böhm-Bawerk and Friedrich von Wieser, major figures of the Austrian School, he was not accepted among the Austrian School because he was critical of its essentialism and psychologism. In 1908, he published *Das Wesen und der Hauptinhalt der theoretischen Nationalökonomie*, which was the recapitulation of neoclassical economics on the lines of the general equilibrium theory of Léon Walras. The book was a methodological work that aimed to make a contribution to the solution of the *Methodenstreit* between Carl Menger, the leader of the Austrian School, and Gustav von Schmoller, the leader of the younger German Historical School. Schumpeter ingeniously adapted the philosophy of science of Ernst Mach to economics and developed the methodology of instrumentalism, the view that theories are not descriptions but instruments for deriving useful results and are neither true nor false. According to this methodology, it is of no use to quarrel about the superiority of historical and theoretical methods because they are designed for different purposes. Schumpeter's methodological work can be compared to that of Max Weber, who was also devoted to the solution of the conflict between history and theory at the time.

In 1912, Schumpeter published *Theorie der wirtschaftlichen Entwicklung*, which was a unique attempt to establish a dynamic theory on the basis of neoclassical static theory. Static theory had explored the logic of economic behavior that formulated the most pervasive adaptive forces of an economy in response to changes in exogenous factors, and had been applied to the circular flow and the steady process of economic growth. In contrast, Schumpeter's economic dynamics or theory of economic development was concerned with destruction of the circular flow by the introduction of innovation that includes new products, new techniques, new markets, new sources of supply and new forms of organization. He defined economic development by reference to innovation (the cause of development), entrepreneurs (the carriers of development) and bank credit (the means of development). He emphasized the role of entrepreneurs because he sought an endogenous explanation for economic changes that addresses changes originating from an economic system itself rather than changes emerging from external disturbances.

When Schumpeter explained the nature of his theory of economic development, he referred to two great figures, Léon Walras and Karl Marx, to whom he had been indebted (Schumpeter, 1937). According to him, the former provided 'a pure logic of the interdependence between economic quantities' and the latter 'a vision of economic evolution as a distinct process generated by the economic system itself'. Schumpeter's basic idea of evolutionary economic changes is that both a cause of changes in economic system and a response mechanism to changes are endogenous; thus he regarded entrepreneurial innovation as the cause of economic development and formulated the phenomenon of business cycles as the process spreading and absorbing the impact of innovation through a response mechanism of the economy. It is important to observe that Schumpeter's concept of the entrepreneur was a special case of the leader as the carrier of innovation in a wider area of social life.

Schumpeter soon shifted his interest to economic sociology and developed a theory of social classes that would serve as the crucial link between the concept of leadership in various areas of social life, on the one hand, and the overall concept of civilization or the *Zeitgeist*, on the other. In other words, social classes mediate the interrelationships between the economic and the non-economic areas. This shaped the skeleton of his economic sociology that was later developed in *Capitalism, Socialism and Democracy* (1942), in which he presented his famous thesis on the demise of capitalism as the result of its success: according to him, the very success of capitalist economy will produce non-economic factors that are inconsistent with it; these factors will, in turn, worsen the economic performance of capitalism.

Schumpeter taught at the University of Czernowitz (now Ukraine) in 1909–11 and at the University of Graz in 1911–18. After World War I, he was Minister of Finance in the socialist government of Austria for seven months of 1919. His experience in the socialist government gave him a realistic view of socialism in operation. He was against overall socialization because the time was not ripe, but he did predict the eventual fall of capitalism. After his unsuccessful involvement in politics he became president of a private bank in Vienna which went bankrupt in 1924. During 1925–32, he was a professor at the University of Bonn. In 1932, Schumpeter emigrated to America to become a professor at Harvard University and worked there until his death in 1950.

He published *Business Cycles* (1939), in two massive volumes, with the subtitle 'A Theoretical, Historical and Statistical Analysis of the Capitalist Process'. This book was intended as an expansion and elaboration of the theory of economic development in historical and statistical context, but it was not a success. Schumpeter's *tour de force* was *History of Economic Analysis* (1954), which demonstrated that he was perhaps the last of the great polymaths. This work was not a hobby of the social scientist; there was a deeper reason for his interest in the history of economics. For him, the development of an economy and society and the development of thought and science are two aspects of the same evolutionary process. Corresponding to three branches of social studies, economic statics, economic dynamics and economic sociology, he worked on the philosophy of science (the methodology for the rules of scientific procedure), the history of science (the development of scientific apparatus) and the sociology of science (the nature of scientific activity carried out in social circumstance). These two sets of work and their interrelationships constitute Schumpeter's universal social science, which was a substitute for Marx's economic interpretation of history concerning the relationships between the substructure and the superstructure of a society. During the latter half of Schumpeter's life, the Keynesian revolution prevailed so overwhelmingly that his long-term and wide-ranging perspective was neglected, but his rich vision in various fields of social science has certainly given a stimulus to broadening the scope of economics.

YUICHI SHIONOYA

See also:

Business Cycle Theory (I) and (II); Keynes, John Maynard; Keynesian Revolution; Lausanne, The School of.

Bibliography

Allen, Robert Loring (1991), *Opening Doors: The Life and Work of Joseph Schumpeter*, 2 vols, New Brunswick: Transaction Publishers.

Schumpeter, Joseph Alois (1908), *Das Wesen und der Hauptinhalt der theoretischen Nationalökonomie*, Leipzig: Duncker & Humblot.

Schumpeter, Joseph Alois (1912), *Theorie der wirtschaftlichen Entwicklung*, Leipzig: Duncker & Humblot; 2nd rev. edn, 1926.

Schumpeter, Joseph Alois (1934), *The Theory of Economic Development*, abridged translation of the German 2nd edn, trans. Redvers Opie, Cambridge, Mass.: Harvard University Press.

Schumpeter, Joseph Alois (1937), Preface to Japanese edition of *Theorie der wirtschaftlichen Entwicklung*.

Schumpeter, Joseph Alois (1939), *Business Cycles*, 2 vols, New York: McGraw-Hill.

Schumpeter, Joseph Alois (1942), *Capitalism, Socialism and Democracy*, New York: Harper & Brothers; 2nd rev. edn, 1947; 3rd rev. edn, 1950.

Schumpeter, Joseph Alois (1951), *Imperialism and Social Classes*, trans. Heinz Norden, New York: Augustus M. Kelley.

Schumpeter, Joseph Alois (1954), *History of Economic Analysis*, New York: Oxford University Press.

Shionoya, Yuichi (1997), *Schumpeter and the Idea of Social Science*, Cambridge: Cambridge University Press.

Swedberg, Richard (1991), *Joseph A. Schumpeter: His Life and Work*, Cambridge: Polity Press.

Schwartz, Anna J.

Anna Jacobson Schwartz was born on 11 November 1915 in New York City. She earned her BA from Barnard College in 1934. In 1936 she married Isaac Schwartz, earned her MA from Columbia University and went to work for the US Department of Agriculture. After one year at the Department she returned to Columbia, where she was employed by the Social Science Research Council. During her five-year stay at the Council she worked with Arthur D. Gayer, Isaiah Finkelstein and Walt W. Rostow, and, in collaboration with her colleagues, developed several basic statistical series, three of which will be discussed below. In 1941, she changed jobs again, moving to the National Bureau of Economic Research. Periodically she would venture into the world of academia to teach – Brooklyn College (1952), Baruch College (1959–60), Hunter College (1967–8), and New York University (1969–70) – but in the end she always returned to the Bureau. In 1985, the Bureau bestowed on her the title of Associate Researcher Emeritus in recognition of over 40 years of working for the Bureau and for her scholarly achievements.

Schwartz's scholarly output can be divided into four areas. The first deals with the development of basic statistical series, three of which are noteworthy: the British share price index developed with Gayer and Finkelstein (Gayer *et al.*, 1940), the commodity price index for Britain developed with Gayer and Rostow (Gayer *et al.*, 1953) and the monetary and economic series for the United States and the United Kingdom (Friedman and Schwartz, 1963, 1970, 1982). Given the initial controversy which greeted the publication of Friedman and Schwartz's *Monetary History*, the third basic statistical series has become the most famous. The second area deals with economic history. In her writings about the Great Depression, Schwartz argues that the dramatic decline in real gross domestic product was the direct result of the substantial decline in the stock of money. In the short run discretionary monetary policy does have a significant impact on real income (Friedman and Schwartz, 1963; Schwartz, 1981). She concludes that the Fed needs to drop its reliance on discretionary policy because the principal effect of discretionary policy is a decrease in the stability and welfare of the economy. The third area is international monetary arrangements. After examining the effects of discretionary monetary policy in the United States and the United Kingdom,

Schwartz turned her attention to economic events in the international arena. Her contributions to this area include, but are not limited to, a thorough examination of the return to gold conducted while she was a member of the US Gold Commission (Schwartz, 1982).

The fourth, and probably the most important, area of her scholarship is monetary policy. Her work in the development of the basic statistical series for the United States and the United Kingdom and her extensive collaboration with Friedman convinced Schwartz of the critical importance of the three long-run monetary facts associated with the quantity theory of money. These facts are that the correlation between the rate of growth of the money supply and the rate of inflation is very high, that the correlation between the rate of growth of the money supply and the rate of growth of real output is very low, and that the correlation between the rate of inflation and the rate of growth of real output is very low. These conclusions follow from the subtle yet powerful model developed by Friedman in which key variables are denoted as being either 'measured' or 'transitory'. Friedman (1957) first used this model to examine the theory of consumption and the result was the permanent income hypothesis. In *Monetary History*, this model is used to examine monetary theory and policy and the result is the monetarist counter revolution.

The model developed by Friedman and Schwartz can be expressed in the following manner:

$$M = (K)(Y - \mu_y)^a + \mu_m \tag{1}$$

where M is the nominal stock of money (currency plus commercial bank deposits) or 'measured money', K is the reciprocal of the 'normal' income velocity of money (assumed to be constant), Y is measured money income, a is the 'normal' income elasticity of demand for money balances ($a > 1$ and assumed to be constant) and μ_y and μ_m are 'transitory' income and money, respectively (Clower, 1964). The model postulates the existence of a stable demand for real cash balances and an independently determined supply of money. Any change in the level, or in the rate of growth, of the supply of money effects a change in the level, or in the rate of growth, of nominal income. These changes are the result of the adjustment process undertaken by society to equate actual real cash balances to desired cash balances. These changes will be accompanied by variable lags in the affected variables. From this analysis flow two conclusions in which Schwartz believes: that discretionary management of the money supply leads to economic instability and that a constant rate of growth of the money supply will result in economic stability (Friedman and Schwartz, 1963; Schwartz and Cagan, 1975; Schwartz and Bordo, 1983).

Friedman and Schwartz argue that (1) is a stable relationship. The irregular movements in income employment and output are the direct result of the unintended consequences of discretionary monetary policy. From this premise their policy conclusion follows: follow rules and avoid discretionary policy. In the *Tract on Monetary Reform* (1924), Keynes, using principles developed in *A Treatise on Probability* (1922), shows that a thorough examination of the factors which affect the demand for money yields the induction of an unstable pattern. Keynes's statement that the long-run conclusions of the quantity theory are not practical guides for monetary policy follows from such an investigation.

One final remark is required if one is to do justice to Schwartz's scholarship and her role in the professional community. A perusal of her work reveals that the arguments developed and the theses defended are always accurate, precise and thoughtful (Friedman, 1989). A higher tribute a colleague cannot receive.

TOM CATE

See also:

Clower, Robert W.; Friedman, Milton; Monetarist School of Economics; Monetary Policy; Money; Quantity Theory of Money.

Bibliography

Clower, Robert W. (1964), 'Monetary History and Positive Economics', *Journal of Economic History*, **24**, (3), September, pp. 364–80.

Gayer, Arthur D., Anna Jacobson and Isaiah Finkelstein (1940), 'British Share Prices, 1811–1850', *Review of Economics and Statistics*, **2**, (2), May, pp. 78–93.

Gayer, Arthur D., Walt W. Rostow and Anna J. Schwartz (1953), *The Growth Fluctuation of the British Economy, 1790–1850*, 2 vols; reprinted Brighton: Harvester Press, 1975.

Friedman, Milton (1957), *A Theory of the Consumption Function*, Princeton: Princeton University Press.

Friedman, Milton (1989), 'Collaboration in Economics', in Michael D. Bordo (ed.), *Money, History and International Finance: Essays in Honor of Anna J. Schwartz*, Chicago: University of Chicago Press.

Friedman, Milton and Anna J. Schwartz (1963), *A Monetary History of the United States, 1867–1960*, Princeton: Princeton University Press for the National Bureau of Economic Research.

Friedman, Milton and Anna J. Schwartz (1970), *Monetary Statistics of the United States*, National Bureau of Economic Research, New York: Columbia University Press.

Friedman, Milton and Anna J. Schwartz (1982), *Monetary Trends in the United States and the United Kingdom: Their Relation to Income, Prices, and Interest Rates, 1867–1975*, Chicago: University of Chicago Press for the National Bureau of Economic Research.

Keynes, John Maynard (1922), *A Treatise on Probability*, London: Macmillan.

Keynes, John Maynard (1924), *A Tract on Monetary Reform*, London: Macmillan.

Schwartz, Anna J. (1981), 'Understanding 1929–1933', in Karl Brunner (ed.), *The Great Depression Revisited*, The Hague: Martinus Nijhoff.

Schwartz, Anna J. (1982), *Report to Congress*, vol. 1, Commission on the Role of Gold in the Domestic and International Monetary Systems, Washington, DC: US Printing Office.

Schwartz, Anna J. and Michael D. Bordo (1983), 'The Importance of Stable Money: Theory and Evidence', *Cato Journal*, **3**, (1), spring, pp. 63–82.

Schwartz, Anna J. and Phillip Cagan (1975), 'How Feasible is a Flexible Monetary Policy?', in R.T. Seldon (ed.), *Capitalism and Freedom: Problems and Prospects*, Charlottesville: University of Virginia Press.

Shackle, G.L.S.

George Shackle was born in Cambridge on 14 July 1903, but the family moved to the nearby village of Great Shelford when he was two years of age; he only finally left there in 1930. After his retirement from the Brunner Chair of Economic Science, University of Liverpool, in September 1969, he returned to his native East Anglia, residing in Aldeburgh, Suffolk, until his death on 3 March 1992.

George Shackle's father, Robert, was a first-class mathematician who had coached Keynes for his scholarship to Eton. In his schooldays George emulated his father: he too attended the Perse School, Cambridge and looked destined for a career in mathematics (though he also had leanings towards the Romance languages). Just when he was to follow further in his father's footsteps by entering St Catherine's College, Cambridge, the family encountered financial difficulties which meant that George had to find paid employment. This he did, in a bank where he remained a clerk for four years. Thereafter he worked for a tobacco company for one year, followed by almost ten (as he said, happy) years as a schoolmaster in Wales and in Lichfield. While in the bank he had begun the study of economics, having in view an external degree from the University of London. His spell as a schoolteacher enabled him to fulfill that ambition and, in 1931, he was awarded a degree, in Latin, French and economics. He recalls, (Shackle, 1983) how in that year, having read Keynes's *A Treatise on Money* (1930) and Hayek's *Production and Prices* (1931), he determined to pursue an academic career in economics. In 1934, the opportunity to do so came in the form of a Leverhulme Scholarship at the London School of Economics, where in 1935 he began work on a doctorate, under the supervision of Hayek. At the LSE he had contact with a generation of the most gifted of economists, besides Hayek himself: for example, Hicks, Kaldor, Lerner, Meade, Robbins and Brinley Thomas (who seems to have exercised the greatest influence on him by introducing him to the ideas of the Stockholm School). Shackle was awarded his doctorate in 1937. He joined the University of Oxford in December of that year to work with Henry Phelps Brown at New College and at the (now named) Oxford Institute of Economics and Statistics. On the basis of his research there he was awarded an Oxford doctorate (1940).

Following the outbreak of World War II in September 1939, having only recently left Oxford to take up a lectureship at St Andrews in Scotland, Shackle was asked to join a team of economists formed by Churchill's special scientific adviser (Lindemann, afterwards, Lord Cherwell). After that team was disbanded in 1945, Shackle moved to the Economic Section of the Cabinet Secretariat, initially headed by Meade. In 1950, Shackle returned to academic pastures when he was invited by A.J. Brown to accept the readership in economic theory at the University of Leeds. Shortly afterwards, he was appointed to his chair at the University of Liverpool.

Like the celebrated philosopher, Henri Bergson (to whose work his own was likened – a comparison that George Shackle himself denied), Shackle's writings were composed of many themes (for a comprehensive bibliography, see Ford, 1994), but these were derived from a basic thread: time is real (and not the mechanical time of the scientist) and consequently the development of the world should be envisaged as one of creative evolution rather than as deterministic, with God at the center of creation. The world is driven by the imagination and thoughts of humankind; those thoughts can engender novelty and hence the economic or wider social world cannot be predicted. This theme was pursued most pellucidly in his *Time in Economics* (1958), his favorite amongst his own books, which contained his 1957 de Vries lectures. This led to his being associated with a Keynesian nihilist view of macroeconomics. The pivotal role that he believed must be accorded in economics to time, expectations and uncertainty resulted in critical attacks on general equilibrium theory; attacks which found their fullest and most meticulous expression in his *magnum opus, Epistemics and Economics* (1972), where he was critical also of the reliance that economic theory placed upon mathematics. An extensive critique of the treatment of time in economic models and their inadequate attention to expectations and uncertainty, especially within the theory of cycles and growth in aggregate output, is presented in the course of his *A Scheme of Economic Theory* (1965).

Shackle's views on real time meant that the macroeconomic implications of time, expectations and uncertainty figured prominently in his writings more or less from the time of his first publication, on monetary theories of the trade cycle (in the first issue of the *Review of Economic Studies*, 1933; published, we note, before he had even been accepted for doctoral research at the LSE). It was that research that launched him into the study of the trade cycle, where he adopted a Keynesian stance, emphasizing the crucial part played by the expectations–real investment nexus in determining the path of macroeconomic activity. His doctoral thesis was published as his first monograph, *Expectations, Investment and Income* (1938, 1968), one of his most original works, in which he advanced two theories of the trade cycle. One theory had the economy's dynamic path determined by the response of businessmen to a divergence between their expectations of returns to newly installed plant and equipment and the actual returns on that real investment. Owing to the fact that the entrepreneurs will not have made allowance in their calculations of investment returns for the multiplier effects that will arise from the fact that all entrepreneurs will have been expanding their plant and their stocks of machinery, they will be the recipients of unanticipated profits from that new investment. This will encourage further bouts of real investment. Once entrepreneurs have learnt the 'rational expectations' multiplier effect of their investment expenditures, the boom is brought to an end. In the course of his analysis of this theory of the trade cycle, Shackle introduces (some years ahead of Duesenberry) the ratchet effect in consumption to demonstrate that there will be an asymmetry between the time profiles of the boom and the slump.

Despite the fact that the unanticipated multiplier effect can be discerned in Aftalion, Shackle's first theory of the trade cycle contains seminal contributions to the literature. His second theory is less innovative and is based on a clustering of investment, or a swarm of investments, as Schumpeter would say (Shackle's theory was advanced at just about the same time as Schumpeter's, of which he was unaware). That clustering initiates the boom through the concomitant multiplier mechanism and when the investment (maybe innovation) effects are diffused the slump begins.

Output, employment, interest and money in a Keynesian world continued to occupy Shackle's thoughts through the years and he was especially concerned with what he called 'Keynes's true meaning' and with defending what he regarded as Keynes's greatest innovation, the liquidity preference theory of the rate of interest. His writings on this topic enabled him to bequeath to us in one cover examples of his finest literary contributions to economics in the form of his *Years of High Theory* (1967). At the same time that book enabled him to demonstrate his consummate skills as an historian of economic theory; for in that work he provides exegeses of all the major developments in economic theory in the period from 1926 to the outbreak of World War II, besides those contained in Keynes's *A Treatise on Money* (1930) and *The General Theory* (1936) – a period of innovation in economic theory hardly matched since. A later, succinct, version of Shackle's ideas on the economics of Keynes is to be found in his *Keynesian Kaleidics* (1974).

From the late 1940s, Shackle's interest in the role of expectations and uncertainty in individual decision making, especially in the context of the investment in real capital undertaken by entrepreneurs, began to dominate his thinking and it permeated all his subsequent writings. His earlier published ideas on decision making under uncertainty were developed to the full in his most original monograph, *Expectation in Economics* (1949, 1952). It is this very distinctive and, many have felt, idiosyncratic, analytical work with which Shackle is most identified. He propounded a new means of encapsulating uncertainty, namely, degrees of potential surprise, together with a new paradigm of choice of action by the individual when faced with a set of uncertain prospects (in general, 'gambles'; specifically, for example, type of plant, mixture of financial assets in a portfolio). These innovations were the product of his dissatisfaction with the orthodox theory, wherein prospects on any action scheme were epitomized in a probability distribution of outcomes, and where the optimal choice of action scheme was made on the basis of 'mathematical expectation'; in current language, this would be the maximization of subjective expected utility.

To Shackle, it is not admissible to use the concept of probability in situations of uncertainty; it can only be utilized in situations which are characterized by risk. Furthermore the classical notion of probability has several undesirable features; notably it is what he called a 'distributional variable'. To be specific, this means that, if the universe of discourse alters (so that an individual now believes that another event (outcome) additional to the original set of events (outcomes) could occur) he or she must alter the probability previously assigned to at least one of the original events (outcomes) to accommodate the fact that the probabilities assigned to each event (outcome) in a set of exhaustive events (outcomes) must sum to unity. Furthermore it is possible that an individual is not sure about the feasible events (outcomes) that could occur; he or she might therefore introduce the notion of a residual hypothesis to encapsulate the possibility that some event (outcome) other than those now imagined might materialize. In terms of the orthodox paradigm, the universe of discourse might be incomplete. Shackle's notion of a 'degree of potential surprise' avoids these pitfalls. It measures the surprise, at the decision date, that the individual would feel if the particular hypothesis (outcome) should materialize.

In his decision model the individual was assumed to assign to every outcome (say, returns on a portfolio of assets) a degree of potential surprise. The prospect (the given portfolio) was thus epitomized by a potential surprise distribution, as it were, rather than by a probability distribution as in subjective expected utility theory. The selection of the best such prospect (hence of asset portfolio) was founded upon some psychological premises, the most important of which were that (1) the individual would separate gain (positive) outcomes from loss (negative) outcomes for any prospect (for example, asset portfolio); (2) the gain elements and the loss elements in the prospect were each to be encapsulated by one pair of outcomes being labelled primary focus outcomes; these were focused upon by the individual, gaining 'ascendancy' in her or his mind; (3) those outcomes were standardized which, if they were to be assigned a zero degree of potential surprise, would produce the same level of ascendancy as its primary counterpart; and (4) any prospect (say, asset portfolio) would be epitomized by its pair of standardized focus outcomes. The resultant hope of gain and the fear of loss would be weighed to give, as it were, a utility level, which lay on one of the individual's 'gambler-preference curves', as Shackle named them. The prospect that lay on the highest preference curve would be chosen, provided that its pair of standardized focus outcomes lay upon an indifference curve above that which went through the origin of the Cartesian diagram in (focus-gain, focus-loss) space. The pair of outcomes at the origin represent a 'do nothing' (or as the case might be, a 'no change') solution.

The dissatisfaction with the subjective expected utility theory that has been engendered by the results of numerous laboratory experiments over the last 40 or so years has spawned many alternative explanations of choice under uncertainty and risk. Most of these are within the spirit of the expected utility paradigm, in that they postulate that the individuals' preference function utilizes an 'averaging' mechanism, as Shackle called it: all outcomes in the prospects promised by an action scheme play a part in its evaluation. The 'utility' each outcome provides is multiplied by its probability or by some weighting function based on that probability, and the results are summed across the set of outcomes. By offering a radical alternative to that kind of approach, apart from proposing an alternative measure of uncertainty, Shackle's theory remains unique half a century later.

J.L. FORD

See also:
Business Cycle Theory (I) and (II); Economics of Keynes and of his Revolution, Key Elements of the; Expectations, Theories of; Keynes, John Maynard; Keynes, The Influence of Burke and Moore on; Keynesian Revolution; Relative Income Hypothesis; Schumpeter, Joseph A.; von Hayek, Friedrich A.

Bibliography
Carter, C.F., G.P. Meredith and G.L.S. Shackle (eds) (1954, 1957), *Uncertainty and Business Decisions*, Liverpool: Liverpool University Press.

Ford, J.L. (1993), 'G.L.S. Shackle (1903–1992): A Life with Uncertainty', *Economic Journal*, **103**, (418), May, pp. 683–97.

Ford, J.L. (1994), *G.L.S. Shackle: The Dissenting Economist's Economist*, Aldershot/Brookfield, VT: Edward Elgar.

Frowen, S.F. (ed.) (1990), *Unknowledge and Choice in Economics*, London: Macmillan.

Harcourt, G.C. (1981), 'Notes on an economic querist: G.L.S. Shackle', *Journal of Post Keynesian Economics*, **4**, (1), Fall, pp. 136–44.

Hayek, F.A. (1931), *Prices and Production*, London: Routledge and Sons.

Keynes, John M. (1930), *A Treatise on Money*, London: Macmillan.

Shackle, G.L.S. (1938, 1968), *Expectations, Investment and Income*, Oxford: Oxford University Press.

Shackle, G.L.S. (1949, 1952), *Expectation in Economics*, Cambridge: Cambridge University Press.

Shackle, G.L.S. (1958), *Time in Economics*, Amsterdam: North-Holland.

Shackle, G.L.S. (1965), *A Scheme of Economic Theory*, Cambridge: Cambridge University Press.

Shackle, G.L.S. (1967), *The Years of High Theory. Invention and Tradition in Economic Thought 1926–1939*, Cambridge: Cambridge University Press.

Shackle, G.L.S. (1972), *Epistemics and Economics*, Cambridge: Cambridge University Press.

Shackle, G.L.S. (1974), *Keynesian Kaleidics*, Edinburgh: Edinburgh University Press.
Shackle, G.L.S. (1983), 'A student's pilgrimage', *Banca del Lavoro Quarterly Bulletin*, **35**, (145), September, pp. 108–16.
Symposium (1959), 'A symposium on Shackle's theory of decision', *Metroeconomica*, **10**, (I–II), April/August.
Symposium (1985), 'Expectation, possibility and interest: an appraisal of the economics of G.L.S. Shackle', *Journal of Economic Studies*, **12**, (1/2).

Sharpe, William F.

William F. Sharpe received the Nobel Memorial Prize in Economic Science, together with Merton H. Miller and Harry M. Markowitz, for their pathbreaking work in the field of financial economics. Among his contributions to the field, Sharpe is most well known for his work on the capital asset pricing model (CAPM).

Sharpe spent most of his youth in southern California. He received both his undergraduate degree and doctorate from the University of California–Los Angeles. While pursuing his doctorate, he worked as an economist for the RAND Corporation where he met Markowitz who had worked on a theory of optimal portfolio allocation. Sharpe explored the market equilibrium implications of Markowitz's (1952) portfolio allocation model in his dissertation. This work became the basis of Sharpe's famous (1964) paper on the CAPM. After receiving his doctorate in 1961, Sharpe moved to the University of Washington in Seattle. In 1968, he moved to the University of California at Irvine, then to Stanford University Graduate School of Business in 1970. He has been affiliated with Stanford University ever since. In 1989, he became professor emeritus and now devotes his efforts to the firm he founded in 1986 to provide research and consulting services to institutional investors. Sharpe and his wife Kathryn have two children.

The CAPM predicts the relationship between an asset's expected return and its risk. To derive this relationship, investors are assumed to follow Markowitz's strategy of selecting a portfolio that maximizes return while minimizing risk (measured by the variance of returns). They are assumed to plan only one period ahead and to have common information regarding assets' expected returns and covariances. All securities are assumed to be publicly traded and investors' positions in securities, including a riskless security, can be positive or negative. Under these assumptions, Sharpe showed that market equilibrium has several key implications. The portfolio of all traded assets, called the market portfolio, is an efficient portfolio, which is one that yields the maximum expected return for a given level of risk. Secondly, combinations of positions in the market portfolio and the riskless asset can duplicate the expected risk and return characteristic of any efficient portfolio. Thirdly, the difference between the return on the market portfolio and the return on the riskless asset, called the risk premium, is proportional to the variance of the return on the market portfolio. Finally, the most well known result is that the risk premium on an individual security is proportional to its beta, that is, the covariance of its return with the return on the market portfolio. This latter relationship, called the security market line, is

$$E(R_i) = R_f + \beta_{im}[E(R_m) - R_f] \tag{1}$$

where R_i, R_m, R_f are the returns on the individual security, the market portfolio and the riskless security; β_{im} is $\text{cov}[R_m, R_i]/\text{var}(R_m)$; and E is the expectations operator.

Although numerous subsequent studies of the CAPM show that modification of some of the assumptions weakens these powerful conclusions, the insights provided by the CAPM are sufficiently accurate to have fundamentally affected financial practice. For example, investors now assess the riskiness of an investment by its contribution to the risk of the market portfolio and its return is compared with the return predicted by the security market line. Increasingly money managers implement portfolio strategies with index funds, that is, mutual funds that capture the behavior of the market portfolio.

In a well-known critique of empirical tests of the CAPM, Roll (1977) pointed out that the implications of CAPM stem from a single hypothesis, that the market portfolio is efficient. Since the true market portfolio is unobservable, this means that empirical tests depend on the characteristics of the proxy for the market portfolio, not the market portfolio itself. Therefore testing cannot conclusively confirm the CAPM. Nevertheless there is an indirect test. A central assumption is that investors have identical information, so they construct identical efficient portfolios. Trade leads to the mean-variance efficiency of the market portfolio and to asset prices that reflect all information. Assuming informational efficiency, a proxy that adequately reflects the market portfolio will outperform professionally managed portfolios on a risk-adjusted basis.

Sharpe evaluated the performance of 34 mutual funds in a (1966) paper that pioneered research on portfolio performance evaluation. He used the (now named) Sharpe's measure:

$$S = [E(R_p) - R_f]/\text{var}(R_p) \tag{2}$$

where R_p equals the return on the mutual fund portfolio. This risk-adjusted measure of return is now a common criterion for the performance of professionally managed portfolios. Sharpe's study and subsequent studies by others showed that the performance of professionally managed mutual funds is not significantly superior to proxies of the market portfolio.

Among the many other contributions Sharpe has made to the field of finance is his textbook on investments, first published in 1978, in which he was the first to propose the now widely used binomial option pricing method which is a numerical method of valuing complex options whose value cannot be derived analytically. His more recent research focused on institutional investment policy and asset allocation, that is, the allocation of funds between major asset categories. He also continues to disseminate the results of research in financial economics to its practitioners through his research and consulting company, William F. Sharpe Associates.

STACIE E. BECK

See also:

Expectations, Theories of; Interest, Theories of; Markowitz, Harry M.; Minsky, Hyman P.

Bibliography

Markowitz, Harry (1952), 'Portfolio Selection', *Journal of Finance*, **7**, (1), March, pp. 77–91.

Roll, Richard (1977), 'A Critique of the Asset Pricing Theory's Tests: Part I On Past and Potential Testability of the Theory', *Journal of Financial Economics*, **4**, (2), March, pp. 129–76.

Sharpe, William (1964), 'Capital Asset Prices – A Theory of Market Equilibrium Under Conditions of Risk', *Journal of Finance*, **19**, (3), September, pp. 425–42.

Sharpe, William (1966), 'Mutual Fund Performance', *Journal of Business*, **39**, (1, Part II), January, pp. 119-38.

Sharpe, William (1978), *Investments*, Englewood Cliffs, NJ: Prentice-Hall.

Solow, Robert M.

Robert Solow is a Nobel laureate and president emeritus of the American Economic Association. He has written about growth theory and macroeconomic policy, and has made fundamental contributions to neo-Keynesianism. Solow's published works include well over 100 articles and several books.

Solow was born in 1924. He is a self-avowed neo-Keynesian who is admired almost as much for his rapier wit and readable prose as for his deep insight into matters economic. In fact, his 1975 piece 'The Intelligent Citizen's Guide to Inflation' encapsulates much of his approach to economics: his explanations are clear enough for the layman and yet piercing enough to entrance the professional. He is clearly 'The Intelligent Citizen' of economics, so much so that he is one of the few economists who purports never to have had an article rejected (Gans and Shepherd, 1994).

Solow entered Harvard in 1940. He had originally intended to study botany, biology or genetics, but quickly determined that these subjects were not his forte. World War II interrupted his studies and he joined the army before graduating. Following his return from the war, he married his girlfriend, who had recently graduated from Radcliffe with an economics degree. Her endorsement of the economics major prompted him to take up the subject. The rest, as they say, is history. Solow received his bachelor's degree in 1947, his master's in 1949 and his PhD in 1951 (all from Harvard). His academic career has been spent primarily within sight of the Charles River in Cambridge, Massachusetts. In 1949, he joined the MIT faculty as an assistant professor, was promoted to associate in 1954, and became Institute Professor of Economics in 1958.

Solow's seminal work in modern growth theory won him the 1987 Nobel Prize in Economics. His primary contribution is to insert the proposition that labor and capital are substitutes. Contrary to the original Harrod–Domar conclusion of a single, unstable equilibrium growth path, Solow's work shows a range of possible stable equilibria. Without a fixed proportion production function, diminishing returns ensure that the long-run output growth rate is entirely dependent upon technological progress. The level, however, may depend upon the societal rate of savings. For example, an economy that succeeds in increasing its savings (and hence investment) rate will move to a higher output level so that the growth rate of output is temporarily higher. After reaching the higher level of output, the economy returns to the previous rate of growth. Showing the robustness of his conclusion with various production functions, Solow spawned a sizeable literature analysing the role of the production function in such models.

His early work in the area of growth also opened the door for the analysis of various behavioral postulates in the long-run economy, such as rigid real wages, liquidity preferences, variable savings rates, variable population growth and labor supply variability. These extensions of the main model imply that there is an important role to be played by policy. Indeed, in his Nobel lecture, he remarks that 'growth theory provides a framework within which one can seriously discuss macroeconomic policies that not only achieve and maintain full employment but also make a deliberate choice between current consumption and current investment, and therefore between current consumption and future consumption' (Solow, 1988, pp. 309–10). Solow suggests that observed fluctuations in economic growth are not deviations *in* economic growth trends but *from* economic growth trends. Therefore he sees in these models an open arena for government intervention.

Solow devoted an increasing amount of his attention to short-run fluctuations in the decades following his initial foray into growth modeling. Writing with Alan Blinder in 1973, Solow produced a classic article entitled 'Does Fiscal Policy Matter?' (Blinder and Solow, 1973) which analyses the wealth effect for implications about fiscal policy crowding out. This effect arises when fiscal policy is bond-financed. Some consumer wealth is transformed into government bonds with their stream of interest payments. This increase in wealth gives rise to a net increase in consumption, increasing the government spending multiplier. There is a countervailing effect of an increase in money demand that puts upward pressure on interest rates and reduces interest-sensitive spending. While Solow and Blinder concede that the net effect of these two opposing effects is an empirical matter, they show that the contractionary effect can only dominate in a system that is inherently unstable, so that bond-financed government spending would ultimately drive output to zero. They are able to conclude that fiscal policy does, indeed, matter. They are not able to conclude on the extent of this effect, however.

Solow continues his efforts to study the cause and cure of short-run fluctuations in his American Economic Association presidential address entitled 'Theories of Unemployment' (Solow, 1980) in which he discusses the characteristics of the labor market that cause it to deviate from 'thorough-going competition'. He concludes that labor market fluctuations are more likely to arise from entrenched tendencies towards disequilibrium than from temporary, self-correcting market inefficiencies. These characteristics include labor market segmentation (not only by skill but by geography, industry, job classification and even by employer), trade unionism, unemployment insurance and a socially enforced code of reasonable behavior. These last three will tend to prevent wages from adjusting downwards quickly, or perhaps at all. An imperfectly adjusting labor market means that disequilibria will not always be self-correcting, so that government policy will not only matter but will sometimes be essential.

A summary of Solow's work can be distilled down to the following words, taken from his own address to the American Economic Association: 'All I claim is that a reasonable theory of economic policy ought to be based on a reasonable theory of economic life' (Solow, 1980, p. 10).

NANCY J. BURNETT

See also:
Crowding Out; Demand Management; Domar Evsey D.; Fiscal Policy; Harcourt, Geoff; Harrod, Sir Roy; Keynesian Revolution; Neoclassical Synthesis (Bastard Keynesianism); Robinson, Joan; Samuelson, Paul A.; Swan, Trevor W.; Technological Change.

Bibliography
Blinder, Alan S. and Robert M. Solow (1973), 'Does Fiscal Policy Matter?', *Journal of Public Economics*, **2**, (3), June, pp. 319-37.
Gans, Joshua A. and George B. Shepherd (1994), 'How are the Mighty Fallen: Rejected Classic Articles by Leading Economists', *Journal of Economic Perspectives*, **8**, (1), February, pp. 165–79.
Klamer, Arjo (1983), *Conversations with Economists*, Totowa, NJ: Rowman & Allenheld.
Solow, Robert M. (1956), 'A Contribution to the Theory of Economic Growth', *Quarterly Journal of Economics*, **70**, (3), June, pp. 65-94.

Solow, Robert M. (1970), *Growth Theory: An Exposition*, Oxford: Clarendon.

Solow, Robert M. (1975), 'The Intelligent Citizen's Guide to Inflation', *Public Interest*, **38**, Winter, pp. 30–66.

Solow, Robert M. (1980), 'On Theories of Unemployment', *American Economic Review*, **70**, (1), March, pp. 1–11.

Solow, Robert M. (1988), 'Growth Theory and After', *American Economic Review*, **78**, (3), June, pp. 307–17.

Sraffa, Piero

Piero Sraffa was born in 1898 in Turin, the son of a successful law professor. With the educational advantages that prosperous families offer their progeny, Sraffa was himself able to join the professoriate. His lifelong sympathy for socialist movements can be traced to his years as a student. These sympathies would be reflected in his mature works as an economist.

While attending lectures at the London School of Economics in 1921, he had the good fortune to meet Keynes. Sraffa's early interests were of an applied nature. His work on banking in the period of reconstruction following World War I caught the eye of Keynes, who engaged the young Sraffa to write on the subject for British publications. The candor with which he wrote of the banking situation in his homeland earned the wrath of Mussolini's regime. The Fascist government insisted that the Home Secretary deny Sraffa entry into Britain, a decree rescinded in 1924 through the intercession of Keynes.

Paul Samuelson argues that no other economist with so limited an output has had 'so great an impact on economic science as Piero Sraffa', whose work consists of a handful of masterful contributions. A common theme runs throughout: the neoclassical mode of analysis must be rejected in favor of one resembling the classical approach. Sraffa gained widespread professional attention in 1926 with the publication of his critique of the Marshallian competitive equilibrium in the *Economic Journal*. Marshall's fusion of the classical law of diminishing returns with the law of increasing returns was called into question. Sraffa believed decreasing returns to scale to be rarely observed because factors of production are not often fully employed. He thought increasing returns to scale to be a commonplace, but inconsistent with a perfectly competitive equilibrium. Increasing returns imply an industry characterized by fewer firms operating at higher levels of production. Perfect competition could exist only under constant returns to scale. Yet in many industries, increasing, not constant, returns to scale govern.

What determines the size of the firm? Sraffa looked to demand: firms develop clienteles by selling differentiated products that are close, if not perfect, substitutes for competing products. Firms face downward-sloping demand; they are price makers, not the price takers of the perfectly competitive model.

Firm size is influenced, not just by cost of production, but also by the need to lower price to sell more. Firms produce to the point at which marginal revenue and marginal cost are equated, a point reached before constant returns take hold. Sraffa believed he had undermined a centerpiece of neoclassical theory. Further elaboration was left to Joan Robinson and Edward H. Chamberlin, who ushered in the 'monopolistic competition revolution' with separate works in 1933. Sraffa may have been disappointed with the outcome. His ideas in the form of the monopolistically competitive model were absorbed into neoclassical thought. The neoclassical paradigm survived his critique.

This work prompted Keynes to offer Sraffa a lectureship at King's College, Cambridge in 1927. He taught courses on value and banking. His teaching style pursued a dialogue with students, unheard of in the Cambridge of his day. A highly regarded lecturer known to agonize into the wee hours the night before a class, he tired of his teaching duties and was granted permission to relinquish them. He was appointed librarian of the Marshall Library and director of research at King's College. In 1930, Keynes made him editor of the Royal Economic Society's edition of *The Works and Correspondence of David Ricardo*.

Sraffa was a founding member of the Cambridge 'Circus' of young economists who met from 1931 to 1935 to discuss the ideas in Keynes's *Treatise on Money* as they evolved into those of *The General Theory*. Austin Robinson recalls Sraffa not as an original thinker in the Circus, but as a critic of the ideas of others. In the 1930s, Sraffa formed an important intellectual relationship with the philosopher Ludwig Wittgenstein, who credited him with facilitating his transition from the ideas in his *Tractatus Philosophicus* to the more mature ones of his *Philosophical Investigations*. Legend has it that Wittgenstein experienced his philosophical epiphany on a train with Sraffa, who made a familiar obscene gesture and inquired of its meaning. According to Schick, Sraffa's inquiry led Wittgenstein to discard his picture theory of meaning in favor of a use theory of meaning, the basis of the ordinary language philosophy that dominated Cambridge and Oxford for decades.

In 1932, at Keynes's behest, Sraffa reviewed Hayek's *Prices and Production*. He noted Hayek's failure to account for the distributional effects that price level changes can have on nominal contracts. He thought monetary policy could be used as an instrument of class conflict since it can effect wealth transfers between classes. Blaug believes Sraffa's review effectively demolished the Austrian theory of business cycles, leaving the stage to Keynes. The relationship between Sraffa and Keynes is an intriguing one. They were both avid bibliophiles and together discovered and saw to the publication of a work by David Hume. They remained close even after Sraffa left King's in 1939 to become a fellow at Trinity. It was Keynes who won Sraffa's release from internment by the British government as an enemy alien in 1940.

Sraffa's attack on the neoclassical view led Keynes to invite him to Cambridge. Yet Keynes did not fully share his misgivings about the Marshallian view. He thought Sraffa's attempt to restore the classical approach faced serious obstacles. Though Sraffa was an active member of the Circus who saw Keynes frequently, his influence on *The General Theory* was limited to the 'own rate of return' concept developed in his review of Hayek. Keynes was unsympathetic to parts of the Ricardian legacy. Writing on Malthus in his *Essays in Biography*, he described Ricardo's dismissal of Malthus's underemployment equilibrium as 'a disaster for the progress of economics' that 'constrained the subject for a full hundred years'. Keynes's enthusiasm for Sraffa's editorship of Ricardo was partly motivated by the belief that Sraffa would relegate some parts of Ricardo's work to a well-deserved obscurity. The two men differed on Karl Marx, with Sraffa a serious scholar of Marx, and Keynes dismissive. To Keynes, Marxian socialism 'was a doctrine so illogical and so dull' and the works of Marx were 'the turbid rubbish of the cheap book stores'. Lorie Tarshis recounts that Keynes teased Sraffa, asking if 'there is anything to that Marx chap?' Ironically Sraffa's editorship of Ricardo and his subsequent work heralded a major revival in Ricardian economics, giving life to the Post Keynesian school and renewing interest in Marxian analysis.

In 1933, in his essay on Malthus, Keynes had noted the imminent publication of *The Works and Correspondence of David Ricardo* under Sraffa's editorship. In truth, the preparation and final publication of *The Works and Correspondence* had one of the longest gestation periods in the history of ideas. After many false starts, the first ten volumes were finally published between 1951 and 1955; an index came as the eleventh volume in 1971. In the 1930s and 1940s Sraffa's work was disrupted by the discovery of new papers by Ricardo. Progress on his undertaking was greatly facilitated from 1948 onwards, when Maurice Dobb collaborated with him on the introductions to the various volumes. The publication was greeted with universal praise; reviewers declared Sraffa's work to be the very model of scholarly achievement. Economists had declared Ricardo either a quaint curiosity or largely irrelevant. While some of his work, such as the doctrine of comparative advantage, had survived, the bulk of it had been supplanted by neoclassical theory. Sraffa's introductions and commentaries provided new interpretations of Ricardo and led in time to his rehabilitation. Sraffa argued that Ricardo never abandoned his labor theory of value or his search for an invariable standard of value, and claimed Ricardo's corn model showed profits to be determined independently of valuation. Sraffa's views were embraced by enthusiasts of the surplus approach to value and those favorably disposed to Marx, whose work was indebted to Ricardian principles.

Sraffa's editorship served as the genesis for his own most lasting work, *Production of Commodities by Means of Commodities*, published in 1960. He demonstrated that, given the real wage, relative prices are determined by the technical means of production and the manner in which the surplus is distributed. Herein lies a striking departure from the neoclassical view: prices are determined without reference to demand. An idea central to the classical scheme had been revived. The usual relationship between wages and profits in the classical model is reversed. Rather than let wages be determined by subsistence needs, profits, made to follow the rate of interest, are exogenously determined by the actions of monetary institutions and the intervention of the state. An economic explanation of distribution is not offered; labor's share in output is a residual that depends on the relative power of the various social classes. The appeal to Marxists is clear: wages and profits are not determined by the neoclassical notion of marginal productivity, but rather by the struggle for power between the laboring and capitalist classes; class conflict could not be denied its rightful place as a means to understand social relations. Sraffa's analytical insights also fit nicely the emerging Post Keynesian school's critique of capitalism. Led by Kalecki, Robinson and others, this critique asserts that the distribution of income is determined by macroeconomic forces, such as the willingness of the capitalist class to spend its profits. With the incorporation of his ideas into the Post Keynesian explanation of macroeconomic performance, some thought Sraffa's death blow to the neoclassical apologia for market capitalism to be complete.

While mainstream microeconomics continues to evolve along general equilibrium lines, Sraffa has presented a compelling heterodoxy in *Production of Commodities*: commodity and factor prices are not simultaneously determined. His rehabilitation of Ricardian economics argues for the restoration of a classical chain of causality, wherein a consideration of distribution must come first, and out of which the determination of prices then follows. He wished to free economic analysis from the need to rely on subjective elements such as consumer preferences and work–leisure preferences and, at least in principle, to ground theory on the objective considerations which he believed informed the classical approach.

His work unleashed a storm of controversy. His adherents saw in it the opportunity, as Roncaglia has said, to 'eliminate a false scheme of knowledge' that served to justify the capitalist system. They regarded continued reliance on the neoclassical model as disreputable. His critics labeled his work a special case of the neoclassical view, superseded by the linear models developed by others. The debate goes on, one from which Sraffa, in his characteristic fashion, remained detached. He kept his silence right up to his death in 1983.

JAMES N. MARSHALL

See also:

Cambridge Circus; Classical Economics; Kahn, Lord Richard F.; Keynes, John Maynard; Keynesian Revolution; Marshall, Alfred; Post Keynesian School of Economics; Robinson, Joan.

Bibliography

Blaug, Mark (1985), 'Sraffa, Piero (1898–1983)', in *Great Economists since Keynes*, Cambridge: Cambridge University Press.

Blaug, Mark (1986), 'Ricardo, David (1772–1823)', in *Great Economists before Keynes*, Cambridge: Cambridge University Press.

Eatwell, John and Carlo Panico (1987), 'Sraffa, Piero (1898–1983)', in John Eatwell, Murray Milgate and Peter Newman (eds), *The New Palgrave: A Dictionary of Economics*, Vol. 4, New York: Stockton Press.

Pasinetti, L.L. (1979), 'Sraffa, Piero', in D.L. Sills (ed.), *International Encyclopaedia of the Social Sciences*, Vol. 18, New York: The Free Press.

Patinkin, Don and J. Clark Leith (eds) (1978), *Keynes, Cambridge and the General Theory*, London: Macmillan.

Roncaglia, Alessandro (1981), 'Piero Sraffa's Contribution to Political Economy', in J.R. Shackleton and G. Locksley (eds), *Twelve Contemporary Economists*, London: Macmillan.

Samuelson, Paul A. (1987), 'Sraffian economics', in John Eatwell, Murray Milgate and Peter Newman (eds), *The New Palgrave: A Dictionary of Economics*, Vol. 4, New York: Stockton Press.

Sraffa, P. (1926) 'The Laws of Returns under Competitive Conditions', *Economic Journal*, **36**, (144), December, pp. 535–50.

Sraffa, P. (1932), 'Dr. Hayek on Money and Capital', *Economic Journal*, **42**, (165), March, pp. 42-53.

Sraffa, P. (ed.) (1951–73), *The Works and Correspondence of David Ricardo*, 11 vols, Cambridge: Cambridge University Press.

Sraffa, P. (1960), *Production of Commodities by Means of Commodities: Prelude to a Critique of Economic Theory*, Cambridge: Cambridge University Press.

Stein, Herbert

Herbert Stein, who was born in Detroit, Michigan, on 27 August 1916, would be included in any list of the dozen most influential macroeconomic policy advisers for America in the post-World War II period. Since scarcity of talent makes for preciousness, Stein was one of the few most valuable advisers to centrist Republican administrations who ruled much of the time in the White House and Congress.

Stein was typical of America's new meritocracy. Growing up in a working-class family, he was able in the worst years of the Great Depression to attend Williams College (1931–5), then mostly a school for the elite establishment. During his four vacations from college his search for a needed job resulted in only one day of work, so it was natural that he would drift into economic study with the excellent undergraduate faculty there. And it was natural, too, for a bright student to go on to the University of Chicago to work towards a PhD in economics.

Although the Chicago of Frank Knight and Jacob Viner did not become an early hotbed of Keynesianism, Henry C. Simons had a great and lasting impact on Stein. Simons was a devotee of economic freedoms and market mechanisms' efficiency, but he also had creative understandings of the pathologies for monetary policy during great depressions and stubborn inflations, and believed that the state had three important roles in accomplishing what laissez faire itself could not be counted on to achieve: workably effective competition required anti-trust and other supervisory monitoring by government; positive rules and measures to attenuate macroeconomic instabilities of inflation and slump were also needed; and important to Simons was the desirability of an effective and efficient tax-transfer structure that would mitigate the extremes of inequality of incomes and opportunity inseparable from a truly automatic market system. Thus the First Chicago School (of Knight, Viner and Simons) differed systematically from the Second Chicago School (of Milton Friedman, George Stigler, Aaron Director and Gary Becker).

After his Chicago sojourn (1935–8), Herbert Stein began a six-decade career in the Washington, DC environs (interrupted only by two war years as a junior naval officer and in 1974–84 as a mostly full-time professor at the nearby University of Virginia). He achieved first real prominence, outside the circle of the Federal Deposit Insurance Corporations (FDIC), War Planning Board (WPB), and varied war agencies, when he won first prize in the prestigious Pabst Post-War Employment competition. (Its financial worth at the time almost matched then current Nobel Prizes; he beat some thousand competitors, including Alvin Hansen and Paul Samuelson; secondary prize-winners included Leon Keyserling, of later Truman administration fame, and Everett Hagen, the chief coordinator of the US government's disastrously pessimistic forecast of a postwar recession.)

From age 31 to 53, Stein worked as an economist for the liberal business group the CED (Committee on Economic Development), for the last ten years as Director of Research. The CED was first influential in pressing the case for a non-recessionary postwar conversion and it did much to advocate prudent postwar macro policies along centrist Keynesian lines – a viewpoint much needed in the American business climate.

A sage policy adviser need not be a creative innovator in economic science, but Herbert Stein earned distinction as a forceful architect of the CED's 'budget balance at full employment' concept. Stein was skeptical of the feasibility of fine fiscal tuning that varied expenditures countercyclically and sought short-term fluctuations in tax rates. The CED instead accepted a failure of the budget to balance in every year and in every phase of the business cycle. Pragmatically it counted on built-in fiscal stabilizers that would operate under a relatively stable tax structure set with rates adequate to cover desired long-run governmental services. Also Stein's two editions of

The Fiscal Revolution in America constitute an indispensable economic history of that subject in the mid-century era.

Herbert Stein was an eclectic Keynesian (or eclectic Simons–Keynesian). He believed money mattered but doubted that *only* money mattered. He found unconvincing both Milton Friedman monetarism and the Robert Lucas new-classical notion that macro policy's systematic effects could be (even in short runs of time) only on price levels rather than real outputs. But he had to dissent from popular Keynesians who advocated whatever demand stimulus was needed to maintain really full levels of employment. And increasingly over time, Stein stressed the need to preserve microeconomic incentives conducive to efficiency and growth. More than most end-of-century American economists, Herbert Stein insisted upon the importance and feasibility of a level of defense expenditures adequate for America's security needs and to which good macro policy could and should adjust.

Finally Herbert Stein has been a prolific and fine writer. His attractive style is not a mere rhetorical frosting to enhance persuasion towards his viewpoint; rather it reflects the clarity and depth of his analyses. In *The Wall Street Journal* and syndicated economic columns, in books and in testifying before Congressional committees, Stein's wit has been proverbial. (Perhaps apocryphally, he has been credited with the witticism concerning the August 1971 Nixon decisions to suspend Bretton Woods gold convertibility and institute price–wage controls: 'George Shultz and Herbert Stein were the contractors who carried out the Nixon–Connolly program, but they were not its architects.')

Herbert Stein's 1969–74 stint on the Nixon and Ford Councils of Economic Advisers (including 1972–4 as chairman of the CEA) merits his place on the CEA honor roll (along with Heller–Tobin–Gordon, Arthur Burns and Martin Feldstein) and on any honor roll that includes such names as Henry Wallich, Paul McCracken, Gottfried Haberler and Alan Greenspan. Herbert Stein's two-decade association with the American Enterprise Institute is tribute to the need for such diversified think-tanks by the American society.

PAUL A. SAMUELSON

See also:

Automatic Stabilizers; Business Cycle Theory (I) and (II); Demand Management; Fiscal Policy; Full Employment Budget; Keynesian Revolution; Keynesianism in America; Lucas Critique; Monetarist School of Economics; Viner, Jacob.

Bibliography
Stein, Herbert (1969), *The Fiscal Revolution in America*, Chicago: University of Chicago Press; rev. edn, Washington, DC: American Enterprise Institute, 1990.
Stein, Herbert (1984,1985), *Presidential Economics*, New York: Simon & Schuster; rev. edns, Washington, DC: American Enterprise Institute, 1988, 1994.
Stein, Herbert (1989), *Governing the $5 Trillion Economy*, New York: Twentieth Century Fund.

Stein, Herbert and Murray Foss (1992), *An Illustrated Guide to the American Economy*, Washington, DC: The American Enterprise Institute.

Stockholm School of Economics

The founding father of the Stockholm School was Knut Wicksell. Its leading names were Erik Lindahl, Gunnar Myrdal, Bertil Ohlin and Erik Lundberg, whose contributions all appeared within the 1930s. Stockholm theory generalized Wicksell's (1898) cumulative process of prices into cumulative processes of prices *and* quantities. The motive force of a cumulative process was the revision of plans at the end of a period caused by disappointed expectations. Disappointment came in two forms.

In the first form, called 'temporary equilibrium' by Lindahl (1930), markets always cleared within the period but not always at the expected price. The disappointed expectations, then, were *price* expectations. In the second form, called 'disequilibrium' by Lindahl (1939), a price was announced at the beginning of the period and adhered to throughout the period. At that price markets might not clear: inventory might pile up or be depleted. Here the disappointed expectations were *sales* expectations.

Two years ahead of Keynes (1936), Ohlin (1934) applied three Keynesian tools: the propensity to consume, the multiplier and liquidity preference. To these he added a non-Keynesian one, the accelerator. The four tools would interact as follows in a feedback mechanism. With consumption demand being stimulated, output would rise and generate new income. The propensity to consume would link consumption to the *level* of output and thus generate a consumption feedback. The accelerator would link investment to a *change* in output and thus generate an investment feedback. The two feedbacks would interact in a cumulative process of quantities.

Asked by a Royal Commission to consider measures against unemployment, Ohlin (1934) and Myrdal (1934) were forced to treat quantities of output and employment as variables – as Keynes was to do two years later. But they went one better than Keynes: the *General Theory* had nothing to say about fiscal policy – that had to wait for Hansen (1941) – but seven years ahead of Hansen, Ohlin and Myrdal recommended government investment in infrastructure, say highways or electrification of state railways, not competing with private investment. Tax financing would discourage consumption. Fiscal deficits financed by selling government bonds in the open market would depress bond prices and so discourage private investment. That left fiscal deficits financed by central bank discounting of Treasury bills.

Ohlin and Myrdal reached their policy conclusions by verbal intuition alone. A big step forward – and the crowning achievement of the Stockholm

School – was Lundberg's (1937) difference equations. Lundberg offered recursive solutions in a number of cases: first, the case of a pure Keynesian multiplier with exogenous investment; second, several cases of interaction between a multiplier and an exogenous accelerator; third, a case of interaction between a multiplier and an endogenous accelerator seen as a function of the rate of interest.

Let us round off by modernizing and generalizing a Stockholm cumulative process. Lags are its essence. Stockholm lags were the rigid lags of Lundberg's difference equations. Differential equations can handle lags in the more general and flexible form of continuously distributed lags, as follows. First, let desired consumption be the propensity to consume c times actual level of output X. Let there be a continuously distributed lag in the response of consumption C to level of output X. Specifically let the response dC/dt be in proportion to the gap between desired and actual consumption:

$$\frac{dC}{dt} = \alpha(cX - C) \tag{1}$$

where α is the speed of response of consumption to that gap. Next, let desired investment be the accelerator b times actual change in output dX/dt. Let there be a continuously distributed lag in the response of investment I to change in output dX/dt. Specifically let the response dI/dt be in proportion to the gap between desired and actual investment:

$$\frac{dI}{dt} = \beta\left(b\frac{dX}{dt} - I\right) \tag{2}$$

where β is the speed of response of investment to that gap.

Actual output adjusts to actual demand for it:

$$X = C + I \tag{3}$$

Differentiate (3) with respect to time, insert (1) and (2), use (3) upon the result, and express I in terms of dX/dt and X alone:

$$I = \frac{1-b\beta}{\alpha-\beta}\frac{dX}{dt} + \frac{\alpha(1-c)}{\alpha-\beta}X \tag{4}$$

which is meaningful if and only if $\alpha \gtrless \beta$. Differentiate (4) with respect to time and express dI/dt in terms of d^2X/dt^2 and dX/dt. Insert I and dI/dt into (2) and find the system reduced to the linear homogeneous second-order differential equation:

$$\frac{d^2 X}{dt^2} + A\frac{dX}{dt} + BX = 0, \text{ where}$$

$$A \equiv \frac{\alpha(1-c)+(1-\alpha b)\beta}{1-b\beta} \tag{5}$$

$$B \equiv \frac{\alpha\beta(1-c)}{1-b\beta}$$

Depending on the orders of magnitude of parameters α, β, b, and c output may be fluctuating, growing or decaying.

Indeed our continuously distributed lags are flexible enough to include equilibrium as the special case of instant response. To see how, insert A and B into (5), multiply both sides by $1 - b\beta$, divide both sides by $\alpha\beta$, let α and β rise beyond bounds, and find (5) approaching the limit:

$$-b\frac{dX}{dt} + (1-c)X = 0, \text{ or} \tag{6}$$

$$g_x \equiv \frac{dX}{dt}\frac{1}{X} = \frac{1-c}{b}$$

Such equilibrium growth at a rate g_x equaling the propensity to save divided by the accelerator was formulated for the first time by Cassel (1918, 1932, pp. 61-2). It was formulated a second time when Keynes (1937), for once in his life and without knowing Cassel's formulation, considered a secular problem. In a little-noticed essay in the *Eugenics Review*, Keynes estimated a secular propensity to save $1 - c$ of between 8 and 15 per cent, estimated a secular accelerator $b = 4$ and found output growing at a rate g_x of between 2 and 4 per cent per annum.

The Stockholm School anticipated much of Keynes and certainly was richer and more general. Both are history now. But in their heyday Keynes was the winner, and he won on his simplicity and his operational significance: there was so much you could *do* by shifting *IS* and *LM* curves, and you could do it so sure-footedly.

HANS BREMS

See also:

Accelerator Principle; Business Cycle Theory (I) and (II); Keynes, John Maynard; Keynesian Revolution; Lundberg, Erik; Multiplier Effect; Myrdal, Gunnar; Ohlin, Bertil.

Bibliography

Cassel, Gustav (1918), *Theoretische Sozialökonomie*, Leipzig: Wintersche Verlagshandlung; trans. 1932, S.L. Barron, *The Theory of Social Economy*, New York: Harcourt, Brace.

Hansen, Alvin H. (1941), *Fiscal Policy and Business Cycles*, New York: Norton.

Keynes, John M. (1936), *The General Theory of Employment, Interest and Money*, London: Macmillan.

Keynes, John M. (1937), 'Some Economic Consequences of a Declining Population', *Eugenics Review*, April, pp. 13–17; reprinted in Moggridge (ed.) (1973), *The Collected Writings of John Maynard Keynes*, Vol. XIV, ii, London: Macmillan/St Martin's Press, pp. 124–33.

Lindahl, Erik (1930), *Penningpolitikens medel*, Lund: Gleerup; trans. 1939, 'The Rate of Interest and the Price Level', *Studies in the Theory of Money and Capital*, II, London: Allen & Unwin.

Lindahl, Erik (1939), 'The Dynamic Aspect to Economic Theory', *Studies in the Theory of Money and Capital*, I, London: Allen & Unwin.

Lundberg, Erik (1937), *Studies in the Theory of Economic Expansion*, London: King.

Myrdal, Gunnar (1934), *Finanspolitikens ekonomiska verkningar* (The Economic Effects of Fiscal Policy), Stockholm: Norstedt.

Ohlin, Bertil (1934), *Penningpolitik, offentliga arbeten, subventioner och tullar som medel mot arbetslöshet* (Monetary Policy, Public Works, Subsidies and Customs Duties as Measures against Unemployment), Stockholm: Norstedt.

Wicksell, Knut (1898), *Geldzins und Güterpreise*, Jena: Gustav Fischer, trans. 1936, R.F. Kahn, *Interest and Prices*, London: Macmillan.

Stone, Sir John Richard N.

When Sir Richard Stone was awarded the Nobel Memorial Prize in Economic Science in 1984, he was arguably the most obscure of the economist laureates up to that time. It was close to five decades since Keynes had launched the *General Theory* and few of his contemporaries who knew him well in their roles as disciples or adversaries were alive and/or still functioning. Joan Robinson had died the previous year. R.F. Harrod, Keynes's first biographer, had died six years earlier. Hawtrey had passed from the scene almost a decade before. Pigou and Robertson were long gone. Only Richard Kahn, James Meade and Austin Robinson were still in harness. But Richard Stone, who had once worked tirelessly as an assistant to Keynes in the early 1940s, was still working, if a little less earnestly, in 1984, no matter that he is the least known economist named in this paragraph.

John Richard Nicholas Stone was born 13 August 1913, in London and died 6 December 1991, in Cambridge, England. Educated at Westminster School and Gonville and Caius College, Cambridge, Stone first studied law at his father's urging, but soon switched to economics, graduating with a BA in 1935 and an MA in 1938. It was at Cambridge that Stone encountered Colin Clark who was lecturing in statistics. Clark was one of the pioneers in the modeling, measurement and estimation of national income. This work made a deep impression on Stone.

After graduation Stone worked for a London stock brokerage firm for which he turned out a monthly economic newsletter. In connection with this task he began to gain a deeper awareness of the complexity of the economic system. In 1939, at the beginning of World War II, he joined the Ministry of Economic Warfare, leaving the next year for the offices of the War Cabinet where he joined forces with future Nobel laureate James Meade to work on national accounting problems. By this time John Maynard Keynes had become involved in the measurement of national income, making use of Colin Clark's statistics, in working out Keynes's overall plan to aid in the British war effort. But Keynes needed vast amounts of data in order to give persuasive advice on how to run the war economy and he encouraged Stone and Meade to come to his assistance. It was under this stimulus that Stone attempted to generate a complete set of data in order to get a better understanding of the true extent of Britain's resources available for the war effort. The results of this research were published in the 1941 Government White Paper, *An Analysis of the Sources of War Finance and an Estimate of the National Income and Expenditure in 1938 and 1940.*

Stone and Meade jointly had produced a structure for showing how a nation's income and expenditure fitted together into a logically connected system of national accounts. Stone was mainly responsible for the methodological breakthrough that made this possible. What was his innovation? Stone's insight was his recognition of the national income as an interlocking system of accounts in which the concept of double-entry bookkeeping must be maintained. Keynes's emphasis on the equality of income and expenditure in his theoretical analysis of national income has its counterpart in Stone's statistical formulation. The double-entry format revealed that every income item on one side of the national ledger required an expenditure item on the other side. This meant that every outflow item must be matched somewhere else by an inflow item. Stone's systematic framework ensured internal consistency and has become the world standard for organizing national income statistics. It is the work for which Stone received the 1984 Nobel Prize in Economics.

Following the war, Stone returned to Cambridge where, at Keynes's urging, the Department of Applied Economics had been founded. With Keynes's strong backing, Stone was appointed its first director, a position he held until 1955, when he became P.D. Leake Professor of Finance and Accounting at Cambridge. He retired from this position in 1980. During the postwar years Stone turned out a steady flow of papers and books. Most of this work consisted of contributions to applied econometrics, the capstone of which was his massive study, *The Measurement of Consumers' Expenditure and Behaviour in the United Kingdom, 1920–1938* (Stone et al., 1954; Stone and Rowe, 1966). This work continued to build on Keynes's insight that a country's income was a product of consumption, investment and government spending. Keynes's influence on Richard Stone had already been revealed in one of Stone's earliest publications (Stone and Stone, 1938), in which he had attempted empirically to estimate the marginal propensity to consume and the multiplier, concepts that played such a large role in Keynes's *General Theory*. Now Stone devoted intense effort to measure carefully aggregate economic activity by showing the interactions between the various elements that Keynes had previously identified. In so doing, Stone provided a careful and detailed exposition of consumer demand. The work became a classic of econometric literature.

In the 1960s, Richard Stone shifted his attention to the problem of economic growth. Great Britain's relatively sluggish performance in the postwar period had caused alarm and a feeling that a better understanding of the forces making for economic growth was imperative. Accordingly Stone spearheaded a project in the Department of Applied Economics to examine the ways economic policy affected the British growth rate. The Cambridge Growth Project made advances in economic modeling by examining the economy sector by sector rather than by using the standard technique of a highly aggregated model. Stone's disaggregated procedure was a valuable contribution to large-scale empirical modeling techniques and laid the groundwork for further research in this area (Stone and Brown, 1962).

Although Richard Stone was knighted in 1978 and was the recipient of many professional honors, including the presidency of the Econometric Society in 1955 and of the Royal Economic Society from 1978 to 1980, he remained relatively unknown among economists outside Great Britain until the Nobel Prize in 1984 catapulted him into prominence. There are a number of probable reasons for the relative obscurity of someone whose work had such a profound influence on the way economic measurement is carried out. For one thing, research in applied economics did not have the professional prestige accorded to those engaged in high theory. The early Keynesians who achieved great fame among their peers were typically theorists whose work was unburdened by masses of data and sophisticated statistical techniques. As a consequence, the abstract theoretical work of Joan Robinson, Abba Lerner, Paul Samuelson and other leading Keynesian scholars tended to eclipse the contributions of an unglamorous 'number cruncher' like Richard Stone. For another thing, Stone was modest and shunned the limelight. Never a self-promoter, he was not given to recruiting disciples or forming a school of thought. In his entry in *Who's Who*, for example, he listed as his chief recreation 'staying at home'. He and his wife, Lady Giovanna, often spent time reading to each other from their large personal library or attending the theater. To the end Sir Richard Stone remained unimpressed by the weight of his own accomplishments.

WILLIAM BREIT

See also:

Clark, Colin; Keynes, John Maynard; Keynes's Economics, National Income Accounting Activism and; Keynesian Revolution; Kuznets, Simon; Meade, James E.

Bibliography

Houthakker, H.S. (1985), *Richard Stone and the Analysis of Consumer Demand*, Cambridge, Mass.: Harvard Institute of Economic Research.

Johansen, Leif (1987), 'Richard Stone's Contribution to Economics', *Scandinavian Journal of Economics*, **87**, (1), pp. 4–32.

Stone, Sir Richard (1985), 'The Accounts of Society', *Journal of Applied Econometrics*, **1**, (1), January–March, pp. 5–28 (1984 Nobel Memorial Lecture).

Stone, Richard and Alan Brown (1962), *A Computable Model of Economic Growth*, vol. 1 in *A Programme for Growth*, London: Chapman & Hall.

Stone, Richard and D.A. Rowe (1966), *The Measurement of Consumers' Expenditure and Behaviour in the United Kingdom, 1920–1938*, Volume 2, Cambridge: Cambridge University Press.

Stone, Richard and W.M. Stone (1938), 'The Marginal Propensity to Consume and the Multiplier', *Review of Economic Studies*, **6**, (1), October, pp. 1–24.

Stone, Richard, D.A. Rowe, W.J. Corlett, Renée Hurstfield and Muriel Potter (1954), *The Measurement of Consumers' Expenditure and Behaviour in the United Kingdom, 1920–1938*, Volume 1, Cambridge: Cambridge University Press.

Swan, Trevor W.

Deep in our hearts, we know that economists (and no doubt other academics) write too much. Who should know better than we that it is all a matter of incentives? If I try to think of macroeconomists who wrote either just enough or too little, the first names that come to mind are A.W. Phillips and Trevor Swan. Maybe there is something about the southern hemisphere. The limited space available here will be used to describe only two of Swan's major contributions. One is very well known: 'Economic Growth and Capital Accumulation' (1956). The other is essentially unknown: 'The Principle of Effective Demand – A "Real Life" Model', written in 1945 but published in the *Economic Record* only in December 1989. The second of these is a truly remarkable, precocious and pioneering exercise in empirical Keynesianism. The first is Swan's independent version of the standard neoclassical growth model. It serves also as a reminder that one can be a Keynesian for the short run and a neoclassical for the long run, and that this combination of commitments may be the right one.

The 1945/89 paper is an explicit realization of the aggregate supply–aggregate demand model of the *General Theory*. At this late date it has a slightly archaic air, probably because it sticks firmly to Keynes's conventions of measuring everything in wage units, and using employment rather than income as the equilibrating variable. On the demand side, Swan's consumption and investment functions quite naturally use (lagged) income as the main independent variable. So the conversion to employment requires going back to the aggregate supply relation between last period's realized proceeds (=realized income) and last period's actual employment. Thus in the end the aggregate demand curve is not independent of the aggregate supply curve. This does no harm to the model, but one is reminded why the Keynesian tradition shifted to income as the carrier of effective demand.

Apart from the *General Theory*, Swan's guides are Lange's 1938 translation into equations, Kalecki's 1939 *Essays* (especially 'Investment and Income'), Kaldor's 1940 model of the trade cycle and even Pigou's *Employment and Equilibrium*, but he puts them all to shame by virtue of the clarity of his thinking and his use of the macroeconomic data of the Australian economy, 1928–39, to give empirical substance to the analytical structure.

The aggregate supply function is derived from a concave production function (involving employment alone, the stock of capital being fixed) together with profit maximization. Concretely this takes the form of a convex (quadratic) function specifying the dependence of labor requirements on output. Aggregate demand is the sum of consumption demand (a strictly concave function of lagged income, so that the marginal propensity to consume is falling gently), investment demand (linear in lagged income, though Swan mentions the possibility of introducing the acceleration principle), government purchases and net exports. The last two are exogenous and are described as the ultimate determinants.

The out-of-equilibrium mechanism is simple and straightforward. The underlying presumption is that the aggregate demand schedule shifts – driven by autonomous spending on public investment and exports, and also by price-driven changes in imports – along a stable aggregate supply schedule. As the volume of sales varies, firms employ the appropriate number of workers along aggregate supply. From this decision arises a new realized income and the process repeats. Equilibrium would persist, if the demand schedule were unchanged, at its intersection with aggregate supply, because then and only then the volume of spending generates employment decisions that keep the volume of spending unchanged. Since Swan's aggregate demand curve intersects his aggregate supply curve from above, the equilibrium would be stable if only the demand curve did not shift. This combination of equilibrium thinking and sequence analysis is child's play now. For the time, its 26-year-old author is producing a virtuoso performance. The model works and Swan's commentary on it is very sophisticated.

The 1956 paper contains the germ of neoclassical growth theory. But the author has not abandoned Keynesianism. He says: 'When Keynes solved "the great puzzle of Effective Demand", he made it possible for economists once more to study the progress of society in long-run classical terms – with a clear conscience.' In other words, the assumption is that effective demand is so regulated that 'all savings are profitably invested, productive capacity is fully utilized, and the level of employment can never be increased simply by raising the level of spending'.

The model works exclusively in Cobb–Douglas terms (mostly with constant returns to scale). This allows an exposition entirely in terms of growth rates. Although this formulation fits in well with the literature of the time, it obscures the general-equilibrium character of the model. Between them, the limited generality and the preoccupation with growth rates may account for the fact that Swan's mode of exposition did not catch on.

As is now very familiar, under Cobb–Douglas, the growth rate of output is a weighted average of the given growth rate of employment and the growth rate of capital. The latter can be expressed as the product of the saving rate and the output–capital ratio. Swan then shows diagrammatically that there is only one steady-state value of the output–capital ratio, at which output and capital are growing at the same rate as employment, and that all paths converge to this steady state. These are equilibrium paths, but Swan's mode of exposition does not emphasize this point. All of the standard neoclassical results follow from the model; and Swan observes that technical progress is needed to generate a steady state with rising income per head, and can be incorporated in his diagram.

To crown this achievement, Swan notices that the model makes technological progress a powerful way of improving the standard of living and capital accumulation a disconcertingly weak reed. He looks for an answer to 'this anti-accumulation, pro-technology line of argument' and mentions two possibilities. One is very classical: if higher output per head will induce faster growth of the labor force, then something like Arthur Lewis's unlimited supply of labor is present, and additional capital accumulation becomes much more powerful. His second idea is that 'the rate of technical progress may not be independent of the rate of accumulation of capital, or … accumulation may give rise to external economies, so that the true social yield of capital is greater than any "plausible" figure based on common private experience. This point would have appealed to Adam Smith, but it will not be pursued here.' Of course that point is now being pursued by an army of economists.

ROBERT M. SOLOW

See also:
Aggregate Demand–Aggregate Supply Model and Diagram; Domar, Evsey D.; Econometric Models, Macroeconomic; Harcourt, Geoff; Harrod, Sir Roy; Keynes, John Maynard; Keynesian Revolution; Samuelson, Paul A.; Solow, Robert M.

Bibliography
Kaldor, Nicholas (1940), 'A Model of the Trade Cycle', *Economic Journal*, **50**, (197), March, pp. 78–92.

Keynes, John M. (1936), *The General Theory of Employment, Interest and Money*, London: Macmillan.

Lange, O. (1939), *Essays in the Theory of Economic Fluctuations*, New York: Farrar & Rinehart.

Pigou, A.C. (1941), *Employment and Equilibrium*, London: Macmillan.

Swan, Trevor (1956), 'Economic Growth and Capital Accumulation', *Economic Record*, **32**, November, pp. 334–61.

Swan, Trevor (1989), 'The Principle of Effective Demand: A "Real Life" Model', *Economic Record*, **65**, (191), December, pp. 378–98.

Tarshis, Lorie

Lorie Tarshis (born Singer) was born in Toronto, Ontario, on 22 March 1911. After the death of his natural father of typhoid in 1915, Tarshis's mother remarried and Lorie took the surname of his stepfather.

Tarshis earned a BComm in 1932 from the University of Toronto, where he read the *Treatise on Money* under the tutelage of A.F.W. (Wynne) Plumptre and Vincent Bladen. Subsequently he traveled to Cambridge to study with Keynes, taking the BA (1934), MA (1938) and PhD (1939) from Trinity College, Cambridge. In his 1947 obituary article on Keynes, Austin Robinson remembers Tarshis as a member of the Cambridge Circus. This group consisted of Austin and Joan Robinson, James Meade, Richard Kahn, Piero Sraffa, Charles Gifford, Wynne Plumptre, Tarshis and several others, with varying composition from term to term. This circle offered critical remarks to Keynes on his *Treatise* which many of the members later felt were influential in assisting him in making the transition from the thinking of that book to the thinking of the *General Theory*.

Tarshis's dissertation, which incorporated some of the short-run analysis of Joan Robinson and Richard Kahn, was entitled 'The Determinants of Labor Income'. It presaged his important 1938 and 1939 papers on the movement of real wages across the cycle which (along with John T. Dunlop's work) convinced Keynes that he needed to rethink the competitive assumptions in the *General Theory*. In the 1939 paper, for example, Tarshis specifically highlights three major assumptions of Keynes: (1) that money wages begin to rise only after unemployment has fallen to a very low level; (2) that increases in output beyond this point are associated with rising marginal costs even in the absence of increases in money wages; and (3) that the character of competition does not change appreciably between the lower and upper turning points of the cycle. Tarshis argues that these assumptions are not borne out by US data and hence that they are not realistic.

Tarshis's academic positions include Tufts University, Stanford University, University of Toronto and York University. He was also a Carnegie Fellow at the National Bureau of Economic Research and held a number of positions during World War II, including stints with the War Production Board, the Ninth and Twelfth Bomber Commands and the Fifteenth Air Force in Italy during which he learned much about the methodology of natural scientists. He has also held the position of research director with the Ontario Economic Council.

Tarshis is best known as a meticulous student and proselytizer of Keynesian economics. His notes on Keynes's lectures form an integral part of Thomas

Rymes's reconstruction of Keynes's thinking during the formative years of the *General Theory*. It is based on the classroom notes of nine of Keynes's students. The two students in this group who kept notes for more Michaelmas terms under Keynes than any of the others included in Rymes's book were Tarshis and fellow Canadian Robert Bryce. While Bryce is generally given credit for having more to do with bringing Keynes to America, Tarshis, after his return to the United States, assumed a position at Tufts University which allowed him to attend seminars at Harvard and to play an important role in bringing Keynesian economics to Cambridge, Massachusetts.

Tarshis's work on the aggregate supply function is held in high regard by Keynesian economists. More recently his writings have ranged over such widely diverse issues as problems with international debt (especially those of LDCs), the relationship between deficits, debt and interest rates and essays in the history of economic thought. An extensive bibliography of Tarshis's work is given in Cohen and Harcourt (1986).

Tarshis was an exceptional classroom performer and pioneered the teaching of Keynesian economics in the United States with his *The Elements of Economics* (1947), now recognized as the first fully Keynesian textbook designed for the college and university market. The book had an early success but became embroiled in charges that it and its author were a part of a dangerous socialist trend in the teaching of economics. In fact, William F. Buckley, Jr., in *God and Man at Yale*, refers to Tarshis no fewer than ten times in this context. For this reason the book never achieved the best-seller status that slightly later Keynesian treatments of macroeconomics (such as that of Paul Samuelson) would enjoy. There is little doubt as to Tarshis's eminence as teacher and researcher. But it is also true that his biographers uniformly refer to him as a caring man with an easy ability to make friends and one who was quick to offer valuable assistance to colleagues. Tarshis died 4 October 1993.

BEN W. BOLCH

See also:

Cambridge Circus; Currie, Lauchlin; Hansen, Alvin H.; Kahn, Lord Richard F.; Keynesian Revolution; Keynesianism in America; Robinson, Joan.

Bibliography

Cohen, Jon S. and G.C. Harcourt (1986), 'Introduction', in Jon S. Cohen and G.C. Harcourt (eds), *International Monetary Problems and Supply-Side Economics: Essays in Honor of Lorie Tarshis*, New York: St Martin's Press.

Harcourt, G.C. (1982). 'An Early Post Keynesian: Lorie Tarshis (or: Tarshis on Tarshis by Harcourt)', *Journal of Post Keynesian Economics*, **4**, (4), summer, pp. 609–19.

Robinson, Austin (1947), 'John Maynard Keynes', *Economic Journal*, **57**, (225), March, pp. 1–68.

Rymes, Thomas K. (ed.) (1989), *Keynes's Lectures, 1932–35, Notes of a Representative Student*, Ann Arbor: University of Michigan Press.

Tarshis, Lorie (1938), 'Real Wages in the United States and Great Britain', *Canadian Journal of Economics and Political Science*, **4**, pp. 362–76.

Tarshis, Lorie (1939), 'Changes in Real and Money Wages', *Economic Journal*, **49**, (103), March, pp. 150–54.

Tarshis, Lorie (1947), *The Elements of Economics: An Introduction to the Theory of Price and Employment*, Boston: Houghton Mifflin.

Tarshis, Lorie. (1967), *Modern Economics: An Introduction*, Boston, Mass.: Houghton Mifflin Company.

Tarshis, Lorie (1978), 'Keynes as Seen by His Students in the 1930s', in Don Patinkin and J.C. Leith (eds), *Keynes, Cambridge and the General Theory*, Toronto: University of Toronto Press, pp. 48–63.

Tarshis, Lorie (1979), 'The Aggregate Supply Function in Keynes's *General Theory*', in Michael J. Boskin (ed.), *Economics and Human Welfare: Essays in Honour of Tibor Scitovsky*, New York: Academic Press, pp. 369–93.

Tarshis, Lorie (1984), *World Economy in Crisis: Unemployment. Inflation and International Debt*, Toronto: James Lorimer.

Tarshis, Lorie (1988), 'The International Debt of the LDCs', in Omar F. Hamouda and John Born Smithin (eds), *Keynes and Public Policy After Fifty Years*, vol. 2, New York: Columbia University Press.

Technological Change

Technological change, a change in the level of technical knowledge, is typically interpreted in an incremental or positive sense. Knowledge ordinarily advances or progresses rather than retreats or regresses, and consequently the notions of change and progress are virtually synonymous. Progress can be readily thought of in a production function context, where it has three dichotomous dimensions. It is either neutral or non-neutral, either disembodied or embodied, and either exogenous or endogenous. The first dimension refers to the pattern of the isoquant shift prompted by progress. Isoquants shift towards the origin, and neutrality – or unbiasedness – in the Hicksian taxonomy means that they shift in a parallel fashion. Hicks non-neutral – or biased – progress means that the shifts occur in a non-parallel fashion, thereby 'saving' one input and 'using' another. Neutrality in Hicks's view can also be understood as progress that augments, or expands, the various inputs at the same rate. By contrast, Harrod neutrality is progress that augments only the labor input, whereas Solow neutrality augments only the capital input. However, under the production function developed by Charles Cobb and Paul Douglas (1928), Hicks, Harrod and Solow neutralities are all equivalent.

The second dimension refers to the mechanism by which progress enters the productive process. Can technical progress be captured in the absence of new capital goods, or can it enter only on the back of new capital? In the former case, progress is called disembodied. Isoquants shift even if no new capital is acquired. Progress is organizational in nature. In other words, it applies uniformly to all capital goods regardless of their age and, hence, from the standpoint of technology, capital goods are homogeneous. In the latter case, progress is embodied: isoquants shift only if new capital is acquired. To take advantage of the latest advances in robotics, a firm must purchase a new robot. Reorganizing capital by moving a screwdriver from one side of the assembly line to another would miss entirely the improvement in know-how. Similarly, to take advantage of the latest breakthroughs in avionics, an airline must buy new equipment. Relocating a fire extinguisher from starboard to port in a ten-year-old aircraft would be ineffective in seizing those developments. By embodying the technology of the date of their construction, capital goods do not share uniformly in progress. They are heterogeneous rather than homogeneous.

Dimension three, exogeneity versus endogeneity, refers to the control that entrepreneurs exert over progress. Exogenous progress is progress whose features such as speed and bias remain beyond the influence of entrepreneurs. By comparison, endogenous progress is progress that responds to business preferences shaped perhaps by the movement of prices or by the behavior of factor shares.

As regards dimension two, disembodiment versus embodiment, John Maynard Keynes (1936) offers some early insights in *The General Theory of Employment, Interest and Money*. In fact, certain passages there constitute a basic 'how to' guide for later practitioners. Commenting in Chapter 4 on Professor Pigou's treatment of the net National Dividend or net output, Keynes notes the distinction between new and old capital attributable to physical deterioration. As he says (p. 38), 'we have to find some basis for a quantitative comparison between the new items of equipment produced during the period and the old items which have perished by wastage'. Soon thereafter he stresses the idea that capital is heterogeneous owing to technical progress. In his words (p. 39), Professor Pigou 'is unable to devise any satisfactory formula to evaluate new equipment against old when, owing to changes in technique, the two are not identical'. Keynes further observes (p. 39) that 'calculating net output by setting off new items of equipment against the wastage of old items presents conundrums which permit, one can confidently say, of no solution'. To this point he later adds that the notions of the quantity of output as a whole and the quantity of capital equipment as a whole are vague ones (p. 43). According to Keynes, then, new capital should be distinguished from old capital because of decay, capital is heterogeneous owing to progress, and calculating something as vague as output and capital aggregates entails unsolvable conundrums.

Yet Keynes goes on to suggest how capital might be aggregated. He introduces the methodology in terms of labor by arguing that the quantities of employment, when heterogeneous, can be made homogeneous (p. 41) 'by taking an hour's employment of ordinary labour as our unit and weighting an hour's employment of special labour in proportion to its remuneration; *i.e.* an hour of special labour remunerated at double ordinary rates will count as two units'. For capital that is heterogeneous by virtue of embodiment, this Keynesian method advises taking capital at some initial point in time, say time zero, as 'our unit' with a technology weight of one and calibrating proportionally the quality improvements built into the newer capital: machinery embodying twice the technical know-how of the base stock commanding a technology weight of two.

But Keynes provides even more guidance concerning aggregation. In Chapter 11 of *The General Theory*, he refers to what has come to be called 'vintage production functions'. To quote (p. 141), 'The output from equipment produced to-day will have to compete, in the course of its life, with the output from equipment produced subsequently, perhaps at a lower labour cost, perhaps by an improved technique.' Each layer or vintage of capital generates a layer of output. That is, output is set out at the vintage level, and aggregate output results from a summation across vintages.

Precision can be injected into this reasoning by specifying, for manageability, the vintage production function to be Cobb–Douglas and thus progress to be equivalently Hicks, Harrod and Solow neutral. Moreover progress may be modeled both as disembodied at the exponential rate γ and as embodied at the exponential rate μ. Exogeneity prevails, making

$$Y_{vt} = \beta e^{\gamma t} L_{vt}^{\alpha} (e^{\mu v} K_{vt})^{1-\alpha}, \tag{1}$$

whose β is a constant. Y_{vt} denotes the quantity of output produced from capital of vintage v at time t, L_{vt} symbolizes the quantity of labor employed on capital of vintage v at t, and K_{vt} signifies the stock of capital of vintage v surviving at t. Necessarily $v \leq t$. Consonant with the Keynesian method, vintage zero equipment has an embodiment index $e^{\mu v}$ of one whereas, under a 3 per cent embodiment rate ($\mu = 0.03$), vintage 23 has an index of two. Inasmuch as the capital and labor exponents sum to unity, the vintage function exhibits constant returns to scale. Furthermore it involves both variable factor proportions and a diminishing marginal product of labor, two properties held by Keynes (1936, pp. 17–18).

Proceeding from vintages to aggregates can be done by following Robert Solow (1960, pp. 91–3) or James Gapinski (1982, pp. 287–90). Homogeneous labor is allocated over heterogeneous capital to equalize labor's marginal product across vintages:

$$\partial Y_{vt} / \partial L_{vt} = m_t, \tag{2}$$

m_t being the common marginal product at t. The motivation behind this equimarginal-product rule is the maximization of aggregate output. Such output Y_t is the sum of the outputs across vintages, and aggregate labor L_t is the corresponding sum of homogeneous labor across vintages. Arithmetically

$$Y_t = \int_{-\infty}^{t} Y_{vt}\,dv, \tag{3}$$

$$L_t = \int_{-\infty}^{t} L_{vt}\,dv, \tag{4}$$

where, for convenience, the set of surviving vintages consists of all vintages ever constructed.

Expanding relation (2) using equation (1) and substituting results into expressions (3) and (4) eventually yield

$$Y_t = \beta e^{\pi t} L_t^{\alpha} J_t^{1-\alpha}, \tag{5}$$

$$J_t = \int_{-\infty}^{t} e^{\mu v} K_{vt}\,dv. \tag{6}$$

The J_t factor can be seen as the aggregate capital stock under embodiment. Through K_{vt} it distinguishes new equipment from old equipment that has not 'perished by wastage'. In addition, it weights the heterogeneous capital by the embodiment index to create a homogeneous measure $e^{\mu v} K_{vt}$, which is then summed. Correspondingly, expression (5) can be recognized as the aggregate production function: it ties aggregate output to aggregate labor and aggregate capital. Given the precision of equations (5) and (6), aggregate output and aggregate capital are not as vague as one might infer from reading Keynes. Alvin Hansen (1953, p. 44) concurs.

Three points might be mentioned in connection with this mathematical exercise. First, when progress is entirely disembodied with $\mu = 0$, the aggregate capital stock J_t reduces to a simple, uncorrected sum of the vintage stocks. In other words, capital is homogeneous. Each vintage is identical to every other vintage as all vintages share equally in the advancing know-how. Second, the derivation of the aggregate relationships from the vintage counterparts is not automatic. Instead it occurs under restrictive conditions. As Franklin Fisher (1965, pp. 264–5, 269–72) shows, the equimarginal-product rule (2) must hold, and embodiment must take a form that enables the vintage production function to be specified with capital-generalized constant returns; namely, under embodiment the function must display constant returns to scale in labor and any technology-induced monotonic transformation of capital. Fixed factor proportions, which undermine restriction (2), represent only one threat to the aggregation process. Third, embodiment need not invalidate the standard growth-theoretic conclusion that steady equilibrium growth occurs at Harrod's natural rate, which depends directly on the growth rates of labor and technology.

This third property can be verified by postulating that the surviving stock of vintage v capital K_{vt} is linked to the total amount of vintage v produced I_v, the link being the deterioration schedule $K_{vt} = I_v e^{-\delta(t-v)}$, where δ is the rate of physical decay and where $t-v$ is the age of vintage v at time t. For equilibrium $I_t = sY_t$, s denoting the saving rate. It therefore follows that steady equilibrium growth requires that $\hat{Y} = \hat{I} = \zeta$, the circumflex indicating a growth rate and the ζ representing a constant. Imposing these conditions on relations (5) and (6) and positing aggregate labor L_t to expand at the exponential rate η ultimately leaves $\zeta = \eta + \gamma/\alpha + \mu(1 - \alpha)/\alpha$ confirming that steady equilibrium growth takes place at the natural rate.

An interesting sidelight to the embodiment discussion can be found in the work of Nicholas Kaldor. One of Keynes's countrymen, Kaldor (1957, pp. 595–8; 1961, pp. 207–9, 215) saw embodiment as being incompatible with the premise of a production function because, in his view, capital acquisitions under embodiment confused movements across stationary isoquants with shifts in isoquants. Striking out in a supposedly different direction, Kaldor proposed a technical progress function, which related the growth rate of output per head to the growth rate of capital per head. Nevertheless, when postulated in linear fashion, the technical progress function reduced to an aggregate production function analogous to equation (5). Thus, despite Kaldor's intention, the two concepts proved to exhibit a fairly close kinship.

JAMES H. GAPINSKI

See also:

Business Cycle Theory (I) and (II); Domar, Evsey D.; Harcourt, Geoff; Harrod, Sir Roy; Hicks, Sir John R.; Kaldor, Lord Nicholas; Robinson, Joan; Samuelson, Paul A.; Schumpeter, Joseph A.; Solow, Robert M.; Swan, Trevor W.

Bibliography

Cobb, Charles W. and Paul H. Douglas (1928), 'A Theory of Production', *American Economic Review*, **18**, (1), Supplement, March, pp. 139–65.
Fisher, Franklin M. (1965), 'Embodied Technical Change and the Existence of an Aggregate Capital Stock', *Review of Economic Studies*, **32**, (92), October, pp. 263–88.
Gapinski, James H. (1982), *Macroeconomic Theory: Statics, Dynamics and Policy*, New York: McGraw-Hill.
Hansen, Alvin H. (1953), *A Guide to Keynes*, New York: McGraw-Hill.
Kaldor, Nicholas (1957), 'A Model of Economic Growth', *Economic Journal*, **67**, (268), December, pp. 591–624.
Kaldor, Nicholas (1961), 'Capital Accumulation and Economic Growth', in F.A. Lutz and D.C. Hague (eds), *The Theory of Capital*, London: Macmillan.
Keynes, John Maynard (1936), *The General Theory of Employment, Interest and Money*, London: Macmillan.
Solow, Robert M. (1960), 'Investment and Technical Progress', in K.J. Arrow, S. Karlin and P. Suppes (eds), *Mathematical Methods in the Social Sciences, 1959*, Stanford: Stanford University Press.

Tobin, James

James Tobin was born in Champaign, Illinois, in 1918. He received his bachelor's degree in 1939 and his master's degree in 1940, both from Harvard. Following naval service during the years 1942–6, he returned to his graduate studies and received his PhD from Harvard in 1947. In 1950, he joined the economics department at Yale University, and he has largely remained at Yale and has been identified with this institution throughout his career. He twice directed the Cowles Foundation for Research in Economics, first from 1955 to 1961, and then from 1964 to 1965. He also served for two years, 1961–2, as a member of President Kennedy's Council of Economic Advisors. In 1981, he was awarded the Nobel Prize in Economics for his many important and diverse contributions to economic theory.

Tobin's most fundamental contributions to economics are in the fields of monetary and macroeconomic theory. His first published paper (in 1941), 'A Note on the Money Wage Problem', addresses the problem of whether a cut in money wages exerts an independent influence on aggregate employment. This question was at the heart of Keynes's criticism of classical economics. Tobin demonstrates his gift for critical thought and logical consistency by criticizing Keynes's notion of an unemployment equilibrium. He points out that a reduction in money wages will diminish the transactions demand for money and lead to a fall in interest rates, causing a rise in investment, output and employment. Tobin does not believe, however, that this removes the need for government intervention during recessions. According to Tobin, all that is required to justify Keynesian demand management policies is sluggish wage and price adjustments. From this early paper, it is clear that Tobin was destined not merely to *follow*, but to extend and refine Keynes's analysis.

Tobin's seminal 1958 paper, 'Liquidity Preference as Behavior Towards Risk', provides a new framework to deal with a question raised by Hicks in his 1935 paper, 'A Suggestion for Simplifying the Theory of Money'. Hicks asks why people would hold zero interest assets (money) when other interest-bearing assets are available. In his response to this question, Tobin revolutionized monetary theory by providing a choice-theoretic model of money demand. This model was required to execute Sir John Hicks's famous 'Suggestion'. In addition, in this same paper, he established a whole new discipline, financial economics, by introducing the 'separation theorem'. This theorem explains that risk-averse people will diversify their portfolios by holding both money (a safe asset with a zero yield) and risky assets with potential positive returns. Another important prediction of Tobin's model is that the demand for money will fall as the return on the risky asset increases. In this one paper, Tobin was able to provide a firmer theoretical justification for Keynes's liquidity preference theory, advance monetary theory by utilizing a choice-theoretic framework to analyse the demand for money, and become the 'father' of financial economics.

Tobin has made important contributions to the theory of economic growth. His 1965 paper, 'Money and Economic Growth', deals with the interaction between monetary factors and the degree of capital intensity in the economy. His analysis leads him to the conclusion that monetary policy can effect the ratio of capital to labor in long-run equilibrium. This is due to the fact that an increase in the rate of money growth leads to an increase in the equilibrium inflation rate. The higher inflation rate causes individuals to substitute away from money and towards capital in their portfolios. This illustrates how Tobin's portfolio balance approach to economic questions has provided interesting answers to a variety of economic questions.

However it was not until the publication of his 1969 paper, 'A General Equilibrium Approach to Monetary Theory', that Tobin presented a complete formal summary of his theoretical framework. In that paper he spells out a full model of asset equilibrium and relates asset yields to the flow of investment. In the model, the ratio of the market value of the firm's capital to the replacement cost of the firm's capital (Tobin's Q) was the key variable determining the flow of investment. Furthermore the theory points out that stock prices contain information, because they are good indicators of the market value of firms' capital.

Throughout his career Tobin has been a vocal critic of monetarism. His 1970 paper, 'Money and Income: Post Hoc Ergo Propter Hoc?', presented an effective criticism of the reduced-form evidence showing a link between money and income often used to support monetarist conclusions. Tobin was able to demonstrate that a simplified Keynesian model could generate the same temporal relationships between money and income which monetarists claimed supported their views. He warned against the danger of 'accepting timing evidence as empirical proof of propositions about causation'. Ironically the Tobin-type 'reverse causality' argument has recently become popular among proponents of Real Business Cycle Theory. These economists use the criticism to explain away evidence showing that nominal shocks have real output effects.

Looking back on Tobin's career, it is clear that his contributions to economic science have been enormous. He has also been a consistent and vocal advocate of Keynesian stabilization policies. This seems appropriate since Tobin had done more than anyone else to extend and refine the analysis first presented in *The General Theory*.

TONY CAPORALE

See also:

Business Cycle Theory (I) and (II); Demand Management; Friedman, Milton; Hicks, Sir John R.; Kahn, Lord Richard F.; Keynesian Revolution; Lausanne The School of; Markowitz, Harry M.; Monetarist School of Economics; Monetary Policy; Sharpe, William F.

Bibliography

Hicks, John (1935), 'A Suggestion for Simplifying the Theory of Money', *Economica*, NS, **2**, (5), February, pp. 1–19.
Tobin, James (1941), 'A Note on the Money Wage Problem', *Quarterly Journal of Economics*, **50**, (3), May, pp. 508–16.
Tobin, James (1958), 'Liquidity Preference as Behaviour Towards Risk', *Review of Economic Studies*, **25**, (67), February, pp. 65–86.
Tobin, James (1965), 'Money and Economic Growth', *Econometrica*, **33**, (4), October, pp. 671–84.
Tobin, James (1969), 'A General Equilibrium Approach to Monetary Theory', *Journal of Money, Credit and Banking*, **1**, (1), February, pp. 15–29.
Tobin, James (1970), 'Money and Income: Post Hoc Ergo Propter Hoc?', *Quarterly Journal of Economics*, **84**, (335), May, pp. 301–17.

Townsend, Robert

Born in 1948, Robert Townsend earned his PhD from the University of Minnesota at Minneapolis in 1975 with his dissertation of 'Essays on Markets Under Uncertainty'. The son of an economist, he admitted to initially resisting going into the study of economics, but his interest in the social sciences prevailed and his fondness for economics was strengthened by the contrast it offers with other social science disciplines. In his own words, he admired economics as a discipline for its explanatory, rather than descriptive and encyclopedic, aspect. He portrayed economics as a 'search for explanations ... for abstractions that shed light on existing arrangements'. In a December 1982 interview (Klamer, 1984), he credited Neil Wallace and Thomas Sargent as two major influences in the early development of his career as an economist. He is a well-published author with works dealing principally with information and contracts.

During the same 1982 interview, Townsend expressed his interest in the availability of information and the differences of available information as important facets of his research. The volume of articles he has written on this topic attests to his continued interest and research on this issue: 'Optimal Contracts and Competitive Markets with Costly State Verification' (Townsend, 1979): 'Allocation Mechanisms, Asymmetric Information and the Revelation Principle' (Townsend and Harris, 1985); 'Resource Allocation Under Asymmetric Information' (Townsend and Harris, 1981); 'Information Constrained Insurance' (Townsend, 1988). These articles explored models where asymmetric information can only be transmitted at some cost, where agents are asymmetrically informed prior to trading and, thus, the cost of information asymmetries imposes certain incentive compatibility constraints on achievable allocation, and the application of statistical decision theory that explicitly incorporates information availability and transmittal to characterizing efficient allocation processes.

His latest work (Townsend, 1990) deals with the way agents organize themselves for economic purposes and how financial arrangements develop out of these economic conditions. The book consists of 15 previously published articles organized into topics representative of Townsend's varied interests. These articles discuss the role of spatial separation, uncertainty, private information, limited communication and limited commitment as essential ingredients in the development of the financial arrangements, contracts and economic organization. An interesting aspect of this book is his attempt to match 'key features in environments of theories with key features in actual historical environments' as these features apply to the early European economy. The inspiration for this book was his observation that the evolution of the European economy as described in the historical materials seems closely to parallel stylized economic models. Separation in terms of space and time, the uncertainty related to production, the primitive (or, lack of) communication that cultivated the prevalence of private information and the difficulties of forming arrangements during those times are important characterizations of the early economy and the stylized facts in some economic models. The early European economy provided a good research agenda for studying economic organizations resulting from spatial separation and financial arrangements and instruments resulting from uncertainty.

RUTH I. OBAR

See also:

Friedman, Milton; Lucas, Jr., Robert E.; Markowitz, Harry M.; New Classical School of Economics; Tobin, James; von Hayek, Friedrich A.

Bibliography

Feiwel, George R. (ed.) (1985), *Issues in Contemporary Microeconomics and Welfare*, New York: State University of New York Press.

Klamer, Arjo (1984), *Conversations with Economists*, Totowa, NJ: Rowman and Allanheld.

Townsend, Robert (1979), 'Optimal Contracts and Competitive Markets with Costly State Verification', *Journal of Economic Theory*, **21**, (2), October, pp. 265–93.

Townsend, Robert (1988), 'Information Constrained Insurance', *Journal of Monetary Economics*, **21**, (2/3), March/May, pp. 411–50.

Townsend, Robert (1990), *Financial Structure and Economic Organization: Key Elements and Patterns in Theory and History*, Oxford: Basil Blackwell.

Townsend, Robert and Milton Harris (1981), 'Resource Allocation Under Asymmetric Information', *Econometrica*, **49**, (1), January, pp. 33–69.

Townsend, Robert and Milton Harris (1985), 'Allocation Mechanisms, Asymmetric Information and the Revelation Principle', in George R. Feiwel (ed.), *Issues in Contemporary Microeconomics and Welfare*, New York: State University of New York Press.

Treasury View

The 'Treasury view' is the name given to a tenet held by the British Treasury Department during the 1920s and 1930s concerning the effectiveness and appropriateness of public works expenditures as an employment policy. The economic environment of the time was a general decline towards the Great Depression and the position arose as Treasury officials made public their opposition to the use of public works expenditures. The 'Treasury view' represents a focal point in the debate between Keynes and various Treasury officials.

The position was first publicly taken by Treasury Assistant Secretary Ralph Hawtrey in 1925. Winston Churchill, in his role as chancellor of the exchequer, asserted the 'Treasury view' in 1929 that 'very little additional employment and no permanent employment' can be created by loan financed public works. The Treasury's position in opposition to public works expenditures seems to have originated as a response to actions taken by the Lloyd George government in the very early 1920s and was outlined in various oral testimonies before Parliament and in some written statements.

The position amounts to a denial of public works expenditures as a policy tool in the government's pursuit of lower unemployment rates. The 'Treasury view' is a broad summary of the official attitude towards the management and direction of the British economy, prompted by a firm belief among Treasury officials and policy makers in balanced national budgets that resulted in an attack on public works schemes. The attack resides on the ground that, owing to a crowding out effect, public works expenditures would not stimulate macroeconomic activity. The view was ultimately abandoned in 1937, when the Treasury embraced countercyclical policy and the extensive use of loan-financed public works projects.

The theoretical basis of the 'Treasury view', in addition to the perceived result of crowding out, included the relationship between saving and investing. Keynes held that identity to be true prior to 1920, but Treasury officials held tenaciously to the idea that saving determined investment during periods of relatively high unemployment. In addition to a general wariness of inflation, the Treasury position also required strict adherence to a quantity theory of money, as expressed primarily by Hawtrey in other writings. The term 'Treasury view' could have been coined by Keynes himself as he wrote and spoke against it, although it was most likely used by Treasury officials in describing and defending their various policies. In 1925, the term was used in Treasury communications with the International Labour Organization. The 'Treasury view' was the subject of a White Paper published by the Conservative government in 1929. Keynes, Joan Robinson and A.C. Pigou all used the term freely in opposing the policy.

The opposition to the 'Treasury view' was led by Keynes and supported by a wide range of contemporaries within both the economics community and the party not in power, in this case the Liberals. Keynes's opposition to the official position limiting public works expenditures developed prior to the publication of *The General Theory* and represented an evolution in his economic and political thinking. Because he was outside the government, he could easily ignore or underestimate concerns about public confidence as a contributor to the success of policy. The positions Keynes took in opposing the 'Treasury view' included apparent shifts in his thinking, primarily on budget deficits, the relationship between saving and investment and exchange rates. He defended these shifts on the grounds that the essence of being both a scholar and an economist was continually to question previously held positions, including one's own.

Keynes took public written positions in favor of public works expenditures as a way to mitigate unemployment in journal articles as early as 1924. His answer to the crowding out problem relied upon his faith in the role of interest rates in the relationship between saving and investment and a *reductio ad absurdum* argument, familiar in later writings, that it is incumbent upon government to create unemployment when the private sector cannot. He was also concurrently moving away from a philosophy of permanently balanced budgets and towards the position that there were times when it was not practicable for the government to reduce government expenditures, especially during deep recessions. By 1929, he was prepared to admit that public works would not bring unemployment levels back up to those seen prior to 1914. Instead Keynes believed that employment, which by then was being regularly monitored using standard definitions, would certainly increase above current levels. The debate also included acceptance by both sides of the emerging multiplier concept, although interpretations of the effect of the multiplier varied.

The debate over the proper role of public works expenditures and particularly the method of financing those expenditures has continued at various times since the 1930s in both the United States and Great Britain. Most recently the narrow interpretation of crowding out was used within the context of supply-side writings.

In terms of the policies actually augmented by the Treasury during the course of their adherence to the 'Treasury view', there is a modest mix of tax-financed and loan-financed public works expenditures. Thus there was not strict adherence to a prohibition against public works. However the evaluation of the policies by Keynes and his sympathetic contemporaries was that actual expenditures were too small to have a significant macroeconomic impact. It is important to recall that Keynes was reacting in almost all of his writings and speeches in the late 1920s and 1930s to the Great Depression that spread through most industrialized economies. Because of the enormity of economic problems faced at the time, it is difficult to see in his writings a position that would be compatible with the new classical economics. The main criticism of rational expectations by the followers of Keynes is the failure of the new theory to explain prolonged periods of economic depression. Keynes's advocacy of budget deficits resulting from public works expenditures to reduce unemployment is clearly a discretionary policy rather than a 'rule'.

HAROLD R. CHRISTENSEN

See also:

Classical Economics; Government Investment Programs (the Socialization of Investment); Hawtrey, Sir Ralph; Keynes, John Maynard; Keynesian Revolution; Niemeyer, Sir Otto E.; Robertson, Sir Dennis H.

Bibliography

Dimand, Robert W. (1988), *The Origins of the Keynesian Revolution: The development of Keynes' theory of employment and output*, Stanford: Stanford University Press.

Keynes, John Maynard (1930), *A Treatise on Money*, London: Macmillan.

Keynes, John M. (1936), *The General Theory of Employment, Interest and Money*, London: Macmillan.

Keynes, John Maynard and Hubert Henderson (1929), 'Can Lloyd George Do It? The Pledge Examined'; reprinted in *The Collected Writings of John Maynard Keynes*, Vol. IX.

Middleton, Roger (1985), *Towards the Managed Economy: Keynes, the treasury and the fiscal policy debate of the 1930s*, New York: Methuen.

Patinkin, Don (1976), *Keynes' Monetary Thought: A study of its development*, Durham: Duke University Press.

Patinkin, Don (1982), *Anticipations of the General Theory? and other essays on Keynes*, Chicago: University of Chicago Press.

Peden, G.C. (1984), 'The "Treasury View" on Public Works and Employment in the Interwar Period', *The Economic History Review*, **25**, (2), May, pp. 167–82.

Weeks, John (1989), *A Critique of Neoclassical Macroeconomics*, New York: St Martin's Press.

Viner, Jacob

Jacob Viner was born on 3 May 1892 in Montreal and died on 12 September 1970. He graduated from McGill University in 1914 and completed his doctoral dissertation under the direction of his mentor, Frank W. Taussig, at Harvard in 1922. The dissertation, *Canada's Balance of International Indebtedness, 1900–1913*, was published by Harvard University Press in 1924. Viner began his career, well before obtaining his PhD, at the University of Chicago in 1916. In 1921, he published his first major contribution to economic theory; in 1925, at the age of 32, he was promoted to full professor; and in 1929, he was named co-editor of the *Journal of Political Economy* with Frank Knight, raising it to 'the peak of its distinction' (Baumol and Seiler, 1979, p. 783). During his tenure at Chicago, Viner also held several positions in government. In 1950, he moved to Princeton to become the third Walker Professor of International Finance. He retired from teaching in 1960, but remained intellectually active until his death.

Viner made major contributions to all fields in which he wrote. However his major accomplishments can be summarized in the areas of economic theory, international economics and the history of economic thought. He was a sympathetic critic of Keynes and an early advocate of active countercyclical fiscal policy. The first major contribution to economic theory came in Viner's 1921 article, 'Price Policies: The Determination of Market Price' (reprinted in Viner, 1958). This remarkable five-page article contains the basic elements of both the theory of monopolistic competition and the kinked demand curve within the theory of a 'follow-the-leader method of price determination' (Viner, 1958, p. 6). As Spiegel (1987) observes, Viner's article was published five years before Sraffa (1926), 12 years before Robinson (1933) and Chamberlin (1933) and 18 years before Sweezy (1939). While this first article was largely ignored by the profession, Viner's other great achievement in economic theory, his 1931 article, 'Cost Curves and Supply Curves', immediately changed the profession. This article contains much of what is still considered the modern theory of cost, including Viner's famous (famous partly for its mistake) development of the envelope curve. As is well known, Viner wanted his draftsman, Dr Wong, to draw each tangency of the short-run and long-run cost curves at the minimum point of the short-run curves. Samuelson reports that, as of 1935, Viner was willing to admit to his class that he had been wrong both mathematically and economically. However Samuelson also recounts a light-hearted exchange with Viner that, 'he [Viner] said to me privately just as the class bell rang, "although there seems to be some esoteric mathematical reason why the envelope cannot be drawn so that it passes smoothly through the declining bottoms of the U-shaped cost curves, nevertheless *I* can do it!" "Yes," I replied impishly, "with a good *thick* pencil, you can do it"' (Samuelson, 1972, p. 9).

While Jacob Viner made significant contributions to advance pure economic theory, he is best known for his contributions to the history of economic thought and international trade theory. He should be ranked among the top historians of thought of his generation. Viner's method in writing the history of thought was to evaluate previous writers through the lens of modern theory. Given that, as Viner saw the world, economic theory has progressed with each passing generation towards a clearer understanding of the fundamental relations guiding the path of all economies, older doctrines were evaluated by the closeness with which they conformed to modern theory. This approach is best illustrated in his masterpiece, *Studies in the Theory of International Trade*, in which he provides 'an inventory of English ideas, good and bad ... classified and examined in the light of modern monetary and trade theory' (Viner, 1975, p. 2).

This approach to the history of thought provided Viner with what he saw as a powerful critique of Keynes's assessment of mercantilist doctrine as outlined in Chapter 23 of the *General Theory*. As viewed in the light of the modern theory of comparative cost, Viner found that almost all mercantilist doctrine should be rejected, along with the 'modern apologies for mercantilism' (ibid., p. 110). When Keynes lauded mercantilist writers for never supposing 'that there was a self-adjusting tendency by which the rate of interest would be established at the appropriate level' (Keynes, 1964, p. 341), Viner questioned his objectivity: 'As a historian of thought in areas in which he was emotionally involved as a protagonist and prophet, Keynes seemed to me to be seriously lacking in the unexciting but essential qualities for the intellectual historian of objectivity and of judiciousness' (Lekachman, 1964, p. 254). The truth seems to be that Keynes was using Viner's methodology of evaluation; he merely held different modern theories as his measuring rod.

Viner wrote two extensive reviews of Keynes's *General Theory*. The first appeared in the *Quarterly Journal of Economics* in 1936; the second, which extended the scope of the first, was published in Lekachman (1964). His evaluation of Keynes was both respectful and highly critical. The original review began with high praise: 'The indebtedness of economists to Mr. Keynes has been greatly increased by this latest addition to his series of brilliant, original and provocative books, whose contribution to our enlightenment will prove, I am sure, to have been greater in the long run than in the short run' (Viner, 1936, p. 235). However general praise quickly turned to specific criticism as Viner saw Keynes's monetary cure of involuntary unemployment as 'a constant race between the printing press and the business agents of the trade unions, with the problem of unemployment largely solved if the printing press could maintain a constant lead' (ibid., p. 237).

The second review more clearly outlined what Viner saw as the most important difference between himself and Keynes. Keynes had not given long-run equilibrium analysis the credit it deserved for the advances that it had made. Viner was more than willing to agree that traditional classical theory gave inadequate guidance in dealing with persistent unemployment. However he was proud of the fact that he had recognized this by 1930, long before the *General Theory* appeared. In this context Viner referred to his and the Chicago School's 1931 policy memorandum which called for an active countercyclical policy of deficit spending and public works projects that would act as a 'business pump' to bring the economy back to full employment. While the memorandum did call for economic policies that were not inspired by classical theory, it would be, as Samuelson (1972, p. 11) points out, 'a perversion of history to believe that there was an oral tradition at the University of Chicago which had already anticipated the valid nucleus of Keynesian analysis'.

Viner would probably agree with Samuelson's assessment: reference to a 'Keynesian Revolution in economics' was 'permissible' because of the true innovations that had been made in short-run analysis. Viner's ultimate concern centered on Keynes's denial of classical equilibrating mechanisms working even in the long run: 'On its [Keynes's analysis] adequacy as long-run analysis, and especially on its denial that (in a truly competitive economy) there exist powerful automatic forces which in the log run... will restore "equilibrium", I still remain skeptical at least, with some propensity to be hostile' (Lekachman, 1964, p. 255). While Viner can be counted as a critic of Keynes, it would be a complete misrepresentation to classify him as one of the many economists of his generation who refused to acknowledge the validity of even the smallest Keynesian cracks in the walls surrounding classical theory. His intellectual honesty would not allow that assessment.

BRUCE T. ELMSLIE

See also:

Cassel, Karl G.; Classical Economics; Demand Management; Keynes, John Maynard; Keynesian Revolution; Marshall, Alfred; Meade, James E.; Ohlin, Bertil; Schumpeter, Joseph A.

Bibliography

Baumol, William and E.V. Seiler (1979), 'Jacob Viner', *International Encyclopedia of the Social Sciences*, Vol. 18, New York: Free Press.
Bloomfield, Arthur I. (1992), 'On the Centenary of Jacob Viner's Birth: A Retrospective View of the Man and his Work', *Journal of Economic Literature*, **30**, (4), pp. 2052–87.
Chamberlin, Edward (1933), *The Theory of Monopolistic Competition*, Cambridge, Mass.: Harvard University Press.

Irwin, Douglas (1991), 'Introduction', in Douglas Irwin (ed.), *Essays on the Intellectual History of Economics*, Princeton: Princeton University Press.

Keynes, John M. (1964), *The General Theory of Employment, Interest and Money*, New York: Harcourt Brace Jovanovich (first published 1936).

Lekachman, Robert (ed.) (1964), *Keynes' General Theory: Reports of Three Decades*, New York: St Martin's Press.

Robinson, Joan (1933), *The Economics of Imperfect Competition*, London: Macmillan.

Rotwein, Eugene (1983), 'Jacob Viner and the Chicago Tradition', *History of Political Economy*, **15**, (2), summer, pp. 265–80.

Samuelson, Paul A. (1972), 'Jacob Viner, 1892–1970', *Journal of Political Economy*, **80**, (1), January/February, pp. 5–11

Spiegel, Henry W. (1987), 'Jacob Viner', in John Eatwell, Murray Milgate and Peter Newman (eds), *The New Palgrave: A Dictionary of Economics*, Vol. 4, New York: Stockton Press.

Sraffa, Piero (1926), 'The Laws of Return under Competitive Conditions', *Economic Journal*, **36**, (144), December, pp. 535–50.

Sweezy, Paul (1939), 'Demand under Conditions of Oligopoly', *Journal of Political Economy*, **47**, (4), August, pp. 568–73.

Viner, Jacob (1921), 'Price Policies: The Determination of Market Price', in L.C. Marshall (ed.), *Business Administration*, Chicago: University of Chicago Press.

Viner, Jacob (1936), 'Mr. Keynes on the Cause of Unemployment', *Quarterly Journal of Economics*, **51**, (1), November.

Viner, Jacob (1958), *The Long View and the Short: Studies in Economic Theory and Policy*, Glencoe, Ill.: Free Press.

Viner, Jacob (1975), *Studies in the Theory of International Trade*, Clifton, NJ: Augustus M. Kelley (first published 1937).

von Hayek, Friedrich A.

Friedrich August von Hayek was born in Vienna, the center of political and cultural life of the Austro-Hungarian empire, on 8 May 1899. His father, August Edler von Hayek, was a doctor and amateur botanist. Hayek's educational training was demanding but typical of the Viennese upper classes; in his Gymnasium (second school), rigorous emphasis was put on languages and mathematics. During World War I, Hayek was required to interrupt his schooling and devote one year to military service on the Italian front as an artillery officer. In 1918, he entered the University of Vienna, where he came under the influence of the Austrian school of economic theory and adopted some aspects of Friedrich von Wieser's methodological approach. In 1921, after earning degrees in law and political science, he was introduced to Ludwig von Mises who, Hayek later confessed, taught him 'more than…any other man'. Mises is also credited with turning Hayek away from Fabian socialist doctrine towards his appreciation of the market system. Mises helped Hayek get a job with the Austrian government, negotiating and settling war debts. This position, his first, made use of Hayek's practical skills as an economist, lawyer and linguist.

During the 1920s, Hayek managed to travel and experience other ideas and other cultures. In 1919–20, during the awful fuel shortages in Vienna that necessitated the closing of the university, Hayek travelled to Zurich and worked in the laboratory of the distinguished anatomist von Monakow, who had made pioneering discoveries about the human brain. During this period Hayek's strong interest in psychology and epistemology colored all of his ideas, especially about economics and its methods of analysis. His early thoughts on the subject reached fruition in his remarkable *The Sensory Order*, published in 1952. This book has attracted much attention, not only because of its contributions to cognitive psychology but because some believe it contains the key to appreciating Hayek's entire contribution to economics, psychology, law, political science and philosophy. According to William N. Butos, Hayek's scientific output over a long career can be understood as an inquiry about the status of knowledge, how it is acquired and transmitted, an investigation into the various structures in which it adheres and the mechanisms that encourage its utilization. Also Hayek's epistemology is a peculiar blend of Immanuel Kant and David Hume. Like Kant, Hayek insists that we experience the world through certain categories or mental structures but, unlike Kant, he goes on to point out that the structures themselves are constantly evolving and cannot be fully understood: we can detect patterns and the general shape of things, but that is all.

Hayek traveled to New York in 1923–4 and attended classes at both New York University and Columbia College. At Columbia College, he learned first-hand of Wesley Clair Mitchell's pioneering efforts to measure and chart the course of the business cycle, especially at the newly created National Bureau of Economic Research in New York City. Mitchell's efforts, along with those of Arthur F. Burns, led to the creation of the famed 'reference cycles', which distilled many statistical indicators of booms and slumps into a single indicator that would identify the turning-points in business cycles; that is, identify when booms turn into recessions and recessions into revivals. When Hayek returned to Vienna in 1924, he joined the famous Privatseminar conducted by Ludwig von Mises in the Austrian Chamber of Commerce. At these meetings distinguished economists such as Fritz Machlup, Oskar Morgenstern, Gottfried Haberler, Gerhard Tintner, Karl Schlesinger, Erich Schiff, Martha Stefanie Braun, Ilse Mintz, Felix Kaufmann and Alfred Schutz tested ideas and debated the leading methodological issues of the day. In addition, Hayek – along with Hans Mayer, Fritz Machlup and Oskar Morgenstern – was influential in founding the Austrian Economic Society, which invited distinguished speakers to Vienna. The Englishman Lionel Robbins, for example, was familiar with the Society and Mises's seminar, and in turn he developed a strong interest in the revolutionary ideas of several of the Austrian thinkers, including Hayek. Within a decade and a half, nearly all of the aforementioned economists would have emigrated safely in advance of Hitler's armies.

In 1927, Hayek joined Mises in establishing the Austrian Institute for Business Cycle Research. Although Hayek strenuously disagreed with Mitchell's claim that measurement was more important than theoretical explanation, he worked hard to organize and publish the Institute's statistical reports. Hayek's commitment to questions surrounding monetary theory and the business cycle was apparent in his brilliant papers on intertemporal equilibrium and the monetary causes that set the trade cycle in motion. Perhaps because of the originality of this work, Robbins invited Hayek to present a series of lectures at the London School of Economics in 1931. Hayek's lectures, later published under the title *Prices and Production*, created quite a stir in London academic circles. According to one veteran observer, the Nobel Laureate John R. Hicks, '*Prices and Production* was in English, but it was not English economics'. In the midst of all this academic excitement, Hayek accepted the London School's offer to occupy the prestigious Tooke chair, and by 1938 he had become a British subject. In London, Hayek continued his seminal research on economic theory, history and methodology and somehow managed to attract the wrath of the fledgling Keynesian school. To Keynes and his circle, Hayek became the chief representative of economic orthodoxy: the Hayekian dragon had to be slain to make way for Keynes and 'new economics'. Hayek's nemeses during the 1930s included Piero Sraffa, John Maynard Keynes and Nicholas Kaldor. Many of the younger generation of economists, such as Abba Lerner, John R. Hicks, Sho-Chieh Tsiang, Kaldor and George Shackle, were intrigued by Hayek's teachings but, as time wore on, they defected, one by one, and joined the Keynesian camp.

During the 1930s, despite some serious disagreements with Ludwig von Mises on the problem of general equilibrium and its proper definition, Hayek adopted and defended many of Mises's characteristic positions on economics and policy. Together, Mises and Hayek battled against socialist writers such as H.D. Dickinson, Oskar Lange and Fred Taylor in what has been termed the 'economic calculation debate'. Hayek's opponents thought that the best features of the market system could be preserved if the economy were managed and planned as if it were a giant household under the control of a patriarch-like Central Planning Ministry; that planners in such a system would set and enforce abstract rules about the types of decisions managers of factories should undertake. Hayek rejected the household management view of economics, which largely dominates the teaching and practice of economics throughout the world.

In his most popular book, *The Road to Serfdom* (1944), Hayek argued that attempts to plan the economy would bring the worst criminal behavior into politics and either force the abandonment of the plan or else set the stage for totalitarian takeover and rule. Even the American *Reader's Digest* published excerpts from the book, thereby making Hayek something of a media economist. This media recognition was frowned upon by Hayek's academic colleagues and his cries against the socialist planners were dismissed in academic circles as unnecessarily alarmist.

Other personal pressures in Hayek's life made him think about finding a more attractive financial position. When such an offer came in 1950, he left the London School of Economics for the University of Chicago, where he would become part of the celebrated Committee on Social Thought. In Chicago, Hayek continued his efforts to reconstruct a form of classical liberalism that emphasized the importance of human liberty while at the same time it criticized those who made extraordinary claims about human reasoning and what it was capable of achieving. According to Hayek, the human mind could detect only broad patterns in social life: it could 'never aspire to an exhaustive description of concrete social facts'. The idea that social scientists could uncover laws of the form 'If A then B' was most improbable, if not epistemologically impossible, even if it were granted that the variables denoted 'A' and 'B' referred to human intentions and subjectively held meanings. This meant that the widespread claim that economists could 'engineer' better social outcomes, by promulgating regulations or instituting administrative agency, was without any basis in fact. The best economists could do, in Hayek's opinion, was to recognize the limits of reason when it comes to complex social phenomena. Economists should be humble and advocate only those broad institutional arrangements that were more likely than not to promote 'coordination' in human affairs. One such collection of institutions that was highly recommended is, of course, the market system. In *The Constitution of Liberty* and *Law, Legislation and Liberty*, Hayek argued that adherence to broad, abstract, procedural-type laws – laws that treated citizens anonymously and equally without trying to redistribute or 'correct' the inequalities in a citizen's initial endowments or subsequent fortunes – would produce prosperity for the masses. Hayek's system of thought leads to an important restatement of classical liberalism, one much more qualified and conservative than has been found in either the natural rights or the utilitarian camps, respectively. Indeed Hayek's notorious reputation as a 'right-wing' economist may be traced back to his consistent opposition to the macroeconomic approach of Keynes and textbook treatments of so-called 'Keynesian' economics that requires a more activist government in its practical applications.

Hayek returned to Europe in 1962 with an appointment at the University of Freiburg. In 1969, he moved to the University of Salzburg in Austria, and it was in his native Austria that he learned, in 1974, that he had been awarded the Nobel Prize in Economic Science. In 1977, Hayek moved back to Freiburg, where he spent the remainder of his career and where he died on 23 March 1992. Hayek's literary output spans more than six decades and reaches into fields as diverse as economic analysis, psychology, political science, law and biology. A large and growing army of Hayek scholars now scrutinizes each of his 18 books, 235 journal articles and 41 edited books and pamphlets.

The theme of coordination

Social sciences study both the actions of the individual and interactions among individuals. The abstractions of economics help us to evaluate institutions and structures for their likelihood to enhance or diminish a typical citizen's chances of achieving his or her most cherished plans and objectives. Economic reasoning also warns us against those institutions that confuse actors and promote the discoordination of plans. In the case of modern monetary institutions which include central banks and practices designed to allow fractional-reserve banks, the prevailing policy instruments discoordinate human plans in ways not recognized by most economists. The majority of economists watch statistical aggregates and chart the behavior of the aggregates: popular charts include those that feature gross domestic product, the consumer or producer price indexes, the unemployment index, and so on. Stability in these indexes is considered to be consistent with economic stability itself. According to Hayek, stability in the aggregate often masks changes in relative prices and resource allocation that reflect certain non-measurable, deep-seated features of the economic system. Disregarding these deep preferences and structures promotes discoordination even when the macroeconomic averages appear to be constant. One especially damaging form of discoordination was the business depression, such as the Great Depression of the 1930s, which followed a cluster of business errors or malinvestments due to the distortion of the price signals in the market-place.

Ludwig von Mises had indicted modern banking practices for hyperinflation and the insidious expansion of credit that enters the economy through the capital goods markets. Hayek continued this line of thought. The lowered interest rate tricks entrepreneurs into believing that capital-intensive methods of production are now more profitable. They may then resort to more roundabout or time-consuming methods of production. Mises believed that pressure groups (such as organized labor) force democratic legislatures into budgetary deficits and the central banks try to keep borrowing costs down by encouraging the sale of government debt. The lowering of interest rates raises the present-discounted value of all capital goods projects but especially those where the benefits take longer to accrue. These tend to be capital-intensive methods of production. Thus the lowering of interest rates encourages the utilization of more roundabout and time-consuming methods of production, even though the true underlying preferences of the public have not authorized such an extension or deepening of the capital structure.

Unless the real, voluntary saving of the community has expanded to make the construction of the capital goods possible, a surge in credit-financed investment must create a cyclical boom that ends in crisis and disaster. The economist cannot say exactly on what date the crisis will occur, or which particular capital-using industries will be hardest hit, but a broad pattern of events leading towards crisis and the clustering of malinvestments in the capital goods industry can be detected and explained. Hayek expanded on Mises's teachings about an inevitable 'reverse movement' and rejected macroeconomic methods of reasoning in favor of a sequence of relative price changes. Once set in motion, these relative changes would guarantee that, if the boom financed by credit expansion does not end for any other reason, it must end when consumer goods prices race ahead of money wages, encouraging a switch towards labor-intensive investment projects. Hayek termed this sequence of price changes, 'The Ricardo effect'. In his 1931 London School lectures – and periodically after that, in publication after publication, even as late as 1969 in the *Journal of Political Economy* – Hayek tried to explain why the boom had to end in crisis so long as the voluntary saving of the community had not also increased to make the financing of the new capital goods both profitable and possible.

Microeconomic foundations of macroeconomic claims

The majority of economists in the twentieth century (and the list includes not only Keynes but Joseph A. Schumpeter as well) believed that the monetarization of credit and the use of modern methods of finance could succeed in intensifying capital goods structures (that is, raising the amount of capital goods per man employed in production) even if the voluntary saving of the community was inadequate or slow in growing. 'Forced saving', it was sometimes alleged, could finance any target level of investment. The way the forced saving mechanism works is worth recalling: the new investment expenditure expands aggregate spending and, under conditions of full capacity utilization, the extra spending pushes prices upwards. Consumers experiencing the surge in prices find that their incomes command a smaller purchasing power than they had expected, so they actually end up spending less in real terms than they had intended – hence the label 'forced saving'. The issue for Hayek was not whether the phenomenon of forced saving existed but whether the magnitude of the effect could be enough to sustain a more intensified capital goods structure.

One of Hayek's earliest critics on this point, Piero Sraffa, reviewed Hayek's *Prices and Production* and pointed out errors in his reasoning. Sraffa's main argument was that Hayek had not proved what he had set out to prove. If increased bank credit permitted the intensification of capital structures before the bank credit runs out and the credit market tightens then there was no reason why the intensified capital structures and higher output per worker could not remain permanently intact. Sraffa's argument was later developed further by Nicholas Kaldor, who successfully demonstrated that Hayek's argument could not be justified by using comparative–static equilibrium analysis. Hayek's main point was that the process that he termed 'the Ricardo effect' was a sequence of events in historical time designed to demonstrate why, whether or not one started out in a situation of fully coordinated equilibrium, the economy could not successfully reach a second coordinated situation in which capital per unit of labor was greater. According to Hayek, Kaldor was a prisoner of his own comparative–static equilibrium methodology. That methodology caused Kaldor to assume away precisely the sort of disequilibrium market process problem that intrigued Hayek.

Hayek on equilibrium constructions
As early as 1937, Hayek had detected that the general equilibrium constructions that informed economics were dangerously ambiguous at certain critical points. For example, the claim that 'everybody knows everything' – the perfect knowledge assumption – is used to justify the conclusion that the market system leads to the same results as if it were deliberately managed by a benevolent omniscient dictator. But the process by which the 'division of knowledge' in society produces this remarkable general equilibrium result was not explained. According to Hayek, this process is often ignored or simply assumed away by abstract mathematical constructs. In his view, however, the problem of how knowledge is acquired and communicated remains the critically important unresolved problem in economics. What economics requires is attention to the division of knowledge in society and how that knowledge is mobilized in market settings. Any advances in this area would be just catching up with the attention paid to the division of labor in society, which has received the overwhelming bulk of attention by economists both past and present.

This perspective led Hayek to the gradual abandonment of the household management model of macroeconomics. Indeed one of his most far-reaching and still barely understood contributions has to do with his vision of what a market system was and what lay in the future. Hayek was the first of the Austrian writers explicitly to reject the methodological approach that he learned from Wieser. The view that the economy is essentially similar to a gigantic household managed by a benevolent, omniscient dictator eventually became anathema to Hayek. The market system did not maximize any magnitude, whether it be total utility, the monetary value of gross domestic product or the number employed. Instead the market system was a collection of customs, abstract rules and working institutions that created incentives for individuals to utilize practical bits and pieces of practical information in ever more valuable ways. Competition, along with profit-and-loss accounting, kept any one group from utilizing information in unprofitable ways. Entrepreneurs continuously reshuffle the means of production in ways that produce opportunities for other market participants to achieve their most important plans. The economy is not a place where known resources are allocated to their most valued uses. Rather the economy is a dynamic knowledge-coordinating arrangement through which individuals are motivated to grasp and apply bits and pieces of circumstantially relevant information in ever more profitable ways. A vast coordination of sorts is constantly taking shape as incentives are created for individuals to utilize decentralized information in ways that permit an alignment of their privately held plans and objectives.

In later writings, starting at least as early as 1967, Hayek groped for a vocabulary that would properly capture and communicate his insights. The economy was definitely unlike a household, because a household manager must organize the goals and objectives of its members. In a market system, no Procrustean hierarchy of plans and purposes need be established. Experimentation with new methods of production, consumption and distribution in a framework of rivalrous competition and secure property rights was, roughly speaking, the 'vision' that increasingly characterized Hayek's writings about the market system. He broke new ground when he distinguished between the character and order found in an organization formed for explicit purposes and with explicit rules (what the Greeks called a 'taxis') and the character and order represented by a spontaneously formed market (what the Greeks called a 'cosmos'). Hayek later termed the latter a 'catallaxy' (roughly meaning a network of exchanges), thereby rejecting the household management metaphor once and for all.

The battle over saving

Early in his tenure at the London School of Economics, Hayek began an argument with the Cambridge economists. In 1931, he published his erudite review of Keynes's *Treatise on Money*, hammering away at the logical foundations of Keynes's approach. According to Hayek, Keynes had not described what he meant by production. The investment that Keynes spoke of must lead to the construction of capital goods, but how are the new capital goods integrated into the continuing production structures? On these important matters Keynes was silent. Instead Keynes was apparently content to put his emphasis on mere monetary flows and how they do and do not balance, creating entrepreneurial profits and losses. This analysis was, in Hayek's view, terribly unsophisticated and out of line with the standards of inquiry established by continental writers such as Böhm-Bawerk, Knut Wicksell and others.

There was some merit to Hayek's criticism. In his *Treatise* (and later in his *General Theory*) Keynes concentrated on flows of spending and the income they generated. The emphasis was on the balance between them, and the deep-seated coordinating processes that underlay the market process were skipped over or not discussed at all. Thus, for Keynes, the interest rate is formed in the money market and has mostly to do with the demand for and supply of money. For Austrians, the interest rate is formed by the demand for and supply of loanable funds, but the sources and uses of these funds reflect still more fundamental relationships stemming from the subjective time preferences of the community. Hayek made some progress in relating the Austrian structure-of-production approach to some of Keynes's speculations about money and interest in Part IV of his *Theory of Capital*. Whatever progress was made in reconciling the approaches pale by comparison with the modern Austrian School's outright rejection of Keynes's most celebrated work, *The General Theory of Employment, Interest and Money*.

Hayek surely read Keynes's 1936 book, but perhaps not as carefully as he had read the *Treatise*. Indeed, years after it had been published, he recollected his state of mind in 1936 and confessed that he was sorry he had not taken the time to prepare a full-length review of the arguments contained in that volume. To Hayek (and to other Austrian writers as well), the *General Theory* was an economically naive tract that advocated inflation as a method of job creation. The *General Theory* has been dismissed by Hayek as mostly a mercantilist-style political tract. He seldom read it from any other vantage point. The efforts of the post Keynesian writers to emphasize the subtle subjectivist insights contained in the *General Theory*, especially regarding the incentive to invest, did not make an impression on Hayek. Seen through the lens of the Austrian School, the *General Theory* recommends a discredited method of maintaining employment in a world where labor is organized into powerful unions that threaten politicians with the loss of patronage and votes. Keynes explained how to pacify the union demands for wage increases in excess of productivity while at the same time not risking political failure. The secrete is inflation: that is, surprise inflation to create jobs.

The Austrians view the Keynesian contribution as part of a modern inflationist scenario. First, the unions raise nominal wages by threatening strikes and supporting nativist legislation to keep out immigrants. The factory owners cave in and concede the higher nominal wages in order to avoid violence, but they work behind the scenes and ultimately through their representatives at the central bank to expand the money supply to bolster aggregate spending and reduce unemployment. The large money supply leads to a rise in consumer goods prices, and the money paid to the workers is stripped of its purchasing power. Jobs remain intact, but there are many losers in this scenario. Those rentier–creditors who loaned money at interest rates that prove in retrospect to have been too low complain. The rentiers caught by the surprise inflation lose wealth but, since the workers are more important, these redistributions have little or no economic significance. Indeed Keynes himself spoke of the 'euthanasia' of the rentier class.

Most significantly, Keynes treated investment expenditure as a form of expenditure much like consumption expenditure except that it has the special 'autonomous' characteristic of generating increases in income. Indeed, as the famous multiplier formula shows, the income will increase by enough to generate exactly enough new saving to equal the increase in investment expenditure: the investment spending automatically generates its own financing. The income multiplier process contradicts the traditional Austrian claim that, in order for investment to be effective in raising living standards, saving must occur *first*. According to Keynes and the later Keynesians, investment should come first and the right amount of saving will follow later. The Keynesian attitude suggested that traditional sentimental bourgeois values such as thrift and the avoidance of luxury were, at times of unemployment and unused capacity, antisocial values. For this reason, Hayek's approach of emphasizing austerity during depressions and limited government involvement in the economy became the symbol of the 'old-school' macroeconomic policy that the 'new economics' of Keynes and his followers was trying to supplant. With much less justification, Hayek was branded a pawn of those right-wing politicians who wished to suppress the labor movement as it was developing in the west, thereby coloring the Keynes–Hayek debate with hidden nativist and political agendas.

After World War II, Keynes and Hayek were sharply divided on matters of international political reform. Keynes and his students despised the gold exchange standard in particular and commodity exchange standards in general because they acted to limit the discretionary authority of the national central banks. A government had its first responsibility to its home labor movement and therefore the new international payments mechanisms, whatever their exact shape and size, had to give pride of place to the concept of 'domestic autonomy'. Forced to choose between austerity and inflation, Keynesians would under most circumstances choose inflation. At the 1944 Bretton Woods conference, Keynes's particular arrangement for the restoration of the world order was not the one chosen, but the values and norms that he advocated came to dominate postwar economics. The original Bretton Woods agreement, and its successor modifications, institutionalized the norm that price and wage deflation were something to avoid. The deflation of the 1930s was to be avoided at almost all costs. Also to be avoided was the economic isolationism of the 1930s.

When a national government is experiencing a loss of foreign exchange reserves, a central bank should have the means to follow an expansionary domestic policy that will curtail the foreign drain, and it should have the international cooperation of other governments to keep their currencies from appreciating. This is the practical meaning of the expression 'international monetary cooperation'.

International economic policy

There are three cherished goals of international economic policy: (1) to free the central banks from the day-to-day pressures of maintaining exchange rate convertibility at relatively fixed exchange ratios; (2) to open borders to the free movement of commodities and selected services (not the movement of labor) and flows of financial capital; and (3) to keep a nation's currency from being repeatedly devalued or re-evaluated vis-à-vis the currencies of its major trading partners. It is generally agreed that not all three of these goals can be achieved simultaneously. One or more has to be dropped, or at least seriously compromised. Which one will it be?

Keynes wanted to preserve domestic monetary autonomy above all else. This would give the central bank the freedom to try to neutralize labor union activity so as to preserve domestic peace. If, for example, the trade unions were to demand wage concessions in excess of productivity growth, the Keynesians would prefer not to fight the unions but to orchestrate a mild inflation coupled with a currency devaluation to preserve export sales. This implies that Keynesians demonstrate a willingness to jettison (3) and even (2) in order to preserve (1).

Hayek, true to Mises's teachings and traditional classical liberal attitudes, preferred (2) and (3) to (1). And so, if the union leaders and the rank and file demanded and received wage increases in certain industries far in excess of productivity, foreign sales or exports would diminish and foreign-owned claims against local financial institutions would increase. Jobs would be lost in the export sector, and layoffs and bankruptcies would teach the unions and their leaders an important lesson about wage increases that can be justified by productivity gains and those that cannot. For Austrians like Hayek, trying to pacify the unions and then inflating the local economy to neutralize the unions' gains is cowardly, deceptive and would only hasten and intensify a dreadful outcome everyone fears. Thus Hayek spoke of the attempts to grant nominal wage increases and then neutralize their effects with price inflation as nothing short of trying to 'catch a tiger by the tail'. During the 1970s, prominent Keynesian economists such as Abba Lerner advocated wage and price controls to use the full power of the state to regulate the growth of nominal income. At this time the events of western economies seemed to bear out what Hayek had forecast. Efforts to lower unemployment by inflation produced more of both and required ever-stronger doses of inflation. Ironically high rates of unemployment returned.

In his later writings Hayek was willing to consider even more radical solutions, such as a return to international commodity standards under the control of local central banks and government. In 1978, he advocated private money in the form of 'trade mark' money: private firms would issue promises and stick by their promises or else go belly up; over time competition and selection by market forces would leave only a small number of money issuers that would survive because of the integrity of their issue. Hayek did not take the next logical step of considering a monetary payments mechanism, in which the 'unit of account' function of money is completely severed from its 'medium of exchange' characteristic. This idea, which is of major concern to modern Austrian writers, nevertheless has roots in the norms and values that Hayek preserved in his writings on international payments mechanisms.

Hayek and the 'right-wing' label

Hayek has been repeatedly labeled a 'right-winger', especially by the journalists. According to one *Financial Times* book reviewer, Lionel Robbins brought Hayek to the London School of Economics to 'bias' the faculty towards 'right-wing' economics. That article goes on to say that Hayek was one of a group – which included Edwin Cannan, Lionel Robbins and, later on, Harry Johnson and Alan Walters – that has been the 'most consistently free-market, anti-Keynesian, even right-wing of any [faculty] in the UK'. Such talk is likely to distract students from what is important about Hayek's work, but since the view is so widespread it deserves investigation. As Hayek himself explained to an American audience in 1960, a conservative wishes to preserve existing customs, social practices and institutions. Hayek's 1960s-style conservatism extended only to those institutions that expand and protect human dignity. According to Hayek, the institutions he wished to preserve were those closely associated with the American form of government – namely, those which personified the procedural safeguards of the 'rule of law' – and other institutions consonant with the market system and rivalrous competition. Perhaps fortuitously, those institutions that protect human dignity and freedom of expression are also the ones that promote the coordination of human plans and therefore make the market economy more effective at raising living standards. Some of the institutions that have worked the best are what are termed 'spontaneous social formations'. Spontaneous social formations, like language, money and other means of debt transfer, law and customs, emerge gradually over time. They promote the achievement of human plans and can be appreciated only in terms of their broad patterns. A spontaneous social formation cannot be simulated by experiments or super-imposed on a community by administrative fiat. Rather such institutions must grow organically and this necessitates slow, gradual evolution.

Hayek's insistence that human reason is limited in its abilities and can never reinvent a social order without causing much chaos, poverty and suffering does, however, lead to a different sort of conservatism. Although Hayek preferred to call himself a 'classical liberal' or 'Burkean Whig', it is unclear how his political philosophy could ever lead him to support radical revolutionary change. The conservatism became especially apparent in his last book, *The Fatal Conceit*, where he pleads for a greater appreciation and respect for old norms and customs, even religious beliefs. These traditions, in his view, survived because they coordinate privately held plans in ways that no single human mind can ever hope to fully comprehend. According to Hayek, an index of the success of a society's traditions is available: population growth. Those norms and customs that promote population growth will tend to flourish as cultures copy other cultures that are seen to be more successful. It can be argued that Hayek moved sharply away from his 1960s-style conservative position towards a traditional European conservative position in his last book.

To be sure, pre-communist China was able to sustain large gains in population in the face of customs that included a preference for (female) suicide over divorce and the binding of the feet of upper-class girls. To many liberal observers, these customs were rejected as ugly and worth eliminating from Chinese society as quickly as the surgeon's knife of legislative reform would allow. It is not clear whether Hayek's political philosophy would permit a forceful attack on these particular customs and practices if they were still in operation. In the west, the wholesale entailment of large estates and other barriers that left women unable to pass on landed property were only gradually eliminated over the centuries, mostly through the development of the common law, bolstered by occasional legislative acts. If gradual reform is what Hayek would have preferred in China, he would have *opposed* those forceful reforms, first by the Chinese Nationalist Party and later continued by Mao's Communist Party, which only in the twentieth century legalized divorce and outlawed foot-binding.

But branding Hayek a 'right-winger' and lumping him in the same league with the anti-labor policies of Augusto Pinochet, and the restrictionary rhetoric of Ronald Reagan and Margaret Thatcher trivializes his contribution. Still the characterization of Hayek as a 'right-wing' conservative is perhaps not entirely unfair.

LAURENCE S. MOSS

See also:

Austrian School of Economics; Business Cycle Theory (I) and (II); Chicago School of Economics; Interest, Theories of; Keynes, John Maynard; Keynesian Revolution; Machlup, Fritz; Robbins, Lord Lionel; Wicksell, Knut.

Bibliography
Bator, Francis (1957), 'General Equilibrium, Welfare and Allocation', *American Economic Review*, **46**, (1), March, pp. 22–59.

Blaug, Mark (1985), *Great Economists Since Keynes: An Introduction to the Lives & Works of One Hundred Modern Economists*, New York: Cambridge University Press.

Boettke, Peter J. (1994), *The Elgar Companion to Austrian Economics*, Aldershot: Edward Elgar.

Butos, W.N. (1991), 'Mind and Market in Hayek's Theory of Cognition', mimeo.

Cowen, Tyler and Randall Kroszner (1994), *Explorations in the New Monetary Economics*, New York: Basil Blackwell.

Garrison Roger W. and Israel M. Kirzner (1987), 'Friedrich August von Hayek', *The New Palgrave: A Dictionary of Economics*, Vol. 2, New York: Stockton Press.

Gray, John (1984), *Hayek on Liberty*, New York: Basil Blackwell.

Hayek, Friedrich A. (1937), 'Economics and Knowledge', *Economica*, **4**, (13), February, pp. 33–54.

Hayek, Friedrich A. (1941), *The Pure Theory of Capital*, London: Routledge & Kegan Paul.

Hayek, Friedrich A. (1944), *The Road to Serfdom*, Chicago: University of Chicago Press.

Hayek, Friedrich A. (1945), 'The Use of Knowledge in Society', *American Economic Review*, **35**, (4), September, pp. 519–30.

Hayek, Friedrich A. (1948), *Individualism and Economic Order*, London: Routledge & Kegan Paul.

Hayek, Friedrich A. (1952), *The Sensory Order – An Inquiry into the Foundations of Theoretical Psychology*, Chicago: University of Chicago Press.

Hayek, Friedrich A. (1967), 'The Confusion of Language in Political Thought' (lecture), reprinted in F.A. Hayek (ed.), *New Studies in Philosophy, Politics, Economics and the History of Ideas*, Chicago: University of Chicago Press.

Hayek, Friedrich A. (1960), *The Constitution of Liberty*, Chicago: University of Chicago Press.

Hayek, Friedrich A. (1969), 'The Theory of Complex Phenomena', *Studies in Philosophy, Politics and Economics*, New York: Simon & Schuster.

Hayek, Friedrich A. (1972), *The Tiger By the Tail: The Keynesian Legacy of Inflation*, London: Institute of Economic Affairs.

Hayek, Friedrich A. (1973, 1976, 1979), *Law, Legislation and Liberty*, 3 vols, Chicago: University of Chicago Press.

Hayek, Friedrich A. (1978), *The Fatal Conceit: The Errors of Socialism*, Vol. 1 of *Collected Works of F.A. Hayek*, ed. W.W. Bartley, Chicago: University of Chicago Press.

Hayek, Friedrich A. (1994), *Hayek on Hayek: An Autobiographical Dialogue*, S. Kresge and L. Wenar (eds), Chicago: University of Chicago Press.

Hayek, Friedrich A. (1995), *Contra Keynes and Cambridge: Essays, Correspondence*, Vol. 9 of *Collected Works of F.A. Hayek*, ed. Bruce Caldwell, Chicago: University of Chicago.

Hicks, John (1967), *Critical Essays in Monetary Theory*, Oxford: Clarendon.

Lawson, Tony (1995), 'Realism and Hayek: A Case of Continuing Transformation', in M. Colonna, H. Hagemann and O. Hamouda (eds), *Capitalism, Socialism and Knowledge: The Economics of F.A. Hayek* vol. 2, Aldershot: Edward Elgar.

Machlup, Fritz (1974), 'Hayek's Contribution to Economics', *Swedish Journal of Economics*, **76**, (4), December, pp. 498–531.

McMahon, Sir Kit (1995), 'Where Conflict is on the Curriculum' (book review of Ralf Dahrendorf, *LSE: A History of the London School of Economics 1895–1995*), *Financial Times*, 27–8 May, p. xi.

Menger, Karl (1871) [1950], *Principles of Economics*, Glencoe, Ill.: Free Press.

Mises, Ludwig von (1920), 'Economic Calculation in the Socialist Commonwealth'; reprinted in F.A. Hayek (ed.), *Collectivist Economic Planning*, London: Routledge & Kegan Paul, 1963.

Mises, Ludwig von (1949) [1963], *Human Action: A Treatise on Economics*, New Haven, Conn.: Yale University Press.

Moss, Laurence S. (1974), *The Economics of Ludwig von Mises: Toward a Critical Reappraisal*, Mission, Kansas: Sheed Andrews and McMeel.

Moss, Laurence S. (1978), 'Carl Menger and Austrian Economics', *Atlantic Economic Journal*, **6**, (3), September, pp. 17–30.

Moss, Laurence S. (1992), 'Harmony, Conflict and Culture: An Essay About the Praxeological Ideas of Ludwig von Mises', *Cultural Dynamics*, **5**, pp. 371–91.

Moss, Laurence S. (1995), 'Hayek and the Several Faces of Socialism', in M. Colonna, H. Hagemann and O. Hamouda (eds), *Capitalism, Socialism and Knowledge: The Economics of F.A. Hayek*, Vol. 2, Aldershot: Edward Elgar.

Moss, Laurence S. and Karen I. Vaughn (1986), 'Hayek's Ricardo Effect: A Second Look', *History of Political Economy*, **18**, (4), Winter, pp. 545–65.

Vanberg, Viktor J. (1994), 'Friedrich A. Hayek', in G.M. Hodgson, W.J. Samuels and M.R. Tool (eds), *The Elgar Companion to Institutional and Evolutionary Economics*, Aldershot: Edward Elgar.

Vaughn, Karen I. (1994), *Austrian Economics in America: The Migration of a Tradition*, New York: Cambridge University Press.

Weintraub, Sidney

Sidney Weintraub is remembered as a promoter of Post Keynesian economics. He and Paul Davidson were co-founders of the *Journal of Post Keynesian Economics*. Weintraub was born in New York City in 1914. After studying at the London School of Economics he received his PhD from New York University in 1941. He initially worked for the United States government in various positions. In the early 1950s, he joined the faculty at the University of Pennsylvania, where he spent the remainder of his career. During the course of his career he served visiting appointments at numerous national and international universities. He died in 1983. His writings include over 20 books and monographs, 100 professional articles and more than 200 popular press pieces. At one time he had articles simultaneously appearing in the *American Economic Review*, the *Quarterly Journal of Economics* and the *Journal of Political Economy*.

In his first book, *Price Theory* (1949), Weintraub presented a systematic and reasonably complete statement of modern price theory. The work was a revision of his PhD thesis on 'Monopoly and the Economic System'. In the book he focused on the dynamic aspects of the economy and the distinction between partial equilibrium analysis and general equilibrium analysis. This work formed the base for his later work on the microeconomic aspects of macroeconomics. He attempted, in his macroeconomic theory, to find an alternative statement to the equation of exchange ($MV = PQ$). The intent of his theory was to specify the major variables affecting the level of prices. The theory developed by Weintraub was called the wage-cost mark-up model (WCM). Weintraub developed the theory as an alternative to the more traditional Keynesian approach to economics. The WCM model was a distributional model of the economy that showed labor's share of national income and the share of national income going to all other factors (Weintraub, 1951, 1959).

It was common for those, such as Weintraub, who operated within a Post Keynesian framework to recommend the use of incomes policies as a means of controlling inflation. This was particularly true in the 1970s when stagflation represented a new experience for western capitalism. The traditional instruments of monetary and fiscal policy no longer appeared to be effective in coping with simultaneous inflation and unemployment. Economists were asked to provide new policy instruments to cope with the problem.

In the 1970s, Weintraub proposed his own version of an incomes policy (Weintraub, 1978a). The plan proposed by Weintraub was different from its predecessors in that it was an incomes policy with a direct market orientation.

The plan used the corporate tax rate as a lever to induce non-inflationary behavior by business and labor. The plan would have penalized, with increased corporate taxes, those firms which granted wage increases in excess of a national norm. Following the design of previous incomes policies, that norm was the national average increase in productivity per worker. Since corporate taxes would have increased with wage increases in excess of increases in labor productivity, firms would have had an incentive to keep wage settlements to levels equal to or below the rate of increase in the national level of productivity. In Weintraub's view of the world, this would have acted to reduce inflation. To Weintraub the inflation of the day was primarily the cost-push variety. More precisely excessive wage agreements were driving prices upward (Weintraub, 1978b).

A few months prior to Weintraub's first presentation of his incomes policy idea, Leonard Silk, economist for the *New York Times*, described in his column the incomes policy that Weintraub was proposing (Silk, 1970). Silk, who had received an early draft of the proposal from Weintraub, pointed out that Henry C. Wallich of Yale University had made a similar suggestion to the Joint Economic Committee in 1966, as well as expounding a plan in newsprint. Although Wallich and Weintraub were friends they were apparently unaware of each other's work on such similar topics. Working jointly, Weintraub and Wallich pursued the tax-based incomes policy (TIP) approach further (Wallich and Weintraub, 1971). They accepted Weintraub's original premise that, instead of disrupting the market process, market forces should be used to curb inflation, leaving business and labor free to make their own decisions. Like Weintraub's earlier work, their proposal called for an extra surcharge on the corporate profits tax for firms granting wage increases in excess of some guidepost figure. While Wallich and Weintraub realized that certain technical problems existed with TIP – which they claimed tax experts would work out – what TIP offered was a solution to the problem of stagflation that had not been successfully dealt with either by traditional monetary or fiscal policy, or other incomes policies.

One of the greatest contributions of the original TIP plan was to initiate theoretical debate among economists offering similar plans. The number of analysts who examined TIP and its variants was large. There are four individuals, however, whose work was especially influential in the development of TIP: Arthur Okun, Laurence Seidman, Abba P. Lerner and David Colander. Each of these presented either an improvement on, or a variant of, TIP intended to make it better. To solve a problem such as the stagflation of the 1970s, it was important for economists to communicate and build on one another's ideas. The original Wallich–Weintraub TIP was a vital link in the communications process concerning the development of market mechanisms to cure inflation (Hoaas, 1988).

Sidney Weintraub's economic interests were broad. They covered theoretical as well as applied economics and public policy, including problems concerning developing countries. In his scientific work, however, he constantly followed the fundamental aim of breaking down the dichotomy between microeconomics and macroeconomics. His intention was to unify the theories of the price level, income distribution and economic growth.

DAVID J. HOAAS

See also:

Davidson, Paul; Harcourt, Geoff; Incomes Policies; Keynes, John Maynard; Keynesian Revolution; Lerner, Abba P.; Minsky, Hyman P.; Post Keynesian School of Economics; Robinson, Joan.

Bibliography

Hoaas, David J. (1988), 'The Forgotten Contribution of a Wage TIP', *The American Economist*, **32**, (2), fall, pp. 35–40.
Silk, Leonard S. (1970), 'An Incomes Policy?', *New York Times*, 18 November.
Wallich, Henry C. and Sidney Weintraub (1971), 'A Tax-Based Incomes Policy', *Journal of Economic Issues*, **5**, (2), June, pp. 1–19.
Weintraub, Sidney (1949), *Price Theory*, New York: Pitman.
Weintraub, Sidney (1951), *Income and Employment Analysis*, New York: Pitman Publishing Corporation.
Weintraub, Sidney (1959), *A General Theory Of The Price Level, Output, Income Distribution and Economic Growth*, New York: Chilton Company.
Weintraub, Sidney (1978a), 'An Incomes Policy to Stop Inflation', *Keynes, Keynesians and Monetarists*, Pennsylvania: University of Pennsylvania Press.
Weintraub, Sidney (1978b), *Capitalism's Inflation and Unemployment Crisis: Beyond Monetarism and Keynesianism*, Reading, Mass.: Addison-Wesley.

White, Harry D.

Harry Dexter White, the leading American negotiator at the Bretton Woods monetary conference, was born in Boston in 1892, the youngest of seven children of Lithuanian Jewish immigrants. After working for two years in his family's hardware and crockery business and then studying at the Massachusetts Agricultural College (now University of Massachusetts at Amherst), White served in the American Expeditionary Force in France, mustering out as a first lieutenant of infantry. White spent three terms studying government at Columbia but received his AB in economics from Stanford with great distinction in 1924. He was elected to Phi Beta Kappa, and took an MA in economics at Stanford in 1925. After six years as a graduate student and instructor at Harvard, White won the David A. Wells Prize for his doctoral dissertation, published as *The French International Accounts 1880–1913* in the Harvard Economic Studies series (1933) and dedicated to his teacher, Frank Taussig. White's book, like volumes in the same series by such Taussig students as Jacob Viner and John Williams, attempted an empirical verification of the classical theory of balance of payments adjustment, in White's case for a capital-exporting country under the gold standard.

White was hired to teach economics by Lawrence College, Appleton, Wisconsin, in 1932, with promotion to full professor in 1933, and reviewed works on international trade by Ohlin and Haberler for Taussig's *Quarterly Journal of Economics*, but soon left academic economics. An invitation from Viner to spend the summer of 1934 at the Treasury studying the choice of a monetary standard led to 13 years in Washington. White rose through the Treasury ranks, meeting Keynes on a Treasury mission to London in April 1935 and becoming Director of Monetary Research in 1938, although he was not classified as an established civil servant until January 1942. From August 1941, White was also an assistant to Treasury Secretary Henry Morgenthau, Jr. and on 8 December 1941 he was given charge of all Treasury matters touching foreign relations, with the status of Assistant Secretary of the Treasury (but without the formal title until January 1945). As such, White helped draft the Morgenthau plan for a partitioned, deindustrialized Germany, and was Keynes's counterpart in negotiations for the postwar international monetary settlement. White's intellectual influence on Morgenthau and Morgenthau's long friendship with President Roosevelt gave White a position of exceptional importance, which vanished in 1945 with the death of Roosevelt and resignation of Morgenthau.

The Keynes and White plans for postwar monetary cooperation for exchange stability and international liquidity became public on 7 April 1943. Lord Keynes's proposal, for an international currency (bancor) and an International Clearing Union providing large overdraft facilities to member countries, was less orthodox and less prone to deflationary pressure than White's plan for a Bank for Reconstruction and a Stabilization Fund with fixed quotas. From informal discussions in London in October 1942 and a meeting of experts in Atlantic City in June 1944 to the United Nations Monetary and Financial Conference at Bretton Woods, New Hampshire, in July 1944, Keynes and White were the principal negotiators who produced a revised version of the White plan, creating the International Monetary Fund and the World Bank (the International Bank for Reconstruction and Development). The main modification of the White plan was American acceptance of a scarce currency clause, which placed more of the pressure for balance of payments adjustment on creditor countries. Keynes wished the Clearing Union to be obliged passively to accommodate overdraft demands, while White advocated a degree of Fund discretion on letting deficit countries draw on their reserve quotas. Their negotiations were characterized by great mutual respect, but also by extreme rudeness: White addressed Keynes as 'Your Royal Highness', while Keynes contrasted his Christian English with the

Cherokee of American drafts. In recommending White's formal nomination as Assistant Secretary, Morgenthau stressed that 'White has been more than a match for people like Lord Keynes' (Rees, 1973, p. 297). Keynes (Vol. XXV, p. 356) wrote of White:

> Any reserves we may have about him are a pale reflection of what his colleagues feel. He is over-bearing, a bad colleague, always trying to bounce you, with harsh rasping voice, aesthetically oppressive in mind and manner; he has not the faintest conception of how to behave or observe the rules of civilised intercourse. At the same time, I have a very great respect and even liking for him. In many respects he is the best man here. A very able and devoted public servant, carrying an immense burden of responsibility and initiative, of high integrity and of clear sighted idealistic international purpose, genuinely intending to do his best for the world. Moreover, his over-powering will combined with the fact that he has constructive ideas mean that he does get things done, which few else here do. He is not open to flattery in any crude sense. The best way to reach him is to respect his purpose, arouse his intellectual interest (it is a great softener to intercourse that it is easy to arouse his genuine interest in the merits of any issue) and to tell him off frankly and firmly without any finesse when he has gone off the rails of relevant argument or appropriate behaviour.

White left the Treasury in May 1946 to become the first US representative on the IMF Board of Executive Directors, but, to Keynes's surprise, White was not nominated as the first IMF managing director. Even his nomination as an executive director would have been withdrawn had Senate confirmation been a day slower, as Elizabeth Bentley and Whittaker Chambers accused White of ties to Communist underground groups. White left the IMF in May 1947 and rebutted the allegations vigorously before a House committee in August 1948, a few days before he died of a heart attack. Of his accusers, Bentley never met White, while Chambers (whom White did not recall meeting) extended his charges from Communist sympathies to espionage only after White's death. John Morton Blum (1967, p. 90) concluded that White 'appointed some assistants who were almost certainly members of the Communist Party, though Morgenthau did not know they were, and those assistants, in White's view, were as free to pass along information about Treasury policy to the Russians as was Averell Harriman, for example, free to talk to the British'.

ROBERT W. DIMAND

See also:
Bretton Woods.

Bibliography
Blum, John Morton (1967), *From the Morgenthau Diaries*, Vol. III, *Years of War 1941–1945*, Boston, Mass.: Houghton Mifflin.

Gardner, Richard N. (1969), *Sterling–Dollar Diplomacy*, rev. edn, New York/London: McGraw-Hill.

Horsefield, J. Keith (ed.) (1969), *The International Monetary Fund, 1945–1965*, 3 vols, Washington, DC: International Monetary Fund.

Keynes, John Maynard (1971–89), *Collected Writings*, 30 vols, managing eds D.E. Moggridge and E.A.G. Robinson, volume eds D.E. Moggridge and E.S. Johnson, Vols XXV–XXVII, *Shaping the Post-War World*, London: Macmillan/New York: Cambridge University Press for the Royal Economic Society.

Rees, David (1973), *Harry Dexter White: A Study in Paradox*, New York: Coward, McCann & Geoghegan.

United States Senate, Judiciary Committee, Internal Security Subcommittee (1956). *Interlocking Subversion in Government Departments*, Part 30: 'H.D. White Papers, Concord Files', pp. 2415–2816. Hearings, 84th Congress, Washington, DC: Government Printing Office.

Whipple, Charles L. (1953), 'The Life and Death of Harry Dexter White', *Boston Globe*, 12 parts, beginning 15 November.

White, Harry D. (1933), *The French International Accounts 1880–1913*, Harvard Economic Studies no. 40, Cambridge, Mass.: Harvard University Press.

White, Harry D. (1943), 'Postwar Currency Stabilization', *American Economic Review Papers and Proceedings*, **33**, (1), March, pp. 382–7.

Wicksell, Knut

Knut Wicksell was born on 20 December 1851 in Stockholm. He attended Uppsala University where he earned his BA in mathematics and physics (1872) and his philosophiae licentiatus in mathematics (1885). Rather than pursue his studies in mathematics, he chose to study economics. Given the structure of the university system in Sweden, economics was part of the law curriculum, so additional years of study were required. Thus not until 1900, at the age of 49, did Wicksell secure a permanent appointment, a position at the University of Lund. While he did not follow the normal path to prominence within the university system, his writings had a profound impact on economic theory in Sweden, where he is considered to be the founder of the Stockholm School of Economics, and in England, where his writings influenced Keynes. After a lively and distinguished career Wicksell died on 2 May 1926.

In this entry we examine three of Wicksell's more important contributions to economics: the exhaustion theorem, the cumulative process and 'the Wicksell effect'. Neoclassical theory states that factors of production are paid their marginal products. The exhaustion theorem, an element of neoclassical theory, shows that, if factors of production are paid their marginal products, the product will be completely exhausted. Wicksell (1893) argues that the product exhaustion theorem is an equilibrium condition, occurs when the production function is tangent to a linearly homogeneous function and, given the existence of perfect competition, the market mechanism ensures that the product is exhausted. Wicksteed (1894) develops a logical argument for this theorem and Flux (1894), in his review of Wicksteed's *Essay*, provides a mathematical proof of the theorem, one which combines the ideas of Wicksell, Wicksteed and Euler's theorem. Flux criticized Wicksell's book and praised Wicksteed's, with the result that Wicksteed was given credit for solving the exhaustion theorem.

Associated with the exhaustion theorem are three assumptions of neoclassical theory: cost curves are U-shaped, the level of income is given, and consumer demand curves are invariant with respect to costs of production. The two revolutions that occurred at Cambridge attacked these assumptions. Sraffa (1926) and Kahn (1929) argue that cost curves are reversed L-shaped and firms are interdependent. This work forms the basis of the microeconomic revolution culminating in Robinson's (1933) theory of imperfect competition. Keynes attacked the other two assumptions. He did not dispute the fact that at the microeconomic level consumer demand curves are invariant with respect to the prices paid for the factors of production; at the macroeconomic level, however, aggregate consumer demand is not invariant with respect to costs of production. Specifically Keynes argued that a reduction in the costs of production translates into a reduction in income. This argument forms the basis of the macroeconomic revolution, the economics of Keynes and the origin of the debate between Keynes and the 'Classics'.

The second contribution of Wicksell is the cumulative process. Gibson's paradox deals with the movements in the market rate of interest and the price level. Monetary theory suggests that they move in opposite directions, whereas empirical evidence shows them moving in the same direction. Prior to Wicksell, the quantity theory of money tried to explain this paradox using a direct mechanism coupled with a real balance effect. Wicksell explains this paradox using an indirect mechanism. He examines the effects of central bank activity within the context of a pure cash economy and a pure credit economy. In a pure cash economy the rise in the general level of prices cannot become cumulative because the existence of reserve requirements for the banking system will stop the process. Such is not the case in a pure credit economy. Here the changes in the general level of price can become cumulative, with the result that the central bank can establish any price level it desires. The real world, however, lies somewhere between these two extremes. In the *Treatise on Money*, Keynes employed a procedure similar to Wicksell's cumulative process. This procedure may be found in the series of macroeconomic stories associated with the Fundamental Equations. The members of the Cambridge Circus took Keynes to task over an essential feature of these stories – namely, the fact that the level of output did not vary. Out of that discussion came the essential elements of the *General Theory*.

Wicksell's explanation of the cumulative process relies on two rates of interest, the money or the market rate of interest which is the cost of borrowing money and the natural rate of interest which is the yield on newly created capital or the internal rate of return. More precisely, for Wicksell the real or natural rate of interest is the marginal productivity of physical capital. Wicksell argues that the economic system is in equilibrium when three conditions are met: (1) the market rate of interest is equal to the natural rate of interest; (2) the demand for loanable funds is equal to the supply of loanable funds; and (3) the rate of change in the general level of prices is equal to zero. At least two problems emerge from this discussion, both of which were acknowledged by Wicksell. First, if net investment is greater than zero, new capacity is present and there is a tendency for the general level of prices to decline. In order to stabilize the general level of price the bank rate may have to decline, which has implications for Wicksell's conditions for equilibrium. Second, the economic consequences of potential difference between expected outcomes and actual outcomes need to be examined. For example, if planned saving is less than planned investment then realized income will be greater than planned income, or inventories will decrease, or both. The movements in these variables may affect the price level, which affects Wicksell's equilibrium.

His third contribution is known as 'the Wicksell effect'. This effect deals with the revaluation of the existing capital stock as net investment affects wages and the market rate of interest. If the stock of capital is defined to be goods in progress, and real wages increase and the rate of interest declines, the value of the total stock of capital in terms of product will increase. If, however, the stock of capital is defined to be goods in progress and durable goods, and real wages increase and the rate of interest declines, the value of the total stock of capital expressed in terms of product may increase or decrease. The Wicksell effect may be broken down into two component parts: the price aspect, which deals with the change in the value of the capital stock when there is no technological change, and the real aspect, which deals with the value of the capital stock when a change in technique is induced by a change in the rate of interest. A positive real Wicksell effect implies that, as the rate of interest declines, more capital-intensive methods of production will be employed and that investment is a well-behaved function of the rate of interest. A negative real Wicksell effect implies that, as the rate of interest declines, less capital-intensive methods of production will be employed and that investment is not a well-behaved function of the rate of interest. In their critique of the neoclassical theory of capital, Robinson (1953–4) and Sraffa (1960) argued that firms could 'switch' and 'reswitch' between more and less capital-intensive techniques as the rate of interest declined. Samuelson (1966) conceded this point in his summary of the Cambridge Controversy.

TOM CATE

See also:
Business Cycle Theory (I) and (II); Classical Economics; Inflation; Keynes, John Maynard; Monetary Policy; Post Keynesian School of Economics.

Bibliography
Blaug, Mark (1983), *Economic Theory in Retrospect*, Cambridge: Cambridge University Press.
Flux, A.W. (1894), 'A Review of Wicksell's Value, Capital and Rent and Wicksteed's Essay', *Economic Journal*, **4**, (14), June, pp. 305–13.
Harcourt, Geoff C. (1972), *Some Cambridge Controversies in the Theory of Capital*, Cambridge: Cambridge University Press.
Kahn, R.F. (1929), *The Economics of the Period*; reprinted 1989, New York: St Martin's Press.
Robinson, Joan (1933), *The Economics of Imperfect Competition*, London: Macmillan.
Robinson, Joan (1953–4), 'The Production Function and the Theory of Capital', *Review of Economic Studies*, **21**, (55), pp. 81–106.
Robinson, Joan (1962), *Essays in the Theory of Economic Growth*, New York: Macmillan.
Samuelson, Paul A. (1966), 'Paradoxes in Capital Theory: A Symposium. A Summing Up', *Quarterly Journal of Economics*, **80**, (4), November, pp. 568–83.
Sraffa, Piero (1926), 'The Laws of Return Under Competitive Conditions', *Economic Journal*, **36**, (144), December, pp. 535–60.
Sraffa, Piero (1960), *The Production of Commodities by Commodities*, Cambridge: Cambridge University Press.
Uhr, Carl G. (1951), 'Knut Wicksell – A Centennial Evaluation', *American Economic Review*, **41**, (5), December, pp. 829–60.
Wicksell, Knut (1893), *Value, Capital and Rent*; reprinted 1970, New York: Augustus M. Kelley.
Wicksell, Knut (1896), *Public Finance*; a 1958 partial translation appears as Chapter 6 in R.A. Musgrave and A.T. Peacock (eds), *Classics of Public Finance*, London: Macmillan.
Wicksell, Knut (1898), *Interest and Prices*; reprinted 1936, London: Macmillan.
Wicksell, Knut (1901), *Lectures on Political Economy*, vol. I: *General Theory*; reprinted 1934, London: Routledge & Kegan Paul.
Wicksell, Knut (1906), *Lectures on Political Economy*, vol. II: *Money*; reprinted 1935, London: Routledge & Kegan Paul.
Wicksteed, Philip (1894), *An Essay on the Co-ordination of the Laws of Distribution*, reprinted 1932, London: London School of Economics.